Lerwick

Kirkwall

Wick

Sunderland

York

Kingston upon Hull

Leeds

Sheffield

DLANDS

Nottingham

erby

Leicester

Coventry

Northampton

Cambridge

Ipswich

Luton

Oxford

LONDON

SOUTHEAST ENGLAND

Dover

outhampton

Portsmouth

Brighton

0 kilometres

0 miles

EYEWITNESS TRAVEL GUIDES

GREAT
BRITAIN

EYEWITNESS TRAVEL GUIDES

GREAT
BRITAIN

Main contributor: MICHAEL LEAPMAN

LONDON, NEW YORK,
MELBOURNE, MUNICH AND DELHI
www.dk.com

ART EDITOR Stephen Bere
PROJECT EDITOR Marian Broderick
EDITORS Carey Combe, Sara Harper, Elaine Harries,
Kim Inglis, Ella Milroy, Andrew Szudek, Nia Williams
DESIGNERS Susan Blackburn, Elly King,
Colin Loughrey, Andy Wilkinson

CONTRIBUTORS
Josie Barnard, Christopher Catling,
Juliet Clough, Lindsay Hunt, Polly Phillimore,
Martin Symington, Roger Thomas

MAPS
Jane Hanson, Phil Rose, Jennifer Skelley (Lovell Johns Ltd)
Gary Bowes (Era-Maptec Ltd)

PHOTOGRAPHERS
Joe Cornish, Paul Harris, Rob Reichenfeld, Kim Sayer

ILLUSTRATORS
Gary Cross, Richard Draper, Jared Gilby (Kevin Jones Assocs),
Paul Guest, Roger Hutchins, Chris Orr & Assocs,
Maltings Partnership, Ann Winterbotham, John Woodcock

Reproduced by Colourscan (Singapore)
Printed and bound by South China Printing Co. Ltd., China

First published in Great Britain in 1995
by Dorling Kindersley Limited
80 Strand, London WC2R 0RL

**Reprinted with revisions 1996, 1997, 1998, 1999, 2000, 2001,
2002, 2003, 2004, 2005**

Copyright 1995, 2005 © Dorling Kindersley Limited, London
A Penguin Company

A CIP CATALOGUE RECORD IS AVAILABLE FROM THE BRITISH LIBRARY.

ISBN 1 4053 0779 X

FLOORS ARE REFERRED TO THROUGHOUT IN ACCORDANCE WITH BRITISH
USAGE; IE, THE "FIRST FLOOR" IS ABOVE GROUND LEVEL.

**The information in this
Dorling Kindersley Travel Guide is checked annually**.
Every effort has been made to ensure that this book is as up-to-date
as possible at the time of going to press. Some details, however,
such as telephone numbers, opening hours, prices, gallery hanging
arrangements and travel information are liable to change. The
publishers cannot accept responsibility for any consequences arising
from the use of this book, nor for any material on third-party
websites, and cannot guarantee that any website address in this
book will be a suitable source of travel information. We value the
views and suggestions of our readers highly. Please write to:
Publisher, DK Eyewitness Travel Guides,
Dorling Kindersley, 80 Strand, London, Great Britain WC2R 0RL.

CONTENTS

A 14th-century illustration
of two knights jousting

INTRODUCING GREAT BRITAIN

Beefeater at the Tower of London

LONDON

Eilean Donan Castle on Loch Duich in the Scottish Highlands

Jacobean "Old House"
in Hereford

View of the Usk Valley and the
Brecon Beacons, Wales

HOW TO USE THIS GUIDE

THIS GUIDE helps you to get the most from your holidays in Great Britain. It provides both detailed practical information and expert recommendations. *Introducing Great Britain* maps the country and sets it in its historical and cultural context. The six regional chapters, plus *London*, describe important sights, using maps, pictures and illustrations. Features cover topics from houses and famous gardens to sport. Hotel, restaurant, and pub recommendations can be found in *Travellers' Needs*. The *Survival Guide* has practical information on everything from transport to personal safety.

LONDON

The centre of London has been divided into four sight-seeing areas. Each has its own chapter, which opens with a list of the sights described. The last section, *Further Afield*, covers the most attractive suburbs. All sights are numbered and plotted on an area map. The information for each sight follows the map's numerical order, making sights easy to locate within the chapter.

Sights at a Glance lists the chapter's sights by category: Historic Streets and Buildings; Museums and Galleries; Churches and Cathedrals; Shops; Parks and Gardens.

2 Street-by-Street Map
This gives a bird's-eye view of the key areas in each chapter.

Stars indicate the sights that no visitor should miss.

All pages relating to London have red thumb tabs.

A locator map shows where you are in relation to other areas of the city centre.

1 Area Map
For easy reference, the sights are numbered and located on a map. Sights in the city centre are also marked on the Street Finder *on pages 135–43.*

A suggested route for a walk is shown in red.

3 Detailed information
The sights in London are described individually. Addresses, telephone numbers, opening hours, admission charges, tours and wheelchair access are also provided, as well as public transport links.

1 Introduction

The landscape, history and character of each region is outlined here, showing how the area has developed over the centuries and what it has to offer the visitor today.

GREAT BRITAIN AREA BY AREA

Apart from London, Great Britain has been divided into 14 regions, each of which has a separate chapter. The most interesting towns and places to visit have been numbered on a *Pictorial Map*.

Each area of Great Britain can be identified quickly by its colour coding, shown on the inside front cover.

2 Pictorial Map

This shows the main road network and gives an illustrated overview of the whole region. All entries are numbered and there are also useful tips on getting around the region by car, train and other forms of transport.

3 Detailed information

All the important sights, towns and other places to visit are described individually. They are listed in order, following the numbering on the Pictorial Map. *Within each entry, there is detailed information on important buildings and other sights.*

Story boxes explore related topics.

For all the top sights, a Visitors' Checklist provides the practical information you need to plan your visit.

4 The top sights

These are given one or more full pages. Three-dimensional illustrations reveal the interiors of historic buildings. Interesting town and city centres are given street-by-street maps, featuring individual sights.

INTRODUCING
GREAT BRITAIN

Putting Great Britain on the Map

LYING IN NORTHWESTERN EUROPE, Great Britain is bounded by the Atlantic Ocean, the North Sea and the English Channel. The island's landscape and climate are varied, and it is this variety that even today affects the pattern of settlement. The remote shores of the West Country peninsula and the inhospitable mountains of Scotland and Wales are less populated than the relatively flat and fertile Midlands and Southeast, where the vast majority of the country's 58 million people live. Due to this population density, the south is today the most built-up part of the country.

KEY

═══	Motorway
━━━	Major road
- - -	Ferry route
•••	Channel Tunnel
▬ ▬	National border

◁ *Salisbury Cathedral: from the meadows* by John Constable (1776–1837)

Regional Great Britain: London, the South, the Midlands and Wales

GREAT BRITAIN has airline connections with most cities in the world. London is the main transport hub with three major international airports, including Heathrow, the world's busiest. Southern England, Britain's most populous area, is divided, within this book, into four regions – Southeast England, the West Country, Wales and the Midlands – with a separate chapter for London. Road and rail links to the North and Scotland *(see pp14–15)* are plentiful, as are links between all main towns.

KEY TO COLOUR-CODING

- London

Southeast England

- The Downs and Channel Coast
- East Anglia
- Thames Valley

The West Country

- Wessex
- Devon and Cornwall

Wales

- North Wales
- South and Mid-Wales

The Midlands

- The Heart of England
- East Midlands

KEY TO MAP

- Ferry port
- Airport
- Motorway
- Major road
- Railway line
- Channel Tunnel

Europe

Great Britain is situated in the northwest corner of Europe. Its nearest neighbours are Ireland to the west, and the Netherlands, Belgium and France across the Channel. Denmark, Norway and Sweden are also easily accessible.

Shetland and Orkney islands

These islands form the northern-most part of Great Britain, with the Shetlands lying six degrees south of the Arctic Circle. There are transport links to the mainland.

GREATER LONDON

Greater London

Greater London, the area within the M25 motorway ring, is home to 7 million people and covers an area of 600 sq miles (1,580 sq km).

Regional Great Britain: The North and Scotland

THIS PART OF GREAT BRITAIN is divided into two sections in this book. Although it is far less populated than the southern sector of the country, there are good road and rail connections, and ferry services link the islands with the mainland.

KEY TO COLOUR-CODING

The North Country

- Lancashire and the Lakes
- Yorkshire and Humber Region
- Northumbria

Scotland

- The Lowlands
- The Highlands and Islands

Isle of Lewis

Stornoway

Tarbert

Ullapool

Lochmaddy

Uig

Western Isles

Isle of Skye

Kyle of Lochalsh

Lochboisdale

Castlebay

Mallaig

Fort William

Hebrides

Arinagour

Tobermory

Scarinish

Craignure

Oban

Crainlarich

Inner Hebrides

Scalasaig

Jura

Greenock

Kennacraig

Paisley

Ardrossan

Islay

Brodick

Irvine

Port Ellen

Ayr

Campbeltown

Isle of Arran

Larne

Belfast

Cairnryan

Stranraer

Isle of Man

Douglas

Dub

Holyhead

MILEAGE CHART

10 = Distance in miles
10 = Distance in kilometres

LONDON										
111 / **179**	*BIRMINGHAM*									
150 / **241**	102 / **164**	*CARDIFF*								
74 / **119**	185 / **298**	228 / **367**	*DOVER*							
372 / **599**	290 / **466**	373 / **600**	442 / **711**	*EDINBURGH*						
389 / **626**	292 / **470**	374 / **602**	466 / **750**	45 / **72**	*GLASGOW*					
529 / **851**	448 / **721**	530 / **853**	600 / **966**	158 / **254**	167 / **269**	*INVERNESS*				
184 / **296**	81 / **130**	173 / **278**	257 / **414**	213 / **343**	214 / **344**	371 / **597**	*MANCHESTER*			
274 / **441**	204 / **328**	301 / **484**	343 / **552**	107 / **172**	145 / **233**	265 / **426**	131 / **211**	*NEWCASTLE*		
112 / **180**	161 / **259**	235 / **378**	167 / **269**	360 / **579**	383 / **616**	517 / **832**	185 / **298**	260 / **418**	*NORWICH*	
212 / **341**	206 / **332**	152 / **261**	287 / **462**	427 / **784**	426 / **785**	545 / **1038**	250 / **451**	427 / **655**	324 / **521**	*PLYMOUTH*

0 kilometres 100

0 miles 100

ORKNEY AND
SHETLAND
ISLANDS

Shetland Islands

Unst

Yell

Mainland

Foula

Lerwick

Fair
Isle

Westray

Mainland

Sanday

Stromness

Stronsay

Kirkwall

Orkney
Islands

Hoy

Scrabster

Thurso

WICK

Aberdeen

Scrabster
Thurso
Wick

Stromness

Lerwick

Elgin
Fraserburgh
Peterhead
Inverness
Aberdeen
Braemar
Montrose
Forfar
Arbroath
Dundee
Perth
St Andrews
Stirling
Kirkcaldy
Dunfermline
EDINBURGH
Glasgow
East Kilbride
Berwick-Upon-Tweed
Galashiels
Peebles
Holy
Island
Farne Islands
Hawick
Jedburgh
Bamburgh
Alnwick
Warkworth
Dumfries
Morpeth
Castle
glas
Hexham
Corbridge
Newcastle
Upon Tyne
Sunderland
Carlisle
Durham
Cockermouth
Middleton-in-
Teesdale
Hartlepool
Whitehaven
Keswick
Penrith
Barnard
Castle
Middlesbrough
Grasmere
Appleby-in-
Westmorland
Darlington
Hawkshead
Windermere
Richmond
Goathland
Whitby
Kendal
Helmsley
Scarborough
Barrow-in-
Furness
Thirsk
Flamborough Head
Heysham
Ripon
Bridlington
Lancaster
Skipton
Harrogate
Clitheroe
York
Beverley
Blackpool
Burnley
Leeds
Kingston
Upon Hull
Preston
Blackburn
Bradford
Wakefield
Southport
Halifax
Huddersfield
Scunthorpe
Grimsby
Bolton
Rochdale
Wigan
Manchester
Barnsley
Doncaster
Liverpool
Stockport
Sheffield
Chester
Lincoln

Stavanger
Bergen

Zeebrugge
Rotterdam

KEY TO MAP

Ferry port

Airport

Motorway

Major road

Railway line

A PORTRAIT OF GREAT BRITAIN

B RITAIN HAS BEEN ASSIDUOUS *in preserving its traditions, but offers the visitor much more than stately castles and pretty villages. A diversity of landscape, culture, literature, art and architecture, as well as its unique heritage, results in a nation balancing the needs of the present with those of its past.*

Britain's character has been shaped by its geographical position as an island. Never successfully invaded since 1066, its people have developed their own distinctive traditions. The Roman invasion of AD 43 lasted 350 years but Roman culture and language were quickly overlain with those of the northern European settlers who followed. Ties with Europe were loosened further in the 16th century when the Catholic church was replaced by a less dogmatic established church.

Tudor rose

Although today a member of the European Union, Britain continues to delight in its non-conformity, even in superficial ways such as driving on the left-hand side of the road instead of the right. The opening of the rail tunnel to France is a topographical adjustment that does not necessarily mark a change in national attitude.

The British heritage is seen in its ancient castles, cathedrals and stately homes with their gardens and Classical parklands. Age-old customs are renewed each year, from royal ceremonies to Morris dancers performing on village greens.

For a small island, Great Britain encompasses a surprising variety in its regions, whose inhabitants maintain distinct identities. Scotland and Wales are separate countries from England with their own legislative assemblies.

Walking along the east bank of the River Avon, Bath

◁ Punting, a popular pastime on the River Cam, Cambridge

Widecombe-in-the-Moor, a Devon village clustered round a church and set in hills

They have different customs, traditions, and, in the case of Scotland, different legal and educational systems. The Welsh and Scots Gaelic languages survive and are sustained by their own radio and television networks. In northern and West Country areas, English itself is spoken in a rich variety of dialects and accents, and these areas maintain their own regional arts, crafts, architecture and food.

The landscape is varied, too, from the craggy mountains of Wales, Scotland and the north, through the flat expanses of the Midlands and eastern England to the soft, rolling hills of the south and west. The long, broad beaches of East Anglia contrast with the picturesque rocky inlets along much of the west coast.

Scottish coat of arms at Edinburgh Castle

Despite the spread of towns and cities over the last two centuries, rural Britain still flourishes. Nearly three-quarters of Britain's land is used for agriculture. The main commercial crops are wheat, barley, sugar beet and potatoes, though what catches the eye in early summer are the fields of bright yellow rape or slate-blue flax.

The countryside is dotted with farms and charming villages, with picturesque cottages and lovingly tended gardens – a British passion. A typical village is built around an ancient church and a small, friendly pub. Here the pace of life slows. To drink a pint of ale in a cosy, village inn and relax before a fire is a time-honoured British custom. Strangers will be welcomed cordially, though perhaps with caution; for even if strict formality is a thing of the past, the British have a tendency to be reserved.

In the 19th and early 20th centuries, trade with the extensive British Empire, fuelled by abundant coal supplies, spurred manufacturing and created wealth. Thousands of people moved from the countryside to towns and cities near mines, mills and factories. By 1850 Britain was the world's strongest industrial nation. Now many

Lake and gardens at Petworth House, Sussex

of these old industrial centres have declined, and today manufacturing employs only 22 per cent of the labour force, while 66 per cent work in the growing service sector. These service industries are located mainly in the southeast, close to London, where modern office buildings bear witness to comparative prosperity.

Crowds at Petticoat Lane market in London's East End

SOCIETY AND POLITICS

British cities are melting-pots for people not just from different parts of the country but also from overseas. Irish immigration has long ensured a flow of labour into the country, and since the 1950s hundreds of thousands have come from former colonies in Africa, Asia and the Caribbean, many of which are now members of the Commonwealth. Nearly five per cent of Britain's 58 million inhabitants are from nonwhite ethnic groups – and about half of these were born in Britain. The result

is a multi-cultural society that can boast a wide range of music, art, food and religions. However, prejudice does exist and in some inner-city areas where poorer members of different communities live, racial tensions can occasionally arise. Even though discrimination in housing and employment on the grounds of race is against the law, it does occur in places.

Britain's class structure still intrigues and bewilders many visitors, based as it is on a subtle mixture of heredity and wealth. Even though many of the great inherited fortunes no longer exist, some old landed families still live on their

Bosses in Norwich Cathedral cloisters

large estates, and many now open them to the public. Class divisions are further entrenched by the education system. While more than 90 per cent of children are educated free by the state, richer parents often opt for private schooling, and the products of these private schools are disproportionately represented in the higher echelons of government and business.

The monarchy's position highlights the dilemma of a people seeking to preserve its most potent symbol of national unity in an age that is suspicious of inherited privilege. Without real political power, though still head of the Church of England, the Queen and her family are subject to increasing public scrutiny. Following a spate of personal scandals, some citizens advocate the abolition of the monarchy.

Democracy has deep foundations in Britain: there was even a parliament of sorts in London in the 13th century.

Priest in the Close at Winchester Cathedral

Yet with the exception of the 17th-century Civil War, power has passed gradually from the Crown to the people's elected representatives. A series of Reform Acts between 1832 and 1884 gave the vote to all male citizens, though women were not enfranchised on an equal basis until 1928. Margaret Thatcher – Britain's first woman Prime Minister – held office for 12 years from 1979. During the 20th

Afternoon tea on the back lawn at the Thornbury Castle Hotel, Avon

century, the Labour (left wing) and Conservative (right wing) parties have, during their periods in office, favoured a mix of public and private ownership for industry and ample funding for the state health and welfare systems.

The position of Ireland has been an intractable political issue since the 17th century. Part of the United Kingdom for 800 years, but divided in 1921, it has seen conflict between Catholics and Protestants for many years. The Good Friday Peace Agreement of 1998 was a huge step forward but the path to lasting peace is a rocky one.

CULTURE AND THE ARTS
Britain has a famous theatrical tradition stretching back to the 16th century and William Shakespeare. His plays

The House of Lords, in Parliament

have been performed on stage almost continuously since he wrote them and the works of 17th- and 18th-century writers are also frequently revived. Contemporary British playwrights such as Tom Stoppard, Alan Ayckbourn and David Hare draw on this long tradition with their vivid language and by using comedy to illustrate serious themes. British actors such as Vanessa Redgrave, Ian McKellen, Ralph Fiennes and Anthony Hopkins have international reputations.

While London is the focal point of British theatre, fine drama is to be seen in many other parts of the country. The Edinburgh Festival and its Fringe are the high point of Great Britain's cultural calendar with theatre and music to suit all tastes. Other music festivals are held across the country, chiefly in summer, while there are annual

Schoolboys at Eton, the famous public school

festivals of literature at Hay-on-Wye and Cheltenham. Poetry has had an enthusiastic following since Chaucer wrote the *Canterbury Tales* in the 14th century: poems from all eras can even be read on the London Underground, where they are interspersed with the advertisements in the carriages and on the station platforms.

In the visual arts, Britain has a strong tradition in portraiture, caricature, landscape and watercolour. In modern times David Hockney and Lucian Freud, and sculptors Henry Moore and Barbara Hepworth, have enjoyed worldwide recognition. Architects including

Christopher Wren, Inigo Jones, John Nash and Robert Adam all created styles that define British cities; and today, Norman Foster and Richard Rogers carry the standard for Post-Modernism. Britain is becoming famous for its innovative fashion designers, many of whom now show their spring and autumn collections in Paris.

Reading the newspaper in Kensington Gardens

The British are avid newspaper readers. There are 11 national newspapers published from London on weekdays: the standard of the broadsheets is very high and newspapers such as *The Times* are read the world over because of their reputation for strong international reporting. Most popular, however, are the tabloids packed with gossip, crime and sport, which account for some 80 per cent of the total.

The indigenous film industry, although squeezed by Hollywood, produces a few international hits such as *The Full Monty* and *Notting Hill*. British television is famous for the quality of its news, current affairs and drama programmes. The publicly funded British Broadcasting Corporation (BBC), which controls five national radio networks and two terrestrial television channels, as well as additional radio stations and television channels via digital technology, is widely admired.

The British are great sports fans, and soccer, rugby, cricket and golf are popular. An instantly recognizable English image is that of the cricket match on a village green. Nationwide, fishing is the most popular sporting pastime, and the British make good use of their national parks as keen walkers.

British food used to be derided for a lack of imagination. The cuisine relied on a limited range of quality ingredients, plainly prepared. But recent influences from abroad have introduced a wider range of ingredients and more adventurous techniques. Typical English food – plain home cooking and regional dishes – can still be found but they are being supplemented by a tastier modern British cuisine.

Naomi Campbell, a British supermodel

In this, as in other respects, the British are doing what they have done for centuries: accommodating their own traditions to influences from other cultures, while leaving the essential elements of their national life and character intact.

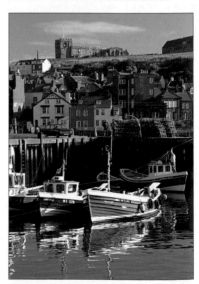

Whitby harbour and St Mary's Church, Yorkshire

Gardens Through the Ages

STYLES OF GARDENING in Britain have expanded alongside architecture and other evolving fashions. The Elizabethan knot garden became more elaborate and formal in Jacobean times, when the range of plants greatly increased. The 18th century brought a taste for large-scale "natural" landscapes with lakes, woods and pastures, creating the most distinctively English style to have emerged. In the 19th century, fierce debate raged between supporters of natural and formal gardens, developing into the eclecticism of the 20th century when "garden rooms" in differing styles became popular.

Monumental column

A grotto and cascade brought romance and mystery.

Capability Brown (1715–83) *was Britain's most influential garden designer, favouring the move away from formal gardens to man-made pastoral settings.*

Blackthorn

Classical temples were a much appreciated feature in 18th-century gardens and were often exact replicas of buildings that the designers had seen in Greece.

Elaborate parterres *were a feature of aristocratic gardens of the 17th century, when the fashion spread from Europe. This is the Privy Garden at Hampton Court Palace, restored in 1995 to its design under William III.*

Maple

Winding paths were carefully planned to allow changing vistas to open out as visitors strolled around the garden.

IDEAL LANDSCAPE GARDEN

Classical Greece and Rome inspired the grand gardens of the early 18th century, such as Stourhead and Stowe. Informal clumps of trees played a critical part in the serene, manicured landscapes.

DESIGN AND FORMALITY

A flower garden is a work of artifice, an attempt to tame nature rather than to copy it. Growing plants in rows or regular patterns, interspersed with statues and ornaments, imposes a sense of order. Designs change to reflect the fashion of the time and the introduction of new plants.

Medieval gardens usually had a herber (a turfed sitting area) and a vine arbour. A good reconstruction is Queen Eleanor's Garden, Winchester.

Tudor gardens featured edged borders and sometimes mazes. The Tudor House Garden, Southampton, also has beehives and heraldic statues.

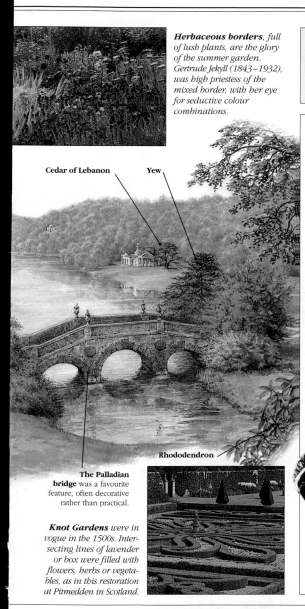

Herbaceous borders, full of lush plants, are the glory of the summer garden. Gertrude Jekyll (1843–1932), was high priestess of the mixed border, with her eye for seductive colour combinations.

Cedar of Lebanon   **Yew**

Rhododendron

The Palladian bridge was a favourite feature, often decorative rather than practical.

Knot Gardens were in vogue in the 1500s. Intersecting lines of lavender or box were filled with flowers, herbs or vegetables, as in this restoration at Pitmedden in Scotland.

DEVELOPMENT OF THE MODERN PANSY

All garden plants derive from wild flowers, bred over the years to produce qualities that appeal to gardeners. The story of the pansy, one of our most popular flowers, is typical.

The wild pansy *(Viola tricolor)* native to Britain is commonly known as heartsease. It is a small-flowered annual which can vary considerably in colour.

The mountain pansy (*Viola lutea*) is a perennial. The first cultivated varieties resulted from crossing it with heartsease in the early 19th century.

The Show Pansy was bred by florists after the blotch appeared as a chance seedling in 1840. It was round in form with a small, symmetrical blotch.

The Fancy Pansy, developed in the 1860s, was much larger. The blotch covered all three lower petals save for a thin margin of colour.

Modern hybrids of pansies, violas and violettas, developed by selective breeding, are varied and versatile in a wide range of vibrant new colours.

17th-century gardening was more elaborate. Water gardens like those at Blenheim were often combined with parterres of exotic foreign plants.

Victorian gardens, their formal beds a mass of colour, were a reaction to the landscapes of Capability Brown. Alton Towers has a good example.

20th-century gardens mix historic and modern styles, as at Hidcote Manor, Gloucestershire. Growing wild flowers is becoming a popular choice.

Stately Homes

THE GRAND COUNTRY HOUSE reached its zenith in the 18th and 19th centuries, when the old landed families and the new captains of industry enjoyed their wealth, looked after by a retinue of servants. The earliest stately homes date from the 14th century, when defence was paramount. By the 16th century, when the opulent taste of the European Renaissance spread to England, houses became centres of pleasure and showplaces for fine art *(see pp290–91)*. The Georgians favoured chaste Classical architecture with rich interiors, the Victorians flamboyant Gothic. Due to 20th-century social change many stately homes have been opened to the public, some administered by the National Trust.

Adam sketch (c.1760) for ornate panel

The saloon, a domed rotunda based on the Pantheon in Rome, was designed to display the Curzon family's Classical sculpture collection to 18th-century society.

The Drawing Room, the main room for entertaining, contains the most important pictures and some exquisite plasterwork.

The Marble Hall is where balls and other social functions took place among Corinthian columns of pink alabaster.

The Family Wing is a self-contained "pavilion" of private living quarters; the servants lived in rooms above the kitchen. The Curzon family still live here.

The Music Room is decorated with musical themes. Music was the main entertainment on social occasions.

TIMELINE OF ARCHITECTS

1650

1750

Sir John Vanbrugh *(see p384)* was helped by **Nicholas Hawksmoor** (1661–1736) on Blenheim Palace *(see pp216–17)*

Colen Campbell (1676–1729) designed Burlington House *(see p83)*

William Kent (1685–1748) built Holkham Hall *(see p185)* in the Palladian style

Robert Adam (1728–92), who often worked with his brother James (1730–94) was as famous for decorative details as for buildings

John Carr (1723–1807) designed the Palladian Harewood House *(see p396)*

Henry Holland (1745–1806) designed the Neo-Classical south range of Woburn Abbey *(see p218)*

Castle Howard (1702) by Sir John Vanbrugh

Adam fireplace, Kedleston Hall, adorned with Classical motifs

NATIONAL TRUST

At the end of the 19th century, there were real fears that burgeoning factories, mines, roads and houses would obliterate much of Britain's historic landscape and finest buildings. In 1895 a group that included the social reformer Octavia Hill formed the National Trust, to preserve the nation's valuable heritage. The first

National Trust oak leaf design

building acquired by the trust was the medieval Clergy House at Alfriston in Sussex, in 1896 *(see p168)*. Today the National Trust is a charity that runs many historic houses and gardens, and vast stretches of countryside and coastline *(see p617)*. It is supported by more than two million members nationwide.

A corridor links the kitchen to the main house.

The 13th-century church is all that is left of Kedleston village, moved in 1760 to make way for the new house and its grounds.

KEDLESTON HALL

This Derbyshire mansion *(see p324)* is an early work of the influential Georgian architect Robert Adam, who was a pioneer of the Neo-Classical style derived from ancient Greece and Rome. It was built for the Curzon family in the 1760s.

***Life Below Stairs* by Charles Hunt (c.1890)**

LIFE BELOW STAIRS

A large community of resident staff was essential to run a country house smoothly. The butler was in overall charge, ensuring that meals were served on time. The housekeeper supervised uniformed maids who made sure the place was clean. The cook ran the kitchen, using fresh produce from the estate. Ladies' maids and valets acted as personal servants.

1800	1850

Dining Room, Cragside, Northumberland

Norman Shaw (1831–1912) was an exponent of Victorian Gothic, as in Cragside (above), and a pioneer of the Arts and Crafts movement *(see p316)*

Philip Webb (1831–1915) was a leading architect of the influential Arts and Crafts movement *(see p316)*, whose buildings favoured the simpler forms of an "Old English" style, instead of flamboyant Victorian Gothic

Sir Edwin Lutyens (1869–1944) designed the elaborate Castle Drogo in Devon *(see p283)*, one of the last grand country houses

Standen, West Sussex (1891–94) by Philip Webb

Heraldry and the Aristocracy

Order of the Garter medal

THE BRITISH ARISTOCRACY has evolved over 900 years from the feudal obligations of noblemen to the Norman kings, who conferred privileges of rank and land in return for armed support. Subsequent monarchs bestowed titles and property on their supporters, establishing new aristocratic dynasties. The title of "earl" dates from the 11th century; that of "duke" from the 14th century. Soon the nobility began to choose their own symbols, partly to identify a knight concealed by his armour: these were often painted on the knight's coat (hence the term "coat of arms") and also copied onto his shield.

The College of Arms, London: housing records of all coats of arms and devising new ones

ROYAL COAT OF ARMS

The most familiar British coat of arms is the sovereign's. It appears on the royal standard, or flag, as well as on official documents and on shops that enjoy royal patronage. Over nearly 900 years, various monarchs have made modifications. The quartered shield in the middle displays the arms of England (twice), Scotland and Ireland. Surrounding it are other traditional images including the lion and unicorn, topped by the crown and the royal helm (helmet).

Edward III (1327–77) was the founder of the chivalric Order of the Garter. The garter, bearing the motto, Honi soit qui mal y pense *(evil be to him who thinks of evil), goes round the central shield.*

The lion is the most common beast in heraldry.

The red lion is the symbol of Scotland.

The unicorn is a mythical beast, generally regarded as a Scottish royal beast in heraldry.

Henry II (1154–89) formalized his coat of arms to include three lions. This was developed by his son Richard I to become the "Gules three lions passant guardant or" seen on today's arms.

The royal helm with gold protective bars was introduced to the arms by Elizabeth I (1558–1603).

Dieu et mon droit (God and my right) has been the royal motto since the reign of Henry V (1413–22).

Henry VII (1485–1509) devised the Tudor rose, joining the white and red roses of York and Lancaster.

ADMIRAL LORD NELSON

When people are ennobled they may choose their own coat of arms if they do not already have one. Britain's naval hero (1758–1805) was made Baron Nelson of the Nile in 1798 and a viscount in 1801. His arms relate to his life and career at sea; but some symbols were added after his death.

A seaman supports the shield.

The motto means "Let him wear the palm (or laurel) who deserves it".

A tropical scene shows the Battle of the Nile (1798).

The San Joseph was a Spanish man o'war that Nelson daringly captured.

TRACING YOUR ANCESTRY

Records of births, deaths and marriages in England and Wales since 1837 are at the **Family Records Centre,** 1 Myddelton St, London (020-8392 5300), and in Scotland at **New Register House**, 3 West Register St, Edinburgh EH1 3YT (0131 314 4433). For help in tracing family history, consult **Society of Genealogists**, 14 Charterhouse Bldgs, London EC1 (020-7251 8799).

Inherited titles usually pass to the eldest son or the closest male relative, but some titles may go to women if there is no male heir.

The Duke of Edinburgh (born 1921), husband of the Queen, is one of several dukes who are members of the Royal Family.

The Marquess of Salisbury (1830–1903), Prime Minister three times between 1885 and 1902, was descended from the Elizabethan statesman Robert Cecil.

Earl Mountbatten of Burma (1900–79) was ennobled in 1947 for diplomatic and military services.

Viscount Montgomery (1887–1976) was raised to the peerage for his military leadership in World War II.

Lord Byron (1788–1824), the Romantic poet, was the 6th Baron Byron: the 1st Baron was an MP ennobled by Charles I in 1625.

PEERS OF THE REALM

There are nearly 1,200 peers of the realm. In 1999 the process began to abolish the hereditary system in favour of life peerages which expire on the death of the recipient *(see left and below)*. All peers are entitled to sit in the House of Lords, including the Lords Spiritual – archbishops and senior bishops of the Church of England – and the Law Lords. In 1958 the Queen expanded the list of life peerages to honour people who had performed notable public service. From 1999 the system of "peoples peerages" began to replace inherited honours.

KEY TO THE PEERS

☐ 25 dukes

☐ 35 marquesses

☐ 175 earls and countesses

☐ 100 viscounts

☐ 800+ barons and baronesses

THE QUEEN'S HONOURS LIST

Twice a year several hundred men and women nominated by the Prime Minister and political leaders for outstanding public service receive honours from the Queen. Some are made dames or knights, a few receive the prestigious OM (Order of Merit), but far more receive lesser honours such as OBEs or MBEs (Orders or Members of the British Empire).

Mother Theresa received the OM in 1983 for her work in India.

Terence Conran, founder of Habitat, was knighted for services to industry.

The Beatles were given MBEs in 1965. Paul McCartney was knighted in 1997.

Rural Architecture

FOR MANY, THE ESSENCE OF BRITISH LIFE is found in villages. Their scale and serenity nurture a way of life envied by those who live in towns and cities. The pattern of British villages dates back some 1,500 years, when the Saxons cleared forests and established settlements, usually centred around a green or pond. Most of today's English villages existed at the time of the *Domesday Book* in 1086, though few actual buildings survive from then. The settlements evolved organically around a church or manor; the cottages and gardens were created from local materials. Today, a typical village will contain structures of various dates, from the Middle Ages onward. The church is usually the oldest, followed perhaps by a tithe barn, manor house and cottages.

Abbotsbury, in Dorset – a typical village built up around a church

A steep-pitched roof covers the whole house.

Timbers are of Wealden oak.

Eaves are supported by curved braces.

Wealden Hall House in Sussex is a medieval timber-framed house, of a type found in southeast England. It has a tall central open hall flanked by bays of two floors and the upper floor is "jettied", overhanging the ground floor.

A tiled roof keeps the grain dry.

Holes let in air – and birds.

The entrance is big enough for ox-wagons.

Walls and doors are weatherboarded.

The medieval tithe barn stored produce for the clergy – each farmer was required to donate one tenth (tithe) of his annual harvest. The enormous roofs may be supported by crucks, large curved timbers extending from the low walls.

THE PARISH CHURCH

The church is the focal point of the village and, traditionally, of village life. Its tall spire could be seen – and its bells heard – by travellers from a distance. The church is also a chronicle of local history: a large church in a tiny village indicates a once-prosperous settlement. A typical church contains architectural features from many centuries, occasionally as far back as Saxon times. These may include medieval brasses, wall paintings, misericords *(see p329)*, and Tudor and Stuart carvings. Many sell informative guide books inside.

Slender spire from the Georgian era

West elevation

Pinnacled towers dating from the 15th century are situated at the west end.

Bells summon the congregation.

Buttresses support old walls.

Norman arches are rounded.

Stone cottages such as this Pennine longhouse are built from hard, local granite, keeping out the severe winter weather. Farm animals were housed in the barn (on right), and the family home was at the other end (see far right).

Chimneys come in various shapes.

The roof is made from slabs of Lake District stone.

Windows were often small in cold areas.

The roof is surfaced with tiles.

Type of stone used depends on locality. In Cumbria blue-grey Pennine stone was used.

Weatherboard houses were built chiefly in southeast England in the 18th and 19th centuries; the timber boarding acted as cladding to keep out the cold and rain.

Bay windows add light and space.

Thatch is made from reeds or straw.

Thatched cob cottages of the 17th century have a cob covering a timber frame. The cob is made from a mixture of wet earth, lime, dung, chopped reed, straw, gravel, sand and stones.

Walls are 1 m (3 ft) thick.

BUILDING MATERIALS

The choice of materials depended on local availability. A stone cottage in east Scotland or Cornwall would be granite, or in the Cotswolds, limestone. Timber for beams was often oak. Flint and pebble were popular in the chalky south and east. Slate is quarried in Wales and brick was widely used from Tudor times.

Welsh slate, making a durable roof

Tiles made from fired clay

Flint and pebble – common in Norfolk

Wood planks used for weatherboarding

Brick, widely used since Tudor times

Local hard granite from South Wales

South elevation

The nave is often the oldest part of the building, with extensions added in later centuries.

Towers are often later additions, due to their tendency to collapse.

Ropes used by bell-ringers.

The font, where babies are baptized, is often a church's oldest feature.

Pointed arches date from the 13th century.

Many pulpits are Jacobean.

A screen separates nave from chancel.

The chancel houses the choir and altar.

The Countryside

Common Blue butterfly

FOR ITS SIZE, Britain contains an unusual variety of geological and climatic conditions that have shaped diverse landscapes, from treeless windswept moorland to boggy marshes and small hedged cattle pastures. Each terrain nurtures its typical wildlife and displays its own charm through the seasons. With the reduction in farming and the creation of footpaths and nature reserves, the countryside is becoming more of a leisure resource.

INDIGENOUS ANIMALS AND BIRDS

There are no large or dangerous wild animals in Britain but a wealth of small mammals, rodents and insects inhabit the countryside, and the rivers and streams are home to many varieties of fish. For bird-watchers there is a great range of songbirds, birds of prey and seabirds.

Livestock graze on low pastures.

Trees provide shelter and protection for wildlife.

Higher land is uncultivated.

Bushes and trees grow between rocks.

Streams flow over a stony bed from mountain springs.

The highest ground is often covered in snow until spring.

WOODED DOWNLAND

Chalk downland, seen here at Ditchling Beacon on the Downs *(see p169),* has soil of low fertility and is grazed by sheep. However crops are sometimes grown on the lower slopes. Distinctive wild flowers and butterflies thrive here, while beech and yew predominate in the woods.

WILD HILLSIDE

Large tracts of Britain's uplands remain wild terrain, unsuitable for crops or forestry. Purple heather is tough enough to survive in moorland, the haunt of deer and game birds. The highest craggy uplands, such as the Cairngorms *(see p530–31)* in Scotland, pictured here, are the habitat of birds of prey, such as the golden eagle.

***Spear thistle** has pink heads in summer that attract several species of butterfly.*

***The dog rose** is one of Britain's best-loved wild flowers; its pink single flower is widely seen in hedgerows.*

***Ling,** a low-growing heather with tiny pink bell-flowers, adds splashes of colour to peaty moors and uplands.*

***Tormentil** has small yellow flowers. It prefers moist, acid soil and is found near water on heaths and moors in summer.*

***Hogweed** has robust stems and leaves with large clusters of white flowers.*

***Meadow cranesbill** is a wild geranium with distinctive purple flowers.*

Swallows, swifts and house martins are all summer visitors.

Kestrels are small falcons that prey on mammals such as voles.

Rabbits are often spotted feeding at the edge of fields or near woods.

Robins, common in gardens and hedgerows, have distinctive red breast feathers.

Foxes, little bigger than domestic cats, live in hideaways in woods, near farmland.

Cereal crops ripen in small fields.

Hedgerows provide refuge for wildlife.

Small mixed woods break up the field pattern.

Sheep graze on salty marshes.

Culverts drain water from the field.

Reed beds edge the water.

TRADITIONAL FIELDS

The patchwork fields here in the Cotswolds *(see p292)* reflect generations of small-scale farming. A typical farm would produce silage, hay and cereal crops, and keep a few dairy cows and sheep in enclosed pastures. The tree-dotted hedgerows mark boundaries that may be centuries old.

MARSHLAND

Flat and low-lying wetlands, criss-crossed with dykes and drainage canals, provide the scenery of Romney Marsh *(see also p170)* as well as much of East Anglia. Some areas have rich, peaty soil for crops, or salty marshland for sheep, but there are extensive uncultivated sections, where reed beds shelter wildlife.

The oxeye daisy is a larger relative of the common white daisy, found in grassland from spring to late summer.

Sea lavender is a saltmarsh plant that is tolerant of saline soils. It flowers in late summer.

Orchids are among the rarer wild flowers. This species is the Common Spotted Orchid.

Cowslips belong to the primrose family. In spring they are often found in the grass on open meadowlands.

Poppies glow brilliant red in cornfields.

Buttercups are among the most common wild flowers. They brighten meadows in summer.

Walkers' Britain

WALKERS OF ALL LEVELS of ability and enthusiasm are well served in Britain. There is an unrivalled network of long-distance paths through some spectacular scenery, which can be tackled in stages with overnight stays en route, or dipped into for a single day's walking. For shorter walks, Britain is dotted with signposts

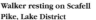

Walker resting on Scafell Pike, Lake District

showing public footpaths across common or private land. You will find books of walk routes in local shops and a large map will keep you on track. Choose river routes for easy walking or take to the hills for a greater challenge.

The West Highland Way is an arduous 95 mile (153 km) route from Milngavie, near Glasgow, to north of Fort William, across mountainous terrain with fine lochs and moorland scenery *(see p480)*.

The Pennine Way was Britain's first designated long-distance path. The 268 mile (431 km) route from Edale in Derbyshire to Kirk Yetholm on the Scottish border is a challenging upland hike, with long, lonely stretches of moorland. It is only for experienced hill walkers.

Offa's Dyke Footpath follows the boundary between Wales and England. The 168 mile (270 km) path goes through the beautiful Wye Valley (see p447) in the Welsh borders.

Dales Way runs from Ilkley in West Yorkshire to Bowness-on-Windermere in the Lake District, 81 miles (130 km) of delightful flat riverside walking and valley scenery.

Pembrokeshire Coastal path is 186 miles (299 km) of rugged cliff-top walking from Amroth on Carmarthen Bay to the west tip of Wales at Cardigan.

ORDNANCE SURVEY MAPS

The best maps for walkers are published by the Ordnance Survey, the official mapping agency (08456 050505). Out of a wide range of maps the most useful are the *Explorer* series, which include the more popular regions and cover a large area, on a scale of 1:25,000, and the *Landranger* series, on a scale of 1:50,000.

The Southwest Coastal Path offers varied scenery from Minehead on the north Somerset coast to Poole in Dorset, via Devon and Cornwall – in all a marathon 630 mile (1,014 km) round trip.

Fort William

Glasgow

St Bees Head

Prestatyn

St Dogmaels

Amroth

Minehead

SIGNPOSTS

Long-distance paths are well
signposted, some of them with an
acorn symbol (or with a thistle in Scotland). Many
shorter routes are marked with coloured arrows by
local authorities or hiking groups. Local councils
generally mark public footpaths with yellow arrows.
Public bridleways, marked by blue arrows, are
paths that can be used by both walkers and horse
riders – remember, horses churn up mud. Signs
appear on posts, trees and stiles.

TIPS FOR WALKERS

Be prepared: The weather can
change very quickly: dress for the
worst. Always take a compass, a
proper walking map and get
local advice before undertaking
any ambitious walking. Pack
some food and drink if the map
does not show a pub en route.
On the walk: Always keep to
the footpath and close gates
behind you. Never feed or upset
farm animals, leave litter, pick
flowers or damage plants.
Where to stay: The International
Youth Hostel Federation (see
pp616–17) has a network of
hostels which cater particularly
for walkers. Bed-and-breakfast
accommodation is also available
near most routes (see p539).
Further information: The
Ramblers' Association (020-7339
8500; www.ramblers.org.uk) is a
national organization for walkers,
with a guide to accommodation.

**The Coast to Coast
Walk** crosses the Lake
District, Yorkshire Dales
and North York Moors,
on a 190 mile (306 km)
route. This demanding
walk covers a spectacular
range of North Country
landscapes. All cross-
country routes are best
walked from west to east
to take advantage of the
prevailing wind.

The Ridgeway is a
fairly easy path that
follows an ancient
track once used by
cattle drovers. Start-
ing near Avebury
(see p251) it covers
85 miles (137 km) to
Ivinghoe Beacon.

**Peddars Way and the Norfolk
Coast Path** together make 94 miles
(151 km) of easy lowland walking,
from Thetford, north to
the coast then east
to Cromer.

Icknield Way, the
most ancient
prehistoric road in
Britain, is 105 miles
(168 km) long and
links the Ridgeway
to Peddars Way.

The Thames Path
follows the river
for 213 miles (341
km) from central
London to Kemble,
its source in
Gloucestershire.

The South Downs Way is a
varied 101 mile (162 km) walk
from Eastbourne on the south
coast to Winchester (see p158–9).
It can be completed in a week.

The Isle of Wight Coastal Path
circles the entire island on an
easy 65 mile (105 km) footpath.

The North Downs Way is an
ancient route through 141 miles
(227 km) of low-lying hills from
Farnham in Surrey to Dover or
Folkestone in Kent.

Kirk Yetholm
Windermere
Ilkley
Robin Hood's Bay
Edale
Kemble
Chepstow
Avebury
Farnham
Winchester
Poole Harbour
Ivinghoe
London
Dover
Eastbourne
Sheringham
Thetford

The Traditional British Pub

Beer label
c.1900

EVERY COUNTRY HAS ITS BARS, but Britain is famous for its pubs or "public houses". Ale was brewed in England in Roman times – mostly at home – and by the Middle Ages there were inns and taverns which brewed their own. The 18th century was the heyday of the coaching inn as stage coaches brought more custom. In the 19th century came railway taverns for travellers and "gin palaces" for the new industrial workers. Today, pubs come in all styles and sizes and many cater to families, serving food as well as drink (see pp608–11).

Early 19th-century coaching inn – also a social centre and post office

THE VICTORIAN PUB

A century ago, many pubs in towns and cities had smart interiors, to contrast with the poor housing of their clients.

Elaborately etched glass is a feature of many Victorian interiors.

Pub games, *such as cribbage, bar billiards, pool and dominoes are part of British pub culture. Here some regular customers are competing against a rival pub's darts team.*

Beer gardens *outside pubs are a favourite venue for family summer treats.*

Pint glasses (containing just over half a litre) are used for beer.

The Red Lion pub name is derived from Scottish heraldry (see p26).

Old-fashioned cash register contributes to the period atmosphere of the bar.

Pewter tankards, seldom used by drinkers today, add a traditional touch.

WHAT TO DRINK

Draught bitter is the most traditional British beer. Brewed from malted barley, hops, yeast and water, and usually matured in a wooden cask, it varies from region to region. In the north of England the sweeter mild ale is popular, and lagers served in bottles or on tap are also widely drunk. Stout, made from black malt, is another variation.

Beer pump

Draught bitter is drunk at cellar temperature.

Draught lager is a light-coloured, carbonated beer.

Guinness is a thick, creamy Irish stout.

Pavement tables, crowded with city drinkers during the summer months

A village pub, offering a waterside view and serving drinks in the garden

Bottles of spirits, as well as the popular port and sherry, are ranged behind the bar.

Glass lamps imitate the Victorian style.

Wine, once rarely found in pubs, is now increasingly popular.

A deep-toned mahogany bar forms part of the traditional setting.

Draught beer, served from pumps or taps, comes from national and local brewers.

Optics dispense spirits in precise measures.

Mild may be served by the pint or in a half-pint tankard (as above).

Top cocktails are gin-and-tonic (right) and Pimm's.

Pub Signs

Early medieval inns used vines or evergreens as signs – the symbol of Bacchus, the Roman god of wine. Soon pubs acquired names that signalled support for monarchs, or noblemen, or celebrated victories in battle. As many customers could not read, pub signs had vivid images.

The George may derive from one of the six English kings of that name, or, as here, from England's patron saint.

The Bat and Ball celebrates cricket, and may be sited near a village green where the game can be played.

The Green Man is a woodland spirit from pagan mythology, possibly the basis for the legend of Robin Hood (see p324).

The Magna Carta sign commemorates and illustrates the "great charter" signed by King John in 1215 (see p48).

The Bird in Hand refers to the ancient country sport of falconry, traditionally practised by noblemen.

A Flavour of British Food

BRITAIN'S UNIQUE contributions to gastronomy include its cooked breakfasts, afternoon teas and satisfying puddings. Fast food and take-aways were pioneered here with fish and chips, the sandwich and the Cornish pasty. Modern British cuisine is innovative and varied, but it is also worth seeking out traditional dishes which use first-rate ingredients: beef, lamb and game figure prominently. As an island, Britain has historically been a fish-eating nation, although shellfish, once cheap, has become pricier.

Fish and chips (French fries) are made from white sea fish, batter-coated and fried in oil, with chipped potatoes, salt and vinegar.

A full English breakfast can include fried bacon and egg, mushrooms, sausage, tomatoes, fried bread and black pudding.

Cockles and whelks remain cheap compared with larger shellfish. They are sold from small stalls outside pubs, and can be awkward to eat.

Laverbread is a Welsh speciality made from dark-coloured seaweed. It is served cold with seafood, or, as here, hot with bacon, toast and tomato.

Cornish pasties are filled with meat and vegetables baked in a pastry crust. They originated as a handy way for farm labourers to take their lunch to work.

TEA TIME

Afternoon tea, taken at around 4pm, is a British tradition enacted in tea-shops and grand hotels. The tea is usually from India or Sri Lanka, served with optional milk and sugar; but it could be scented China or herbal tea served with or without lemon. Small, delicately cut sandwiches are eaten first: cucumber is a traditional filling. These may be followed by scones, jam and cream, especially in the west of England *(see p275)*. Other options include buttered toast or crumpets, but leave room for a slice of fruit cake or jam sponge, a chocolate éclair or a regional speciality such as Scottish shortbread.

Eccles cake

Bakewell tart

Barra brith or Welsh tea bread

Welsh cakes

Ginger cake

Victoria sponge

Cucumber sandwiches

Ceylon tea

Lapsang Souchong tea

Ploughman's lunch is served in many pubs. It consists of bread, cheese (often Cheddar), and pickles, garnished with salad. Ham or pâté may be substituted for cheese.

Horseradish sauce

Gravy

Roast beef

Yorkshire pudding

Broccoli

Roast potatoes

Shepherd's pie is made from minced lamb baked with a potato topping. If minced (ground) beef is used, the dish is called cottage pie.

Roast beef is Britain's traditional Sunday lunch. It usually comes with Yorkshire pudding (savoury batter baked with the meat), roast potatoes and seasonal vegetables. A rich gravy enhances the flavour, and horseradish sauce is a favourite relish.

Dover sole is Britain's most prized flat fish. Served on the bone or filleted, it is firm fleshed and delicately flavoured.

Cumberland sausage, a regional speciality, is in a coil. Sausages and mashed potatoes are called "bangers and mash".

Steak and kidney pie is beef and kidney in thick gravy baked in pastry or in a suet crust, when it is known as a pudding.

Strawberries and cream are the delight of early summer, associated with outdoor social occasions of all types. Later, raspberries come into season. Both fruits make excellent jam.

Cheese is often served to finish lunch and dinner. Mature Cheddar is one of the most popular regional varieties. Blue-veined cheeses such as Stilton are an acquired taste.

Stilton

Cheddar

Treacle pudding is a steamed sponge pudding, topped with syrup and served with custard. It is a popular dessert in winter.

Cornish Yarg

Sage Derby

Sherry trifle was originally sponge cake soaked in sweet sherry and served with custard. Modern versions may include sponge fingers covered with fruit, jelly and a layer of cream, and decorated with angelica and cherries.

Cheshire

Red Leicester

THE HISTORY OF GREAT BRITAIN

BRITAIN BEGAN TO assume a cohesive character as early as the 7th century, with the Anglo-Saxon tribes absorbing Celtic and Roman influences and finally achieving supremacy. They suffered repeated Viking incursions and were overcome by the Normans at the Battle of Hastings in 1066. Over centuries, the disparate cultures of the Normans and Anglo-Saxons combined to form the English nation, a process nurtured by Britain's position as an island. The next 400 years saw English kings involved in military expeditions to Europe, but their control over these areas was gradually wrested from them. As a result they extended their domain over Scotland and Wales. The Tudor monarchs consolidated this control and laid the foundations for Britain's future commercial success. Henry VIII recognized the vital importance of sea power and under his daughter, Elizabeth I, English sailors ranged far across the world, often coming into conflict with the Spanish. The total defeat of the Spanish Armada in 1588 confirmed Britain's position as a major maritime power. The Stuart period saw a number of internal struggles, most importantly the Civil War in 1641. But by the time of the Act of the Union in 1707 the whole island was united and the foundations for representative government had been laid. The combination of this internal security with continuing maritime strength allowed Britain to seek wealth overseas. By the end of the Napoleonic Wars in 1815, Britain was the leading trading nation in the world. The opportunities offered by industrialization were seized, and by the late 19th century, a colossal empire had been established across the globe. Challenged by Europe and the rise of the US, and drained by its leading role in two world wars, Britain's influence waned after 1945. By the 1970s almost all the colonies had become independent Commonwealth nations.

Medieval knights, masters of the arts of war

Contemporary map showing the defeat of the Armada (1588), making Britain into a world power

◁ **Henry VIII, founder of the British navy, seen here with his children Edward and Mary**

Kings and Queens

ALL ENGLISH MONARCHS since the Norman Conquest in 1066 have been descendants of William the Conqueror. Scottish rulers, until James VI and the Union of Crowns in 1603 (see pp468–9), have been more diverse. When the Crown passes to someone other than the monarch's eldest son, the name of the ruling family usually changes. The rules of succession have been precisely laid down and strongly favour men over women, but Britain has still had six queens since 1553. In Norman times the monarchy enjoyed absolute power, but today the position is largely symbolic.

1413–22 Henry V

1509–47 Henry VIII

1399–1413 Henry IV

1485–1509 Henry VII

1066–87 William the Conqueror

1087–1100 William II

1100–35 Henry I

1135–54 Stephen

1327–77 Edward III

1483–5 Richard III

1050	1100	1150	1200	1250	1300	1350	1400	1450	1500
NORMAN		**PLANTAGENET**					**LANCASTER**	**YORK**	**TUDOR**
1050	1100	1150	1200	1250	1300	1350	1400	1450	1500

1154–89 Henry II

1189–99 Richard I

1199–1216 John

1216–72 Henry III

1307–27 Edward II

1272–1307 Edward I

1422–61 and 1470–1 Henry VI

1461–70 and 1471–83 Edward IV

1377–99 Richard II

Matthew Paris's 13th-century chronicle showing clockwise from top left, Richard I, Henry II, John and Henry III

1483 Edward V

1553–8 Mary I

1660–85 Charles II

1685–8 James II

1689–1702 William III and Mary II

1702–14 Anne

1714–27 George I

1936 Edward VIII

1603–25 James I

1837–1901 Victoria

1901–10 Edward VII

1727–60 George II

1952– Elizabeth II

1550	1600	1650	1700	1750	1800	1850	1900	1950	2000
	STUART			HANOVER		SAXE-COBURG		WINDSOR	
1550	1600	1650	1700	1750	1800	1850	1900	1950	2000

1649–60 Commonwealth under Lord Protector Oliver Cromwell

1830–37 William IV

1936–52 George VI shown on the George Medal

1820–30 George IV

1910–36 George V

1625–49 Charles I

1558–1603 Elizabeth I

1547–53 Edward VI

1760–1820 George III

Prehistoric Britain

BRITAIN WAS PART of the European landmass until the end of the last Ice Age, around 6000 BC, when the English Channel was formed by melting ice. The earliest inhabitants lived in limestone caves: settlements and farming skills developed gradually through the Stone Age. The magnificent wooden and stone henges and circles are masterworks from around 3000 BC, but their significance is a mystery. Flint mines and ancient pathways are evidence of early trading and many burial mounds (barrows) survive from the Stone and Bronze Ages.

Axe Heads
Stone axes, like this one found at Stonehenge, were used by Neolithic men.

Cup and ring marks
were carved on standing stones, such as this one at Ballymeanoch.

MAPPING THE PAST

Monuments from the Neolithic (New Stone), Bronze and Iron Ages, together with artifacts found from these periods, provide a wealth of information about Britain's early settlers, before written history began with the Romans.

Neolithic Tools
Antlers and bones were made into Neolithic leather-working tools. These were found at Avebury (see p251).

(see p251)

Pottery Beaker
The Beaker People, who came from Europe in the early Bronze Age, take their name from these drinking cups often found in their graves.

Gold Breast Plate
Made by Wessex goldsmiths, its spectacular pattern suggests it belonged to an important chieftain.

Pentre Ifan, an impressive Neolithic burial chamber in South Wales, was once covered with a huge earth mound.

Mold Cape
Gold was mined in Wales and Cornwall in the Bronze Age. This intricately worked warrior's cape was buried in a grave at Mold, Clwyd.

This gold cup,
found in a Cornish barrow, is evidence of the wealth of Bronze Age tribes.

TIMELINE

6000–5000 As the Ice Age comes to an end, sea levels rise, submerging the land-link between Britain and the Continent

Neolithic flint axes

6000 BC	5500 BC	5000 BC	4500 BC	4000 BC

A gold pendant and button (1700 BC), found in Bronze Age graves

3500 Neolithic Age begins. Long barrows and stone circles built around Britain

Skara Brae is a Neolithic village of about 2500 BC (see p514).

Maiden Castle
An impressive Iron Age hill fort in Dorset, its concentric lines of ramparts and ditches follow the contours of the hill top (see p257).

Iron Age Brochs, round towers with thick stone walls, are found only in Scotland.

Iron Age Axe
The technique of smelting iron came to Britain around 700 BC, brought from Europe by the Celts.

Castlerigg Stone Circle is one of Britain's earliest Neolithic monuments (see p349).

Uffington White Horse
Thought to be 3,000 years old, the shape has to be "scoured" to keep grass at bay (see p209).

A chalk figure, thought to be a fertility goddess, was found at Grimes Graves (see p182).

This bronze Celtic helmet (50 BC) was found in the River Thames, London.

Stonehenge was begun around 3,500 years ago (see pp250–51).

WHERE TO SEE PREHISTORIC BRITAIN

Wiltshire, with Stonehenge (p250) and Avebury (p251), has the best group of Neolithic monuments, and the Uffington White Horse is nearby (p209). The Scottish islands have many early sites and the British Museum (pp108–9) houses a huge collection of artefacts.

A circular bank with over 180 stones encloses the Neolithic site at Avebury (see p251).

Snettisham Torc
A torc was a neck ring worn by Celtic men. This one, found in Norfolk, dates from 50 BC and is made from silver and gold.

3000 BC	2500 BC	2000 BC	1500 BC	1000 BC	500 BC
2500 Temples, or henges, are built of wood or stone	**1650–1200** Wessex is at the hub of trading routes between Europe and the mines of Cornwall, Wales and Ireland		**1000** First farmsteads are settled	**550–350** Migration of Celtic people from southern Europe	**500** Iron Age begins. Hill forts are built
	2100–1650 The Bronze Age reaches Britain. Immigration of the Beaker People, who make bronze implements and build ritual temples		*Chieftain's bronze sceptre (1700 BC)* **1200** Small, self-sufficient villages start to appear		**150** Tribes from Gaul begin to migrate to Britain

Roman Britain

Tʜʀᴏᴜɢʜᴏᴜᴛ the 350-year Roman occupation, Britain was ruled as a colony. After the defeat of rebellious local tribes, such as Boadicea's Iceni, the Romans remained an unassimilated occupying power. Their legacy is in military and civil construction: forts, walls, towns and public buildings. Their long, straight roads, built for easy movement of troops, are still a feature of the landscape.

Roman jasper seal

Cavalry Sports Helmet
Found in Lancashire, it was used in tournaments by horsemen. Cavalry races and other sports were held in amphitheatres near towns.

Silver Jug
This 3rd-century jug, the earliest known silver item with Christian symbols, was excavated near Peterborough.

Exercise corridor

Main baths

Fishbourne Palace was built at the site of a natural harbour and ships could moor here.

Entrance hall

Hadrian's Wall
Started in 120 as a defence against the Scots; it marked the northern frontier of the Roman Empire and was guarded by 17 forts housing over 18,500 foot-soldiers and cavalry.

Mithras
This head of the god Mithras was found on the London site of a temple devoted to the cult of Mithraism. The sect demanded of its Roman followers loyalty and discipline.

TIMELINE

54 BC Julius Caesar lands in Britain but withdraws

Julius Caesar (c.102–44 BC)

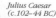

AD 61 Boadicea rebels against Romans and burns their towns, including St Albans and Colchester, but is defeated *(see p183)*

AD 70 Romans conquer Wales and the North

Boadicea (1st century), Queen of the Iceni

140–143 Romans occupy southern Scotland and build Antonine Wall to mark the frontier

55 BC	AD 1	AD 50		150

AD 43 Claudius invades; Britain then becomes part of the Roman Empire

AD 78–84 Agricola advances into Scotland, then retreats

120 Emperor Hadrian builds a wall on the border with Scotland

Flavian Mosaic
Roman floors of the 1st century used patterns in black and white stone. More mosaics survive at Fishbourne than at any other British site.

Courtyard

Guest apartment

Guest bathroom

Box hedges

Aisled hall

WHERE TO SEE ROMAN BRITAIN

Many of Britain's main towns and cities were established by the Romans and have Roman remains, including York *(see pp390–95)*, Chester *(see pp298–9)*, St Albans *(see p220)*, Colchester *(see p193)*, Bath *(see pp246–9)*, Lincoln *(see pp328–9)* and London *(see pp70–123)*. Several Roman villas were built in southern England, favoured for its mild climate and proximity to Europe.

The Roman baths in Bath
(see pp246–9), known as Aquae Sulis, were built between the 1st and 4th centuries around a natural hot spring.

Battersea Shield
Found in the Thames near Battersea, the shield bears Celtic symbols and was probably made at about the time of the first Roman invasion. Archaeologists suspect it may have been lost by a warrior while crossing the river, or offered as a sacrifice to one of the many river gods. It is now at the British Museum (see pp108–9).

FISHBOURNE PALACE
Built during the 1st century for Togidubnus, a pro-Roman governor, the palace (here reconstructed) had sophisticated functions such as under-floor heating and indoor plumbing for baths *(see p159)*.

Chi-Rho Symbol
This early Christian symbol is from a 3rd-century fresco at Lullingstone Roman villa in Kent.

---

206 Tribes from northern Scotland attack Hadrian's Wall

254 St Alban is beheaded, and becomes Britain's first Christian martyr

Aberlemno Pictish stone in Scotland

410 Romans withdraw from Britain

| 200 | 250 | 300 | 350 | 400 |

209 Septimius Severus arrives from Rome with reinforcements

306 Roman troops in York declare Constantine emperor

350–69 Border raids by Picts and Scots

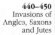

440–450 Invasions of Angles, Saxons and Jutes

Anglo-Saxon Kingdoms

**King Canute
(1016–35)**

B Y THE MID-5TH CENTURY, Angles and Saxons from Germany had started to raid the eastern shores of Britain. Increasingly they decided to settle, and within 100 years Saxon kingdoms, including Wessex, Mercia and Northumbria, were established over the entire country. Viking raids throughout the 8th and 9th centuries were largely contained, but in 1066, the last invasion of England saw William the Conqueror from Normandy defeat the Anglo-Saxon King Harold at the Battle of Hastings. William then went on to assume control of the whole country.

Viking Axe
The principal weapons of the Viking warriors were spear, axe and sword. They were skilled metal-workers with an eye for decoration, as seen in this axe-head from a Copenhagen museum.

Vikings on a Raiding Expedition
Scandinavian boat-building skills were in advance of anything known in Britain. People were terrified by these large, fast boats with their intimidating figureheads, which sailed up the Thames and along the coasts.

ANGLO-SAXON CALENDAR
These scenes from a chronicle of seasons, made just before the Norman invasion, show life in late Anglo-Saxon Britain. At first people lived in small farming communities, but by the 7th century towns began to spring up and trade increased. Saxon kings were supported by nobles but most of the population were free peasants.

TIMELINE

c.470–495
Saxons and Angles settle in Essex, Sussex and East Anglia

c.556 Saxons move across Britain and set up seven kingdoms

St Augustine (d.604)

635 St Aidan establishes a monastery on Lindisfarne

730–821
Supremacy of Mercia, whose king, Offa (d.796), builds a dyke along the Mercia–Wales border

450	500	550	600	650	700	750

450 Saxons first settle in Kent

563 St Columba lands on Iona

617–85 Supremacy of Northumbrian kingdom

597 St Augustine sent by Rome to convert English to Christianity

Mercian coin which bears the name of King Offa

Ox-drawn plough for tilling

Alfred Jewel
This 9th-century gold ornament in the Ashmolean Museum (see p212) has the inscription: "Alfred ordered me made". This may refer to the Saxon King Alfred.

WHERE TO SEE ANGLO-SAXON BRITAIN

The best collection of Saxon artefacts is from a burial ship unearthed at Sutton Hoo in Suffolk in 1938 and now on display at the British Museum *(see pp108–9)*. There are fine Saxon churches at Bradwell in Essex and Bosham in Sussex *(see p159)*. In York the Viking town of Jorvik has been excavated *(see p394)* and actual relics are shown alongside models of people and dwellings.

The Saxon church of St Laurence (see p243) was built in the late 8th century.

Minstrels entertaining at a feast

Edward the Confessor
In 1042, Edward – known as "the Confessor" because of his piety – became king. He died in 1066 and William of Normandy claimed the throne.

Hawks, used to kill game

Harold's Death
This 14th-century illustration depicts the victorious William of Normandy after King Harold was killed with an arrow in his eye. The Battle of Hastings (see p169) was the last invasion of Britain.

Legend of King Arthur
Arthur is thought to have been a chieftain who fought the Saxons in the early 6th century. Legends of his knights' exploits appeared in 1155 (see p273).

802–839 After the death of Cenwulf (821), Wessex gains control over most of England

867 Northumbria falls to the Vikings

An invading Norman ship

878 King Alfred defeats Vikings but allows them to settle in eastern England

1016 Danish King Canute *(see p159)* seizes English crown

800	850	900	950	1000	1050	1100

843 Kenneth McAlpin becomes king of all Scotland

c.793 Lindisfarne sacked by Viking invaders; first Viking raid on Scotland about a year later

926 Eastern England, the Danelaw, is reconquered by the Saxons

1042 The Anglo-Saxon Edward the Confessor becomes king (d.1066)

1066 William of Normandy claims the throne, and defeats Harold at the Battle of Hastings. He is crowned at Westminster

The Middle Ages

Noblemen stag hunting

REMAINS OF Norman castles on English hill tops bear testimony to the military might used by the invaders to sustain their conquest – although Wales and Scotland resisted for centuries. The Normans operated a feudal system, creating an aristo-cracy that treated native Anglo-Saxons as serfs. The ruling class spoke French until the 13th century, when it mixed with the Old English used by the peasants. The medieval church's power is shown in the cathedrals that grace British cities today.

Magna Carta
To protect themselves and the church from arbitrary taxation, the powerful English barons compelled King John to sign a "great charter" in 1215 (see p223). This laid the foundations for an inde-pendent legal system.

Craft Skills
An illustration from a 14th-century manuscript depicts a weaver and a copper-beater – two of the trades that created a wealthy class of artisans.

Becket is received into heaven.

Henry II's knights murder Becket in Canterbury Cathedral.

MURDER OF THOMAS À BECKET
The struggle between church and king for ultimate control of the country was brought to a head by the murder of Becket, the Archbishop of Canterbury. After Becket's canonization in 1173, Canterbury became a major centre of pilgrimage.

Ecclesiastical Art
Nearly all medieval art had religious themes, such as this window at Canterbury Cathedral (see pp174–5) depicting Jeroboam.

Black Death
A plague swept Britain and Europe several times in the 14th century, killing mil-lions of people. This illustration, in a religious tract, produced around 100 years later, represents death taking its heavy toll.

TIMELINE

1071 Hereward the Wake, leader of the Anglo-Saxon resistance, defeated at Ely

1154 Henry II, the first Plantagenet king, demolishes castles, and exacts money from barons instead of military service

1170 Archbishop of Canterbury, Thomas à Becket, is murdered by four knights after quar-relling with Henry II

| 1100 | 1150 | 1200 | 1250 |

1086 The *Domesday Book*, a survey of every manor in England, is compiled for tax purposes

Domesday Book

1215 Barons compel King John to sign the *Magna Carta*

1256 First Parliament to include ordinary citizens

Battle of Agincourt

In 1415, Henry V took an army to France to claim its throne. This 15th-century chronicle depicts Henry beating the French army at Agincourt.

This casket (1190), in a private collection, is said to have contained Becket's remains.

Becket takes his place in Heaven after his canonization.

Two clergymen look on in horror at Becket's murder.

Richard III

Richard, shown in this 16th-century painting, became king during the Wars of the Roses: a bitter struggle for power between two factions of the royal family – the houses of York and Lancaster.

John Wycliffe *(1329–84)*

This painting by Ford Madox Brown (1821–93) shows Wycliffe with the Bible he translated into English to make it accessible to everyone.

WHERE TO SEE MEDIEVAL BRITAIN

The university cities of Oxford *(pp210–15)* and Cambridge *(pp198–203)* contain the largest concentrations of Gothic buildings. Magnificent cathedrals rise high above many historic cities, among them Lincoln *(pp328–9)* and York *(pp390–95)*. Both cities still retain at least part of their ancient street pattern. Military architecture is best seen in Wales *(pp424–5)* with the formidable border castles of Edward I.

All Souls College *in Oxford (see p214), which only takes graduates, is a superb blend of medieval and later architecture.*

Castle Life

Every section of a castle was allotted to a baron whose soldiers helped defend it. This 14th-century illustration shows the coats of arms (see p26) of the barons for each area.

1282–3 Edward I conquers Wales	**1314** Scots defeat English at the Battle of Bannockburn *(see p468)*	**1387** Chaucer starts writing the *Canterbury Tales* *(see p174)*		**1485** Battle of Bosworth ends Wars of the Roses
	1348 Europe's population halved by Black Death			*Geoffrey Chaucer (c.1345–1400)*

1300 | **1350** | **1400** | **1450**

1296 Edward I invades Scotland but Scots resist stoutly

Edward I (1239–1307)

1381 Peasants' revolt after the imposition of a poll tax on everyone in the country over 14

1415 English victory at Agincourt

1453 End of Hundred Years' War against France

Tudor Renaissance

Hawking, a popular pastime

AFTER YEARS OF DEBILITATING civil war, the Tudor monarchs established peace and national self-confidence, reflected in the split from the church of Rome – due to Henry VIII's divorce from Catherine of Aragon – and the consequent closure of the monasteries. Henry's daughter, Mary I, tried to re-establish Catholicism but under her half-sister, Elizabeth I, the Protestant church secured its position. Overseas exploration began, provoking clashes with other European powers seeking to exploit the New World. The Renaissance in arts and learning spread from Europe to Britain, with playwright William Shakespeare adding his own unique contribution.

Curtains behind the queen are open to reveal scenes of the great English victory over the Spanish Armada in 1588.

Sea Power
Henry VIII laid the foundations of the powerful English navy. In 1545, his flagship, the Mary Rose *(see p157), sank before his eyes in Portsmouth harbour on its way to do battle with the French.*

Theatre
Some of Shakespeare's plays were first seen in purpose-built theatres such as the Globe (see p122) in south London.

The globe signifies that the queen reigns supreme far and wide.

Monasteries
With Henry VIII's split from Rome, England's religious houses, like Fountains Abbey (see pp376–7), were dissolved. Henry stole their riches and used them to finance his foreign policy.

TIMELINE

1497 John Colet denounces the corruption of the clergy, supported by Erasmus and Sir Thomas More

1533–4 Henry VIII divorces Catherine of Aragon and is excommunicated by the Pope. He forms the Church of England

1542–1567 Mary, Queen of Scots rules Scotland

1490	1510	1530

1497 John Cabot *(see p244)* makes his first voyage to North America

1513 English defeat Scots at Flodden *(see p468)*

1535 Act of Union with Wales

1536–40 Dissolution of the Monasteries

1549 First Book of Common Prayer introduced

Henry VIII (1491–1547)

Mary, Queen of Scots
As great-granddaughter of Henry VII, she laid claim to the English throne in 1559. But in 1567, Elizabeth I had her imprisoned for 20 years until her execution for treason in 1587.

Jewels symbolize triumph.

DEFEAT OF THE ARMADA
Spain was England's main rival for supremacy on the seas, and in 1588 Philip II sent 100 powerfully armed galleons towards England, bent on invasion. The English fleet – under Lord Howard, Francis Drake, John Hawkins and Martin Frobisher – sailed from Plymouth and destroyed the Spanish navy in a famous victory. This commemorative portrait of Elizabeth I by George Gower (d.1596) celebrates the triumph.

WHERE TO SEE TUDOR BRITAIN

Hampton Court Palace *(p161)* has been altered over the centuries but remains a Tudor showpiece. Part of Elizabeth I's former home at Hatfield *(p219)* still survives. In Kent, Leeds Castle, Knole *(pp176–7)* and Hever Castle *(p177)* all have connections with Tudor royalty. Burghley House *(pp330–31)* and Hardwick Hall *(p290)*, both Midlands mansions, retain their 16th-century character.

This astronomical clock
at Hampton Court (see p161), with its intriguing zodiac symbols, was installed in 1540 by Henry VIII.

Protestant Martyrs
Catholic Mary I reigned from 1553 to 1558. Protestants who opposed her rule were burned, such as these six churchmen at Canterbury in 1555.

William Shakespeare (1564–1616)

1570 Sir Francis Drake's first voyage to the West Indies

1584 Sir Walter Raleigh tries to colonize Virginia after Drake's first unsuccessful attempt

1591 First play by Shakespeare performed

1600 East India Company founded, beginning British involvement on the Indian continent

1550 | **1570** | **1590**

1553 Death of Edward VI; throne passes to the Catholic Mary I

1559 Mary, Queen of Scots lays claim to English throne

1558 Elizabeth I ascends the throne

1587 Execution of Mary, Queen of Scots on the orders of Elizabeth I

1588 Defeat of the Spanish Armada

Sir Walter Raleigh (1552–1618)

1603 Union of Crowns. James VI of Scotland becomes James I of England

Stuart Britain

THE END of Elizabeth I's reign signalled the start of internal turmoil. The throne passed to James I, whose belief that kings ruled by divine right provoked clashes with Parliament. Under his son, Charles I, the conflict escalated into Civil War that ended with his execution. In 1660 Charles II regained the throne, but after his death James II was ousted for Catholic leanings. Protestantism was reaffirmed with the reign of William and Mary, who suppressed the Catholic Jacobites *(see p469).*

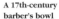

A 17th-century barber's bowl

Science

Sir Isaac Newton (1642–1727) invented this reflecting telescope, laying the foundation for a greater understanding of the universe, including the law of gravity.

Charles I stayed silent at his trial.

Oliver Cromwell

A strict Protestant and a passionate champion of the rights of Parliament, he led the victorious Parliamentary forces in the Civil War. He became Lord Protector of the Commonwealth from 1653 to 1658.

On the way to his death, the king wore two shirts for warmth, so onlookers should not think he was shivering with fright.

Theatre

After the Restoration in 1660, when Parliament restored the monarchy, theatre thrived. Plays were performed on temporary outdoor stages.

EXECUTION OF CHARLES I

Cromwell was convinced there would be no peace until the king was dead. At his trial for treason, Charles refused to recognize the authority of the court and offered no defence. He faced his death with dignity on 30 January 1649, the only English king to be executed. His death was followed by a republic known as the Commonwealth.

TIMELINE

1605 "Gunpowder Plot" to blow up Parliament thwarted	**1614** "Addled Parliament" refuses to vote money for James I	**1620** Pilgrim Fathers sail in the *Mayflower* to New England	**1642** Civil War breaks out	**1653–8** Cromwell rules as Lord Protector
	1625			**1650**
James I (1566–1625)	**1611** New translation of Bible published, known as King James Version	**1638** Scots sign National Covenant, opposing Charles I's Catholic leanings	**1649** Charles I executed outside Banqueting House and Commonwealth declared by Parliament	**1660** Restoration of the monarchy under Charles II

Restoration of the Monarchy

This silk embroidery celebrates the fact that Charles II escaped his father's fate by hiding in an oak tree. There was joy at his return from exile in France.

WHERE TO SEE STUART BRITAIN

The best work of the two leading architects of the time, Inigo Jones and Christopher Wren, is in London, and includes St Paul's Cathedral *(pp116–17)*. In the southeast two classic Jacobean mansions are Audley End *(p196)* and Hatfield House *(p219)*. The Palace of Holyrood *(p496)*, in Edinburgh, is another example.

The headless body kneels by the block.

The axeman holds the severed head of Charles I.

Plague

Bills of mortality showed the weekly deaths as bubonic plague swept London in 1665. Up to 100,000 Londoners died.

Hatfield House (p219) *is a splendid Jacobean mansion.*

Onlookers soaked up the king's blood with their handkerchiefs to have a memento.

Anatomy

By dissecting corpses, physicians began to gain an understanding of the working of the human body – a crucial step towards modern surgery and medicine.

Pilgrim Fathers

In 1620 a group of Puritans sailed to America. They forged good relations with the native Indians; here they are shown being visited by the chief of the Pokanokets.

1665–6 Great Plague

The Great Fire of London

1666 Great Fire of London

1688 The Glorious Revolution: Catholic James II deposed by Parliament

1707 Act of Union with Scotland

1675

1700

1690 Battle of the Boyne: William's English/Dutch army defeats James II's Irish/French army

1692 Glencoe Massacre of Jacobites (Stuart supporters) by William III's forces

William III (1689–1702)

Georgian Britain

THE 18TH CENTURY saw Britain, now recovered from the trauma of its Civil War, develop as a commercial and industrial powerhouse. London became a centre of banking, and a mercantile and professional class grew up. Continuing supremacy at sea laid the foundations of an empire; steam engines, canals and railways heralded the Industrial Revolution. Growing confidence was reflected in stately architecture and elegant fashions but, as cities became more crowded, conditions for the underclass grew worse.

Actress Sarah Siddons (1785), Gainsborough

Slate became the preferred tile for Georgian buildings. Roofs became less steep to achieve an Italian look.

A row of sash windows is one of the most characteristic features of a Georgian house.

Battle of Bunker Hill
In 1775 American colonists rebelled against British rule. The British won this early battle in Massachusetts, but in 1783 Britain recognized the United States of America.

Oak was used in the best dwellings for doors and stairs, but pine was standard in most houses.

The saloon was covered in wallpaper, a cheaper alternative to hanging walls with tapestries or fabrics.

The drawing room was richly ornamented and used for entertaining visitors.

The dining room was used for all family meals.

Watt's Steam Engine
The Scottish engineer James Watt (1736–1819) patented his engine in 1769 and then developed it for locomotion.

Lord Horatio Nelson
Nelson (see p27) became a hero after his death at the Battle of Trafalgar fighting the French.

Steps led to the servants' entrance in the basement.

TIMELINE

1720 "South Sea Bubble" bursts: many speculators ruined in securities fraud

The Dutch Bubblers

1746 Bonnie Prince Charlie *(see p521),* Jacobite claimant to throne, defeated at the Battle of Culloden

	1715		1730		1745		1760

1714 George, Elector of Hanover, succeeds Queen Anne, ending the Stuart dynasty and giving Britain a German-speaking monarch

George I (1660–1727)

1721 Robert Walpole (1646–1745) becomes the first Prime Minister

Satirical engraving about the South Sea Bubble, 1720

1757 Britain's first canal completed

The attics were where children and servants slept.

The master bedroom often had a mahogany four-poster bed.

Furniture was often carved, depicting animal heads and legs.

GEORGIAN TOWN HOUSE

Tall, terraced dwellings were built to house wealthy families. The main architects of the time were Robert Adam *(see p24)* and John Nash *(see p107)*.

The servants lived and worked in the basement during the day.

Kitchen

Canal Barge *(1827)*
Canals were a cheap way to carry the new industrial goods but were gradually superseded by railways during the 19th century.

Chippendale Armchair *(1760)*
Thomas Chippendale (1718–79) designed elegant furniture in a style still popular today.

WHERE TO SEE GEORGIAN BRITAIN

Bath *(see pp246–9)* and Edinburgh *(see pp490–7)* are two of Britain's best-preserved Georgian towns. The Building of Bath Museum in Bath *(see p249)* has a real Georgian flavour and Brighton's Royal Pavilion *(see pp166–7)* is a Regency extravaganza by John Nash.

Charlotte Square (see p490) in Edinburgh has fine examples of Georgian architecture.

Hogarth's Gin Lane
Conditions in London's slums shocked William Hogarth (1697–1764), who made prints like this to urge social reform.

1776 American Declaration of Independence

1788 First convict ships are sent to Australia

1805 The British, led by Lord Nelson, beat Napoleon's French fleet at Battle of Trafalgar

1811–17 Riots against growing unemployment

1815 Duke of Wellington beats Napoleon at Waterloo

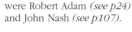

Caricature of Wellington (1769–1852)

| 1775 | 1790 | 1805 | 1820 |

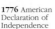
Silver tureen, 1774

1783 Steam-powered cotton mill invented by Sir Richard Arkwright (1732–92)

1807 Abolition of slave trade

1811 Prince of Wales made Regent during George III's madness

1825 Stockton to Darlington railway opens

1829 Catholic Emancipation Act passed

Victorian Britain

WHEN VICTORIA BECAME QUEEN in 1837, she was only 18. Britain was in the throes of its transformation from an agricultural country to the world's most powerful industrial nation. The growth of the Empire fuelled the country's confidence and opened up markets for Britain's manufactured goods. The accelerating growth of cities created problems of health and housing and a powerful Labour movement began to emerge. But by the end of Victoria's long and popular reign in 1901, conditions had begun to improve as more people got the vote and universal education was introduced.

Victoria and Disraeli, 1887

Florence Nightingale *(1820–1910)*
Known as the Lady with the Lamp, she nursed soldiers in the Crimean War and pioneered many improvements in army medical care.

Glass walls and ceiling

Prefabricated girders

Newcastle Slum *(1880)*
Rows of cheap houses were built for an influx of workers to the major industrial cities. The awful conditions spread disease and social discontent.

UNITED SOCIETY OF BOILERMAKERS AND IRON AND STEEL SHIPBUILDERS
ESTD 1834

UNITY IS STRENGTH

LONDON DISTRICT COMMITTEE

Union Banner
Trade unions were set up to protect industrial workers against unscrupulous employers.

As well as silk textiles exhibits included carriages, engines, jewels, glass, plants, cutlery and sculptures.

Ophelia by Sir John Everett Millais *(1829–96)*
The Pre-Raphaelite painters chose Romantic themes, reflecting a desire to escape industrial Britain.

TIMELINE

1832 Great Reform Bill extends the vote to all male property owners

1841 London to Brighton railway makes resort accessible

Vase made for the Great Exhibition

1851 Great Exhibition

1867 Second Reform Act gives the vote to all male householders in towns

1830	1840	1850	1860

1834 Tolpuddle Martyrs transported to Australia for forming a union

1833 Factory Act forbids employment of children for more than 48 hours per week

1854–6 Britain victorious against Russia in Crimean War

1863 Opening of the London Underground

Triumph of Steam and Electricity
This picture from the Illustrated London News *(1897) sums up the feeling of optimism engendered by industrial advances.*

Elm trees were incorporated into the building along with sparrows, and sparrow hawks to control them.

WHERE TO SEE VICTORIAN BRITAIN

The industrial cities of the Midlands and the North are built around grandiose civic, commercial and industrial buildings. Notable Victorian monuments include the Manchester Museum of Science and Industry *(p361)* and, in London, the vast Victoria and Albert Museum *(pp100–101).*

The Rotunda, Manchester
is a stately Victorian building.

Cycling Craze
The bicycle, invented in 1865, became immensely popular with young people, as illustrated by this photograph of 1898.

GREAT EXHIBITION OF 1851

The brainchild of Prince Albert, Victoria's consort, the exhibition celebrated industry, technology and the expanding British Empire. It was the biggest of its kind held up till then. Between May and October, six million people visited Joseph Paxton's lavish crystal palace, in London's Hyde Park. Nearly 14,000 exhibitors brought 100,000 exhibits from all over the world. In 1852 it was moved to south London where it burned down in 1936.

1872 The Ballot Act introduces secret voting

1874 Benjamin Disraeli becomes Prime Minister

1884 Telephones introduced

1893 Gladstone's Irish Home Rule Bill defeated

1901 Queen Victoria dies

Cartoon of Gladstone, Vanity Fair *(1869).*

1870   1880   1890   1900

1870 Education Act makes school compulsory for children up to the age of 11

1877 Queen Victoria created Empress of India

Early telephone

1892 First Labour MP elected

1899–1902 Britain defeats South African Dutch settlers in Boer War

Britain from 1900 to 1950

**Playwright
Noel Coward**

WHEN QUEEN VICTORIA'S REIGN ended in 1901, British society threw off many of its 19th-century inhibitions, and an era of gaiety and excitement began. This was interrupted by World War I. The economic troubles that ensued, which culminated in the Depression of the 1930s, brought misery to millions. In 1939 the ambitions of Germany provoked World War II. After emerging victorious from this conflict, Britain embarked on an ambitious programme of social, educational and health reform.

Suffragettes
Women marched and chained themselves to railings in their effort to get the vote; many went to prison. Women over 30 won the vote in 1919.

Welwyn Garden City was based on the Utopian ideals of Sir Ebenezer Howard (1850–1928), founder of the garden city movement.

The Roaring Twenties
Young flappers discarded the rigid social codes of their parents and instead discovered jazz, cocktails and the Charleston.

NEW TOWNS
A string of new towns was created on the outskirts of London, planned to give residents greenery and fresh air. Welwyn Garden City was originally founded in 1919 as a self-contained community, but fast rail links turned it into a base for London commuters.

World War I
British troops in Europe dug into deep trenches protected by barbed wire and machine guns, only metres from the enemy, in a war of attrition that cost the lives of 17 million.

Wireless
Invented by Guglielmo Marconi, radios brought news and entertainment into homes for the first time.

TIMELINE

1903 Suffragette movement founded	**1911** MPs are given a salary for the first time, allowing working men to be elected	**1914–18** World War I	**1924** First Labour government

1905	1910	1915	1920

Henry Asquith (1852–1928), Prime Minister

1908 Asquith's Liberal government introduces old age pensions

1918 Vote given to all women over 30

1922 First national radio service begins

Marching for Jobs
These men were among thousands who marched for their jobs after being put out of work in the 1920s. The stock market crash of 1929 and the ensuing Depression caused even more unemployment.

Garden cities all had trees, ponds and open spaces.

World War II
German night-time air raids targeted transport, military and industrial sites and cities, such as Sheffield, in what was known as the "Blitz".

Cheap housing and the promise of a cleaner environment attracted many people to these new cities.

Family Motoring
By the middle of the century, more families could afford to buy mass-produced automobiles, like the 1950s Hillman Minx pictured in this advertisement.

Modern Homes
Labour-saving devices, such as the vacuum cleaner, invented by William Hoover in 1908, were very popular. This was due to the virtual disappearance of domestic servants, as women took jobs outside the home.

| 1926 General Strike | | 1936 Abdication of Edward VIII | 1944 Education Act: school leaving age raised to 15; grants provided for university students | 1948 National Health Service introduced |
| *Edward VIII (1894–1972) and Wallis Simpson (1896–1986)* | | | | 1947 Independence for India and Pakistan |

| 1925 | 1930 | 1935 | 1940 | 1945 |

| | 1929 Stock market crashes | 1936 First scheduled television service begins | 1939–45 Winston Churchill leads Britain to victory in World War II | 1945 Majority Labour government; nationalization of railways, road haulage, civil aviation, Bank of England, gas, electricity and steel |
| | 1928 Votes for all men and women over 21 | | *Food ration book* | |

Britain Today

WITH THE DEPRIVATIONS of war receding, Britain entered the Swinging Sixties, an explosion of youth culture characterized by the mini-skirt and the emergence of pop groups. The Age of Empire came to an end as most colonies gained independence by the 1970s – although Britain went to war again in 1982 when Argentina sought to annexe the tiny Falkland Islands.

Designer Vivienne Westwood and Naomi Campbell

People were on the move; immigration from the former colonies enriched British culture – though it also gave rise to social problems – and increasing prosperity allowed millions of people to travel abroad. Britain joined the European Community in 1973, and forged a more tangible link when the Channel Tunnel opened in 1994.

1960s The mini-skirt takes British fashion to new heights of daring – and Flower Power arrives from California

1951 Winston Churchill comes back as Prime Minister as Conservatives win general election

1958 Campaign for Nuclear Disarmament launched, reflecting young people's fear of global annihilation

1965 Death penalty is abolished

1950	1955	1960	1965	1970
1950	1955	1960	1965	1970

1953 Elizabeth II crowned in first televised Coronation

1963 The Beatles pop group from Liverpool captures the spirit of the age with numerous chart-topping hits

1959 First motorway, the M1, built from London to the Midlands

1957 First immigrants arrive from the Caribbean by boat

1951 Festival of Britain lifts postwar spirits

VOTE!

...GET BRITAIN OUT

1973 After years of negotiation, Britain joins the European Community

1970s The outlandish clothes, hair and make-up of Punk Rockers shock the country

1990 Mrs Thatcher forced to resign by Conservative MPs; replaced by John Major

1991 Britain's tallest building, Canada Tower *(see p133)*, erected as part of the huge Docklands development – London's new financial centre

1982 British troops set sail to drive the Argentinians from the British-owned Falkland Islands

1992 Conservative Government elected for fourth term – a record for this century

1997 New Labour ends 18 years of Conservative government

1976 Supersonic Concorde makes first commercial flight

1984 Year-long miners' strike fails to stop pit closures and heralds decline in trade union power

1975	1980	1985	1990	1995	2000

1975	1980	1985	1990	1995	2000

1981 Charles, Prince of Wales, marries Lady Diana Spencer in "fairytale" wedding at St Paul's Cathedral

1999 Formation of Scottish Parliament and Welsh Assembly

1975 Drilling begins for North Sea oil

1979 The "Iron Lady" Margaret Thatcher becomes Britain's first woman Prime Minister; her right-wing Conservative Government privatizes several state-owned industries

1985 Concern for famine in Africa gives rise to giant Live Aid pop concert to raise money for the starving

1994 Channel Tunnel opens to give direct rail link between Britain and Continental Europe

GREAT BRITAIN
THROUGH THE YEAR

Film festival sign

EVERY BRITISH SEASON has its particular charms. Most major sights are open all year round, but many secondary attractions may be closed in winter. The weather is changeable in all seasons and the visitor is as likely to experience a crisp, sunny February day as to be caught in a cold, heavy shower in July. Long periods of adverse weather and extremes of temperature are rare. Spring is characterized by daffodils and bluebells, summer by roses and autumn by the vivid colours of changing leaves. In wintertime, country vistas are visible through the bare branches of the trees. Annual events and ceremonies, many stemming from age-old traditions, reflect the attributes of the seasons.

Bluebells in spring in Angrove woodland, Wiltshire

SPRING

AS THE DAYS get longer and warmer, the countryside starts to come alive. At Easter many stately homes and gardens open their gates to visitors for the first time, and during the week before Whit Sunday, or Whitsun (the seventh Sunday after Easter), the Chelsea Flower Show takes place. This is the focal point of the gardening year and spurs on the nation's gardeners to prepare their summer displays. Outside the capital, many music and arts festivals mark the middle months of the year.

MARCH

Ideal Home Exhibition *(second week)*, Earl's Court, London. New products and ideas for the home.
Crufts Dog Show, National Exhibition Centre, Birmingham.
International Book Fair *(third week)*, Olympia, London.
St Patrick's Day *(17 March)*. Musical events in major cities celebrate the feast day of Ireland's patron saint.

APRIL

Maundy Thursday (Thursday before Easter), the Queen gives money to pensioners.
St George's Day *(23 April)*, English patron saint's day.
Antiques for Everyone *(last week)*, National Exhibition Centre, Birmingham.

Water garden exhibited at the Chelsea Flower Show

MAY

Furry Dancing Festival *(8 May)*, Helston, Cornwall. Spring celebration *(see p268)*.
Well-dressing festivals *(Ascension Day)*, Tissington, Derbyshire *(see p325)*.
Chelsea Flower Show *(May)*, Royal Hospital, London.
Brighton Festival *(last three weeks)*. Performing arts.
Glyndebourne Festival Opera Season *(mid-May–end Aug)*, near Lewes, East Sussex. Opera productions.
International Highland Games *(last weekend)*, Blair Atholl, Scotland.

Yeomen of the Guard conducting the Maundy money ceremony

SUMMER

LIFE MOVES OUTDOORS in the summer months. Cafés and restaurants place tables on the pavements and pub customers take their drinks outside. The Queen holds garden parties for privileged guests at Buckingham Palace while, more modestly, village fêtes – a combination of a carnival and street party – are organized. Beaches and swimming pools become crowded and office workers picnic in city parks at lunch. The rose, England's national flower, bursts into bloom in millions of gardens. Cultural treats include open-air theatre performances, outdoor concerts, the Proms in London, the National Eisteddfod in Wales, Glyndebourne's opera festival, and Edinburgh's festival of the performing arts.

Glastonbury music festival, a major event attracting thousands of people

Deck chair at Brighton

JUNE

Royal Academy Summer Exhibitions *(Jun–Aug)*. Large and varied London show of new work by many artists.
Bath International Festival *(late May–early Jun)*, various venues. Arts events.
Beaumaris Festival *(27 May–4 Jun)*, various venues. Concerts, craft fairs plus fringe activities.
Trooping the Colour *(Sat closest to 10 Jun)*, Whitehall,

London. The Queen's official birthday parade.
Glastonbury Festival *(late June)*, Somerset.
Aldeburgh Festival *(second and third weeks)*, Suffolk. Arts festival with concerts and opera.
Royal Highland Show *(third week)*, Ingliston, near Edinburgh. Scotland's agricultural show.
Leeds Castle *(last week)*. Open-air concerts.
Glasgow International Jazz Festival *(last weekend)*. Various venues.

JULY

Royal Show *(first week)*, near Kenilworth, Warwickshire. National agricultural show.
International Eisteddfod *(first week)*, Llangollen, North Wales. International music and dance competition *(see p436)*.
Hampton Court Flower Show *(early July)*, Hampton Court Palace, Surrey.
Summer Music Festival *(third weekend)*, Stourhead, Wiltshire.
International Henley Royal Regatta *(first week)*, Henley-on-Thames. Rowing regatta on the Thames.
Cambridge Folk Festival *(last weekend)*. Music festival with top international artists.
Royal Welsh Show *(last weekend)*, Builth Wells, Wales. Agricultural show.
International Festival of Folk Arts *(late Jul–early Aug)*, Sidmouth, Devon *(see p277)*.

Assessment of sheep at the Royal Welsh Show, Builth Wells

AUGUST

Royal National Eisteddfod *(early in month)*. Traditional arts competitions, in Welsh *(see p421)*. Various locations.

Reveller in bright costume at the Notting Hill Carnival

Henry Wood Promenade Concerts *(mid-Jul–mid-Sep)*, Royal Albert Hall, London. Famous concert series popularly known as the Proms.
Edinburgh International Festival *(mid-Aug–mid-Sep)*. The largest festival of theatre, dance and music in the world *(see p495)*.
Edinburgh Festival Fringe. Alongside the festival, there are 400 shows a day.
Brecon Jazz *(mid-Aug)*, jazz festival in Brecon, Wales.
Beatles Festival *(last weekend)*, Liverpool. Music and entertainment related to the Fab Four *(see p363)*.
Notting Hill Carnival *(last weekend)*, London. West Indian street carnival with floats, bands and stalls.

Boxes of apples from the autumn harvest

AUTUMN

A FTER THE HEADY escapism of summer, the start of the new season is marked by the various party political conferences held in October and the royal opening of Parliament. All over the country on 5 November, bonfires are lit and fireworks let off to celebrate the foiling of an attempt to blow up the Houses of Parliament by Guy Fawkes and his co-conspirators in 1605. Cornfields become golden, trees turn fiery yellow through to russet and orchards

are heavy with apples and other autumn fruits. In churches throughout the country, thanksgiving festivals mark the harvest. The shops stock up for the run-up to Christmas, their busiest time of the year.

SEPTEMBER

Blackpool Illuminations *(beg Sep–end Oct).* A 5 mile (8 km) spectacle of lighting along Blackpool's seafront.
Royal Highland Gathering *(first Sat),* Braemar, Scotland. Kilted clansmen from all over the country toss cabers, shot putt, dance and play the bagpipes. The royal family usually attends.
International Sheepdog Trials *(14 – 16 Sep),* all over Britain, with venues changing from year to year.
Great Autumn Flower Show *(third weekend),* Harrogate, N Yorks. Displays by nurserymen and national flower organizations.
Oyster Festival *(Sat at beginning of oyster season),* Colchester. Lunch hosted by the mayor to celebrate the beginning of the oyster season.

Shot putting at Braemar

Harvest Festivals *(whole month),* all over Britain especially in farming areas.
Horse of the Year Show *(6–10 Oct),* NEC, Birmingham.
Nottingham Goose Fair *(second weekend).* One of Britain's oldest traditional fairs now has a funfair.
Canterbury Festival *(second and third weeks).* Music, drama and the arts.
Aldeburgh Britten Festival *(third weekend).* Concerts with music by Britten *(see p189)* and other composers.

Procession leading to the state opening of Parliament

NOVEMBER

Opening of Parliament *(Oct or Nov).* The Queen goes from Buckingham Palace to Westminster in a state coach, to open the new parliamentary session.
London Film Festival *(end Oct–beg Nov).* Forum for new films, various venues.
Lord Mayor's Procession and Show *(second Sat).* Parade in the City, London.
Remembrance Day *(second Sun).* Services and parades at the Cenotaph in Whitehall, London, and all over Britain.
RAC London to Brighton Veteran Car Rally *(first Sun).* A 7am start from Hyde Park, London to Brighton, East Sussex.
Guy Fawkes Night *(5 Nov),* fireworks and bonfires all over the country.
Regent Street Christmas Lights *(mid-Nov),* London.

Fireworks over Edinburgh on Guy Fawkes Night

Winter landscape in the Scottish Highlands, near Glencoe

WINTER

BRIGHTLY COLOURED fairy lights and Christmas trees decorate Britain's principal shopping streets as shoppers rush to buy their seasonal gifts. Carol services are held in churches across the country, and pantomime, a traditional entertainment for children deriving from the Victorian music hall, fills theatres in major towns.

Brightly lit Christmas tree at the centre of Trafalgar Square

Many offices close between Christmas and the New Year. Shops reopen for the January sales on 27 December – a paradise for bargain-hunters.

DECEMBER

Christmas Tree *(first Thu)*, Trafalgar Square, London. The tree is donated by the people of Norway and is lit by the Mayor of Oslo; this is followed by carol singing.
Carol concerts *(whole month)*, all over Britain.
Grand Christmas Parade *(beg Dec)*, London. Parade with floats to celebrate myth of Santa Claus.
Midnight Mass *(24 Dec)*, in churches everywhere around Britain.
Allendale Tarbaal Festival *(31 Dec)*, Northumberland. Parade by villagers with burning tar barrels on their heads to celebrate the New Year.

Sprig of holly

JANUARY

Hogmanay and **New Year** *(31 Dec, 1 Jan)*, Scottish celebrations. **Burns Night** *(25 Jan)*. Scots everywhere celebrate poet Robert Burns' birth with poetry, feasting and drinking.

FEBRUARY

Chinese New Year *(late Jan or early Feb)*. Lion dances, firecrackers and processions in Chinatown, London.

PUBLIC HOLIDAYS

New Year's Day (1 Jan).
2 Jan (Scotland only).
Easter weekend (March or April). In England it begins on **Good Friday** and ends on **Easter Monday**; in Scotland there is no Easter Monday holiday.
May Day (usually first Mon in May).
Late Spring Bank Holiday (last Mon in May).
Bank Holiday (first Mon in August, Scotland only).
August Bank Holiday (last Mon in August, except Scotland).
Christmas and Boxing Day (25 26 December).

Morris dancing on May Day in Midhurst, Sussex

The Sporting Year

MANY OF THE WORLD'S major competitive sports, including soccer, cricket and tennis, were invented in Britain. Originally devised as recreation for the wealthy, they have since entered the arena of mass entertainment. Some, however, such as the Royal Ascot race meeting and Wimbledon tennis tournament, are still valued as much for their social prestige as for the sport itself. Other delightful sporting events in Britain take place at a local level: village cricket, point-to-point racing and the Highland Games are all popular amateur events.

Kelly Holmes

Royal Ascot is the four-day social highlight of the horse racing year. The high class of the thoroughbreds is matched by the high style of the fashions, with royalty attending.

Oxford and Cambridge Boat Race, *first held in 1829 at Henley, has become a national event, with the two university eights now battling it out between Putney and Mortlake on the Thames.*

The FA Cup Final is the apex of the football season.

Derby Day horse races, Epsom

January	February	March	April	May	June

Cheltenham Gold Cup steeplechase *(see p316)*

Grand National steeple-chase, Aintree *(see p362)*, Liverpool

Rugby League Cup Final, Wembley

Embassy World Snooker Championships, Sheffield

Wimbledon Lawn Tennis Tournament is the world's most prestigious lawn tennis championship.

Henley Royal Regatta (see p222) is an international rowing event on the Thames (first held in 1839). It is also a glamorous social occasion.

Six Nations Rugby Union *is an annual contest between England, France, Italy, Ireland (left), Scotland (right) and Wales. This league-based competition runs through winter ending in March.*

London Marathon *attracts thousands of long-distance runners, from the world's best to fancy-dressed fund raisers.*

British Grand Prix, held at Silverstone, is Britain's round of the Formula One World Championship.

TICKETS AND TOUTS

For many big sporting events, the only official source of tickets is the club concerned. Booking agencies may offer hard-to-get tickets – though often at high prices. Unauthorized touts may lurk at popular events but their expensive tickets are not always valid. Check carefully.

Tickets for the Grand Prix

British Open Golf Championship, a major golf event, is held at one of several British courses. Here, Nick Faldo putts.

The Cheltenham and Gloucester Trophy is the final of a season of competition to find the year's county cricket champions. It takes place at Lord's (see p129).

Cowes week *(see p156)*, a yachting festival, covers all classes of racing.

Horse of the Year Show brings together top show-jumpers to compete on a tough indoor course *(see p64)*.

Oxford versus Cambridge rugby union, Twickenham

ly	August	September	October	November	December

European Showjumping Championships at Hickstead

Braemar Highland Games *(see p64)*

British Figure Skating and Ice Dance Championships are a feast of elegance on ice (various venues).

Winmau World Masters Darts Championships

Gold Cup Humber powerboat race, Hull

KEY TO SPORT SEASONS

Cricket

River fishing

Football (soccer)

Hunting and shooting

Rugby (union and league)

Flat racing

Jump racing

Athletics – track and field

Road running and cross-country

Polo

Cartier International Polo, at the Guards Club, Windsor (see p223), is one of the main events for this peculiarly British game, played mainly by royalty and army officers.

Steven Cousins

The Climate of Great Britain

BRITAIN HAS A TEMPERATE CLIMATE. No region is far from the sea, which exerts a moderating influence on temperatures. Seldom are winter nights colder than -15°C, even in the far north, or summer days warmer than 30°C in the south and west: a much narrower range than in most European countries. Despite Britain's reputation, the average annual rainfall is quite low – less than 100 cm (40 inches) – and heavy rain is rare. The Atlantic coast is warmed by the Gulf Stream, making the west slightly warmer, though wetter, than the east.

Wick
Inverness
The Highlands and Islands
EDINBURGH
Glasgow
The Lowlands
Lancashire and the Lakes

LANCASHIRE AND THE LAKES

°C/°F

19/66
12/54 13/55 14/57
5/41   8/46 6/43
                    2/36

5.5 hrs	6 hrs	3 hrs	1.5 hrs
53 mm	85 mm	104 mm	90 mm
month	Apr	Jul	Oct	Jan

THE HEART OF ENGLAND

°C/°F

20/68
12/54 13/55 13/55
5/41   8/46 6/43
                    2/36

4.5 hrs	5.5 hrs	3 hrs	1.5 hrs
53 mm	69 mm	69 mm	74 mm
month	Apr	Jul	Oct	Jan

Average monthly maximum temperature

Average monthly minimum temperature

Average daily hours of sunshine

Average monthly rainfall

Liverpool
North Wales
Caernarfon
South and Mid-Wales
CARDIFF
Bris
West Country
Exeter
Devon and Cornwall

SOUTH AND MID-WALES

°C/°F

20/68
13/55 13/55 14/57
5/41   8/46 7/45
                    2/36

5.5 hrs	6 hrs	3.5 hrs	1.5 hrs
65 mm	89 mm	109 mm	108 mm
month	Apr	Jul	Oct	Jan

NORTH WALES

°C/°F

17/63
11/52 11/52 14/57
5/41   8/46 6/43
                    1/34

3 hrs	3.5 hrs	2.5 hrs	1.5 hrs
144 mm	206 mm	261 mm	252 mm
month	Apr	Jul	Oct	Jan

DEVON AND CORNWALL

°C/°F

19/66
13/55 13/55 15/59
6/43   9/48 8/46
                    4/39

6 hrs	6.5 hrs	3.5 hrs	2 hrs
53 mm	70 mm	91 mm	99 mm
month	Apr	Jul	Oct	Jan

WEST COUNTRY

°C/°F

21/70
14/57 14/57 15/59
6/43   9/48 7/45
                    2/36

5.5 hrs	6.5 hrs	3.5 hrs	2 hrs
49 mm	65 mm	85 mm	74 mm
month	Apr	Jul	Oct	Jan

THAMES VALLEY

°C/°F

22/72
14/57 13/55 15/59
5/41   7/45 7/45
                    1/34

5.5 hrs	6 hrs	3 hrs	1.5 hrs
41 mm	55 mm	64 mm	61 mm
month	Apr	Jul	Oct	Jan

Northumbria

● Newcastle upon Tyne

Yorkshire

● York

● Manchester

East Midlands

● Birmingham

Heart of England

● Norwich

● Cambridge

Thames Valley   *East Anglia*

● Oxford

● London

Downs and Channel Coast

● Dover

● Portsmouth

THE HIGHLANDS AND ISLANDS

°C/°F			
11/52	17/63	13/55	
3/37	10/50	7/45	7/45
			1/34
4.5 hrs	3.5 hrs	2 hrs	1 hrs
111 mm	137 mm	215 mm	200 mm
month	Apr	Jul	Oct	Jan

THE LOWLANDS

°C/°F			
11/52	19/66	14/57	
4/39	11/52	7/45	6/43
			1/34
5 hrs	5.5 hrs	3 hrs	1.5 hrs
38 mm	69 mm	56 mm	47 mm
month	Apr	Jul	Oct	Jan

NORTHUMBRIA

°C/°F			
11/52	18/64	13/55	
5/41	13/55	8/46	6/43
			2/36
5 hrs	5.5 hrs	3 hrs	1.5 hrs
38 mm	64 mm	61 mm	62 mm
month	Apr	Jul	Oct	Jan

YORKSHIRE

°C/°F			
13/55	21/70	14/57	
5/41	12/54	7/45	6/43
			1/34
5 hrs	5.5 hrs	3 hrs	1.5 hrs
41 mm	62 mm	56 mm	59 mm
month	Apr	Jul	Oct	Jan

EAST MIDLANDS

°C/°F			
13/55	21/70	14/57	
4/39	12/54	6/43	6/43
			0/32
5 hrs	5.5 hrs	3 hrs	1.5 hrs
38 mm	58 mm	56 mm	56 mm
month	Apr	Jul	Oct	Jan

THE DOWNS AND CHANNEL COAST

°C/°F			
14/57	22/72	14/57	
4/39	12/54	6/43	6/43
			0/32
5.8 hrs	7.3 hrs	4 hrs	2 hrs
38 mm	58 mm	56 mm	56 mm
month	Apr	Jul	Oct	Jan

LONDON

°C/°F			
13/55	22/72	16/61	
7/45	15/59	10/50	8/46
			4/39
5 hrs	6 hrs	3.5 hrs	1.5 hrs
39 mm	45 mm	50 mm	44 mm
month	Apr	Jul	Oct	Jan

EAST ANGLIA

°C/°F			
14/57	22/72	15/59	
4/39	12/54	6/43	7/45
			1/34
5 hrs	6 hrs	3.5 hrs	2 hrs
37 mm	58 mm	51 mm	49 mm
month	Apr	Jul	Oct	Jan

LONDON

London at a Glance

THE LARGEST CITY IN EUROPE, London is home to about seven million people and covers 625 sq miles (1,600 sq km). The capital was founded by the Romans in the first century AD as a convenient administrative and communications centre and a port for trade with Continental Europe. For a thousand years it has been the principal residence of British monarchs as well as the centre of business and government, and it is rich in historic buildings and treasures from all periods. In addition to its diverse range of museums, galleries and churches, London is an exciting contemporary city, packed with a vast array of entertainments and shops. The attractions on offer are virtually endless but this map highlights the most important of those described in detail on the following pages.

Buckingham Palace (pp88–9) *is London home and office to the monarchy. The Changing of the Guard takes place on the palace forecourt.*

REGENT'S PARK AND BLOOMSBURY *(see pp104–109)*

WEST END AND WESTMINSTER *(see pp78–95)*

SOUTH KENSINGTON AND HYDE PARK *(see pp96–103)*

Hyde Park (p77), *the largest central London park, boasts numerous sports facilities, restaurants, an art gallery and Speakers' Corner. The highlight is the Serpentine Lake.*

0 kilometres 1

0 miles 0.5

GREATER LONDON

Watford, Enfield, Barnet, Edgware, Ruislip, Finchley, Walthamstow, Hampstead, Uxbridge, Ealing, Bethnal Green, Barking, Dagenham, London City, Greenwich, Heathrow, Richmond, Wandsworth, Dulwich, Bexley, Dartford, Staines, Kingston-Upon-Thames, Wimbledon, Beckenham, Bromley, Orpington, Epsom

0 kilometres 15

0 miles 15

The Victoria and Albert Museum (pp100–101) *is the world's largest museum of decorative arts. This German cup is 15th century.*

KEY

Main sightseeing area

◁ **Nelson's Column (1843) and the National Gallery, Trafalgar Square**

The British Museum's (pp108–9) *vast collection of antiquities from all over the world includes this Portland Vase from the 1st century BC.*

The National Gallery's (pp84–5) *world-famous collection of paintings includes works such as* Christ Mocked *(c.1495) by Hieronymus Bosch.*

THAMES

THE CITY AND
SOUTHWARK
(see pp110–123)

St Paul's (pp116–17) *huge dome is the cathedral's most distinctive feature. Three galleries around the dome give spectacular views of London.*

Westminster Abbey (pp94–5) *has glorious medieval architecture and is crammed with impressive tombs and monuments to some of Britain's greatest public figures.*

Tate Britain (p93) *displays an outstanding collection of British art ranging from stylized Elizabethan portraiture, such as* The Cholmondeley Sisters, *to cutting edge installation and film.*

The Tower of London (pp120–21) *is most famous as the prison where enemies of the Crown were executed. The Tower houses the Crown Jewels, including the Imperial State Crown.*

A River View of London

THE RIVER THAMES was the artery for much of the country's commerce from Roman times until the 1950s. Today the river is one of London's foremost leisure amenities, with wharves and warehouses converted into riverside marinas, bars and restaurants. One of the most enjoyable ways to see the capital is by boat, and the most popular river trips travel downstream from the Houses of Parliament to Tower Bridge. This 30-minute cruise gives a different perspective on some of London's historic buildings and sights.

St Paul's Cathedral (pp116–17), *Wren's masterpiece, dominates the north bank of the river.*

Temple and the Inns of Court (p114) *have been the offices of lawyers and barristers for over 500 years.*

Millennium Bridge

Shell Mex House *was built in 1931 on the site of the vast Cecil Hotel.*

Savoy Hotel (p544)

Somerset House (p82)

Blackfriars Millennium Pier

Savoy Pier

Blackfriars

Cleopatra's Needle

Temple

Hungerford Bridge

THAMES

Charing Cross

Oxo Tower

Tate Modern (p123)

Embankment

Waterloo Bridge

The Globe (p122)

The South Bank Centre (p128)

Blackfriars Bridge

Bankside Pier

Festival Pier

The British Airways London Eye (p83) *is the tallest observation wheel in the world. The wheel moves slowly but continuously at the gentle pace of 26cm (10in) per second. A full revolution takes 30 minutes.*

Embankment Pier

Waterloo Millennium Pier

County Hall

Westminster

Westminster Millennium Pier

Westminster Bridge

The Houses of Parliament (p92) *were designed by Charles Barry after a fire burnt down the 14th-century Palace of Westminster in 1834. The tall tower housing Big Ben dominates the skyline.*

THAMES CRUISES

The most popular boat trips run through central London round the year, with reduced schedules in winter. During the summer, sailing times are frequent between Westminster *(pp90–91)* and Greenwich *(p133)*, with a boat arriving every half hour to an hour. Often accompanied by witty commentary, a cruise along this fascinating stretch of the Thames should not be missed.

Trips can also be taken further afield, with launches heading downstream from Greenwich to the Thames Barrier, an awe-inspiring work of modern engineering. The cruise takes 30 minutes one-way and sails past industrial sites. Heading upstream to picturesque Kew *(p134)* from Westminster (2 hrs) leaves the city behind, after sailing through Hammersmith and passing some of the city's most startling landmarks, including Battersea Power Station and the MI6 building, headquarters of the internal security service. It's possible to head even further upstream to Richmond *(p134)* and Hampton Court *(p161)*, but be forewarned that tidal conditions can hamper the journey.

Kew Pier

Richmond
St Helena Pier
Richmond
Landing Stage

Hampton Court

Chelsea
Harbour Pier

Cadogan
Pier

Millbank
Millennium
Pier

*See enlarged
area below*

Thames
Barrier

Canary
Wharf Pier

Hilton
Docklands
Nelson Dock
Pier

Greenland
Pier

Masthouse
Terrace

Greenwich
Pier

TIMES AND TICKETS Transport for London produces a comprehensive *River Thames Boat Service Guide*, available at tube stations, listing cruise times and operators. Tickets for most cruises are available from kiosks at the piers themselves.

London
Bridge

Cannon
Street

Fishmongers'
Hall

Monument
(p118)

Old
Billingsgate

Monument

Tower of London
(pp120–21) *has the eerie Traitors' Gate, where prisoners entered the Tower by boat.*

Custom
House

Tower
Millennium Pier

St Katharine's
Dock

St Katharine's
Pier

Southwark
Bridge

London
Bridge

St Olave's House

Southwark
Cathedral
(p122)

London Bridge
City Pier

Hay's
Galleria

GLA City Hall

Victorian
warehouses

Design
Museum
(p119)

HMS Belfast
(p119) *is a World War II cruiser built in 1939. It opened as a naval museum in 1971.*

KEY

⊖	Underground station
⇥	Railway station
▭	River boat pier

Tower Bridge (p118) *was built in 1886–94 and is an easily recognized landmark. It still opens to allow tall ships to pass underneath.*

London's Parks and Gardens

Camellia japonica

LONDON HAS ONE OF THE WORLD'S greenest city centres, full of tree-filled squares and large expanses of grass, some of which have been public land since medieval times. From the elegant terraces of Regent's Park to the botanic gardens of Kew, every London park and garden has its own charm and character. Some are ancient crown or public land, while others were created from the grounds of private houses or disused land. Londoners make the most of these open spaces: for exercise, listening to music, or simply escaping the bustle of the city.

Holland Park (see pp130–31) *offers acres of peaceful woodland, an open-air theatre (see p127) and a café.*

Kew Gardens (see p134) *are the world's premiere botanic gardens. An amazing variety of plants from all over the world is complemented by an array of temples, monuments and a landscaped lake.*

Richmond Park (see p134), *London's largest royal park, remains unspoiled with roaming deer and magnificent river views.*

0 kilometres   1

0 miles   0.5

SEASONAL BEST

As winter draws to a close, spectacular drifts of crocuses, daffodils and tulips are to be found peeping above the ground in Green Park and Kew. Easter weekend marks the start of outdoor events with funfairs on many commons and parks. During the summer months the parks are packed with picnickers and sunbathers and you can often catch a free open-air concert in St James's or Regent's parks. The energetic can play tennis in most

Winter in Kensington Gardens, adjoining Hyde Park

parks, swim in Hyde Park's Serpentine or the ponds on Hampstead Heath, or take rowing boats out on the lakes in Regent's and Battersea parks. Autumn brings a different atmosphere, and on 5 November firework displays and bonfires celebrate Guy Fawkes Night *(see p64)*. Winter is a good time to visit the tropical glasshouses and the colourful outdoor winter garden at Kew. If the weather gets really cold, the Round Pond in Kensington Gardens may be fit for ice-skating.

Hampstead Heath *(see p132)* is a breezy open space embracing a variety of landscapes.

Regent's Park (see p105) *has a large boating lake, an open-air theatre (see p127) and London Zoo. Surrounded by Nash's graceful buildings, it is one of London's most civilized retreats.*

St James's Park, *in the heart of the city, is a popular escape for office workers. It is also a reserve for wildfowl.*

THAMES

Green Park, *with its shady trees and benches, offers a cool, restful spot in the heart of London.*

Battersea Park is a pleasant riverside site with a man-made boating lake.

Greenwich Park (see p133) *is dominated by the National Maritime Museum. There are fine views from the Old Royal Observatory on the hill top.*

Hyde Park and Kensington Gardens *(see p103) are both popular London retreats. There are sporting facilities, a lake and art gallery in Hyde Park. This plaque is from the ornate Italian Garden in Kensington Gardens.*

HISTORIC CEMETERIES

In the late 1830s, a ring of private cemeteries was established around London to ease the pressure on the monstrously overcrowded and unhealthy burial grounds of the inner city. Today the cemeteries, notably **Highgate** *(see p132)* and **Kensal Green,** are well worth visiting for their flamboyant Victorian monuments.

Kensal Green cemetery on the Harrow Road

WEST END AND WESTMINSTER

T HE WEST END is the city's social and cultural centre and the London home of the royal family. Stretching from the edge of Hyde Park to Covent Garden, the district bustles all day and late into the night. Whether you're looking for art, history, street- or café-life, it is the most rewarding area in which to begin an exploration of the city.

Westminster has been at the centre of political and religious power for a thousand years. In the 11th century, King Canute founded Westminster Palace and Edward the Confessor built Westminster Abbey, where all English monarchs have been crowned since 1066. As modern government developed, the great offices of state were established in the area.

Horse Guard on Whitehall

SIGHTS AT A GLANCE

Historic Streets and Buildings
Banqueting House **18**
Buckingham Palace pp88–9 **13**
Cabinet War Rooms **16**
Downing Street **17**
Houses of Parliament pp92–3 **19**
Piccadilly Circus **8**
Ritz Hotel **10**
Royal Mews **15**
The Mall **12**
The Piazza and Central Market **1**

Museums and Galleries
London's Transport Museum **2**
National Gallery pp84–5 **6**
National Portrait Gallery **7**
Queen's Gallery **14**
Royal Academy **9**
Somerset House **4**
Tate Britain **21**
Theatre Museum **3**

Churches
Queen's Chapel **11**
Westminster Abbey pp94–5 **20**

Attractions
British Airways London Eye **5**

KEY

- Street-by-Street map *pp80–81*
- Street-by-Street map *pp86–7*
- Street-by-Street map *pp90–91*
- Underground station
- Railway station
- Parking
- River boat pier

GETTING THERE
This area is the hub of the city's public transport system, served by virtually all tube lines and scores of buses (*see pp642–3*). The most convenient tube and railway station is Charing Cross.

0 metres   500
0 yards   500

◁ **Big Ben and the Houses of Parliament**

Street-by-Street: Covent Garden

Until 1973, COVENT GARDEN was an area of decaying streets and warehouses, which only came alive after dark when the fruit and vegetable market traders packed up for the day. Since then the Victorian market and elegant buildings nearby have been converted into stylish shops, restaurants, bars and cafés, creating an animated district which attracts a lively young crowd, night and day.

Seven Dials is a replica of a 17th-century monument marking the crossroads.

Covent Garden

Neal Street and Neal's Yard are lined with many specialist shops converted from former warehouses.

St Martin's Theatre (see p127) is home to the world's longest running play, *The Mousetrap*.

Stanfords map shop

The Lamb and Flag, built in 1623, is one of London's oldest pubs.

New Row is lined with little shops and cafés.

St Paul's Church was designed in 1633 by Inigo Jones (see p53), in the style of the Italian Renaissance architect, Andrea Palladio. Jones also designed the original Covent Garden Piazza.

Theatre Museum
This houses a collection of theatrical memorabilia ❸

The Royal Opera House
(see p128) is where many of the greatest opera singers and ballet dancers have performed.

LOCATOR MAP
See Street Finder map 4

KEY

– – – Suggested route

| 0 metres | 100 |
| 0 yards | 100 |

London's Transport Museum
This museum's intriguing collection brings to life the history of the city's tubes, buses and trains. It also displays examples of 20th-century commercial art ❷

Jubilee Market

★ **Piazza and Central Market**
One of the Piazza's many cafés ❶

STAR SIGHTS

★ **Piazza and Central Market**

The Piazza and Central Market ❶

Covent Garden WC2. **Map** 4 F5.
🚇 *Covent Garden.* ♿ *cobbled streets.* **Street performers in Piazza:** *10am–dusk daily.*

THE 17TH-CENTURY ARCHITECT Inigo Jones *(see p53)* planned the Piazza in Covent Garden as an elegant residential square, modelled on the piazza in the Tuscan town of Livorno, which he had seen under construction during his travels in Italy. For a brief period, the Piazza became one of the most fashionable addresses in London, but it was superseded by the even grander St James's Square *(see p87)* which lies to the southwest.

Decline accelerated when a fruit and vegetable market developed. By the mid-18th century, the Piazza had become a haunt of prostitutes and most of its houses had turned into seedy lodgings, gambling dens, brothels and taverns.

A mid-18th-century view of Covent Garden's Piazza

Meanwhile the wholesale produce market became the largest in the country and in 1828 a market hall was erected to ease congestion. The market, however, soon outgrew its new home and despite the construction of new buildings, such as Floral and Jubilee halls, the congestion grew worse. In 1973 the market moved to a new site in south London, and over the next two decades Covent Garden was redeveloped. Today only St Paul's Church remains of Inigo Jones's buildings, and Covent Garden, with its many small shops, cafés, restaurants, market stalls and street entertainers, is one of central London's liveliest districts.

London's Transport Museum ❷

The Piazza, Covent Garden WC2. **Map** 4 F5. ☎ 020-7379 6344. ⊖ Covent Garden. ○ opening times may be limited due to refurbishment – phone to check. Café and shop will remain open. 🎟 ♿ 🎁 phone in advance. 🅿 ▣ Ⓦ www.ltmuseum.co.uk

Poster by Michael Reilly (1929), London Transport Museum

T HIS COLLECTION of buses, trams and underground trains ranges from the earliest horse-drawn omnibuses to a present-day Hoppa bus. Housed in the Victorian Flower Market of Covent Garden built in 1872, the museum is particularly good for children, who can sit in the driver's seat of a bus or an underground train, operate signals and chat to an actor playing a 19th-century tube-tunnel miner.

London's bus and train companies have long been prolific patrons of artists, and the museum holds a fine collection of 19th- and 20th-century commercial art. Copies of some of the best posters and works by distinguished artists, such as Paul Nash and Graham Sutherland, are on sale at the museum shop.

Theatre Museum ❸

Russell St WC2. **Map** 4 F5. ☎ 020-7943 4700. ⊖ Covent Garden. ○ 10am–6pm Tue–Sun. ● public hols. 🅿 ♿ Ⓦ www.theatremuseum.org

C HILDREN CAN BE MADE UP with gruesome wounds in this museum, and find out how Cyrano de Bergerac's nose was created for the film. An exhibition reveals how a theatre production is mounted, from cast readings of the

author's original script, through videoed rehearsals and back-stage procedures, to the first staged performance.

More conventionally, the intriguing history of show business is traced through a collection of memorabilia – playbills, programmes, props and costumes.

Somerset House ❹

Strand WC2. **Map** 4 F5. ☎ 020-7845 4600. ⊖ Temple. ○ 10am–6pm daily (last adm: 5.15pm). ● 1 Jan, 24–26 Dec. **Ice rink** ○ two months in winter. 🎟 ▣ **Courtauld Institute of Art** ☎ 020-7848 2526. 🅿 🎁 **Gilbert Collection** ☎ 020-7240 9400. 🔊 🎁 **Hermitage Rooms** ☎ 020-7413 3398. 🔊 ▣ 🎁 🎟 all galleries. ♿ all galleries. **Admiralty Restaurant** ☎ 020-7845 4646. Ⓦ www.somerset-house.org.uk

D ESIGNED IN 1770 by William Chambers, Somerset House is home to three great collections of art, the **Courtauld Institute of Art**, the **Gilbert Collection** and the **Hermitage Rooms**. The

Somerset House: Strand façade

courtyard forms an attractive piazza (which becomes an ice rink in winter), and the riverside terrace has a café. The Admiralty Restaurant is highly regarded. Located in Somerset House but famous in its own right is the Courtauld Institute of Art. Its collection includes important Impressionist and Post-Impressionist works. The Gilbert Collection is a major decorative arts museum, with pieces dating from the 16th century, including European silverware. The Hermitage Rooms recreate, in miniature, the splendour of the Winter Palace which now comprises

---

SOHO AND CHINATOWN

Soho has been renowned for pleasures of the table, the flesh and the intellect ever since it was first developed in the late 17th century. At first a fashionable residential area, it declined when high society shifted west to Mayfair and immigrants from Europe moved into its narrow streets. Furniture-makers and tailors set up shop here and were joined in the late 19th century by pubs, nightclubs, restaurants and brothels. In the 1960s, Hong Kong Chinese moved into the area around Gerrard and Lisle streets and they created an aromatic Chinatown, packed with many restaurants and food shops. Soho's raffish reputation has long attracted artists and writers, ranging from the 18th-century essayist Thomas de Quincey to poet Dylan Thomas and painter Francis Bacon. Although strip joints and peep shows remain, Soho has enjoyed something of a renaissance, and today is full of stylish and lively bars and restaurants.

Lion dancer in February's Chinese New Year celebrations

The opulent Palm Court of the Ritz Hotel

the State Hermitage Museum, St Petersburg, and exhibitions are mounted from the museum's collections.

British Airways London Eye ❺

Jubilee Gardens, South Bank, SE1. **Map** 6 F2. *0870 5000 600 (information and 24-hr advance booking – recommended as tickets sell out days in advance).* ⊖ *Waterloo, Westminster.* 🚌 *11, 24, 211.* ⭕ *Sep–Dec & Feb–May: 9.30am–8pm daily; Jun: 9.30am–9pm Mon–Thu, Fri–Sun to 10pm; Jul & Aug: 9.30am–10pm daily.* ⬤ *25 Dec & Jan.* 🏷 *Pick up tickets at County Hall (adjacent to Eye) at least 30 mins before boarding time.* 🅿 🅰 ♿ 🌐 *www.londoneye.com*

THE BRITISH AIRWAYS London Eye is a 135-m (443-ft) observation wheel that was installed on the South Bank to mark the Millennium. Its enclosed passenger capsules offer a gentle, 30-minute ride as the wheel makes a full turn, with breathtaking views over London and for up to 42 km (26 miles) around. Towering over one of the world's most familiar river-scapes, it has understandably captured the hearts of Londoners and visitors alike, and is one of the city's most popular attractions. "Flights" are on the hour and half-hour.

National Gallery ❻

See pp84–5.

National Portrait Gallery ❼

2 St Martin's Place WC2. **Map** 6 E1. *020-7306 0055.* ⊖ *Charing Cross, Leicester Sq.* ⭕ *10am–6pm Sat–Wed, 10am–9pm Thu & Fri.* ⬤ *1 Jan, Good Fri, 24 & 25 Dec.* ♿ 🅰 🍽 🅿 🅰 🌐 *www.npg.org.uk*

THIS MUSEUM celebrates Britain's history through portraits, photographs and sculptures; subjects range from Elizabeth I to Margaret Thatcher. The 20th-century section contains paintings and photographs of the royal family, politicians, rock stars, designers, artists and writers.

Piccadilly Circus ❽

W1. **Map** 6 D1. ⊖ *Piccadilly Circus.*

DOMINATED BY garish neon advertising hoardings, Piccadilly Circus is a hectic traffic junction surrounded by shopping malls. It began as an early 19th-century crossroads between Piccadilly and John Nash's (*see p107*) Regent Street. It was briefly an elegant space, edged by curving stucco façades, but by 1910 the first electric advert-isements had been installed. For years people have con-gregated at its centre, beneath the delicately poised figure of Eros, erected in 1892.

Royal Academy ❾

Burlington House, Piccadilly W1. **Map** 6 D1. *020-7300 8000.* ⊖ *Piccadilly Circus, Green Park.* ⭕ *10am–6pm Sat–Thu, 10am–10pm Fri.* ⬤ *24–25 Dec, Good Fri.* 🏷 ♿ 🏷 *by appointment.* 🍽 🅿 🅰 🌐 *www.royalacademy.org.uk*

FOUNDED IN 1768, the Royal Academy is best known for its summer exhibition, which has been an annual event for over 200 years and comprises a rewarding mix of around 1,200 new works by established and unknown painters, sculptors and architects. During the rest of the year, the gallery shows prestigious touring exhibitions from around the world, and the courtyard in front of Burlington House, one of the West End's few surviving mansions from the early 18th century, is often filled with people waiting to get in. Quite apart from its aesthetic delights, the Royal Academy provides the weary traveller with a little lacuna of tranquillity. Its interior decoration inspires calm, and seems to be cut off from the stresses and strains of modern city life.

The Statue of Eros

Ritz Hotel ❿

Piccadilly W1. **Map** 5 C1. *020-7493 8181.* ⊖ *Green Park.* ♿ See **Where to Stay** p540. 🌐 *www.theritzlondon.com*

CESAR RITZ, the Swiss hotelier who inspired the word "ritzy", had virtually settled down to a quiet retire-ment by 1906 when this hotel was built and named after him. The colonnaded front of the château-style building was erected in 1906 to suggest just the merest whiff of Paris, where the grandest hotels were to be found at the turn of the century. It still maintains its Edwardian air of *fin de siècle* opulence and sophisticated grandeur, and is a popular venue for afternoon tea (reservations are required). A touch of *soigné* danger may be found in the casino.

National Gallery ⑥

THE NATIONAL GALLERY is London's leading art museum, with over 2,300 paintings, most on permanent display. It has flourished since 1824 when George IV persuaded the government to purchase 38 major paintings. These became the core of a national collection of European art that now ranges from Cimabue in the 13th century to 19th-century Impressionists. The gallery's particular strengths are in Dutch, Italian Renaissance and 17th-century Spanish painting. In 1991 the Sainsbury Wing was added to hold the Early Renaissance collection. During 2005 rooms may be closed for renovation.

The Adoration of the Kings *(1564)*
This realistic work is by Flemish artist Pieter Brueghel the Elder (1520–1569).

Education Centre entrance 🦽

Stairs to lower floor
🚶‍♀️🚼‍♂️

★ **The Leonardo Cartoon**
(c.1499–1500)
The genius of Leonardo da Vinci glows through this picture of the Virgin and Child, St Anne and John the Baptist.

Link to main building

Stairs to lower floors 🔼

KEY TO FLOORPLAN

☐	Painting 1250–1500
☐	Painting 1500–1600
☐	Painting 1600–1700
☐	Painting 1700–1900
☐	Special exhibitions
☐	Non-exhibition space

Arnolfini Portrait
Jan van Eyck (1389–1441), one of the pioneers of oil painting, shows his mastery of colour, texture, and minute detail in this portrait of 1434.

Entrance to Sainsbury Wing 🦽

The Annunciation
This refined work of the late 1450s, by Fra Filippo Lippi, forms part of the gallery's exceptional Italian Renaissance collection.

★ **Rokeby Venus**
This is Velázquez's only surviving female nude (1647–51).

Stairs to lower galleries

33
32 34
37 35
36 41
38 40 43 42
39 45 44
13 46
3 1
2 i
4 1

East entrance

Trafalgar Square entrance

VISITORS' CHECKLIST

Trafalgar Sq WC2. **Map** 6 E1.
020-7747 2885. Charing Cross, Leicester Sq, Piccadilly Circus. 3, 6, 9, 11, 12, 13, 15, X15 23, 24, 29, 53, X53, 77A, 88, 91, 94, 109, 139, 159, 176. Charing Cross. 10am–6pm daily (9pm Wed). 1 Jan, 24–26 Dec. via Sainsbury Wing entrance.
www.nationalgallery.org.uk

★ **The Hay-Wain** *(1821)*
The great age of 19th-century landscape painting is represented by Constable and Turner (see p93). This picture shows how Constable caught changing light and shadow.

The Neo-Classical façade is made of Portland stone.

The Ambassadors
The strange shape in the foreground of this Hans Holbein portrait (1533) is a foreshortened skull, a symbol of mortality.

GALLERY GUIDE
Most of the collection is housed on the first floor, divided into four wings. The paintings hang chronologically, with the earliest works, notably the Italian Renaissance collection (1250–1500), in the Sainsbury Wing. Lesser paintings of all periods are displayed on the lower floor of the main building. The better of the two restaurants is on the first floor in the Sainsbury Wing.

STAR PAINTINGS

★ **Cartoon by Leonardo da Vinci**

★ **Rokeby Venus by Diego Velázquez**

★ **The Hay-Wain by John Constable**

At the Theatre *(1876–7)*
Renoir was one of the greatest painters to be influenced by the Impressionist movement. The theatre was a popular subject among artists of the time.

Street-by-Street:
Piccadilly and St James's

AS SOON AS HENRY VIII built St James's
Palace in the 1530s, the surrounding
area became the centre of fashionable court
life. Today Piccadilly forms a contrast
between the bustling commercial district full
of shopping arcades, eateries and cinemas,
with St James's, to the
south, which is still
the domain of the
wealthy and the
influential.

St James's Church was
designed by Sir
Christopher
Wren in
1684.

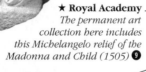

★ **Royal Academy**
*The permanent art
collection here includes
this Michelangelo relief of the
Madonna and Child (1505)* ❾

Fortnum & Mason
(see p124) was
founded in 1707.

The Ritz
*César Ritz
founded
one of
London's
most fam-
ous hotels
in 1906* ❿

Burlington Arcade, an
opulent covered walk,
has fine shops and
beadles on patrol.

St James's Palace
was built on the site
of a leper hospital.

**To the Mall and
Buckingham Palace**
(see pp88–9)

Spencer House, recently
restored to its 18th-century
splendour, contains fine
period furniture and paintings. This Palladian
palace was completed in
1766 for the 1st Earl
Spencer, an ancestor of
the late Princess of Wales.

STAR SIGHTS

★ **Piccadilly
Circus**

★ **Royal Academy**

★ **Piccadilly Circus**
The crowds and dazzling neon lights make this the West End's focal point ❽

LOCATOR MAP
See Street Finder map 5, 6

KEY

- - - Suggested route

0 metres	100
0 yards	100

Piccadilly

Jermyn Street has elegant shops selling antiques, unusual gifts and men's clothing.

Pall Mall is a street of gentlemen's clubs, which admit only members and their guests.

St James's Square has long been the most fashionable address in London.

Queen's Chapel
This was the first Classical church in England ⓫

Royal Opera Arcade is lined with quality shops. Designed by John Nash, it was completed in 1818.

Queen's Chapel ⓫

Marlborough Rd SW1. **Map** 6 D1. 020-7930 4832. ⊖ Green Park. ◯ to the public Sun services (Easter–end Jul) and major Saints' Days only. ♿

THE SUMPTUOUS Queen's Chapel was designed by Inigo Jones for the Infanta of Spain, the intended bride of Charles I (*see pp52–3*). Work started in 1623 but ceased when the marriage negotiations were shelved. The chapel was finally completed in 1627 for Charles's eventual queen, Henrietta Maria. It was the first church in England to be built in a Classical style, with a coffered ceiling based on a reconstruction by Palladio of an ancient Roman temple.

Interior of Queen's Chapel

The Mall ⓬

SW1. **Map** 6 D2. ⊖ Charing Cross, Green Park.

THIS BROAD TRIUMPHAL approach from Trafalgar Square to Buckingham Palace was created by Aston Webb when he redesigned the front of the palace and the Victoria Monument in 1911. The spacious tree-lined avenue follows the course of an old path at the edge of St James's Park. The path was laid out in the reign of Charles II, when it became London's most fashionable and cosmopolitan promenade. The Mall is used for royal processions on special occasions. Flagpoles down both sides fly the national flags of foreign heads of state during official visits. The Mall is closed to traffic on Sundays.

Buckingham Palace ⑬

OPENED TO VISITORS for the first time in 1993 to raise money for repairing fire damage to Windsor Castle *(see pp224–5)*, the Queen's official London home and office is an extremely popular attraction in August and

Queen Elizabeth II

September. John Nash *(see p107)* began converting the 18th-century Buckingham House into a palace for George IV in 1826 but was taken off the job in 1831 for overspending his budget. The first monarch to occupy the palace was Queen Victoria, just after she came to the throne in 1837. The tour takes visitors up the grand staircase and through the splendour of the State Rooms, but not into the royal family's private apartments.

Music Room
State guests are presented and royal babies christened in this room.

White Drawing Room
Green Drawing Room
Grand Staircase
Blue Drawing Room
State Dining Room

Queen's Gallery
Masterpieces from the Royal Collection, such as Vermeer's The Music Lesson *(c.1660), are displayed here in a series of changing exhibitions.*

Throne Room
The Queen carries out many formal ceremonial duties here, under the richly gilded ceiling.

View over the Mall
On special occasions the Royal Family wave to crowds from the balcony.

VISITORS' CHECKLIST

SW1. **Map** 5 C2. **☎** 020-7321 2233. **⊖** St James's Park, Victoria. **🚌** 11, 16, 24, 25, 28, 36, 38, 52, 73, 135, C1. **🚆** Victoria. **State Rooms** ◯ Aug–Sep: 9:30am–5:30pm daily (last adm: 4:15pm). The ticket office is located in Green Park by Canada Gate. Each ticket has a set entry time. 🖼 ♿ phone first. **Changing of the Guard**: 11:30am daily or alternate days. Subject to change without notice. **☎** 020-7321 2233. **w** www.royal.gov.uk

The Royal Standard flies while the Queen is in residence.

The East Wing façade was added by Aston Webb in 1913.

The Changing of the Guard takes place on the palace forecourt.

THE CHANGING OF THE GUARD

Dressed in brilliant scarlet tunics and tall furry hats called bearskins, the palace guards stand in sentry boxes outside the Palace. Crowds gather in front of the railings to watch the colourful and musical military ceremony as the guards march down the Mall from St James's Palace, parading for half an hour while the palace keys are handed by the old guard to the new.

Queen's Gallery ⓮

Buckingham Palace Rd SW1. **Map** 5 C2. **☎** 020-7321 2233. **⊖** St James's Park, Victoria. ◯ 10am–5:30pm daily (last adm for exhibitions: 4:30pm). ● 25, 26 Dec. 🖼 w www.royal.gov.uk

T HE QUEEN'S ART COLLECTION is one of the finest and most valuable in the world, rich in the works of old masters such as Vermeer and Leonardo. A recent major expansion programme has increased the display space for the Collection, enabling the virtual year-round display of many masterpieces, as well as special exhibitions of drawings and decorative arts.

Detail: The Gold State Coach (1762), Royal Mews

Royal Mews ⓯

Buckingham Palace Rd SW1. **Map** 5 C3 **☎** 020-7321 2233. **⊖** Victoria. ◯ Mar–Oct: 11am–4pm daily (last adm: 3:15pm). Extended opening hrs may operate Aug–Sep. 🛍 open 9:30am–5pm daily all year (closed 25, 26 Dec). 🖼 ♿ w www.royal.gov.uk

L OVERS OF HORSES and royal pomp should not miss this working stable and coach house. Designed by John Nash in 1825, it houses horses and state coaches used on official occasions. Among them is the glass coach used for royal weddings and foreign ambassadors. The star exhibit is the ornate gold state coach, built for George III in 1762, which was used by the Queen during the Golden Jubilee celebrations in 2002. The shop sells interesting merchandise.

Street-by-Street: Whitehall and Westminster

THE BROAD AVENUES of Whitehall and Westminster are lined with imposing buildings that serve the historic seat of both government and the established church. On weekdays the streets are crowded with civil servants whose work is based here, while at weekends the area takes on a different atmosphere with a steady flow of tourists.

Downing Street
Sir Robert Walpole was the first Prime Minister to live here in 1732 ⑰

Cabinet War Rooms
Now open to the public, these were Winston Churchill's World War II headquarters ⑯

St Margaret's Church
is a favourite venue for political and society weddings.

★ Westminster Abbey
The abbey is London's oldest and most important church ⑳

Central Hall (1911)
is a florid example of the Beaux Arts style.

Richard I's Statue
is an 1860 depiction of the king, killed in battle in 1199.

Dean's Yard is a secluded grassy square surrounded by picturesque buildings from different periods, many used by Westminster School.

The Burghers of Calais is a cast of Auguste Rodin's 1886 original in France.

To Trafalgar Square

Banqueting House
Inigo Jones designed this elegant building in 1622 **18**

REGENT'S PARK & BLOOMSBURY

THE CITY & SOUTHWARK

WEST END & WESTMINSTER

SOUTH KENSINGTON & HYDE PARK

THAMES

LOCATOR MAP
See Street Finder map 6

The Cenotaph (1920) is a war memorial by Sir Edwin Lutyens.

WHITEHALL

RICHMOND TERRACE

VICTORIA EMBANKMENT

STREET

Westminster

Horse Guards is a parade ground protected by a guard, changed twice each day.

Westminster Pier is the main starting point for river trips *(pp74–5)*.

★ **Houses of Parliament**
The seat of government is dominated by the clock tower, holding the 14-tonne bell Big Ben, hung in 1858. Its deep chimes are broadcast daily on BBC radio **19**

KEY

– – – Suggested route

0 metres 100

0 yards 100

STAR SIGHTS

★ **Westminster Abbey**

★ **Houses of Parliament**

Cabinet War Rooms **16**

Clive Steps, King Charles St SW1. **Map** 6 E2. [020-7930 6961. ⊖ *Westminster.* ◻ *Apr–Sep: 9:30am–6pm; Oct–Mar: 10am–6pm.* ● *24–26 Dec.* ⊠ & ⊡ ⓣ ┴ www.iwb.org.uk

THIS WARREN OF CELLARS below a government office building is where the War Cabinet – first under Neville Chamberlain, then Winston Churchill from 1940 – met during World War II when German bombs were falling on London. The rooms include living quarters for ministers and military leaders and a Cabinet Room, where strategic decisions were taken. They are laid out as they were when the war ended, complete with Churchill's desk, communications equipment, and maps for plotting battles and strategies. The Churchill Museum is a new addition, which records and illustrates Churchill's life and career.

Telephones in the Map Room, Cabinet War Rooms

Downing Street **17**

SW1. **Map** 6 E2. ⊖ *Westminster.* ● *to the public.*

NUMBER 10 Downing Street has been the official residence of the British Prime Minister since 1732. It contains a Cabinet Room in which government policy is decided, an impressive State Dining Room and a private apartment; outside is a well-protected garden.

Next door at No. 11 is the official residence of the Chancellor of the Exchequer, who is in charge of the nation's financial affairs. In 1989, iron gates were erected at the Whitehall end of Downing Street for security purposes.

Banqueting House ⑱

Whitehall SW1. **Map** 6 E1. 020-7839 8919. Charing Cross. 10am–5pm Mon–Sat. public hols & for functions. W www.hrp.org.uk

COMPLETED BY Inigo Jones (see p53) in 1622, this was the first building in central London to embody the Palladian style of Renaissance Italy. In 1629 Charles I commissioned Rubens to paint the ceiling with scenes exalting the reign of his father, James I. They symbolize the divine right of kings, disputed by the Parliamentarians, who executed Charles I outside the building in 1649 (see pp52–3).

Panels from the Rubens ceiling (1629–34), Banqueting House

Houses of Parliament ⑲

SW1. **Map** 6 E2. 020-7219 3000. Westminster. **Visitors' Galleries** 2:30–10:30pm Mon; 11:30am–7:30pm Tue, Wed; 11:30am–6:30pm Thu; 9:30am–3pm sitting Fri. Queue or UK residents may apply in advance to local MP. frequently for parliamentary recesses. see website or call 0870-906 3773 to book tickets for tours. W www.parliament.uk

THERE HAS BEEN a Palace of Westminster here since the 11th century, though only Westminster Hall remains from that time. The present Neo-Gothic structure by Sir Charles Barry was built after the old palace was destroyed by fire in 1834. Since the 16th century it has housed the two Houses of Parliament, the Lords and the Commons. The House of Commons consists of elected Members of Parliament (MPs).

The party with most MPs forms the Government, and its leader becomes Prime Minister. The House of Lords comprises peers, law lords, bishops and archbishops.

Westminster Abbey ⑳

See pp94–5.

Victoria Tower

Central Lobby

The House of Commons' original chamber was destroyed by fire in 1941.

Royal Gallery

St Stephen's entrance for the public

The House of Lords is a lavishly decorated Gothic Hall designed by Pugin in 1836–7.

Members' entrance

Big Ben has kept exact time for the nation almost continuously since 1859.

Westminster Hall

Portico of Tate Britain

Tate Britain ㉑

Millbank SW1. **Map** 6 E4. *020-7887 8000.* Pimlico. 77a, 88, C10. Victoria, Vauxhall. to Tate Modern every 40 mins. 10am–5:50pm daily. 24–26 Dec. for major exhibitions. Atterbury St. W www.tate.org.uk

FORMERLY THE Tate Gallery, Tate Britain is the national gallery of British art, and includes works from the 16th to the 21st century. Displays draw on the enormous Tate Collection, which also includes the international modern art seen at Tate Modern *(p123)*. A new boat, Tate to Tate, takes visitors between the two galleries. Located in the adjoining Clore Gallery is the Turner Bequest (see box).

The permanent collection displays occupy three-quarters of the main floor. The displays follow a broad chronological sweep from the early 16th century to the present. The size of the collection necessitates some rotation of displays, which are organized in various imaginative and innovative ways. Major themes change on a three yearly basis, solo artists rooms and smaller

Recumbent Figure (1938) by Henry Moore

themed rooms more frequently. Loan exhibitions are installed in the ground floor galleries and part of the main floor.

The section on the years 1500–1800 is dominated by portraiture, as seen in an exquisite portrait of Elizabeth I (c.1575) by the miniaturist Nicholas Hilliard, as well as the lively works of William Hogarth and the grand portraiture of Joshua Reynolds and Thomas Gainsborough. The section concludes with the visionary paintings of William Blake.

The 19th-century section is rich in the great landscape works of John Constable, as well as the vibrant images of the Pre-Raphaelites such as John Everett Millais and Dante Gabriel Rossetti.

The period 1900–1960 includes the war imagery of C R W Nevinson, the landscapes of Paul Nash, and the British modernist works of Henry Moore, Barbara Hepworth and Ben Nicholson.

The Tate Collection is outstanding in its wealth of British art from 1960 to the present, and the displays in this section are changed on a regular basis. Works range from the 1960s Pop artists David Hockney, Richard

***Mr. and Mrs. Clark and Percy* (1970–71) by David Hockney**

Hamilton and Peter Blake, through the works of Gilbert and George and the landscape artist Richard Long, to the 1980s paintings of Lucian Freud, Howard Hodgkin and R B Kitaj. The so-called Young British Artists (YBAs) are well represented by the leading figures Damian Hirst, Tracey Emin and Sarah Lucas, as is the contemporary movement of British artists such as Tacita Dean and Douglas Gordon, who use film and video as their medium.

***Captain Thomas Lee* (1594) by Marcus Gheeraerts II**

THE TURNER BEQUEST

The Turner Bequest comprises some 300 oil paintings and 20,000 watercolours and drawings, left to the nation by the great landscape painter J M W Turner on his death in 1851. Turner's will had specified that a special gallery be built to house his pictures and this was finally done in 1987 with the opening of the Clore Gallery, a south-east extension of Tate Britain. The oils are on view in the main galleries, and the wonderful watercolours are the subject of changing displays.

The Scarlet Sunset: A Town on a River (c.1830–40)

Westminster Abbey ⑳

WESTMINSTER ABBEY has been the burial place of Britain's monarchs since the 11th century and the setting for many coronations and royal weddings. It is one of the most beautiful buildings in London, with an exceptionally diverse array of architectural styles, ranging from the austere French Gothic of the nave to the astonishing complexity of Henry VII's chapel. Half national church, half national museum, the abbey aisles and transepts are crammed with an extraordinary collection of tombs and monuments honouring some of Britain's greatest public figures, ranging from politicians to poets.

North Entrance
The mock-medieval stonework is Victorian.

Statesmen's Aisle

Flying buttresses help redistribute the great weight of the roof.

★ Nave
At a height of 31 m (102 ft), the nave is the highest in England. The ratio of height to width is 3:1.

CORONATION

The coronation ceremony is over 1,000 years old and since 1066, with the crowning of William the Conqueror on Christmas Day, the abbey has been its sumptuous setting. The coronation of Queen Elizabeth II, in 1953, was the first to be televised.

Cloisters
Built mainly in the 13th and 14th centuries, the cloisters link the Abbey church with the other buildings.

STAR FEATURES

★ Nave

★ Henry VII Chapel

★ Chapter House

★ **Henry VII Chapel**
The chapel, built in 1503–19, has superb late Perpendicular vaulting and choir stalls dating from 1512.

The Sanctuary, built by Henry III, has been the scene of 38 coronations.

Poets' Corner
A host of great poets are honoured here, including Shakespeare, Chaucer and T S Eliot.

VISITORS' CHECKLIST

Broad Sanctuary SW1. **Map** 6 E2.
020-7222 5152. ⊖ Westminster. 3, 11, 12, 24, 29, 53, 70, 77, 77a, 88, 109, 159, 170. ⊠ Victoria. Westminster Pier. **Cloisters** ⬜ *8am–6pm daily.* **Abbey, including Royal Chapels, Poets' Corner, Choir, Statesmen's Aisle, Nave** ⬜ *9:30am–3:45pm Mon, Tue, Thu, Fri (last adm: 2:45pm), 9:30am–6pm Wed, 9:30am–1:45pm Sat (last adm: 12:45pm).* **Chapter House & Museum** ⬜ *10:30am–4pm daily.* **College Garden** ⬜ *Apr–Sep: 10am–6pm Tue–Thu; Oct–Mar: 10am–4pm Tue–Thu.* **Evensong** *5pm Mon–Fri, 3pm Sat, Sun.* **Concerts.** ⬛ ⬛
W www.westminster-abbey.org

The Museum has many of the abbey's treasures including wood, plaster and wax effigies of monarchs.

The Pyx Chamber is where the coinage was tested in medieval times.

★ **Chapter House**
A beautiful octagonal room, remarkable for its 13th-century tile floor. It is lit by six huge stained glass windows showing scenes from the abbey's history.

HISTORICAL PLAN OF THE ABBEY

The first abbey church was established as early as the 10th century, but the present French-influenced Gothic structure was begun in 1245 at the behest of Henry III. Because of its unique role as the coronation church, the abbey escaped Henry VIII's onslaught on Britain's monastic buildings *(see pp50–51).*

KEY

☐ Built between 1055–1350
☐ Added from 1350–1420
☐ Built between 1500–1512
☐ Towers completed 1745
☐ Restored after 1850

St Edward's Chapel
The shrine of Edward the Confessor is housed here, along with the tombs of many medieval monarchs.

SOUTH KENSINGTON AND HYDE PARK

T HIS EXCLUSIVE district embraces one of London's largest parks and some of its finest museums, shops, restaurants and hotels. Until the mid-19th century it was a genteel, semi-rural backwater of large houses and private schools lying to the south of Kensington Palace. In 1851, the Great Exhibition, until then the largest arts and science event ever staged *(see pp56–7)*, was held in Hyde Park, transforming the area into a celebration of Victorian learning and self-confidence.

Peter Pan statue in Kensington Gardens

The brainchild of Queen Victoria's husband, Prince Albert, the exhibition was a massive success and the profits were used to buy 35 ha (87 acres) of land in South Kensington. Here, Prince Albert encouraged the construction of a concert hall, museums and colleges devoted to the applied arts and sciences; most of them survive. The neighbourhood soon became modish, full of flamboyant red-brick mansion blocks, garden squares and the elite shops still to be found in Knightsbridge.

SIGHTS AT A GLANCE

Historic Buildings
Kensington Palace **7**

Churches
Brompton Oratory **2**

Shops
Harrods **1**

Parks and Gardens
Hyde Park and Kensington
  Gardens **6**

Museums and Galleries
Natural History Museum **5**
Science Museum **4**
*Victoria and Albert Museum
  pp100–101* **3**

GETTING THERE
South Kensington station (accessible from an entrance on Exhibition Road) is on the Piccadilly, Circle and District lines; only the Piccadilly line passes through Knightsbridge and Hyde Park Corner. The No. 14 bus runs direct from Piccadilly Circus to South Kensington, via Knightsbridge.

0 metres   500
0 yards   500

KEY

Street-by-Street map
pp98–9

Underground station

P Parking

◁ **Ennismore Mews in South Kensington, built 1843–6**

Street-by-Street: South Kensington

THE NUMEROUS MUSEUMS and colleges created in the wake of the Great Exhibition of 1851 *(see pp56–7)* continue to give this neighbourhood an air of leisured culture. Visited as much by Londoners as tourists, the museum area is liveliest on Sundays and on summer evenings during the Royal Albert Hall's famous season of classical "Prom" concerts *(see p128).*

The Royal Albert Hall opened in 1870 and was modelled on Roman amphitheatres.

The Memorial to the Great Exhibition is surmounted by a bronze statue of its instigator, Prince Albert.

The Royal College of Music, founded in 1882, exhibits historic musical instruments such as this harpsichord dating from 1531.

★ **Science Museum**
Visitors can experiment with over a thousand interactive displays ❹

★ **Natural History Museum**
The Creepy Crawlies exhibition has proved highly popular ❺

STAR SIGHTS

★ Science Museum

★ Natural History Museum

★ Victoria and Albert Museum

Entrance to South Kensington tube

KEY

– – – Suggested route

0 metres   100

0 yards   100

The Albert Memorial was built in memory of Queen Victoria's husband who died in 1861.

LOCATOR MAP
See Street Finder map 2

REGENT'S PARK & BLOOMSBURY
WEST END & WESTMINSTER
SOUTH KENSINGTON & HYDE PARK

★ **Victoria and Albert Museum**
The museum has a fine collection of applied arts and photography from around the world ❸

Brompton Oratory
This ornate Baroque church is famous for its splendid musical tradition ❷

Brompton Square (1821)

To Knightsbridge and Harrod's

Harrods Food Hall

Harrods ❶

Knightsbridge SW1. **Map** 5 A3.
020-7730 1234. Knightsbridge.
10am–7pm Mon–Sat.
See *Shops and Markets* pp122–3.
www.harrods.com

IN 1849 HENRY CHARLES HARROD opened a small grocery shop on Brompton Road, which soon became famous for its impeccable service and quality. The store moved into these extravagant premises in Knightsbridge in 1905.

Brompton Oratory ❷

Brompton Rd SW7. **Map** 2 F5.
020-7808 0900. South Kensington.
6:30am–8pm daily.
www.bromptonoratory.org.uk

THE ITALIANATE ORATORY is a lavish monument to the 19th-century English Catholic revival. It was established as a base for a community of priests by John Henry Newman (later Cardinal Newman), who introduced the Oratorian movement to England in 1848. The church was opened in 1884, and the dome and façade added in the 1890s.

The sumptuous interior holds many fine monuments. The 12 huge 17th-century statues of the apostles are from Siena Cathedral, the elaborate Baroque Lady Altar (1693) is from the Dominican church at Brescia, and the 18th-century altar in St Wilfred's Chapel is from Rochefort in Belgium.

GORE
ALBERT COURT
ROAD
PRINCES GARDENS
GARDENS
BROMPTON ROAD

Victoria and Albert Museum ❸

THE VICTORIA AND ALBERT MUSEUM (the V&A) contains one of the world's widest collections of art and design, ranging from early Christian devotional objects and the mystical art of southeast Asia to cutting-edge furniture design. Originally founded in 1852 as the Museum of Manufactures to inspire students of design, it was renamed by Queen Victoria in 1899 in memory of Prince Albert. The museum is undergoing a dramatic redisplay of much of its collection,

The Glass Gallery, room 131

and there are currently plans to construct a major new contemporary space, the Spiral, designed by Daniel Libeskind.

Whiteley Silver Galleries
Radiant pieces such as the Burgess Cup (Britain, 1863) fill these stunning galleries.

★ British Galleries
The Great Bed of Ware has been a tourist attraction since 1601, when Shakespeare sparked interest in it by making reference to it in Twelfth Night.

★ Dress Court
In this gallery, European clothing from the mid-1500s to the present day is displayed, such as these famous Vivienne Westwood shoes.

Exhibition Road entrance

KEY TO FLOORPLAN

- ☐ Level 0
- ☐ Level 1
- ☐ Level 2
- ☐ Level 3
- ☐ Level 4
- ☐ Level 6
- ☐ Henry Cole Wing
- ☐ Non-exhibition space

STAR EXHIBITS

- ★ British Galleries
- ★ Dress Court
- ★ Medieval Treasury
- ★ Nehru Gallery of Indian Art

GALLERY GUIDE

The V&A has a 7-mile (11-km) layout spread over six levels. The main floor, level 1, houses the Asian and Islamic galleries, as well as the Dress Court, Sculpture and Cast Courts, and European Medieval and Renaissance displays. The British Galleries are on levels 2 and 4. Level 3 contains the 20th Century galleries and displays of silver, metalwork, arms and jewellery; textiles are also on this floor. The glass and ceramics displays are on levels 4 and 6. Much of the Henry Cole Wing, on the northwest side of the building, is closed for refurbishment; it will house the Print Room, a Learning Centre and the RIBA Drawings and Manuscripts collections.

Stained Glass
Illuminated European stained glass, such as Susannah and the Elders *(c. 1520), is located in rooms 111, 116 and 117.*

VISITORS' CHECKLIST

Cromwell Rd SW7. **Map** 2 F5.
📞 020-7942 2000.
🚇 South Kensington. 🚌 14, 74, 414, C1. 🕐 10am–5:45pm daily (10am–10pm Wed and last Fri of each month). ● 24–26 Dec. ♿ 📷 🍴 🛍 ☕
W www.vam.ac.uk

The Contemporary Space
exhibits all facets of design from fashion to digital media.

T T Tsui Gallery of Chinese Art
This magnificent ancestor portrait is among the many exquisite pieces on show in this gallery.

★ **Medieval Treasury**
The Eltenberg Reliquary (c.1180) is one of the museum's masterpieces of medieval craftsmanship.

Aston Webb's façade (1909) is decorated with 32 sculptures of English craftsmen and designers.

★ **Nehru Gallery of Indian Art**
Considered the greatest collection outside India, it includes Tippoo's Tiger (1795), a pump organ in the form of a man being mauled by a tiger.

Main entrance

Science Museum ❹

Exhibition Rd SW7. **Map** 2 E5. ⚡
020-7942 4000. 🚇 South Kensington. 🕐 10am–6pm daily. ⚫ 24–26
Dec. 🎟 for IMAX, special exhibitions
and simulators only. ♿ 📷 📶 📲
🆆 www.sciencemuseum.org.uk

CENTURIES OF continuing
scientific and technolo-
gical development lie at the
heart of the Science Museum's
massive collections. The hard-
ware displayed is magnificent:
from steam engines to aero-
engines; spacecraft to the very
first mechanical computers.
Equally important is the social

**Newcomen's Steam Engine (1712),
Science Museum**

context of science – what dis-
coveries and inventions mean
for day-to-day life – and the
process of discovery itself.
There are many interactive
and hands-on displays which
are very popular with children.

The museum is spread over
seven floors and includes the
recent Wellcome Wing at the
west end of the museum. The
basement features the excellent
hands-on galleries for children,
including the Launch Pad and
Garden. Power dominates the
ground floor, and is dedicated
to steam power, with the still-
operational Harle Syke Mill
Engine of 1903. Here too are
Space and Making the Modern
World, a highlight of which is
the display of the scarred
Apollo 10 spacecraft, which
carried three astronauts to the
moon and back in May 1969.
In Challenge of Materials,
located on the first floor, our
expectations of
materials are

confounded with exhibits
such as a bridge made of glass
and a steel wedding dress.

The Flight gallery on the
third floor is packed with
early flying contraptions,
fighter planes and aeroplanes.
The fourth and fifth floors
house the medical science
galleries, where Science and
the Art of Medicine has a
17th-century Italian vase for
storing snake bite treatment.

The high-tech Wellcome
Wing offers four floors of interactive technology, including
the digital landscape of Digi-
topolis, where you can explore
a virtual world of sound and
vision. With an IMAX 3D
Cinema and the SIMEX
simulator ride, it is a breathtaking addition to the museum.
The museum cafés and shop
are particularly good.

Natural History Museum ❺

Cromwell Rd SW7. **Map** 2 E5. ⚡ 020-
7942 5000. 🚇 South Kensington. 🕐
10am–5:50pm Mon–Sat, 11am–5:50pm
Sun & public hols. ⚫ 25, 26 Dec.
📲 ♿ 📷 📶 🆆 www.nhm.ac.uk

THIS VAST CATHEDRAL-LIKE
building is the most archi-
tecturally flamboyant of the
South Kensington museums.
Its richly sculpted stonework
conceals an iron and steel
frame; this building technique
was revolutionary when the
museum opened in 1881. The
imaginative displays tackle
fundamental issues such as
the ecology and evolution of
the planet, the origin
of species and the
development of
human beings
– all explained
through a
dynamic
combination

**Relief from a decorative panel in
the Natural History Museum**

of the latest technology, interactive techniques and
traditional displays.

The museum is divided into
the Life and Earth Galleries. In
the former, the Ecology exhibition begins its exploration
of the complex web of the
natural world, and man's role
in it, through a convincing replica of a moonlit rainforest
buzzing with the sounds of
insects. One of the most
popular exhibits is the Dinosaur Gallery, which has life-
like animatronic models of
dinosaurs, as well as skeletons
and fossils. The state-of-the-
art Earth Galleries explore the
history of Earth and its wealth
of natural resources, and the
Power Within offers the opportunity to experience the
rumblings of an earthquake.

**The Tuojiangasaurus
skeleton (about 150
million years old),
Natural History Museum**

Statue of the young Queen Victoria outside Kensington Palace, sculpted by her daughter, Princess Louise

Hyde Park and Kensington Gardens ❻

W2. **Map** 2 F2. 📞 *020-7298 2100.*
Hyde Park 🚇 *Hyde Park Corner,*
Knightsbridge, Lancaster Gate, Marble
Arch. 🕐 *dawn–midnight daily.* ♿
Kensington Gardens 📞 *020-7298*
2117. 🚇 *Queensway, Lancaster Gate.*
🕐 *dawn–dusk daily.* ♿ *See also*
pp76–7. **Diana, Princess of Wales**
Memorial Playground 🚇 *Queens-*
way, Bayswater. 🕐 *10am–dusk daily.*
♿ 📶 🅦 *www.royalparks.org.uk*

T HE ANCIENT MANOR of Hyde was part of the lands of Westminster Abbey seized by Henry VIII at the Dissolution of the Monasteries in 1536 *(see pp50–51)*. James I opened the park to the public in the early 17th century, and it was soon one of the city's most fashionable public spaces. Unfortunately it also became popular with duellists and highwaymen, and consequently

William III had 300 lights hung along Rotten Row, the first street in England to be lit up at night. In 1730, the Westbourne River was dammed by Queen Caroline in order to create the Serpentine, an artificial lake that is today used for boating and swimming, and Rotten Row for horse riding. The park is also a rallying point for political demonstrations, while at Speaker's Corner, in the northeast, anyone has had the right to address the public since 1872. Sundays are particularly lively, with many budding orators and a number of eccentrics revealing their plans for the betterment of mankind.

Adjoining Hyde Park is Kensington Gardens, the former grounds of Kensington Palace. Three great attractions for children are the innovative Diana, Princess of Wales Memorial Playground, the bronze statue of J M Barrie's fictional Peter Pan (1912), by George Frampton, and the Round Pond where people sail model boats. Also worth seeing is the dignified Orangery (1704), once used by Queen Anne as a "summer supper house" and now a summer café.

Detail of the Coalbrookdale
Gate, Kensington Gardens

Kensington Palace ❼

Kensington Palace Gdns W8. **Map** 2
D3. 📞 *020-7937 9561.* 🚇 *High St*
Kensington, Queensway. 🕐 *Nov–Feb:*
10am–5pm daily; Mar–Oct: 10am–6pm
daily (last adm: 1 hr before closing).
⬤ *1 Jan, 24–26 Dec.* 🅿 🎁 ♿
ground floor. 📶 🅦 *www.hrp.org.uk*

K ENSINGTON PALACE was the principal residence of the royal family from the 1690s until 1760, when George III moved to Buckingham Palace. Over the years it has seen a number of important royal events. In 1714 Queen Anne died here from a fit of apoplexy brought on by over-eating and, in June 1837, Princess Victoria of Kent was woken to be told that her uncle William IV had died and she was now queen – the beginning of her 64-year reign. Half of the palace still holds royal apartments, but the other half is open to the public. Among the highlights are the 18th-century state rooms with ceilings and murals by William Kent *(see p24)*. After the death of Princess Diana in 1997, the palace became a focal point for mourners who gathered in their thousands at its gates and turned the area into a field of bouquets.

REGENT'S PARK AND BLOOMSBURY

CREAM STUCCOED terraces built by John Nash *(see p107)* fringe the southern edge of Regent's Park in London's highest concentration of quality Georgian housing. The park, named for the Prince Regent, was also designed by Nash, as the culmination of a triumphal route from the Prince's house in St James's *(see pp86–7)*. Today it is the busiest of the royal parks and boasts a zoo, an open air theatre, boating lake, rose garden, cafés and London's largest mosque. To the northeast is Camden Town *(see p132)* with its popular market, shops and cafés, reached by walking, or taking a boat, along the picturesque Regent's Canal.

Ancient Greek vase, British Museum

Bloomsbury, an enclave of attractive garden squares and Georgian brick terraces, was one of the most fashionable areas of the city until the mid-19th century, when the arrival of large hospitals and railway stations persuaded many of the wealthier residents to move west to Mayfair, Knightsbridge and Kensington. Home to the British Museum since 1753 and the University of London since 1828, Bloomsbury has long been the domain of artists, writers and intellectuals, including the Bloomsbury Group *(see p151)*, George Bernard Shaw, Charles Dickens and Karl Marx. Traditionally a centre for the book trade, it remains a good place for literary browsing.

SIGHTS AT A GLANCE

Historic Streets
Bloomsbury **5**

Museums and Galleries
British Museum pp108–9 **4**

Madame Tussaud's and the Planetarium **1**
Sherlock Holmes Museum **2**
Wallace Collection **3**

KEY

🔵 Underground station

P Parking

0 metres 500
0 yards 500

GETTING THERE

For most of Regent's Park, the nearest tube stations are Regent's Park, Great Portland Street and Baker Street. Buses 13, 139 and 159 run from Trafalgar Square to near Baker Street. The closest station to the zoo is Camden Town. Russell Square tube station is in the heart of Bloomsbury.

◁ St Andrew's Place, Regent's Park

Madame Tussaud's and the Planetarium ❶

Marylebone Rd NW1. **Map** 3 B3.
📞 0870 400 3000. ⊖ Baker St.
🕐 9:30am–5:30pm daily. ⬛ 25 Dec.
🔲 📷 ♿ phone first. ⬛
🌐 www.madame-tussauds.com

MADAME TUSSAUD began her wax-modelling career making death masks of victims of the French Revolution. She moved to England and in 1835 set up an exhibition of her work in Baker Street, near the present site. Traditional techniques are still used to create figures of royalty, politicians, actors, pop stars and sporting heroes. The main sections of the exhibition are:

Wax figure of Elizabeth II

Blush, where visitors get to feel what it is like to be at a celebrity A-list party; Première Night, devoted to the giants of the entertainment world; and the World Stage, a collection of various royalty, statesmen, world leaders, writers and artists, from Shakespeare to Picasso.

The Chamber of Horrors is the most renowned part of Madame Tussaud's. Alongside some of the original French Revolution death masks are recreations of murders and executions. In the Spirit of

Wax model of Luciano Pavarotti (1990), Madame Tussaud's

Conan Doyle's fictional detective Sherlock Holmes

London finale, visitors travel in stylized taxi-cabs through the city's history to "witness" events, from the Great Fire of 1666 to the Swinging 1960s. Next door, the Planetarium, built in 1958, has spectacularly exciting star and laser shows.

Sherlock Holmes Museum ❷

221b Baker St NW1. **Map** 3 A3.
📞 020-7935 8866. ⊖ Baker St. 🕐
9:30am–6pm daily. ⬛ 25 Dec. 📷 🔲
🌐 www.sherlock-holmes.co.uk

SIR ARTHUR CONAN DOYLE's fictional detective was supposed to live at 221b Baker Street, which did not exist. The museum, labelled 221b, actually stands between Nos. 237 and 239, and is the only surviving Victorian lodging house in the street. There is a reconstruction of Holmes's front room, and memorabilia from the stories decorate every room. Visitors can buy plaques, Holmes hats, Toby jugs and meerschaum pipes.

Wallace Collection ❸

Hertford House, Manchester Sq W1.
Map 3 B4. 📞 020-7563 9500. ⊖
Bond St, Baker St. 🕐 10am–5pm
Mon–Sat, noon–5pm Sun. ⬛ 24–26
Dec, Good Fri, 1 Jan. ♿ phone first. 🔲
📷 🌐 www.wallace-collection.org.uk

ONE OF THE WORLD's finest private collections of European art, it has remained intact since 1897. The product of passionate collecting by four generations of the Seymour-Conway family who were Marquesses of Hertford, it was bequeathed to the state on the condition that it would go on permanent public display with nothing added or taken away. Hertford House still retains the atmosphere of a grand 19th-century house, and the recent Centenary Project has created more gallery space and a stunning high-level glass roof for the central courtyard, which now contains a sculpture garden and an elegant restaurant.

The 3rd Marquess (1777–1842), a flamboyant London figure, used his Italian wife's fortune to buy works by Titian and Canaletto, along with numerous 17th-century Dutch paintings including works by Van Dyck. The collection's particular strength is 18th-century French painting, sculpture and decorative arts, acquired by the 4th Marquess (1800–70) and his natural son, Sir Richard Wallace (1818–90).

A 16th-century Italian majolica dish from the Wallace Collection

The Marquess had a taste for lush romanticism, and notable among his acquisitions are Watteau's *Champs Elysées* (1716–17), Fragonard's *The Swing* (1766) and Boucher's *The Rising and Setting of the Sun* (1753).

Other highlights at the Wallace Collection include Rembrandt's *Titus, the Artist's Son* (1650s), Titian's *Perseus and Andromeda* (1554–6) and Hals's famous *Laughing Cavalier* (1624). There is also an important collection of Renaissance armour, and superb examples of Sèvres porcelain and Italian majolica.

John Nash's Regency London

JOHN NASH, the son of a Lambeth millwright, was designing houses from the 1780s. However, it was not until the 1820s that he also became known as an inspired town planner, when his "royal route" was completed. This took George IV from his Pall Mall palace, through Piccadilly Circus and up the elegant sweep of Regent Street to Regent's Park, which Nash bordered with rows of beautiful

Statue of John Nash (1752–1835)

Neo-Classical villas, such as Park Crescent and Cumberland Terrace. Though many of his plans were never completed, this map of 1851, which unusually places the south at the top, shows Nash's overall architectural impact on London. His other work included the revamping of Buckingham Palace *(see pp88–9)*, and the building of several theatres and churches.

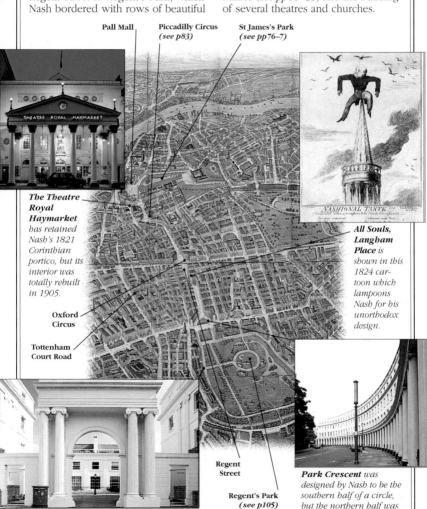

Pall Mall   **Piccadilly Circus** *(see p83)*   **St James's Park** *(see pp76–7)*

The Theatre Royal Haymarket *has retained Nash's 1821 Corinthian portico, but its interior was totally rebuilt in 1905.*

Oxford Circus

Tottenham Court Road

All Souls, Langham Place *is shown in this 1824 cartoon which lampoons Nash for his unorthodox design.*

VASHIONAL TASTE !!!

Cumberland Terrace, *the longest and most ornate of the stuccoed terraces surrounding Regent's Park, was intended to face a royal palace, which was never built.*

Regent Street

Regent's Park *(see p105)*

Park Crescent *was designed by Nash to be the southern half of a circle, but the northern half was never built. The interiors were refurbished in the 1960s but the dramatic façade was kept intact.*

British Museum ❹

Helmet from
Sutton Hoo
ship burial

THE OLDEST public museum in the world, the British Museum was established in 1753 to house the collections of the physician Sir Hans Sloane (1660–1753). Sloane's collection has been added to by gifts and purchases from all over the world, and the museum now contains objects spanning thousands of years. The main part of the building (1823–50) is by architect Robert Smirke, but the architectural highlight is the modern Great Court, with the Reading Room at its centre.

★ **Egyptian Mummies**
Animals such as this cat (30 BC) were preserved alongside humans by the ancient Egyptians.

Upper floors

North entrance

Bronze Figure Shiva Nataraja
This statue of the Hindu God Shiva Nataraja (c.1100) from South India forms part of the fine collection of Oriental art.

The Egyptian Gallery on the main floor houses the Rosetta Stone, the inscription that enabled 19th-century scholars to decipher Egyptian hieroglyphs.

GALLERY GUIDE

The Greek and Roman, and Ancient Near Eastern collections are found on all three levels of the museum, predominantly on the west side. The African collection is located on the lower floor, while Asian exhibits are found on the main and upper floors on the north side of the museum. The Americas collection is located in the northeast corner off the main floor. Egyptian artifacts are found in the large gallery to the west of the Great Court and on the first floor.

★ **Parthenon Sculptures**
These reliefs from the Parthenon in Athens were brought to London by Lord Elgin around 1802 and are housed in a special gallery.

Main floor

Lower floor

STAR EXHIBITS

- ★ **Egyptian Mummies**
- ★ **Parthenon Sculptures**
- ★ **Lindow Man**

KEY TO FLOORPLAN

- ☐ Asian collection
- ☐ Americas collection
- ☐ Coins, medals, prints and drawings
- ☐ Greek and Roman collections
- ☐ Egyptian collection
- ☐ World collection
- ☐ Ancient Near Eastern collection
- ☐ Prehistory and Europe collection
- ☐ African collection
- ☐ Temporary exhibitions
- ☐ Non-exhibition space

First floor

The Great Court is London's largest covered square, with shops, cafés, a restaurant, display areas and educational facilities.

VISITORS' CHECKLIST

Great Russell St WC1. **Map** 4 E4.
020-7323 8000. Holborn,
Russell Sq, Tottenham Court Rd.
7, 8, 10,14, 19, 24, 25, 29,
30, 38, 55, 134,188. Euston,
King's Cross. 10am–5:30pm
daily (selected galleries until
8:30pm Thu & Fri). 1 Jan,
Good Fri, 24–26 Dec.
www.thebritishmuseum.ac.uk

Private gardens of Bedford Square

Bloomsbury 5

WC1. **Map** 4 F4. *Russell Sq, Tottenham Court Rd.* **Charles Dickens Museum** *48 Doughty St WC1.*
020-7405 2127. *10am–5pm Mon–Sat, 11am–5pm Sun (last adm: 4:30pm).*
www.dickensmuseum.com

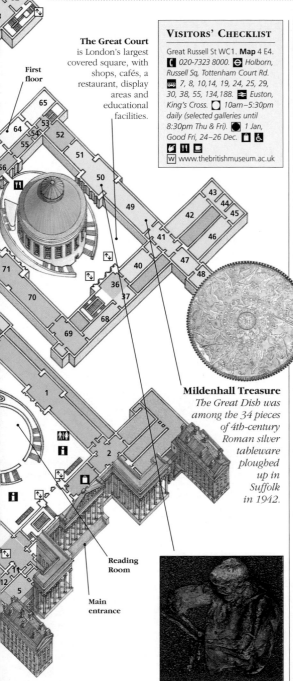

Mildenhall Treasure
The Great Dish was among the 34 pieces of 4th-century Roman silver tableware ploughed up in Suffolk in 1942.

Reading Room

Main entrance

★ Lindow Man
The skin on this 2,000-year-old human body was preserved by the acids of a peat-bog in Cheshire. He was probably killed in an elaborate ritual.

HOME TO numerous writers and artists, Bloomsbury is a traditional centre of the book trade. It is dominated by the British Museum and the University of London and characterized by several fine Georgian squares. These include **Russell Square**, where the poet T S Eliot (1888–1965) worked for a publisher for 40 years; **Queen Square** which contains a statue of Queen Charlotte, wife of George III; and **Bloomsbury Square**, laid out in 1661. A plaque here commemorates members of the Bloomsbury Group *(see p151)*. One of London's best-preserved 18th-century oases is **Bedford Square**. Charles Dickens *(see p177)* lived at 48 Doughty Street during a brief but critical stage in his career, and it was here that he wrote *Oliver Twist* and *Nicholas Nickleby*, both completed in 1839.

Queen Charlotte (1744–1818)

His former home is now the **Charles Dickens Museum**, which has rooms laid out as they were in Dickens's time, with objects taken from his other London homes and first editions of many of his works.

THE CITY AND SOUTHWARK

DOMINATED TODAY BY glossy office blocks, the City is the oldest part of the capital. The Great Fire of 1666 obliterated four-fifths of its buildings. Sir Christopher Wren rebuilt much of it and many of his churches survived World War II *(see pp58–9)*. Commerce has always been the City's lifeblood, and the power of its merchants and bankers secured it a degree of autonomy from state control. Humming with activity in business hours, it empties at night.

In the Middle Ages Southwark, on the south bank of the Thames, was a

Old bank sign on
Lombard Street

refuge for pleasure-seekers, prostitutes, gamblers and criminals. Even after 1550, when the area fell under the jurisdiction of the City, its brothels and taverns thrived. There were also several bear-baiting arenas in which plays were staged until the building of theatres such as the Globe (1598), where many of Shakespeare's works were first performed. Relics of old Southwark are mostly on the waterfront, which has been imaginatively redeveloped and provided with a pleasant walkway.

SIGHTS AT A GLANCE

Historic Sights and Buildings
HMS Belfast ⑫
Lloyd's Building ⑦
Monument ⑧
The Old Operating Theatre ⑭
Temple ③
Tower Bridge ⑩
Tower of London pp120–21 ⑨

Pubs
George Inn ⑮

Museums and Galleries
Design Museum ⑪
London Dungeon ⑬
Museum of London ⑥
Shakespeare's Globe ⑱
Sir John Soane's Museum ④
Tate Modern ⑲

Markets
Borough Market ⑯

Churches and Cathedrals
St Bartholomew-the-Great ⑤
St Paul's Cathedral
  pp116–17 ②
St Stephen Walbrook ①
Southwark Cathedral ⑰

GETTING THERE
The City is served by the Circle, Central, District, Northern and Metropolitan lines and by a number of buses. London Bridge is the main station for Southwark – served by the Northern and Jubilee lines and by trains running from Charing Cross, Cannon Street and Waterloo.

KEY

▧	Street-by-Street map *pp112–13*
⊖	Underground station
⌖	Railway station
P	Parking
⛴	River boat pier

0 metres   500
0 yards   500

◁ **St Paul's Cathedral in the heart of the City, with the NatWest Tower (1980) to the left**

Street-by-Street: The City

Detail: St Paul's Cathedral

THIS IS THE FINANCIAL HEART of London and has been ever since the Romans set up a trading post here 2,000 years ago. For years it was London's main residential area but today very few people live here. The City was severely bombed in World War II and the main clues to its past are streets named after vanished inns and markets. Its numerous churches, many built after the Great Fire of 1666 by the architect Sir Christopher Wren *(see p116)*, are now dwarfed by lavish banks and post-modern developments.

St Mary-le-Bow takes its name from the bow arches in the Norman crypt. Anyone born within earshot of its bells is said to be a true Cockney.

New Change replaces Old Change, a 13th-century street destroyed in World War II.

St Paul's station

Statue of Queen Anne

ST PAUL'S CHURCHYARD

NEW CHANGE

WATLING STREET

BREAD STREET

CANNON STREET

FRIDAY ST

QUEEN VICTORIA

QUEEN

St Nicholas Cole was the first church Wren built in the City (in 1677). Like many others, it had to be restored after World War II bomb damge.

Mansion House station

★ **St Paul's Cathedral** *Built after the Great Fire of 1666, Wren's masterpiece was funded by a tax on coal* ❷

St James Garlickhythe contains unusual sword rests and hat stands, beneath Wren's elegant spire of 1717.

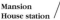
COLLEGE · OF · ARMS

The College of Arms is the official repository of the coats of arms and pedigrees of British families *(see p26)*. It was rebuilt here, on its former site, in the 1670s after the Great Fire.

STAR SIGHTS

★ **St Paul's Cathedral**

★ **St Stephen Walbrook**

Mansion House (1753), designed by George Dance the Elder, is the official home of the Lord Mayor. The Palladian façade is a familiar City landmark.

The Temple of Mithras is an important Roman relic discovered during World War II.

LOCATOR MAP
See Street Finder map 7, 8

Bank of England Museum

The Royal Exchange was founded in 1565 by Sir Thomas Gresham as a centre for commerce. The current building dates from 1844.

Bank station

Lombard Street, named after bankers who came here from Lombardy in the 13th century, retains its traditional banking signs.

KEY

- - - Suggested route

St Mary Abchurch owes its unusually spacious feel to Wren's large dome. The altar carving is by Grinling Gibbons.

★ **St Stephen Walbrook**
This fine Wren church contains a striking white stone altar by Henry Moore ❶

0 metres   100
0 yards   100

Skinners' Hall is an 18th-century Italianate building constructed for the ancient guild that controlled trade in fur and leather.

St Stephen Walbrook [1]

39 Walbrook EC4. **Map** 8 D3.
[020-7626 8242. e *Bank,
Cannon St.* ○ *10am–4pm Mon–Thu,
10am–3pm Fri.* ● *public hols.*

THE LORD MAYOR's parish
church was built by Sir
Christopher Wren in the 1670s
and is among the finest of all
his City churches. The bright,
airy interior is flooded with
light by a huge dome that
appears to float above the
eight columns and arches that
support it. The dome, deep
and coffered with ornate
plasterwork, was a forerunner
of St Paul's. Original fittings,
such as the highly decorative
font cover and pulpit canopy,
contrast with the stark simplicity of Henry Moore's
massive white stone altar
(1987). The best time to see
the church is during one of its
free organ recitals from 12.30
to 1.30pm on Fridays.

St. Paul's [2]

See pp116–17.

Effigies in Temple Church

Temple [3]

Inner Temple, King's Bench Walk EC4.
[020-7797 8250. **Map** 7 A3. e
Temple. ○ *10am–4pm Mon–Fri
(grounds).* & **Middle Temple Hall**,
Middle Temple Ln EC4. [020-7427
4800. ○ *10–11:30am, 3–4pm Mon–
Fri.* & **Temple Church** [020-7353
8559. ○ *11am–4pm daily.* ☑

A CLUSTER of atmospheric
squares form the Inner
and Middle Temples, two of
London's four Inns of Court,
where law students are trained.
The name Temple derives from
the medieval Knights Templar,
a religious order which protected pilgrims to the Holy Land
and was based here until 1312
when it was suppressed by
the Crown. Marble effigies of
knights lie on the floor of the
circular Temple Church, part
of which dates from the 12th
century. Middle Temple Hall
has a fine Elizabethan interior.

St Bartholomew-the-Great [5]

West Smithfield EC1. **Map** 7 B1.
[020-7606 5171. e *Barbican,
St Paul's.* ○ *8:30am–5pm (4pm in
winter) Tue–Fri, 8:30am–1pm Sat,
2.30–8pm Sun.* ● *25, 26 Dec, 1
Jan.* & ☑ *by appt.* **Concerts.**
w www.greatstbarts.com

THE HISTORIC AREA of Smithfield has witnessed a
number of bloody events over
the years, among them the
execution of rebel peasant
leader Wat Tyler in 1381, and,
in the reign of Mary I (1553–
58), the burning of scores
of Protestant martyrs.

Sir John Soane's Museum [4]

13 Lincoln's Inn Fields WC2. **Map** 4 F4.
[020-7405 2107. e *Holborn.* ○
*10am–5pm Tue–Sat, 6–9pm 1st Tue
of month.* ● *1 Jan, 24–26 Dec,
Easter.* & *ground floor only.*
☑ *Sat 2:30pm.* w www.soane.org

ONE OF THE MOST eccentric
museums in London, this
house was left to the nation
by Sir John Soane in 1837,
with a stipulation that nothing
should be changed. The son
of a bricklayer, Soane became
one of Britain's leading late
Georgian architects developing a restrained Neo-Classical
style of his own. After marrying the niece of a wealthy
builder, whose fortune he
inherited, he bought and reconstructed No. 12 Lincoln's
Inn Fields. In 1813 he and his
wife moved into No. 13 and
in 1824 he rebuilt No. 14,
adding a picture gallery and
the mock medieval Monk's

Parlour. Today, true to Soane's
wishes, the collections are
much as he left them – an
eclectic gathering of beautiful,
instructional and often simply
peculiar artifacts. There are
casts, bronzes, vases, antique
fragments, paintings and a
selection of bizarre trivia which
ranges from a giant fungus
from Sumatra to a scold-bridle,
a device designed to silence
nagging wives. Highlights
include the sarcophagus of
Seti I, Soanes's own designs,
including those for the Bank
of England, models by leading Neo-Classical sculptors
and the *Rake's Progress* series
of paintings (1734) by William
Hogarth, which Mrs Soane
bought for £520.

The building itself is full of
architectural surprises and
illusions. In the main ground
floor room, cunningly placed
mirrors play tricks with light
and space, while an atrium
stretching from the basement
to the glass-domed roof
allows light on to every floor.

A glass dome lets light
on to all the floors.

A vast sarcophagus
(1300 BC) stands on
the floor of the crypt.

Hidden in a quiet corner behind Smithfield meat market (central London's only surviving wholesale food market), St Bartholomew-the-Great is one of London's oldest churches. It once formed part of a priory founded in 1123 by a monk named Rahere, whose tomb is here. He was Henry I's court jester until he dreamed that St Bartholomew had saved him from a winged monster.

The 13th-century arch, now topped by a Tudor gatehouse, used to be the entrance to the church until the old nave was pulled down during the Dissolution of the Monasteries (*see pp50–51*). The painter William Hogarth was baptized here in 1697. The church featured in the film *Four Weddings and a Funeral.*

St Bartholomew's gatehouse

Museum of London 6

London Wall EC2. **Map** 7 C2.
📞 0870 444 3851. 🚇 Barbican, St Paul's. 🕐 10am–5:50pm Mon–Sat & public hols, noon–5:50pm Sun.
⬤ 1 Jan, 24–26 Dec. ♿ 🖼 🛍
🌐 www.museumoflondon.org.uk

THIS MUSEUM traces life in London from prehistoric times to the outbreak of World War I. Displays of archaeological finds and domestic objects alternate

Delft plate made in London 1600, Museum of London

with reconstructed street scenes and interiors. The World City galleries chart the birth of modern London from the French Revolution to World War I, and display Nelson's bejewelled sword.

The Roman London gallery has a brightly coloured 2nd-century fresco from a South-wark bath house, while the 17th-century section holds the shirt that Charles I wore on the scaffold (*see pp52–3*). Popular exhibits are the Lord Mayor's State Coach, built in 1757 and still used for the Lord Mayor's Show in November, and the working model of the Great Fire of 1666.

Every wall is covered and every room filled with artifacts from Soane's voluminous collection.

In the picture gallery, panels covered with paintings unfold to reveal more works of art hidden behind them.

The Monk's Parlour is full of grotesque Gothic casts.

St Paul's Cathedral ❷

THE GREAT FIRE OF LONDON in 1666 left the medieval cathedral of St Paul's in ruins. Wren was commissioned to rebuild it, but his design for a church on a Greek Cross plan (where all four arms are equal) met with considerable resistance. The authorities insisted on a conventional Latin cross, with a long nave and short transepts, which was believed to focus the congregation's attention on the altar. Despite the compromises, Wren created a magnificent Baroque cathedral, which was built between 1675 and 1710 and has since formed the lavish setting for many state ceremonies.

★ Dome
At 111 m (360 ft), the elaborate dome is one of the highest in the world.

The balustrade along the top was added in 1718 against Wren's wishes.

★ West Front and Towers
Inspired by the Italian Baroque architect, Borromini, the towers were added by Wren in 1707.

The West Portico consists of two storeys of coupled Corinthian columns, topped by a pediment carved with reliefs showing the Conversion of St Paul.

The Nave
An imposing succession of massive arches and saucer domes open out into the vast space below the cathedral's main dome.

West Porch

Main entrance approached from Ludgate Hill

CHRISTOPHER WREN

Trained as a scientist, Sir Christopher Wren (1632–1723) began his impressive architectural career at the age of 31. He became a leading figure in the rebuilding of London after the Great Fire of 1666, building a total of 52 new churches. Although Wren never visited Italy, his work was influenced by Roman, Baroque and Renaissance architecture, as is apparent in his masterpiece, St Paul's Cathedral.

The lantern weighs a massive 850 tonnes.

The Golden Gallery has splendid views over London.

The oculus is an opening through which the cathedral floor can be seen.

Stone Gallery

The High Altar canopy was made in the 1950s, based on designs by Wren.

★ Whispering Gallery
The dome's unusual acoustics mean that words whispered against the wall can be heard clearly on the opposite side.

Choir
Jean Tijou, a Huguenot refugee, created much of the fine wrought iron-work in Wren's time, including these choir screens.

Entrance to crypt, which has many memorials to the famous.

Entrance to Golden, Whispering and Stone galleries

The South Portico was inspired by the porch of Santa Maria della Pace in Rome. Wren absorbed the detail by studying a friend's collection of architectural engravings.

STAR SIGHTS

★ **West Front and Towers**

★ **Dome**

★ **Whispering Gallery**

Choir Stalls
The 17th-century choir stalls and organ case were made by Grinling Gibbons (1648–1721), a wood-carver from Rotterdam. He and his team of craftsmen worked on these intricate carvings for two years.

Richard Rogers's Lloyd's building

Lloyd's Building ❼

1 Lime St EC3. **Map** 8 E2. 📞 020-7327 1000. 🚇 Monument, Bank, Aldgate. ⬤ to the public.

L LOYD'S WAS FOUNDED in the late 17th century and soon became the world's main insurers, issuing policies on everything from oil tankers to Betty Grable's legs. The present building, designed by Richard Rogers, dates from 1986 and is one of the most interesting modern buildings in London. Its exaggerated stainless steel external piping and high-tech ducts echo Roger's forceful Pompidou Centre in Paris. Lloyds' is well worth seeing floodlit at night.

Monument ❽

Monument St EC3. **Map** 8 D3. 📞 020-7626 2717. 🚇 Monument. ◐ 9:30am–5pm daily. ⬤ 1 Jan, 24–26 Dec. 🈂 🆆 www.towerbridge.org.uk

T HIS DORIC COLUMN, designed by Wren to commemorate the Great Fire of London that devastated the original walled city in September 1666, was, in 1681, the tallest isolated stone column in the world. Topped with a bronze flame, the Monument is 62 m (205 ft) high; the exact distance west to Pudding Lane, where the fire is believed to have started. Reliefs around the column's base show Charles II restoring the city after the tragedy.

The 311 tightly-spiralled steps lead to a tiny, claustrophobia-inducing viewing platform. (In 1842, it was enclosed with an iron cage to prevent suicides.) The steep climb is well worth the effort as the views from the top are spectacular and visitors are rewarded with a certificate.

Tower of London ❾

See pp120–21.

Tower Bridge ❿

SE1. **Map** 8 F4. 📞 020-7403 3761. 🚇 Tower Hill. **The Tower Bridge Exhibition** ◐ Apr–Oct: 10am–6pm daily; Nov–Mar: 9:30am–6pm daily (last adm: 5:30pm). ⬤ 24 & 25 Dec. 🈂 ♿ 🅿 🆆 www.towerbridge.org.uk

T HIS FLAMBOYANT piece of Victorian engineering, designed by Sir Horace Jones, was completed in 1894 and soon became a symbol of London. Its two Gothic towers contain the mechanism for raising the roadway to permit large ships to pass through. The towers are made of a supporting steel framework clad in stone, and are linked by two high level walkways which were closed between 1909 and 1982 due to their popularity with suicides and prostitutes. The bridge now houses The Tower Bridge Exhibition, with interactive displays bringing the bridge's history to life. There are fine river views from the walkways, and a look at the steam engine room that powered the lifting machinery until 1976, when the system was electrified.

Walkways, open to the public, give panoramic views over the Thames and London.

The roadway, when raised, creates a space 40 m (135 ft) high and 60 m (200 ft) wide, big enough for large cargo ships.

Engine room

South Bank

Lifts and 300 steps lead to the top of the towers.

The Victorian winding machinery was originally powered by steam.

Entrance

North Bank

Design Museum ⓫

Butlers Wharf, Shad Thames SE1. **Map** 8 F4. 🅲 *0870-909 9009.* 🚇 *Tower Hill, London Bridge.* 🕐 *10am–5:45pm daily (last adm: 5:15pm), late Fri opening to 9pm Jun–Aug.* ● *25 & 26 Dec.* 🖼 🚻 🍽 **Blueprint Café** *020-7378 7031 for reservations.* 💻 📷 🆆 *www.designmuseum.org*

THIS MUSEUM was the first in the world to be devoted solely to modern and contemporary design when it was founded in 1989. A frequently changing programme of exhibitions explores landmarks in modern design history and the most exciting innovations in contemporary design set against the context of social, cultural, economic and technological changes. The Design Museum embraces every area of design, from furniture and fashion, to household products, cars, graphics, websites and architecture in exhibitions and new design commissions. Each spring the museum hosts Designer of the Year, a national design prize, with an exhibition at which the public can vote for the winner.

The museum is arranged over three floors, with major exhibitions on the first floor. There is a choice of smaller displays on the second, which also houses an Interaction Space, where visitors can play vintage video games and learn about the designers featured in the museum in the Design at the Design Museum online research archive. The shop and café are on the ground floor. On the first floor is the **Blueprint Café** restaurant, which has stunning views of the Thames (booking ahead recommended).

Austin Mini in the Design Museum

The now familiar sight of the naval gunship HMS Belfast on the Thames

HMS Belfast ⓬

Morgan's Lane, Tooley St SE1. **Map** 8 E4. 🅲 *020-7940 6300.* 🚇 *London Bridge, Tower Hill.* 🕐 *Mar–Oct: 10am–6pm daily; Nov–Feb: 10am–5pm daily (last adm: 45 mins before closing).* ● *24–26 Dec.* 🖼 🚻 limited. 💻 📷 🆆 *www.iwm.org.uk*

ORIGINALLY LAUNCHED in 1938 to serve in World War II, the 11,500-ton battle ship HMS *Belfast* was instrumental in the destruction of the German battle cruiser *Scharnhorst* in the battle of North Cape, and also played an important role in the Normandy Landings.

After the war, the battle cruiser, designed for offensive action and for supporting amphibious operations, was sent to work for the United Nations in Korea. The ship remained in service with the British navy until 1965.

Since 1971, the cruiser has been used as a floating naval museum. Part of it has been atmospherically recreated to show what the ship was like in 1943, when it participated in sinking the German battle cruiser. Other displays portray life on board during World War II, and there are also general exhibits which relate to the history of the Royal Navy.

As well as being a great family day out, it is also possible for children to take part in the educational activity weekends that take place on board the ship.

London Dungeon ⓭

Tooley St SE1. **Map** 8 D4. 🅲 *020-7403 7221.* 🚇 *London Bridge.* 🕐 *Jul & Aug 10am–7:30pm; Sep & Oct 10am–5:30pm; Nov–Easter 10:30am–5pm; Easter–Jun 10am–5:30pm; daily.* ● *25 Dec.* 🖼 🚻 💻 📷 🆆 *www.thedungeons.com*

IN EFFECT a much expanded version of the chamber of horrors at Madame Tussaud's *(see p106)*, this museum is a great hit with children. It illustrates the most bloodthirsty events in British history. It is played strictly for terror, and screams abound as Druids perform a human sacrifice at Stonehenge, Henry VIII's wife Anne Boleyn is beheaded, and a room full of people die in agony during the Great Plague. Other displays include torture, murder and witchcraft.

19th-century surgical tools

The Old Operating Theatre ⓮

9a St Thomas St SE1. **Map** 8 D4. 🅲 *020-7955 4791.* 🚇 *London Bridge.* 🕐 *10:30am–5pm daily.* ● *15 Dec–5 Jan.* 🖼 📷 🆆 *www.thegarret.org.uk*

ST THOMAS'S HOSPITAL stood here from its foundation in the 12th century until it was moved west in 1862. At this time most of its buildings were demolished to make way for the railway. The women's operating theatre (The Old Operating Theatre Museum and Herb Garret) survived only because it was located away from the main buildings, in a garret over the hospital church. It lay, bricked up and forgotten, until the 1950s. Britain's oldest operating theatre, dating back to 1822, it has now been fitted out as it would have been in the early 19th century.

Tower of London ❾

Soon after he became king in 1066, William the Conqueror built a fortress here to guard the entrance to London from the Thames Estuary. In 1097 the White Tower, standing today at the centre of the complex, was completed in sturdy stone; other fine buildings have been added over the centuries. The Tower has served as a royal residence, armoury, treasury and most famously as a prison for enemies of the crown. Many were tortured and among those who met their death there were the "Princes in the Tower", the sons and heirs of Edward IV. Today the tower is a popular attraction, housing the Crown Jewels and other exhibits. Its most celebrated residents are seven ravens whose presence is protected by the legend that the kingdom will fall if they desert the tower.

Beauchamp Tower
Many high-ranking prisoners were held here, often with their own retinues of servants. The tower was built by Edward I around 1281.

"Beefeaters"
Thirty-seven Yeoman Warders guard the Tower and live here. Their uniforms hark back to Tudor times.

Two 13th-century curtain walls protect the tower.

Tower Green was the execution site for favoured prisoners, away from crowds on Tower Hill, where many had to submit to public execution. Seven people died here, including two of Henry VIII's six wives, Anne Boleyn and Catherine Howard.

Queen's House
This Tudor building is the sovereign's official residence at the Tower.

Main entrance from Tower Hill

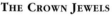

THE CROWN JEWELS

The world's best-known collection of precious objects, now displayed in a splendid exhibition room, includes the gorgeous regalia of crowns, sceptres, orbs and swords used at coronations and other state occasions. Most date from 1661, when Charles II commissioned replacements for regalia destroyed by Parliament after the execution of Charles I (*see pp52–3*). Only a few older pieces survived, hidden by royalist clergymen until the Restoration – notably, Edward the Confessor's sapphire ring, now incorporated into the Imperial State Crown (*see p73*). The crown was made for Queen Victoria in 1837 and has been used at every coronation since.

The Sovereign's Ring (1831)

The Sovereign's Orb (1661), a hollow gold sphere encrusted with jewels

★ **Jewel House**
Among the magnificent Crown Jewels is the Sceptre with the Cross (1660), which now contains the world's biggest diamond.

★ **White Tower**
When the tower was finished in 1097, it was the tallest building in London at 27 m (90 ft) high.

★ **Chapel of St John**
This austerely beautiful Romanesque chapel is a particularly fine example of Norman architecture.

Traitors' Gate
The infamous entrance was used for prisoners brought from trial in Westminster Hall.

Bloody Tower
Edward IV's two sons were put here by their uncle, Richard of Gloucester (subsequently Richard III), after their father died in 1483. The princes, depicted here by John Millais (1829–96), disappeared mysteriously and Richard was crowned later that year. In 1674 the skeletons of two children were found nearby.

VISITORS' CHECKLIST

Tower Hill EC3. **Map** 8 E3.
0870-756 7080 for advance booking. Tower Hill; Tower Gateway (DLR). RV1, 15, X15, 25, 42, 78, 100, D1, D9, D11. Fenchurch Street. Mar–Oct: 9am–6pm Mon–Sat, 10am–6pm Sun; Nov–Feb: 9am–5pm Tue–Sat, 10am–5pm Sun & Mon. 1 Jan, 24–26 Dec. limited, except Jewel House. **Ceremony of the Keys**: 9:30pm daily (book in advance).
W www.tower-of-london.org.uk

STAR SIGHTS

★ **Jewel House**

★ **White Tower**

★ **Chapel of St John**

The George Inn, now owned by the National Trust

George Inn ⑮

77 Borough High St SE1. **Map** 8 D4.
█ 020-7407 2056. ⊖ *London Bridge, Borough.* ◯ *11am–11pm Mon–Sat, noon–10:30pm Sun.* ▯

DATING FROM THE 17th century, this building is the only traditional galleried coaching inn left in London and is mentioned in Dickens's *Little Dorrit*. It was rebuilt after the Southwark fire of 1676 in a style that dates back to the Middle Ages. There were originally three wings around a courtyard, where plays were staged in the 17th century. In 1889 the north and east wings were demolished, so there is only one wing remaining.

The inn is still a restaurant and a popular pub with a well-worn, comfortable atmosphere, perfect on a cold, damp day. In the summer, the yard fills with picnic tables and patrons are occasionally entertained by actors and morris dancers. The house bitter is highly recommended.

Borough Market ⑯

8 Southwark St SE1. **Map** 8 D4.
⊖ *London Bridge.* **Retail market** ◯ *Fri noon–6pm, Sat 9am–4pm.*

BOROUGH MARKET was until recently an exclusively wholesale fruit and vegetable market, which had its origins in medieval times, and moved to its current atmospheric position beneath the railway tracks in 1756. A popular and fine food market has now become well established, selling gourmet foods from Britain and abroad, as well as quality fruit and vegetables, to locals and tourists alike.

Shakespeare window (1954), Southwark Cathedral

Southwark Cathedral ⑰

Montague Close SE1. **Map** 8 D4.
█ 020-7367 6700. ⊖ *London Bridge.* ◯ *8am–6pm daily.* ▯ ▯
▯ www.dswark.org/cathedral

ALTHOUGH SOME PARTS OF this building date back to the 12th century, it was not until 1905 that it became a cathedral. Many original medieval features remain, notably the superb Gothic choir, and the tomb of the poet John Gower (c.1325–1408), a contemporary of Chaucer *(see p172)*. There is a monument to Shakespeare, carved in 1912, and a memorial window *(above)* installed in 1954.

Shakespeare's Globe ⑱

New Globe Walk SE1. **Map** 7 C3.
█ 020-7902 1400. Box office: 020-7401 9919. ⊖ *Southwark, London Bridge.* **Exhibition** ◯ *May–Sep: 9am–5pm daily; Oct–Apr: 10am–5pm daily.* ▯ �& ▯ *every 30 mins. (Rose Theatre tours for groups of 15 or more by appt only).* **Performances** *mid-May–Sep.* �& *limited.* ▯ ▯
▯ ▯ www.shakespeares-globe.org

OPENED IN 1997, this circular building is a faithful reproduction of an Elizabethan theatre, close to the site of the original Globe where many of Shakespeare's plays were first performed. It was built using handmade bricks and oak laths, fastened with wooden pegs rather than metal screws, and has the first thatched roof allowed in London since the Great Fire of 1666. The theatre was erected thanks to a heroic campaign waged by the American actor and director Sam Wanamaker. Open to the elements (although the seats are protected), it operates only in the summer, and seeing a play here can be a thrilling experience, with top-quality acting under the artistic direction of Mark Rylance among others (any performances with him in the cast are well worth seeing).

Beneath the theatre, Shakespeare's Globe Exhibition is open all year and covers many aspects of Shakespeare's work and times. Groups of 15 or more may book to see the foundations of the nearby Rose Theatre.

Shakespeare's *Henry IV* (performed at the Globe Theatre around 1600)

Tate Modern ⑲

Holland St, SE1. **Map** 7 C3. 020-
7887 8000. Blackfriars, Southwark.
to Tate Britain every 40 mins.
Blackfriars 10am–6pm Sun–Thu,
10am–10pm Fri & Sat. 24–26
Dec. major exhibitions.
www.tate.org.uk

LOOMING OVER the southern
bank of the Thames, Tate
Modern occupies the converted
Bankside power station, a
dynamic space for one of the
world's premier collections of
modern art. Tate Modern
draws its main displays from
the expansive Tate Collection
– also shown at the other
Tate galleries: Tate St Ives
(p265), Tate Liverpool (p363)
and Tate Britain (p93). A river
boat, Tate to Tate, transports
visitors between Tate Modern
and Tate Britain. The rotation
of pieces and numerous

special exhibitions result in
compelling displays that
change constantly.
    The gallery's west entrance
leads straight into the massive
Turbine Hall. Each year an
artist is commissioned to
install in this space. Louise
Bourgeois was the first to
install here, creating three
giant towers and a gargantuan
spider, *Maman* (2000). Recently, Olafur Eliasson's *The
Weather Project* lit the Turbine
Hall with a giant glowing sun.
    An escalator whisks visitors
from the Turbine Hall, up to
level 3 where the main
galleries are located. In a break
with convention, Tate Modern
organizes its
displays by
theme rather
than chron-
ology or
school – a
practice that cuts
across movements and
mixes up media. Four
themes based on tradi-
tional genres reveal how
traditions have been
confronted, extended
or rejected by artists
throughout the 20th and
into the 21st centuries.
    Still Life/Object/Real Life
on level 3 includes work
ranging from Cézanne's
paintings to works by
Claus Oldenburg and
Damien Hirst.
Landscape/
Matter/Environ-
ment, also on
Level 3, looks at how artists
have taken up the challenge
of representing our
environment. In one room,
Impressionist Claude Monet's

Standing by the Rags (1988-89) by
Lucian Freud

Water Lilies is placed opposite
Jules Olitski's ethereal abstract
*Instant
Loveland*,
suggesting
both artists'
immersion in
nature.
    In Nude/
Action/Body on level 5,
artists who have attempt-
ed to re-define the body,
such as Lucian Freud,
Pablo Picasso and Lovis
Corinth, are on display.
Also on level 5 is
History/ Memory/
Society. These galleries
contain 20th-century
works by artists such
as Piet Mondrian and
Gilbert and George,
who engage with the
social and
political world.
    To comple-
ment its
permanent collection, Tate
Modern presents a dynamic
programme of temporary
exhibitions, including three
large-scale shows per year.

Death from **Death Hope Life Fear**
(1984) by Gilbert and George

Soft Drainpipe – Blue (Cool)
(1967) by Claes Oldenburg

BANKSIDE POWER STATION

This forbidding fortress was designed in 1947 by Sir Giles
Gilbert Scott, the architect of Battersea Power Station, Waterloo
Bridge and London's famous red telephone boxes. The power
station is of a steel-framed brick skin construction, comprising
over 4.2 million bricks. The Turbine Hall was designed to
accommodate huge oil-burning generators and three vast oil
tanks are still in situ, buried under the ground just south of
the building. The tanks are to be employed in a future stage
of Tate Modern development. The power station itself was converted by Swiss architects Herzog and de Meuron who designed
the two-storey glass box, or lightbeam, which runs the length
of the building. This serves to flood the upper galleries with
light and also provides wonderful views of London.

The façade, chimney and light beam of Tate Modern

SHOPS AND MARKETS

Bags from two famous London department stores

LONDON is one of the great shopping cities of Europe, with bustling, lively street markets, world-famous department stores, and a wide variety of eclectic shops selling clothes, crafts and antiques *(see p627)*. The best shopping areas range from elegant, upmarket districts such as Knightsbridge and Bond Street, which sell expensive designer clothes, to the busy, chaotic stretch of Oxford Street, and the colourful, noisy markets of Covent Garden *(see p81)*, Berwick Street and Brick Lane. The city is best known, however, for its huge range of clothes shops selling everything from traditional tweeds to the latest zany designs of the ever-changing high-street fashions.

CHAIN AND DEPARTMENT STORES

Façade of Liberty (1925)

THE MOST FAMOUS of London's many department stores is **Harrods**, with some 300 departments, 4,000 staff, and a spectacular Edwardian food hall. Nearby **Harvey Nichols** stocks high fashion and boasts the city's most stylish food hall. Gourmets should make a pilgrimage to **Fortnum & Mason**, which has stocked high-quality food for nearly 300 years. Traditional teas are available in the café.

Selfridges sells virtually everything from international fashion labels to household gadgets, while **John Lewis** and its newly revamped Chelsea partner **Peter Jones** specialize in fabrics, china, glass and household items. **Liberty**, set in a beautiful Tudor-style building, still sells the silks and Oriental goods for which it was famous when it opened in 1875, as well as contemporary fashion. **Marks & Spencer** has long been known for its quality own-label clothes, and also has many good food stores.

The best chain store record shops are **Virgin Megastore**, **Tower Records** and HMV.

CLOTHES AND SHOES

BRITISH DESIGNERS range from elegant **Ben de Lisi** to **Vivienne Westwood**, doyenne of the punkish avant-garde. Top British fashion designers **Margaret Howell** and **Paul Smith** sell stylish fashion for men and women, while shops such as **Urban Outfitters** stock adventurous young designer ware for trendy clubbers. More established international designers are stocked at **Browns** and the department stores **Harvey Nichols**, **Liberty** and **Selfridges** (which also has a Top Shop concession with great fashion for girls).

Traditional English clothing – Barbour jackets and Burberry trench coats – is found in outlets such as **Harrods**, **Hackett** (for men), **Burberry** and **Gieves & Hawkes**. Shoes range from traditional mens at **Church's Shoes** and **John Lobb**, to the stylish designs of **Emma Hope** and the more affordable **Hobbs** and **Pied à Terre**.

MARKETS

LONDON'S MARKETS sell everything from street fashion and vintage clothes to fine food, antiques and cheap household goods.

The fashionable markets are **Camden Lock**, **Greenwich**, **Portobello Road** and **Covent Garden** where you can find handmade crafts, old clothes and antiques. For those more serious about antique collecting, go early on a Friday to

Harrods at night, illuminated by 11,500 lights

Bermondsey Market in South London. **Petticoat Lane** is worth a visit for the sheer volume of leather goods and fabric. **Brick Lane** is another authentic East End market where stalls and sheds are piled high with tatty furniture and bric-a-brac. Nearby is **Old Spitalfields Market,** a mecca for the latest street fashions. For a glimpse of spirited costermongers head for **Berwick Street**, which is lined with fruit and vegetables, fabrics and household goods. **Borough Market** is a thriving fine food and farmer's market with a great atmosphere *(see p122)*.

Bustling Petticoat Lane market, officially known as Middlesex Street

---

DIRECTORY

CHAIN AND DEPARTMENT STORES

Fortnum & Mason
181 Piccadilly W1.
Map 6 D1.
020-7734 8040.

Harrods
87–135 Brompton Rd SW1.
Map 5 A3.
020-7730 1234.

Harvey Nichols
109–125 Knightsbridge SW1.
Map 5 B2.
020-7235 5000.

HMV
150 Oxford St W1.
Map 4 D4.
020-7631 3423.

John Lewis
278–306 Oxford St W1.
Map 3 C5.
020-7629 7711.

Liberty
210–20 Regent St W1.
Map 3 C5.
020-7734 1234.

Marks & Spencer
173 & 458 Oxford St W1.
Map 3 C5/3 B5.
020-7935 7954.
Two of many branches.

Peter Jones
Sloane Square SW1
Map 5 A4.
020-7730 3434.

Selfridges
400 Oxford St W1.
Map 3 B5.
0870-837 7377.

Tower Records
1 Piccadilly Circus W1.
Map 6 D1.
020-7439 2500.

Virgin Megastore
14–16 Oxford St W1.
Map 4 E4.
020-7631 1234.

CLOTHES AND SHOES

Ben de Lisi
40 Elizabeth St SW1.
Map 5 B4.
020-7730 2994.

Browns
23–27 South Molton St W1.
Map 3 B5.
020-7514 0000.
One of several branches.

Burberry
21–23 New Bond St W1.
Map 3 C5.
020-7930 3343.
One of three branches.

Church's Shoes
201 Regent St W1.
Map 3 C5.
020-7734 2438.
One of several branches.

Gieves & Hawkes
1 Savile Row W1.
Map 3 C5.
020-7434 2001.

Hackett
87 Jermyn St W1.
Map 6 D1.
020-7930 1300.
One of several branches.

Hobbs
47–48 South Molton St W1. **Map** 3 C5.
020-7629 0750.
One of several branches.

Emma Hope
53 Sloane Sq SW1.
Map 5 B4.
020-7259 9566.
One of three branches.

John Lobb
9 St James's St SW1.
Map 6 D1.
020-7930 3664.

Margaret Howell
34 Wigmore St W1
Map 3 B4.
020-7009 9009.

Paul Smith
40–44 Floral St WC2.
Map 4 E5.
020-7379 7133.
One of several branches.

Pied à Terre
19 South Molton St W1
Map 3 B5.
020-7629 1362.
One of several branches.

Vivienne Westwood
6 Davies St W1.
Map 3 B5.
020-7629 3757.

Urban Outfitters
36–38 Kensington High St W8. **Map** 1 C4.
020-7761 1001.

MARKETS

Bermondsey
Long Lane & Bermondsey St SE1. **Map** 8 E5.
5am–2pm Fri.

Berwick Street
Berwick St W1. **Map** 4 D5.
9am–6pm Mon–Sat.

Borough
8 Southwark St SE1.
Map 8 D4. Fri noon–6pm, Sat 9am–4pm.

Brick Lane
Brick Lane E1.
Liverpool St, Aldgate East. dawn–1pm Sun.

Camden Lock
Chalk Farm Rd NW1.
Camden Town, Chalk Farm.
9:30am–5:30pm daily.

Covent Garden
The Piazza WC2.
Map 4 F5. 9am–5pm daily (antiques: Mon).

Greenwich
College Approach SE10.
Greenwich.
9am–6pm Sat, Sun.

Old Spitalfields
Commercial St E1.
Liverpool St.
9:30am–5:30pm Sun.

Petticoat Lane
Middlesex St E1.
Map 8 E2 Liverpool St.
9am–2pm Sun.

Portobello Road
Portobello Rd W10.
Notting Hill Gate.
7am–5:30pm Sat.

ENTERTAINMENT IN LONDON

LONDON HAS THE ENORMOUS variety of entertainment that only the great cities of the world can provide. The historical backdrop and the lively bustling atmosphere add to the excitement. Whether dancing the night away at a famous disco or making the most of London's varied arts scene, the visitor has a bewildering choice. A trip to London is not complete without a visit to the theatre which ranges from glamorous West End musicals to experimental Fringe plays. There is world-class ballet and opera in fabled venues such as Sadler's Wells and the Royal Opera House. The musical menu covers everything from classical, jazz and rock to rhythm and

Many London cafés have free live music

blues performed in atmospheric basement clubs, old converted cinemas and outdoor venues such as Wembley. Movie buffs can choose from hundreds of films each night. Sports fans can watch cricket at Lord's or participate in a host of activities from water sports to ice skating. *Time Out*, published every Tuesday, is the most comprehensive guide to what's on in London, with detailed weekly listings and reviews. *The Evening Standard*, *The Guardian* (Saturday) and *The Independent* also have reviews and information on events. If you buy tickets from booking agencies rather than direct from box offices, do compare prices – and only buy from ticket touts if you're desperate.

WEST END AND NATIONAL THEATRES

Palace Theatre poster (1898)

THE GLAMOROUS, glittering world of West End theatreland, emblazoned with the names of world-famous performers, offers an extraordinary range of entertainment.

West End theatres (see Directory for individual theatres) survive on their profits and rely on financial backers, known as "angels". Consequently, they tend to stage commercial productions with mass appeal: musicals, classics, comedies

and plays by bankable contemporary playwrights.

The state-subsidized **Royal National Theatre** is based in the South Bank Centre *(see p128)*. It has three auditoriums – the large, open-staged Olivier, the proscenium-arched Lyttelton, and the small studio space of the Cottesloe.

The **Royal Shakespeare Company** (RSC) regularly stages Shakespeare plays, but its repertoire includes Greek tragedies, Restoration comedies and modern works. Based at Stratford-upon-Avon *(see pp313–15)*, its major productions perform at London West End theatres. The RSC ticket hotline has information. **The Old Vic** has been rejuvenated recently under the artistic directorship of Kevin Spacey, whose exciting programme of drama attracts wide audiences.

Theatre tickets generally cost from £5 to £30 and can be bought direct from box offices, by telephone or post. The "tkts" discount theatre ticket booth in Leicester Square sells tickets for a wide range of shows on the day of performance. It is open Monday to Saturday (10am–7pm) for matinees and evening shows, and Sundays (noon–3pm) for matinees only (cash or credit card only).

OFF-WEST END AND FRINGE THEATRES

OFF-WEST END THEATRE is a middle category bridging the gap between West End and Fringe theatre. It includes venues that, regardless of location, have a permanent management team and often provide the opportunity for established directors and actors to turn their hands to more adventurous works in a smaller, more intimate, environment. Fringe theatres, on the other hand, are normally venues hired out to visiting companies. Both offer a vast array of innovative productions, serving as an outlet for new, often experimental writing.

Venues (too numerous to list – see newspaper listings),

The Old Vic, the first home of the National Theatre from 1963

Open-air theatre at Regent's Park

range from tiny theatres or rooms above pubs such as the Gate, which produces neglected European classics, to theatres such as the Donmar Warehouse, which attracts major directors and actors.

OPEN-AIR THEATRE

IN SUMMER, a performance of one of Shakespeare's airier creations such as *A Midsummer Night's Dream*, takes on an atmosphere of pure enchantment among the green vistas of Regent's Park (020-7935 5756) or Holland Park (020-7602 7856). Open-air performances of a different kind are to be had at Shakespeare's Globe (*see p122*), an authentic reproduction of an Elizabethan theatre.

CINEMAS

THE WEST END abounds with multiplex cinema chains (MGM, Odeon, UCI) which show big budget Hollywood films, usually in advance of the rest of the country, although release dates tend to lag well behind the US and many other European countries.

The Odeon Marble Arch has the largest commercial screen in Europe, while the Odeon Leicester Square boasts London's biggest auditorium with almost 2,000 seats.

Londoners are well-informed cinema-goers and even the larger cinema chains include some low-budget and foreign films in their repertoire. The majority of foreign films are

IMAX Cinema, at Waterloo

subtitled, rather than dubbed. A number of independent cinemas, such as the Metro, Renoir and Prince Charles in central London, and the Curzon in Mayfair, show foreign-language and slightly more offbeat art films.

The largest concentration of cinemas is in and around Leicester Square although there are local cinemas in most areas. Just off Leicester Square, the Prince Charles is the West End's cheapest cinema. Elsewhere in the area you can expect to pay between £6 and £9 for an evening performance – almost twice the price of the local cinemas. Monday and afternoon performances in the West End are often cheaper.

The National Film Theatre (NFT), on the South Bank, is London's flagship repertory cinema. Subsidized by the British Film Institute, it screens a wide range of films, old and new, from all around the world. Nearby at Waterloo is the IMAX, with one of the world's largest screens.

DIRECTORY

Adelphi
Strand. **Map** 4 F5.
☎ 020-7344 0055.

Albery
St Martin's Lane. **Map** 4 E5.
☎ 020-7369 1730.

Aldwych
Aldwych. **Map** 4 F5.
☎ 020-7379 3367.

Apollo
Shaftesbury Ave. **Map**
4 E5. ☎ 020-7494 5050.

Cambridge
Earlham St. **Map** 4 E5.
☎ 020-7494 5050.

Comedy
Panton St. **Map** 6 E1.
☎ 020-7369 1731.

Criterion
Piccadilly Circus. **Map**
4 D5. ☎ 020-7413 1437.

Dominion
Tottenham Court Rd. **Map**
4 E4. ☎ 0870-607 7460.

Duchess
Catherine St. **Map** 4 F5.
☎ 020-7494 5050.

Duke of York's
St Martin's Lane. **Map**
4 E5. ☎ 020-7369 1791.

Fortune
Russell St. **Map** 4 F5.
☎ 020-7369 1737.

Garrick
Charing Cross Rd. **Map**
4 E5. ☎ 020-7494 5050.

Gielgud
Shaftesbury Ave. **Map**
4 D5. ☎ 020-7494 5050.

Her Majesty's
Haymarket. **Map** 6 E1.
☎ 020-7494 5050.

Lyceum
Wellington St. **Map** 4 F5.
☎ 0870 243 9000.

Lyric
Shaftesbury Ave. **Map** 4
D5. ☎ 0870-890 1107.

New London
Drury Lane. **Map** 4 E5.
☎ 020-7494 5050.

The Old Vic
Waterloo Rd SE1. **Map**
7 A5. ☎ 0870 060 6628.

Palace
Shaftesbury Ave. **Map**
4 E5. ☎ 020-7494 5050.

Phoenix
Charing Cross Rd. **Map**
4 E5. ☎ 020-7369 1733.

Piccadilly
Denman St. **Map** 4 D5.
☎ 020-7369 1734.

Prince Edward
Old Compton St. **Map** 4
D5. ☎ 020-7447 5400.

Prince of Wales
Coventry St. **Map** 4 D5.
☎ 020-7839 5972.

Queen's
Shaftesbury Ave. **Map**
4 E5. ☎ 020-7494 5050.

Royal National
South Bank. **Map** 7 A4.
☎ 020-7452 3000.

RSC ☎ 0870 609 1110.

Shaftesbury
Shaftesbury Ave. **Map**
4 E4. ☎ 020-7379 3345.

Strand Aldwych. **Map**
4 F5. ☎ 0870-060 2335.

St Martin's
West St. **Map** 4 E5.
☎ 020-7836 1443.

Theatre Royal:
– Drury Lane
Catherine St. **Map** 4 F5.
☎ 020-7494 5050.

–Haymarket
Haymarket. **Map** 6 E1.
☎ 0870-901 3356.

Vaudeville
Strand. **Map** 4 F5.
☎ 020-7494 5050.

Wyndham's
Charing Cross Rd. **Map**
4 E5. ☎ 020-7369 1736.

Royal Festival Hall, South Bank Centre

CLASSICAL MUSIC, OPERA AND DANCE

L ONDON IS ONE of the world's great centres for classical music, with five symphony orchestras, internationally renowned chamber groups such as the Academy of St-Martin-in-the-Fields and the English Chamber Orchestra, as well as a number of contemporary groups. There are performances virtually every week by major international orchestras and artists, reaching a peak during the summer Proms season at the **Royal Albert Hall** *(see p63)*. The newly restored **Wigmore Hall** has excellent acoustics and is a fine setting for chamber music, as is the converted Baroque church (1728) of **St John's, Smith Square**.

Although televised and outdoor performances by major stars have greatly increased the popularity of opera, prices at the **Royal Opera House** are still aimed at corporate entertainment but the policy now is to keep a few cheaper seats. The refurbished building is elaborate and productions are often extremely lavish. English National Opera, based at the **London Coliseum**, has more adventurous productions, appealing to a younger audience (nearly all operas are sung in English). Tickets range from £5 to £200 and it is advisable to book in advance.

The Royal Opera House is also home to the Royal Ballet, and the London Coliseum to the English National Ballet, the two leading classical ballet companies in Britain. Visiting ballets also perform in both. There are numerous young contemporary dance companies, and **The Place** is a dedicated contemporary

dance theatre where many companies perform. Other major dance venues are **Sadler's Wells**, the **ICA**, the **Peacock Theatre** and the **Chisenhale Dance Space**.

The **Barbican Concert Hall** and **South Bank Centre** (comprising the Royal Festival Hall, Queen Elizabeth Hall and Purcell Room) host an impressive variety of events ranging from touring opera and classical music performances to free foyer concerts.

Elsewhere in London many outdoor musical events take place in summer *(see pp62–3)* at venues such as **Kenwood House**. Events to look out for are: the London Opera Festival (June) with singers from all over the world; the City of London Festival (July) which hosts a range of varied musical events; and contemporary dance festivals Spring Loaded (February–April) and Dance Umbrella (October) – see *Time Out* and newspaper listings.

Kenwood House on Hampstead Heath *(see p132)*

DIRECTORY

CLASSICAL MUSIC, OPERA AND DANCE

Barbican Concert Hall
Silk St EC2. **Map** 7 C1.
☎ 020-7638 8891.
ⓦ www.barbican.org.uk

Chisenhale Dance Space
64–84 Chisenhale Rd E3.
ⓔ Bethnal Green, Mile End. ☎ 020-8981 6617.

ICA
The Mall SW1. **Map** 6 E1.
☎ 020-7930 0493.
ⓦ www.ica.org.uk

Kenwood House
Hampstead Lane NW3.
ⓔ Archway.
☎ 020-8348 1286.

London Coliseum
St Martin's Lane WC2. **Map** 4 E5. ☎ 020-7632 8300.
ⓦ www.eno.org

Peacock Theatre
Portugal St WC2. **Map** 4 F5. ☎ 020-7863 8000.

The Place
17 Duke's Rd WC1. **Map** 4 E2. ☎ 020-7387 0031.

Royal Albert Hall
Kensington Gore SW7.
Map 2 E4.
☎ 020-7589 8212. ⓦ www.royalalberthall.com

Royal Opera House
Floral St WC2. **Map** 4 F5.
☎ 020-7304 4000.
ⓦ www.royalopera.org

Sadler's Wells
Rosebery Ave EC1. ⓔ Angel. ☎ 020-7863 8000.
ⓦ www.sadlerswells.com

St John's, Smith Sq
Smith Sq SW1. **Map** 6 E3.
☎ 020-7222 1061.
ⓦ www.sjss.org.uk

South Bank Centre
SE1. **Map** 6 F1. ☎ 020-7921 0600. ⓦ www.southbanklondon.com

Wigmore Hall
Wigmore St W1. **Map** 3 B4.
☎ 020-7935 2141. ⓦ www.wigmore-hall.org.uk

ROCK, POP, JAZZ AND CLUBS

100 Club
100 Oxford St W1. **Map** 4 D5. ☎ 020-7636 0933.

Brixton Academy
211 Stockwell Rd SW9.
ⓔ Brixton.
☎ 0870-771 2000.

Forum
9–17 Highgate Rd NW5.
ⓔ Kentish Town.
☎ 020-7344 0044.

Fridge
Town Hall Parade, Brixton Hill SW2. ⓔ Brixton.
☎ 020-7326 5100.

The Hippodrome, Leicester Square

ROCK, POP, JAZZ AND CLUBS

AN ORDINARY WEEK NIGHT in London features scores of concerts, ranging from rock and pop, to jazz, Latin, world, folk and reggae. Artists guaranteed to fill thousands of seats play large venues such as **Wembley Arena** or the **Royal Albert Hall**. However, many major bands prefer to play the **Brixton Academy** and the **Forum**, both former cinemas.

The number of jazz venues has increased over the last few years. Best of the old crop is **Ronnie Scott's**, while of the newcomers the **100 Club**, **Jazz Café** and **Pizza on the Park** have good reputations.

London's club scene is one of the most innovative in Europe, particularly since 1990, when all-night clubbing (though not drinking) was legalized. It is dominated by big-name DJs, who host different nights in different clubs, and some of the best clubs are one-nighters (see *Time Out* and newspaper listings). The world-famous mainstream discos **Stringfellows** and the **Hippodrome** are glitzy, expensive and very much part of the tourist circuit. In contrast the New York-style **Ministry of Sound**, the camp cabaret of **Madame Jojo's**, the trendy Shoreditch clubs **333** and **Cargo**, and a host of other venues ensure that you will never be short of choice. Alternatives are the excellent laser and light shows at **Heaven**, the glamorous super-club **Pacha London**, or the ska, classic soul and R'n'B at **Gossips** on Thursdays. Heaven and the **Fridge** are among the most popular of London's gay clubs.

Opening times are usually 10pm–3am, but on weekends many clubs open until 6am.

SPORTS

AN IMPRESSIVE variety of public sports facilities are to be found in London and they are generally inexpensive to use. Swimming pools, squash courts, gyms and sports centres, with an assortment of keep-fit classes, can be found in most districts, and tennis courts hired in most parks. Water sports, ice skating and golf are among the variety of activities on offer. Spectator sports range from football and rugby at various club grounds to cricket at **Lord's** or the **Oval**, and tennis at the **All England Lawn Tennis Club**, Wimbledon. Tickets for the most popular matches can often be hard to come by *(see p67)*. More traditional sports include polo at **Guards**, croquet at **Hurlingham** and medieval tennis at **Queen's Club Real Tennis**. See pages 630 to 631 for more information on sporting activities.

Ticket agency, Shaftesbury Avenue

Cargo
83 Rivington St EC2. 🚇
Old St. 📞 *020-7613 7731.*

Gossips
69 Dean St W1. **Map** 4 D4.
📞 *020-7434 4480.*

Heaven
Under the Arches, Villiers St WC2. **Map** 6 E1.
📞 *020-7930 2020.*

Hippodrome
Cranbourne St WC2.
Map 4 E5.
📞 *020-7437 4311.*

Jazz Café
3-5 Parkway NW1.
🚇 *Camden Town.*
📞 *020-7916 6060.*

Madame Jojo's
8–10 Brewer St W1.
Map 4 D5.
📞 *020-7734 3040.*

Ministry of Sound
103 Gaunt St SE1. **Map** 7
C5. 📞 *020-7378 6528.*

Pacha London
Terminus Place, SW1.**Map**
5 C3. 📞 *020-7833 3139.*
🌐 *www.pachalondon.com*

Pizza on the Park
11 Knightsbridge SW1.
Map 5 B2. 📞 *020-7235 5550.* 🌐 *www.*
pizzaonthepark.com

Ronnie Scott's
47 Frith St W1. **Map** 4 D5.
📞 *020-7439 0747.*
🌐 *www.ronniescotts.uk*

Stringfellows
16–19 Upper St Martin's Lane WC2. **Map** 4 E5.
📞 *020-7240 5534.*

333
333 Old St EC1.
📞 *020-7739 5949.*
🌐 *www.333mother.com*

SPORTS

All England Lawn Tennis Club
Church Rd, Wimbledon SW19. 🚇 *Southfields.*
📞 *020-8946 2244.*

Guards Polo Club
Windsor Great Park, Englefield Green, Egham, Surrey. 🚃 *Egham.*
📞 *01784 434212.*

Hurlingham Club
Ranelagh Gdns SW6.
Map 5 B5.
📞 *020-7736 8411.*

Lord's Cricket Ground
St John's Wood NW8.
🚇 *St John's Wood.*
📞 *020-7289 1611.*

Oval Cricket Ground
The Oval, Kennington SE11.
🚇 *Oval.*
📞 *020-7582 6660.*

Queen's Club Real Tennis
Palliser Rd W14.
🚇 *Barons Court.*
📞 *020-7385 3421.*

FURTHER AFIELD

OVER THE CENTURIES London has steadily expanded to embrace the scores of villages that surrounded it, leaving the City as a reminder of London's original boundaries. Although now linked in an almost unbroken urban sprawl, many of these areas have maintained their old village atmosphere and character. Hampstead and Highgate are still distinct enclaves, as are artistic Chelsea and literary Islington. Greenwich, Chiswick and Richmond have retained features that hark back to the days when the Thames was an important artery for transport and commerce, while just to the east of the City the wide expanses of the former docks have, in the last 20 years, been imaginatively rebuilt as new commercial and residential areas.

SIGHTS AT A GLANCE

Camden and Islington **7**	Greenwich **9**	Holland Park **2**
Chelsea **1**	Hampstead **4**	Notting Hill and
Chiswick **10**	Hampstead Heath **5**	Portobello Road **3**
East End and Docklands **8**	Highgate **6**	Richmond and Kew **11**

KEY

▨	Main sightseeing areas
☐	Greater London
☐	Parks
═	Motorway
▬	Major road
═	Minor road

10 miles = 15 km

Chelsea **1**

SW3. ⊖ *Sloane Square.*

RIVERSIDE CHELSEA has been fashionable since Tudor times when Sir Thomas More, Henry VIII's Lord Chancellor

Statue of Sir Thomas More (1478–1535), Cheyne Walk

(see p50), lived here. The river views attracted artists and the arrival of the historian Thomas Carlyle and essayist Leigh Hunt in the 1830s began a literary connection. Blue plaques on the houses of **Cheyne Walk** celebrate former residents such as J M W Turner *(see p93)* and writers George Eliot, Henry James and T S Eliot.

Chelsea's artistic tradition is maintained by its galleries and antique shops, many of them scattered among the clothes boutiques on **King's Road**. This begins at **Sloane Square**, named after the physician Sir Hans Sloane, who bought the manor of Chelsea in 1712. Sloane expanded the **Chelsea Physic Garden** (1673) along Swan Walk to cultivate plants and herbs.

Wren's **Royal Hospital**, on Royal Hospital Road was built in 1692 as a retirement home for old soldiers and still houses 400 Chelsea Pensioners.

Arab Hall, Leighton House (1866)

Holland Park **2**

W8, W14. ⊖ *Holland Park.*

THIS SMALL but delightful park is more intimate than the large royal parks such as Hyde Park *(see p103)*. It was opened in 1952 on the grounds of **Holland House**, a centre of social and political intrigue in its 19th-century heyday.

Around the park are some magnificent late Victorian

houses. **Linley Sambourne House** was built about 1870 and has received a much-needed facelift, though it remains much as Sambourne furnished it, in the Victorian manner, with china ornaments and heavy velvet drapes. He was a political cartoonist for the satirical magazine *Punch* and drawings cram the walls.

Leighton House, built for the Neo-Classical painter Lord Leighton in 1866, has been preserved as an extraordinary monument to the Victorian Aesthetic movement. The highlight is the Arab Hall, which was added in 1879 to house Leighton's stupendous collection of 13th- to 17th-century Islamic tiles. The best paintings include some by Leighton himself and by his contemporaries Edward Burne-Jones and John Millais.

🏛 **Linley Sambourne House**
18 Stafford Terrace W8. ☎ 020-7938 1295. ⊖ *High St Ken.* ◯ *10am–5pm Sat & Sun.* 🎫 ✔ *mandatory. Tours every hr; last tour 3:30pm.* ☒

🏛 **Leighton House**
12 Holland Park Rd W14. ☎ 020-7602 3316. ⊖ *High St Kensington.* ◯ *11am–5:30pm Wed–Mon.* ● *public hols.* ✔ *Wed & Thu.* ☒

Notting Hill and Portobello Road ❸

W11. ⊖ *Notting Hill Gate.*

I N THE 1950s AND 60s, Notting Hill became a centre for the Caribbean community and today it is a vibrant cosmopolitan part of London. It is also home to Europe's largest street carnival *(see p63)* which began in 1966 and takes over the entire area on the August bank holiday weekend, when costumed parades flood through the crowded streets.

Nearby, Portobello Road market *(see pp124–5)* has a bustling atmosphere with hundreds of stalls and shops selling a variety of collectables.

Hampstead ❹

NW3, N6. ⊖ *Hampstead.* ⊠ *Hampstead Heath.*

P OSITIONED ON A high ridge north of the metropolis, Hampstead has always remained aloof from London. Essentially a Georgian village with many perfectly maintained mansions and houses, it is one of London's most desirable residential areas, home to a community of artists and writers since Georgian times.

Situated in a quiet Hampstead street, **Keats House** (1816), is an evocative and memorable tribute to the life and work of the poet John Keats (1795–1821). Keats lived here for two years before his tragic death from consumption at the age of 25, and it was under a plum tree in the garden that he wrote his celebrated *Ode to a Nightingale.*

Georgian house, Hampstead

Mementoes of Keats and of Fanny Brawne, the neighbour to whom he was engaged, are on display.

The **Freud Museum**, which opened in 1986, is dedicated to the dramatic life of Sigmund Freud (1856–1939), the founder of psychoanalysis. At the age of 82, Freud fled from Nazi persecution in Vienna to this Hampstead house where he lived and worked for the last year of his life. His daughter Anna, pioneer of child psychoanalysis, continued to live here until her death in 1982. Inside, Freud's rich Viennese-style consulting rooms remain unaltered, and 1930s home movies show moments of Freud's life, including scenes of the Nazi attack on his home in Vienna.

🏛 **Keats House**
Keats Grove NW3.
☎ 020-7435 2062. ⊖ *Hampstead, Belsize Pk.* ◯ *noon–5pm Tue–Sun.* ☒
ⓦ www.cityoflondon.gov.uk/keats
🏛 **Freud Museum**
20 Maresfield Gdns NW3.
☎ 020-7435 2002. ⊖ *Finchley Rd.* ◯ *noon–5pm Wed–Sun.* 🎫 ♿ *limited.* ☒ ⓦ www.freud.org.uk

Antique shop on Portobello Road

View east across Hampstead Heath to Highgate

Hampstead Heath ❺

N6. 🚇 *Hampstead, Highgate.* ⇄ *Hampstead Heath.*

Separating the hill-top villages of Hampstead and Highgate, the open spaces of Hampstead Heath are a precious retreat from the city. There are meadows, lakes and ponds for bathing and fishing, and fine views over the capital from **Parliament Hill**, to the east.

Situated in landscaped grounds high on the edge of the Heath is the magnificent **Kenwood House**, where classical concerts *(see p128)* are held by the lake in summer. The house was remodelled by Robert Adam *(see p24)* in 1764 and most of his interiors have survived, the highlight of which is the library. The mansion is filled with Old Master paintings, such as works by Van Dyck, Vermeer, Turner *(see p93)* and Romney; the star attraction is Rembrandt's self-portrait of 1663.

🏛 **Kenwood House**
Hampstead Lane NW3. 📞 020-8348 1286. ⬜ *daily.* ♿ 📷 🚻
🌐 www.english-heritage.org.uk

Handmade crafts and antiques, Camden Lock indoor market

Highgate ❻

N6. 🚇 *Highgate, Archway.*

A settlement since the Middle Ages, Highgate, like Hampstead, became a fashionable aristocratic retreat in the 16th century. Today, it still has an exclusive rural feel, aloof from the urban sprawl below, with a Georgian high street and many expensive houses.

Highgate Cemetery *(see p77)*, with its monuments and hidden overgrown corners, has an extraordinary, magical atmosphere. Tour guides (daily in summer, weekends in winter) tell of the many tales of intrigue, mystery and vandalism connected with the cemetery since it opened in 1839. In the eastern section is the tomb of Victorian novelist George Eliot (1819–80) and of the cemetery's most famous incumbent, Karl Marx (1818–83).

🏛 **Highgate Cemetery**
Swains Lane N6. 📞 020-8340 1834.
🚇 *Archway, Highgate.* ⬜ *daily.*
🔴 *during burials, 25–26 Dec.* 📷 ✔
🌐 www.highgate-cemetery.org

Camden and Islington ❼

NW1, N1. **Camden** 🚇 *Camden Town, Chalk Farm.* **Islington** 🚇 *Angel, Highbury & Islington.*

Camden is a lively area packed with restaurants, shops and a busy **market** *(see p124–5)*. Thousands of people come here each weekend to browse among the wide variety of stalls or simply to soak up the atmosphere of the lively cobbled area around the canal, which is enhanced by the buskers and street performers.

Neighbouring Islington was once a fashionable spa but the rich moved out in the late 18th century and the area deteriorated rapidly. In the 20th century, writers such as Evelyn Waugh, George Orwell and Joe Orton lived here. In recent decades, Islington has been rediscovered and is again fashionable as one of the first areas in London to become "gentrified", with many professionals buying the old houses.

East End and Docklands ❽

E1, E2, E14. **East End** 🅔 *Aldgate East, Liverpool St, Bethnal Green.* **Docklands** 🅔 *Canary Wharf.*

IN THE MIDDLE AGES the East End was full of craftsmen practising noxious trades such as brewing, bleaching and vinegar-making, which were banned within the City. The area has also been home to numerous immigrant communities since the 17th century, when French Huguenots, escaping religious persecution moved into Spitalfields, and made it a silk-weaving centre. Even after the decline of the silk industry, textiles and clothing continued to dominate, with Jewish tailors and furriers setting up workshops in the 1880s, and Bengali machinists sewing in cramped premises from the 1950s.

A good way to get a taste of the East End is to explore its Sunday street markets *(see p125)*, and sample freshly baked bagels and spicy Indian food. By way of contrast, anyone interested in contemporary architecture should visit the **Docklands**, an ambitious re-development of disused docks, dominated by the Canada Tower; at 250 m (800 ft) it is London's tallest building. Other attractions include the **Bethnal Green Museum of Childhood**, a toy museum with a good display of toys and dolls' houses and **Dennis Severs' House**, in which you are taken on a historic journey from the 17th to the 19th centuries.

Royal Naval College framing the Queen's House, Greenwich

🏛 **Bethnal Green Museum of Childhood**
Cambridge Heath Rd E2. 🕻 020-8983 5200. ◻ 10am–5:50pm Sat–Thu. ● 1 Jan, 24–26 Dec. ♿ 🖳 🖵 🖺
🆆 www.museumofchildhood.org.uk
🎪 **Dennis Severs' House**
18 Folgate St E1. 🕻 020-7247 4013. ◻ 1st Sun & Mon of month. 🈺
🆆 www.dennissevershouse.co.uk

Greenwich ❾

SE10. 🚃 *Greenwich, Maze Hill.* 🅔 *Cutty Sark (DLR).*

THE WORLD'S TIME has been measured from the **Royal Observatory Greenwich** (now housing a museum) since 1884. The area is full of maritime and royal history, with Neo-Classical mansions, a park, many antique and book shops and various markets *(see pp124–5)*. The **Queen's House**, designed by Inigo Jones for James I's wife, was completed in 1637 for Henrietta Maria, the queen of Charles I. It has now been restored to its original state. The highlights of the Queen's House include the perfectly

Canada Tower, Canary Wharf

cubic main hall and the unusual spiral "tulip staircase".

The adjoining **National Maritime Museum** has exhibits that range from primitive canoes, through Elizabethan galleons, to modern ships. Anyone interested in naval history should visit the **Old Royal Naval College**, which was designed by Christopher Wren *(see p116)* in two halves so that the Queen's House

An 18th-century compass, National Maritime Museum

could retain its river view. It began as a royal palace, became a hospital in 1692, and in 1873 the Old Royal Naval College moved its premises here. The Rococo chapel and the 18th-century *trompe l'oeil* Painted Hall are open to the public.

🏛 **Royal Observatory Greenwich**
Greenwich Park SE10. 🕻 020-8312 6535. ◻ daily. ● 24–26 Dec. 🖺
🆆 www.rog.nmm.ac.uk
🏛 **Queen's House and National Maritime Museum**
Romney Rd SE10. 🕻 020-8312 6565. ◻ daily. ● 24–26 Dec. 🈺 ♿ limited. 🖳 🖺 🆆 www.nmm.ac.uk
🎪 **Old Royal Naval College**
King William Walk, Greenwich SE10. 🕻 020-8269 4747. ◻ 10am–5pm Mon–Sat; 12:30–5pm Sun. ● public hols.

Chiswick ❿

W4. 🚇 *Chiswick.*

CHISWICK IS A PLEASANT suburb of London, with
pubs, cottages and a
variety of birdlife,
such as herons,
along the pictur-
esque riverside.
One of the main
reasons for a visit is
Chiswick House, a
magnificent country villa
inspired by the Renaissance
architecture of Andrea Palladio.
It was designed in the early
18th century by the 3rd Earl
of Burlington as an annexe
to his larger house (demolished in 1758), so that he
could display his collection of
art and entertain friends. The
gardens are now restored to
their former glory.

Heron

🏛 **Chiswick House**
Burlington Lane W4. 📞 *020-8995
0508.* ⭕ *Apr–Oct: daily.* 🎟 ♿ *call
ahead.* 🖥 🚻

Richmond and Kew ⓫

SW15. 🚇 🚆 *Richmond.*

THE ATTRACTIVE village of
Richmond took its name
from a palace built by Henry
VII (the former Earl of Richmond in Yorkshire) in 1500,
the remains of which can be
seen off the green. Nearby is
the expansive **Richmond
Park** *(see p76)*, which was
once Charles I's royal hunting
ground. In summer, boats

sail down the Thames from
Westminster Millennium Pier,
making a pleasant day's
excursion from central
London *(see pp74–5).*
　　The nobility continued to
favour Richmond after royalty
had left, and some of their
mansions have survived. The
Palladian villa, **Marble Hill
House**, was built in 1724–9
for the mistress of
George II and has
been restored to its
original appearance.
On the opposite
side of the
Thames, the brooding
Ham House, built in
1610, had its heyday
later that century when
it became the home of the
Lauderdales. The Countess of
Lauderdale inherited the
house from her father, who
had been Charles I's "whip-
ping boy" – meaning that he
was punished whenever the
future king misbehaved. He
was rewarded as an adult by
being given a peerage and
the lease of Ham estate.
　　A little further north along
the Thames, **Syon House** has
been inhabited by the Dukes
and Earls of Northumberland
for over 400 years. Numerous
attractions here include a butterfly house, a museum of
historic cars and a spectacular
conservatory built in 1830.
The lavish Neo-Classical interiors of the house, created by
Robert Adam in the 1760s *(see
p24)*, remain the highlight.

Brewers Lane, Richmond

On the riverbank to the south,
Kew Gardens *(see p76)*, the
most complete botanic gardens
in the world, are flawlessly
maintained, with examples of
nearly every plant that can be
grown in Britain. There are
also conservatories where
thousands of exotic tropical
blooms are on display.

🏛 **Marble Hill House**
Richmond Rd, Twickenham. 📞 *020-
8892 5115.* ⭕ *Apr–Sep: daily; Oct:
Wed–Sun.* ♿ *limited.* 🍴 🖥 🚻
🏛 **Ham House**
Ham St, Richmond. 📞 *020-8940
1950.* ⭕ *Apr–Oct: Sat–Wed.* 🎟 ♿
🏛 **Syon House**
London Rd, Brentford. 📞 *020-8560
0881.* **House** ⭕ *mid-Mar–Oct: Wed,
Thu, Sun.* **Gardens** ⭕ *daily.* ⬤ *Nov–
mid-Mar.* 🎟 🚫 ♿ *gardens only.* 🖥
🚻 ⓦ *www.syonpark.co.uk*
🌷 **Kew Gardens**
Royal Botanic Gdns, Kew Green,
Richmond. 📞 *020-8332 5655.*
⭕ *daily.* ⬤ *25 Dec, 1 Jan.* 🎟 ♿
🚫 🍴 🖥 🚻 ⓦ *www.kew.org*

**Chiswick
House**

STREET FINDER

THE MAP REFERENCES given with the sights, hotels, restaurants, shops and entertainment venues based in central London refer to the following four maps. All the main places of interest within the central area are marked on the maps in addition to useful practical information, such as tube, railway and coach stations. The key map below shows the area of London that is covered by the *Street Finder*. The four main city-centre areas (colour-coded in pink) are shown in more detail on the inside back cover.

KEY

Major sight	
Other sight	
Other building	
Underground station	
Mainline station	
Coach station	
Bus station	
River boat boarding point	

Tourist information	
Hospital with casualty unit	
Police station	
Church	
Synagogue	
Post office	
Railway line	
Motorway	

One-way street
Pedestrian street
*56 House number (main street)

0 kilometres   1
0 miles   1

SCALE OF MAP PAGES

0 metres   250
0 yards   250

SOUTHEAST ENGLAND

Southeast England at a Glance

T HE OLD SAXON KINGDOMS covered the
areas surrounding London, and today,
while their accessibility to the capital
makes them a magnet for commuters, each
region retains a character and history of its
own. The attractions include England's
oldest universities, royal palaces, castles,
stately homes and cathedrals, many of
which played critical roles in the
nation's early history. The landscape
is soft, with the green and rounded
hills of the south country levelling
out to the flat fertile plains and fens of East
Anglia, fringed by broad, sandy beaches.

Blenheim Palace (see pp216–
17) *is a Baroque masterpiece.
The Mermaid Fountain
(1892) is part of the
spectacular gardens.*

Bedfordshire

Hertford

Buckinghamshire

THAMES VALLEY
(see pp204–25)

Oxfordshire

Oxford University's *buildings* (see pp210–15)
*amount to a textbook of English architecture
from the Middle Ages to the present. Christ Church
College (1525) is the largest in the university.*

Surrey

Hampshire

West Sussex

Windsor Castle (see pp224–5) *is
Britain's oldest royal residence. The
Round Tower was built in the 11th
century when the palace guarded the
western approaches to London.*

Winchester Cathedral (see pp158–9) *was
begun in 1097 on the ruins of a Saxon
church. The city has been an important
centre of Christianity since the 7th century.
The cathedral's northwest door is built
in a characteristic medieval style.*

◁ **The white cliffs of Dover, Kent**

Ely Cathedral's (see pp182–3) *south transept contains some of the finest stone carving in Britain. The octagonal corona was added in the 14th century when the Norman tower collapsed; the replacement tower dominates the surrounding flat fenland.*

Norfolk

Cambridgeshire

EAST ANGLIA
(see pp178–203)

Suffolk

Essex

Cambridge University's (see pp198–203) *buildings are enhanced by the quiet college gardens, the Backs and the public commons. King's College Chapel is the outstanding example of late medieval architecture in the city.*

LONDON
(see pp70–143)

Kent

THE DOWNS AND CHANNEL COAST
(see pp152–77)

East Sussex

Canterbury Cathedral (see pp174–5) *is the spiritual home of the Church of England. It contains some of the country's most exquisite medieval stained glass such as the nave's west window. It also has some well-preserved 12th-century wall paintings.*

Brighton's Royal Pavilion (see pp166–7) *was built for the Prince Regent and is one of the most lavish buildings in the land. Its design by John Nash (see p107) is based on Oriental themes and it has recently been restored to its original splendour.*

0 kilometres   25

0 miles   25

The Garden of England

WITH ITS FERTILE SOIL, mild climate and regular rainfall, the Kentish countryside has flourished as a fruit-growing region ever since its first orchards were planted by the Romans. There has been a recent boom in wine-making, as the vine-covered hillsides around Lamberhurst show, and several vineyards may be visited. The orchards are dazzling in the blossom season, and in the autumn the branches sag with ripening fruit – a familiar sight which inspired William Cobbett (1762–1835) to describe the area as "the very finest as to fertility and diminutive beauty in the whole world". Near Faversham, the fruit research station of Brogdale is open to the public, offering orchard walks, tastings and informative displays.

White wine from the southeast

HOPS AND HOPPING

Hop-picking, a family affair

Oast houses, topped with distinctive angled cowls, are a common feature of the Kentish landscape, and many have now been turned into houses. They were originally

SEASONAL FRUIT

This timeline shows the major crops in each month of the farming year. The first blossoms may appear when the fields are still dusted with snow. As the petals fall, fruit appears among the leaves. After ripening in the summer sun, the fruit is harvested in the autumn.

Raspberries are a luscious soft fruit. Many growers allow you to pick your own from the fields, and then pay by weight.

Peach blossom is usually to be found on south-facing walls, as its fruit requires warm conditions.

Orchards are used to grow plums, pears and apples. The latter (blossoming above) remain Kent's most important orchard crop.

MARCH	APRIL	MAY	JUNE	JULY

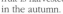

Srawberries are Britain's favourite and earliest soft fruit. New strains allow them to be picked all summer.

Sour cherry blossom is the earliest flower. Its fruit is used for cooking.

Pear blossom has creamy white flowers which appear two or three weeks before apple blossom.

Cherry plum blossom is one of the most beautiful blossoms; the plum is grown more for its flowers than its fruit.

Gooseberries are not always sweet enough to eat raw, though all types are superb in pies and other desserts.

built to dry hops, an ingredient in brewing beer *(see pp34–5)*. Many are still used for that, for although imports have reduced domestic hop-growing, more than four million tonnes are produced in Britain annually, mostly in Kent.

In summer, the fruiting plants can be seen climbing the rect-angular wire frames in fields by the roadside. Until the middle of the 20th century thousands of families from London's East End would move to the Kentish hop fields every autumn for working holidays harvesting the crop and camping in barns. That tradition has faded, because now the hops are picked by machine.

OAST HOUSE

The cowls turn in the wind, pro-viding air which is controlled by trap-doors below.

Hops are dried above a fan which blows hot air from the underlying radiators.

After drying, the hops are cooled and stored.

A press packs the hops into bags, ready for the breweries.

Cherries are the sweetest of Kent's fruit: two popular varieties are Stella (top) and Duke.

Plums are often served stewed, in pies, or dried into prunes. The Victoria plum (left) is the classic English dessert plum and is eaten raw. The Purple plum is also popular.

Greengages are green plums. They have a distinctive taste and can be made into jam.

Bramley Seedling is one of the best cooking apples, but it is not sweet enough to eat raw.

Pears, such as the William (left), should be eaten at the height of ripe-ness. The Conference keeps better.

AUGUST	SEPTEMBER	OCTOBER	NOVEMBER

Currants are among the most assertively flavoured fruit and are used in desserts and jams.

Peaches, grown in China 4,000 years ago, came to England in the 19th century.

Dessert apples, such as Cox's Orange Pippin (right), are some of England's best-loved fruits. The newer Discovery is easier to grow.

The Kentish cob, a variety of hazelnut, is undergoing a revival, having been eclipsed by European imports. Unlike many nuts, it is best picked fresh from the tree.

Vineyards are now a familiar sight in Kent (as well as Sussex and Hampshire). Most of the wine produced, such as Lamberhurst, is white.

Houses of Historical Figures

Visiting the homes of artists, writers, politicians and royalty is a rewarding way of gaining an insight into their private lives. Southeast England, near London, boasts many historic houses that have been preserved as they were when their illustrious occupants were alive. All these houses, from large mansions such as Lord Mountbatten's Broadlands to the more modest dwellings, like Jane Austen's House, contain exhibits relating to the life of the famous people who lived there.

Florence Nightingale *(1820–1910), the "Lady with the Lamp", was a nurse during the Crimean War (see p56). She stayed at Claydon with her sister, Lady Verney.*

Nancy Astor *(1879–1964) was the first woman to sit in Parliament in 1919. She lived at Cliveden until her death and made it famous for political hospitality.*

Claydon House, Winslow, nr Milton Keynes

The Duke of Wellington *(1769–1852) was given this house by the nation in 1817, in gratitude for leading the British to victory at Waterloo (see p55).*

THAMES VALLEY *(see pp204–25)*

Cliveden House, nr Maidenhead

Stratfield Saye, Basingstoke, nr Windsor

Jane Austen *(1775–1817) wrote three of her novels, including* Emma, *and revised the others at this house where she lived for eight years until shortly before her death (see p160).*

Jane Austen's House, Chawton, nr Winchester

Broadlands, nr Southampton

Lord Mountbatten (1900–79), a British naval commander and statesman, was the last Viceroy of India in 1947. He lived here all his married life and remodelled the original house considerably.

Osborne House, Isle of Wight

Queen Victoria (1819–1901) and her husband, Prince Albert, built Osborne House *(see p156)* in 1855 as a seaside retreat for their family because they never truly warmed to the Royal Pavilion in Brighton.

BLOOMSBURY GROUP

A circle of avant-garde artists, designers and writers, many of them friends as students, began to meet at a house in Bloomsbury, London, in 1904 and soon gained a reputation for their Bohemian lifestyle. When Duncan Grant and Vanessa Bell moved to Charleston in 1916 (*see p168*), it became a Sussex outpost of the celebrated group. Many of the prominent figures associated with the circle, such as Virginia Woolf, EM Forster, Vita Sackville-West and JM Keynes paid visits here. The Bloomsbury Group was also known for the Omega Workshops, which made innovative ceramics, furniture and textiles.

Vanessa Bell at Charleston by Duncan Grant (1885–1978)

Gainsborough's House, Sudbury, nr Ipswich

EAST ANGLIA
(see pp178–203)

Thomas Gainsborough *(1727–88), one of Britain's greatest painters, was born in this house (see p194). He was best known for his portraits, such as this one of Mr and Mrs Andrews.*

Charles Darwin *(1809–82), who developed the theory that man and apes have a common ancestor, wrote his most famous book, On the Origin of Species, at the house where he lived.*

Down House, Downe, nr Sevenoaks

THE DOWNS AND CHANNEL COAST
(see pp152–77)

Bleak House, Broadstairs, nr Margate

Charles Dickens (1812–70), the prolific and popular Victorian novelist (*see p177*), had many connections with Kent. He took holidays at Bleak House, later named after his famous novel.

Chartwell, Westerham, nr Sevenoaks

Batemans, Burwash, nr Hastings

Winston Churchill (1874–1965), Britain's inspirational Prime Minister in World War II (*see p177*), lived here for 40 years until his death. He relaxed by rebuilding parts of the house.

Rudyard Kipling *(1865–1936), the poet and novelist, was born in India, but lived here for 34 years until his death. His most famous works include* Kim, *the two* Jungle Books *and the* Just So Stories.

Charleston, Lewes

Vanessa Bell (1879–1961), artist and member of the Bloomsbury Group, lived here until her death in 1961. The 18th-century farmhouse reflects her decorative ideas and is filled with murals, paintings and painted furniture (*see p168*).

THE DOWNS AND CHANNEL COAST

HAMPSHIRE · SURREY · EAST SUSSEX · WEST SUSSEX · KENT

W HEN SETTLERS, *invaders and missionaries came from Europe, the southeast coast was their first landfall. The wooded chalk ridges and lower-lying weald beyond them made an ideal base for settlement and proved to be productive farmland.*

The Romans were the first to build major fortifications along the Channel Coast to discourage potential attackers from the European mainland. The remains of many of these can be seen today, and some, like Portchester Castle just outside Portsmouth, were incorporated into more substantial defences in later centuries. There also exists substantial evidence of Roman domestic buildings, such as Fishbourne Palace, in coastal areas and further inland.

The magnificence of cathedrals such as Canterbury and Winchester bear witness to their role as important bases of the medieval church, then nearly as powerful as the state. Many Kent and Sussex ports grew prosperous on trade with the Continent – as did the hundreds of smugglers who operated from them. From Tudor times on, monarchs, noblemen and courtiers acquired estates and built manor houses in the countryside between London and the coast, appreciating the area's moderate climate and proximity to the capital. Many of these survive and are popular attractions for visitors.

Today the southeast corner of England is its most prosperous and populous region. Parts of Surrey and Kent, up to 20 miles (32 km) from the capital, are known as the Stockbroker Belt: the area has many large, luxurious villas belonging to wealthy people prominent in business and the professions, attracted by the same virtues that appealed to the Tudor gentry.

The fertile area of Kent has long been known as the Garden of England, and despite the incursion of bricks and mortar, it is still a leading area for growing fruit *(see pp148–9)*, being in a prime position for the metropolitan market nearby.

Aerial view of the medieval and moated Leeds Castle

◁ **A lush covering of bluebells in the deciduous woodlands of Kent**

Exploring the Downs and Channel Coast

THE NORTH AND SOUTH DOWNS, separated by the lower-lying Weald are ideal walking country as well as being the site of many stately homes. From Tudor times, wealthy, London-based merchants and courtiers built their country residences in Kent, a day's ride from the capital, and many are open to the public. On the coast are the remains of sturdy castles put up to deter invaders from across the Channel. Today, though, the seashore is largely devoted to pleasure. Some of Britain's earliest beach resorts were developed along this coast, and sea bathing is said to have been invented in Brighton.

View of Brighton's Palace Pier from the promenade

Oast houses at Chiddingstone near Royal Tunbridge Wells

GETTING AROUND

The area is well served, with a network of motorways and A roads from London to the major towns. The A259 is a scenic coast road which offers fine views over the English Channel. Bus and rail transport is also good, with a number of coach companies providing regular tours to the major sites. An InterCity train service runs to all the major towns.

0 kilometres   20

0 miles   10

SEE ALSO

- *Where to Stay* pp545–7
- *Where to Eat* pp582–4

SIGHTS AT A GLANCE

KEY

▬	Motorway
▬	Major road
▬	Minor road
▬	Scenic route
▬	Scenic path
▬	River
※	Viewpoint

Canterbury Cathedral's spire, dominating the skyline

The Victorian Osborne House, Isle of Wight

Isle of Wight ❶

Isle of Wight. 🅰 133,000. 🚢 from
Lymington, Southampton,
Portsmouth. 🅸 Westridge Centre,
Brading Road, Ryde (01983 813818).
🆆 www.islandbreaks.co.uk

A VISIT TO **Osborne House**,
the favoured seaside
retreat of Queen Victoria and
Prince Albert (see p148), is
alone worth the ferry ride from
the mainland. Furnished much
as they left it, the house
provides a marvellous insight
into royal life and is dotted
with family mementos.

The **Swiss Cottage** was
built for the royal children to
play in. It is now a museum
attached to Osborne House.
Adjacent to it you can see the
bathing machine used by the
queen to preserve her modesty
while taking her to the edge
of the sea (see p383).

The other main sight on the
island is **Carisbrooke Castle**,
built in the 11th century. A
walk on its outer wall and the
climb to the top of its keep
provides spectacular views. It
was here that Charles I (see
pp52–3) was held prisoner in
1647; an attempt to escape
was foiled when he got stuck
between the bars of a window.

The island is a base for
ocean sailing, especially during
Cowes Week (see p67). The
scenic highlight is the
Needles – three towers of
rock jutting out of the sea at
the island's western end. This
is only a short walk from

Alum Bay, famous for its
multi-coloured cliffs and sand.

🏛 Osborne House
(EH) East Cowes. 🅲 01983 200022.
⭘ Apr–Oct: daily; Nov–Mar: open
some days for 🅲 only, phone for
details. 🅿 🧺 🦽 limited. 🅳 (also
🅳 in Swiss Cottage Apr–Oct only)
🏰 Carisbrooke Castle
Newport. 🅲 01983 522107.
⭘ daily. ⬤ 1 Jan, 24–26 Dec. 🧺
🦽 limited. 🅿 🅲 🅳

Beaulieu ❷

Brockenhurst, Hampshire. 🅲 01590
612345. 🚆 Brockenhurst then taxi.
⭘ daily. ⬤ 25 Dec. 🅿 🧺 🦽
🧺 by arrangement. 🅳
🆆 www.beaulieu.co.uk

PALACE HOUSE, once the gatehouse of Beaulieu Abbey,
has been the home of Lord
Montagu's family since 1538. It
now contains the finest collection of vintage cars in the
country at the **National Motor
Museum**, along with boats
used in the James Bond films.

There is also an exhibition
of monastic life in the ruined

ancient **abbey**, founded in
1204 by King John (see p48)
for Cistercian monks. The
original abbey church now
serves as the parish church.

ENVIRONS: Just south is the
maritime museum at **Buckler's
Hard**, telling the story of shipbuilding in the 18th century.
The yard employed 4,000
men at its peak but declined
when steel began to be used.

🏛 Buckler's Hard
Beaulieu. 🅲 01590 616203.
⭘ daily. ⬤ 25 Dec. 🧺 🦽 limited.

New Forest ❸

Hampshire. 🚆 Brockenhurst.
🚌 Lymington then bus. 🅸 main car
park, Lyndhurst (023 8028 2269).
🆆 www.thenewforest.co.uk

THIS UNIQUE EXPANSE of heath
and woodland is, at 145
sq miles (375 sq km), the largest area of unenclosed land
in southern Britain.

William the Conqueror's
"new" forest, despite its name,
is one of the few primeval oak
woods in England. It was the
popular hunting ground of
Norman kings, and in 1100
William II was fatally wounded
here in a hunting accident.

Today it is enjoyed by up to
seven million visitors a year
who share it with the New Forest ponies, unique to the area,
and over 1,500 fallow deer.

Southampton ❹

Hampshire. 🅰 220,000. ✈ 🚆 🚌
🚢 🅸 9 Civic Centre Road (023 8083
3333). 🆆 www.southampton.gov.uk

FOR CENTURIES this has been
a flourishing port. The
Mayflower sailed from here
to America in 1620 with the

A 1909 Rolls-Royce Silver Ghost at Beaulieu's National Motor Museum

Pilgrim Fathers, as did the *Titanic* on its maiden and ultimately tragic voyage in 1912.

The **Maritime Museum** has exhibits about both these ships, along with displays on the huge romantic liners that sailed from the port in the first half of the 20th century.

There is a walk around the remains of the medieval city wall. At the head of the High Street stands the old city gate, **Bargate**, the most elaborate gate to survive in England. It still has its 13th-century drum towers and is decorated with intricate, 17th-century armorial carvings. **God's**

The luxurious liner the *Titanic*, which sank in 1912

House Tower Museum of Archaeology consists of a 13th-century gatehouse and 15th-century gallery and tower, and includes displays from the Roman to medieval periods.

🏛 **Maritime Museum**
Town Quay Rd. 📞 023 8063 5904. ○ Tue–Sun (closed 1–2pm). ● 1 Jan, 25, 26 Dec, public hols. 🔾 limited. 🗖

🏛 **God's House Tower Museum**
Winkle St. 📞 023 8063 5904. ○ Tue–Sat (closed noon–1pm), 2–5pm Sun . 🔾 foyer & shop only. 🗖

Portsmouth ❺

Hampshire. 🔢 190,000. 🚢 🚆 ℹ
The Hard (023 9282 6722). 🗓 Thu–Sat. 🔲 www.portsmouthand.co.uk

ONCE A VITAL naval port, with all the nightlife that entails, Portsmouth is today a much quieter town but fascinating for those interested in English naval history.

Under the banner of **Flagship Portsmouth Victorygate**, the city's historic dockyard is the hub of Portsmouth's most important sights. Among these is the hull of the *Mary Rose*, the favourite of Henry VIII *(see p50)*, which capsized on its maiden voyage as it left to fight the French in 1545. It was recovered from the sea bed in 1982 along with thousands of 16th-century objects now on display nearby, giving an absorbing insight into life at sea in Tudor times.

Alongside it is **HMS Victory**, the English flagship on which Admiral Nelson was killed at Trafalgar *(see p27)* and now restored to its former glory. You can also visit the **Royal Naval Museum** which deals with naval history from the 16th century to the Falklands War, the 19th-century **HMS Warrior**, and galleries telling the story of Nelson.

Portsmouth's other military memorial is the **D-Day Museum**. This is centred on the *Overlord Embroidery*, a masterpiece of needlework which was commissioned in 1968 from the Royal School

The figurehead on the bow of HMS *Victory* at Portsmouth

of Needlework and took five years to complete. At 83 m (272 ft), its 34 panels are 12 m (41 ft) longer than the *Bayeux Tapestry* in France, and it depicts the World War II Allied landing in Normandy in 1944.

Portchester Castle, on the north edge of the harbour, was fortified in the third century and is the best example of Roman sea defences in northern Europe. The Normans later used the Roman walls to enclose a castle – only the keep survives – and a church. Henry V used the castle as a garrison to assemble his army before the Battle of Agincourt *(see p49)*. In the 18th–19th centuries it was a prisoner-of-war camp and you can still see where the prisoners carved their names on the walls.

Among less warlike attractions is the **Charles Dickens Museum** *(see p177)*. The house where the author was born in 1812 is furnished in the style of that time.

🏛 **Flagship Portsmouth Victorygate**
The Hard. 📞 023 9286 1512.
○ daily. ● 25 Dec. 🔾 🔾 🍴 🗖

🏛 **D-Day Museum**
Clarence Esplanade. 📞 023 9282 7261. ○ daily. ● 24–26 Dec. 🔾 🔾 🖳 🗖

🏛 **Portchester Castle**
Castle St, Porchester. 📞 023 9237 8291. ○ daily. ● 24–26 Dec, 1 Jan. 🔾 🔾 by arrangement.

🏛 **Charles Dickens Museum**
393 Old Commercial Rd. 📞 023 9282 7261. ○ Apr–Oct: daily, 7 Feb (Dickens's birthday). 🔾 🗖

A wild pony and her foal roaming freely in the New Forest

Winchester ❻

Hampshire. 🏃 *36,000.* 🚉 🚌
ℹ️ *Guildhall, The Broadway (01962 840500).* 🛍️ *Wed–Sat.*
🌐 *www.visitwinchester.com*

CAPITAL of the ancient king-dom of Wessex, the city of Winchester was also the headquarters of the Anglo-Saxon kings until the Norman Conquest *(see p47)*.

William the Conqueror built one of his first English castles here. The only surviving part of the castle is the **Great Hall**, erected in 1235 to replace the original. It is now home to the legendary Round Table. The story behind the table is a mix of history and myth. King Arthur *(see p273)* had it shaped so no knight could claim precedence. It was said to have been built by the wizard Merlin but was actually made in the 13th century.

The **Westgate Museum** is one of the two surviving 12th-century gatehouses in the city wall. The room (once a prison) above the gate has a 16th-century painted ceiling. It was moved here from Winchester College, England's oldest fee-paying, or "public" school. Winchester has been an

The 13th-century Round Table, Great Hall, Winchester

ecclesiastical centre for many centuries. **Wolvesey Castle** (built around 1110) was the home of the **cathedral's** bishops after the Conquest. The **Hospital of St Cross** is an almshouse built in 1446.

Author Izaac Walton *(1593–1683) is depicted in the stained glass Anglers' Window made in 1914.*

These magnificent choir-stalls (c.1308) are England's oldest.

The Lady Chapel was rebuilt by Elizabeth of York (c.1500) after her son was baptized in the cathedral.

The Perpendicular nave is the highlight of the building.

Jane Austen's grave

Main entrance

Visitors' centre

WINCHESTER CATHEDRAL
The Close. 📞 *01962 857202.*
⭕ *daily.* ♿ **Donation** 🔢 📷
🌐 *www.winchester-cathedral.org.uk*
The first church was built here in 648 but the present building was begun in 1097. Originally a Benedictine monastery, much of the Norman architecture remains despite continual modifications until the early 16th century.

The 12
century bla
Tournai marble fo

Weary strangers may claim the "Wayfarer's Dole" a horn (cup) of ale and bread, given out since medieval times.

🏛 Great Hall & Visitor Centre Castle Ave. 📞 *01962 846476.* 🔲 *daily.* ⬤ *25, 26 Dec.* ♿

🏛 Westgate Museum High St. 📞 *01962 848269.* 🔲 *Feb, Mar: Tue–Sun; Apr–Oct: Mon–Sun.* 📷

🏛 Hospital of St Cross St Cross Rd. 📞 *01962 851375.* 🔲 *Mon–Sat.* ⬤ *25 Dec.* 🗺 W *www.stcrosshospital.co.uk*

The Library has over 4,000 books. This "B" from Psalm 1 is found in the Winchester Bible, an exquisite work of 12th-century illumination.

The Norman chapter house ceased to be used in 1580. Only the Norman arches survive.

Prior's Hall

The Close originally contained the domestic buildings for the monks of the Priory of St Swithun – the name before it became Winchester Cathedral. Most of the buildings, such as the refectory and cloisters, were destroyed during the Dissolution of the Monasteries *(see p50).*

Chichester ❼

West Sussex. 🏠 *26,000.* 🚇 🚌 ℹ *29A South St (01243 775888).* 🛒 *Wed, Sat.* W *www.visitsussex.org*

THIS WONDERFULLY preserved market town, with an elaborate early 16th-century market cross at its centre, is dominated by its **cathedral**, consecrated in 1108. The exterior is a lovely mix of greenish limestone and Caen stone and its graceful spire, said to be the only English cathedral spire visible from the sea, dominates the town. The cathedral still contains much of interest, including a unique detached bell tower dating from 1436.

There are two carved stone panels in the choir, dating from 1140. Modern works include paintings by Graham Sutherland (1903–80), and a stained-glass window by Marc Chagall (1887–1985).

ENVIRONS: Just west at Bosham is the Saxon **Holy Trinity Church,** thought to have been used by King Canute *(see p46).* Myth has it that this was where Canute failed to stop the incoming tide and so proved to his courtiers that his powers had limits. The church appears in the *Bayeux Tapestry,* held in France, because Harold heard mass here in 1064 before he was shipwrecked off Normandy and then rescued by William the Conqueror *(see p47).*

Fishbourne Roman Palace *(see p45),* between Bosham and Chichester, is the largest Roman villa in Britain. It covers 3 ha (7 acres) and was discovered in 1960 by a workman digging for drains. Constructed

Chagall's stained glass window (1978), Chichester Cathedral

from AD 75, it was destroyed by fire in 285. The north wing has some of the finest mosaics in Britain, including one of Cupid.

To the north is the 18th-century **Goodwood House**. Its magnificent art collection features works by Canaletto (1697–1768) and Stubbs (1724–1806). This impressive house, home to the Earl of March, has a racecourse on the Downs.

⛪ Chichester Cathedral West St. 📞 *01243 782595.* 🔲 *daily.* ⬤ *during services.* ♿ 🗺
🏛 Fishbourne Roman Palace Fishbourne. 📞 *01243 785859.* 🔲 *Feb–mid-Dec: daily; mid-Dec–Jan (café closed): Sat, Sun.* 🗺 ♿ 🛒 📷 W *www.sussexpast.co.uk*
🏛 Goodwood House Goodwood. 📞 *01243 755048.* 📠 *01243 755040.* 🔲 *Apr–Sep: Sun–Mon (pm); Aug: Sun–Thu (pm).* ⬤ *special events.* 🗺 ♿ 🛒 📷

WILLIAM WALKER

At the beginning of the 20th century, the cathedral's east end seemed certain to collapse unless its foundations were underpinned. But because the water table lies only just below the surface, the work had to be done under water. From 1906 to 1911, Walker, a deep-sea diver, worked six hours a day laying sacks of cement beneath the unsteady walls, until the building was safe.

William Walker in his diving suit

The dominating position of Arundel Castle, West Sussex

Arundel Castle ⑧

Arundel, West Sussex. **(** *01903 883136.* ⌘ *Arundel.* ○ *Apr–Oct: Sun–Fri.* ● *Good Fri.* ▨ ✔ *by arrangement.* 🍴 ▢ ⬜
ⓦ *www.arundelcastle.org*

DOMINATING the small river-side town below, this vast, grey hill-top castle, surrounded by castellated walls, was first built by the Normans.

During the 16th century it was acquired by the powerful Dukes of Norfolk, the country's senior Roman Catholic family, whose descendants still live here. They rebuilt it after the original was virtually destroyed by Parliamentarians in 1643 *(see p52)*, and restored it again in the 19th century.

In the castle grounds is the parish church of **St Nicholas**. The small Catholic Fitzalan chapel (c.1380) was built into its east end by the castle's first owners, the Fitzalans, and can only be entered from the grounds.

Petworth House ⑨

(NT) Petworth, West Sussex.
(*01798 342207.* ⌘ *Pulborough then bus.* **House** ○ *Mar–Nov: Sat–Wed.* **Park** ○ *daily.* ▨ ♿ *limited.* 🍴 ⬜
ⓦ *www.nationaltrust.org.uk/petworth*

THIS LATE 17th-century house was immortalized in a series of famous views by the painter J M W Turner *(see p93)*. Some of his best paintings are on display here and are part of Petworth's

outstanding art collection which also includes works by Titian (1488–1576), Van Dyck (1599–1641) and Gainsborough *(see p151)*. Also extremely well represented is ancient Roman and Greek sculpture, such as the 4th-century BC *Leconfield Aphrodite,* widely thought to be by Praxiteles.

The Carved Room is decorated with intricately carved wood panels of birds, flowers and musical instruments, by Grinling Gibbons (1648–1721).

The large deer park includes some of the earliest work of Capability Brown *(see p22)*.

The Restoration clock on the Tudor Guildhall, Guildford

Guildford ⑩

Surrey. 🏠 *63,000.* ⌘ ● ▤ 🛈 *14 Tunsgate (01483 444333).* ⌂ *Fri, Sat.*
ⓦ *www.guildford.gov.uk*

THE COUNTY TOWN of Surrey, settled since Saxon times, incorporates the remains of a small Norman **castle**. The

attractive High Street is lined with Tudor buildings, such as the impressive **Guildhall**. But it is the huge modern red-brick cathedral, completed in 1954, that dominates the town's skyline.

ENVIRONS: Guildford stands on the end of the North Downs, a range of chalk hills which are popular for walking *(see p33)*. The area also has two famous beauty spots: **Leith Hill** – the highest point in southeast England – and **Box Hill**. The view from the latter is well worth the short, gentle climb from West Humble.

Just to the south of the town is the perfect red brickwork of **Clandon Park**. This 18th-century house has a sumptuous interior, especially the Marble Hall – one of the grandest English interiors of the period. It has an intricate Baroque ceiling, and the hall's side lamps are supported by black ivory forearms jutting from the wall, which represent the Park's West Indian servants.

Southwest is Chawton, where **Jane Austen's House** *(see p150)* is located. This small red-brick house is where she wrote most of her gentle, witty comedies of middle-class manners in Georgian England, such as *Pride and Prejudice*.

🏛 **Clandon Park**
(NT) West Clandon, Surrey. **(** *01483 222482.* ○ *Apr–Oct: Tue–Thu, Sun; public hols.* ▨ ♿ *limited.* 🍴 ⬜
🏛 **Jane Austen's House**
Alton, Hants. **(** *01420 83262.* ○ *Jan–Feb: Sat, Sun; Mar–Dec: daily.* ● *25, 26 Dec.* ▨ ♿ *limited.* ⬜

Hampton Court ⑪

East Molesey, Surrey. ☎ 0870-752 7777. ➤ Hampton Court. ◯ daily. ● 24–26 Dec. 🎫 ♿ 📷 🍴 🛍 W www.hrp.org.uk

THE POWERFUL chief minister and Archbishop of York to Henry VIII (see pp50–51), Cardinal Wolsey, leased a small manor house in 1514 and transformed it into a magnificent country residence. In 1528, to retain royal favour, Wolsey gave it to the king. After the royal takeover, Hampton Court was extended twice, first by Henry himself and in the 1690s by William and Mary, who used Christopher Wren (see p116) as the architect. From the outside the palace is a harmonious blend of Tudor and English Baroque; inside there is a striking contrast between Wren's Classical royal rooms,

Ceiling decoration, Hampton Court

which include the King's Apartments, and Tudor architecture, such as the Great Hall. Many of the state apartments are decorated with paintings and furnishings from the Royal Collection.

The Baroque gardens, with their radiating avenues of majestic limes, collections of rare plants and formal plant beds, have been painstakingly restored.

The Baroque maze is one of the garden's most famous features; visitors often become lost in it.

The Queen's Apartments, including the Presence Chamber and Bedchamber, are arranged around the the north and east sides of Fountain Court.

Fountain Court

The Fountain Garden still has a few of the original yews planted by William and Mary (see p53). Only one fountain remains out of the original 13 built.

Great Hall

Main entrance

Anne Boleyn's Gateway is at the entrance to Clock Court.

River Thames

The Mantegna Gallery houses Andrea Mantegna's nine canvasses depicting *The Triumphs of Caesar* (1490).

Long Water

Broad Walk

The Pond Garden, a sunken water garden, was part of Henry VIII's elaborate designs. The small pond in the middle contains a single-jet fountain.

The Tudor Chapel Royal was completed by Henry VIII. But the superb woodwork, including the massive reredos by Grinling Gibbons, all date from a major refurbishment by Queen Anne (c.1711).

Steyning ⑫

West Sussex. 🏠 5,000 🚉 ℹ️ 9 The
Causeway, Horsham (01403 211661).

THIS LOVELY little town in
the lee of the Downs is
packed with timber-framed
houses from the Tudor period
and earlier, with some built of
flint and others in sandstone.

In Saxon times, Steyning was
an important port and shipbuilding centre on the River
Adur: King Ethelwulf, father
of King Alfred (see p47), was
buried here in 858; his body
was later moved to Winchester.
The Domesday Book (see p48)
records that Steyning had 123
houses, making it one of the
largest towns in the south. The
12th-century church is spacious
and splendid, evidence of the
area's ancient prosperity: the
tower, of chequered stone and
flint, was added around 1600.

In the 14th century the river
silted up and changed course
away from the town, putting
an end to its days as a port.
Later it became an important
coaching stop on the south
coast road: the **Chequer Inn**
recalls this prosperous period,
with its unusual 18th-century
flint and stone façade.

ENVIRONS: The remains of a
Norman castle can be visited
at Bramber, east of Steyning.
This small, pretty village also
contains the timber-framed **St
Mary's House** (1470). It has
fine panelled rooms, including
the Elizabethan Painted Room,
and one of the oldest trees in
the country, a Ginkgo biloba.
Chanctonbury Ring and
Cissbury Ring, on the hills
west of Steyning, were Iron
Age forts and the latter has the
remains of a Neolithic flint
mine. Worthing is the resort
where Oscar Wilde (1854–
1900) wrote The Importance
of Being Earnest.

🏛 **St Mary's House**
Bramber. 📞 01903 816205. ◯
Easter–Sep: Sun, Thu (pm), public
hols. 🅿️ 📷 📹 ♿

Street-by-Street: Brighton ⑬

**A stick of
Brighton rock**

AS THE NEAREST south coast resort to London,
Brighton is perennially popular, but has
always been more refined than its boisterous
rivals further east, such as Margate (see p171)
and Southend. The spirit of the Prince
Regent (see p167) lives on, not only in the
magnificence of his Royal Pavilion, but in
the town's reputation as a
venue for adulterous weekends in
discreet hotels. Brighton has
always attracted actors and
artists – Laurence Olivier
made his final home here.

Old Ship Hotel
*Built in 1559, it
was later bought by
Nicholas Tettersells,
with the money given
to him by Charles II as
a reward for taking him
to France during the
Civil War (see p52).*

★ Palace Pier
*Built in 1899, this typical late-
Victorian pier now caters
for today's visitors
with amusement
arcades.*

KING'S ROAD

BLACK LION

GRAND JUNCTION ROAD

KEY
– – – Suggested route

STAR SIGHTS
★ Palace Pier
★ Royal Pavilion

★ **Royal Pavilion**
*The Prince Regent's fantastic
Oriental palace helped turn
Brighton into a fashionable
resort, and is today its
principal attraction.*

VISITORS' CHECKLIST

East Sussex. 🚗 *154,000.* 🚊
Brighton Central. 🚌 *Pool Valley.*
ℹ️ *10 Bartholomew Sq (0906
7112255).* 🏛 *Mon–Sat.* 🎭
International Arts Festival: May.

Many new plays are first
staged in the charming
Theatre Royal, established
in 1807, before they move
to the West End of London.

The Dome, an Indian-
style building opposite
the Royal Pavilion and
once George IV's
stables, is now a
venue for arts and
exhibitions.

inset

ALBERT STREET

NEW ROAD

NORTH STREET

CHURCH STREET

EET

GRAND PARADE

Art Deco
*This 1920s Art Deco
bronze lamp is on
display at the Brighton
Museum and Art Gallery.*

OLD STEINE

OLD STEINE

| 0 metres | | 100 |
| 0 yards | | 100 |

MARINE PARADE

DEIRA DRIVE

↓ **Eastbourne**

Sea Life Centre
*Built in 1872 as a menagerie,
it became an aquarium in
1929. Don't miss the sharks
and other British marine life.*

THE LANES

BLACK LION ST
PRINCE ALBERT ST
UNION ST
NILE ST
MEETING HOUSE LA
MEETING HOUSE LA
MEETING HOUSE LA
BRIGHTON PL
BARTHOLOMEWS
REGENT ARCADE
MARKET ST
NORTH ST
EAST ST

The Lanes
*Today an engrossing
maze of antique shops,
the Lanes were the ori-
ginal streets of the village
of Brighthelmstone.*

Brighton: Royal Pavilion

As SEA BATHING became fashionable in the mid-18th century, Brighton was transformed into England's first seaside resort. Its gaiety soon appealed to the rakish Prince of Wales, who became George IV in 1820. When, in 1785, he secretly married Mrs Fitzherbert, it was here that they conducted their liaison. He moved to a farmhouse near the shore and had it enlarged by Henry Holland *(see p24)*. As his parties grew more lavish, George needed a suitably extravagant setting for them, and in 1815 he employed John Nash *(see p107)* to transform the house into a lavish Oriental palace. Completed in 1822, the exterior has remained largely unaltered. Queen Victoria sold the Pavilion to the town of Brighton in 1850.

Central Dome
Nash adopted what he called the Hindu Style, as in this delicate tracery on one of the imposing turban domes.

★ **Banqueting Room**
Fiery dragons feature in many of the interior schemes. This colourful one dominates the centre of the Banqueting Room's extraordinary ceiling, and has a huge crystal chandelier suspended from it.

The exterior is partly built in Bath stone.

Banqueting Room Gallery

South Galleries

The banqueting table, which seats 24 people, is laid as for a splendid feast.

The eastern façade of the Pavilion

Standard Lamps
More dragons, along with dolphins and lotus flowers, figure on the Banqueting Room's eight original standard lamps, made of porcelain, ormolu and gilded wood.

STAR SIGHTS
★ Banqueting Room
★ Great Kitchen

★ **Great Kitchen**
The Prince's epic banquets required a kitchen of huge proportions. The vast ranges and long shelves of gleaming copper pans were used by famous chefs of the day.

◁ **Front façade of George IV's extravagant Royal Pavilion, Brighton**

Saloon
The gilded wall decorations were designed on Indian themes, but the Chinese wallpaper harks back to an earlier decorative scheme. The long couch mimics an Egyptian river boat.

Long Gallery
Mandarin figures, which can nod their heads, line the pink and blue walls of this 49 m (162 ft) gallery.

Queen Victoria's Bedroom
This reproduction four-poster is on display in the upper floor apartments that were used by Queen Victoria (see pp56–7).

The Music Room, with its crimson and gold murals, was where a 70-piece orchestra played to the Prince's guests.

The domes are made of cast iron.

Music Room Gallery

Bow Rooms

PLAN OF THE ROYAL PAVILION
Both Holland and Nash made additions and changes to the original farmhouse. The upper floor contains bedrooms, such as the Bow Rooms, which George's brothers used. The shaded areas represent the artwork above.

PRINCE OF WALES AND MRS FITZHERBERT

The Prince of Wales was only 23 years old when he fell in love with Maria Fitzherbert, a 29-year-old Catholic widow, and secretly married her. They lived in the farmhouse together and were the toast of Brighton society until George's official marriage took place to Caroline of Brunswick in 1795. Mrs Fitzherbert moved into a small house nearby.

Upstairs interior of Anne of Cleves House, Lewes

Lewes ⑭

East Sussex. 🏘 16,000. ➌ ⓘ 187
High St (01273 483448).
ⓦ www.visit-lewes.co.uk

THE ANCIENT COUNTY TOWN of
Sussex was a vital strategic
site for the Saxons, because of
its high vantage point looking
out over the coastline. William
the Conqueror built a
wooden castle here in 1067
but this was soon replaced by
a large stone structure whose
remains can be visited today.

In 1264 it was the site of a
critical battle in which Simon
de Montfort and his barons
defeated Henry III, enabling
them to establish the first
English Parliament.

The Tudor **Anne of Cleves
House** is a museum of local
history, although Anne of
Cleves, Henry VIII's fourth
wife, never actually lived here.

On Guy Fawkes Night *(see
p64)* lighted tar barrels are
rolled to the river and effigies
of the pope are burned instead
of the customary Guy Fawkes.
This commemorates the town's
17 Protestant martyrs burnt at
the stake by Mary I *(see p51)*.

ENVIRONS: Nearby are the 16th-
century **Glynde Place**, a fine
courtyard house, and the charming **Charleston**, home to the
Bloomsbury Group *(see p151)*.

🏛 **Anne of Cleves House**
Lewes. ⓒ 01273 474610. ◯ Mar–
Oct: daily; Nov–Feb: Tue–Sat. 🈺 🚻
🏯 **Glynde Place**
Lewes. 🚻 01273 858224. ◯ call
for details. 🈺 🚻 🏯
🏯 **Charleston**
Lewes. ⓒ 01323 811265. ◯ Apr–
Oct: Wed–Sun, Bank Hol Mon. 🈺
🏯 ⓦ www.charleston.org.uk

Eastbourne ⑮

East Sussex. 🏘 93,000. ➌ ⓑ ⓘ
Cornfield Rd (01323 411400). ⓐ
Tue, Sat. ⓦ www.eastbourne.org

THIS VICTORIAN SEASIDE resort
is a popular place for
retirement, as well as a first-
rate centre for touring the
Downs. The South Downs
Way *(see p33)* begins at
Beachy Head, the spectacular
163 m (536 ft) chalk cliff just
on the outskirts of the town.
From here it is a bracing walk
to the cliff top at Birling Gap,
with views to the **Seven
Sisters**, the chalk hills that end
abruptly as they meet the sea.

ENVIRONS: To the west of
Eastbourne is **Seven Sisters
Country Park**, a 285 ha (700
acre) area of chalk cliffs and
Downland marsh. The **Park
Visitor's Centre** contains
information on the local
area, history and geology.

Just north is the pretty
village of **Alfriston**, with an
ancient market cross and a
15th-century inn, **The Star**, in
its quaint main street. Near
the church is the 14th-century
Clergy House that, in 1896,
became the first National
Trust property *(see p25)*. To
the east is the huge prehistoric
chalk carving, the **Long Man
of Wilmington** *(see p209)*.

ⓘ **Park Visitor's Centre**
Exceat, Seaford. ⓒ 01323 870280.
◯ Apr–Oct: daily; Nov–Mar: Sat, Sun.
● 25 Dec. 🏯 🚻 🈴
🏯 **Clergy House**
(NT) Alfriston. ⓒ 01323 870001. ◯
Mar: Sat, Sun; Apr–Oct: Sat–Mon, Wed,
Thu; Nov, Dec: Wed–Sun. 🏯 🈺

The lighthouse (1902) at the foot of Beachy Head, Eastbourne

The meandering River Cuckmere flowing through the South Downs to the beach at Cuckmere Haven

The Downs ⑯

East Sussex. 🚃 🚌 *Eastbourne.*
ℹ️ *Cornfield Rd, Eastbourne (01323 411400).*

T HE NORTH and South
Downs are parallel chalk
ridges that run from east to
west all the way across Kent,
Sussex and Surrey, separated
by the lower-lying and fertile
Kent and Sussex Weald.

The smooth Downland hills
are covered with springy turf,
kept short by grazing sheep,
making an ideal surface for
walkers. The hill above the
precipitous **Devil's Dyke**,
just north of Brighton, offers
spectacular views for miles
across the Downs. The legend
is that the Devil cut the gorge
to let in the sea and flood the
countryside, but was foiled
by divine intervention. The
River Cuckmere runs through
one of the most picturesque
parts of the South Downs.

Located at the highest point of
the Downs is **Uppark House**.
This neat square building has
been meticulously restored to
its mid-18th-century appearance after a fire in 1989.

🏛 Uppark House

(NT) Petersfield, West Sussex.
📞 *01730 825857.* ⏰ *Apr–Oct:
Sun–Thu (pm).* 🏛 ♿ 🍴 📷

Hastings ⑰

East Sussex. 👥 *83,000.* 🚃 🚌
ℹ️ *Queens Square , Priory
Meadow (01424 781111).*
🌐 *www.hastings.gov.uk*

T HIS FASCINATING seaside
town was one of the first
Cinque Ports *(see p170)* and
is still a thriving fishing port.
The town is characterized by
the unique tall wooden "net
shops" on the beach, where
for hundreds of years fishermen have stored their nets. In

the 19th century, the area to
the west of the Old Town was
built up as a seaside resort,
which left the narrow,
characterful streets of the old

The wooden net shops, on
Hastings' shingle beach

fishermen's quarter intact.
There are two cliff railways
and smugglers' caves
displaying where contraband
used to be stored *(see p268).*

ENVIRONS: Seven miles (11
km) from Hastings is Battle.
The centre square of this small
town is dominated by the
gatehouse of **Battle Abbey**.
William the Conqueror built
this on the site of his great
victory, reputedly placing the
high altar where Harold fell,
But the abbey was destroyed
in the Dissolution *(see p50)*.
There is an evocative walk
around the actual battlefield.

⋂ Battle Abbey

High St, Battle. 📞 *01424 773792.*
⏰ *Easter–Sep: 10am–6pm; Oct:
10am–5pm; Nov–Easter: 10am–4pm
daily.* 🌑 *1 Jan, 24–26 Dec.* 🏛 ♿

BATTLE OF HASTINGS

In 1066, William the Conqueror's *(see p47)* invading army
from Normandy landed on the south coast, aiming to take
Winchester and London. Hearing that King Harold and his
army were camped just inland from Hastings, William confronted them. He won the battle after Harold was mortally
wounded by an
arrow in his eye. This
last successful in-
vasion of England is
depicted on the
Bayeux Tapestry in
Normandy, France.

King Harold's death,
Bayeux Tapestry

The fairy-tale 14th-century Bodiam Castle surrounded by its moat

Bodiam Castle ⑱

(NT) Nr Robertsbridge, East Sussex.
◎ *01580 830436.* ≋ *Robertsbridge then taxi.* ○ *mid-Feb–Oct: daily; Nov–mid-Feb: Sat–Sun.* ● *24–26 Dec.*
◎ & *limited.* ▢ 🖂

S URROUNDED BY its wide, glistening moat, this late 14th-century castle is one of the most romantic in England.
It was previously thought to have been built as a defence against French invasion, but is now believed to have been intended as a home for a Sussex knight. The castle saw action during the Civil War *(see p52),* when it was damaged in an assault by Parliamentary soldiers. They removed the roof to reduce its use as a base for Charles I's troops.

It has been uninhabited since, but its grey stone has proved indestructible. With the exception of the roof, it was restored in 1919 by Lord Curzon who gave it to the nation.

ENVIRONS: To the east is **Great Dixter**, a 15th-century manor house restored by Sir Edwin Lutyens in 1910. Christopher Lloyd created a magnificent garden with an Edwardian blend of terraces and borders.

🏛 **Great Dixter**
Northiam, Rye. ◎ *01797 252878.*
○ *Apr–Oct: 2–5:30pm Tue–Sun & public hols.* ◎ 🖂
🗔 www.greatdixter.co.uk

Rye ⑲

See pp170–71.

Romney Marsh ⑳

Kent. ≋ *Ashford.* ▣ *Ashford, Hythe.*
🚹 *Magpies Church Approach, New Romney (01797 364044).*

U NTIL ROMAN TIMES Romney Marsh and its southern neighbour Walland Marsh were entirely covered by the sea at high tide. The Romans drained the Romney section, and Walland Marsh was gradually reclaimed during the Middle Ages. Together they formed a large area of fertile land, particularly suitable for the bulky Romney Marsh sheep bred for the quality and quantity of their wool.
Dungeness, a desolate and lonely spot at the southeastern tip of the area, is dominated by a lighthouse and two nuclear power stations that

---

COASTAL DEFENCE AND THE CINQUE PORTS

Before the Norman Conquest *(see pp46–7),* national government was weak and, with threats from Europe, it was important for Saxon kings to keep on good terms with the Channel ports. So, in return for keeping the royal fleet supplied with ships and men, five ports – Hastings, Romney, Hythe, Sandwich and Dover – were granted the right to levy taxes; others were added later. "Cinque" came from the old French word for five. The privileges were revoked during the 17th century. In 1803, in response to the growing threat from France, 74 fixed defences were built along the coast. Only 24 of these Martello towers still exist.

The cliff-top position of Dover Castle

A Martello tower, built as part of the Channel's defences

break up the skyline. It is also the southern terminus of the popular **Romney, Hythe and Dymchurch Light Railway** which was opened in 1927. During the summer this takes passengers 14 miles (23 km) up the coast to Hythe on trains a third the conventional size.

The northern edge of the marsh is crossed by the Royal Military Canal, built to serve both as a defence and supply line in 1804, when it was feared Napoleon was planning an invasion *(see p55)*.

Dover ❷

Kent. 🏛 *30,000.* 🚆 🚌 ⛴ 🛈 *Old Town Jail, Biggin St (01304 205108).* 📅 *Sat.* 🌐 *www.dover.gov.uk*

ITS PROXIMITY to the European mainland makes Dover, with its neighbour Folkestone (now the terminal for the Channel Tunnel, *see p632*), the leading port for cross-Channel travel. Its famous white cliffs exert a strong pull on returning travellers.

Dover's strategic position and large natural harbour mean the town has always had an important role to play in the nation's defences.

Built on the original site of an ancient Saxon fortification, **Dover Castle**, superbly positioned on top of the high cliffs, has helped defend the town from 1198, when Henry II first built the keep, right up to World War II, when it was used as the command post for the Dunkirk evacuation. Exhibits in the castle and in the labyrinth of tunnels beneath made by prisoners in the Napoleonic Wars *(see p55)* cover all these periods.

ENVIRONS: One of the most significant sites in England's early history is the ruin of **Richborough Roman Fort**. Now a large grassy site two miles (3 km) inland, this was where, in AD 43, Claudius's Roman invaders *(see p44)* made their first landing. For hundreds of years afterwards, Rutupiae, as it was known, was one of the most important ports of entry and military bases in the country.

♣ **Dover Castle**
Castle Hill. 📞 *01304 211067.* 🕐 *Mar: Wed–Sun; Apr–Oct: daily; Nov–Feb: Sat, Sun.* ● *1 Jan, 24–26 Dec.* 📷
🏰 **Richborough Roman Fort**
Richborough. 📞 *01304 612013.* 🕐 *Oct–Mar: Sat, Sun; Apr–Nov: daily.*

Margate ❷

Kent. 🏛 *40,000.* 🚆 🚌 🛈 *12–13 The Parade (01843 583333 / 583334).* 🌐 *www.tourism.thanet.gov.uk*

TRADITIONALLY the most boisterous of the three seaside resorts on the Isle of Thanet (the other two are Ramsgate and Broadstairs), Margate has long been a popular destination for Londoners, travelling in Victorian times by steam boat and later by train. The town has theme parks and fairground rides.

ENVIRONS: Just south is a 19th-century gentleman's residence, **Quex House,** which has two unusual towers in its grounds. The adjoining museum has a fine collection of African and Oriental art, as well as unique dioramas of tropical wildlife.

Visitors relaxing on Margate's popular sandy beach

To the west is a Saxon church, built within the remains of the bleak Roman coastal fort of **Reculver**. Dramatic twin towers, known as the Two Sisters, were added to the church in the 12th century – these were luckily saved from destruction in 1809 because they were a useful navigational aid for shipping. The church now stands at the centre of a very pleasant, if rather windy, 37 ha (91 acre) camp site.

🏠 **Quex House**
Birchington. 📞 *01843 842168.* 🕐 *Apr–Oct: Tue–Thu, Sun & public hols (Museum only: Nov, Mar: Sun).* 📷 ♿ 🅿 *for groups.* 🍴 🚻
🏰 **Reculver Fort**
Reculver. 📞 *01227 361911 (Herne Bay Tourist Information).* 🕐 *daily.*

A drainage dyke running through the fertile plains of Romney Marsh

Street-by-Street: Rye ⑲

T HIS ANCIENT and delightful fortified town was added to the original Cinque ports *(see p170)* in the 11th century. A huge storm in 1287 diverted the River Rother so that it met the sea at Rye, and for more than 300 years it was one of the most important channel ports. However, in the 16th century the harbour began to silt up and the town is now 2 miles (3 km) inland. Rye was frequently attacked by the French, culminating in 1377 when it was burnt to the ground.

The Mermaid Inn sign

★ **Mermaid Street**
This delightful cobbled street, its huddled houses jutting out at unlikely angles, has hardly altered since it was rebuilt in the 14th century.

The Mint
got its name from the 17th-century minting of tokens.

The Mermaid Inn, founded in the 11th century, is Rye's largest medieval building. In the 1750s it was the headquarters of a notorious and bloodthirsty smuggling gang called the Hawkhursts.

View over the River Tillingham

Strand Quay
The brick and timber warehouses survive from the prosperous days when Rye was a thriving port.

STAR SIGHTS

★ **Mermaid Street**

★ **Ypres Tower**

Lamb House
This fine Georgian house was built in 1722. George I stayed here when stranded in a storm, and author Henry James (1843–1916) lived here.

St Mary's Church
The 16th-century turret contains the oldest working clock in England. The face was added in 1761.

↑ Hastings and railway station

Land Gate
Built in the 14th century this is the only survivor of the old fortified town's four gates.

The 16th-century Flushing Inn

This cistern was built in 1735; horse-drawn machinery was used to raise water to the highest part of the town.

Gun Garden, Ypres Tower

★ Ypres Tower
Built as a fort in 1250, it was turned into a house in 1430. It has since been a prison and mortuary.

KEY

– – – Suggested route

0 metres   50
0 yards   50

VISITORS' CHECKLIST

East Sussex. 👤 4,500. 🚉 Station Approach. 🚌 Station Approach. ℹ️ Strand Quay (01797 226696). 🛒 Wed, Thu. 🎭 Medieval Weekend: Jul or Aug; Rye Festival: Sep. 🌐 www.visitrye.co.uk

ENVIRONS: Just 2 miles (3 km) to the south of Rye is the small town of **Winchelsea**. At the behest of Edward I, it was moved to its present position in 1288, when most of the old town on lower land to the southeast, was drowned by the same storm that diverted the River Rother in 1287.

Winchelsea is probably Britain's first coherently planned new town. Although not all of it was built as originally planned, its rectangular grid survives today, as does the **Church of St Thomas Becket** (begun c.1300) at its centre. Several raids during the 14th century by the French damaged the church and burned down scores of houses. The church has three tombs that probably predate it, having been rescued from the old town before it was submerged. There are also two well-preserved medieval tombs in the chantry. The three windows (1928–33) in the Lady Chapel were designed by Douglas Strachan as a memorial to those who died in World War I. Just beyond the edges of present-day Winchelsea are the remains of three of the original gates – showing just how big a town was first envisaged. The beach below is one of the finest on the southeast coast.

Camber Sands, to the east of the mouth of the Rother, is another excellent beach. Once used by fishermen it is now popular with swimmers and edged with seaside bungalows and a holiday camp.

The ruins of **Camber Castle** are west of the sands, between Rye and Winchelsea. This was one of the forts built along this coast by Henry VIII when he feared an attack by the French. When it was built it was on the edge of the sea but it was abandoned in 1642 when it became stranded inland as the river silted up.

🏰 Camber Castle
(EH) Camber, Rye. 📞 01797 223862. ◯ Jul–Sep: Sat, Sun pm for 🎫 only.

Jesus on Christ Church Gate, Canterbury Cathedral

Canterbury ㉓

Kent. 🚶 *50,000.* 🚆 🚲 ℹ️ *Sun St, Buttermarket (01227 378100).* 🏪 *Wed, Fri.* 🆆 *www.canterbury.co.uk*

I TS POSITION on the London to Dover route meant Canterbury was an important Roman town even before the arrival of St Augustine in 597, sent by the pope to convert the Anglo-Saxons to Christianity. The town rose in importance, soon becoming the centre of the Christian Church in England.

With the building of the **cathedral** and the martyrdom of Thomas à Becket *(see p48),* Canterbury's future as a religious centre was assured.

Adjacent to the ruins of **St Augustine's Abbey**, destroyed in the Dissolution *(see p50),* is **St Martin's Church**, the oldest in England. This was where St Augustine first worshipped and it has impressive Norman and Saxon work.

West Gate Museum, with its round towers, is an imposing medieval gatehouse. It was built in 1381 and contains a display of arms and armoury.

The Poor Priests' Hospital, founded in the 12th century, now houses the **Museum of Canterbury.**

🏛 **West Gate Museum**
St Peter's St. 🅲 *01227 789576.* ⬜ *Mon–Sat.* ⬛ *23 Dec–1 Jan, Good Fri.* 🈶 🅿️

🏛 **Museum of Canterbury**
Stour St. 🅲 *01227 475202.* ⬜ *Jun–Sep: daily; Oct–May: Mon–Sat.* 🈶 🅿️
🆆 *www.canterbury-museum.co.uk*

Canterbury Cathedral

T O MATCH CANTERBURY'S growing ecclesiastical rank as a major centre of Christianity, the first Norman archbishop, Lanfranc, ordered a new cathedral to be built on the ruins of the Anglo-Saxon cathedral in 1070. It was enlarged and rebuilt many times and as a result embraces examples of all styles of medieval architecture. The most poignant moment in its history came in 1170 when Thomas à Becket was murdered here *(see p48).* Four years after his death a fire devastated the cathedral and Trinity Chapel was built to house Becket's remains. The shrine quickly became an important religious site and until the Dissolution *(see p50)* the cathedral was one of Christendom's chief places of pilgrimage.

The nave at 60 m (188 ft) makes Canterbury one of the longest medieval churches.

The South West Porch (1426) may have been built to commemorate the victory at Agincourt *(see p49).*

Main entrance

★ **Medieval Stained Glass**
This depiction of the 1,000-year-old Methuselah is a detail from the southwest transept window.

GEOFFREY CHAUCER

Considered to be the first great English poet, Geoffrey Chaucer (c.1345–1400), a customs official by profession, wrote a rumbustious and witty account of a group of pilgrims travelling from London to Becket's shrine in 1387 in the *Canterbury Tales.* The pilgrims represent a cross-section of 14th-century English society and the tales remain one of the greatest and most entertaining works of early English literature.

Wife of Bath, *Canterbury Tales*

Bell Harry Tower
The central tower, dominating the skyline, was built in 1498 to house a bell donated by Henry of Eastry 100 years before. The fan vaulting is a superb example of the late Perpendicular style.

VISITORS' CHECKLIST

11 The Precincts, Canterbury.
01227 762862. 9am–6:30pm Mon–Sat (till 5pm Oct–Mar); 12:30–2:30pm & 4:30–`5:30pm Sun. during services & concerts; 25 Dec. 8am daily; 11am Sun; 3:15pm Sat, Sun; 5:30pm Mon–Fri.
www.canterbury-cathedral.org

Great Cloister

★ **Site of the Shrine of St Thomas à Becket**
This Victorian illustration (anon) portrays Becket's canonization. The Trinity Chapel was built to house his tomb which stood here until it was destroyed in 1538. The spot is now marked by a lighted candle.

Chapter House

The Great South Window has four stained glass panels (1958) by Erwin Bossanyi.

★ **Black Prince's Tomb**
This copper effigy is on the tomb of Edward III's son, who died in 1376.

STAR FEATURES

★ **Medieval Stained Glass**

★ **Site of the Shrine of St Thomas à Becket**

★ **Black Prince's Tomb**

St Augustine's Chair

The choir, completed in 1184, is one of the longest in England.

Trinity Chapel

The circular Corona Chapel

The keep of Rochester Castle, dominating Rochester and the Medway Valley

Leeds Castle ②④

Maidstone, Kent. **(** 01622 765400.
≥ Bearsted then bus. **○** daily.
● for concerts & 25 Dec. **≥** **&** **Ⅱ**
□ **□** **W** www.leeds-castle.com

SURROUNDED BY A LAKE that
reflects the warm buff
stone of its crenellated turrets,
Leeds is often considered to
be the most beautiful castle in
England. Begun in the early
12th century, it has been
continuously inhabited and its
present appearance is a result
of centuries of rebuilding and
extensions, most recently in
the 1930s. Leeds has royal
connections going back to
1278, when it was given to
Edward I by a courtier
seeking favour.

Henry VIII loved the castle
and visited it often, escaping
from the plague in London.
It contains a life-sized bust of
Henry from the late 16th century. Leeds passed out of royal
ownership when Edward VI
gave it to Sir Anthony St Leger
in 1552 as a reward for helping to pacify the Irish.

Rochester ②⑤

Kent. **♔** 145,000. **≥** **□**
ⓘ 95 High Street (01634 843666).

CLUSTERED AT THE MOUTH of
the River Medway are the
towns of Rochester, Chatham
and Gillingham, all rich in
naval history, but none more

so than Rochester, which
occupied a strategic site on
the London to Dover road.

England's tallest Norman
keep is at **Rochester Castle,**
worth climbing for the views
over the Medway. The town's
medieval history is still visible,
with the original city walls –
which followed the lines of the
Roman fortifications – on view
in the High Street, and some
well-preserved wall paintings
in the **cathedral,** built in 1088.

ENVIRONS: In Chatham, the
Historic Dockyard is now a
museum of shipbuilding and
nautical crafts. **Fort Amherst**
nearby was built in 1756 to
protect the dockyard and river
entrance from attack, and has
1,800 m (5,570 ft) of tunnels
to explore that were hewn by
Napoleonic prisoners of war.

♣ Rochester Castle
The Esplanade. **(** 01634 402276.
○ daily. **●** 1 Jan, 24–27, 31 Dec.
≥ **&** grounds only. **□**

m Historic Dockyard
Dock Rd, Chatham. **(** 01634
823800. **○** mid-Feb–Oct: daily; Nov:
Sat, Sun. **≥** **&**
♠ Fort Amherst
Dock Rd, Chatham. **(** 01634 847747.
○ call for details. **≥** **□**

Knole ②⑥

(NT) Sevenoaks, Kent. **(** 01732
462100. **≥** Sevenoaks then taxi.
House **○** Mar–Nov: Wed–Sun (pm),
Good Fri & public hols. **Park** **○** daily.
≥ **&** limited. **✔** by arrangement.
□ **□**

THIS HUGE TUDOR MANSION
was built in the late 15th
century, and was seized by
Henry VIII from the Arch-
bishop of Canterbury at the
Dissolution (see p50). In 1566
Queen Elizabeth I gave it to
her cousin Thomas Sackville.
His descendants have lived
here ever since, including the
writer Vita Sackville-West,
(1892–1962). The house is
well known for its 17th-
century furniture,
such as the
elaborate bed
made for James II.
The 405-ha (1,000-acre) park
has deer and lovely walks.

ENVIRONS: A small manor
house, **Ightham Mote,** east of
Knole, is one of the finest
examples of English medieval
architecture. Its 14th-century
timber-and-stone building

A gladiator,
Knole

encloses a central court and is encircled by a moat.

At **Sissinghurst Castle Garden** are gardens created by Vita Sackville-West and her husband Harold Nicolson in the 1930s.

Ightham Mote
(NT) Ivy Hatch, Sevenoaks. 📞 01732 810378. ⬜ Apr–Oct: Wed–Fri, Sun, Mon & public hols. 🖼️ ♿ 🚻
🌷 **Sissinghurst Castle Garden**
(NT) Cranbrook. 📞 01580 710700. ⬜ Apr–Oct: 11am–6:30pm Mon, Tue, Fri; 10am–6:30pm Sat, Sun, Good Fri. 🖼️ ♿ limited. 🚻 🛍️

Hever Castle ㉗

Edenbridge, Kent. 📞 01732 861701. 🚆 Edenbridge Town. ⬜ Mar–Nov: daily; **Gardens** 11am–6pm; **Castle** noon–6pm. 🖼️ ♿ limited. 🚻
🎒 groups by arrangement. 🛍️
W www.hevercastle.co.uk

THIS SMALL, MOATED CASTLE is famous as the 16th-century home of Anne Boleyn, the

CHARLES DICKENS

Charles Dickens (1812–70), a popular writer in his own time, is still widely read today. He was born in Portsmouth but moved to Chatham aged five. As an adult, Dickens lived in London but kept up his Kent connections, taking holidays in Broadstairs, just south of Margate – where he wrote *David Copperfield* – and spending his last years at Gad's Hill, near Rochester. The town celebrates the famous connection with an annual Dickens festival.

The façade of Chartwell, Winston Churchill's home

doomed wife of Henry VIII, executed for adultery. She lived here as a young woman and the king often visited her while staying at Leeds Castle. In 1903 Hever was bought by William Waldorf Astor, who undertook a restoration programme, building a Neo-Tudor village alongside it to accommodate guests and servants. The moat and gatehouse date from around 1270.

ENVIRONS: To the northwest of Hever is **Chartwell**, the family home of Sir Winston Churchill (see p59). It remains furnished as it was when he lived here. Some 140 of his paintings are on display.

Chartwell
(NT) Westerham, Kent. 📞 01732 866368. ⬜ mid-Mar–Jun, Sep–Nov: 11am–5pm Wed–Sun & public hols; Jul–Aug: 11am–5pm Tue–Sun & public hols. 🖼️ ♿ limited. 🚻 🛍️

Royal Tunbridge Wells ㉘

Kent. 🏘️ 55,000. 🚆 🚌 ℹ️ Old Fish Market, The Pantiles (0800 393686). 🍴 Wed. W www.visittunbridgewells.com

HELPED BY ROYAL patronage, the town became a popular spa in the 17th and 18th centuries after mineral springs were discovered in 1606. The Pantiles – the colonnaded and paved promenade – was laid out in the 1700s.

ENVIRONS: Nearby is a superb manor house, **Penshurst Place**. Built in the 1340s, it has an 18 m (60 ft) high Great Hall.

Penshurst Place
Tonbridge, Kent. 📞 01892 870307. ⬜ Apr–Oct: daily; Mar: Sat, Sun: **House** noon–5:30pm; **Gardens** 10:30am–6pm; **Toy Museum** noon–5pm. 🖼️ ♿ limited. 🚻 🍴 🛍️

An early 18th-century astrolabe to measure the stars, Hever Castle garden

EAST ANGLIA

NORFOLK · SUFFOLK · ESSEX · CAMBRIDGESHIRE

T HE BULGE OF LAND *between the Thames Estuary and the Wash, flat but far from featureless, sits aside from the main north–south axis through Britain, and for that reason it has succeeded in maintaining and preserving its distinctive architecture, traditions and rural character in both cities and countryside.*

East Anglia's name derives from the Angles, the people from northern Germany who settled here during the 5th and 6th centuries. East Anglians have long been a breed of plain-spoken and independent people. Two prominent East Anglians – Queen Boadicea in the 1st century and Oliver Cromwell in the 17th century – were famous for their stubbornness and their refusal to bow to constituted authority. During the Civil War, East Anglia was Cromwell's most reliable source of support. The hardy people who made a difficult living hunting and fishing in the swampy fens, which were drained in the 17th century, were called the Fen Tigers. After draining, the peaty soil proved ideal for arable farming, and today East Anglia grows about a third of Britain's vegetables. The rotation of crops, heralding Britain's agricultural revolution, was perfected in Norfolk in the 18th century. Many of the region's towns and cities grew prosperous on the agricultural wealth, including Norwich. The sea also plays a prominent role in East Anglian life. Coastal towns and villages support the many fishermen who use the North Sea, rich in herring in former days but now known mainly for flat fish.

In modern times, the area has become a centre of recreational sailing, both off the coast and on the inland waterway system known as the Norfolk Broads. East Anglia is also home to one of Britain's top universities: Cambridge.

Lavender fields in full bloom in July, Heacham, Norfolk

◁ Cley windmill overlooking the sea marshes on the north Norfolk coast

Exploring East Anglia

As you move away from London, you soon reach the countryside immortalized by the painter Constable *(see p192)* and in many ways unchanged since his day, scattered with churches, windmills and medieval agricultural barns. Nature lovers will find it fruitful territory, especially North Norfolk with its bird reserves and seal colonies. Boating enthusiasts, too, are well catered for in this, Britain's driest and sunniest region. The local architecture ranges from a mix of medieval to modern. The distinctive pink-washed cottages in Suffolk, flint cottages in Norfolk and thatched roofs everywhere, are also much in evidence.

Norfolk Coast Path

THE WASH

8 NORTH NORFOLK TOUR

7 SANDRINGHAM

Pedlars Way

A149

A1065

6 KINGS LYNN

A47

Grantham

A47

A1

Leicester

A47

A1(M)

PETERBOROUGH 1

Nene

New Bedford River

Vermuden's Drain

Old Bedford River

Delph

FENS 5

Great Ouse

A10

SWAFFHAM 4

Wensey A

A47

GRIMES GRAVES 3

Little Ouse

THETFORD

A11

A134

A1

A14T

ELY 2

A10

A142

A14(A604)

HUNTINGDON 26

Cam

Great Ouse

A14(A45)

BURY ST EDMUND 23

A134

NEWMARKET 24

ANGLESEY ABBEY 25

27

A45

CAMBRIDGE

Bedford, London

M11

Icknield Way

Stour

A604

LAVENHAM 22 A1

A131

AUDLEY END 28

A120

Colne

COLCHESTER

COGGESHALL 21 A12

A120

Bishop's Stortford

M11

A12

MALDON 30

EPPING FOREST

M25 29

London

A13

SOUTHEND-ON-SEA

Thames Estuary

Punting on the River Cam in Cambridge

SEE ALSO
• *Where to Stay* pp547–9
• *Where to Eat* pp584–5

KEY

- Motorway
- Major road
- Minor road
- Scenic route
- Scenic path
- River
- Viewpoint

GETTING AROUND

The region's more isolated sights can be very difficult to reach by public transport and, for a few people, car rental may be a cheaper and more efficient method of travelling around. The M11 motorway runs from London to Cambridge. The coast road from Aldeburgh to King's Lynn takes you through some of the best countryside in the area. There are frequent mainline trains to Norwich, Ipswich and Cambridge although the local trains are more sporadic. There are international and domestic airports at Stansted *(see p634)* and Norwich.

Beach huts on Wells-next-the-Sea beach, north Norfolk

SIGHTS AT A GLANCE

0 kilometres 10
0 miles 10

Peterborough ❶

Cambridgeshire. 🏛 *156,000.* 🚇 🚌
🛈 *3 Minster Precinct (01733
452336).* 🛍 *Tue–Sat.*
🌐 www.peterborough.gov.uk

ALTHOUGH ONE OF the oldest
settlements in Britain,
Peterborough was designated
a New Town in 1967, and is
now a mixture of ancient
and modern.

The city centre is dominated
by the 12th-century **St Peter's
Cathedral** which gave the city
its name. The interior of this
classic Norman building, with
its vast yet simple nave, was
badly damaged by Cromwell's
troops *(see p52),* but its unique
painted wooden ceiling (1220)
has survived intact. Catherine
of Aragon, the first wife of

**Peterborough's coat of arms with
a Latin inscription: Upon this Rock**

Henry VIII, is buried here,
although Cromwell's troops
also destroyed her tomb.

ENVIRONS: The oldest wheel in
Britain (1,300 BC) was found
preserved in peat at **Flag Fen
Bronze Age Centre**. The site
provides a fascinating glimpse
into prehistory.

**⛏ Flag Fen Bronze Age
Centre**
The Droveway, Northey, Peterborough.
📞 *01733 313414.* ⏰ *daily 10am–
5pm.* ⬤ *Christmas wk.* 🎫 ♿ 📷 🖥

Grimes Graves ❸

(EH) Lynford, Norfolk. 📞 *01842
810656.* 🚉 *Brandon then taxi.* ⬤
daily. ⬤ *1 Jan, 24–26 Dec.* 🎫 🛈

ONE OF THE MOST important
Neolithic sites in England,
this was once an extensive
complex of flint mines – 433
shafts have been located –
dating from before 2000 BC.

Using antlers as pickaxes,
Stone Age miners hacked
through the soft chalk to
extract the hard flint below to
make axes, weapons and tools.
It is possible that the flint was
transported long distances
around England on the
prehistoric network of paths.
You can descend 9 m (30 ft)
by ladder into one of the
shafts and see the galleries

Ely ❷

Cambridgeshire. 🏛 *14,000.*
🚇 🛈 *29 St Mary's St (01353
662062).* 🛍 *Thu (general),
Sat (craft & antiques).*
🌐 www.elyeastcambs.co.uk

BUILT ON A chalk hill, this
small city is thought to be
named after the eels in the
nearby River Ouse. The hill
was once an inaccessible
island in the then marshy and
treacherous Fens *(see p184).*
It was also the last stronghold
of Anglo-Saxon resistance,
under Hereward the Wake
(see p48), who hid in the
cathedral until the Normans
crossed the Fens in 1071.

Today this small prosperous
city, totally dominated by the
huge **cathedral**, is the
market centre for the rich
agricultural area surrounding it.

The lantern's glass
windows admit light
into the dome.

*This painted
wooden angel is
one of hundreds of
bosses that were
carved all over the
south and north
transepts in the 13th
and 14th centuries.*

**Stained glass
museum**

The tomb is that of
Alan de Walsingham,
designer of the
unique Octagon.

*The Octagon,
made of wood, was built
in 1322 when the Norman
tower collapsed. Its roof,
the lantern, took an extra
24 years to build and
weighs 200 tonnes.*

Octagon　　**Area of cutaway**

ELY CATHEDRAL
Ely. 📞 *01353 667735.*
⏰ *daily.* ⬤ *special events.* 🎫 ♿ 🍴 🖥 🛍
Begun in 1083, the cathedral took 268 years to
complete. It survived the Dissolution *(see p50)*
but was closed for 17 years by Cromwell *(see
p52)* who lived in Ely for a time.

where the flint was mined. During excavations, unusual chalk models of a fertility goddess *(see p43)* and a phallus were discovered.

ENVIRONS: Nearby, at the centre of the once fertile plain known as the Breckland, is the small market town of **Thetford**.

Once a prosperous trading town, its fortunes dipped in the 16th century, when its priory was destroyed *(see p50)* and the surrounding land deteriorated due to excessive sheep grazing. The area was later planted with pine trees. A mound in the city marks the site of a pre-Norman castle.

The revolutionary writer and philosopher Tom Paine, author of *The Rights of Man*, was born here in 1737.

Oxburgh Hall surrounded by its medieval moat

Swaffham ❹

Norfolk. 🏘 *6,700.* 🚌 ℹ️ *Apr–Oct: Market Place (01760 722255).* 🛒 *Sat.* 🌐 www.aroundswaffham.co.uk

THE BEST-PRESERVED Georgian town in East Anglia and a fashionable resort during the Regency period, Swaffham is at its liveliest on Saturdays when a market is held in the square around the market cross of 1783. In the centre of the town is the 15th-century **Church of St Peter and St Paul**, with a small spire added in the 19th century. It has a magnificent Tudor north aisle, said to have been paid for by John Chapman, the Pedlar of Swaffham. He is depicted on the two-sided town sign near the market place. Myth has it that he went to London and met a stranger who told him of hidden treasure at Swaffham. He returned, dug it up and used it to embellish the church, where he is shown in a window.

ENVIRONS: Castle Acre, north of the town, has the remains of a massive Cluniac **priory**. Founded in 1090, its stunning Norman front still stands.

A short drive south is **Oxburgh Hall and Garden**, built by Sir Edmund Bedingfeld in 1482. The hall, entered through a huge 24 m (80 ft) fortified gatehouse, displays the velvet Oxburgh Hangings, embroidered by Mary, Queen of Scots *(see p497)*.

Swaffham town sign

🏛 **Castle Acre Priory**
(EH) Castle Acre.
📞 *01760 755394.*
⏰ *Apr–Oct: daily; Nov–Mar: Wed–Sun.* 🔵 *24-26 Dec, 1 Jan.* 💷
♿ *limited.* 📷

🏛 **Oxburgh Hall & Garden**
(NT) Oxborough. 📞 *01366 328258.*
⏰ *Mar–Nov: Sat–Wed (garden also Dec: Sat, Sun).* 💷 ♿ *limited.* 🍴 📷

The huge cathedral spire dominates the flat Fens countryside surrounding Ely.

Painted ceiling, 19th century

The Prior's Door (c.1150)

The south aisle has 12 classic Norman arches at its foot, with pointed Early English windows above.

BOADICEA AND THE ICENI

When the Romans invaded Britain, the Iceni, the main tribe in East Anglia, joined forces with them to defeat the Catuvellauni, a rival tribe. But the Romans then turned on the Iceni, torturing Queen Boadicea (or Boudicca). In AD 61, she led a revolt against Roman rule: her followers burned down London, Colchester and St Albans. The rebellion was put down and the queen took poison rather than submit. At Cockley Cley, near Swaffham, an Iceni camp has been excavated.

Illustration of Queen Boadicea leading her Iceni followers

A windmill on Wicken Fen

The Fens ❺

Cambridgeshire/Norfolk. 🚆 Ely. 🛈
29 St Mary's St, Ely (01353 662062).
🅆 www.eastcambs.gov.uk

THIS IS THE OPEN, flat, fertile
expanse that lies between
Lincoln, Cambridge, Bedford
and King's Lynn. Up until the
17th century it was a swamp,
and settlement was possible
only on "islands", such as Ely
(see p182), raised above their
low-lying surroundings.

Through the 17th century,
speculators, recognizing the
value of the peaty soil for farmland, brought in Dutch experts
to drain the fens. However,
as the peat dried it
contracted, and the
fens have slowly
been getting lower.
Powerful electric
pumps now keep
it drained.

Nine miles (14 km)
from Ely is Wicken
Fen, 243 ha (600
acres) of undrained
fen providing a
habitat for water
life, wildfowl and
wild flowers.

King's Lynn ❻

Norfolk. 👥 42,000. 🚆 🚌
🛈 Custom House, Purfleet Quay
(01553 763044). 🅰 Tue, Fri, Sat.
🅆 www.west-norfolk.gov.uk

FORMERLY BISHOP'S LYNN, its
name was changed at the
Reformation (see p50) to
reflect the changing political
reality. In the Middle Ages
it was one of
England's most
prosperous ports,
shipping grain and
wool from the sur-
rounding countryside
to Europe. There are
still a few warehouses
and merchants'
houses by the River
Ouse surviving
from this period.
At the north end of
the town is **True's**

**Trinity Guildhall,
King's Lynn**

North Norfolk Coastal Tour ❽

THIS TOUR TAKES YOU THROUGH some of the most
beautiful areas of East Anglia; nearly all of the
north Norfolk coast has been designated an Area of
Outstanding Natural Beauty. The sea has dictated the
character of the area. With continuing deposits of silt,
once busy ports are now far inland and the shingle
and sand banks that have been built up are home to
a huge variety of wildlife. Do bear in mind when
planning your journey that this popular route can get
congested during summer.

TIPS FOR DRIVERS

Tour length: 28 miles (45 km).
Stopping-off points: Holkham
Hall makes a pleasant stop for a
picnic lunch. There are some good
pubs in Wells-next-the-Sea. (See
also pp636–7.)

Hunstanton Cliffs ②
These magnificent
cliffs tower 18 m
(60 ft) above the
beach. Their three
bands of colour are
made from car-
stone and red and
white chalk.

Caley Mill ①
The largest producer of English
Lavender, this whole area is at
its best in July and August when
the fields are a blaze of purple.

Lord Nelson pub ③
Nelson (p54), born near Burnham Market, dined here befor
he went to sea for the last tim

Yard, a relic of the old fishermen's quarter.

The **Trinity Guildhall**, located in the Saturday Market Place, dates back to the 15th century and was formerly a prison. The handsome **Customs House**, overlooking the river, was built in the 17th century as a merchant exchange. It is now a museum dedicated to the town's colourful maritime history. The Tourist Information Centre is also located here. **St Margaret's Church**, on the Market Place, dates back to 1101, and the interior includes a fine Elizabethan screen. In 1741 the tall spire on the southwest tower collapsed in a storm.

⚏ Customs House
Purfleet Quay. 📞 *01553 763044.*
◯ *daily.* 🚫 ♿ *ground floor.*

Sandringham House, where the Royal Family spend every Christmas

Sandringham ❼

Norfolk. 📞 *01553 772675.* 🚌 *from King's Lynn.* ◯ *Easter–Oct: daily.* ● *two wks Jul–Aug.* 🚫 ♿ 🍴 🎁 W www.sandringhamestate.co.uk

THIS SIZEABLE NORFOLK estate has been in royal hands since 1862 when it was bought by the Prince of Wales, who later became Edward VII. The 18th-century house was elaborately embellished and refurbished by the prince and now retains an appropriately Edwardian atmosphere.

The large stables are now a museum and contain several trophies that relate to hunting, shooting and horse racing – all favourite royal activities. A popular feature is a display of royal motor cars spanning nearly a century. In the park there are scenic nature trails.

Holkham Hall ④
This Palladian home is magnificent. Set in a beautiful landscaped park, it houses an impressive collection of art and Classical sculptures.

KEY

▬ Tour route
═ Other roads
🔆 Viewpoint

Cley Windmill ⑦
This famous landmark overlooks Cley Marshes which became, in 1926, the first nature and bird reserve in Britain.

Blakeney Marshes ⑥
In the 13th century, Blakeney was a substantial trading port. Today, the marsh is inhabited by a seal colony and hundreds of sea birds.

Wells-next-the-Sea ⑤
ue to silting, this port is now a le (1.5 km) from the sea. Its ng sandy beach is popular and ed with colourful beach huts.

0 kilometres   5

0 miles   3

The symmetrical red-brick façade of the 17th-century Blickling Hall

Blickling Hall ❾

(NT) Aylsham, Norfolk. 📞 *01263 738030.* 🚆 *Norwich, then bus.*
House ◯ *Apr–Oct: 1–5pm Wed–Sun & public hols.* **Garden** ◯ *Apr–Oct: 10:15am–5:15pm Wed–Sun & public hols; Aug daily.* **Park** ◯ *daily.* 📷 ♿
🍴 🏠 🆆 www.nationaltrust.org.uk

APPROACHED FROM the east, its symmetrical Jacobean front framed by trees and flanked by two yew hedges, Blickling Hall offers one of the most impressive vistas of any country house in the area.

Anne Boleyn, Henry VIII's tragic second queen, spent her childhood here, but very little of the original house remains. Most of the present structure dates from 1628, when it was home to James I's Chief Justice Sir Henry Hobart. Later in 1767 the 2nd Earl of Buckinghamshire, John Hobart, celebrated the Boleyn connection with reliefs in the Great Hall depicting Anne and her daughter, Elizabeth I.

The Long Gallery is the most spectacular room to survive from the 1620s. Its ceiling depicts symbolic representations of learning.

The Peter the Great Room marks the 2nd earl's service as ambassador to Russia and was built to display a huge spectacular tapestry (1764) of the tsar on horseback, a gift from, Catherine the Great. It also has portraits (1760) of the ambassador and his wife by Gainsborough *(see p151)*.

Norwich ❿

See pp188–9.

The Broads ⓫

Norfolk. 🚆 *Hoveton, Wroxham.* 🚌 *Norwich, then bus.* 🛈 *Station Rd, Hoveton (01603 782281) Apr–Oct.* 🆆 www.broads/authority.gov.uk

THESE SHALLOW LAKES and waterways south and northeast of Norwich, joined by six rivers – the Bure, Thurne, Ant, Yare, Waveney and Chet – were once thought to have been naturally formed, but in actual fact they are medieval peat diggings which flooded when the water level rose in the 13th century.

During summer the 125 miles (200 km) of open waterways, uninterrupted by locks, teem with thousands of boating enthusiasts, from devotees of pure sail to those who prefer motorboats. You can either hire a boat yourself or take one of the many trips on offer to view the plants and wildlife of the area. Look out for Britain's largest butterfly, the swallowtail. Wroxham, the unofficial capital of the Broads, is the starting point for many of these excursions.

The waterways support substantial beds of strong and durable reeds, much in demand for thatching *(see p29)*. They are cut in winter and carried to shore in the distinctive Broads punts.

For a more detailed look at the origins of the Broads and their varied wildlife, visit the **Norfolk Wildlife Trust** – a large thatched floating information centre on Ranworth Broad, with displays on all aspects of the area, and a bird-watching gallery.

In the centre of Ranworth is **St Helen's Church** which has a painted medieval screen, a well-preserved 14th-century illuminated manuscript and spectacular views over the entire area from its tower.

🦋 **Norfolk Wildlife Trust**
Ranworth. 📞 *01603 270479.*
◯ *Apr–Oct: daily.* ♿ 🏠

Sailing boat, Wroxham Broad, Norfolk

Great Yarmouth ⑫

Norfolk. 🏠 90,000. 🚢 🚉 🚌 ℹ️ *Town Hall (01493 846345); Apr–Oct: Marine Parade (01493 842195).* 🗓️ *Wed, Fri (summer), Sat.*
🆆 www.great-yarmouth.co.uk

HERRING FISHING was once the major industry of this port, with 1,000 boats engaged in it just before World War I. Over-fishing led to a depletion of stocks and, for the port to survive, it started to earn its living from servicing container ships and North Sea oil rigs.

It is also the most popular seaside resort on the Norfolk coast and has been since the 19th century, when Dickens (*see p177*) gave it useful publicity by setting part of his novel *David Copperfield* here.

The **Elizabethan House Museum** has a large, eclectic display which illustrates the social history of the area.

In the old part of the town, around South Quay, are a number of charming houses including the 17th-century **Old Merchant's House**. It retains its original patterned plaster ceilings as well as examples of old ironwork

Fishing trawlers at Lowestoft's quays

and architectural fittings from nearby houses, which were destroyed during World War II. The guided tour of the house includes a visit to the adjoining cloister of a 13th-century friary.

🏛️ **Elizabethan House Museum**
(EH) 4 South Quay. 📞 *01493 855746.*
🕐 *Apr–Oct: daily.* 🎟️ 📷
🏚️ **Old Merchant's House**
(NT) South Quay. 📞 *01493 857900.*
🕐 *Apr–Oct: daily.* 🎟️ 📷

Lowestoft ⑬

Suffolk. 🏠 55,000. 🚢 🚉
ℹ️ *East Point Pavilion, Royal Plain (01502 533600).* 🗓️ *Tue, Fri, Sat.*
🆆 www.visit/lowestoft.co.uk

THE MOST EASTERLY TOWN in Britain was long a rival to Great Yarmouth, both as a holiday resort and a fishing port. Its fishing industry has only just survived.

The coming of the railway in the 1840s gave the town an advantage over other resorts, and the solid Victorian and Edwardian boarding houses are evidence of its popularity.

Lowestoft Museum, in a 17th-century house, has a good display of the fine porcelain made here in the 18th century, as well as exhibits on local archaeology and domestic life.

ENVIRONS: Somerleyton Hall is built in Jacobean style on the foundations of a smaller mansion. Its gardens are a real delight, and there is a genuinely baffling yew hedge maze.

🏛️ **Lowestoft Museum**
Oulton Broad. 📞 *01502 568560.*
🕐 *Mar (last Mon)–Oct (1st Sun) 10:30am–5pm Mon–Fri, 2–5pm Sat & Sun.* 🎟️ ♿ *limited.* 📷 *by arrangement.*
🏚️ **Somerleyton Hall**
(EH) On B1074. 📞 *01502 730224.*
🕐 *Easter Sun–Oct: Thu, Sun & public hols (Jul–Aug: Tue–Thu, Sun & public hols).* 🎟️ 📷 ♿ 📷 *by arrangement.*
📷 🆆 www.somerleyton.co.uk

Corn mill at Saxtead Green, near Framlingham

Herringfleet Smock Mill, near Lowestoft

WINDMILLS ON THE FENS AND BROADS

The flat, open countryside and the stiff breezes from the North Sea made windmills an obvious power source for East Anglia well into the 20th century, and today they are an evocative and recurring feature of the landscape. On the Broads and Fens, some were used for drainage, while others, such as that at Saxtead Green, ground corn. On the boggy fens they were not built on hard foundations, so few survived, but elsewhere, especially on the Broads, many have been restored to working order. The seven-storey Berney Arms Windmill is the tallest on the Broads. Thurne Dyke Drainage Mill is the site of an exhibition about the occasionally idiosyncratic mills and their more unusual mechanisms.

Norwich ⑩

IN THE HEART of the fertile East Anglian countryside, Norwich, one of the best-preserved cities in Britain, is steeped in a relaxed provincial atmosphere. The city was first fortified by the Saxons in the 9th century and still has the irregular street plan of that time. With the arrival of Flemish settlers in the early 12th century and the establishment of a textile industry, the town soon became a prosperous market and was the second city of England until the Industrial Revolution in the 19th century *(see pp56–7)*.

The cobbled street, Elm Hill

Exploring Norwich
The oldest parts of the city are Elm Hill, one of the finest medieval streets in England, and Tombland, the old Saxon market place by the cathedral. Both have well-preserved medieval buildings, which are now incorporated into pleasant areas of small shops.

With a trading history spanning hundreds of years, the colourful market in the city centre is well worth a visit. A good walk meanders around the surviving sections of the 14th-century flint city wall.

⛪ Norwich Cathedral
The Close. 📞 *01603 218321.*
🕐 *daily.* **Donations.** 🚻 ♿ 📷 🍴
Ⓦ www.cathedral.org.uk
This magnificent building was founded in 1096 by Bishop Losinga and built with stone from Caen in France and Barnack.

The precinct originally included a monastery, and the surviving cloister is the most extensive in England. The thin cathedral spire was added in the 15th century, making it, at 96 m (315 ft), the second tallest in England after Salisbury *(see pp252–3)*. In the majestic

nave, soaring Norman pillars and arches support a 15th-century vaulted roof whose stone bosses, many of which illustrate well-known Bible stories, have recently been beautifully restored.

Easier to appreciate at close hand is the elaborate wood carving in the choir – the canopies over the stalls and the misericords beneath the seats, one showing a small boy being smacked. Not to be missed is the 14th-century Despenser Reredos in St Luke's Chapel. It was hidden for years under a carpenter's table to prevent its destruction by Puritans.

Two gates to the cathedral close survive: **St Ethelbert's**,

One of over a thousand carved bosses in the cathedral cloisters

a 13th-century flint arch, and the **Erpingham Gate** at the west end, built by Sir Thomas Erpingham, who led the triumphant English archers at the Battle of Agincourt in 1415 *(see p49)*.

Beneath the east outer wall is the grave of Edith Cavell, the Norwich-born nurse who was arrested and executed in 1915 by the Germans for helping Allied soldiers escape from occupied Belgium.

🏛 Castle Museum
Castle Meadow. 📞 *01603 493648.*
🕐 *daily (Sun pm only).* ● *1 Jan, 25 & 26 Dec.* ♿ Ⓦ www.norfolk.gov.uk/tourism/museums
The brooding keep of this 12th-century castle has been a museum since 1894, when it ended 650 years of service as a prison. The most important Norman feature is a carved door that used to be the main entrance.

Exhibits include significant collections of archaeology,

A view of Norwich Cathedral's spire and tower from the southeast

It's nicer with
MUSTARD

COLMAN'S MUSTARD

It was said of the Colmans that they made their fortune from what diners left on their plate. In 1814 Jeremiah Colman started milling mustard at Norwich because it was at the centre of a fertile plain where mustard was grown. Today at 15 Royal Arcade a shop sells mustard and related items, while a small museum illustrates the history of the company.

A 1950s advertisement for Colman's Mustard

VISITORS' CHECKLIST

Norfolk. 🏘 *125,000.* 🚉 ⛴
Thorpe Road. 🚌 *Surrey St.* ℹ
Millennium Plane (01603 727927).
🌐 *www.visitnorwich-area.co.uk*

🏛 Strangers' Hall

Charing Cross. ◯ *Wed, Sat for* 🎟
*only. Tickets from Castle Museum
(01603 493648).*
This 14th-century merchant's house gives a glimpse into English domestic life through the ages. The costume display features a unique collection of underwear. The house was lived in by immigrant weavers – the "strangers". It has a fine 15th-century Great Hall.

natural history, fine art as well as the world's largest collection of ceramic teapots.

The art gallery is dominated by works from the Norwich School of painters. This group of early 19th century land-scape artists painted directly from nature, getting away from the stylized studio land-scapes that had been fashion-able up to then. Chief among the group were John Crome (1768–1821), whom many compare with Constable *(see p192)*, and John Sell Cotman (1782–1842), known for his watercolours. There are also regular exhibitions held here which are brought from the Tate Gallery in London.

🔒 Church of St Peter Mancroft

Market Place. ◯ *01603 610443.*
◯ *10am–4pm Mon–Sat; 10am–4pm
Sat (summer), 10am–1pm (winter); Sun
(services only).* **Donations.** ♿
This imposing Perpendicular church, built around 1455, so dominates the city centre that many visitors assume it is the cathedral. John Wesley *(see p267)* wrote of it, "I scarcely ever remember to have seen a more beautiful parish church".

The large windows make the church very light, and the dramatic east window still has most of its 15th-century glass. The roof is unusual in having wooden fan tracery – it is normally in stone – covering the hammerbeam construction. The famous peal of 13 bells rang out in 1588 to celebrate the defeat of the Spanish

Armada *(see p51)* and is still heard every Sunday.

Its name derives from the Latin *magna crofta* (great meadow) which described the area in pre-Norman times.

🏛 Bridewell Museum

Bridewell Alley. ◯ *01603 629127.*
◯ *10am–5pm Mon–Sat.* 🎟 📷
One of the oldest houses in Norwich, this 14th-century flint-faced building was for years used as a jail. It now houses an exhibition of local industries, with displays of old machines, advertisements and reconstructed shops.

🏛 Guildhall

Gaol Hill. 🚻
Above the city's ancient market place is the imposing 15th-century flint and stone Guild-hall with its gable of check-ered flushwork (now a café).

🏛 The Sainsbury Centre for Visual Arts

University of E Anglia (on B1108). ♿
01603 593199. ◯ *Tue–Sun.* ● *23
Dec–2 Jan.* 🎟 ♿ 🎟 *by arrangement.*
🍴 🛍 🌐 *www.uea.ac.uk/scva*
This important art gallery was built in 1978 to house the collection of Robert and Lisa Sainsbury given to the University of East Anglia in 1973.

The collection's strength is in its modern European paintings, including works by Modigliani, Picasso and Bacon, and in its sculptures by Giacometti and Moore. There are also displays of ethnographic art from Africa, the Pacific and the Americas.

The centre, designed by Lord Norman Foster, one of Britain's leading and most innovative architects, was among the first to display its steel structure openly.

***Back of the New Mills* (1814) by John Crome of the Norwich School**

Purple heather in flower on Dunwich Heath

Southwold ⑭

Suffolk. 🚶 3,900. 🚉 ℹ️ High Street
(01502 724729). 🚢 Mon, Thu.
W www.visit-southwold.co.uk

THIS PICTURE-POSTCARD seaside resort, with its charming white-washed villas clustered around small greens has, largely by historical accident, remained unspoiled. The railway line which connected it with London was closed in 1929, which effectively isolated this Georgian town from an influx of day-trippers.

That this was also once a large port can be judged by the size of the 15th-century **St Edmund King and Martyr Church**, worth a visit for the 16th-century painted screens. On

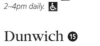

Jack o'the Clock,
Southwold

its tower is a small figure dressed in the uniform of a 15th-century soldier and known as Jack o'the Clock. **Southwold Museum** tells the story of the Battle of Sole Bay, which was fought offshore between the English and Dutch navies in 1672.

ENVIRONS: The pretty village of **Walberswick** lies across the creek. By road it is a long detour and the only alternatives are a rowing-boat ferry across the harbour (summer only) or a footbridge across the river half a mile inland. Further inland at Blythburgh, the 15th-century **Holy Trinity Church** dominates the surrounding land. In 1944 a US bomber blew up over the church, killing Joseph Kennedy Jr, brother of the future American president.

🏛 **Southwold Museum**
9–11 Victoria St. ◐ Easter–Oct:
2–4pm daily. ♿

Dunwich ⑮

Suffolk. 🚶 1,400.

THIS TINY VILLAGE is all that remains of a "lost city" consigned to the sea by erosion. In the 7th century Dunwich was the seat of the powerful East Anglian kings. In the 13th century it was still the biggest port in Suffolk and some 12 churches were built. But the land was being eroded at about a metre (3 ft) a year, and the last original church collapsed into the sea in 1919.

Dunwich Heath, to the south, runs down to a sandy beach and is an important nature reserve. **Minsmere Reserve** has observation hides for watching a huge variety of birds.

🦋 **Dunwich Heath**
(NT) Nr Westleton. 📞 01728 648505.
◐ phone for details. 🅿️ 🚻 🎁
🦋 **Minsmere Reserve**
Minsmere, Westleton. 📞 01728
648281.◐ Wed–Mon. ● 25, 26 Dec.
🅿️ ♿ 🚻 🎁 W www.rspb.org.uk

Aldeburgh ⑯

Suffolk. 🚶 2,500. 🚉 ℹ️ High St
(01728 453637).
W www.aldeburgh-uk.com

BEST KNOWN TODAY for the music festivals at Snape Maltings just up the River Alde, Aldeburgh has been a

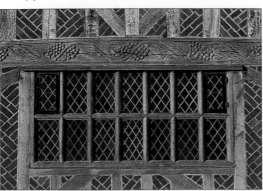

Intricate carving on the exterior of the Tudor Moot Hall, Aldeburgh

port since Roman times (the Roman area is under water).

Erosion has resulted in the fine Tudor **Moot Hall**, once far inland, now being close to the beach and promenade. Its ground floor, originally the market, is now a museum. The large timbered court room above can only be reached by the original outside staircase.

The **church**, also Tudor, contains a large stained glass window placed in 1979 as a memorial to Benjamin Britten.

🎧 Moot Hall
Market Cross Pl. ◯ Apr, May: Sat, Sun (pm); Jun: daily (pm); Jul, Aug: daily. 🏷 ◻

Framlingham Castle ⓱

(EH) Framlingham, Suffolk. 🎧 01728 724189. 🚃 Wickham Market then taxi. ◯ daily. ● 24–26 Dec, 1 Jan. ◻ 🏷

PERCHED ON A HILL, the small village of Framlingham has long been an important strategic site, even before the present castle was built in 1190 by the Earl of Norfolk.

Little of the castle from that period survives except the powerful curtain wall and its towers; walk round the top of it for fine views of the town.

Mary Tudor, daughter of Henry VIII, was staying here in 1553 when she heard she was to become queen.

ENVIRONS: To the southeast, on the coast, is the 27 m (90 ft) keep of **Orford Castle**, built for Henry II as a coastal defence at around the same time as Framlingham. It is an early example of an English castle with a 16-sided keep; earlier they were square and later round. A short climb to the top of the castle gives fantastic views.

🏰 Orford Castle
(EH) Orford. 🎧 01394 450412. ◯ Apr–Oct: daily; Nov–Mar: Wed–Sun. ● 24–26 Dec, 1 Jan. 🏷 ◻

Ipswich ⓲

Suffolk. 🏙 120,000. 🚃 ◻ 🛈 St Stephen's Lane (01473 258070). ● Tue, Fri, Sat. ⓦ www.ipswich.gov.uk

SUFFOLK'S COUNTY TOWN has a largely modern centre but several buildings remain from earlier times. It rose to prominence after the 13th century as a port for the rich Suffolk wool trade *(see p195)*. Later, with the Industrial Revolution, it began to export coal.

The **Ancient House** in Buttermarket has a superb example of pargeting – the ancient craft of ornamental façade plastering. The town's museum and art gallery,

Christchurch Mansion, is a Tudor house from 1548, where Elizabeth I stayed in 1561. It also boasts the best collection of Constable's paintings out of London *(see p192)*, including four marvellous Suffolk landscapes, as well as pictures by the Suffolk-born painter Gainsborough *(see p151)*.

Ipswich Museum contains replicas of the Mildenhall and Sutton Hoo treasures, the originals being in the British Museum *(see pp108–9)*.

In the centre of the town is **St Margaret's**, a 15th-century church built in flint and stone with a double hammerbeam roof and 17th-century painted ceiling panels. **Wolsey's Gate**, a Tudor gateway of 1527, provides a link with Ipswich's most famous son, Cardinal Wolsey *(see p161)*. He started to build an ecclesiastical college in the town, but fell from royal favour before it was finished.

🏛 Christchurch Mansion
Soane St. 🎧 01473 433554. ◯ 10am–5pm Tue–Sat & public hols; 2:30–4:30pm Sun. ● 1 Jan, Good Fri, 24–26 Dec. ♿ limited. 🏷 by arrangement ◻

🏛 Ipswich Museum
High St. 🎧 01473 433550. ◯ Tue–Sat. ◻

Pargeting on the Ancient House in Ipswich

Constable Walk ⑲

THIS WALK in Constable country follows one of the most picturesque sections of the River Stour. The route taken would have been familiar to the landscape painter John Constable (1776–1837). Constable's father, a wealthy merchant, owned Flatford Mill, which was depicted in many of the artist's important paintings. Constable claimed to know and love "every stile and stump, and every lane" around East Bergholt.

The River Stour, used as a backdrop for Constable's *Boatbuilding* **(1814)**

TIPS FOR WALKERS

Starting point: *Park off Flatford Lane, East Bergholt (charge to park).* ℹ️ *01206 299460;* **(NT)** *Bridge Cottage (01206 298260).* **Getting there:** *A12 to Ipswich, then B1070 to East Bergholt, follow signs to Flatford.* 🚆 *Manningtree is within walking distance of Flatford.* 🚌 *from Ipswich or Colchester.* **Stopping-off point:** *Dedham.* **Length:** *3 miles (5 km).* **Difficulty:** *Flat trail along riverside footpath with kissing gates.*

Viewpoint ⑤
The view over the valley from the top of the hill shows Constable country at its best.

Car Park ①
Follow the signs to Flatford Mill then cross the footbridge.

Dedham Mill

Stour

Dedham

EAST BERGHOLT

Gosnalls Farm

Fen Bridge ③
This modern foot-bridge replaced one that Constable used as a focus for many of his paintings.

Ram Lock

Flatford Mill

Dedham Church ④
The tall church tower appears in many of Constable's pictures including the *View on the Stour near Dedham* (1822).

KEY

▬ ▬	Route
▭	B road
▭	Minor road
🌿	Viewpoint
🅿	Parking

0 metres		500
0 yards		500

Willy Lott's Cottage ②
This cottage remains much the same as it did when featured in Constable's painting *The Hay-Wain (see p85).*

Colchester ⑳

Essex. 🏘 150,000. 🚅 🚌 ℹ Queen St (01206 282920). 🛒 Fri, Sat.

THE OLDEST recorded town in Britain, Colchester was the effective capital of south-east England when the Romans invaded in AD 43, and it was here that the first permanent Roman colony was established.

After Boadicea (see p183) burnt the town in AD 60, a 2 mile (3 km) defensive wall was built, 3 m (10 ft) thick and 9 m (30 ft) high, to deter any future attackers. You can still see these walls and the surviving Roman town gate, which is the largest in Britain.

During the Middle Ages Colchester developed into an important weaving centre. In the 16th century, a number of immigrant Flemish weavers settled in an area west of the castle, known as the **Dutch Quarter**, which still retains the original tall houses and steep, narrow streets.

Colchester was besieged for 11 weeks during the Civil War (see p52) before being captured by Cromwell's troops.

🏛 Tymperleys
Trinity St. 📞 01206 282943. 🕐 Apr–Oct: Tue–Sat. 🅿 ♿
Clock-making was an important craft in Colchester, and it is celebrated in this restored half-timbered, 15th-century mansion, also worth visiting for its formal Tudor garden.

🏛 Hollytrees Museum
Castle Park. 📞 01206 282940. 🕐 daily 🚫 24–26 Dec, 1 Jan. 🅿 ♿
W www.colchestermuseums.org.uk
This elegant Georgian town-house was built in 1719. Now a charming museum of social history, you can experience the day-to-day lives of Col-chester people and changing technology over 300 years.

🏛 Castle Museum
High St. 📞 01206 282939. 🕐 daily; 11am–5pm Sun. 🚫 24–27 Dec. 🅿 🎦 ♿ 🎟
W www.colchestermuseums.org.uk
This is the oldest and largest Norman keep still standing in England. Twice the size of the White Tower at the Tower of London (see pp120–21), it was

The Norman keep of the Castle Museum, Colchester

built in 1076 on the platform of a Roman temple dedicated to Claudius (see p44), using stones and tiles from other Roman buildings. Today, the museum is packed full of exhibits relating the story of the town from prehistoric times to the Civil War. You can also visit the medieval prison.

🏰 Layer Marney Tower
Off B1022. 📞 01206 330784. 🕐 Apr–Sep: Sun–Fri (pm). 🅿 🎦 ♿ limited. 🎟 by arrangement. 📷
W www.layermarneytower.co.uk
This remarkable Tudor gate-house is the tallest in Britain: its pair of six-sided, eight-storey turrets reach to 24 m (80 ft). It was intended to be part of a larger complex but the designer, Sir Henry Marney, died before it was completed. The brickwork and terracotta ornamentation around the roof and windows arc models of Tudor craftsmanship.

🌿 Beth Chatto Garden
Elmstead Market. 📞 01206 822007. 🕐 Mar–Oct: 9am–5pm Mon–Sat; Nov–Feb: 9am–4pm Mon–Fri. 🚫 24 Dec–6 Jan. 🅿 🎦 📷
W www.bethchatto.co.uk
One of Britain's most eminent gardening writers began this experiment in the 1960s to test her belief that it is possible to create a garden in the most adverse conditions. The dry and windy slopes, boggy patches, gravel beds and wooded areas all support an array of plants best suited to that particular environment.

Coggeshall ㉑

Essex. 🏘 4,000. 🛒 Thu.

THIS SMALL TOWN has two of the most important and best-preserved medieval and Tudor buildings in the country. Dating from 1140, **Coggeshall Grange Barn** is the oldest surviving timber-framed barn in Europe. Inside is a display of historic farm wagons. The half-timbered merchant's house, **Paycocke's**, was built around 1500 and has a beauti-fully panelled interior. There is a display of Coggeshall lace.

🏰 Coggeshall Grange Barn
(NT) Grange Hill. 📞 01376 562226. 🕐 Apr–Oct: Tue, Thu, Sun & public hols (pm). 🚫 Good Fri. 🎦 ♿
🏰 Paycocke's
(NT) West St. 📞 01376 561305. 🕐 Apr–Oct: Tue, Thu, Sun & public hols (pm). 🚫 Good Fri. 🎦 ♿

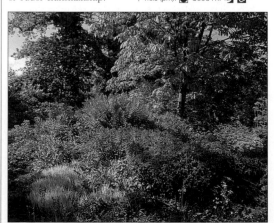
Beth Chatto Garden, Colchester, in full summer bloom

Lavenham ㉒

Suffolk. 🏠 1,700. 🛈 Lady St (01787 248207).

OFTEN CONSIDERED the most perfect of all English small towns, Lavenham is a treasure trove of black and white timber-framed houses ranged along streets whose pattern is virtually unchanged from medieval times. For 150 years, between the 14th and 16th centuries, Lavenham was the prosperous centre of the Suffolk wool trade. It still has many outstanding and well-preserved buildings; indeed no less than 300 of the town's buildings are listed, including the magnificent **Little Hall**.

ENVIRONS: Gainsborough's House, Sudbury, is a museum on this painter (see p151).

🏛 **Little Hall** Market Place. 📞 01787 247179. ⬜ Apr–Oct: Wed, Thu, Sat, Sun (all pm); public hols. 🅿
🏛 **Gainsborough's House** Sudbury. 📞 01787 372958. ⬜ Tue–Sun. ⬛ 24 Dec–1 Jan, Good Fri. 🎟
🅿 🅦 www.gainsborough.org

LITTLE HALL

The solar bedroom was the best and sunniest room in the house.

Communal dormitory

The crown-post roof is a superb feat of medieval engineering.

An Egyptian bronze cat represents the Goddess Bastet.

Library

Entrance

Dining room

The herringbone-style timber on the exterior was used often in the 14th century.

Bury St Edmunds ㉓

Suffolk. 🏠 34,000. 🚆 🚌 🛈 Angel Hill (01284 764667). ⬛ Wed, Sat. 🅦 www.stedmundsbury.gov.uk

ST EDMUND was the last Saxon king of East Anglia, decapitated by Danish raiders in 870. Legend has it that a wolf picked up the severed head – an image that appears in a number of medieval carvings. Edmund was canonized in 900 and buried in Bury, where in 1014 King Canute (see p159) built an **abbey** in his honour, the wealthiest in England until its destruction in the Dissolution of the Monasteries (see p339). The abbey ruins now lie in the town centre.

Nearby are two large 15th-century churches, built when the wool trade made the town wealthy. **St James's** was designated a cathedral in 1914. The best features of **St Mary's** are the north porch and the hammerbeam roof over the nave. A stone slab in the northeast corner marks the tomb of Mary Tudor (see pp50–51).

Illustration of St Edmund

Just below the **market cross** in Cornhill – remodelled by Robert Adam (see p24) in 1714 – stands the large 12th-century **Moyse's Hall**, a merchant's house that serves as the local history museum, displaying archaeology from the area.

ENVIRONS: Three miles (5 km) southwest of Bury is the late 18th-century **Ickworth House**. This eccentric Neo-Classical mansion features an unusual rotunda with a

The 18th-century rotunda of Ickworth House, Bury St Edmunds

domed roof flanked by two huge wings. The art collection includes works by Reynolds and Titian. There are also fine displays of silver, porcelain and sculpture, for example, John Flaxman's (1755–1826) moving *The Fury of Athamas*. The house is set in a large park.

🏛 **Moyse's Hall**
Cornhill. 📞 *01284 706183.* ⏰ *daily.*
⬤ *24–26 Dec, Good Fri.* 🎦 ♿ 🚻
🚌 **Ickworth House**
Horringer. 📞 *01284 735270.* ⏰
Apr–Nov: Fri–Tue, public hols (pm).
🎦 ♿ 🚻 🚻

Newmarket ㉔

Suffolk. 🏠 *17,000.* 🚆 🚌
ℹ *Palace House, Palace St (01638 667200).* 🛒 *Tue, Sat.*

A WALK DOWN the short main street tells you all you need to know about this busy and wealthy little town. The shops sell horse feed and all manner of riding accessories; the clothes on sale are tweeds, jodhpurs and the soft brown hats rarely worn by anyone except racehorse trainers.

Newmarket has been the headquarters of British horse racing since James I decided that its open heaths were ideal for testing the mettle of his fastest steeds against those of his friends. The first ever

The stallion unit at the National Stud, Newmarket

recorded horse race was held here in 1622. Charles II shared his grandfather's enthusiasm and after the Restoration *(see p53)* would move the whole court to Newmarket, every spring and summer, for the sport – he is the only British king to have ridden a winner.

A horse being exercised on Newmarket Heath

The modern racing industry began to take shape here in the late 18th century. There are now over 2,500 horses in training in and around the town, and two racecourses staging regular race meetings from around April to October *(see pp66–7)*. Training stables are occasionally open to the public but you can view the horses being exercised on the heath in the early morning. Tattersall's, the auction house for thoroughbreds, is in the centre of Newmarket.

The **National Stud** can also be visited. You will see the five or six stallions on stud, mares in foal and if you are lucky a newborn foal – most likely in April or May.

The **National Horseracing Museum** tells the history of the sport and contains many offbeat exhibits such as the skeleton of Eclipse, one of the greatest horses ever, unbeaten in 18 races and the ancestor of most of today's fastest performers. It also has a large display of sporting art.

🔵 **National Stud**
Newmarket. 📞 *01638 663464* ⏰
Mar–Sep: daily. 🎦 ♿ 🎦 🖥 🚻
🌐 *www.nationalstud.co.uk*
🏛 **National Horseracing Museum**
99 High St, Newmarket. 📞 *01638 667333.* ⏰ *Apr–Oct: Tue–Sun.* 🎦
♿ 🎦 🖥 🚻 🌐 *www.nhrm.co.uk*

St Mary's Church, Stoke-by-Nayland, southeast of Bury St Edmunds

THE RISE AND FALL OF THE WOOL TRADE

Wool was a major English product from the 13th century and by 1310 some ten million fleeces were exported every year. The Black Death *(see p48)*, which swept Britain in 1348, perversely provided a boost for the industry: with labour in short supply, land could not be cultivated and was grassed over for sheep. Around 1350 Edward III decided it was time to establish a home-based cloth industry and encouraged Flemish weavers to come to Britain. Many settled in East Anglia, particularly Suffolk, and their skills helped establish a flourishing trade. This time of prosperity saw the construction of the sumptuous churches, such as the one at Stoke-by-Nayland, that we see today – East Anglia has more than 2,000 churches. The cloth trade here began to decline in the late 16th century with the development of water-powered looms. These were not suited to the area, which never regained its former wealth. Today's visitors are the beneficiaries of this decline, because the wool towns such as Lavenham and Bury St Edmunds never became rich enough to destroy their magnificent Tudor halls and houses and construct new buildings.

The façade of Anglesey Abbey

Anglesey Abbey ㉕

(NT) Lode, Cambridgeshire. 📞
01223 810080. ≈ Cambridge then
bus. **House** ○ Apr–Oct: Wed–Sun;
Garden ○ Wed–Sun. 📷 ♿
limited. 🍴 🎁

THE ORIGINAL ABBEY was built
in 1135 for an Augustinian
order. But only the crypt – also
known as the monks' parlour
– with its vaulted ceiling on
marble and stone pillars, survived the Dissolution (see p50).
This was later incorporated
into a manor house whose
treasures include furniture
from many periods and a rare

seascape by Gainsborough
(see p194). The superb garden
was created in the 1930s by
Lord Fairhaven as an ambitious, Classical landscape of
trees, sculptures and borders.

Huntingdon ㉖

Cambridgeshire. 🏠 18,000. ≈ 🚌
🅸 Princes St (01480 388588). 🛒
Wed, Sat. 🅆 www.huntsleisure.org

MORE THAN 300 YEARS
after his death, Oliver
Cromwell (see p52) still dominates this small town. Born here
in 1599, a record of his baptism
can be seen in the County
Records Office in Huntingdon.
You can see his name and
traces of ancient graffiti
scrawled all over it which says
"England's plague for five
years". **Cromwell Museum**,
his former school, traces his
life with pictures and mementoes, including his death mask.
Cromwell remains one of
the most disputed figures in
British history. An MP before

he was 30, he quickly became
embroiled in the disputes
between Charles I and Parliament over taxes and religion.
In the Civil War (see p52) he
proved an inspired general
and – after refusing the title
of king – was made Lord
Protector in 1653, four years
after the King was beheaded.
But just two years after his
death the monarchy was restored by popular demand,
and his body was taken out
of Westminster Abbey (see
pp94–5) to hang on gallows.
There is a 14th-century
bridge across the River Ouse
which links Huntingdon with
Godmanchester, the site of a
Roman settlement.

🏛 Cromwell Museum
Grammar School Walk. 📞 01480
375830. ○ Apr–Oct: Tue–Sun; Nov–
Mar: Tue–Sun (pm only except Sat). ●
24–27 Dec, 1 Jan, some public hols. 🎁

Cambridge ㉗

See pp198–203.

Audley End ㉘

Saffron Walden, Essex. 📞 01799
522399. ≈ Audley End then taxi. ○
Apr–Sep: Wed–Sun & public hols noon–
5pm ; Oct: 11am–3pm. ● 24–26
Dec. 📷 ♿ limited. 🎥 🍴 🖥 🎁

THIS WAS THE largest house
in England when built in
1614 for Thomas Howard,
Lord Treasurer and 1st Earl of
Suffolk. James I joked that
Howard's house was too big
for a king but not for a Lord
Treasurer. Charles II, his grandson, disagreed and bought it
in 1667 as an extra palace; but
he and his successors seldom
went there and in 1701 it was
given back to the Howards,
who demolished two thirds of
it to make it more manageable.
What remains is a Jacobean
mansion, retaining its original
hall and many fine plaster ceilings. Robert Adam (see p24)
remodelled most of the interior
in the 1760s and many rooms
have been restored to his original designs. At the same
time, Capability Brown (see
p22) landscaped the magnificent 18th-century park.

The Chapel was completed
in 1772 to a Gothic design.
The furniture was made to
complement the wooden
pillars and vaulting which
are painted to imitate stone.

The painted window,
built in 1768, represents
the Last Supper.

Main entrance

The Great Hall,
hung with family
portraits, is the highlight
of the house, with the
massive oak screen and
elaborate hammerbeam
roof surviving in their
Jacobean form.

Epping Forest ㉙

Essex. 🚃 Chingford. 🚉 Loughton, Theydon Bois. 🛈 High Beach, Loughton (020-8508 0028).

AS ONE OF THE LARGE open spaces near London, the 2,400 ha (6,000 acre) forest is popular with walkers, just as, centuries ago, it was a favourite hunting ground for kings and courtiers – the word forest denoted an area for hunting.

Epping Forest contains oaks and beeches up to 400 years old

A depiction of the Battle of Maldon (991) on the *Maldon Embroidery*

Henry VIII had a lodge built in 1543 on the edge of the forest. His daughter Elizabeth I, also a keen hunter, often used the lodge and it soon became known as **Queen Elizabeth's Hunting Lodge**.

This three-storey timbered building has been fully renovated and now houses an exhibition explaining the lodge's history and other aspects of the forest's life.

The tracts of open land and woods interspersed with a number of lakes, make an ideal habitat for a variety of plant, bird and animal life: deer roam the northern part, many of a special dark strain introduced by James I. The Corporation of London bought the forest in the mid-19th century to ensure it remained open to the public.

🏛 Queen Elizabeth's Hunting Lodge
Rangers Rd, Chingford. 📞 020-8529 6681. ◯ Wed–Sun (pm). ● 24–26 Dec, 1 Jan. 🎟 ♿ limited. 📷 by appointment.

Maldon ㉚

Essex. 🏘 21,000. 🚃 Chelmsford then bus. 🛈 Coach Lane (01621 856503). 🖥 Thu, Sat. 🖥 www.maldon.gov.uk

THIS DELIGHTFUL old town on the River Blackwater, its High Street lined with shops and inns from the 14th century on, was once an important harbour. One of its best-known industries is the production of Maldon sea salt, panned in the traditional way.

A fierce battle here in 991, when Viking invaders defeated the Saxon defenders, is told in *The Battle of Maldon,* one of the earliest known Saxon poems. The battle is also celebrated in the *Maldon Embroidery* on display in the **Maeldune Centre**. This 13 m (42 ft) long embroidery, made by locals, depicts the history of Maldon from 991 to 1991.

ENVIRONS: East of Maldon at Bradwell-on-Sea is the sturdy Saxon church of **St Peter's-on-the-Wall**, a simple stone building that stands isolated on the shore. It was built in 654, from the stones of a former Roman fort, by St Cedd, who used it as his cathedral. It was restored in the 1920s.

🏛 Maeldune Centre
High St. 📞 01621 851628. ◯ Oct–Mar: Thu–Sat; Apr–Sep: Mon–Sat; pm only. ● 24–26 Dec, 1 Jan. 🎟

***Thomas Howard**, the 1st Earl of Suffolk (1561–1626), painted here by Biagio Rebecca, spent over £200,000 on the house.*

Jacobean wooden screen (1708)

Saloon

Little Drawing Room

The Great Drawing Room shows Adam's work at its finest.

Street-by-Street: Cambridge ㉗

Carving, King's College Chapel

CAMBRIDGE HAS BEEN an important town since Roman times as it was sited at the first navigable point on the River Cam. In the 11th century religious orders began to be established in the town and, in 1209, a group of religious scholars broke away from Oxford University *(see pp210–15)* after academic and religious disputes and came here. Student life dominates the city but it is also a thriving market centre serving a rich agricultural region.

Cyclists in Cambridge

Newmarket

BRIDGE STREET

ST JOHN'S STREET

Magdalene Bridge carries Bridge Street across the Cam from the city centre to Magdalene College.

St John's College has superb Tudor and Jacobean architecture.

Kitchen Bridge

★ Bridge of Sighs
Built in 1831 in imitation of its namesake in Venice, it is best viewed from the Kitchen Bridge.

Trinity College

Trinity Avenue Bridge

The Backs
This is the name given to the grassy strip lying between the backs of the big colleges and the banks of the Cam – a good spot to enjoy this classic view of King's College Chapel.

Clare College

Clare Bridge

KEY

– – – Suggested route

STAR SIGHTS

★ **Bridge of Sighs**

★ **King's College Chapel**

Grantchester

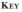

| 0 metres | 75 |
| 0 yards | 75 |

St Mary's Church
This clock is over the west door of the university's official church. Its tower offers fine views.

Round Church
The 12th-century Church of the Holy Sepulchre has one of the few round naves in the country. Its design is based on the Holy Sepulchre in Jerusalem.

Gonville and Caius
(pronounced "keys"), founded in 1348, is one of the oldest colleges.

★ King's College Chapel
This late medieval masterpiece took 70 years to build (see pp200–1).

Market square

Coach station →

King's College
Henry VIII, king when the chapel was completed in 1515, is commemorated in this statue near the main gate.

Queens' College
Its Tudor courts are among the university's finest. This 17th-century sundial is over the old chapel – now a reading room.

Corpus Christi College

To London and railway station

Mathematical Bridge
Linking the two parts of Queens' College across the Cam, the bridge was first built without nuts or bolts.

🏛 Fitzwilliam Museum

Trumpington St. 📞 *01223 332900.*
⏱ *Tue–Sun; public hols.* ⬤ *24 Dec–
1 Jan. Good Fri, May Day.* **Donation.**
♿ 📷 *Sun pm.* 📱 📷
🌐 www.fitzmuseum.cam.ac.uk
One of Britain's oldest public
museums, this massive Classical building has works of
exceptional quality and rarity,
especially antiquities, ceramics,
paintings and manuscripts.

The core of the collection
was bequeathed in 1816 by
the 7th Viscount Fitzwilliam.
Other gifts have since greatly
added to the exhibits.

Works by Titian (1488–1576)
and the 17th-century Dutch
masters, including Hals, Cuyp
and Hobbema's *Wooded
Landscape* (1686), stand out
among the paintings. French
Impressionist gems include
Monet's *Le Printemps* (1866)
and Renoir's *La Place Clichy*
(1880), while Picasso's *Still
Life* (1923) is notable among
the modern works. Most of
the important British artists
are represented, from
Hogarth in the 18th century
through Constable in the 19th
to Ben Nicholson in the 20th.

The miniatures include the
earliest surviving depiction of
Henry VIII. In the same gallery
are some dazzling illuminated
manuscripts, notably the 15th-
century *Metz Pontifical*, a
French liturgical work.

The impressive Glaisher
collection of European
earthenware and stoneware
includes a unique display of
English delftware from the
16th and 17th centuries.

Handel's bookcase contains
folios of his work, and nearby
is Keats's original manuscript
for *Ode to a Nightingale* (1819).

**Portrait of Richard James
(c.1740s) by William Hogarth**

Cambridge: King's College

**King's College
Coat of Arms**

H ENRY VI FOUNDED this college in
1441. Work on the chapel – one
of the most important examples of late
medieval English architecture – began
five years later, and took 70 years to
complete. Henry himself decided that
it should dominate the city and gave
specific instructions about its dimensions: 88 m (289 ft) long, 12 m (40 ft)
wide and 29 m (94 ft) high. The detailed design is
thought to have been by master stonemason Reginald
Ely, although it was altered in later years.

★ Fan Vaulted Ceiling
*This awe-inspiring ceiling,
supported by 22 buttresses,
was built by master stonemason John Wastell in 1515.*

The Fellows' Building was
designed in 1724 by James
Gibbs, as part of an
uncompleted design for
a Great Court.

Henry VI's statue
*This bronze statue of the college's
founder was erected in 1879.*

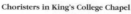

KING'S COLLEGE CHOIR

When he founded the chapel,
Henry VI stipulated that a choir
of six lay clerks and 16 boy
choristers – educated at the
College school – should sing
daily at services. This still
happens in term time but today
the choir also gives concerts all
over the world. Its broadcast
service of carols has become a
much-loved Christmas tradition.

Choristers in King's College Chapel

Crown and Tudor Rose
This detail of Tudor heraldry on the west door of the Chapel reflects Henry VII's vision of English supremacy.

VISITORS' CHECKLIST

King's Parade. **C** *01223 331212.*
○ *Oct–Jul: 9:30am–3:30pm daily;*
Aug–Sep: 9:30am–4:30pm daily.
● *for events ring first.* 🈲
✝ *term-time: 5:30pm Mon–Sat,*
10:30am & 3:30pm Sun 🅱 📷
W *www.cam.ac.uk*

Stained Glass Windows
The 16th-century windows in the chapel all depict biblical scenes. This one shows Christ baptizing his followers.

Organ
The massive 17th-century organ case above the screen is decorated with two angels playing trumpets.

One of four octagonal turrets

Side chapels

The screen is a superb example of Tudor woodwork and divides the chapel into antechapel and choir.

Gothic gatehouse, 19th-century

Main entrance

★ Altarpiece by Rubens
Painted in 1634 for the convent of the White Nuns in Belgium, The Adoration of the Magi was privately donated to King's in 1961.

STAR SIGHTS

★ **Fan Vaulted Ceiling**

★ **Altarpiece by Rubens**

Exploring Cambridge University

CAMBRIDGE UNIVERSITY HAS 31 COLLEGES *(see also pp198–9)*, the oldest being Peterhouse (1284) and the newest being Robinson (1979). Clustered around the city centre, many of the older colleges have peaceful gardens backing onto the River Cam, which are known as the "Backs". The layout of the older colleges, as at Oxford *(see pp214–15)*, derives from their early connections with religious institutions, although few escaped heavy-handed modification in the Victorian era. The college buildings are generally grouped around squares called courts and offer an unrivalled mix of over 600 years of architecture from the late medieval period through Wren's masterpieces and up to the present day.

The nave of the Wren Chapel at Pembroke College

The imposing façade of Emmanuel College

Emmanuel College
Built in 1677 on St Andrew's Street, Sir Christopher Wren's *(see p116)* chapel is the highlight of the college. Some of the intricate interior details, particularly the plaster ceiling and Amigoni's altar rails (1734), are superb. Founded in 1584, the college has a Puritan tradition. One notable graduate was the clergyman John Harvard, who emigrated to America in 1636 and left all his money to the Massachusetts college that now bears his name.

Senate House
King's Parade is the site of this Palladian building, which is used primarily for university ceremonies. It was designed by James Gibbs in 1722 as part of a grand square of university buildings – which was never completed.

Corpus Christi College
Just down from Senate House, this was founded in 1352 by the local trade guilds, anxious to ensure that education was not the sole prerogative of

church and nobility. Its Old Court is remarkably well preserved and looks today much as it would have done when built in the 14th century.
The college is connected by a 15th-century gallery of red brick to St Bene't's Church (short for St Benedict's), whose large Saxon tower is the oldest structure in Cambridge.

King's College
See pp200–1.

Pembroke College
The college chapel was the first building completed by Wren *(see pp116–17)*. A formal classical design, it replaced a 14th-century chapel that was turned into a library. The college, just off Trumpington Street, also has fine gardens.

Jesus College
Although founded in 1497, some of its buildings on Jesus Lane are older, as the college took over St Radegond's nunnery, built in the 12th century. There are traces of Norman columns, windows and a well-preserved hammerbeam roof in the college dining hall.
The chapel keeps the core of the original church but the stained glass windows are modern and contain work by William Morris *(see pp208–9)*.

Queens' College
Built in 1446 on Queens' Land, the college was endowed in 1448 by Margaret of Anjou, queen of Henry VI, and again in 1465 by Elizabeth Woodville, queen of Edward IV, which explains the position of the apostrophe. Queens' has a

PUNTING ON THE CAM

Punting captures the essence of carefree college days: a student leaning on a long pole, lazily guiding the flat-bottomed river craft along, while others stretch out and relax. Punting is still popular both with students and visitors, who can hire punts from boat-yards along the river – with a chauffeur if required. Punts do sometimes capsize, and novices should prepare for a dip.

Punting by the King's College "Backs"

marvellous collection of Tudor buildings, notably the half-timbered President's Gallery, built in the mid-16th century on top of the brick arches in the charming Cloister Court. The Principal Court is 15th century, as is Erasmus's Tower, named after the Dutch scholar.

Pepys Library in Magdalene College

The college has buildings on both sides of the Cam, linked by the bizarre Mathematical Bridge, built in 1749 to hold together without the use of nuts and bolts – although they have had to be used in subsequent repairs.

Magdalene College
Pronounced "maudlin" – as is the Oxford college *(see p214)* – the college, on Bridge Street, was established in 1482. The diarist Samuel Pepys (1633–1703) was a student here and left his large library to the college on his death. The 12 red-oak bookcases have over 3,000 books. Magdalene was the last all-male Cambridge college and it admitted women students only in 1987.

St John's College
Sited on St John's Street, the imposing turreted brick and stone gatehouse of 1514, with its colourful heraldic symbols, provides a fitting entrance to the second largest Cambridge college and its rich store of 16th- and 17th-century build-s. Its hall, most of it lizabethan, has portraits of the college's famous alumni, such as the poet William Wordsworth *(see p354)* and the statesman Lord Palmerston. St John's spans the Cam and boasts two bridges, one built in 1712 and the other, the Bridge of Sighs, in 1831, based on its Venetian namesake.

Peterhouse
The first Cambridge college, on Trumpington Street, is also one of the smallest. The hall still has original features from 1286 but its best details are later – a Tudor fireplace which is backed with 19th-century tiles by William Morris *(see pp208–9)*. A gallery connects the college to the 12th-century church of St Mary the Less, which used to be called St Peter's Church – hence the college's name.

William Morris tiles, Peterhouse

VISITORS' CHECKLIST

Cambridge Colleges can usually be visited from 2–5pm daily, but there are no set opening hours. See noticeboards at each college for daily opening times. Some colleges charge admission.

Trinity College
The largest college, situated on Trinity Street, was founded by Henry VIII in 1547 and has a massive court and hall. The entrance gate, with statues of Henry and James I (added later), was built in 1529 for King's Hall, an earlier college incorporated into Trinity. The Great Court features a late Elizabethan fountain – at one time the main water supply. The chapel, built in 1567, has life-size statues of college members, notably Roubiliac's statue of the scientist Isaac Newton (1755).

University Botanic Garden
A delightful place for a leisurely stroll, just off Trumpington Street, as well as an important academic resource, the garden has been on this site since 1846. It has a superb collection of trees and a sensational water garden. The winter garden is one of the finest in the country.

The Bridge of Sighs over the River Cam, linking the buildings of St John's College

THAMES VALLEY

BUCKINGHAMSHIRE · OXFORDSHIRE · BERKSHIRE
BEDFORDSHIRE · HERTFORDSHIRE

T HE MIGHTY TIDAL RIVER *on which Britain's capital city was founded has modest origins, meandering from its source in the hills of Gloucestershire through the lush countryside towards London. Almost entirely agricultural land in the 19th century, the Thames Valley maintains its pastoral beauty despite the incursion of modern industry.*

There are ancient royal connections with the area. Windsor Castle has been a residence of kings and queens for more than 900 years, and played a critical role in history in 1215, when King John set out from here to sign the *Magna Carta* at Runnymede on the River Thames. Further north, Queen Anne had Blenheim Palace built for her military commander, the 1st Duke of Marlborough. Elizabeth I spent part of her childhood at Hatfield House, and part of the Tudor palace still stands.

Several towns in this region, most notably Burford in Oxfordshire, developed as coach staging posts on the important trunk routes between London and the West Country. With the introduction of commuter transportation in the early 20th century, much of the area became an extension of suburbia and saw some imaginative experiments in Utopian town planning such as the garden city of Welwyn and the Quaker settlement at Jordons.

Oxford, the Thames Valley's principal city, owes its importance to the foundation of Britain's first university there in 1167; many of its colleges are gems of medieval architecture. In the 17th century, a number of battles during the Civil War *(see p52)* were fought around Oxford, which for a time was the headquarters of King Charles I, who was supported by the students. When the royalists were forced to flee Oxford, Cromwell made himself chancellor of the university.

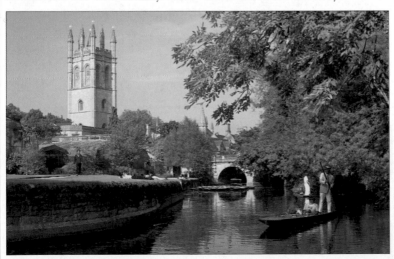

Punting on the River Cherwell, Oxford

◁ **Medieval staircase in Christchurch College, Oxford**

Exploring the Thames Valley

THE PLEASANT COUNTRYSIDE of the Chiltern Hills and of the Thames Valley itself appealed to aristocrats who built stately homes close to London. Many of these are among the grandest in the country, including Hatfield House and Blenheim. Around these great houses grew picturesque villages, with half-timbered buildings and, as you move towards the Cotswolds, houses built in attractive buff-coloured stone. That the area has been inhabited for thousands of years is shown by the number of prehistoric remains, including the most remarkable chalk hillside figure, the White Horse of Uffington.

SIGHTS AT A GLANCE

Blenheim Palace pp216–17 **6**
Burford **2**
Gardens of the Rose **14**
Great Tew **1**
Hatfield House **12**
Hughenden Manor **15**
Kelmscott **3**
Knebworth House **11**
Oxford pp210–15 **5**
St Albans **13**
Stowe **7**
Vale of the White Horse **4**
Waddesdon Manor **9**
Whipsnade Wild Animal Park **10**
Windsor pp223–5 **17**
Woburn Abbey **8**

Walks and Tours
Touring the Thames **16**

A thatched cottage, Upper Swarford, Banbury

GETTING AROUND

As an important commuter belt, the Thames Valley is well served by public transport, as well as a good network of motorways and major roads into London. Mainline trains travel to all the major towns and there are many coach services that run from London to the major sights and attractions.

0 kilometres 10

0 miles 10

Peterborough

Great Ouse

A428

BEDFORD

A6

A1

Cam Rhee

Marlow Bridge, spanning the Thames

8 WOBURN ABBEY

A4012

Icknield Way

A505

M1

LUTON

A1(M)

A100

11 KNEBWORTH HOUSE

A602

WHIPSNADE WILD ANIMAL PARK 10

Ridgeway

Lee

A418

HILTERN HILLS

ST ALBANS 13

12 HATFIELD HOUSE

GARDENS OF THE ROSE 14

A10

15 HUGHENDEN MANOR

M25

M1

A1

Dartford tunnel

A413

A404

HIGH WYCOMBE

M25

M40

London

SEE ALSO

• **Where to Stay** pp549–51

• **Where to Eat** pp586–7

A4

BURNHAM BEECHES

M4

17 WINDSOR

KEY

	Motorway
	Major road
	Scenic route
	Scenic path
	River
	Viewpoint

Radcliffe Camera, surrounded by Oxford's spires

Great Tew ●

Oxfordshire. 🏘 250. 🚆 Oxford or Banbury then taxi. ℹ Spiceball Park Rd, Banbury (01295 259855).
🌐 www.banburytown.co.uk

THIS SECLUDED village of ironstone was founded in the 1630s by Lord Falkland for estate workers. It was heavily restored between 1809 and 1811 in the Gothic style. Thatched cottages stand in gardens with clipped box hedges, and in the centre of the village is the 16th-century pub, the **Falkland Arms**, which retains its original period atmosphere.

ENVIRONS: Five miles (8 km) west are the **Rollright Stones**, three Bronze Age monuments. They comprise a stone circle of 77 stones, about 30 m (100 ft) in diameter, known as the King's Men; the remains of a burial chamber called the Whispering Knights; and the solitary King Stone.

Further north is **Banbury**, well known for its spicy flat cakes and its market cross, immortalized in the nursery rhyme, *Ride a Cock-horse to*

The 19th-century Banbury Cross

Banbury Cross. The original medieval cross was destroyed but it was replaced in 1859.

🍺 **Falkland Arms**
Great Tew. 📞 01608 683653.
⬜ daily. ⬛ 25 Dec. 🍴

Burford ●

Oxfordshire. 🏘 1,000. ℹ Sheep St (01993 823558).

A CHARMING SMALL town, Burford has hardly changed from Georgian times, when it was an important coach stop between Oxford and the West Country. Cotswold stone houses, inns and shops, many built in the 16th century, line its main street. **Tolsey Hall** is a Tudor house with an open ground floor where stalls are still set up. The house is located on the corner of Sheep Street, itself a reminder of the importance of the medieval wool trade *(see p195)*.

ENVIRONS: Just east of Burford is **Swinbrook**, whose church contains the Fettiplace Monuments, six carved figures from the Tudor and Stuart periods.

Two miles (3 km) beyond are the ruins of **Minster Lovell Hall**, a 15th-century manor house whose unusual dovecote survives intact.

Witney, further west, has a town hall dating from 1730. On its outskirts lies **Cogges Manor Farm**, a working farm and museum of rural life, restored to its Victorian state.

🏛 **Minster Lovell Hall**
Minster Lovell. ⬜ daily.
🏛 **Cogges Manor Farm**
Witney. 📞 01993 772602. ⬜ mid-Mar–Nov: Tue–Sun (Sat & Sun pm) & public hols. 🐾 ♿ limited. 📷 📖

Kelmscott ●

Oxfordshire. 🏘 100. ℹ 7a Market Place, Faringdon (01367 242191).
🌐 www.faringdon.org

THE IMAGINATIVE designer and writer William Morris lived in this pretty Thameside village from 1871 until his death in 1896. He shared his house, the classic Elizabethan **Kelmscott Manor**, with fellow painter Dante Gabriel Rossetti (1828–82), who left after an affair with Morris's wife Jane – the model for many pre-Raphaelite paintings.

Morris and his followers in the Arts and Crafts movement were attracted by the

Cotswold stone houses, Burford, Oxfordshire

The formal entrance of the Elizabethan Kelmscott Manor

medieval feel of the village and several cottages were later built in Morris's memory.

Today Kelmscott Manor has works of art by members of the movement – including some William de Morgan tiles. Morris is buried in the village churchyard, with a tomb designed by Philip Webb.

Two miles (3 km) to the east is **Radcot Bridge**, thought to be the oldest bridge still standing over the Thames. Built in the 13th century from the local Taynton stone, it was a strategic river crossing, and in 1387 was damaged in a battle between Richard II and his barons.

🏰 Kelmscott Manor
Kelmscott. ☎ 01367 252486.
⬤ Apr–Jun, Sep: Wed, 3rd Sat;
Jul–Aug: Wed, 1st & 3rd Sat. 📷 ♿
limited.
W www.kelmscottmanor.co.uk

Vale of the White Horse ❹

Oxfordshire. 🚆 Didcot. 🛈 25 Bridge St, Abingdon (01235 522711); 19 Church St, Wantage (01235 760176).

THIS LOVELY VALLEY gets its name from the huge chalk horse, 100 m (350 ft) from nose to tail, carved into the hillside above Uffington. It is believed to be Britain's oldest hillside carving and has sparked many legends: some say it was cut by the Saxon leader Hengist (whose name means stallion in German), while others believe it is to do with Alfred the Great, thought to have been born nearby.

It is, however, a great deal older than either of these stories suggest, having been dated at around 1000 BC.

Nearby is the Celtic earth ramparts of the Iron Age hill fort, **Uffington Castle**. A mile (1.5 km) west along the Ridgeway, an ancient trade route, (see p33), is an even older monument, a large Stone Age burial mound which is known as **Wayland's Smithy**. This is immersed in legends that Sir Walter Scott (see p498) used in his novel *Kenilworth*.

The best view of the horse is to be had from Uffington village, which is also worth visiting for the **Tom Brown's School Museum**. This 17th-century school house contains exhibits devoted to the author Thomas Hughes (1822–96). Hughes set the early chapters of his Victorian novel, *Tom Brown's Schooldays*, here. The museum also contains material about excavations on White Horse Hill.

🏛 Tom Brown's School
Broad St, Uffington. 🛈 01367 820259. ⬤ Easter–Oct: Sat, Sun & public hols (pm). 📷 ♿ limited.
W www.uffington.net/museum

HILLSIDE CHALK FIGURES

It was the Celts who first saw the potential for creating large-scale artworks on the chalk hills of southern England. Horses – held in high regard by both the Celts and later the Saxons, and the objects of cult worship – were often a favourite subject, but people were also depicted, notably Cerne Abbas, Dorset (see p257) and the Long Man of Wilmington (see p168). The figures may have served as religious symbols or as landmarks by which tribes identified their territory. Many chalk figures have been obliterated, because without any attention they are quickly overrun by grass. Uffington is "scoured", to prevent encroachment by grass, a tradition once accompanied by a fair and other festivities. There was a second flush of hillside carving in the 18th century, especially in Wiltshire. In some cases – for instance at Bratton Castle near Westbury – an 18th-century carving has been superimposed on an ancient one.

Britain's oldest hillside carving, the White Horse of Uffington

Street-by-Street: Oxford ❺

Oxford has long been a strategic point on the western routes into London – its name describes its position as a convenient spot for crossing the river (a ford for oxen). The city's first scholars, who founded the university, came from France in 1167. The development of England's first university created the spectacular skyline of tall towers and "dreaming spires".

Old Ashmolean
Now the Museum of the History of Science, this resplendent building was designed in 1683 to show Elias Ashmole's collection of curiosities. The displays were moved in 1845.

The Ashmolean Museum displays one of Britain's foremost collections of fine art and antiquities.

St John's College

Balliol College

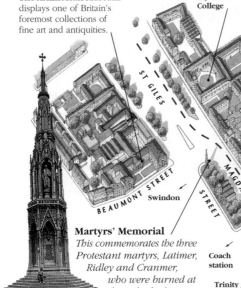

ST GILES

BEAUMONT STREET

MAGDALEN STREET

Swindon

BROAD STREET

TURL

BRA

Martyrs' Memorial
This commemorates the three Protestant martyrs, Latimer, Ridley and Cranmer, who were burned at the stake for heresy.

Coach station

Trinity College

CORNMARKET STREET

MARKET STREET

STR

| 0 metres | 100 |
| 0 yards | 100 |

Oxford Story

KEY

― ― ― ―　Suggested route

Jesus College

Lincoln College

Covered market

Railway station

Lincoln College Library

ST ALD

Museum of Oxford

PERCY BYSSHE SHELLEY

Shelley (1792–1822), one of the Romantic poets *(see p354)*, attended University College, Oxford, but was expelled after writing the revolutionary pamphlet *The Necessity of Atheism.* Despite that disgrace, the college has put up a marble memorial to him.

Sheldonian Theatre
The first building designed by Wren (see p116) is the scene of Oxford University's traditional graduation ceremonies.

STAR SIGHTS

★ **Radcliffe Camera**

★ **Christ Church**

★ Radcliffe Camera
This Classical rotunda is Oxford's most distinctive building and is now a reading room of the Bodleian. It was one of the library's original buildings (see p215).

Bridge of Sighs
A copy of the steeply arched bridge in Venice, this picturesque landmark, built in 1914, joins the old and new buildings of Hertford College.

New College

St Mary the Virgin Church

Queen's College

All Souls College

London

University College

Botanic Garden and Magdalen College

Oriel College

Merton College

QUEEN'S LANE

...ATTE STREET

HIGH STREET

ORIEL STREET

MAGPIE LANE

LOGIC LANE

MERTON STREET

BEAR LANE

DEAD MAN'S WALK

Corpus Christi College

★ Christ Church
Students still eat at long tables in all the college halls. Senior academics sit at the high table and grace is always said in Latin.

Exploring Oxford

A bust on the Sheldonian Theatre

OXFORD IS MORE than just a university city; it has one of Britain's most important car factories in the suburb of Cowley. Despite this, Oxford is dominated by institutions related to its huge academic community: like Blackwell's bookshop which has over 20,000 titles in stock. The two rivers, the Cherwell and the Isis (the name given to the Thames as it flows through the city), provide lovely riverside walks, or you can hire a punt and spend an afternoon on the Cherwell.

🏛 Ashmolean Museum

Beaumont St. **[** 01865 278000.
○ Tue–Sun (Sun pm only) & public hols. ● 1 Jan, Good Fri, 25–28 Dec.
🔵 🗹 Tue, Fri, Sat. ▢ ▯
🔲 www.ashmole.ox.ac.uk

One of the best museums in Britain outside London, the Ashmolean – the first purpose-built museum in England – opened in 1683, based on a display known as "The Ark" collected by the two John Tradescants, father and son.

On their many voyages to the Orient and the Americas they collected stuffed animals and tribal artifacts, the like of which had never before been displayed in England. The collection was acquired on their death by the antiquarian Elias Ashmole, who donated it to the university and had a building made for the exhibits on Broad Street – the Old Ashmolean, now the Museum of the History of Science.

During the 19th century part of the Tradescant collection was moved to the University Galleries, a magnificent Neo-Classical building of 1845. This greatly expanded museum is now known as the Ashmolean.

However, what is left of the original curio collection is overshadowed by the other exhibits in the museum, in particular the paintings and drawings. These include Bellini's *St Jerome Reading in a Landscape* (late 15th century); Raphael's *Heads of Two Apostles* (1519); Turner's *Venice: The Grand Canal* (1840); Rembrandt's *Saskia Asleep* (1635); Michelangelo's *Crucifixion* (1557), Picasso's *Blue Roofs* (1901) and a large group of Pre-Raphaelites, including Rossetti, Millais and Holman Hunt. There are also fine Greek and Roman carvings and a collection of stringed musical instruments. Items of more local interest include a Rowlandson watercolour of Radcliffe Square in about 1790 and the Oxford Crown. This silver coin was minted here during the Civil War in 1644 *(see p52)* when Charles I was based in Oxford, and forms part of the second largest coin collection in Britain. Perhaps the single most important item is the gold enamelled ring known as the Alfred Jewel *(see p47)*, which is over 1,000 years old.

The entrance to the Ashmolean Museum

🌷 Botanic Garden

Rose Lane. **[** 01865 286690.
○ daily. ● 25 Dec, Good Fri.
🔵 Apr–Aug. **Donation** Sep–Mar.
🔵 🔲 www.botanic-garden.ox.ac.uk

Britain's oldest botanic garden was founded in 1621 – one ancient yew tree survives from that period. The entrance gates were designed by Nicholas Stone in 1633 and paid for, like the garden itself, by the Earl of Danby. His statue adorns the gate, along with those of Charles I and II. This small garden is a delightful spot for a stroll, with well-labelled flower beds in the original walled garden and a newer section with a herbaceous border and rock garden.

The 17th-century Botanic Gardens

🔒 Carfax Tower

Carfax Sq. **[** 01865 792653.
○ Apr–Oct daily. 🔵 ▯

The tower is all that remains of the 14th-century Church of St Martin, demolished in 1896 so that the adjoining road could be widened. Be there to watch the clock strike the quarter hours, and climb to the top for a panoramic view of the city. Carfax was the crossing point of the original north-to-south and east-to-west routes through Oxford and the word comes from the French *quatre voies,* or "four ways".

🎵 Holywell Music Room

Holywell St. ○ concerts only. 🔵 🔵

This was the first building in Europe designed, in 1752, specifically for public musical performances. Previously, concerts had been held in private houses for invited guests only. Its two splendid chandeliers originally adorned Westminster Hall at the coronation of George IV in 1820, and were given by the king to Wadham College, of which the music room technically forms a part. The room is regularly used for contemporary and classical concerts.

🏛 Museum of Oxford

St Aldate. 📞 01865 815559. 🕐 Tue–Sun. ● 25, 26 Dec, 1 Jan. 🈯

A well-organized display in the Victorian town hall illustrates the long history of Oxford and its university. Exhibits include a Roman pottery kiln and a town seal from 1191.

The main features are a series of well-reconstructed rooms, including one from an Elizabethan inn and an 18th-century student's room.

🏛 Martyrs' Memorial

Magdalen St.

This commemorates the three Protestants burned at the stake on Broad Street – Bishops Latimer and Ridley in 1555, and Archbishop Cranmer in 1556. On the accession of Queen Mary in 1553 (see p51), they were committed to the Tower of London, then sent to Oxford to defend their views before the doctors of divinity who, after the hearing, condemned them as heretics.

The memorial was designed in 1843 by George Gilbert Scott and based on the Eleanor crosses erected in 12 English towns by Edward I (1239–1307) to honour his queen.

🏛 Oxford Story

6 Broad St. 📞 01865 728822. 🕐 daily. ● 25 Dec. 🏠 🈯 ♿ limited.

This audio-visual account of the city's history has a train ride through exhibits which are brought to life with animated, life-size models of major historical characters.

🏛 St Mary the Virgin Church

High St. 📞 01865 279111. 🕐 daily. ● Good Fri, 25, 26 Dec. 🏠 🏠
🌐 www.university-church.ox.ac.uk

This, the official church of the university, is said to be the most visited parish church in England. The oldest parts date from the early 13th century and include the tower, from the top of which you can enjoy a fine view. Its Convocation House, of the same date, served as the university's first library until the Bodleian was founded in 1488 (see p215). The church is where the three Oxford Martyrs were pronounced heretics in 1555. An architectural highlight of the church is the Baroque south porch.

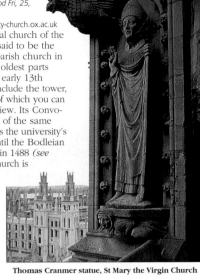

Thomas Cranmer statue, St Mary the Virgin Church

🏛 University Museum

Parks Rd. 📞 01865 272950. 🕐 daily (pm). ● 24–26 Dec, Easter. 🏠
🌐 www.oum.ox.ac.uk

🏛 Pitt Rivers Museum

Parks Rd. 📞 01865 270927. 🕐 daily (pm). ● 24–26 Dec, Easter. 🏠
🌐 www.prm.ox.ac.uk

Two of Oxford's most interesting museums adjoin each other. The first is a museum of natural history containing relics of dinosaurs as well as a stuffed dodo. This flightless bird has been extinct since the 17th century, but was immortalized by Lewis Carroll (an Oxford mathematics lecturer whose real name was Charles Dodgson) in his book Alice in Wonderland (see p387). The exhibits are housed in a large Victorian building with cast-iron columns which support a glass roof leading to a cavernous interior. This leads into the Pitt Rivers Museum, which has one of the world's most extensive ethnographic collections – masks and totems from Africa and the Far East – and archaeological displays, including exhibits collected by the explorer Captain Cook.

🏛 Sheldonian Theatre

Broad St. 📞 01865 277299. 🕐 call for details. ● Christmas period, Easter & public hols. 🈯 ♿ limited.
🌐 www.sheldon.ox.ac.uk

Completed in 1669, this building was designed by Sir Christopher Wren (see p116). It was paid for by Gilbert Sheldon, the Archbishop of Canterbury, as a place to hold university degree ceremonies. The Classical design of the D-shaped building is based on the Theatre of Marcellus in Rome. The octagonal cupola – larger than the original – was built in 1838 and there is a very famous view from its huge Lantern. In the theatre the beautifully painted ceiling depicts the triumph of religion, art and science over envy, hatred and malice.

The impressive frontage of the University Museum and Pitt Rivers Museum

Exploring Oxford University

MANY OF THE 36 COLLEGES which go to make up the university were founded between the 13th and 16th centuries and cluster around the city centre. As scholarship was then the exclusive preserve of the church, the colleges were designed along the lines of monastic buildings but were often surrounded by beautiful gardens. Although most colleges have been altered over the years, many still incorporate a lot of their original features.

The spectacular view of All Souls College from St Mary's Church

All Souls College
Founded in 1438 on the High Street by Henry VI, the chapel on the college's north side has a classic hammerbeam roof, unusual misericords *(see p329)* on the choir stalls and 15th-century stained glass.

Christ Church College
The best way to view this, the largest of the Oxford colleges, is to approach through the meadows from St Aldate's. Christ Church dates from 1525 when Cardinal Wolsey founded it as an ecclesiastical college to train cardinals. The upper part of the tower in Tom Quad – a rectangular courtyard – was built by Wren *(see p116)* in 1682 and is the largest in the

city. When its bell, Great Tom, was hung in 1648, the college had 101 students, which is why the bell is rung 101 times at 9:05pm, to mark the curfew for students (which has not been enforced since 1963). The odd timing is because night falls here five minutes later than at Greenwich *(see p133)*. Christ Church has produced 16 British prime ministers in the last 200 years. Beside the main quad is the 12th-century Christ Church Cathedral, one of the smallest in England.

Lincoln College
One of the best-preserved of the medieval colleges, it was founded in 1427 on Turl Street, and the front quad and façade

are 15th century. The hall still has its original roof, including the gap where smoke used to escape. The Jacobean chapel is notable for its stained glass. John Wesley *(see p267)* was at college here and his rooms, now a chapel, can be visited.

Magdalen College
At the end of the High Street is perhaps the most typical and beautiful Oxford college. Its 15th-century quads in contrasting styles are set in a park by the Cherwell, crossed by Magdalen Bridge. Every May Day at 6am, the college choir sings from the top of Magdalen's bell tower (1508) – a 16th-century custom to mark the start of summer.

New College
One of the grandest colleges, it was founded by William of Wykeham in 1379 to educate clergy to replace those killed by the Black Death of 1348 *(see p49)*.

Magdalen Bridge spanning the River Cherwell

Its magnificent chapel on New College Lane, restored in the 19th century, has vigorous 14th-century misericords and El Greco's (1541–1614) famous painting of *St James*.

Queen's College
Most of the college buildings date from the 18th century and represent some of the finest work from that period in Oxford. Its superb library was built in 1695 by Henry Aldrich (1647–1710) The front screen with its bell-topped gatehouse is a feature of the High Street.

STUDENT LIFE

Students belong to individual colleges and usually live in them for the duration of their course. The university gives lectures, sets exams and awards degrees but much of the students' tuition and social life is based around their college. Many university traditions date back hundreds of years, like the graduation ceremonies at the Sheldonian which are still held in Latin.

Graduation at the Sheldonian *(see p212)*

Merton College seen from Christ Church Meadows

St John's College
The impressive frontage on St Giles dates from 1437, when it was founded for Cistercian scholars. The old library has lovely 17th-century bookcases and stained glass, while the Baylie Chapel has a display of 15th-century vestments.

Trinity College
The oldest part of the college on Broad Street, Durham Quad, is named after the earlier college of 1296 which was incorporated into Trinity in 1555. The late 17th-century chapel has a magnificent reredos and wooden screen.

Corpus Christi College
The whole of the charming front quad on Merton Street dates from 1517, when the college was founded. The quad's sundial, topped by a pelican – the college symbol – bears an early 17th-century calendar. The chapel has a rare 16th-century eagle lectern.

Merton College
Off Merton Street, this is the oldest college (1264) in Oxford. Much of its hall dates from then, including a sturdy decorated door. The chapel choir contains allegorical reliefs representing music, arithmetic, rhetoric and grammar. Merton's Mob Quad served as a model for the later colleges.

BODLEIAN LIBRARY
Founded in 1320, the library was expanded in 1426 by Humphrey, Duke of Gloucester (1391–1447) and brother of Henry V, when his collection of manuscripts would not fit into the old library. It was refounded in 1602 by Thomas Bodley, a wealthy scholar, who insisted on strict rules: the keeper was forbidden to marry. The library is one of the six copyright deposit libraries in the country – it is entitled to receive a copy of every book published in Britain.

The Radcliffe Camera (1748), a domed Baroque rotunda, was built by James Gibbs as a memorial to the physician Dr John Radcliffe (1650–1714).

Main entrance

This extension was built in 1630 and was used for university exams until 1880.

The Divinity School (1488) has a unique vaulted ceiling with 455 carved bosses representing biblical scenes and both mythical and real beasts – one of the country's finest Gothic interiors.

Duke Humphrey's Library (1602) has ceiling panels that carry the university crest and Latin motto Dominus Illuminatio Mea – *the Lord, my Light.*

Blenheim Palace ❻

AFTER JOHN CHURCHILL, the 1st Duke of Marlborough, defeated the French at the Battle of Blenheim in 1704, Queen Anne gave him the Manor of Woodstock and had this palatial house built for him in gratitude. Designed by both Nicholas Hawksmoor and Sir John Vanbrugh *(see p384)*, it is a Baroque masterpiece. It was also the birthplace of Britain's World War II leader, Winston Churchill, in 1874.

★ **Long Library**
*This 55 m (183 f[...]
room was design[...]
by Vanbrugh as [...]
picture gallery. T[...]
portraits include [...]
of Queen Anne b[...]
Sir Godfrey Knel[...]
(1646–1723). T[...]
stucco on the
ceiling is by Isa[...]
Mansfield (1725[...]*

**Winston Churchill
and his wife,
Clementine**

The Grand Bridge was built in 1708. It has a 31 m (101 ft) main span and contains rooms within its structure.

Chapel
The marble monument to the 1st Duke of Marlborough and his family was sculpted by Michael Rysbrack in 1733.

Water Terrace Gardens
These magnificent gardens were laid out in the 1920s by French architect Achille Duchêne in 17th-century style, with detailed patterned beds and fountains.

STAR SIGHTS

★ **Long Library**

★ **Saloon**

★ **Park and Gardens**

Great Hall

This splendid ceiling by Thornhill in 1716, shows the 1st Duke of Marlborough presenting his plan for the Battle of Blenheim to Britannia.

VISITORS' CHECKLIST

Woodstock, Oxfordshire. 📞 01993 811325. 🚌 from Oxford. 🚉 Oxford. **Palace & Gardens** 🕐 mid-Mar–Oct: 10:30am–5:30pm daily (last admission: 4:45pm). **Park** 🕐 9am–5pm daily. 📷 🎫 🍴 ♿

The Italian Garden contains the Mermaid Fountain (1892) by US sculptor Waldo Story.

East gate

First State Room

Entrance

Grinling Gibbons lions (1709)

Clock tower

Great Court

The Green Drawing Room has a full-length portrait of the 4th Duke by George Romney (1734–1802).

Red Drawing Room

Green Writing Room

Second State Room

Third State Room

★ PARK AND GARDENS

Column of Victory

Grand Bridge

Triumphal Arch

Palace

Woodstock

Water Terrace Gardens

Car park

Italian Garden

Temple of Diana

Narrow-gauge railway

Rose Garden

Car park

Butterfly House

Arboretum

Marlborough Maze

Adventure playground

A house fit for a victorious general had to be surrounded by a park with suitably heroic monuments. They were kept when Capability Brown *(see p22)* re-landscaped the park in 1764 and created the lake.

★ Saloon

French artist Louis Laguerre (1663–1721) painted the detailed scenes on the walls and ceiling of the state dining room.

Canaletto's *Entrance to the Arsenal* (1730) hangs at Woburn Abbey

Stowe ❼

(NT) Buckingham, Buckinghamshire. 📞 01280 822850. 🚇 Milton Keynes then bus. 🕐 Mar–22 Dec: Wed–Sun, public hols. 🅿 🛒 limited. 🅿 🛍 🌐 www.nationaltrust/stowegardens

THIS IS THE MOST ambitious and important landscaped garden in Britain, as well as being one of the finest examples of the 18th-century passion for improving on nature to make it conform to fashionable notions of taste.

In the space of nearly 100 years the original garden, first laid out around 1680, was enlarged and transformed by the addition of monuments, Greek and Gothic temples, grottoes, statues, ornamental bridges, artificial lakes and "natural" tree plantings.

Most of the leading designers and architects of the period contributed to the design, including Sir John Vanbrugh, James Gibbs and Capability Brown *(see p22)*, who was head gardener at Stowe for 10 years, at the start of his career.

From 1593 to 1921 the huge property was owned by the Temple and Grenville families – later the Dukes of Buckingham – until the large Palladian house at its centre was sold and converted into an elite boys' public school (tours can be arranged in school holidays).

The family were soldiers and politicians in the liberal tradition, and many of the buildings and sculptures in the garden symbolize Utopian ideals of democracy and freedom. There are temples of British Worthies, of Ancient Virtue and the Fane (temple) of Pastoral Poetry. Some features deteriorated in the 19th century and statues were sold. But a major restoration programme has meant that statues have been bought back and copies made of others.

Woburn Abbey ❽

Woburn, Bedfordshire. 📞 01525 290666. 🚇 Flitwick then taxi. 🕐 Apr–Sep: daily; Jan–Mar, Oct: Sat, Sun. 🅿 🛒 🛍 ring first. 🚗 by arrangement. 🍴 🌐 www.woburnabbey.co.uk

THE DUKES OF BEDFORD have lived here for over 350 years and were among the first owners of an English stately home to open their house to the public some 40 years ago.

The abbey was built in the mid-18th century on the foundations of a large 12th-century Cistercian monastery. Its mix of styles range from Henry Flitcroft and Henry Holland *(see p24)*. It is also popular for its 142 ha (350 acre) safari park and attractive deer park

with nine species including the Manchurian Sika deer from China.

Its magnificent state apartments house an important private art collection with works by Reynolds (1723–92) and Canaletto (1697–1768).

Waddesdon Manor ❾

nr Aylesbury, Buckinghamshire. 📞 01296 653 203. 🚇 Aylesbury then taxi. **House** 🕐 Apr–Oct: 11am–4pm Wed–Sun & bank hol Mon. **Grounds** 🕐 Mar–23 Dec: 10am–5pm Wed–Sun & bank hol Mon. **Bachelors' Wing** 🕐 Mar–Oct: 11am–4pm Wed–Fri. 🛒 🍴 🅿 🛍 🌐 www.waddesdon.org.uk

WADDESDON MANOR was built between 1874–89 by Baron Ferdinand de Rothschild and designed by French architect Gabriel-Hippolyte Destailleur. The garden was originally laid out by French landscape gardener Elie Lainé.

Built in the style of a French 16th-century chateau, Waddesdon Manor houses one of the world's finest collections of French 18th-century decorative art. It also contains renowned collections of French furniture, Savonnierie carpets, Sèvres porcelain and 17th-century paintings.

The garden is renowned for its seasonal displays and over the next five years, displays are being designed by contemporary artists. Wine tasting events are also hosted in the comprehensive Wine Cellars.

The 17th-century Palladian bridge over the Octagon Lake in Stowe Park

Hatfield House, one of the largest Jacobean mansions in the country

Whipsnade Wild Animal Park ⓾

Nr Dunstable, Bedfordshire. 📞
01582 872171. 🚉 Hemel Hempsted
then bus or Whipsnade (from Victoria
Station, London) ⭘ daily. 📷 ♿ 🖃
🌐 www.whipsnade.co.uk

THE RURAL BRANCH of London
Zoo, this was one of the first zoos to minimize the use of cages, confining animals safely but without constriction.

At 240 ha (600 acres), it is Europe's largest conservation park, with more than 2,500 species. You can drive through some areas or go by steam train. Also popular are the adventure playground and sea lions' underwater display.

Knebworth House ⓫

Knebworth, Hertfordshire.
📞 01438 812661. 🚉 Stevenage
then taxi. ⭘ Sat, Sun; two weeks at
Easter: daily; Jul–Sep: daily. 📷 📷
♿ limited. 📷 🖃
🌐 www.knebworthhouse.com

A NOTABLE TUDOR mansion,
with a beautiful Jacobean banqueting hall, Knebworth was overlain with a 19th-century Gothic exterior by Lord Lytton, the head of one of the most colourful families in Victorian England.

His eldest son, the 1st Earl of Lytton, was Viceroy of India, and several exhibits illustrate the Delhi Durbar of 1877, when Queen Victoria became Empress of India.

Hatfield House ⓬

Hatfield, Hertfordshire. 📞 01707
287010. 🚉 Hatfield. ⭘ Easter
Sat–Sep: daily. 📷 📷 ♿ 🍴
🌐 www.hatfield-house.co.uk

ONE OF ENGLAND's finest
Jacobean houses, it was built between 1607 and 1611 for the powerful statesman Robert Cecil.

Its chief historical interest, though, lies in the surviving wing of the original Tudor Hatfield Palace, where Queen Elizabeth I (see pp50–51) spent much of her childhood. She held her first Council of State here when she was crowned in 1558. The palace was partly demolished in 1607 to make way for the new house, which contains mementoes of her life, including the *Rainbow* portrait painted around 1600 by Isaac Oliver. Visitors can attend medieval banquets in the old palace's Great Hall.

Originally laid out by Robert Cecil with help from John Tradescant, the gardens have been restored to reflect these Jacobean origins.

FAMOUS PURITANS

Three major figures connected with the 17th-century Puritan movement are celebrated in the Thames area. John Bunyan (1628–88), who wrote the allegorical tale *The Pilgrim's Progress*, was born at Elstow, near Bedford. A passionate Puritan orator, he was jailed for his beliefs for 17 years. The Bunyan Museum in Bedford is a former site of Puritan worship. William Penn (1644–1718), founder of Pennsylvania in the USA, lived, worshipped

18th century engraving of John Bunyan

and is buried at Jordans, near Beaconsfield. A bit further north at Chalfont St Giles is the cottage where the poet John Milton (1608–74) stayed to escape London's plague. There he completed his greatest work, *Paradise Lost*. The house is now a museum based on his life and works.

William Penn, founder of Pennsylvania

John Milton painted by Pieter van der Plas

St Albans ⓭

TODAY A THRIVING MARKET TOWN and a base for London commuters, St Albans was for centuries at the heart of some of the most stirring events in English history. A regional capital of ancient Britain, it became a major Roman settlement and then a key ecclesiastical centre – so important that during the Wars of the Roses *(see p49)*, two battles were fought for it. In 1455 the Yorkists drove King Henry VI from the town and six years later the Lancastrians retook it.

The martyr St Alban

Exploring St Albans

Part of the appeal of this ancient and fascinating town, little more than an hour's drive from London, is that its 2,000-year history can be traced vividly by visiting a few sites within easy walking distance of one another. There is a large car park within the walls of the Roman city of Verulamium, between the museum and St Michael's Church and across the road from the excavated theatre. From there it is a pleasant lakeside walk across the park, passing more Roman sites, Ye Olde Fighting Cocks inn, the massive cathedral and the historic High Street. Marking the centre of the town, the High Street is lined with several Tudor buildings and a clock tower dating from 1412, from which the curfew bell used to ring at 4am in the morning and 8:30pm at night.

⋔ Verulamium

Just outside the city centre are the walls of Verulamium, one of the first British cities the Romans established after their invasion of Britain in AD 43. Boadicea *(see p183)* razed it

to the ground during her unsuccessful rebellion against the Romans in AD 62, but its position on Watling Street, an important trading route, meant that it was quickly rebuilt on an even larger scale and the city flourished until 410.

🏛 Verulamium Museum

St Michael's. ⟨ 01727 751810.
○ daily. ● 25, 26 Dec. 🖼 🖐 🏠
ⓦ www.stalbansmuseum.org.uk
This excellent museum tells the story of the city, but its main attraction is its splendid collection of well-preserved Roman artefacts, notably some breathtaking mosaic floors, including one depicting the head of a sea god, and another of a scallop shell. Other finds included burial urns and lead coffins.

On the basis of excavated plaster fragments, a Roman room has been painstakingly recreated, its walls painted in startlingly bright colours and geometric patterns.

Between here and St Albans Cathedral are a bath house with a mosaic, remnants of the ancient city wall and one of the original gates.

🍺 Ye Olde Fighting Cocks

Abbey Mill Lane. ⟨ 01727 869152.
○ daily. ● 25 Dec. 🖐
Believed to be England's oldest surviving pub, Ye Olde Fighting Cocks is certainly, with its

One of the oldest surviving pubs in England

octagonal shape, one of the most unusual. It originated as the medieval dovecote of the old abbey and moved here after the Dissolution *(see p50)*.

⋔ Roman Theatre

St Michael's. ⟨ 01727 835035.
○ daily. ● 25, 26 Dec. 🖼 🏠
ⓦ www.romantheatre.co.uk
Just across the road from the museum are the foundations of the open-air theatre, first built around AD 140 but enlarged several times. It is one of only six known to have been built in Roman Britain. Alongside it are traces of a row of Roman shops and a house, from which many of the museum's treasures – such as a bronze statuette of Venus – were excavated in the 1930s.

⛪ St Michael's Church

St Michael's. ⟨ 01727 835037.
○ Apr–Sep: phone for details. 🖐
This church was first founded during the Saxon reign and is built partly with bricks taken from Verulamium, which by then was in decline. Numerous additions have been made since then, including a truly splendid Jacobean pulpit.

The church contains an early 17th-century monument to the statesman and writer Sir Francis Bacon; his father owned nearby Gorhambury, a large Tudor house, now in ruins.

A scallop shell, one of the mosaic floors at the Verulamium Museum

⚑ St Albans Cathedral

Sumpter Yard. ⓒ *01727 860780.*
◯ *daily.* ♿ 🎥 *11:30am & 2:30pm.*
This outstanding example of
medieval architecture has
some classic features such as
the 13th- and 14th-century wall
paintings on the Norman piers.

It was begun in 793, when
King Offa of Mercia founded
the abbey in honour of St
Alban, Britain's first Christian
martyr, put to death by the
Romans in the third century
for sheltering a priest. The
oldest parts, which still stand,

**The imposing west side of
St Albans Cathedral**

were first built in 1077 and
are easily recognizable as
Norman by the round-headed
arches and windows. They
form part of the 84 m (276 ft)
nave – the longest in England.

The pointed arches further
east are Early English (13th
century), while the decorated
work of the 14th century was
added when some of the
Norman arches collapsed.

East of the crossing is
what remains of St Alban's
shrine – a marble pedestal
made up of more than
2,000 tiny fragments. Next
to it is the tomb of Humphrey,
Duke of Gloucester *(see p215).*

It was also here at the
cathedral that the English
barons drafted the *Magna
Carta* document *(see p48),*
which King John was then
forced to sign.

The splendour of the Gardens of the Rose in June

Gardens of the Rose ⓮

Chiswell Green, Hertfordshire. ⓒ
01727 850461. 🚌 *St Albans then
bus.* ◯ *Jun–Sep: 9am–5pm Mon–Sat,
10am–6pm Sun & public hols.* 🅿 🎥
♿ 🛍 Ⓦ www.rosesociety.org.uk

Aₛ WELL AS BEING England's
national symbol, the rose
is the most popular flower
with British gardeners.

The 5 ha (12 acre) garden
of the Royal National Rose
Society, with over 30,000
plants and 1,700 varieties, is
at its peak in late June. The
gardens trace the history of
the flower as far back as the
white rose of York, the red
rose of Lancaster *(see p49)*
and the Rosa Mundi – named
by Henry II for his mistress
Fair Rosamond after she was
poisoned by Queen Eleanor
in 1177. The nuns who buried
Rosamond implied in verse on
her tomb that her reputation
did not smell of roses.

Hughenden Manor ⓯

High Wycombe, Buckinghamshire.
ⓒ *01494 755565.* 🚌 *High Wycombe
then bus.* ◯ *Mar: Sat, Sun; Apr–Nov:
Wed–Sun & public hols.* ◐ *Good Fri.*
🅿 🎥 ♿ *limited.* 🍴

THE VICTORIAN STATESMAN and
novelist Benjamin Disraeli,
Prime Minister from 1874 to
1880, lived here for 33 years
until his death. Originally a
Georgian villa, Disraeli adapted
it in 1862 to the Gothic style.
Furnished as it was in his day,
the house gives an idea of
the life of a wealthy Victorian
gentleman and shows some
portraits of his contemporaries.

GEORGE BERNARD SHAW

Although a controversial playwright and known
as a mischievous character, the Irish-born
George Bernard Shaw (1856–1950) was a man
of settled habits. He lived near St Albans in a
house at Ayot St Lawrence, now called
Shaw's Corner, for the last 44 years of
his life, working until his last weeks
in a summer-house at the bottom
of his large garden. His plays,
combining wit with a powerful
political and social message, still
seem fresh today. One of the most
enduring is *Pygmalion* (1913),
on which the musical *My Fair
Lady* is based. The house and
garden are now a museum
of his life and works.

Touring the Thames ⑯

THE THAMES between Pangbourne and Eton is leafy and romantic and best seen by boat. But if time is short, the road keeps close to its bank for much of the way. Swans glide gracefully below ancient bridges, voles dive into the water for cover, and elegant herons stand impassive at the river's edge. Huge beech trees overhang the banks which are lined with fine houses, their gardens sloping to the water. The tranquil scene has inspired painters and writers through the ages as well as operating, until recently, as an important transport link.

Hambledon Mill ⑥
The white weather-boarded mill, which was operational until 1955, is one of the largest on the Thames as well as one of the oldest in origin. There are traces of the original 16th-century mill.

Beale Park ①
The philanthropist Gilbert Beale (1868–1967) created a 10 ha (25 acre) park to preserve this beautiful stretch of river intact and breed endangered birds like owls, ornamental water fowl, pheasants and peacocks.

Henley ⑤
This lovely old river town boasts houses and churches dating from the 15th and 16th centuries and an important regatta, first held in 1829 *(see p66).*

Pangbourne ②
Kenneth Grahame (1859–1932), author of *The Wind in the Willows,* lived here. Pangbourne was used as the setting by artists Ernest Shepard in 1908 and Arthur Rackham in 1951 to illustrate the book.

Sonning Bridge ④
The 18th-century bridge is made up of 11 brick arches of varying width.

TIPS FOR DRIVERS

Tour length: 50 miles (75 km).
Stopping-off points: The picturesque town of Henley has a large number of riverside pubs which will make good stops for lunch. If you are boating you can often moor your boat alongside the river bank. (See also pp636–7.)

Whitchurch Mill ③
This charming village, linked to Pangbourne by a Victorian toll bridge, has a picturesque church and one of the many disused watermills that once harnessed the power of this stretch of river.

Cookham ⑦

This is famous as the home of Stanley Spencer (1891–1959), one of Britain's leading 20th-century artists. The former Methodist chapel, where Spencer worshipped as a child, has been converted into a gallery that contains some of his paintings and equipment. This work, entitled *Swan Upping* (1914–19), recalls a Thames custom.

Cliveden Reach ⑧
The beech trees lining this attractive stretch of river are in the grounds of Cliveden House *(see p150).*

Eton College ⑨
Founded by Henry VI in 1440, Eton is Britain's most famous public school. It has a superb Perpendicular chapel (1441) with a series of English wall paintings (1479–88).

KEY

▬▬ Tour route

═══ Other roads

⁂ Viewpoint

0 kilometres 10

0 miles 5

Boating Tours

In summer, scheduled river services run between Henley, Windsor, Runnymede and Marlow. Several companies operate from towns along the route. You can hire boats by the hour or the day or, for a longer tour, you can rent cabin cruisers and sleep on board *(see also p641).* Ring Salter Bros on 01753 865 832 for more information.

Salter Bros hire boats, moored at Henley

Windsor ⑰

Berkshire. 🏚 *30,000.* 🚆
🛈 *HighSt (01753 743900).*
ⓦ www.windsor.gov.uk

THE TOWN of Windsor is dwarfed by the enormous **castle** *(see pp224–5)* on the hill above – appropriately enough because its original purpose was to serve the castle's needs. The town is full of quaint Georgian shops, houses and inns. The most prominent building on the High Street is the **Guildhall** completed by Wren *(see p116)* in 1689. The **Household Cavalry Museum** has an extensive collection of arms and uniforms.

The huge 1,940-ha (4,800-acre) **Windsor Great Park** stretches straight from the castle three miles (5 km) to Snow Hill, where there is a statue of George III.

ENVIRONS: Four miles (7 km) to the southeast is the level grassy meadow known as **Runnymede**. This is one of England's most historic sites, where in 1215 King John was forced by his rebellious barons to sign the *Magna Carta (see p48)*, thereby limiting his royal powers. The dainty memorial pavilion at the top of the meadow was erected in 1957.

🏛 Household Cavalry Museum

St Leonard's Rd. 📞 *01753 755112.* ⭕ *Mon–Fri.* ⬤ *public hols.* **Donation** 🔘

King John signing the *Magna Carta*, Runnymede

Windsor Castle

Henry II rebuilt the castle

THE OLDEST CONTINUOUSLY inhabited royal residence in Britain, the castle, originally made of wood, was built by William the Conqueror in 1070 to guard the western approaches to London. He chose the site because it was on high ground and just a day's journey from his base in the Tower of London. Successive monarchs have made alterations that render it a remarkable monument to royalty's changing tastes. King George V's affection for it was shown when he chose Windsor for his family surname in 1917. The castle is an official residence of the Queen and her family who stay here many weekends.

Albert Memorial Chapel
First built in 1240, it was rebuilt in 1485 and finally converted into a memorial for Prince Albert in 1863.

King Henry VIII Gate and main exit

★ St George's Chapel
The architectural highlight of the castle, it was built between 1475 and 1528 and is one of England's outstanding Perpendicular churches. Ten monarchs are buried here.

The Round Tower was first built in wood by William the Conqueror. In 1170 it was rebuilt in stone by Henry II *(see p48)*. It now houses the Royal Archives and Photographic Collection.

Statue of Charles II

Albert Memorial Chapel (1485)

The Round Tower (1080)

Waterloo Chamber (1220s)

St George's Hall (1362–65)

Lower Ward

Middle Ward

Upper Ward

St George's Chapel (1475–1528)

KEY

▓	11th–13th centuries
▓	14th century
▢	15th–18th centuries
▢	19th–20th centuries

WINDSOR CASTLE'S HISTORY
Founded in 1070 as a motte and bailey (see p472), Henry II and Edward III were responsible for the bulk of the work until the castle was remodelled by George IV in 1823.

Drawings Gallery
This chalk etching of Christ by Michelangelo is part of the Royal Collection. Various pieces in the collection are on display here in changing exhibitions, including works by Holbein among others.

VISITORS' CHECKLIST

Castle Hill. 020-7321 2233.
Mar–Oct: 9:45am–5:15pm;
Nov–Feb: 9:45am–4:15pm (last
adm: 1 hr before close). 25 &
26 Dec, Good Fri. St
Georges Chapel – call for times.
www.royal.gov.uk

The Audience Chamber is where the Queen greets her guests.

The Queen's Ballroom

Queen Mary's Dolls' House, designed by Sir Edwin Lutyens, was given to Queen Mary in 1924. The wine cellar contains genuine vintage wine.

Waterloo Chamber
The walls of this banqueting hall, first built in the 13th century, are lined with portraits of the leaders who played a part in Napoleon's defeat (see p55).

Brunswick Tower

The East Terrace Garden was created by Sir Jeffry Wyatville for King George IV in the 1820s.

★ **State Apartments**
These rooms contain many treasures, such as this 18th-century bed in the King's State Bedchamber, hung in its present splendour for the visit in 1855 of Napoleon III.

STAR SIGHTS

★ **St George's Chapel**

★ **State Apartments**

The Fire of 1992
A devastating blaze began during maintenance work on the State Apartments. St George's Hall was destroyed but has been rebuilt.

THE WEST COUNTRY

The West Country at a Glance

THE WEST COUNTRY forms a long peninsula bounded by the Atlantic to the north and the English Channel to the south, tapering down to Land's End, mainland Britain's westernmost point. Whether exploring the great cities and cathedrals, experiencing the awesome solitude of the moors and their prehistoric monuments, or simply enjoying the miles of coastline and mild climate, this region has an enduring appeal for holiday-makers.

Exmoor's (see pp238–9) *heather-clad moors and wooded valleys, grazed by wild ponies and red deer, lead down to some of Devon and Somerset's most dramatic cliffs and coves.*

Wells (see pp240–41) *is a charming town nestling at the foot of the Mendip Hills. It is famous for its exquisite three-towered cathedral with an ornate west façade, featuring an array of statues. Alongside stand the moated Bishop's Palace and the 15th-century Vicar's Close.*

St Ives (see p265) *has a branch of the Tate Gallery that shows modern works by artists associated with the area. Patrick Heron's bold coloured glass (1993) is on permanent display.*

Devon

DEVON AND CORNWALL
(see pp260–83)

Cornwall

Dartmoor (see pp282–83) *is a wilderness of great natural beauty covering an area of 365 sq miles (945 sq km). Stone clapper bridges, picturesque villages and weathered granite tors punctuate the landscape.*

◁ **Stunning views of the Lizard Peninsula**

Bath (see pp246–9) is named after the Roman baths that stand at the heart of the old city next to the splendid medieval abbey. It is one of Britain's liveliest and most rewarding cities, full of elegant Georgian terraces, built in local honey-coloured limestone by the two John Woods (Elder and Younger).

Stonehenge (see pp250–51), the world-famous prehistoric monument, was built in several stages from 3000 BC. Moving and erecting its massive stones was an extraordinary feat for its time. It is likely that this magical stone circle was a place of worship to the sun.

WESSEX
(see pp234–59)

Wiltshire

Somerset

Dorset

Salisbury's (see pp252–3) cathedral with its soaring spire, was the inspiration for one of John Constable's best-loved paintings. The picturesque Cathedral Close has a number of fine medieval buildings.

0 kilometres   25

0 miles   25

Stourhead garden (see pp254–5) was inspired by the paintings of Claude and Poussin. Created in the 18th century, the garden is itself a work of art. Contrived vistas, light and shade and a mixture of landscape and gracious buildings, such as the Neo-Classical Pantheon at its centre, are vital to the overall effect.

Coastal Wildlife

THE LONG AND VARIED West Country coastline, ranging from the stark, granite cliffs of Land's End to the pebble-strewn stretch of Chesil Bank, is matched with an equally diverse range of wildlife. Beaches are scattered with colourful shells, while rock pools form miniature marine habitats teeming with life. Caves are used by larger creatures, such as grey seals, and cliffs provide nest sites for birds. In the spring and early summer, an astonishing range of plants grow on the foreshore and cliffs which can be seen at their best from the Southwest Coastal Path *(see p32)*. The plants in turn attract numerous moths and butterflies.

Cliff-tops of Land's End with safe ledges for nesting birds

Chesil Bank is an unusual ridge of pebbles (see p256) *stretching 18 miles (29 km) along the Dorset coast. The bank was created by storms and the pebbles increase in size from northwest to southeast due to varying strengths of coastal currents. The bank encloses a lagoon called the Fleet, habitat of the Abbotsbury swans, as well as a large number of wildfowl.*

The Painted Lady, often seen on cliff-top coastal plants, migrates to Britain in the spring.

High tides wash up driftwood and shells

Cliff-top turf contains many species of wild flowers.

Thrift, in bummocks of honey-scented flowers, is a familiar sight on cliff ledges in spring.

Yellowhammers are to be seen perched on cliff-top bushes.

Marram grass roots help hold back sand against wind erosion.

Grey seals come on land to give birth to their young. They can be spotted on remote beaches.

A BEACHCOMBER'S GUIDE

The best time to observe the natural life of the sea shore is when the tide begins to roll back, before the scavenging seagulls pick up the stranded crab, fish and sandhoppers, and the seaweed dries up. Much plant and marine life can be found in the secure habitat provided by rock pools.

Durdle Door *was formed by waves continually eroding the weaker chalk layers of this cliff (see p258) in Dorset, leaving the stronger oolite to create a striking arch, known in geology as an eyelet.*

COLLECTING SHELLS

Most of the edible molluscs, such as scallops and cockles, are known as bivalves; others, such as whelks and limpets, are known as gastropods.

Great scallop   **Common cockle**

Common whelk   **Common limpet**

Seaweed, such as bladder wrack, can resemble coral or lichen when in water.

Rocks are colonized by clusters of barnacles, mussels and limpets.

Oystercatchers *have a distinctive orange beak. They hunt along the shore, feeding on all kinds of shellfish.*

Starfish *can be aggressive predators on shellfish. The light-sensitive tips of their tentacles help them to "see" the way.*

Mussels *are widespread and can be harvested for food.*

Rock pools teem with crabs, mussels, shrimps and plant life.

The Velvet Crab, *often found hiding in seaweed, is covered with fine downy hair all over its shell.*

Grey mullet, *when newly hatched, can often be seen in rock pools.*

West Country Gardens

GARDENERS HAVE LONG BEEN ATTRACTED to the West Country. Its mild climate is perfect for growing tender and exotic plants, many of which were brought from Asia in the 19th century. As a result, the region has some of England's finest and most varied gardens, covering the whole sweep of garden styles and history *(see pp22–3)*, from the clipped formality of Elizabethan Montacute, to the colourful and crowded cottage-garden style of East Lambrook Manor.

Lanhydrock's *(p272) clipped yews and low box hedges frame a blaze of colourful annuals.*

Trewithen *(p269) is renowned for its rare camellias, rhododendrons and magnolias, grown from seed collected in Asia. The huge garden is at its most impressive in March and June.*

Cotehele *(p281)* has a lovely lush valley garden.

DEVON AND CORNWALL *(see pp260–8)*

Trelissick *(p269)* has memorable views over the Fal Estuary through shrub-filled woodland.

Glendurgan *(p269)* is a plant-lover's paradise set in a steep, sheltered valley.

Mount Edgcumbe *(p280)* preserves its 18th-century French, Italian and English gardens.

Trengwainton (p264) *has a fine stream garden, whose banks are crowded with moisture-loving plants, beneath a lush canopy of New Zealand tree ferns.*

Overbecks *(near Salcombe) enjoys a spectacular site overlooking the Salcombe Estuary. There are secret gardens, terraces and rocky dells.*

CREATIVE GARDENING

Gardens are not simply collections of plants; they rely for much of their appeal on man-made features. Whimsical topiary, ornate architecture, fanciful statuary and mazes help to create an atmosphere of adventure or pure escapism. The many gardens dotted around the West Country offer engaging examples of the vivid imagination of designers.

Mazes *were created in medieval monasteries to teach patience and persistence. This laurel maze at Glendurgan was planted in 1833.*

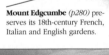

Fountains *and flamboyant statuary have adorned gardens since Roman times. Such eye-catching embellishments add poetic and Classical touches to the design of formal gardens, such as Mount Edgcumbe.*

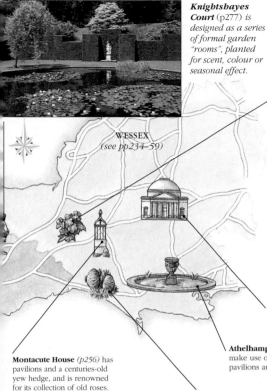

***Knightshayes
Court*** (p277) *is
designed as a series
of formal garden
"rooms", planted
for scent, colour or
seasonal effect.*

WESSEX
(see pp234–59)

East Lambrook Manor *(near
South Petherton) is a riot of
colours, as old-fashioned cottage
plants grow without restraint.*

Stourhead *(see pp254–5)* is a
magnificent example of 18th-
century landscape gardening.

Athelhampton's *(p257)* gardens
make use of fountains, statues,
pavilions and columnar yews.

Montacute House *(p256)* has
pavilions and a centuries-old
yew hedge, and is renowned
for its collection of old roses.

0 kilometres   25

0 miles   25

Parnham *(near Beaminster), like many West
Country gardens, has several parts devoted to
different themes. Here conical yews complement the formality of the stone balustrade;
elsewhere there are woodland, kitchen,
shade and Mediterranean gardens.*

Many garden buildings
*are linked by an element
of fantasy; while country
houses had to conform to
everyday practicalities, the
design of many smaller
buildings gave more scope
for imagination. This
fanciful Elizabethan
pavilion on the forecourt
at Montacute House was
first and foremost decorative, but sometimes served
as a lodging house.*

Topiary *can be
traced back to the
Greeks. Since that
time the sculpting
of trees into
unusual, often
eccentric shapes
has been developed
over the centuries.
The yew topiary of
1920s Knightshayes features a fox being
chased by a pack of hounds. The figures form a
delightful conceit and come into their own in
winter when little else is in leaf.*

WESSEX

WILTSHIRE · SOMERSET · DORSET

THE NATURAL AND DIVERSE BEAUTY *of this predominantly rural region is characterized by rolling hills and charming villages. The area is enriched by a wealth of historical and architectural attractions, ranging from the prehistoric stone circle of Stonehenge to the Roman baths and magnificent Georgian townscape of Bath.*

Vast swathes of bare windswept downland give way to lush river valleys, and the contrast between the two may explain the origin in medieval times of the saying, "as different as chalk and cheese". The chalk and limestone hills provided pasture for sheep whose wool was exported to Europe or turned to cloth in mill towns such as Bradford-on-Avon. Meanwhile the rich cow-grazed pastures of the valleys produced the Cheddar cheese for which the region has become famous.

The area's potential for wealth was first exploited by prehistoric chieftains whose large, mysterious monuments, such as Stonehenge and Maiden Castle, are striking features of the landscape. From this same soil sprang King Arthur *(see p273)* and King Alfred the Great, about whom there are numerous fascinating legends. It was King Arthur who is thought to have led British resistance to the Saxon invasion in the 6th century. The Saxons finally emerged the victors and one of them, King Alfred, first united the West Country into one political unit, called the Kingdom of Wessex *(see p47)*.

Wilton House and Lacock Abbey, both former monasteries, were turned into splendid stately homes during the 16th century, due to the Dissolution of the Monasteries *(see pp50–51)*. Today, their previous wealth can be gauged by the size and grandeur of their storage barns.

Matching the many man-made splendours of the region, Wessex is rich in rare wildlife and plants.

Two visitors enjoying the Elizabethan gardens of Montacute House, Somerset

◁ Eighteenth-century cottages lining Gold Hill, Shaftesbury

Exploring Wessex

FROM THE ROLLING CHALK PLAINS around Stonehenge to the rocky cliffs of Cheddar Gorge and the heather-covered uplands of Exmoor, Wessex is a scenically varied microcosm of England. Reflecting the underlying geology, each part of Wessex contributes its own distinctive architecture, with the Neo-Classically inspired buildings of Bath giving way to the mellow brick and timber of Salisbury and the thatched flint-and-chalk cottages of the Dorset landscape.

Wales
Severn Estuary
M4/M48
BRISTOL 6
A38
WESTON-SUPER-MARE
BRISTOL CHANNEL
M5
CHEDDAR GORGE 5
A38
South West Coast Path
A371
EXMOOR 1
MINEHEAD
A39
3 WEL
Brue
A39
GLASTONBURY 4
A39
A37
A372
A3
A358
Tone
TAUNTON 2
Parrett
Yeo
Exeter
M5
A303
SHERBORNE
A30
A37
Axe
Sidmouth
A35
A35
LYME REGIS
B3157 DORCHEST
18
ABBOTSB
WEYMOU

Bath's abbey and Georgian townscape

| 0 kilometres | 20 |
| 0 miles | 10 |

KEY

- Motorway
- Major road
- Scenic route
- Scenic path
- River
- Viewpoint

Exmoor National Park

SIGHTS AT A GLANCE

Huge sarsen stones of Stonehenge, dating from around 3000 BC

GETTING AROUND

Bath and Bristol are served by fast mainline trains, other major towns and seaside resorts by regional railways and long-distance bus services. Popular sights such as Stonehenge feature on many tour operators' bus excursions. The rural heart of Wessex, however, has little in the way of public transport and unless you have the time to walk the region's footpaths, you will need a car.

Exmoor National Park ❶

T HE MAJESTIC CLIFFS plunging into the Atlantic along Exmoor's northern coast are interrupted by lush, wooded valleys carrying rivers from the high moorland down to sheltered fishing coves. Inland, wild rolling hills are grazed by sturdy Exmoor ponies, horned sheep and the local wild **Curlew** red deer. Buzzards are also a common sight wheeling over the bracken-clad terrain looking for prey. For walkers, Exmoor offers 1,000 km (620 miles) of wonderful footpaths and varied, dramatic scenery, while the tamer perimeters of the National Park offer less energetic attractions – everything from traditional seaside entertainments to picturesque villages and ancient churches.

View east along the Southwest Coast Path

Combe Martin is a pretty setting for the Pack of Cards Inn *(see p274)*.

Parracombe church has a Georgian interior with a complete set of wooden furnishing

Combe Martin
Parracombe
Heddon
A39
West Lyn
Lynton
Lynmouth
A399

BARNSTAPLE

B3358

TIVERTON

Heddon's Mouth
The River Heddon passes through woodland and meadows down to this attractive point on the coast.

The Valley of Rocks
Gritstone outcrops, eroded into fantastical shapes, characterize this natural gorge.

KEY

ℹ️	Tourist information
▬	A road
▭	B road
═	Minor road
- -	Coast path
☼	Viewpoint

Lynmouth
Above the charming fishing village of Lynmouth stands hill-top Lynton. The two villages are connected by a cliff railway (see p274).

Watersmeet
The East Lyn and Hoar Oak Water join together in a tumbling cascade at this spot in the middle of a beautifully wooded valley. There is also a tearoom with a pretty garden.

Culbone church, a mere 10.6 m (35 ft) in length, claims to be Britain's smallest parish church.

Malmsmead has a Natural History Centre illustrating local wildlife.

Oare's church commemorates the writer R D Blackmore, whose romantic novel *Lorna Doone* (1869) is set in the area.

Porlock
The flower-filled village of Porlock has retained its charm, with steep winding streets, thatched houses and a fascinating old church.

Selworthy is a picturesque village of thatched cottages.

Minehead is a major resort built around a pretty quay. A steam railway runs all the way from here to Bishop's Lydeard.

DUNKERY BEACON
520 m
1,704 ft

B R E N D O N
H I L L S

TAUNTON

TIVERTON

Dunster has an ancient castle and an unusual octagonal Yarn Market (1609) where local cloth was once sold.

WIMBLEBALL LAKE

Simonsbath is a good starting point for walkers. The Exmoor ponies found locally are thought to descend from prehistoric ancestors.

TIVERTON

Tarr Steps is an ancient "clapper" bridge built of stone slabs.

Dunkery Beacon
Rising to a height of 520 m (1,700 ft), this is the highest point on Exmoor.

0 kilometres   5

0 miles   3

Taunton ❷

Somerset. 🏛 *77,000.* ✈ 🚍 🚉 **ℹ**
Paul St (01823 336 344). 🛒 *Tue &*
Sat (livestock).
W *www.heartofsomerset.com*

TAUNTON LIES at the heart of a fertile region famous for its apples and cider, but it was the prosperous wool industry that financed the massive church of **St Mary Magdalene** (1488–1514) with its glorious tower. Taunton's **castle** was the setting for the notorious Bloody Assizes of 1685 when "Hanging" Judge Jeffreys dispensed harsh retribution on the Duke of Monmouth and his followers for an uprising against King James II. The

12th-century building now houses the **Somerset County Museum**. A star exhibit is the Roman mosaic from a villa at Low Ham, Somerset, showing the story of Dido and Aeneas.

ENVIRONS: Hestercombe Garden is one of Sir Edwin Lutyens and Gertrude Jekyll's great masterpieces.

🏛 **Somerset County Museum**
Castle Green. **(** *01823 355504.* ○ *Tue–Sat, public hols.* 🚫 👥 *ground floor.* 📷 W *www.somersetgov.uk/museums*

🌸 **Hestercombe Garden**
Cheddon Fitzpaine. **(** *01823 413923.* ○ *daily.* 🚫 📷 📷
W *www.hestercombegardens.com*

Wells ❸

Somerset. 🏛 *10,000.* 🚉 **ℹ** *Market Place (01749 672552).* 🛒 *Wed, Sat.*

WELLS IS NAMED after St Andrew's Well, the sacred spring that bubbles up from the ground near the 13th-century **Bishop's Palace**, residence of the Bishop of Bath and Wells. A tranquil city, Wells is famous for its magnificent cathedral which was begun in the late 1100s. Penniless Porch, where beggars once received alms, leads from the bustling market place to the calm of the cathedral close. **Wells Museum** has prehistoric finds from nearby Wookey Hole and other caves.

Cathedral clock (1386–92)

ENVIRONS: To the northeast of Wells lies the impressive cave complex of **Wookey Hole**, which has an extensive range of popular amusements.

🏛 **Wells Museum**
8 Cathedral Green. **(** *01749 673477.* ○ *Easter–Oct: daily; Nov–Easter: Wed–Mon.* 👥 *limited.* 📷
🕳 **Wookey Hole**
Off A371. **(** *01749 672243.* ○ *daily.* 🚫 📷 🍴 📷 W *www.wookey.co.uk*

The West Front features 300 fine medieval statues of kings, knights and saints – many of them life-size.

The Vicars' Close, built in the 14th century for the Vicars' Choir, is one of the oldest complete streets in Europe.

The Chain Gate (1460)

Cloisters

Path leading round the moat

This graceful flight of steps curves up to the octagonal Chapter House which has delicate vaulting dating from 1306. The 32 ribs springing from the central column create a beautiful palm-tree effect.

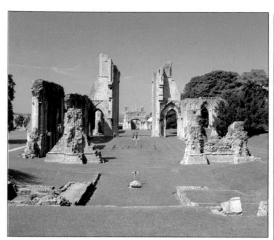

Glastonbury Abbey, left in ruins in 1539 after the Dissolution

Glastonbury ❹

Somerset. 👥 9,000. 🚉 ℹ️ Tribunal,
High St (01458 832954). 🚌 Tue.
🌐 www.glastonbury.co.uk

SHROUDED in Arthurian myth
and rich in mystical association, the town of Glastonbury
was once one of the most
important destinations for pilgrims in England. Now thousands flock here for the annual
rock festival (see p63) and for
the summer solstice on Midsummer's Day (21 June).

Over the years history and
legend have become inter-
twined, and the monks who
founded **Glastonbury Abbey**,
around 700, found it profitable
to encourage the association
between Glastonbury and the
mythical "Blessed Isle" known
as Avalon – alleged to be the
last resting place of King Arthur
and the Holy Grail (see p273).

The great abbey was left in
ruins after the Dissolution of
the Monasteries (see p50).
Even so, some magnificent
relics survive, including parts
of the vast Norman abbey
church, the unusual Abbot's
Kitchen, with its octagonal
roof, and the Victorian farmhouse, now the **Somerset
Rural Life Museum**.

Growing in the abbey
grounds is a cutting from the
famous Glastonbury thorn
which is said to have miracu-
lously grown from the staff
of St Joseph of Arimathea.
According to myth, he was
sent around AD 60 to convert
England to Christianity. The
English hawthorn flowers at
Christmas as well as in May.

The **Lake Village Museum**
has some interesting finds from
the Iron Age settlements that
once fringed the marshlands
around **Glastonbury Tor**.
Seen for miles around, the Tor
is a hill crowned by the remains of a 14th-century church.

🏛 **Somerset Rural Life
Museum**
Chilkwell St. 📞 01458 831197.
🔲 Apr–Oct: Tue–Sun; Nov–Apr:
Tue–Sat & public hols. ● 24–26 Dec,
1 Jan, Good Fri. ♿ limited. 🔲
closed winter.
🏛 **Lake Village Museum**
Tribunal, High St. 📞 01458 832954.
🔲 daily. ● 25, 26 Dec. 📷

*Bishops' tombs circle the
chancel. This sumptuous marble tomb, in the south aisle, is
that of Bishop Lord Arthur
Hervey, who was Bishop of
Bath and Wells (1869–94).*

*The palace moat is home to
swans which ring a bell by the
gatehouse when they want to
be fed. Feeding times are
at 11am and 4pm.*

**The Bishop's
Palace (1230–40)**

WELLS
CATHEDRAL
AND THE
BISHOP'S PALACE
The Close. 📞 01749 674483.
🔲 daily. ♿ limited.
Bishop's Palace 📞 01749 678691.
🔲 Apr–Oct: Tue– Fri, Sun & public hols
(Aug: daily). 📷 ♿
Wells has maintained much of its
medieval character with its cathedral,
Bishop's Palace and other buildings
around the close forming a harm-
onious group. The most striking
features of the cathedral are the west
front and the "scissor arches" installed
in 1338 to support the tower.

**13th-century ruins of
the Great Hall**

Cheddar Gorge ❺

D ESCRIBED AS A "deep frightful chasm" by novelist Daniel Defoe in 1724, Cheddar Gorge is a spectacular ravine cut through the Mendip plateau by fast-flowing streams during the glacial phases of the last Ice Age. Cheddar has given its name to a rich cheese which originates from here and is now produced worldwide. The caves in the gorge once provided the perfect environment of constant temperature and high humidity for storing and maturing the cheese.

The Cheddar Gorge Cheese Company is part of the Cheddar Gorge Rural Village, where you can visit a 1920s working dairy, among many other attractions, and see cheesemakers at work.

The B3135 road winds round the base of the 3 mile (5 km) gorge.

"Cheddar Man", a 9,000-year-old skeleton, is on display in the museum.

A footpath follows the top of the gorge on its southern edge.

Gough's Cave is noted for its cathedral-like proportions.

Tourist information

The gorge is a narrow, winding ravine with limestone rocks rising almost vertically on either side to a height of 120 m (400 ft).

Cox's Cave contains unusually shaped stalactites and stalagmites.

Jacob's Ladder has 274 steps leading to the top of the gorge.

The rare Cheddar Pink is among the astonishing range of plant and animal life harboured in the rocks.

Lookout Tower has far-reaching views over the area to the south and west.

Bristol ❻

See pp244–5.

Bath ❼

See pp246–9.

Bradford-on-Avon ❽

Wiltshire. 🏛 *9,500.* 🚋 🛈 *St Margaret St (01225 865797).* 🚌 *Thu.* 🖰 *www.bradfordonavontown.com*

THIS LOVELY COTSWOLD-STONE town with its steep flagged lanes is full of flamboyant houses built by wealthy wool and cloth merchants in the 17th and 18th centuries. One fine Georgian example is **Abbey House**, on Church Street. A little further along, **St Laurence Church** is a remarkably complete Saxon building founded in 705 *(see p47)*. The

Typical Cotswold-stone architecture in Bradford-on-Avon

church was converted to a school and cottage in the 12th century and was rediscovered in the 19th century when a vicar recognized the characteristic cross-shaped roof.

At one end of the medieval **Town Bridge** is a small stone cell, built as a chapel in the 13th century but later used as a lock-up for 17th-century vagrants. A short walk away, near converted mill buildings and a stretch of the Kennet and Avon Canal, is the massive 14th-century **Tithe Barn** *(see p28)*.

🏛 **Tithe Barn**
Pound Lane. ⬜ *daily.* ⬛ *25, 26 Dec.* ♿

Corsham ❾

Wiltshire. 🏛 *12,000.* 🛈 *High St (01249 714660).* 🖰 *www.northwilts.gov.uk*

THE STREETS of Corsham are lined with stately Georgian houses in Cotswold stone. **St Bartholomew's Church** has an elegant spire and a lovely carved alabaster tomb (1960) to the late Lady Methuen, whose family founded Methuen publishers. The family acquired **Corsham Court** in 1745 with its picture gallery and a remarkable collection of Flemish, Italian and English paintings, including works by Van Dyck, Lippi and Reynolds. Peacocks wander through the grounds, adding their colour and elegance to the façade of the Elizabethan mansion.

Peacock in grounds, Corsham Court

🏛 **Corsham Court**
off A4. ☎ *01249 701610.* ⬜ *mid-Mar– Sep: Tue–Sun (pm); Oct–mid-Mar: Sat, Sun (pm).* ⬛ *Dec.* 🎫 ♿ *limited.*

Lacock ❿

Wiltshire. 🏛 *1,000.*

MAINTAINED in its pristine state by the National Trust, with very few modern intrusions, Lacock is a picturesque and delightful village to explore. The meandering River Avon forms the boundary to the north side of the churchyard, while humorous stone figures look down from **St Cyriac Church**. Inside the 15th-century church is the splendid Renaissance-style tomb of Sir William Sharington (1495–1553). He acquired **Lacock Abbey** after the Dissolution of the Monasteries *(see p50)*, but it was a later owner, John Ivory Talbot, who had the buildings remodelled in the Gothic

revival style, in vogue in the early 18th century.

The abbey is famous for the window (in the south gallery) from which his descendant William Henry Fox Talbot, an early pioneer of photography, took his first picture in 1835, and for the sheets of snowdrops which cover the abbey grounds in early spring. A 16th-century barn at the abbey gates has been converted to the **Fox Talbot Museum**, which has displays on his experiments.

ENVIRONS: Designed by Robert Adam *(see pp24–5)* in 1769, **Bowood House** includes the laboratory where Joseph Priestley discovered oxygen in 1774, and a rich collection of sculpture, costumes and paintings. Italianate gardens surround the house while the lake-filled grounds, landscaped by Capability Brown *(see p22)*, contain a Doric temple, grotto, cascade and now a large adventure playground.

🏰 **Lacock Abbey**
(NT) Lacock. ☎ *01249 730227.* ⬜ *Mar–Oct: Wed–Mon (pm).* ⬛ *Good Fri.* 🎫 ♿ *limited in house.*
🏛 **Fox Talbot Museum**
(NT) Lacock. ☎ *01249 730459.* ⬜ *Mar–Oct: daily.* ⬛ *Good Fri.* 🎫 ♿
🏛 **Bowood House**
Derry Hill, nr Calne. ☎ *01249 812102.* ⬜ *Apr–Oct: daily.* 🎫 ♿ 🍴 🛒 🏛

William Henry Fox Talbot (1800–77)

Bristol ❻

I T WAS IN 1497 that John Cabot sailed from Bristol on his historic voyage to North America. The city, at the mouth of the Avon, became the main British port for transatlantic trade, pioneering the era of the ocean-going steam liner with the construction of SS *Great Britain*. The city flourished as a major trading centre, growing rich on the distribution of wine, tobacco and, in the 17th century, slaves.

King Brennus, St John's Gate
Because of its docks and aero-engine factories, Bristol was heavily bombed duringWorld War II and the city centre bears witness to the ideas of post-war planners. The docks have been shifted to deeper waters at Avonmouth and the old dock area has been transformed, taking on new life characterized by waterside cafés, shops and art galleries.

Exploring Bristol

The most interesting part of the city lies around Broad, King and Corn streets, known as the Old Quarter. There is a lively covered market, part of which occupies the **Corn Exchange**, built by John Wood the Elder *(see p246)* in 1743. Outside are the famous Bristol Nails, four bronze 16th–17th-century pedestals which Bristol merchants used as tables when paying for goods – hence the expression "to pay on the nail". **St John's Gate**, at the head of Broad Street, has medieval statues of Bristol's two mythical founders, King Brennus and King Benilus. Between Lewins Mead and Colston Street, **Christmas Steps** is a steep lane lined with specialist shops and cafés. The **Chapel of the Three Kings** at the top was founded in 1504.

A group of buildings around the cobbled King Street include the 17th-century timber-framed **Llandoger Trow** inn. It is here that Daniel Defoe is said to have met Alexander Selkirk, whose true-life island

The Two Sisters (c.1889) by Renoir, City Museum and Art Gallery

exile served as the inspiration for Defoe's novel *Robinson Crusoe* (1719). Just up from here is the **Theatre Royal**, built in 1766, and home to the famous Bristol Old Vic.

Not far away the renowned **Arnolfini Gallery** on Narrow Quay is a showcase for contemporary art, drama, dance and cinema (closed for refurbishment until spring 2005).

On the Harbourside, **At-Bristol** combines the interactive science centre Explore, the wildlife centre Wildwalk and an IMAX cinema.

To the west of the city, the elegant suburbs of **Clifton** revel in ornate Regency crescents. The impressive **Clifton Suspension Bridge** by Brunel, completed in 1864, perfectly complements the drama of the steep Avon gorge. **Bristol Zoo Gardens**, nearby, concentrate on breeding and conserving endangered species.

The bow of SS *Great Britain*

Memorial to William Canynge the Younger (1400–74)

🔒 St Mary Redcliffe

Redcliffe Way. 📞 *0117 9291487.*
⭕ *daily.* ♿ 🅿 *by arrangement.* ▢
This magnificent 14th-century church was claimed by Queen Elizabeth I to be "the fairest in England". The church owes much to the generosity of William Canynge the Elder and Younger, both famous mayors of Bristol. Inscriptions on the tombs of merchants and sailors tell of lives devoted to trade in Asia and the West Indies. Look out for the Bristol maze in the north aisle.

🏛 SS *Great Britain*

Gas Ferry Rd. 📞 *0117 9260680.*
⭕ *daily.* ● *24, 25 Dec.* 🅿 🔖 ♿
limited. 🅿 *by arrangement.* ▢
🅆 www.ss-great-britain.com
Designed by Isambard Kingdom Brunel, this is the world's first large iron passenger ship. Launched in 1843, she travelled 32 times round the world before she was abandoned in the Falkland Islands in 1886. The ship is being restored until 2005 but remains open, with hard-hat tours to see work in progress.

🏛 Georgian House

7 Great George St. 📞 *0117 9211362.*
⭕ *Apr–Oct: Sat–Wed.*
Life in a wealthy Bristol merchant's house of the 1790s is illustrated by furnishings in the elegant drawing room and the servants' area.

🏛 British Empire & Commonwealth Museum

Station Approach, Temple Meads. 📞
0117 9254980. ⭕ *daily.* ● *25, 26 Dec.* 🅿 🔖 ♿ 🅿 ▢
🅆 www.empiremuseum.co.uk
This major new national museum is located in the 1841 railway terminus by Brunel, and presents the dramatic 500-year history of the British empire and the emergence of the modern Commonwealth, in over 20 themed galleries, special exhibitions, a library and archive.

Warehouses overlooking the Floating Harbour

VISITORS' CHECKLIST

Bristol. 👥 *450,000.* ✈ *7 miles (11 km) SW Bristol.* ➔ *Temple Meads.* 🚌 *Marlborough St.* ⓘ *The Annexe, Wildscreen Walk, Harbourside (0906-586 2313).* 🛥 *daily.* 🎉 *Harbour Festival: Jul–Aug; Balloon Festival: Aug.* Ⓦ *www.visitbristol.co.uk*

🏛 Bristol Industrial Museum

Prince's Wharf. 📞 *0117 9251470.* ◯ *Apr–Oct: Sat–Wed; Nov–Mar: Sat–Sun.* ⬤ *25, 26 Dec.* ♿ 🛒 📷 Ⓦ www.bristol-city.co.uk/museums
The museum's collection of vehicles and models illustrates the huge range of products made in Bristol over the last 300 years. Among them are luxurious Bristol cars, the Bristol bus, the world's first touring caravan and Concorde, represented by a full-scale model of the pilot's cockpit.

🏛 City Museum and Art Gallery

Queen's Rd. 📞 *0117 922 3571.* ◯ *daily.* ⬤ *24, 25 Dec.* ♿ *limited.* 📷 🛒
Ⓦ www.bristol-city.gov.uk/museums
Varied collections include Egyptology, dinosaur fossils, Roman tableware, the largest collection of Chinese glass outside China and a fine collection of European paintings including works by Renoir and Bellini. Bristol artists include Sir Thomas Lawrence and Francis Danby.

✝ Bristol Cathedral

College Green. 📞 *0117 9264879.* ◯ *daily.* **Donation.** ♿ *limited.*
Ⓦ www.bristol-cathedral.co.uk
Bristol's cathedral, begun in 1140, took an unusually long time to build. Rapid progress was made between 1298 and 1330, when the inventive choir was rebuilt; the transepts and tower were finished in 1515, and another 350 years passed before the Victorian architect, G E Street, built the nave. Humorous medieval carving abounds – a snail crawling across the stone foliage in the Berkeley Chapel, musical monkeys in the Elder Lady Chapel, and a fine set of wooden misericords in the choir.

BRISTOL CITY CENTRE

Bristol Cathedral ③
Bristol Industrial Museum ⑤
City Museum and Art Gallery ①
Georgian House ②
St Mary Redcliffe ⑥
SS *Great Britain* ④

KEY

🅿 Parking
ⓘ Tourist information
✝ Church

0 metres   250
0 yards   250

Street-by-Street: Bath ●

BATH OWES ITS MAGNIFICENT Georgian
townscape to the bubbling pool of
water at the heart of the Roman Baths.
The Romans transformed Bath into England's first spa resort and it regained fame
as a spa town in the 18th century. At this
time the two brilliant John Woods (Elder
and Younger), both architects, designed
the city's fine Palladian-style buildings.
Many houses bear plaques recording the
numerous famous
people who have
resided here.

The Circus
*This is a daring
departure from th
typical Georgian
square, by John W
the Elder (1705–5*

No. 1 Royal Crescent

No. 17 is where the 18th-
century painter Thomas
Gainsborough lived *(see p151).*

**Assembly Rooms and
Museum of Costume**

★ Royal Crescent
*Hailed the most majestic street in Britain, this graceful
arc of 30 houses (1767–74) is the masterpiece of John
Wood the Younger. West of the Royal Crescent, Royal
Victoria Park (1830) is the city's largest open space.*

Jane Austen
(see p150), the
writer, stayed at
No. 13 Queen
Square on one
of many visits to
Bath in her youth.

Milsom Street and
New Bond Street con-
tain some of Bath's
most elegant shops.

Theatre Royal (1805)

KEY

– – – Suggested route

0 metres   100

0 yards   100

STAR SIGHTS

★ **Royal Crescent**

★ **Roman Baths**

★ **Bath Abbey**

Pump Rooms
*These tearooms once formed the
social hub of the 18th-century spa
community. They contain this
decorative drinking fountain.*

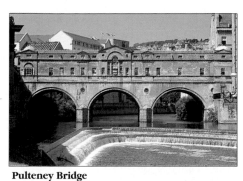

Pulteney Bridge
This charming bridge (1769–74), designed by Robert Adam, is lined with shops and links the centre with the magnificent Great Pulteney Street. Look out for a rare Victorian pillar box on the east bank.

The Building of Bath Museum

★ Roman Baths
Built in the 1st century, this bathing complex is one of Britain's greatest memorials to the Roman era.

★ Bath Abbey
The splendid abbey stands at the heart of the old city in the Abbey Church Yard, a paved courtyard enlivened by buskers. Its unique façade features stone angels climbing Jacob's Ladder to heaven.

Holburne Museum

Parade Gardens
Courting couples came to this pretty riverside park for secret liaisons in the 18th century.

Sally Lunn's House (1482) is one of Bath's oldest houses.

Rail & coach stations

Exploring Bath

THE BEAUTIFUL AND COMPACT CITY OF BATH is set among the rolling green hills of the Avon valley, and wherever you walk you will enjoy spendid views of the surrounding countryside. The traffic-free heart of this lively city is full of street musicians, museums, cafés and enticing shops, while the elegant honey-coloured Georgian houses, so characteristic of Bath, **Piazza cellist** form an elegant backdrop to city life.

Bath Abbey, at the heart of the old city, begun in 1499

🔒 Bath Abbey

13 Kingston Bldgs, Abbey Churchyard.
📞 01225 422462. ⏱ daily. ●
during services. **Donation.** ♿ ▮
🔲 www.bathabbey.org
This splendid abbey was supposedly designed by divine agency. According to legend, God dictated the form of the church to Bishop Oliver King in a dream; this story has been immortalized in the wonderfully eccentric carvings on the west front. The bishop began work in 1499, rebuilding a church that had been founded in the 8th century. Memorials cover the walls and the varied Georgian inscriptions make fascinating reading. The spacious interior is remarkable for the fan vaulting of the nave, an addition made by Sir George Gilbert Scott in 1874.

🏛 Assembly Rooms and Museum of Costume

Bennett St. 📞 01225 477789.
⏱ daily. ● 25, 26 Dec. ▮ 🎟 ♿
🔲 www.museumofcostume.co.uk
The Assembly Rooms were built by Wood the Younger in 1769, as a meeting place for the fashionable elite and as an elegant backdrop for many glittering balls. Jane Austen's novel *Northanger Abbey* (1818) describes the atmosphere of gossip and flirtation here.

In the basements is a collection of costumes in authentic period **Gilded bronze head** settings. The display **of Sulis Minerva** illustrates changing fashions from the 16th century to the present day.

🏛 No. 1 Royal Crescent

Royal Crescent. 📞 01225 428 126. ⏱ Tue–Sun & public hols.
● Dec, Jan, Good Fri. ▮ 🎟
🔲 www.bath-preservation-trust.org.uk
This museum lets you inside the first house of this beautiful Georgian crescent, giving a glimpse of what life was like for 18th-century aristocrats, such as the Duke of York, who probably lived here. It is furnished down to such details as the dog-powered spit used to roast meat in front of the fire.

🏛 Holburne Museum of Art

Great Pulteney St. 📞 01225 466669.
⏱ daily (Nov–Easter: Tue–Sat, Sun pm). ● mid-Dec–mid-Feb. 🎟 ♿
🔲 www.bath.ac.uk/holburne
This historic building is named after William Holburne of Menstrie (1793–1874), whose collections form the nucleus of the display of fine and decorative arts. Paintings can be seen by British artists such as Gainsborough and Stubbs.

ROMAN BATHS MUSEUM

Entrance in Abbey Churchyard.
🏛 01225 477784. ⏱ daily.
● 25, 26 Dec. 🎟 ♿ limited.
🔲 www.romanbaths.co.uk
According to legend, Bath owes its origin to the Celtic King Bladud who discovered the curative properties of its natural hot springs in 860 BC. Cast out from his kingdom as a leper, Bladud cured himself by imitating his swine and rolling in the hot mud at Bath.

In the first century, the Romans built baths around the spring, and a temple dedicated to the goddess Sulis Minerva, who combined the attributes of the Celt water goddess Sulis and the Roman goddess Minerva. Among the Roman relics is a bronze head of the goddess.

Medieval monks of Bath Abbey also exploited the springs' properties, but it was when Queen Anne visited in 1702–3 that Bath reached its zenith as a fashionable watering place.

🏛 Building of Bath Museum

The Vineyards. 📞 01225 333895.
🕐 Tue–Sun & public hols.
⬤ end-Nov–mid-Feb. 💷 ♿ limited.
🌐 www.bath-preservation-trust.org.uk

This museum, housed in an old Methodist chapel, is an excellent starting point for exploring the city. It shows how, in the 18th century, Bath was transformed from a medieval wool town into one of Europe's most elegant spas. John Wood and his son designed the Classically inspired stone fronts of the Royal Crescent and the Circus, leaving individual property speculators to develop the houses behind. While the façades speak of harmony and order, the houses behind show the result of rampant individualism, with no two houses alike. The museum looks at every aspect of the buildings, from their construction to a new gallery of Georgian interiors.

🏛 American Museum

Claverton Manor, Claverton Down.
📞 01225 460503. 🕐 Aug:
daily (pm); Mar–Oct, mid-Nov–mid-Dec: Tue–Sun (pm). 🅿 💷 ♿
limited. 🍴
🌐 www.americanmuseum.org

Founded in 1961, this was the first American museum to be established in this country. Rooms in the 1820 manor house are decorated in many styles, from the rudimentary dwellings of the first settlers to opulent 19th-century homes. There are special sections on Shaker furniture, quilts and Native American art, and a replica of George Washington's Mount Vernon garden of 1785.

A 19th-century American Indian weathervane

The dome (1897) is based on St Stephen Walbrook church in London (see p114).

The Great Bath

The open-air Great Bath, which stands at the heart of the Roman spa complex, was not discovered until the 1870s. Leading off this magnificent pool were various bathing chambers which became increasingly sophisticated over the four centuries the Romans were here. The baths fell into ruin, but extensive excavations have revealed the remarkable skill of Roman engineering.

Around the edges of the bath are the bases of piers that once supported a barrel-vaulted roof

York Street

A late 19th-century terrace bears statues of famous Romans such as Julius Caesar.

The sacred spring is enclosed by a reservoir now named the King's Bath.

The water flows from the spring into the corner of the bath at a constant temperature of 46° C (115° F).

The lead-lined bath, steps, column bases and paving stones around the edge all date from Roman times.

Stonehenge ⑪

BUILT IN SEVERAL STAGES from about 3000 BC, Stonehenge is Europe's most famous prehistoric monument. We can only guess at the rituals that took place here, but the alignment of the stones leaves little doubt that the circle is connected with the sun and the passing of the seasons, and that its builders possessed a sophisticated understanding of both arithmetic and astronomy.

Despite popular belief, the circle was not built by the Druids, an Iron Age priestly cult that flourished in Britain from around 250 BC – more than 1,000 years after Stonehenge was completed.

Finds from a burial mound near Stonehenge (Devizes Museum)

Stonehenge as it is today

The Heel Stone casts a long shadow straight to the heart of the circle on Midsummer's day.

The Avenue forms a ceremonial approach to the site.

The Slaughter Stone, named by 17th-century antiquarians who believed Stonehenge to be a place of human sacrifice, was in fact one of a pair forming a doorway.

The Outer Bank, dug around 3000 BC, is the oldest part of Stonehenge.

BUILDING OF STONEHENGE

Stonehenge's monumental scale is more impressive given that the only tools available were made of stone, wood and bone. The labour involved in quarrying, transporting and erecting the huge stones was such that its builders must have been able to command immense resources and vast numbers of people. One method is explained below.

RECONSTRUCTION OF STONEHENGE

This illustration shows what Stonehenge probably looked like about 4,000 years ago.

A sarsen stone was moved on rollers and levered into a pit.

With levers supported by timber packing, it was gradually raised.

The stone was then pulled upright by about 200 men hauling on ropes.

The pit round the ba was packed tightly wi stones and chalk.

Avebury Stone Circle
A4 · Marlborough
Silbury Hill
West Kennet Long Barrow · A4
A360
Devizes
A342
A342
A360 · A345
A303
Stonehenge
A360 · Avon · A345 · A303
A90 · Salisbury · Old Sarum
A30

WILTSHIRE'S OTHER PREHISTORIC SITES

The open countryside of the Salisbury Plain made this area an important centre of prehistoric settlement, and today it is covered in many ancient remains. Ringing the horizon around Stonehenge are scores of circular barrows, or burial mounds, where members of the ruling class were honoured with burial close to the temple site. Ceremonial bronze weapons and other finds excavated around Stonehenge and the other local prehistoric sites can be seen in the museum at Salisbury *(see pp252–3)* and the main museum at Devizes.

Silbury Hill (NT) is Europe's largest prehistoric earthwork,

Silbury Hill

but despite extensive excavations its purpose remains a mystery. Built out of chalk blocks around 2750 BC, the hill covers 2 ha (5 acres) and rises to a height of 40 m (131 ft). Nearby **West Kennet Long Barrow** (NT) is the biggest

The **Sarsen Circle** was erected around 2300 BC and is capped by lintel stones held in place by mortice and tenon joints.

The **Bluestone Circle** was built around 2000 BC out of some 80 slabs quarried in south Wales. It was never completed.

Horseshoe of Bluestones

Horseshoe of Sarsen Trilothons

Alternate ends of the lintel were levered up.

The weight of the lintel was supported by a timber platform.

The lintel was then levered sideways on to the uprights.

Sarsen stone forming part of the Avebury Stone Circle

Avebury ⑫

Wiltshire. 600. Swindon then bus. Green St (01672 539424).

BUILT AROUND 2500 BC, the **Avebury Stone Circle** (EH/NT) surrounds the village of Avebury and was probably once some form of religious centre. Although the stones used are smaller than those at Stonehenge, the circle itself is wider. Superstitious villagers smashed many of the stones in the 18th century, believing the circle to have been a place of pagan sacrifice.

The original form of the circle is best appreciated by a visit to the excellent **Alexander Keiller Museum** to the west of the site, which illustrates in detail the construction of the circle. There is also a fascinating exhibition entitled "6,000 Years of Mystery", which explains the changing landscape of Avebury.

St James's Church has a Norman font carved with sea monsters, and a rare 15th-century choir screen.

ENVIRONS: A few minutes drive east, **Marlborough** is an attractive town with a long and broad High Street lined with colonnaded Georgian shops.

🏛 Alexander Keiller Museum
(NT) Off High St. 01672 539250. daily. 24, 25 Dec.

chambered tomb in England, with numerous stone-lined "rooms" and a monumental entrance. Built as a communal cemetery around 3250 BC, it was in use for several centuries – old bodies were taken away to make room for newcomers.

Old Sarum is set within the massive ramparts of a 1st-century Romano-British hill fort. The Norman founders of Old Sarum built their own motte and bailey castle inside this ready-made fortification, and the remains of this survive along with the foundations of the huge cathedral of 1075. Above ground nothing remains of the town that once sat within the ramparts. The town's occupants moved to the fertile river valley site that became Salisbury during the early 12th century (see pp252–3).

♙ Old Sarum
(EH) Castle Rd. 01722 335398. daily. 24–26 Dec, 1 Jan.

The chambered tomb of West Kennet Long Barrow (c.3250 BC)

Salisbury ⓭

SALISBURY WAS FOUNDED IN 1220, when the old hill-top settlement of Old Sarum *(see p251)* was abandoned, being too arid and windswept, in favour of a new site among the lush water meadows where the rivers Avon, Nadder and Bourne meet. Purbeck marble may have been floated down the Nadder from Chilmark, 12 miles (20 km) west of Salisbury, for the construction of a new cathedral which was built mostly in the early 13th century, over the remarkably short space of 38 years. Its magnificent landmark spire – the tallest in England – was an inspired afterthought added in 1280–1310.

The 15th-century house of John A'Port, Queen's Street

Bishop's Walk and a sculpture by Elisabeth Frink (1930–93), Cathedral Close

Exploring Salisbury

The spacious and tranquil **Close**, with its schools, almshouses and clergy housing, makes a fine setting for Salisbury's cathedral. Among the numerous elegant buildings here are the **Matrons' College**, built in 1682 as a home for clergy widows, and 13th-century **Malmesbury House** with its splendid early Georgian façade (1719), fronted by lovely wrought-iron gates. Other buildings of interest include the 13th-century **Deanery**, the 13th-century **Wardrobe**, now a regimental museum, and the **Cathedral School**, housed in the 13th-century Bishop's Palace and famous for the quality of its choristers.

Beyond the walls of the Cathedral Close, Salisbury developed its chessboard layout, with areas devoted to different trades, perpetuated in street names such as Fish Row and Butcher Row. Leaving the Close through **High Street Gate**, you reach the busy High Street leading to the 13th-century **Church of St Thomas**, which has a lovely carved timber roof (1450), and a late 15th-century Doom painting, showing Christ seated in judgement and demons seizing the damned. Nearby in Silver Street, **Poultry Cross** was built in the 15th century as a covered poultry market. An intricate network of

alleys fans out from this point with a number of fine timber-framed houses. In the large bustling **Market Place** the **Guildhall** is an unusual cream stone building from 1788–95, used for civic functions. More attractive are the brick and tile-hung houses on the north side of the square, many with Georgian façades concealing medieval houses.

FISH ROW

Street signs reflecting trades of 13th-century Salisbury

The Cloisters are the largest in England. They were added between 1263 and 1284 in the Decorated style.

The Chapter House has an original of the *Magna Carta*. Its walls have stone friezes of the Old Testament.

The Trinity Chapel contains the grave of St Osmund who was bishop of Old Sarum from 1078–1099.

Choir stalls

Bishop Audley's Chantry, a magnificent 16th-century monument to the bishop, is one of several small chapels clustered round the altar.

🏠 Mompesson House

(NT) The Close. 📞 *01722 335659.*
🕐 *Apr–Oct: 11am–5pm Sat–Wed.*
📷 🚻 *limited.* 📷

Built by a wealthy Wiltshire family in 1701, the handsomely furnished rooms of this house give an indication of life for the Close's inhabitants in the 18th century. The delightful garden, bounded by the north wall of the Close, has fine herbaceous borders.

The graceful spire soars to a height of 123 m (404 ft).

The West Front is decorated by rows of lavish symbolic figures and saints in niches.

A roof tour takes you up to an external gallery at the base of the spire with views of the town and Old Sarum.

🏛 Salisbury and South Wiltshire Museum

The Close. 📞 *01722 332151.* 🕐 *Mon–Sat (Jul–Aug: Sun pm).* 📷 📷
📷 🔲 www.salisburymuseum.org.uk

In the medieval King's House, this museum has displays on early man, Stonehenge and nearby Old Sarum *(see p251)*.

SALISBURY CATHEDRAL

The Close. 📞 *01722 555120.* 🕐 *daily.* **Donation.** 🚻 📷
📷 🔲 www.salisburycathedral.org.uk

The cathedral was mostly built between 1220 and 1258. It is a fine example of Early English Gothic architecture, typified by tall, sharply pointed lancet windows.

The clock dating from 1386 is the oldest working clock in Europe.

The nave is divided into ten bays by columns of polished Purbeck marble.

Northwest transept

Numerous windows add to the airy and spacious atmosphere of the interior.

ENVIRONS: The town of Wilton is renowned for its carpet industry, founded by the 8th Earl of Pembroke using French Huguenot refugee weavers. The town's ornate **church** (1844) is a brilliant example of Neo-Romanesque architecture, incorporating genuine Roman columns, Flemish Renaissance woodwork, German and Dutch stained glass and Italian mosaics.

Wilton House has been home to the Earls of Pembroke since it was converted from a nunnery after the Dissolution *(see p50)*. The house, largely rebuilt by Inigo Jones in the 17th century, includes one of the original Tudor towers, a fine collection of art and a landscaped park with a Palladian bridge (1737). The glories of the house are the Single and Double Cube State Rooms. Both have magnificently frescoed ceilings and gilded stucco work and were designed to hang a series of family portraits by Van Dyck.

🏠 Wilton House

Wilton. 📞 *01722 746729.*
🕐 *Easter–Oct: daily.* 📷 🚻 🍴 📷
🔲 www.wiltonhouse.com

Double Cube room, designed by Inigo Jones in 1653

The Longleat Tree tapestry (1980)
depicting a 400-year history

Longleat House ⑭

Warminster, Wiltshire. **☎** 01985
844400. **▤** Warminster then taxi.
House ◯ daily. ● 25 Dec.
Safari Park ◯ Apr–Nov: daily. 🏞
♿ 🍴 🖭 🅿
W www.longleat.co.uk

T HE ARCHITECTURAL HISTORIAN
John Summerson coined
the term "prodigy house" to
describe the exuberance and
grandeur of Elizabethan
architecture that is so well
represented at Longleat. The
house was started in 1540,
when John Thynne bought
the ruins of a priory on the
site for £53. Over the
centuries subsequent owners
have added their own
touches. These include the
Breakfast Room and Lower
Dining Room (dating from
the 1870s), modelled on the
Venetian Ducal Palace, and
erotic murals painted by the
present owner, the 7th
Marquess of Bath. Today, the
Great Hall is the only
remaining room which
belongs to Thynne's time.

In 1949, the 6th Marquess
was the first landowner in
Britain to open his stately
home to the public, in order
to fund the maintenance and
preservation of the house and
its estate. Parts of the grounds,
landscaped by Capability
Brown *(see p22)*, were turned
into an expansive safari park
in 1966, where lions, tigers
and other wild animals roam
freely. This, along with other
additions such as the world's
longest hedge maze, the
Adventure Castle and Blue
Peter Maze, and special
events, now draw even more
visitors than the house.

Stourhead ⑮

S TOURHEAD IS AMONG THE FINEST EXAMPLES of 18th-century
landscape gardening in Britain *(see pp22–3)*. The garden was begun in the 1740s by Henry Hoare (1705–85),
who inherited the estate and transformed it into a breathtaking work of art. Hoare created the lake, surrounding
it with rare trees and plants, and Neo-
Classical Italianate temples, grottoes and
bridges. The Palladian-style house, built by
Colen Campbell *(see p24)*, dates from 1724.

Pantheon
*Hercules is among the
statues of Roman gods
housed in the elegant
Pantheon (1753).*

Gothic Cottage
(1806)

**Iron
Bridge**

A walk of 2 miles
(3 km) round the
lake provides
artistically
contrived
vistas.

The lake was created from
a group of medieval fishponds.
Hoare dammed the valley to
form a single expanse of water.

**Turf
Bridge**

**Temple of
Flora (1744)**

**★ Temple
of Apollo**
*The Classical
temples that dot the
garden were all
designed by
influential archi-
tect Henry Flitcroft
(1679–1769).*

Grotto
Tunnels lead to an artificial cave with a pool and a life-size statue of the guardian of the River Stour, sculpted by John Cheere in 1748.

VISITORS' CHECKLIST

(NT) Stourton, Wiltshire.
☎ 01747 841152. 🛈 0891 335205. 🚂 Gillingham (Dorset) then taxi. **House** ◻ Apr–Oct: 11am–5pm Fri–Tue (last adm: 4:30pm). **Gardens** ◻ 9am–7pm (or dusk if earlier) daily. 🌐 ♿ limited. ◻ 🍴 ◻ ◻

★ **Stourhead House**
Reconstructed after a fire in 1902, the house contains fine Chippendale furniture. The art collection reflects Henry Hoare's Classical tastes and includes The Choice of Hercules (1637) *by Nicolas Poussin.*

Colourful shrubs around the house include fragrant rhododendrons in spring.

Stourton village was incorporated into Hoare's overall design. 🍴 ◻

Pelargonium House is a historical collection of over 100 species and cultivars.

The reception contains exhibitions illustrating the story of Stourhead.

Entrance and car park

🍴 ◻
St Peter's Church
The parish church contains monuments to the Hoare family. The medieval monument nearby was brought from Bristol in 1765.

STAR SIGHTS

★ **Temple of Apollo**

★ **Stourhead House**

Shaftesbury **16**

Dorset. 👥 8,000. 🚉 ℹ️ *8 Bell St (01747 853514).* 🛒 *Thu.*
W www.shaftesburydorset.co.uk

HILLTOP SHAFTESBURY, with its cobbled streets and 18th-century cottages is often used as a setting for films to give a flavour of Old England. Picturesque **Gold Hill** is lined on one side by a wall of the demolished **abbey**, founded by King Alfred in 888. Only the excavated remains of the abbey church survive, and many masonry fragments are found in the local museum.

The Almshouse (1437) adjoining the Abbey Church, Sherborne

Sherborne **17**

Dorset. 👥 9,500. 🚉 🚌 ℹ️ *Digby Rd (01935 815341).* 🛒 *Thu, Sat.*
W www.westdorset.com

FEW OTHER TOWNS in Britain have such a wealth of unspoilt medieval buildings. Edward VI *(see p41)* founded the famous Sherborne School in 1550, saving intact the splendid **Abbey Church** and other monastic buildings that might otherwise have been demolished in the Dissolution *(see p50)*. Remains of the Saxon church can be seen in the abbey's façade, but the most striking feature is the 15th-century fan-vaulted ceiling.

Sherborne Castle, built by Sir Walter Raleigh *(see p51)* in 1594, is a wonderfully varied building that anticipates the flamboyant Jacobean style. Raleigh also lived briefly in the early 12th-century **Old Castle**, which now stands in ruins, demolished during the Civil War *(see p52)*.

ENVIRONS: West of Sherborne, past Yeovil, is the magnificent Elizabethan **Montacute House** *(see p233)*, set in 120 ha (300 acres) of grounds. It is noted for tapestries, and for the Tudor and Jacobean portraits in the vast Long Gallery.

♠ Sherborne Castle
Off A30. ☎ *01935 813182.* **Castle** 🕐 *Apr–Oct: Tue–Thu, Sat, Sun & bank hols (pm).* **Grounds** 🕐 *Apr–Oct: Thu–Tue.* 📷 🚻 🅿️
W www.sherbornecastle.com

♠ Old Castle
(EH) Off A30. ☎ *01935 812730.* 🕐 *Easter–Oct: daily; Nov–Easter: Wed–Sun.* 🔴 *25, 26 Dec, 1 Jan.* 📷 ♿ 🅿️

♦ Montacute House
(NT) Montacute. ☎ *01935 823289.* **Grounds** 🕐 *Apr–Nov: Wed–Mon.* 📷 🚻 🅿️

Abbotsbury **18**

Dorset. 👥 400. ℹ️ *Bakehouse, Market St.* W www.abbotsbury-tourism.co.uk

THE NAME ABBOTSBURY recalls the town's 11th-century Benedictine abbey of which little but the huge tithe barn, built around 1400, remains.

Nobody knows when the **Swannery** here was founded, but the earliest record dates to 1393. Mute swans come to nest in the breeding season, attracted by the reed beds which spread along the Fleet, a brackish lagoon protected from the sea by a high

The Swannery at Abbotsbury

ridge of pebbles called **Chesil Bank** *(see p230)*. Its wild atmosphere makes an appealing contrast to the south coast resorts, although strong currents make swimming too dangerous. **Abbotsbury Sub-Tropical Gardens** are the frost-free home to many new plants, discovered by botanists travelling in South America and Asia in the last 30 years.

🦢 Swannery
New Barn Rd. ☎ *01305 871858.* 🕐 *Apr–Nov: daily.* 📷 ♿ 🚻 🅿️

🌿 Abbotsbury Sub-Tropical Gardens
Off B3157. ☎ *01305 871387.* 🕐 *daily.* 🔴 *25, 26 Dec, 1 Jan.* 📷 ♿ 🚻 🅿️

Weymouth **19**

Dorset. 👥 62,000. 🚉 🚌 ⛴️ ℹ️ *King's Statue, The Esplanade (01305 785747).* 🛒 *Thu.*
W www.jurassiccoast.com

WEYMOUTH'S POPULARITY as one of Britain's earliest seaside resorts began in 1789 when George III paid the first of many summer visits here. The king's bathing machine

Weymouth Quay, Dorset's south coast

can be seen in the **The Esplanade**, and his statue is a prominent feature on the seafront. Here gracious Georgian terraces and hotels look across to the beautiful expanse of Weymouth Bay. Different in character is the old town around Custom House Quay with its fishing boats and old seamen's inns.

🏛 **The Esplanade**
Hope Sq. 📞 01305 777622. ⭕ daily. ⬤ 25, 26 Dec, 2 wks in Jan. 🈂

Dorchester 🟑

Dorset. 🏘 16,000. 🚋 🛈 Antelope Walk (01305 267992). 🖼 Wed. 🅦 www.westdorset.com

DORCHESTER, the county town of Dorset, is still recognizably the town in which Thomas Hardy based his novel *The Mayor of Casterbridge* (1886). Here, among the many 17th- and 18th-century houses lining the High Street, is the **Dorset County Museum**, where the original manuscript of the novel is displayed. Dorchester has the only example of a **Roman town house** in Britain. The remains reveal architectural details including a fine mosaic. There are also finds from Iron Age and Roman sites on the outskirts of the

A 55 m (180 ft) giant carved on the chalk hillside, Cerne Abbas (NT)

town. **Maumbury Rings** (Weymouth Avenue), is a Roman amphitheatre, originally a Neolithic henge. To the west, many Roman graves have been found below the Iron Age hill fort, **Poundbury Camp**.

ENVIRONS: Just southwest of Dorchester, **Maiden Castle** *(see p43)* is a massive monument dating from around 100 BC. In AD 43 it was the scene of a battle when the Romans fought the Iron Age people of southern England.
 To the north lies the charming village of **Cerne Abbas** with its magnificent medieval tithe barn and monastic buildings. The huge chalk figure of a giant on the hillside here is a fertility figure thought to represent either the Roman god Hercules or an Iron Age warrior.
 East of Dorchester are the churches, thatched villages and rolling hills immortalized in Hardy's novels. Picturesque **Bere Regis** is the Kingsbere of *Tess of the D'Urbervilles*, where the tombs of the family whose name inspired the novel may be seen in the Saxon **church**. **Hardy's Cottage** is where the writer was born and **Max Gate** is the house he designed and lived in from 1885 until his death. His heart is buried with

Hardy's statue, Dorchester

his family at **Stinsford** church – his body was given a public funeral at Westminster Abbey *(pp94–5)*.
 There are beautiful gardens *(see p233)* and a magnificent medieval hall at 15th-century **Athelhampton House**.

🏛 **Dorset County Museum**
High West St. 📞 01305 262735. ⭕ Nov–Apr: Mon–Sat; May–Oct: daily. ⬤ 25, 26 Dec. 🈂 ♿ limited. 🅿 🅦 www.dorsetcountymuseum.org
🏚 **Hardy's Cottage**
(NT) Higher Bockhampton. 📞 01305 262366. ⭕ Apr–Oct: Thu–Mon. 🈂 ♿ garden only.
🏚 **Max Gate**
(NT) Alington Ave, Dorchester. 📞 01305 262538. ⭕ Apr–Sep: Sun, Mon & Wed (pm). 🈂 ♿ 🅿
🏚 **Athelhampton House**
Athelhampton. 📞 01305 848363. ⭕ Mar–Oct: Sun–Fri. 🈂 ♿ gardens only. 🈂 🍽 🅿

THOMAS HARDY (1840–1928)

The vibrant, descriptive novels and poems of Thomas Hardy, one of England's best-loved writers, are set against the background of his native Dorset. The Wessex countryside provides a constant and familiar stage against which his characters enact their fate. Vivid accounts of rural life record a key moment in history, when mechanization was about to destroy ancient farming methods, just as the Industrial Revolution had done in the towns a century before *(see pp54–5)*. Hardy's powerfully visual style has made novels such as *Tess of the D'Urbervilles* (1891) popular with modern film-makers, and drawn literary pilgrims to the villages and landscapes that inspired his fiction.

Nastassja Kinski in Roman Polanski's film *Tess* (1979)

Corfe Castle ㉑

(NT) Dorset. 📞 *01929 481294.* 🚃
Wareham then bus. ⭘ *daily.* ● *25
& 26 Dec.* 📷 ♿ *limited.* 🎫
Mar–Oct; Nov–Feb by arrangement.
🖥 📷 W *www.corfecastle.org.uk*

T HE SPECTACULAR RUINS of
Corfe Castle romantically
crown a jagged pinnacle of
rock above the charming unspoilt village that shares its
name. The castle has dominated the landscape since the
11th century, first as a royal
fortification, then as the dramatic ruins seen today. In
1635 the castle was purchased
by Sir John Bankes, whose
wife and her retainers – mostly
women – courageously held
out against 600 Parliamentary
troops, in a six-week siege
during the Civil War *(see
pp52–3)*. The castle was
eventually taken through trea-
chery and in 1646 Parliament
voted to have it "slighted" –
deliberately blown up to
prevent it being used again.
From the ruins there are far-
reaching views over the Isle of
Purbeck and its coastline.

The ruins of Corfe Castle, dating mainly from Norman times

Isle of Purbeck ㉒

Dorset. 🚃 *Wareham.* ⛴ *Shell Bay,
Studland.* ℹ *Swanage (01929
422885).* W *www.swanage.gov.uk*

T HE ISLE OF PURBECK, which
is in fact a peninsula, is
the source of the grey shelly
limestone, known as Purbeck
marble, from which the castle
and surrounding houses were
built. The geology changes to
the southwest at **Kimmeridge**,
where the muddy shale is rich
in fossils and recently

discovered oil reserves. The
Isle is fringed with unspoilt
beaches. **Studland Bay** (NT)
– with its white sand and its
sand-dune nature reserve,
rich in birdlife – has been
rated one of Britain's best
beaches. Sheltered **Lulworth
Cove** is almost encircled by
white cliffs and there is a fine
clifftop walk to Durdle Door
(see p231), a natural chalk
arch eroded by the waves.

The main resort in the area
is **Swanage**, the port where
Purbeck stone was trans-
ported by ship to London, to
be used for everything from
street paving to church building. Unwanted masonry from
demolished buildings was
shipped back and this is how
Swanage got its wonderfully
ornate **Town Hall** façade, designed by Wren around 1668.

Poole ㉓

Dorset. 🏠 *142,000.* 🚃 🚌 ⛴
ℹ *High St (01202 253253).*
W *www.pooletourism.com*

S ITUATED ON ONE of the largest
natural harbours in the
world, Poole is an ancient, still
thriving, seaport. The quay is
lined with old warehouses,
modern apartments and a
marina, overlooking a safe
sheltered bay. The **Waterfront Museum**, partly housed
in 15th-century cellars on the
quay, tells the seafaring history
of the port and town, and has
a range of changing exhibitions. Nearby **Brownsea
Island** (reached by boat from
the quay) is given over to a
woodland nature reserve with

Beach adjoining Lulworth Cove, Isle of Purbeck

a waterfowl and heron sanctuary. The fine views of the
Dorset coast add to the appeal
of the island.

🏛 Waterfront Museum
High St. 📞 *01202 262600.*
⭕ *daily.* ⚫ *25, 26 Dec, 1 Jan.* ♿
🌐 *www.poole.gov.uk*

🌿 Brownsea Island
(NT) Poole. 📞 *01202 707744.* ⭕
*Apr–Nov: daily (boat trips leave the
quayside every 30 mins during the
season).* 📷 ♿ 🚻 🖼 🍴

Boats in Poole harbour

Wimborne
Minster ㉔

Dorset. 🏘 *6,500.* 🚉 🛈 *29 High St
(01202 886116).* 📅 *Fri–Sun.*
🌐 *www.visiteastdorset.com*

THE FINE COLLEGIATE CHURCH of
Wimborne's **Minster** was
founded in 705 by Cuthburga,
sister of King Ina of Wessex. It
fell prey to marauding Danish
raiders in the 10th century,
and the imposing grey church
we see today dates from the
refounding by Edward the
Confessor *(see p47)* in 1043.
Stonemasons made use of the
local Purbeck marble, carving
beasts, biblical scenes, and a
mass of zig-zag decoration.

The 16th-century **Priest's
House Museum** has rooms
furnished in the style of
different periods and an
enchanting hidden garden.

ENVIRONS: Designed for the
Bankes family after the destruction of Corfe Castle,
Kingston Lacy was acquired
by the National Trust in 1981.
The estate has always been
farmed by traditional methods

and is astonishingly rich in
wildlife, rare flowers and butterflies. This quiet, forgotten
corner of Dorset is grazed by
rare Red Devon cattle and
can be explored using paths
and "green lanes" that date
back to Roman and Saxon
times. The fine 17th-century
house on the estate contains
an outstanding collection of
paintings, including works by
Rubens, Velázquez and Titian.

🏛 Priest's House Museum
High St. 📞 *01202 882533.* ⭕ *Apr–
Oct: Mon–Sat.* 📷 ♿ *limited.* 🖼 🍴

🏰 Kingston Lacy
(NT) on B3082. 📞 *01202 883402.*
House ⭕ *Apr–Oct: Sun–Wed.*
Gardens ⭕ *Apr–Oct: daily; Nov–Mar:
Sat & Sun.* 📷 ♿ *gardens only.* 🍴 🍴

Bournemouth ㉕

Dorset. 🏘 *165,000.* ✈ 🚆 🛈
🛈 *Westover Rd (0906 8020234).*
🌐 *www.bournemouth.co.uk*

BOURNEMOUTH'S POPULARITY as
one of England's favourite
seaside resorts is due to an
almost unbroken sweep of
sandy beach, extending from
the mouth of Poole Harbour
to Hengistbury Head. Most of
the seafront is built up, with
many large seaside villas and
exclusive hotels. To the west
there are numerous clifftop
parks and gardens, interrupted
by beautiful wooded river
ravines, known as "chines".
The varied and colourful garden of **Compton Acres** was
conceived as a museum of
many different garden styles.

In central Bournemouth the
amusement arcades, casinos,
nightclubs and shops cater
for the city's many visitors.
During the summer, pop
groups, TV comed-
ians and the

**A toy train on the popular seafront
at Bournemouth**

Marchesa Maria Grimaldi by Sir
Peter Paul Rubens (1577–1640),
Kingston Lacy

highly regarded Bournemouth
Symphony Orchestra perform
at various venues in the city.
The **Russell-Cotes Art Gallery
and Museum**, housed in a late
Victorian villa, has an extensive
collection with many fine
Oriental and Victorian artefacts.

ENVIRONS: The magnificent
Christchurch Priory, east of
Bournemouth, is 95 m (310
ft) in length – the longest
church in England. It was
rebuilt between the 13th and
16th centuries and presents a
sequence of different styles.
The original nave, built around
1093, is an impressive example
of Norman architecture, but the
highlight is the intricate stone
reredos which features a Tree
of Jesse, tracing the lineage of
Christ. Next to the Priory are
the ruins of a Norman **castle**.

Between Bournemouth and
Christchurch, **Hengistbury
Head** is well worth climbing
for grassland flowers, butterflies and sea views, while
Stanpit Marsh, to the west
of Bournemouth, is an excellent spot for viewing herons
and other wading birds.

🌿 Compton Acres
Canford Cliffs Rd. 📞 *01202 700
778.* ⭕ *daily.* 📷 📷 ♿ 🍴
🌐 *www.comptonacres.co.uk*

🏛 Russell-Cotes Art Gallery
and Museum
Eastcliff. 📞 *01202 451800.* ⭕
Tue–Sun. ♿ 🍴 🍴 🌐 *www.
russell-cotes.bournemouth.gov.uk*

DEVON AND CORNWALL

DEVON · CORNWALL

MILES OF MAGNIFICENTLY VARIED COASTLINE *dominate this magical corner of Britain. Popular seaside resorts alternate with secluded coves and unspoilt fishing villages rich in maritime history. In contrast there are lush, exotic gardens and the wild terrain of the moorland interior, dotted with tors and historic remains.*

Geographical neighbours, the counties of Devon and Cornwall are very different in character. Celtic Cornwall, with its numerous villages named after early Christian missionaries, is mostly stark and treeless at its centre. In many places it is still scarred by the remains of tin and copper mining that has played an important part in the economy for some 4,000 years. Yet this does not detract from the beauty and variety of the coastline dotted with lighthouses and tiny coves, and penetrated by deep tidal rivers.

Devon, by contrast, is a land of lush pasture divided into a patchwork of tiny fields and threaded with narrow lanes, whose banks support a mass of flowers from the first spring primroses to summer's colourful mixture of campion, foxglove, oxeye daisies and blue cornflowers. The leisurely pace of rural life here, and in Cornwall, contrasts with life in the bustling cities. Exeter with its magnificent cathedral, historic Plymouth, elegant Truro and Elizabethan Totnes are urban centres brimming with life and character.

The spectacular coastline and the mild climate of the region attract families, boating enthusiasts and surfers. For those in search of solitude, the Southwest Coastal Path provides access to the more tranquil areas. There are fishing villages and harbours whose heyday was in the buccaneering age of Drake and Raleigh *(see p51)*, and inland the wild moorland of Bodmin and Dartmoor, which provided inspiration for many romantic tales. Many of these are associated with King Arthur *(see p273)* who, according to legend, was born at Tintagel on Cornwall's dramatically contorted north coast.

Beach huts on the seafront at Paignton, near Torquay

◁ **Fishing boats in Port Isaac, on Cornwall's north coast**

Exploring Devon and Cornwall

Romantic moorland dominates the inland parts of Devon and Cornwall, ideal walking country with few roads and magnificent views stretching for miles. By contrast the extensive coastline is indented by hundreds of sheltered river valleys, each one seemingly isolated from the rest of the world – one reason why Devon and Cornwall can absorb so many visitors and yet still seem uncrowded. Wise tourists get to know one small part of Devon or Cornwall intimately, soaking up the atmosphere of the region, rather than rushing to see everything in the space of a week.

Key

▭	Motorway
▭	Major road
▭	Minor road
▭	Scenic route
--	Scenic path
～	River
🔆	Viewpoint

Sights at a Glance

AppledNore **16**
Barnstaple **17**
Bideford **15**
Bodmin **11**
Buckfastleigh **23**
Buckland Abbey **26**
Bude **13**
Burgh Island **24**
Clovelly **14**
Cotehele **27**
Dartmoor pp282–3 **29**
Dartmouth **21**
Eden Project pp270–71 **9**
Exeter **19**
Falmouth **6**
Fowey **10**
Helston and the
   Lizard Peninsula **5**
Lynton and Lynmouth **18**
Morwellham Quay **28**
Penzance **3**
Plymouth **25**
St Austell **8**
St Ives **2**
*St Michael's Mount
   pp266–7* **4**
Tintagel **12**
Torbay **20**
Totnes **22**
Truro **7**

Walks and Tours
Penwith Tour **1**

The dramatic cliffs of Land's End, England's most westerly point

See Also

- *Where to Stay* pp553–5
- *Where to Eat* pp589–91

Sub-tropical gardens at Torquay, the popular seaside resort

GETTING AROUND

Large numbers of drivers, many towing caravans (trailers), travel along the M5 motorway and A30 trunk road from mid-July to early September and travel can be slow, especially on Saturdays. Once in Devon and Cornwall, allow ample time if you are travelling by car along the region's narrow and high-banked lanes.

The regular train services, running from Paddington to Penzance, along Brunel's historic Great Western Railway, stop at most major towns. Aside from this, you are dependent on taxis or infrequent local buses.

Typical thatched, stone cottages, Buckland-in-the-Moor, Dartmoor

LYNTON & LYNMOUTH ⑱

● ILFRACOMBE

Minehead

BARNSTAPLE

E X M O O R

⑰

⑯ APPLEDORE

⑮

BIDEFORD

A39

Taunton

● TIVERTON

Yeovil

● HONITON

OKEHAMPTON

⑲ EXETER

● SIDMOUTH

● EXMOUTH

DARTMOOR

㉙

㉘ MORWELLHAM QUAY

㉗ COTEHELE

㉖ BUCKLAND ABBEY

BUCKFASTLEIGH

㉓

● TORQUAY

⑳ TORBAY

㉒ TOTNES

㉕ PLYMOUTH

㉑

DARTMOUTH

㉔ BURGH ISLAND

0 kilometres   15

0 miles   10

Penwith Tour ❶

THIS TOUR PASSES THROUGH a spectacular, remote Cornish landscape, dotted with relics of the tin mining industry, picturesque fishing villages and many prehistoric remains. The magnificent coastline varies between the gentle rolling moorland in the north and the rugged, windswept cliffs that characterize the dramatic south coast. The beauty of the area, combined with the clarity of light, has attracted artists since the late 19th century. Their work can be seen in Newlyn, St Ives and Penzance.

TIPS FOR DRIVERS

Tour length: 31 miles (50 km)
Stopping-off points: There are pubs and cafés in most villages. Sennen Cove makes a pleasant mid-way stop. (See also pp636–7.)

Zennor ①
The carved mermaid in the church recalls the legend of the mermaid who lured the local squire's son to her ocean lair.

Lanyon Quoit ②
One of many prehistoric monuments, this chambered tomb is visible on the left from the road to Madron.

Botallack Mine ⑧
Derelict enginehouses clinging to the cliffside are a vivid reminder of the region's former industry of tin-mining.

Land's End ⑦
England's most westerly point is noted for its dramatic and wild landscape. A local exhibition reveals its history, geology and wildlife.

Trengwainton ③
These gardens are noted for their luxuriance (*p232*).

Merry Maidens ⑤
This Bronze Age stone circle is said to be 19 girls turned to stone for dancing on Sunday.

Minack Theatre ⑥
This Ancient Greek-style theatre (1923) overlooks a magical bay of Porthcurno. It forms a magnificent backdrop for productions in summer.

Newlyn ④
Cornwall's largest fishing port gave its name to a school of artists founded in the 1880s (*p266*). Examples of their work can be seen in the art gallery here.

0 kilometres   3

0 miles   2

KEY

▬▬ Tour route

═══ Other roads

᠊ᢧ᠊ Viewpoint

St Ives ❷

Cornwall. 👥 11,000. 🚂 🚌
ℹ️ Street-an-Pol (01736 796297).
🌐 www.go-cornwall.com

S T IVES is renowned for the **Barbara Hepworth Museum and Sculpture Garden** and **Tate St Ives**, which together celebrate the work of a group of artists who set up a seaside art colony here from the 1920s. Tate St Ives, designed to frame a panoramic view of Porthmeor Beach, reminds visitors of the natural surroundings that inspired the art on display within. The Barbara Hepworth Museum presents the sculptor's work in the house and garden where she lived and worked for many years.

The town of St Ives remains a typical English seaside resort,

The Lower Terrace, Tate St Ives

surrounded by a crescent of golden sands. Popular taste rules in the many other art galleries tucked down winding alleys with names such as Teetotal Street, a legacy of

the town's Methodist heritage. Many galleries are converted cellars and lofts where fish were once salted and packed. In between are whitewashed cottages with tiny gardens brimming with marigolds, sunflowers and trailing lobelia, their vibrant colours made intense by the unusually clear light that first attracted artists to St Ives.

🏛 Barbara Hepworth Museum and Sculpture Garden

Barnoon Hill. 📞 01736 796226. ◯ Mar–Oct: daily; Nov–Feb: Tue–Sun. ● 24–26 Dec; occasionally for rehanging – phone to check. 🎟 ♿ by arrangement. 📷

🏛 Tate St Ives

Porthmeor Beach. 📞 01736 796226. ◯ Mar–Oct: daily; Nov–Feb: Tue–Sun. ● 24–26 Dec. 🎟 ♿ 🍴 📷
🌐 www.tate.org.uk/stives

TWENTIETH-CENTURY ARTISTS OF ST IVES

Ben Nicholson and Barbara Hepworth formed the nucleus of a group of artists that made a major contribution to the development of abstract art in Europe. In the 1920s, St Ives together with Newlyn *(see p264)* became a place for aspiring artists. Among the prolific artists associated with the town are the potter Bernard Leach (1887–1979) and the painter Patrick Heron (1920–99), whose *Coloured Glass Window (see p228)* dominates the Tate St Ives entrance. Much of the art on display at Tate St Ives is abstract and illustrates new responses to the rugged Cornish landscape, the human figure and the ever-changing patterns of sunlight on sea.

Barbara Hepworth *(1903–75)* was one of the foremost abstract sculptors of her time. Madonna and Child *(1953)* can be seen in the church of St Ia.

John Wells' *(1907–2000)* key interests are in light, curved forms and birds in flight, as revealed in Aspiring Forms *(1950)*.

Ben Nicholson's *(1894–1982)* work shows a change in style from simple scenes, such as the view from his window, to a preoccupation with shapes – as seen in this painting St Ives, Cornwall *(1943–5)*. Later, his interest moved towards pure geometric blocks of colour.

Penzance ❸

Cornwall. 🏠 *15,000*. ᴇ 🚉 🚌
ℹ *Station Approach (01736 362207).*
ᴡ *www.go-cornwall.com*

PENZANCE IS A BUSTLING resort with a climate so mild that palm trees and sub-tropical plants grow happily in the lush **Morrab Gardens**. The town commands fine views of St Michael's Mount and a great sweep of clean sandy beach.

The main road through the town is Market Jew Street, at the top of which stands the magnificent domed Market House (1837), fronted by a statue of Sir Humphrey Davy (1778–1829). Davy, who came from Penzance, invented the miner's safety lamp which detected lethal gases.

Chapel Street is lined with curious buildings, none more striking than the flamboyant **Egyptian House** (1835), with its richly painted façade and lotus bud decoration. Just as curious is **Admiral Benbow Inn** (1696) on the same street, which has a pirate perched on the roof looking out to sea. The town's **Museum and Art Gallery** has pictures by the Newlyn School of artists.

ENVIRONS: A short distance south of Penzance, **Newlyn** *(see p264)* is Cornwall's largest fishing port, which has given its name to the local school of artists founded by Stanhope Forbes (1857–1947). They painted outdoors, aiming to capture the fleeting impressions of wind, sun and sea. Continuing south, the coastal road ends at **Mousehole** (pronounced Mowzall), a pretty, popular village with a

The Egyptian House (1835)

tiny harbour, tiers of cottages and a maze of narrow alleys.

North of Penzance, overlooking the magical Cornish coast, **Chysauster** is a fine example of a Romano-British village. The site has remained almost undisturbed since it

St Michael's Mount ❹

(NT) Marazion, Cornwall. ᴄ *01736 710233.* 🚌 *from Marazion (Apr–Oct) or on foot at low tide.* ◯ *Apr–Oct: Mon–Fri; Nov–Mar guided tours only (phone to arrange).* 🎫 🍴 🛍
📷 ᴡ *www.stmichaelsmount.co.uk*

ST MICHAEL'S MOUNT emerges dramatically from the waters of Mount Bay, opposite the small village of Marazion.

According to ancient Roman historians, the mount was the island of Ictis, an important centre for the Cornish tin trade during the Iron Age. It is dedicated to the archangel St Michael who, according to legend, appeared here in 495.

When the Normans conquered England in 1066 *(see pp46–7)*, they were struck by the island's resemblance to their own Mont-St-Michel, whose Benedictine monks were invited to build a small abbey here. The abbey was absorbed into a fortress at the Dissolution *(see p339)*, when Henry VIII set up a chain of coastal defences to counter an expected attack from France.

In 1659 St Michael's Mount was purchased by Sir John St Aubyn whose descendants subsequently turned the fortress into a magnificent house.

View of St Michael's Mount from Marazion

Harbourside village

Access to the island is by boat from Marazion or on foot by a cobbled causeway at low tide.

The rocky slopes were planted with sub-tropical trees and shrubs by the St Aubyn family.

PLAN OF MAIN FLOOR

Exit
Entrance
Sir John's Room
Armoury
Library

Priory Church
North Terrace
Staircase to Museum and Exit
Chevy Chase Room

Choir
South Terrace

Blue Drawing Room
Hall
Map Room
Long Passage
Smoking Room

was abandoned during the 3rd century.

From Penzance, regular boat and helicopter services depart for the **Isles of Scilly**, a beautiful archipelago forming part of the same granite mass as Land's End, Bodmin Moor and Dartmoor. Along with tourism, flower-growing forms the main source of income here.

🏛 **Penlee House Gallery and Museum**
Morrab Rd.
📞 01736 363625. 🕐 May–Sep: 10am–5pm Mon–Sat; Oct–Apr: 10:30am–4:30pm Mon–Sat.
🚫 25–26 Dec, 1 Jan. 🎫 📷
♿ 🅿
W www.penleehouse.org.uk
🏛 **Chysauster**
Off B3311.
📞 07831 757934.
🕐 Apr–Oct: daily. 📷

THE GROWTH OF METHODISM

The hard-working and independent mining and fishing communities of the West Country had little time for the established church, but they were won over by the new Methodist religion, with its emphasis on hymn singing, open-air preaching and regular or "methodical" Bible reading. When John Wesley, the founder of Methodism, made the first of many visits to the area in 1743, sceptical Cornishmen pelted him with stones. His persistence, however, led to many conversions and by 1762 he was preaching to congregations of up to 30,000 people. Simple places of worship were built throughout the county; one favoured spot was the amphitheatre **Gwennap Pit**, at Busveal, south of Redruth. Methodist memorabilia can be seen in the Royal Cornwall Museum in Truro (see p269).

John Wesley (1703–91)

Castle entrance

The South Terrace forms the roof of the large Victorian wing. Beneath it there are five floors of private quarters.

The Blue Drawing Room was formed from the Lady Chapel in the mid-18th century and is decorated in charming Rococo Gothic style. It contains fine plaster work, furniture and paintings by Gainsborough and Thomas Hudson.

The Armoury displays sporting weapons and military trophies brought back by the St Aubyn family from various wars.

The Priory Church, rebuilt in the late 14th century, forms the summit of the island. Beautiful rose windows are found at both ends.

The Chevy Chase Room takes its name from a plaster frieze (1641) representing hunting scenes.

Pinnacles of serpentine rock at Kynance Cove (NT), Lizard Peninsula

Helston and the Lizard Peninsula **5**

Cornwall. ▨ *from Penzance.*
ℹ *79 Meneage St (01326 565431).*
Ⓦ www.go-cornwall.com

THE ATTRACTIVE TOWN of Helston makes a good base for exploring the windswept coastline of the Lizard Peninsula. The town is famous for its Furry Dance which welcomes spring with dancing through the streets *(see p62);* the **Folk Museum** explains the history of this ancient custom. The Georgian houses and inns of Coinagehall Street are a reminder that Helston was once a thriving stannary town where tin ingots were brought for weighing and stamping before being sold. Locally mined tin was brought down river to a harbour at the bottom of this street until access to the sea was blocked in the 13th century by a sand and shingle bar which formed across the estuary. The bar created the freshwater lake, Loe Pool, and an attractive walk skirts its wooded shores. In 1880, Helston's trade was taken over by a new harbour created to the east on the River Helford, at Gweek. Today, Gweek is the home of the **National Seal Sanctuary**, where sick seals are nursed back to health before being released into the sea.

Cornwall's tin mining industry, from Roman to recent times, is covered at the **Poldark Mine** where under-ground tours reveal the working conditions of miners in the 18th century. Another major attraction is **Flambards Village Theme Park,** with its recreation of a Victorian village and of Britain during the Blitz.

Further south, huge satellite dishes rise from the heath-land. The **Goonhilly Earth Station** visitors' centre here explores the world of satellite communications.

Local shops sell souvenirs carved from serpentine, a soft greenish stone which forms the unusual-shaped rocks that rise from the sandy beach at picturesque **Kynance Cove**.

🏛 Folk Museum
Market Place, Helston. **ℂ** *01326 564027.* ◯ *Mon–Sat* ⬤ *Christmas Week.* ▨ ♿ *limited.* ◻

✕ National Seal Sanctuary
Gweek. **ℂ** *01326 221361.* ◯ *daily.*
⬤ *25 Dec.* ▨ ♿ ◻ ◻
Ⓦ www.sealsanctuary.co.uk

🏛 Poldark Mine
Wendron. **ℂ** *01326 573173.*
◯ *Nov–Mar, Jul, Aug: daily; May, Jun, Sep, Oct: Sun–Fri.* ▨ ◻ ◻
◻ Ⓦ www.poldark-mine.co.uk

🏛 Flambards Village Theme Park
Culdrose Manor, Helston. **ℂ** *0845 6018684.* ◯ *Easter–Oct: daily.* ▨
♿ 🍴 ◻ Ⓦ www.flambards.co.uk

🏛 Goonhilly Earth Station
Nr Helston, off B3293. **ℂ** *0800 679593.* ◯ *Apr–Oct: daily.* ▨
♿ ◻ ◻
Ⓦ www.goonhilly.bt.com

Falmouth **6**

Cornwall. ▨ *22,000.* ▤ ▨ ▤
ℹ *28 Killigrew St (01326 312300).*
Ⓦ www.go-cornwall.com

FALMOUTH stands at the point where seven rivers flow into a long stretch of water called the **Carrick Roads**. The drowned river valley is so deep that huge ocean-going ships can sail up almost as far as Truro. Numerous creeks are ideal for boating excursions to view the varied scenery and birdlife.

Falmouth has the third largest naturally deep harbour after Sydney and Rio de Janeiro, and it forms the most interesting part of this seaside resort. On the

---

CORNISH SMUGGLERS

In the days before income tax was invented, the main form of government income came from tax on imported luxury goods, such as brandy and perfume. Huge profits were to be made by evading these taxes, which were at their height during the Napoleonic Wars (1780–1815). Remote Cornwall, with its coves and rivers penetrating deep into the mainland, was prime smuggling territory; estimates put the number of people involved, including women and children, at 100,000. Some notorious families resorted to deliberate wrecking, setting up deceptive lights to lure vessels onto the sharp rocks, in the hope of plundering the wreckage.

harbour waterfront stands the recently constructed **National Maritime Museum Cornwall**, part of a projected large new waterside complex, to include cafés, shops and restaurants. With an exterior that is oak-clad to reflect the history of wooden boat sheds in the area, the museum is dedicated to the great maritime tradition of Cornwall, and contains Britain's finest public collection of historic and contemporary small craft. The building is designed to bring to life the stories of boats, maritime themes and Cornwall's heritage, as well as the story of the people whose lives depended on the sea. It aims to be accessible to the whole family.

The many old houses on the harbour include the striking **Customs House** and the chimney alongside, known as the "King's Pipe" because it was used for burning contraband tobacco seized from smugglers in the 19th century. **Pendennis Castle** and St Mawes Castle opposite, were built by King Henry VIII.

ENVIRONS: To the south, **Glendurgan** (*see p232*) and **Trebah** gardens are both set in sheltered valleys leading down to delightful sandy coves on the Helford River.

Truro Cathedral, designed by J L Pearson and completed in 1910

🏛 National Maritime Museum Cornwall

Discovery Quay, Falmouth.
📞 01326 313388. 🚪 daily.
⬤ public hols. 💺 ♿ 🖥 📷
W www.nmmc.co.uk

♟ Pendennis Castle

(EH) The Headland.
📞 01326 316594. 🚪 daily.
⬤ 24–26 Dec, 1 Jan. 💺 ♿
limited. 💺 📷 🎟

♣ Glendurgan

(NT) Mawnan Smith.
📞 01326 250906. 🚪 mid-Feb–mid-Nov: Tue–Sat & public hols. ⬤ Good Fri. 💺 🖥 📷
W www.nationaltrust.org.uk

♣ Trebah

Mawnan Smith. 📞 01326 250448.
🚪 daily. 🎟 💺 ♿ 🖥
W www.trebah-garden.co.uk

Truro ❼

Cornwall. 🏛 19,000. 🚆 🚌
🛈 Boscawen St (01872 274555).
🛒 Wed (cattle), Wed & Sat (farmers' market). W www.truro.gov.uk

ONCE A market town and port, Truro is now the administrative capital of Cornwall. Truro's many gracious Georgian buildings reflect its prosperity during the tin mining boom of the 1800s. In 1876 the 16th-century parish church was rebuilt to create the first new **cathedral** to be built in England since Wren built St Paul's (*see pp116–17*) in the 17th century. With its central tower, lancet windows and spires, the cathedral is an exuberant building that looks more French than English.

Truro's cobbled streets and alleys lined with craft shops are also a delight to explore. The **Royal Cornwall Museum** provides an excellent introduction to the history of the county with displays on tin mining, Methodism (*see p267*), and smuggling.

ENVIRONS: On the outskirts of the city lie **Trewithen** and **Trelissick** gardens (*see p232*). The former has a rich collection of Asiatic plants.

🏛 Royal Cornwall Museum

River St. 📞 01872 272205. 🚪 Mon–Sat. ⬤ public hols. 💺 ♿ 🖥 📷
W www.royalcornwallmuseum.org.uk

♣ Trewithen

Grampound Rd. 📞 01726 883647.
🚪 Mar–Sep: Mon–Sat (Apr, May: daily). 💺 ♿ 💺 by arrangement. 🖥
📷 W www.trewithengardens.co.uk

♣ Trelissick

(NT) Feock. 📞 01872 862090.
🚪 mid-Feb–Oct: daily. 💺 ♿ 🎟
W www.nationaltrust.org.uk

The "Cornish Alps": china-clay spoil tips north of St Austell

St Austell ❽

Cornwall. 🏛 20,000. 🚆 🚌
🛈 BP Service Station, Southbourne Rd (0870 445 0244). 🛒 Fri–Sun.
W www.cornish-riviera.co.uk

THE BUSY INDUSTRIAL town of St Austell is the capital of the local china-clay industry which rose to importance in the 18th century. Clay is still a vital factor here; until recently, China was the only other place where such quality and quantity of clay could be found. Spoil tips are a prominent feature; on a sunny day they look like snow-covered peaks, meriting the local name the "Cornish Alps".

ENVIRONS: The famous **Lost Gardens of Heligan** are an amazing restoration project to recreate the extraordinary gardens created by the Tremayne family from the 16th century to World War I. At the **Wheal Martyn China Clay Museum**, nature trails weave through clay works that operated from 1878 until the 1920s.

♣ Lost Gardens of Heligan

Pentewan. 📞 01726 845100. 🚪 daily. 💺 ♿ limited. 🎟 🖥 📷
W www.heligan.com

🏛 Wheal Martyn China Clay Museum

Carthew. 📞 01726 850362. 🚪 daily.
💺 ♿ limited. 🖥 📷
W www.wheal-martyn.com

Ship's figure-head, Falmouth

Eden Project ⑨

BUILT INTO THE WALLS OF an abandoned china clay pit, the Eden Project is a global garden for the 21st century and a dramatic setting in which to tell the fascinating story of mankind's dependence on plants. Two futuristic conservatories called biomes have been designed to mimic the environments of warmer climes: one hot and humid, the other warm and dry. Outside, the walls of the pit are planted with species that thrive in the Cornish climate. Unlike a standard conservatory where plants are set out to be admired as species, the Eden Project seeks to educate by telling the story of plants and habitats. The relationship between humans and nature is interpreted by storytellers and artists throughout the site.

④ Tropical South America
Some plants in Amazonia reach massive proportions. The giant waterlilies (Victoria cruziana) *will stretch to 2 m (6 ft) wide.*

③ West Africa
Iboga is central to the African religion Bwiti. Highly hallucinogenic, it is an integral part of initiation ceremonies.

② Malaysia
The Titan arum grows within this rainforest display. The flower will grow to 1.5 m (4 ft) and smell of rotting flesh.

① Oceanic Islands
Set apart from the rest of the world, these islands have many fascinating plants. The rare Madagascar Periwinkle (Catharanthus roseus) *is thought to help cure leukemia.*

THE SITE

Access to the landscape and the biomes is via the visitor centre.

Humid Tropics Biome
① Oceanic Islands
② Malaysia
③ West Africa
④ Tropical South America
⑤ Crops & cultivation

Warm Temperate Biome
⑥ The Mediterranean
⑦ South Africa
⑧ California
⑨ Crops & cultivation

Building Eden

Cornwall's declining china clay industry has left behind many abandoned pits. The Eden Project makes ingenious use of this industrial landscape. After partly infilling a pit, the massive biomes were nestled into its base and walls.

Transparent hexagons made of ultra-light hi-tech plastic

⑤ **Crops and cultivation**
The coffee plant (Coffea arabica) is one of the many plants on display that are used in the manufacture of everyday products.

The entrance to both the Humid Tropics and Warm Temperate Biomes is via The Link, where two restaurants are located.

ᴴUMID TROPICS BIOME

ᴵs vast conservatory houses a lush jungle of 8,000
ᵉs and plants. The dome is high enough to allow
ᵉ rainforest trees to grow to their full height.

ᴵᵗdoor Landscape
- Plants & pollinators
- Plants for Cornish crops
- Plants for taste
- Potatoes
- Sunflowers
- Plants for rope & fibre
- Hemp
- Steppe & prairie
- Eco-engineering
- Beer & brewing
- Tea
- Lavender
- Wheat
- Apples
- Plants for fuel

㉕ Plants in myth & folkore
㉖ Wild Cornwall
㉗ Indigo
㉘ Garden flowers
㉙ Plants for tomorrow's industries
㉚ Flowerless garden
㉛ Plants for fodder
㉜ The Story of the Eden Project
㉝ Wild Chile

KEY

Land Train

0 metres 150
0 yards 150

Lake
Eden Arena
Visitor Centre

View of Polruan across the estuary from Fowey

Fowey ⑩

Cornwall. 🏘 *2,000.* 🚤
🛈 *4 Custom House Hill (01726
833616).* 🅆 *www.fowey.co.uk*

FOWEY (pronounced Foy),
has been immortalized
under the name of Troy Town
in the humorous novels of Sir
Arthur Quiller-Couch (1863–
1944), who lived here in a
house called **The Haven**.
A resort favoured by many
wealthy Londoners with a taste

DAPHNE DU MAURIER

The period romances of
Daphne du Maurier (1907–
89) are inextricably linked
with the wild Cornish landscape where she grew up.
Jamaica Inn established
her reputation in 1936, and
with the publication of
Rebecca two years later
she found herself one of
the most popular authors
of her day. *Rebecca* was
made into a film directed
by Alfred Hitchcock, star-
ring Joan Fontaine and
Lord Laurence Olivier.

for yachting and expensive
seafood restaurants, Fowey is
the most gentrified of the
Cornish seaside towns. The
picturesque charm of the
flower-filled village is undeniable, with its tangle of tiny
steep streets and its views
across the estuary to Polruan.
The church of **St Fimbarrus**
marks the end of the ancient
Saint's Way footpath from
Padstow – a
reminder of the
Celtic missionaries
who arrived on the
shores of Cornwall
to convert people to
Christianity. Its
flower-lined path
leads to a majestic
porch and carved
tower. Inside there
are some fine 17th-
century memorials to
the Rashleigh family
whose seat, Menabilly,
became Daphne du Maurier's
home and featured as Mander-
ley in *Rebecca* (1938).

Jamaica Inn,
Bodmin Moor

ENVIRONS: For a closer look at
the town of **Polruan** and the
ceaseless activity of the harbour there is a number of
river trips up the little creeks.
At the estuary mouth are the
twin towers from which
chains were once hung to de-
mast invading ships – an
effective form of defence.
A fine stretch of coast leads
further east to the picturesque
fishing villages of **Polperro**,
nestling in a narrow green ravine, and neighbouring **Looe**.
Upriver from Fowey is the
tranquil town of **Lostwithiel**.
Perched on a hill just to the
north are the remains of the
Norman **Restormel Castle**.

⚓ **Restormel Castle**
(EH) Lostwithiel. 📞 *01208 872687.*
🕐 *Apr–Oct: daily.* 🏷

Bodmin ⑪

Cornwall. 🚆 *Bodmin Parkway.*
🚌 *Bodmin.* 🛈 *Mount Folly Sq,
Bodmin (01208 76616).*
🅆 *www.bodminlive.com*

BODMIN, CORNWALL'S ancient
county town, lies on the
sheltered western edge of the
great expanse of moorland
that shares its name. The
history and archaeology of
the town and moor is covered by **Bodmin Town
Museum**, while **Bodmin
Jail**, where public executions
took place until 1909, has been
turned into a gruesome tourist attraction. The churchyard
is watered by the ever-gushing
waters of a holy spring, and it
was here that St Guron established a Christian cell in the
6th century. The **church** is
dedicated to St
Petroc, a Welsh
missionary who
founded a mona-
stery here in the
same period, as well
as many others in
the region. The
monastery has dis-
appeared, but the
bones of St Petroc
remain, housed in
a splendid 12th-
century ivory casket in
the church.
  South of Bodmin is the
Lanhydrock estate. Amid its
extensive wooded acres and
formal gardens *(see p232)* lies
the massive house, rebuilt
after a fire in 1881, but retaining some Jacobean features.
The labyrinth of corridors and
rooms illustrates life in a
Victorian manor house and
the fine 17th-century plaster
ceiling in the Long Gallery
depicts scenes from the Bible.
  The desolate wilderness of
Bodmin Moor is noted for its
network of prehistoric field
boundaries. The main attraction, however, is the 18th-
century **Jamaica Inn**, made
famous by Daphne du
Maurier's tale of smuggling
and romance. Today there is
a restaurant and bar based on
du Maurier's novel, and a
small museum. A 30-minute
walk from the Inn is **Dozmary
Pool**, reputed to be bottom-
less until it dried up in 1976.

The ruins of Tintagel Castle on the north coast of Cornwall

According to legend, the dying King Arthur's sword Excalibur was thrown into the pool.

To the east is **Altarnun**. Its spacious 15th-century church of **St Nonna** is known as the "Cathedral of the Moor".

🏛 **Bodmin Town Museum**
Mt Folly Sq, Bodmin. ⌷ 01208 77067. ◯ Easter–Oct: Mon–Sat, Good Fri. ● public hols. 🚻 limited. 🅿
🚽 **Bodmin Jail**
Berrycombe Rd, Bodmin. ⌷ 01208 76292. ◯ daily. ● 25 Dec. 🅿
🎬 🍴
🚽 **Lanhydrock**
(NT) Bodmin. ⌷ 01208 73320.
House ◯ Apr–Oct: Tue–Sun & public hols. **Gardens** ◯ daily. 🅿
🎬 🚻 🍴

Tintagel ⓬

Cornwall. 🏠 1,700. 🛈 01840 779084. 🚌 Thu (summer).
🌐 www.tintagelweb.co.uk

THE ROMANTIC and mysterious ruins of **Tintagel Castle**, built around 1240 by Earl Richard of Cornwall, sit high on a hill-top surrounded by slate cliffs. Access to the castle is via two steep staircases clinging to the cliffside where pink thrift and purple sea lavender abound.

The earl was persuaded to build in this isolated, windswept spot by the popular belief, derived from Geoffrey of Monmouth's fictitious *History of the Kings of Britain,* that this was the birthplace of the legendary King Arthur.

Large quantities of fine eastern Mediterranean pottery dating from around the 5th century have been discovered, indicating that the site was an important trading centre, long before the medieval castle was built. Whoever lived here, perhaps the ancient Kings of Cornwall, could evidently afford a luxurious lifestyle.

A clifftop path leads from the castle to Tintagel's **church**, which has Norman and Saxon masonry. In Tintagel village the **Old Post Office** is a rare example of a 14th-century Cornish manor house, restored and furnished with 17th-century oak furniture.

ENVIRONS: A short distance to the east, **Boscastle** is a pretty National Trust village. The River Valency runs down the middle of the main street to the fishing harbour, which is sheltered from the sea by high slate cliffs. Access from the harbour to the sea is via a channel cut through the rocks.

♠ **Tintagel Castle**
Off High St. ⌷ 01840 770328. ◯ daily. ● 24–26 Dec, 1 Jan. 🎬
🚽 **Old Post Office**
(NT) Fore St. ⌷ 01840 770024. ◯ Apr–Oct: daily. 🅿 🎬

Bude ⓭

Cornwall. 🏠 9,000. 🛈 Crescent car park (01288 354240). 🚌 Fri (summer). 🌐 www.visitbude.co.uk

WONDERFUL beaches around this area make Bude a popular resort for families. The expanse of clean golden sand that attracts visitors today once made Bude a bustling port. Shelly, lime-rich sand was transported along a canal to inland farms where it was used to neutralize the acidic soil. The canal was abandoned in 1880 but a short stretch survives, providing a haven for birds such as kingfishers and herons.

Kingfisher

KING ARTHUR

Historians think the legendary figure of King Arthur has some basis in historical fact. He was probably a Romano-British chieftain or warrior who led British resistance to the Saxon invasion of the 6th century *(see pp46–7).* Geoffrey of Monmouth's *History of the Kings of Britain* (1139) introduced Arthur to literature with an account of the many legends connected with him – how he became king by removing the sword Excalibur from a stone, his final battle with the treacherous Mordred, and the story of the Knights of the Round Table *(see p158).* Other writers, such as Alfred, Lord Tennyson, took up these stories and elaborated on them.

King Arthur, from a 14th-century chronicle by Peter of Langtoft

Clovelly ⓮

Devon. ⚇ 350. 📞 01237 431781.
Town & Visitors' Centre ☐ daily.
⬤ 25 Dec. ♿ ⚓ Visitors' Centre.
🆆 www.clovelly.co.uk

CLOVELLY has been a noted
beauty spot since the novelist Charles Kingsley (1819–
75) wrote about it in his
stirring story of the Spanish
Armada, *Westward Ho!* (1855).
The whole village is privately
owned and has been turned
into a tourist attraction, with
little sign of the flourishing
fishing industry to which it
owed its birth. It is a charming,
picturesque village with
steep, traffic-free cobbled
streets rising up the cliff from
the harbourside, white-washed
houses and gardens brimming
with brightly coloured flowers.
There are superb views from
the lookout points and fine
coastal paths to explore from
the tiny quay.

Hobby Drive is a scenic 3-
mile (5-km) approach on foot
to the village which runs
through woodland along the
coast. The road was con-
structed in 1811–29 to give

Bideford's medieval bridge, 203 m (666 ft) long with 24 arches

employment to local men who
had been made redundant at
the end of the Napoleonic
Wars *(see pp54–5)*.

Bideford ⓯

Devon. ⚇ 14,000. 🚌 ⓘ *Victoria
Park (01237 477676).* �
Tue, Sat.

STRUNG OUT along the boat-
filled estuary of the River
Torridge, Bideford grew and
thrived on importing tobacco
from the New World. Some
17th-century merchants'
houses survive in Bridgeland
Street, including the splendid
bay-windowed house at No. 28
(1693). Beyond is Mill Street,

leading to the parish church
and the fine medieval bridge.
The quay stretches from here
to a pleasant park and a
statue which commemorates
Charles Kingsley, whose novels
helped bring visitors to the
area in the 19th century.

ENVIRONS: To the west of
Bideford, the village **Westward
Ho!** was built in the late 19th
century and named after
Kingsley's popular novel. The
development failed and the
Victorian villas and hotels are
now part of a holiday resort.
Rudyard Kipling *(see p151)*
was at school here and the
hill to the south, known as
Kipling Tors, was the background for *Stalky & Co* (1899).

Also to the west is **Hartland
Abbey**, built as a monastery
c.1157, now a family home.
Visitors can enjoy a museum,
art and antiques collections as
well as informal gardens and
a woodland walk.

Henry Williamson's *Tarka
the Otter* (1927) describes the
otters of the **Torridge Valley**
and naturalists are hoping to
reintroduce otters here. Part
of a Tarka Trail has been laid
out along the Torridge and
bicycles can be hired from the
old railway station. The trail
passes close to the magnificent **Rosemoor Garden**.

Day trips run from either
Bideford or Ilfracombe (depending on the tide) to **Lundy**
island, which is abundant in
birds and wildlife.

🌿 **RHS Rosemoor Garden**
Great Torrington. 📞 01805 624067.
☐ daily. ⬤ 25 Dec. ♿ ⚓ 🍴 ☐
🆆 www.rhs.org.uk
🏛 **Hartland Abbey** nr. Bideford.
📞 01237 441264. ☐ Apr–Oct:
2–5:30pm Tue (Jul–Aug only), Wed,
Thu, Sun, public hols. ♿ ☐

Fishing boats in Clovelly's harbour

Fishermen's cottages, Appledore

Appledore ⑯

Devon. 🎫 3,000. 🚉 Bideford
(01237 477676).

APPLEDORE'S remote position at the tip of the Torridge Estuary has helped to preserve its charms intact. Busy boatyards line the long riverside quay, which is also the departure point for fishing trips and ferries to the sandy beaches of Braunton Burrows on the opposite shore. Timeworn Regency houses line the main street which runs parallel to the quay, and behind is a network of narrow cobbled lanes with 18th-century fishermen's cottages. Several shops retain their original bow-windows and sell an assortment of crafts, antiques and souvenirs.

Uphill from the quay is the **North Devon Maritime Museum**, with an exhibition on the experiences of Devon emigrants in Australia and displays explaining the work of local shipyards. The tiny **Victorian Schoolroom** which is affiliated to the museum, shows various documentary videos on local trades such as fishing and shipbuilding.

🏛 **North Devon Maritime Museum**
Odun Rd. 📞 01237 474852. 🕐 May–Sep: daily; Apr, Oct: pm. 🅿 limited.
📷 🖥 www.devonmuseums.net

Barnstaple ⑰

Devon. 🎫 33,000. 🚉 🚌 🚇 The Square (01271 375000). 🛍 Mon–Sat.
🖥 www.staynorthdevon.co.uk

ALTHOUGTH BARNSTAPLE is an important distribution centre for the whole region, its town centre remains calm due to the exclusion of traffic. The massive glass-roofed **Pannier Market** (1855) has stalls of organic fruit and vegetables, honey and eggs, much of it produced by farmers' wives to supplement their income. Nearby is **St Peter's Church** with its twisted broach spire, said to have been caused by a lightning strike which warped the timbers in 1810.

On the Strand is a wonderful arcade topped with a statue of Queen Anne, now the **Heritage Centre**. This was built as an exchange where merchants traded the contents of their cargo boats moored on the River Taw alongside. Nearby is the 15th-century bridge and the **Museum of Barnstaple and North Devon**, where displays cover local history and the 700-year-old pottery industry, as well as local wildlife, such as the otters. The 180-mile (290 km) Tarka Trail circuits around Barnstaple; 35 miles (56 km) of it can be cycled.

ENVIRONS: Just west of Barnstaple, **Braunton "Great Field"** covers over 120 ha (300 acres) and is a well-preserved relic of medieval open-field cultivation. Beyond lies **Braunton Burrows**, one of the most extensive wild-dune reserves in Britain. It is a must for plant enthusiasts who would like to spot sea kale, sea holly, sea lavender and horned poppies growing in their natural habitat. The sandy beaches and pounding waves at nearby Croyde and Woolacombe, are favourites among surfing enthusiasts, but there are also calmer areas of warm shallow water and rock pools.

Arlington Court, north of Barnstaple, has a collection of model ships, magnificent perennial borders and a lake. The stables house a collection of horse-drawn vehicles. Carriage rides are available.

Statue of Queen Anne (1708)

🏛 **Museum of Barnstaple and North Devon**
The Square. 📞 01271 346747. 🕐 Mon–Sat. 🔴 24 Dec–1 Jan. ♿ limited.
🖥 www.devonmuseums.net
🏛 **Arlington Court**
(NT) Arlington. 📞 01271 850296.
🕐 Apr–Oct: Wed–Mon. 🅿 ♿ limited. 📷 📱

Barnstaple's Pannier Market

The village of Lynmouth

Lynton and Lynmouth ⑱

Devon. 👥 2,000. 🚉 ℹ️ *Town Hall, Lee Rd (015987 52225). See pp238–9.* 🌐 www.lyntourism.co.uk

Sɪᴛᴜᴀᴛᴇᴅ ᴀᴛ ᴛʜᴇ ᴘᴏɪɴᴛ where the East and West Lyn rivers meet the sea, Lynmouth is a picturesque, though rather commercialized, fishing village. The pedestrianized main street, lined with shops selling clotted cream and seaside souvenirs, runs parallel to the Lyn, now made into a canal with high embankments as a precaution against flash floods. One flood devastated the town at the height of the holiday season in 1952. The scars caused by the flood, which was fuelled by heavy rain on Exmoor, are now overgrown by trees in the pretty **Glen Lyn Gorge**, which leads north out of the village. Lynmouth's sister town, Lynton, is a mainly Victorian village perched on the clifftop 130 m (427 ft) above, giving lovely views across the Bristol Channel to the Welsh coast. It can be reached from the harbour front by a cliff railway, by road or by a steep path.

Environs: Lynmouth makes an excellent starting point for walks on Exmoor. There is a 2 mile (3 km) trail that leads southeast to tranquil **Watersmeet** *(see p239)*. On the western edge of Exmoor, **Combe Martin** *(see p238)* lies in a sheltered valley. On the main street, lined with Victorian villas, is the 18th-century Pack of Cards Inn, built by a gambler with 52 windows, for each card in the pack.

Exeter ⑲

Eᴇ̲xᴇᴛᴇʀ ɪs ᴅᴇᴠᴏɴ's ᴄᴀᴘɪᴛᴀʟ, a bustling and lively city with a great deal of character, despite the World War II bombing that destroyed much of its city centre. Built high on a plateau above the River Exe, the city is encircled by substantial sections of Roman and medieval wall, and the street plan has not changed much since the Romans first laid out what is now the High Street. Elsewhere the Cathedral Close forms a pleasant green, and there are cobbled streets and narrow alleys which invite leisurely exploration. For shoppers there is a wide selection of big stores and smaller speciality shops.

Exploring Exeter

The intimate green and the close surrounding Exeter's distinctive cathedral were the setting for Anthony Trollope's novel *He Knew He Was Right* (1869). Full of festive crowds listening to buskers in the summer, the close presents an array of architectural styles. One of the finest buildings here is the Elizabethan **Mol's Coffee House**. Among the other historic buildings that survived World War II are the magnificent **Guildhall** (1330) on the High Street (one of Britain's oldest civic buildings), the opulent **Custom House** (1681) by the quay, and the elegant 18th-century **Rougement House** which stands near the remains of a Norman **castle** built by William the Conqueror *(see pp46–7)*.

The port area has been transformed into a tourist attraction with its early 19th-century warehouses converted into craft shops, antique galleries and cafés. Boats can be hired for cruising down the short stretch of canal. The **Quay House Interpretation Centre**

The timber-framed Mol's Coffee House (1596), Cathedral Close

West front and south tower, Cathedral Church of St Peter

(open daily April–October; weekends November–March) has audio-visual and other displays on the history of Exeter.

🏛 Cathedral Church of St Peter

Cathedral Close. 📞 01392 255573. 🕐 *daily.* 🏛 ♿ 🍴
Exeter's cathedral is one of the most gloriously ornamented in Britain. Except for the two Norman towers, the cathedral is mainly 14th century and built in the style aptly known as Decorated because of the swirling geometric patterns of the stone work. The West Front, the largest single collection (66) of medieval figure sculptures in England, includes kings, apostles and prophets. Started in the 14th century, it was completed by 1450. Inside, the splendid Gothic vaulting sweeps from one end of the church to the other, impressive in its uniformity and punctuated by gaily painted ceiling bosses.

Among the tombs around the choir is that of Edward II's treasurer, Walter de Stapledon (1261–1326), who was murdered by a mob in London. Stapledon raised much of the money needed to fund the building of this cathedral

Collection of shells and other objects in the library of A La Ronde

VISITORS' CHECKLIST

Devon. 🏠 111,000. ✈ 5 miles
(8 km) east. 🚆 Exeter St David's,
Bonhay Rd; Exeter Central, Queen
St. 🚌 Paris St. ℹ Paris St
(01392 265700). 🚋 daily.
Ⓦ www.exeter.gov.uk

North of Sidmouth lies the magnificent church at **Ottery St Mary**. Built in 1338–42 by Bishop Grandisson, the church is clearly a scaled-down version of Exeter Cathedral, which he also helped build. A memorial in the churchyard wall recalls the fact the poet Coleridge was born in the town in 1772.

Nearby **Honiton** is famous for its extraordinarily intricate and delicate lace, made here since Elizabethan times.

To the north of Exeter, **Killerton** is home to the National Trust's costume collection. Here, displays of bustles and corsets and vivid tableaux illustrate aristocratic fashions from the 18th century to the present day.

Further north near Tiverton, is **Knightshayes Court**, a Victorian Gothic mansion with fine gardens (see p233).

and for Exeter College in Oxford (see pp210–15).

🏛 **Underground Passages**
Roman Gate Passage. 📞 01392 665 887. ☐ Jul–Sep: Mon–Sat; Oct–Jun: Tue–Fri (pm), Sat. ● 25, 26 Dec, 1 Jan. 🚻 🎫

Under the city centre lie the remains of Exeter's medieval water-supply system. An excellent video and guided tour explain how the stone-lined tunnels were built in the 14th and 15th centuries on a slight gradient to bring in fresh water from springs outside the town.

🏛 **St Nicholas Priory**
The Mint. 📞 01392 265858. ☐ Easter–Oct: Mon, Wed & Sat pm.

Built in the 12th century, this building has retained many original features and rooms. These trace its fascinating history from austere monastic beginnings, through its secular use as a Tudor residence for wealthy merchants, to its 20th-century incarnation as five separate premises occupied by various tradesmen including a bootmaker and an upholsterer.

🏛 **Royal Albert Memorial Museum and Art Gallery**
Queen St. 📞 01392 265858. ☐ Mon–Sat. ● 24–26 Dec, 1 Jan, Good Fri, public hols. 🚻 🛗 ▭

This museum has a wonderfully varied collection, including Roman remains, a zoo of stuffed animals, West Country art and a particularly good ethnographic display. Highlights include displays on silverware, watches and clocks.

19th-century head of an Oba, Royal Albert Museum

ENVIRONS: South of Exeter on the A376, the eccentric **A La Ronde** is a 16-sided house built in 1796 by two spinster cousins, who decorated the interior with shells, feathers and souvenirs gathered while on tour in Europe.

Further east, the unspoilt Regency town of **Sidmouth** lies in a sheltered bay. There is an eclectic array of architecture, the earliest buildings dating from the 1820s when Sidmouth became a popular summer resort. Thatched cottages stand opposite huge Edwardian villas, and elegant terraces line the seafront. In summer the town hosts the famous International Festival of Folk Arts (see p63).

🏠 **A La Ronde**
(NT) Summer Lane, Exmouth. 📞 01395 265514. ☐ Apr–Oct: Sun–Thu. 🎫 ▭ 🚻

🏠 **Killerton**
(NT) Broadclyst. 📞 01392 881345. **House** ☐ Apr–Oct: daily. **Garden** ☐ daily all year. 🎫 🛗 ▭ 🚻

🌿 **Knightshayes Court**
(NT) Bolham. 📞 01884 254665. ☐ Apr–Nov: Sat–Thu, Good Fri (gardens Apr–Nov daily). 🎫 🛗 limited. 🚻 🚻

Mexican dancer at Sidmouth's International Festival of Folk Arts

Torbay ⑳

Torbay. 🚂 ✈ *Torquay, Paignton.*
ℹ *Vaughan Parade, Torquay*
(01803 297428).
🌐 www.theenglishriviera.co.uk

T HE THREE SEASIDE TOWNS of Torquay, Paignton and Brixham form an almost continuous resort around the great sweep of sandy beach and calm blue waters of Torbay. Because of its mild climate, extensive semi-tropical gardens and exuberant Victorian hotel architecture, this popular coastline has been dubbed the English Riviera. In its heyday, Torbay was patronized by the wealthy, especially during Victorian times. Today, mass entertainment is the theme and there are plenty of attractions of this type, mostly in and around Torquay.

Torre Abbey includes the remains of a monastery founded in 1196 and now serves as an art gallery. There is a magnificent barn in the grounds where prisoners captured from the Spanish

Armada of 1588 were once held. **Torquay Museum** nearby covers natural history and archaeology, including finds from **Kents Cavern**, on the outskirts of the town. This is one of England's most important prehistoric sites and the spectacular caves serve as the background for displays on people and animals who lived here up to 350,000 years ago.

The charming miniature town of **Babbacombe Model Village** lies to the north of Torquay, while a mere mile (1.5 km) inland is the lovely little village of **Cockington**. Visitors travel by horse-drawn carriage to view the preserved Tudor manor house, church, thatched cottages and forge.

In Paignton, the celebrated **Paignton Zoo** teaches children about the planet's wildlife, and from here you can take the steam railway – an ideal way to visit Dartmouth.

Continuing south from Paignton, the pretty town of Brixham was once England's most prosperous fishing port.

Bayards Cove, Dartmouth

🏛 **Torre Abbey**
King's Drive, Torquay. 🕻 *01803*
293593. ◯ *Apr–Oct: daily.* 🎫 🖥
🏛 **Torquay Museum**
Babbacombe Rd, Torquay. 🕻 *01803*
293975. ◯ *daily (Nov–Easter: Mon–Sat).* ● *Christmas wk.* 🎫 ♿ 🖥 📷
🏛 **Kents Cavern**
Ilsham Rd, Torquay. 🕻 *01803 294059.*
◯ *daily.* ● *25 Dec.* 🎫 ♿ 📷 🖥
🏛 **Babbacombe Model Village**
Hampton Ave, Torquay. 🕻 *01803*
315315. ◯ *daily.* 🎫 ♿ 🖥
🐾 **Paignton Zoo**
Totnes Rd, Paignton. 🕻 *01803*
557479. ◯ *daily.* 🎫 ♿ 🍴 📷

Dartmouth ㉑

Devon. 🏘 *5,500.* 🚂 ℹ *Mayors Ave*
(01803 834224). 🚌 *Tue–Fri am.*
🌐 www.dartmouth-information.co.uk

S ITTING HIGH ON THE HILL above the River Dart is the **Royal Naval College**, where British naval officers have trained since 1905. Dartmouth has always been an important port and it was from here that English fleets set sail to join the Second and Third Crusades. Some 18th-century houses adorn the cobbled quay of Bayards Cove, while carved timber buildings line the 17th-century Butterwalk, home to **Dartmouth Museum**. To the south is **Dartmouth Castle** (1388).

🏛 **Dartmouth Museum**
Butterwalk. 🕻 *01803 832923.*
◯ *Mon–Sat.* ● *25, 26 Dec, 1 Jan.*
🎫 📷 🌐 www.devonmuseums.net
⚓ **Dartmouth Castle**
(EH) Castle Rd. 🕻 *01803 833588.*
◯ *daily (Nov–Easter: Wed–Sun).*
● *24–26 Dec, 1 Jan.* 📷 🎫 🖥

Torquay, on the "English Riviera"

Stained glass window in Blessed Sacrament Chapel, Buckfast Abbey

Totnes ㉒

Devon. 🏔 7,500. 🚂 🚌 ⛴
ℹ Coronation Rd (01803 863168).
🗓 Tue am (May–Sep), Fri, Sat.
🌐 www.totnesinfo.org.uk

Totnes sits at the highest navigable point on the River Dart with a Norman **castle** perched high on the hill above. Linking the two is the steep High Street, lined with bow-windowed Elizabethan houses. Bridging the street is the **Eastgate**, part of the medieval town wall. Life in the town's heyday is explored in the **Totnes Elizabethan Museum**, which also has a room devoted to the mathematician Charles Babbage (1791–1871), who is regarded as the pioneer of modern computers. There is a **Guildhall**, and a **church** with a delicately carved and gilded rood screen. On Tuesdays in the summer, market stallholders dress in Elizabethan costume.

Environs: A few miles north of Totnes, **Dartington Hall** has 10 ha (25 acres) of lovely gardens and a famous music school where concerts are held in the timbered 14th-century Great Hall.

Stallholders in Totnes market

♣ Totnes Castle
(EH) Castle St. 📞 01803 864406.
🕐 Apr–Oct: daily. 🎟
🏛 Totnes Elizabethan Museum
Fore St. 📞 01803 863821. 🕐 Easter–Oct: Mon–Fri. 🎟 ♿ limited.
⛪ Guildhall
Rampart Walk. 📞 01803 862147.
🕐 Apr–Oct: Mon–Fri. 🎟
♣ Dartington Hall Gardens
📞 01803 862367. 🕐 daily.
🌐 www.dartingtonhalltrust.com

Buckfastleigh ㉓

Devon. 🏔 3,300. 🚂 ℹ Fore St (01364 644522).

This market town, situated on the edge of Dartmoor *(see pp282–3)*, is dominated by **Buckfast Abbey**. The original abbey, founded in Norman times, fell into ruin after the Dissolution of the Monasteries and it was not until 1882 that a small group of French Benedictine monks set up a new abbey here. Work on the present building was financed by donations and carried out by the monks. The abbey was completed in 1938 and lies at the heart of a thriving community. The fine mosaics and modern stained glass window are also the work of the monks.

Nearby is the **Buckfast Butterfly Farm and Otter Sanctuary,** and the **South Devon Steam Railway** terminus where steam trains leave for Totnes.

🏰 Buckfast Abbey
Buckfastleigh. 📞 01364 645500.
🕐 daily. 🌑 25–27 Dec, Good Fri. ♿
🍴 🚻 🌐 www.buckfast.org.uk
✗ Buckfast Butterfly Farm and Otter Sanctuary
Buckfastleigh. 📞 01364 642916.
🕐 Easter–Nov: daily. 🎟 ♿ 🌐
www.ottersandbutterfliestrust.com

Burgh Island ㉔

Devon. 🚂 Plymouth, then taxi.
ℹ Kingsbridge (01548 853195).
🌐 www.kingsbridgeinfo.co.uk

The short walk across the sands at low tide from Bigbury-on-Sea to Burgh Island takes you back to the era of the 1920s and 1930s. It was here that the millionaire Archibald Nettlefold built the luxury **Burgh Island Hotel** *(see p553)* in 1929. Created in Art Deco style with a natural rock sea-bathing pool, this was the exclusive retreat of figures such as the Duke of Windsor and Noel Coward. The restored hotel is worth a visit for the photographs of its heyday and the Art Deco fittings. You can also explore the island and **Pilchard Inn** (1336), reputed to be haunted by the ghost of a smuggler.

The Art Deco style bar in Burgh Island Hotel

Plymouth 25

Plymouth. 🏙 250,000. ✈ ⛴ 🚉
🚌 🛈 *Island House, The Barbican.*
(01752 304849). 🗓 *daily.*
w www.plymouth.gov.uk

THE TINY PORT from which
Drake, Raleigh, the Pilgrim
Fathers, Cook and Darwin all
set sail on pioneering voyages
has now grown to a substantial city, much of it boldly
rebuilt after wartime
bombing. Old
Plymouth clusters
around the **Hoe**,
the famous patch of
turf on which Sir
Francis Drake is
said to have calmly
finished his game
of bowls as the
Spanish Armada
approached the port in 1588
(see pp50–51). Today the Hoe
is a pleasant park and parade
ground surrounded by mem-
orials to naval men, including
Drake himself. Alongside is
Charles II's **Royal Citadel**,
built to guard the harbour in

Drake's coat of arms

the 1660s. A popular attraction
is **Plymouth Dome**, a visitor
centre which uses high-tech
displays to explain Plymouth's
past and present, including
live satellite weather pictures
and radar screens for monitor-
ing ships. On the harbour is
the **National Marine
Aquarium**. Nearby is the
Mayflower Stone and Steps,
the spot where the Pilgrim
Fathers set sail for the New
World in England's
third and success-
ful attempt at colo-
nization in 1620.

ENVIRONS: A boat
tour of the harbour
is the best way to
see Plymouth's
dockyards where
warships have been
built since the Napoleonic
Wars. There are also splendid
views of various fine gardens,
such as **Mount Edgcumbe
Park** *(see p232),* scattered
around the coastline of the
Plymouth Sound. East of the
city, the 18th-century **Saltram**

**Mid-18th-century carved wood
chimneypiece, Saltram House**

House has two rooms by
Adam *(see pp24–5)* and portraits by Reynolds, who was
born in nearby Plympton.

🏰 **Royal Citadel**
(EH) The Hoe. 📞 *0117 9750700.*
🗓 *call for details.* 🎟 *only.* ♿

🏛 **Plymouth Dome**
The Hoe. 📞 *01752 603300.* 🗓 *Apr–
Oct: daily; Nov–Mar: Tue–Sat.* 🎟 ♿
🖥 🍴

🐟 **National Marine Aquarium**
Rope Walk, Coxside. 📞 *01752
600301.* 🗓 *daily.* ⬤ *25 Dec.* 🎟 ♿
w www.national-aquarium.co.uk

⚓ **Mount Edgcumbe Park**
Cremyll, Torpoint. ⛴ *from Torpoint
car park.* 📞 *01752 822236.* **House**
🗓 *Mar–Nov: Sun–Thu.* **Grounds** 🗓
all year. 🎟 ♿ 🖥 🍴

🏰 **Saltram House**
(NT) Plympton. 📞 *01752 333500.*
Gallery 🗓 *Mar–Dec: Sat–Thu; Jan,
Feb: Sat, Sun.* **Gardens** 🗓 *all year.*
🎟 ♿ 🍴 🖥 *open all year.* 🍴

Buckland Abbey 26

(NT) Yelverton, Devon. 📞 *01822
853607.* 🚌 *from Yelverton.* 🗓
Fri–Wed (Nov–Mar: Sat & Sun pm).
⬤ *call for details.* 🎟 ♿ 🍴 🍴

FOUNDED BY the Cistercian
monks in 1278, Buckland
Abbey was converted to a
house after the Dissolution of
the Monasteries and became
the home of Drake from
1581–96. Many of the monastic buildings survive in a
garden setting, the most
impressive being the 14th-
century tithe barn *(see p28).*
Part of the house explains
Drake's life and times through
paintings and memorabilia.

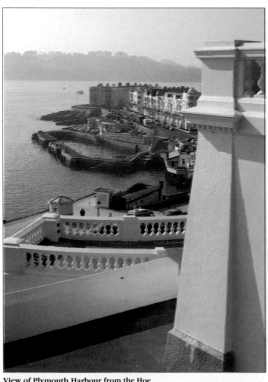

View of Plymouth Harbour from the Hoe

Cotehele 27

(NT) St Dominick, Cornwall. **[** *01579 351346.* **≢** *Calstock.* **House** ○ *Apr–Oct: Sat–Thu & Good Fri.* **Grounds** ○ *daily.* 🅿 ♨ ♿ *limited.* 🍴 ▯

MAGNIFICENT WOODLAND and lush river scenery make Cotehele (pronounced Coteal) one of the most delightful spots on the River Tamar and a rewarding day can be spent exploring the estate. Far from civilization, tucked into its wooded fold in the Cornish countryside, Cotehele has slumbered for 500 years. The main attraction is the house and valley garden at its centre. Built mainly between 1489 and 1520, it is a rare example of a medieval house, set around three courtyards with a magnificent open hall, kitchen, chapel and a warren of private parlours and chambers. The romance of the house is enhanced by colourful terraced gardens to the east, leading via a tunnel into a richly planted valley garden. The path through this garden passes a large domed medieval dovecote and descends to a quay, to which lime and coal were once shipped. There are fine views up and down the winding reed-fringed Tamar from Prospect Tower, and a gallery on the quayside specializes in local arts and crafts. The estate includes a village, a quay with a small maritime museum, working mill buildings, ancient lime kilns and workshops with 19th-century equipment.

Spanish Armada and British fleets in the English Channel, 1588

SIR FRANCIS DRAKE

Sir Francis Drake (c.1540–1596) was the first Englishman to circumnavigate the globe and he was knighted by Elizabeth I in 1580. Four years later he introduced tobacco and potatoes to England, after bringing home 190 colonists who had tried to establish a settlement in Virginia. To many, however, Drake was no more than an opportunistic rogue, renowned for his exploits as a "privateer", the polite name for a pirate. Catholic Spain was the bitter enemy and Drake further endeared himself to queen and people by his part in the victory over Philip II's Armada *(see pp50–51)*, defeated by bad weather and the buccaneering spirit of the English.

Morwellham Quay 28

Near Tavistock, Devon. **[** *01822 832766.* **≢** *Gunnislake.* ○ *Easter–Oct: daily; Nov–Mar: groups only.* 🅿 ♨ ♿ *limited.* 🍴 ▯ Ⓦ *www.morwellham-quay.co.uk*

MORWELLHAM QUAY was a neglected and overgrown industrial site until 1970, when members of a local trust began restoring the abandoned cottages, schoolhouse, farmyards, quay and copper mines to their original condition.

Today, Morwellham Quay is a thriving and rewarding industrial museum, where you can easily spend a whole day partaking in the typical activities of a Victorian village, from preparing the shire horses for a day's work, to riding a tramway deep into a copper mine in the hillside behind the village. The museum is brought to life by characters in costumes, some of whom give demonstrations throughout the day. You can watch, or lend a hand to the

Industrial relics at Morwellham Quay in the Tamar Valley

cooper while he builds a barrel, attend a lesson in the schoolroom, take part in Victorian playground games or dress up in 19th-century hooped skirts, bonnets, top hats or jackets. The staff, who convincingly play the part of villagers, lead you through their lives and impart a huge amount of information about the history of this small copper-mining community.

Medieval dovecote in the gardens of Cotehele estate

Dartmoor National Park ㉘

THE WILD AND OPEN MOORLAND of Dartmoor's bleak and isolated heart provided the eerie background for Conan Doyle's thriller, *The Hound of the Baskervilles* (1902). Here at Princetown, surrounded by gaunt weathered outcrops of granite tors is Britain's most secure prison. Also dotting the landscape are scores of prehistoric remains which have survived because of the durability of granite. Elsewhere the mood is very different. Streams tumble through wooded and boulder-strewn ravines forming pretty cascades and waterfalls, and cosy thatched cottages nestle in the sheltered valleys around the margins of the moor offering cream teas and warming fires to weary walkers.

Buzzard

Characteristic moorland near Drewsteignton

Okehampton has the Museum of Dartmoor Life and a ruined 14th-century castle.

Lydford Gorge (open Apr–Oct) is a dramatic wooded ravine, leading to a waterfall.

Brentor
This volcanic hill crowned by a tiny church (first built in 1130) is visible for miles.

The Ministry of Defence uses much of this area for training but access is available most days.

Main information centre

KEY

![info]	Tourist information
▬▬	A road
▭▭	B road
┄┄	Minor road
☀	Viewpoint

0 kilometres   5

0 miles   5

MELDON RESERVOIR

High Willhays
621 m
2,038 ft

MINISTRY OF DEFENCE FIRING RANGE

Postbridge

Two Bridges

Merrivale

Blackbrook

Princetown

BURRATOR RESERVOIR

Yelverton

PLYMOUTH

LAUNCESTON

Lydford

Tavistock

LISKEARD

West Okement

Walkham

Meavy

Plym

A386

Okehampton

Postbridge
Dartmoor's northern moor can be explored from the village of Postbridge. The gently rolling moorland is crossed by many drystone walls.

PLYMOUTH
Ivyb

Dartmoor Ponies
These small, tough ponies have lived wild on the moor since at least the 10th century.

Grimspound is the impressive site of Bronze Age huts built nearly 4,000 years ago.

Castle Drogo is a magnificent mock-castle built by the architect Sir Edwin Lutyens *(see p25)* in 1910–30.

(see p25)

(see p159)

VISITORS' CHECKLIST

Devon. 🚉 🚌 *Exeter, Plymouth, Totnes then bus.* ℹ️ *High Moorland, Princetown (01822 890414).* **Okehampton Castle**, Castle Lane, Okehampton. (*01837 52844.* ◯ *Apr–Oct: daily.* ● *Nov–Mar.* 🖼️ **Museum of Dartmoor Life**, West St, Okehampton. (*01837 52295.* ◯ *Easter–Oct: Mon–Sat (Jun–Sep: daily); Nov–Easter: Mon–Fri.* ● *24 Dec–1 Jan.* 🖼️ 🚻 *limited.* **Castle Drogo (NT)**, Drewsteignton. (*01647 433306.* ◯ *Apr–Nov: Wed–Mon.* **Gardens** ◯ *daily.* 🖼️ 🚻 *gardens only.* 🚻 🔲 🔲 W www.dartmoor-npa.gov.uk

Becky Falls is a 22 m (72 ft) waterfall set in delightful woodlands.

EXETER Drewsteignton · Teign · EXETER · Moretonhampstead · WORTHY OTR · Bovey · Manaton · A382 · EXETER · Bovey Tracey · Buckland-in-the-Moor · A38 · ENFORD ESEVOIR · Ashburton · Buckfastleigh · Dart · VON DAM ESEVOIR · A38

Bovey Tracey has an extensive woodland reserve.

Haytor Rocks is one of the most accessible of the many tors.

South Devon Steam Railway

Buckfast Abbey was founded by King Canute *(see p159)* in 1018.

Dartmoor Butterfly and Otter Sanctuary

Dartmeet marks the lovely confluence point of the East and West Dart rivers.

Buckland-in-the-Moor
This is one of the most picturesque thatch-and-granite villages on Dartmoor.

Hound Tor
This tor (a pile of rocks, probably Celtic in origin) includes the remains of a medieval settlement which was inhabited from Saxon times until around 1300.

THE
MIDLANDS

The Midlands at a Glance

T HE MIDLANDS IS AN AREA that embraces wonderful landscapes and massive industrial cities. Visitors come to discover the wild beauty of the rugged Peaks, cruise slowly along the Midlands canals on gaily painted narrowboats and explore varied and enchanting gardens. The area encompasses the full range of English architecture from mighty cathedrals and humble churches to charming spa towns, stately homes and country cottages. There are fascinating industrial museums, many in picturesque settings.

Cheshire

Staffordshire

Tissington Trail (see p325) *combines a walk through scenic Peak District countryside with an entertaining insight into the ancient custom of well-dressing.*

Shropshire

THE HEART OF ENGLAND
(see pp292–317)

Worcestershire

Ironbridge Gorge (see pp302–3) *was the birthplace of the Industrial Revolution (see pp336–7). Now a World Heritage Centre, the site is a reminder of the lovely countryside in which the original factories were located.*

Herefordshire

Gloucestershire

The Cotswolds (see pp292–93) *are full of delightful houses built from local limestone, on the profits of the medieval wool trade. Snowshill Manor (left) is situated near the unspoilt village of Broadway.*

0 kilometres   25

0 miles   25

| The front of the half-timbered Lord Leycester Hospital, Warwick

Chatsworth House (see pp322–3), *a magnificent Baroque edifice, is famous for its gorgeous gardens. The "Conservative" Wall, a greenhouse for exotic plants, is pictured above.*

Nottinghamshire

Lincolnshire

Lincoln Cathedral *(see p329), a vast, imposing building, dominates the ancient town. Inside are splendid misericords and the superb 13th-century Angel Choir, which has 30 carved angels.*

Derbyshire

EAST MIDLANDS
(see pp318–331)

Leicestershire

Burghley House *(see pp330–31) is a dazzling landmark for miles around in the flat East Midlands landscape, with architectural motifs from the European Renaissance.*

rwickshire

Warwick Castle (see pp310–11) *is an intriguing mixture of medieval power base and country house, complete with massive towers, battlements, a dungeon and state apartments, such as the Queen Anne Bedroom.*

Northamptonshire

Stratford-upon-Avon *(see pp312–15) has many picturesque houses connected with William Shakespeare's life, some of which are open to visitors. These black and white timber-framed buildings, which abound in the Midlands, are a typical example of Tudor architecture (see pp290–91).*

Canals of the Midlands

O NE OF ENGLAND'S FIRST CANALS was built by the 3rd Duke of Bridgewater in 1761 to link the coal mine on his Worsley estate with Manchester's textile factories. This heralded the start of a canal-building boom and by 1805, a 3,000 mile (4,800 km) network of waterways had been dug across the country, linking into the natural river system. Canals provided the cheapest, fastest way of transporting goods, until competition began to arrive from the railways in the 1840s. Cargo transport ended in 1963 but today nearly 2,000 miles (3,200 km) of canals are still navigable, for travellers who wish to take a leisurely cruise on a narrowboat.

The Grand Union Canal (pictured in 1931) is 300 miles (485 km) long and was dug in the 1790s to link London with the Midlands.

Lock-keepers were provided with canalside houses.

Lockside inns cater for narrowboats.

The Farmer's Bridge is a flight of 13 locks in Birmingham. Locks are used to raise or lower boats from one level of the canal to another. The steeper the gradient, the more locks are needed.

Heavy V-shaped timber gates close off the lock.

Water pressing against the gate keeps it shut.

The towpath is where horses pulled the canal boats before engines were invented. They were changed periodically for fresh animals.

Narrowboats have straight sides and flat bottoms and are pointed at both ends. Cargo space took up most of the boat, with a small cabin for the crew. Exteriors were brightly painted.

NO 7   BILL O TOMS   NEW MARTON LOCK

MIDLANDS CANAL NETWORK

The industrial Midlands was the birthplace of the English canal system and still has the biggest concentration of navigable waterways.

KEY

━━ Canal

━━ River

Canal

Footbridge

A windlass fills or lowers water levels.

A balance beam swings the gates open.

CANAL LOCKS

Canals used tunnels, embankments and locks for the speedy transportation of goods across country. Locks were used to convey boats up or down hills.

***The Edstone Aqueduct**, just north of Stratford-upon-Avon, carries the canal in a cast iron trough. This is supported on brick piers for 180 m (495 ft), over roads and a busy railway line.*

CANAL ART

Canal boat cabins are very small and every inch of space is utilized to make a comfortable home for the occupants. Interiors were enlivened with colourful paintings and attractive decorations.

Furniture was designed to be functional and to brighten up the cramped cabin.

Narrowboats are often decorated with ornamental brass.

Water cans were also painted. The most common designs were roses and castles, with local variations in style.

Tudor Manor Houses

MANY STRIKING MANOR HOUSES were built in central England during the Tudor Age *(see pp50–51)*, a time of relative peace and prosperity. The abolition of the monasteries meant that vast estates were broken up and sold to secular landowners, who built houses to reflect their new status *(see p24)*. In the Midlands, wood was the main building material, and the gentry flaunted their wealth by using timber panelling for flamboyant decorative effect.

The Lucy family arms

The decorative moulding on the south wing dates from the late 16th century. Ancient motifs, such as vines and trefoils, are combined with the latest imported Italian Renaissance styles.

The rectangular moat was for decoration rather than defence. It surrounds a recreated knot garden (see p22) that was laid out in 1975 using plants known to have been available in Tudor times.

The Long Gallery, the last part of the Hall to be built (1580), was used for exercise. It has original murals portraying Destiny (left) and Fortune.

Brickwork chimney

Jetties (overhanging upper stories)

TUDOR MANSIONS AND TUDOR REVIVAL

There are many sumptuously decorated Tudor mansions in the Midlands. In the 19th century Tudor Revival architecture became a very popular "Old English" style, intended to invoke family pride and values rooted in the past.

Hardwick Hall in Derbyshire, whose huge kitchen is pictured, is one of the finest Tudor mansions in the country. These buildings are known as "prodigy" houses (see p330) due to their gigantic size.

Charlecote Park, Warwickshire, is a brick mansion built by Sir Thomas Lucy in 1551–59. It was heavily restored in Tudor style in the 19th century, but has a fine original gatehouse. According to legend, the young William Shakespeare (see pp312–15) was caught poaching deer in the park.

*The **Parlour** was an informal reception room. Biblical scenes such as Susannah and the Elders (right) expressed religious faith and learning.*

Entrance

*The **Great Hall** (c.1440) is the oldest part of the house, and in Tudor times was the most important. The open-plan hall was the main communal area for dining and entertainment.*

Wood panelling

Courtyard

LITTLE MORETON HALL

The Moreton family home (see p299) was built between 1440 and 1580, from a number of box-shapes, fitted together. Wood panelling and jetties displayed the family's wealth.

*The **patterned glazing** in the great bay window is typically 16th century: small pieces of locally made glass were cut into diamond shapes and held in place by lead glazing bars.*

*The **Packwood House** in Warwickshire is a timber-framed mid-Tudor house with extensive 17th-century additions. The unusual garden of clipped yew trees dates from the 17th century and is supposed to represent the Sermon on the Mount.*

*The **Moseley Old Hall**, Staffordshire, has a red brick exterior concealing its early 17th-century timber frame. The King's Room is where Charles II hid after the Battle of Worcester (see pp52–3).*

*The **Wightwick Manor**, West Midlands, was built in 1887–93. It is a fine example of Tudor Revival architecture and has superb late 19th-century furniture and decorations.*

Building with Cotswold Stone

The COTSWOLDS are a range of limestone hills running over 50 miles (80 km) in a northeasterly direction from Bath *(see pp246–9)*. The thin soils are difficult to plough but ideal for grazing sheep, and the wealth engendered by the medieval wool trade was poured into building majestic churches and opulent town houses. Stone quarried from these hills was used to build London's St Paul's Cathedral *(see pp116–17)*, as well as the villages, barns and manor houses that make the landscape so picturesque.

Dragon, Deerhurst Church

Arlington Row Cottages *in Bibury, a typical Cotswold village, were built in the 17th century for weavers whose looms were set up in the attics.*

Windows were taxed and glass expensive. Workers' cottages had only a few, not very large windows made of small panes of glass.

A drip mould keeps rain off the chimney.

The roof is steeply pitched to carry the weight of the tiles. These were made by master craftsmen who could split blocks of stone into sheets by using natural fault lines.

COTSWOLD STONE COTTAGE

The two-storey Arlington Row Cottages are asymmetrical and built of odd-shaped stones. Small windows and doorways make them quite dark inside.

Timber lintels and doors

Timber framing was cheaper than stone, and was used for the upper rooms in the roof.

VARIATIONS IN STONE

Cotswold stone is warmer-toned in the north, pearly in central areas and light grey in the south. The stone seems to glow with absorbed sunlight. It is a soft stone that is easily carved and can be used for many purposes, from buildings to bridges, headstones and gargoyles.

"Tiddles" *is a cat's gravestone in Fairford churchyard.*

Lower Slaughter *gets its name from the Anglo-Saxon word* slough, *or muddy place. It has a low stone bridge, over the River Eye.*

COTSWOLD STONE TOWNS AND VILLAGES

The villages and towns on this map are prime examples of places built almost entirely from stone. By the 12th century almost all of the villages in the area were established. Huge deposits of limestone resulted in a wealth of stone buildings. Masons worked from distinctive local designs that were handed down from generation to generation.

① Winchcombe
② Broadway
③ Stow-on-the-Wold
④ Upper and Lower Slaughter
⑤ Bourton-on-the-Water
⑥ Sherborne
⑦ Northleach
⑧ Painswick
⑨ Bibury
⑩ Fairford

Wool merchants' houses were built of fine ashlar (dressed stone) with ornamental cornerstones, doorframes and windows.

The eaves here have a dentil frieze, so-called because it resembles a row of teeth.

STONE GARGOYLES

In Winchcombe's church, 15th-century gargoyles reflect a combination of pagan and Christian beliefs.

Pagan gods warded off pre-Christian evil spirits.

Fertility figures, always important in rural areas, were incorporated into Christian festivals.

Human faces often caricatured local church dignitaries.

Animal gods represented qualities such as strength in pagan times.

COTSWOLD STONE HOUSE

This early Georgian merchant's house in Painswick shows the fully developed Cotswold style, which borrows decorative elements from Classical architecture.

The door frame has a rounded pediment on simple pilasters.

Dry-stone walling is an ancient technique used in the Cotswolds. The stones are held in place without mortar.

A stone cross (16th century) in Stanton village, near Broadway, is one of many found in the Cotswolds.

Table-top and "tea caddy", fine 18th-century tombs, can be found in Painswick churchyard.

The Cotswold Arms

Bar Snacks
Restaurant
Beer Garden
Morning Coffee

THE HEART OF ENGLAND

CHESHIRE · GLOUCESTERSHIRE · HEREFORDSHIRE
SHROPSHIRE · STAFFORDSHIRE · WARWICKSHIRE · WORCESTERSHIRE

RITAIN'S GREAT ATTRACTION *is its variety, and nowhere is this more true than at the heart of the country, where the Cotswold hills, enfolding stone cottages and churches, give way to the flat, fertile plains of Warwickshire. Shakespeare country borders on the industrial heart of England, once known as the workshop of the world.*

Coventry, Birmingham, the Potteries and their hinterlands have been manufacturing iron, textiles and ceramics since the 18th century. In the 20th century these industries have declined, and a new type of museum has developed to commemorate the towns' industrial heyday and explain the manufacturing processes which were once taken for granted. Ironbridge Gorge and Quarry Bank Mill, Styal, where the factories are now living museums, are fascinating industrial sites and enjoy beautiful surroundings.

These landscapes may be appreciated from the deck of a narrowboat, making gentle progress along the Midlands canals, to the region on the border with Wales known as the Marches. Here the massive walls of Chester and the castles at Shrewsbury and Ludlow recall the Welsh locked in fierce battle with Norman barons and the Marcher Lords. The Marches are now full of rural communities served by the peaceful market towns of Leominster, Malvern, Ross-on-Wye and Hereford. The cities of Worcester and Gloucester both have modern shopping centres, yet their majestic cathedrals retain the tranquillity of an earlier age.

Cheltenham has Regency terraces, Cirencester a rich legacy of Roman art and Tewkesbury a solid Norman abbey. Finally, there is Stratford-upon-Avon, where William Shakespeare, the Elizabethan dramatist, lived and died.

Leisurely village pastimes, reminiscent of a more tranquil age

◁ Cotswold stone: an extremely popular building material in the Heart of England

Exploring the Heart of England

The HEART OF ENGLAND, more than any other region, takes its character from the landscape. Picturesque houses, pubs and churches, made from timber and Cotswold stone, create a harmonic appearance that delights visitors and adds greatly to the pleasures of exploration. The area around Birmingham and Stoke-on-Trent, however – once the industrial hub of England – contrasts sharply. The bleak concrete skyline may not appeal, but the area has a fascinating history that is reflected in the self-confident Victorian art and architecture, and a series of award-winning industrial heritage museums.

Arlington Row: stone cottages in the Cotswold village of Bibury

SIGHTS AT A GLANCE

Walks and Tours

GETTING AROUND

The Heart of England is easily reached by train, with mainline rail services to Cheltenham, Worcester, Birmingham, and Coventry. The M5 and M6 motorways are the major road routes but are frequently congested. Long-distance buses provide regular shuttle services to Cheltenham and Birmingham. Travelling within the region is best done by car. Rural roads are delightfully empty, although major attractions, such as Stratford-upon-Avon, may be very crowded during the summer.

SEE ALSO

Wigan
Liverpool
Mersey
Birkenhead
M53
M56
A54
CHESTER ❷
Dee
A41
Wrexham
Llan
A495
A495 ● ELLESMERE
A49
Welshpool
A458
SHREWSBURY ❹
SHROPSHIRE HILLS
Offa's Dyke Path
LUDLOW ❻
A4113
A4110
Llandrindod Wells
LEOMINSTER ❼
A438
Wye
HEREFORD ❽
ROSS-ON-W

0 kilometres   10

0 miles   10

Manchester

① QUARRY BANK MILL STYAL

Buxton

PEAK DISTRICT NATIONAL PARK

Macclesfield Canal

STOKE-ON-TRENT ③

A52

Derby

UTTOXETER

Dove

STAFFORD

Trent

Nottingham

CANNOCK CHASE

Coventry Canal

IRONBRIDGE

BLACK COUNTRY

Leicester

M69

⑬ BIRMINGHAM

M6

Northampton

KIDDERMINSTER

⑭ COVENTRY

RUGBY

Northampton

M45

WARWICK ⑯

⑮ MIDLANDS GARDEN TOUR

VALE OF EVESHAM

⑫ WORCESTER

⑰ STRATFORD-UPON-AVON

GREAT MALVERN

⑪

Oxford Canal

LEDBURY

⑱ CHIPPING CAMPDEN

Banbury, Oxford, London

⑲ TEWKESBURY

M50

GLOUCESTER

⑳

⑳ CHELTENHAM

Cotswold Way

COTSWOLDS

Oxford

⑳ CIRENCESTER

Swindon

Bristol

Bath

View of the Wye Valley, near Ross-on-Wye

KEY

	Motorway
	Major road
	Scenic route
--	Scenic path
	River
☀	Viewpoint

Reader's House, Ludlow, opposite
St Laurence's Church

Quarry Bank Mill, a working reminder of the Industrial Revolution

Quarry Bank Mill, Styal ❶

(NT) Cheshire. 🎫 *01625 527468.*
🚇 *Wilmslow then bus.* 🕐 *Apr–Sep: daily; Oct–Mar: Tue–Sun.* 🔴 *23-25 Dec.* 🎫 🔥 *limited.* 🚽 🏠
🌐 *www.quarrybankmill.org.uk*

THE HISTORY of the Industrial Revolution *(see pp54–5)* is brought vividly to life at Quarry Bank Mill, an early factory now transformed into a museum. Here, mill master Samuel Greg first used the waters of the Bollin Valley in 1784 to power the water frame, a machine for spinning raw cotton fibres into thread. By the 1840s, the Greg cotton empire was one of the biggest in Britain, and the mill produced bolts of material to be exported all over the world.

Today the massive old mill buildings have been restored to house a living museum of the cotton industry. This dominated the Manchester area for nearly 200 years, but was finally destroyed by foreign competition. The entire process, from the spinning and weaving to the bleaching, printing and dyeing, is shown through a series of reconstructions, demonstrations and hands-on displays.

The weaving shed is full of clattering looms producing textiles. There are fascinating contraptions that demonstrate how water can be used to drive machinery, including an enormous wheel, 50 tons in weight and 7 m (24 ft) high, that is still used daily to provide power for the looms.

The Greg family realized the importance of having a healthy, loyal and stable work-force. A social history exhibition explains how the mill workers were housed in the purpose-built village of Styal, in spacious cottages which had vegetable gardens and toilets. Details of their wages, working con-ditions and medical facilities are displayed on information boards.

There are guided tours of the nearby **Apprentice House**. Local orphans lived here, and were sent to work up to 12 hours a day at the mill when they were just six or seven years old. Visitors can try the beds in the house and even sample the medicine they were given. Quarry Bank Mill is surrounded by over 115 ha (284 acres) of woodland.

Chester ❷

Cheshire. 🏛 *125,000.* 🚉 🚌
🅸 *Town Hall, Northgate St (01244 402111).* 🛒 *Mon–Sat.*
🌐 *www.chestertourism.com*

FIRST SETTLED BY THE ROMANS *(see pp44–5),* who estab-lished a camp in AD 79 to defend fertile land near the River Dee, the main streets of Chester are now lined with timber buildings. These are the **Chester Rows**, which, with their two tiers of shops and continuous upper gallery, anticipate today's multi-storey shops by several centuries.

Although their oriel windows and decorative timber-work are mostly 19th century, the Rows were first built in the 13th and 14th centuries, and the original structures can be seen in many places. The façade of the 16th-century **Bishop Lloyd's House** in Watergate Street is the most richly carved in Chester. The Rows are at their most varied and attractive where Eastgate Street meets Bridge Street. Here, views of the cathedral and the town walls give the impression of a perfectly preserved medieval city. This illusion is helped by the Town Crier, who calls the hour and announces news in summer from the Cross, a reconstruc-tion of the 15th-century stone crucifix that was destroyed in the Civil War *(see pp52–3).*

Chester's 1897 clocktower

The **Grosvenor Museum**, south of the Cross, explains the town's history. To the north is the **cathedral**. The choir stalls have splendid misericords *(see p329),* with

Examples of the intricate carving on Bishop Lloyd's House, a Tudor building in Watergate Street, Chester

The Chester Rows, where shops line the first-floor galleries

scenes including a quarrelling couple. In sharp contrast are the delicate spire-lets on the stall canopies. The cathedral is surrounded on two sides by the **city walls**, originally Roman but rebuilt at intervals. The best stretch is from the cathedral to Eastgate, where a wrought-iron **clock** was erected in 1897. The route to Newgate leads to a **Roman amphitheatre** built in AD 100.

🏛 Grosvenor Museum
Grosvenor St. 📞 01244 402008.
⬜ Mon–Sat, Sun pm. ● 24–26
Dec, 1 Jan, Good Fri. 🔓
♿ limited

♙ Roman Amphitheatre
Little St John St. 📞 01244 402009.
⬜ daily.

Stoke-on-Trent ❸

Stoke-on-Trent. 🕧 252,000. 🚆 🚌
🛈 Quadrant Rd, Hanley (01782
236000). 🛒 Mon–Sat.
W www.visitstoke.co.uk

FROM THE MID-18TH CENTURY, Staffordshire became a leading centre for mass-produced ceramics. Its fame arose from the fine bone china and porcelain products of Wedgwood,

Minton, Doulton and Spode, but the Staffordshire potteries also make a wide range of utilitarian products such as baths, toilets and wall tiles.

In 1910 a group of six towns – Longton, Fenton, Hanley, Burslem, Tunstall and Stoke – merged to form the conurbation of Stoke-on-Trent, also known as the Potteries. Fans of the writer Arnold Bennett (1867–1931) may recognise this area as the "Five Towns",

a term he used in a series of novels about the region (Fenton was excluded).

The **Gladstone Pottery Museum** is a Victorian complex of workshops, kilns, galleries and an engine house. There are demonstrations of traditional pottery techniques. The **Potteries Museum and Art Gallery** in Hanley has historic and modern ceramics.

Josiah Wedgwood began his earthenware firm in 1769 and built a workers' village, Etruria. The last surviving steam-powered pottery mill is on display at the **Etruria Industrial Museum**.

ENVIRONS: About 10 miles (16 km) north of Stoke-on-Trent is **Little Moreton Hall** *(see p291)*, a half-timbered early Tudor manor house.

🏛 Gladstone Pottery Museum
Uttoxeter Rd, Longton. 📞 01782
319232. ⬜ daily. 🚫 ♿ 🍴 🔓
W www.stoke.gov.uk/gladstone
🏛 Potteries Museum and Art Gallery Bethesda St, Hanley. 📞
01782 232323. ⬜ daily. ♿ 🖥 🔓
W www.stoke.gov.uk/museums
🏛 Etruria Industrial Museum
Lower Bedford St, Etruria. 📞 01782
233144. ⬜ Jan–Mar: Mon–Wed;
Apr–Dec: Sat–Wed. ● 25 Dec–1
Jan. 🚫 🎫 by arrangement. 🖥 🔓
♜ Little Moreton Hall
(NT) Congleton, off A34. 📞 01260
272018. ⬜ Mar–Oct: Wed–Sun &
public hols; last week Nov–22 Dec:
Sat, Sun. 🚫 🎫 ♿ limited. 🍴 🔓

STAFFORDSHIRE POTTERY

An abundance of water, marl, clay and easily mined coal to fire the kilns enabled Staffordshire to develop as a ceramics centre; and local supplies of iron, copper and lead were used for glazing. In the 18th century, pottery became widely accessible and affordable. English bone china, which used powdered animals' bones for strength and translucence, was shipped all over the world, and Josiah Wedgwood (1730–95) introduced simple, durable crockery – though his best known design is the blue jasperware decorated with white Classical themes. Coal-powered bottle kilns fired the clay until the 1950s Clean Air Acts put them out of business. They have been replaced by electric or gas-fired kilns.

Wedgwood candlesticks, 1785

Timber-framed, gabled mansions in Fish Street, Shrewsbury

Shrewsbury ❹

Shropshire. 🏘 *96,000.* 🚆 🚌
🛈 *The Square (01743 281200).*
🛒 *Tue, Wed, Fri, Sat.*
W *www.shrewsbury.ws*

SHREWSBURY is almost an island, enclosed by a great loop of the River Severn. A gaunt **castle** of red sandstone, first built in 1083, guards the entrance to the town, standing on the only section of land not surrounded by the river. Such defences were necessary on the frontier between England and the wilder Marches of Wales, whose inhabitants fiercely defied Saxon and Norman invaders *(see pp46– 7)*. The castle, rebuilt over the centuries, now houses the Shropshire Regimental Museum.

In AD 60 the Romans *(see pp44–5)* built the garrison town of Viroconium, modern Wroxeter, 5 miles (8 km) east of Shrewsbury. Finds from the excavations are displayed at **Shrewsbury Museum and Art Gallery**, including a decorated silver mirror from the 2nd century and other luxury goods imported by the Roman army.

The town's medieval wealth as a centre of the wool trade is evident in the many timber-framed buildings found along the High Street, Butcher Row,

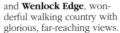

Roman silver mirror in Rowley's House Museum

and Wyle Cop. Two of the grandest High Street houses, **Ireland's Mansions** and **Owen's Mansions**, are named after Robert Ireland and Richard Owen, the wealthy wool merchants who built them in 1575 and 1570 respectively. Similarly attractive buildings in Fish Street frame a view of the **Prince Rupert Hotel**, which was briefly the headquarters of Charles I's nephew, Rupert, in the English Civil War *(see pp52–3)*.

Outside the loop of the river, the **Abbey Church** survives from the medieval monastery. It has a number of interesting memorials, including one to Lieutenant WES Owen MC, better known as the war poet Wilfred Owen (1893–1918), who taught at the local Wyle Cop school and was killed in the last days of World War I.

ENVIRONS: To the south of Shrewsbury, the road to Ludlow passes through the landscapes celebrated in the 1896 poem by AE Housman (1859–1936), *A Shropshire Lad*. Highlights include the bleak moors of **Long Mynd**, with 15 prehistoric barrows, and **Wenlock Edge**, wonderful walking country with glorious, far-reaching views.

♣ **Shrewsbury Castle**
Castle St. 📞 *01743 358516.* ⏰
Easter–Sep: daily; Oct–Easter: Wed–Sat. ● *22 Dec–mid-Feb.* ♿ 📷
🏛 **Shrewsbury Museum and Art Gallery**
Barker St. 📞 *01743 361196.* ⏰
Oct–May: Tue–Sat; Jun–Sep: daily. ●
2 wks over Christmas. ♿ *limited.* 📷
W *www.shrewsburymuseums.com*

Ironbridge Gorge ❺

See pp302–3.

Ludlow ❻

Shropshire. 🏘 *10,000.* 🚆 🛈
Castle St (01584 875053). 🛒 *Mon, Fri, Sat.* W *www.ludlow.org.uk*

LUDLOW ATTRACTS large numbers of visitors to its splendid castle, but there is much else to see in this town, with its small shops and its lovely Georgian and half-timbered Tudor buildings. Ludlow is an important area of geological research and the **museum**, just off the town centre, has fossils of the oldest known animals and plants.

The ruined **castle** is sited on cliffs high above the River Teme. Built in 1086, it was damaged in the Civil War *(see pp52–3)* and abandoned in 1689. *Comus,* a court masque using music and drama and a precursor of opera, by John Milton (1608–74) was first performed here in 1634 in the Great Hall.

The 13th-century south tower and hall of Stokesay Castle, near Ludlow

Prince Arthur (1486–1502), elder brother of Henry VIII (*see pp50–51*), died at Ludlow Castle. His heart is buried in **St Laurence Church** at the other end of Castle Square, as are the ashes of the poet A E Housman. The east end of the church backs onto the **Bull Ring**, with its ornate timber buildings. Two inns vie for attention across the street: **The Bull**, with its Tudor back yard, and **The Feathers**, with its flamboyant façade, whose name recalls the feathers used in arrow-making, once a local industry.

ENVIRONS: About 5 miles (8 km) north of Ludlow, in a lovely setting, is **Stokesay Castle**, a fortified manor house with a colourful moated garden.

♠ **Ludlow Castle**
The Square. 📞 *01584 873355.* ◯ *daily (Jan: Sat, Sun only).* 🎟 📷 ♿ *limited.* W *www.ludlowcastle.com*

🏛 **Ludlow Museum**
Castle St. 📞 *01584 873857.* ◯ *Apr–Oct: Mon–Sat (Jun–Aug: daily).* 📷 ♿

♠ **Stokesay Castle**
Craven Arms, A49. 📞 *01588 672544.* ◯ *Apr–Oct: daily; Nov–Mar: Wed–Sun.* ● *24–26 Dec, 1 Jan.* 📷 📷 🎟

Leominster ❼

Herefordshire. 🏘 *11,000.* 🚋 🏨 *Corn Sq (01568 616460).* 🛒 *Fri.* W *www.visitorlinks.com*

FARMERS COME TO LEOMINSTER (pronounced "Lemster") from all over this rural region to buy supplies. There are two buildings of note in the town, which has been a wool-manufacturing centre for 700 years. In the town centre stands the magnificent **Grange Court**, carved with bold and bizarre figures in 1633. Nearby is the **priory**, whose imposing Norman portal is carved with an equally strange mixture of mythical birds and beasts. The lions, at least, can be explained: medieval monks believed the name of Leominster was derived from *monasterium leonis*, "the monastery of the lions". In fact, *leonis* probably comes from medieval, rather than

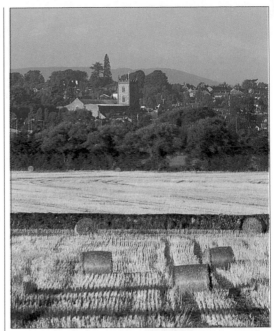

A view of Leominster, set on the River Lugg in rolling border country

Classical Latin, and it means "of the marshes". The aptness of this description can readily be seen in the green lanes around the town, following the lush river valleys.

ENVIRONS: South of the town, the magnificent gardens and parkland at **Hampton Court** have recently been restored and include island pavilions and a maze. To the west of the town, along the River Arrow, are the villages of **Eardisland** and **Pembridge**, with their well-kept gardens and timber-framed houses. **Berrington Hall**, 3 miles

Gatehouse of Stokesay Castle, near Ludlow

(5 km) north of Leominster, is a Neo-Classical house set in grounds by Capability Brown. Inside are beautifully pre-served ceiling decorations and period furniture.

To the northeast of Leo-minster is **Tenbury Wells**, which enjoyed brief popular-ity as a spa in the 19th century. The River Teme flows through it, full of minnows, trout and other fish and beloved of the composer Sir Edward Elgar (*see p305*), who came to seek inspiration on its banks. The river also feeds **Burford House Gardens**, on the western outskirts of Tenbury Wells, where the water is used to create streams, fountains and pools that are rich in unusual moisture-loving plants.

🌼 **Hampton Court Gardens**
nr Hope Under Dinmore. 📞 *01568 797 777.* ◯ *Apr–21 Dec: 11am–5pm (to 4pm Nov–Dec) Tue–Sun.* 📷 ♿ 🏨 🎟 W *www.hamptoncourt.org.uk*

🏛 **Berrington Hall**
Berrington. 📞 *01568 615721.* ◯ *Apr–Oct: daily.* 📷 🏨 🎟

🌼 **Burford House Gardens**
Tenbury Wells. 📞 *01584 810777.* ◯ *daily.* ● *1 Jan, 25, 26 Dec.* 📷 ♿ 🏨 🎟 W *www.burford.co.uk*

Ironbridge Gorge ❺

I RONBRIDGE GORGE was one of the most important
centres of the Industrial Revolution *(see pp54–5)*.
It was here, in 1709, Abraham Darby I (1678–1717)
pioneered the use of inexpensive coke, rather than
charcoal, to smelt iron ore. The use of iron in bridges,
ships and buildings transformed Ironbridge Gorge into
one of the world's great iron-making centres. Industrial
decline in the 20th century led to the Gorge's decay,
although today it has been restored as an exciting complex of industrial archaeology, with several museums
strung along the wooded banks of the River Severn.

VISITORS' CHECKLIST

Shropshire. 🏠 *2,900.* 🚆 *Telford
then bus (Telford Travelink 01952
200005).* 🚌 *01952 433522.*
🚶 *Ironbridge town (01952
432166).* ◯ *mid-Apr–Oct: daily;
Nov–mid-Apr: call for details.*
● *1 Jan, 24, 25 Dec. Some sites
closed Nov–Apr, call for details.*
👤 *most sites.* 📷 🎫 *by arrangement.* 🅿 🍴 🏠
Ⓦ www.ironbridge.org.uk

**Wrought-iron clock (1843) on the
roof of the Museum of Iron**

MUSEUM OF IRON

T HE HISTORY OF IRON and
the men who made it
is traced in this remark-
able museum. Abraham
Darby I's discovery of how
to smelt iron ore with coke
allowed the mass produc-
tion of iron, paving the
way for the rise of large-
scale industry. His original
blast furnace forms the
museum's centrepiece.

One of the museum's
themes is the history of
the Darby dynasty, a
Quaker family who had
a great impact on the
Coalbrookdale community.
The social and working
conditions faced by the
labourers, who sometimes
had to toil for 24 hours at
a stretch, are also illustrated.

Ironbridge led the world
in industrial innovation, producing the first iron wheels
and cylinders for the first
steam engine. A restored
locomotive and cast-iron
statues, many of them

commissioned for the 1851
Great Exhibition *(see pp56–7)*,
are among the many Coal-
brookdale Company products
on display.

One of the Darby family's
homes in the nearby village
of Coalbrookdale, **Rosehill
House**, has been furnished in
mid-Victorian style.

MUSEUM OF THE GORGE

T HIS PARTLY CASTELLATED,
Victorian building was a
warehouse for storing products from the ironworks before
they were shipped down the
River Severn. The warehouse
is now home to the Museum
of the Gorge, and has displays illustrating the
history of the Severn
and the development of
the water industry.

Until the arrival of the
railways in the mid-19th
century, the Severn was the
main form of transport and
communication to and from
the Gorge. Sometimes
too shallow, at other
times in flood, the
river was not a par-
ticularly reliable
means of transport-
ation; by the 1890s
river trading had
stopped completely.

The highlight of
the museum is a
wonderful 12 m
(40 ft) model of the
Gorge as it would
have appeared in
1796, complete with
foundries, cargo boats
and growing villages.

Europe **(1860), statue in
the Museum of Iron**

JACKFIELD TILE MUSEUM

T HERE HAVE BEEN POTTERIES
in this area since the 17th
century, but it was not until
the Victorian passion for decorative tiles that Jackfield became
famous. There were two tile-
making factories here – Maw
and Craven Dunnill – that produced a tremendous variety of
tiles from clay mined nearby.

**Peacock Panel (1928), one of the
tile museum's star attractions**

Talented designers created an
astonishing range of images.
The newly refurbished
Jackfield Tile Museum, in the
old Craven Dunnill works, has
a collection of the decorative
floor and wall tiles that were
produced here from the 1850s
to the 1960s. Visitors can watch
small-scale demonstrations of
traditional methods of tile-
making in the old factory buildings, including the kilns and
the decoration workshops.

IRONBRIDGE GORGE SIGHTS

Blists Hill Museum ⑥
Coalport China
 Museum ⑤
Iron Bridge ③
Jackfield Tile
 Museum ④
Museum of Iron ①
Museum of the Gorge ②

0 kilometres 2

0 miles 1

COALPORT CHINA MUSEUM

IN THE MID-19TH CENTURY the Coalport Works was one of the largest porcelain manufacturers in Britain, and its name was synonymous with fine china. The Coalport Company still makes porcelain but has long since moved its operations to Stoke-on-Trent (see p299). Today the china workshops have been converted into a museum, where visitors can watch demonstrations of the various stages of making porcelain, including the skills of pot-throwing, painting and gilding. There is a superb collection of 19th-century china housed in one of the museum's distinctive bottle-shaped kilns.

Coalport China Museum with its bottle-shaped kiln

Nearby is the **Tar Tunnel**, an important source of natural bitumen discovered 110 m (360 ft) underground in the 18th century. It once yielded 20,500 litres (4,500 gal) of tar every week; visitors can still explore part of the tunnel.

THE IRON BRIDGE

Abraham Darby III (grandson of the first man to smelt iron with coke) cast the world's first iron bridge in 1779, revolutionizing building methods in the process. Spanning the Severn, the bridge is a monument to the ironmasters' skills. The toll-house on the south bank charts its construction.

BLISTS HILL MUSEUM

THIS ENORMOUS OPEN-AIR museum recreates Victorian life as it would have been in an Ironbridge Gorge town. A group of 19th-century buildings has been reconstructed on the 20 ha (50 acre) site of Blists Hill, an old coal mine that used to supply the ironworks in the Gorge. Here, people in period costume enact roles and perform tasks such as iron forging.

The site has period housing, a church and even a Victorian school. Visitors can change money into old coinage to buy items from the baker or even pay for a drink in the local pub.

The centrepiece of Blists Hill is a complete foundry that still produces wrought iron. One of the most spectacular sights is the Hay Inclined Plane, which was used to transport canal boats up and down a steep slope. Other attractions include steam engines, a saddlers, a doctors, a chemist, a candlemakers and a sweetshop.

Hereford ❽

Herefordshire. 🏘 *50,000.* ✈ 🚃
ℹ️ *King St (01432 268430).*
🏪 *Wed (cattle, general), Sat (general).*
🅦 www.visitorlinks.com

O NCE THE CAPITAL of the
Saxon kingdom of West
Mercia, Hereford is today an
attractive town which serves
the needs of a primarily rural
community. A cattle market is
held here every Wednesday,
and local produce is sold at
the covered market in the
town centre. Almost opposite,
the timber-framed **Old House**
of 1621 is now a museum of
local history.

In the **cathedral**, only a
short stroll away, interesting
features include the Lady
Chapel, in richly ornamented
Early English style, the
Mappa Mundi (see below)
and the Chained Library,
whose 1,500 books are
tethered by iron chains to
bookcases as a precaution
against theft. The
story of these
national treasures is
told through models,
original artifacts and
interactive computer
technology. The best
place for an overall
view of the cathedral
is at the Bishop's
Meadow, south of
the centre, leading
down to the banks
of the Wye.

**Detail of figures on
Kilpeck Church**

Hereford's many
rewarding museums include
the **City Museum and Art
Gallery**, noted for its Roman
mosaic and for watercolours
by local artists, and the **Cider

Hereford's 17th-century Old House, furnished in period style

**Museum and King Offa
Distillery**. In the museum,
visitors can discover the
history of traditional cider
making. The King Offa
Distillery, which is open for
visits and tastings,
is the first distillery
licensed to produce
cider brandy for
200 years.

ENVIRONS: During the
12th century, Oliver
de Merlemond made
a pilgrimage from
Hereford to Spain.
Impressed by
several churches he
saw on the way, he
brought French
masons over to England and
introduced their techniques to
this area. One result was
Kilpeck Church, 6 miles (10
km) southwest, covered in

lustful figures showing their
genitals, and tail-biting
dragons. At **Abbey Dore**,
4 miles (6 km) west, the
Cistercian abbey church is
complemented by the serene
riverside gardens of **Abbey
Dore Court**.

🚪 **Old House**
High Town. 📞 *01432 260694.* ⭕
*Apr–Sep: Tue–Sun; Oct–Mar: Tue–Sat;
public hols.* ⬤ *25, 26 Dec, 1 Jan,
Good Fri.* ♿ *limited.* 📷 🅦 *www.
herefordshire.gov.uk/museums*
🏛 **City Museum and Art
Gallery**
Broad St. 📞 *01432 260692.* ⭕ *Apr–
Sep: Tue–Sun; Oct–Mar: Tue–Sat, public
hols.* ⬤ *25, 26 Dec, 1 Jan, Good Fri.*
♿ 🅦 *www.cidermuseum.com*
🏛 **Cider Museum and
King Offa Distillery**
Ryelands St.
📞 *01432 354207.*
⭕ *Apr–Oct: daily; Jan–Mar:
Tue–Sun & public hols.* ⬤ *25, 26
Dec, 1 Jan.* 💰 ♿ *limited.* 🎥 *by
arrangement.* 🖥 🎁

Ross-on-Wye ❾

Herefordshire. 🏘 *10,000.* 🚃
ℹ️ *Eddie Cross St (01989 562768).*
🏪 *Thu, Sat.*
🅦 *www. countrysideatitsbest.com*

T HE FINE TOWN of Ross sits
on a cliff of red sandstone
above the water meadows of
the River Wye. There are wonderful views over the river
from the cliff-top gardens,

MEDIEVAL VIEW

Hereford Cathedral's most
celebrated treasure is the
Mappa Mundi, the Map of
the World, drawn in 1290
by a clergyman, Richard of
Haldingham. The world is
depicted here on Biblical
principles: Jerusalem is at
the centre, the Garden of
Eden figures prominently
and monsters inhabit the
margins of the world.

Central detail, *Mappa Mundi*

The wooded Wye Valley near Ross

given to the town by a local benefactor, John Kyrle (1637–1724). Kyrle was lauded by the poet Alexander Pope (1688–1744) in his *Moral Essays on the Uses of Riches* (1732) for using his wealth in a practical way, and he came to be known as "The Man of Ross". There is a memorial to Kyrle in **St Mary's Church**.

ENVIRONS: From Hereford to Ross, the **Wye Valley Walk** follows 16 miles (26 km) of gentle countryside. From Ross it continues south for 33 miles (54 km), over rocky ground in deep, wooded ravines.

   Goodrich Castle, 5 miles (8 km) south of Ross, is a 12th-century red sandstone fort on a rock above the river.

⚓ **Goodrich Castle**
(EH) Goodrich. 【 *01600 890538.*
⚪ *daily (Nov–Mar: Wed–Sun).* ●
24–26 Dec, 1 Jan. 🚫 ☐ *(Apr–Sep).*

Ledbury ❿

Herefordshire. 👥 *8,000.* �im 🚌
ℹ *The Homend (01531 636147).*
🔲 *www.countrysideatitsbest.com*

LEDBURY'S MAIN STREET is lined with timbered houses, including the **Market Hall** which dates from 1655. Church Lane, a cobbled lane running up from the High Street, has lovely 16th-century buildings: the **Heritage Centre** and **Butcher Row House** are both now museums. **St Michael and All Angels Church** has a massive detached bell tower, ornate Early English decoration and interesting monuments.

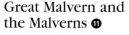

Medieval tile from the Priory at Great Malvern

🏛 **Heritage Centre**
Church Lane. ⚪ *Easter–Oct: daily.*
♿
🏛 **Butcher Row House**
Church Lane. ⚪ *Easter–Oct: daily.*

Great Malvern and the Malverns ⓫

Worcestershire. 👥 *35,000.* 🚉 🚌
ℹ *21 Church St (01684 892289).*
📅 *Fri.* 🔲 *www.malvernhills.gov.uk*

THE ANCIENT GRANITE ROCK of the Malvern Hills rises from the plain of the River Severn, its 9 miles (15 km) of

glorious scenery visible from afar. Composer Sir Edward Elgar (1857–1934) wrote many of his greatest works here, including the oratorio *The Dream of Gerontius* (1900), inspired by what the diarist John Evelyn (1620–1706) described as "one of the goodliest views in England". Elgar's home was in **Little Malvern**, whose truncated Church of St Giles, set on a steep, wooded hill, lost its nave when the stone was stolen during the Dissolution (*see p339*). **Great Malvern**, capital of the hills, is graced with 19th-century buildings which look like Swiss sanitoria: patients would stay at institutions such as Doctor Gulley's Water Cure Establishment. The water gushing from the hillside at St Ann's Well, above the town, is bottled and sold throughout Britain. The town is home to the famous Morgan cars (contact Tourist Information to arrange a factory visit).

   Malvern's highlight is the **Priory**, with its 15th-century stained-glass windows and medieval misericords. The old monastic fishponds below the church form the lake of the **Winter Gardens**. Here the theatre hosts performances of Elgar's music and plays by George Bernard Shaw.

A view of the Malverns range, formed of hard Pre-Cambrian rock

Worcester ⑫

Worcestershire. 🚶 95,000. 🚉
🚌 ℹ️ High St (01905 722480).
🏛️ Mon–Sat.
🌐 www.cityofworcester.gov.uk

WORCESTER is one of many English cities whose character has been transformed by modern development. The architectural highlight remains the **cathedral**, off College Yard, which suffered a collapsed tower in 1175 and a disastrous fire in 1203, before the present structure was started in the 13th century.

The nave and central tower were completed in the 1370s, after building was severely interrupted by the Black Death, which decimated the labour force (see p48). The most recent and ornate addition was made in 1874, when Sir George Gilbert Scott (see p451) designed the High Gothic choir, incorporating 14th-century carved misericords.

There are many interesting tombs, including King John's,

Charles I holding a symbol of the Church on Worcester's Guildhall

a masterpiece of medieval carving, in front of the altar. Prince Arthur, Henry VIII's brother (see p301), who died at the age of 15, is buried in the chantry chapel south of the altar. Underneath, the huge Norman crypt survives from the first cathedral (1084).

From the cathedral cloister, a gate leads to College Green and out into Edgar Street and

its Georgian houses. Here the **Museum of Worcester Porcelain** displays Royal Worcester porcelain dating back to 1751. On the High Street, north of the cathedral, the **Guildhall** of 1723 is adorned with statues of Stuart monarchs, reflecting the city's Royalist allegiances. In Cornmarket is **Ye Olde King Charles House**, in which Prince Charles, later Charles II, hid after the Battle of Worcester in 1651 (see pp52–3).

Some of Worcester's finest timber buildings are found in Friar Street: **Greyfriars**, built around 1480, has been restored in period style. The **Commandery** was originally an 11th-century hospital. It was rebuilt in the 15th century and used by Prince Charles as a base during the Civil War. Now a museum, it has a fine hammerbeam roof.

Elgar's Birthplace was the home of composer Sir Edward Elgar (see p305) and contains memorabilia of his life.

🏛️ **Museum of Worcester Porcelain**
Severn St. 📞 01905 23221.
⭕ daily. 🚪 🔲 ♿ 🎫 🍴
🌐 www.royalworcester.com
🏛️ **Greyfriars**
(NT) Friar St. 📞 01905 23571. ⭕
Apr–Oct: Wed–Sat (public hols pm only). 🎫
🏛️ **Commandery**
Sidbury. 📞 01905 361821.
⭕ daily (Sun: pm). ● 25–26 Dec, 1 Jan. 🚪 🎫
🏛️ **Elgar's Birthplace**
Lower Broadheath. 📞 01905 333224.
⭕ daily. ● 24 Dec–mid-Jan. 🚪
🎫 🌐 www.elgarmuseum.org

Birmingham ⑬

Birmingham. 🚶 1,000,000. ✈️ 🚉
🚌 ℹ️ 0121 2025099. 🏛️ Mon–Sat.
🌐 www.birmingham.org.uk

BRUM, as it is affectionately known to its inhabitants, grew up as a major centre of the Industrial Revolution in the 19th century. A vast range of manufacturing trades was based in Birmingham and was responsible for the rapid development of grim factories and cramped housing. Since the clearance of several of

Worcester Cathedral, overlooking the River Severn

The Last of England, Ford Madox Brown, Birmingham Art Gallery

these areas after World War II, Birmingham has raised its cultural profile. The city succeeded in enticing Sir Simon Rattle to conduct the City of Birmingham Symphony Orchestra, and persuaded the former Royal Sadler's Wells Ballet (now the Birmingham Royal Ballet) to leave London for the more up-to-date facilities of Birmingham. The **National Exhibition Centre**, 8 miles (13 km) east of the centre, draws thousands of people to its conference, lecture and exhibition halls.

Set away from the massive Bullring shopping centre, Birmingham's 19th-century civic buildings are excellent examples of Neo-Classical architecture. Among them are the **City Museum and Art Gallery**, where the collection includes outstanding works by pre-Raphaelite artists such as Sir Edward Burne-Jones (1833–98), who was born in Birmingham, and Ford Madox Brown (1821–93). The museum also organizes some interesting temporary exhibitions of art, such as

works by J M W Turner (1775–1851).

Birmingham's extensive canal system is now used mainly for leisure boating (*see pp288–9*), and several former warehouses have been converted into museums and galleries. **Thinktank – the Birmingham Museum of Science and Discovery** celebrates the city's contributions to the world of railway engines, aircraft, and the motor trade. The old jewellery quarter has practised its traditional crafts here since the 16th century.

Suburban Birmingham has many attractions, including the **Botanical Gardens** at Edgbaston, and **Cadbury World** at Bournville, where there is a visitor centre dedicated to chocolate (booking ahead is advisable). Bournville village was built in 1890 by the Cadbury brothers for their workers and is a pioneering example of a garden suburb.

🏛 **City Museum and Art Gallery**
Chamberlain Sq. ☎ 0121 303 2834.
☐ daily (Sun: pm). ♿ 🖥 🛍
🏛 **Thinktank**
Millennium Point. ☎ 0121 202222.
☐ Sat–Thu. ● 24–26 Dec.
🌷 **Botanical Gardens**
Westbourne Rd, Edgbaston.
☎ 0121 454 1860. ☐ daily.
● 25 Dec. 🅿 📷 ♿ 🛍 by arrangement. 🔢
🏛 **Cadbury World**
Linden Rd, Bournville. ☎ 0121 4514159. ☐ 20 Jan–Oct: daily; Nov, Dec: call for details. ● first two weeks Jan. 📷 ♿

Stately civic office buildings in Victoria Square, Birmingham

Coventry ⑭

Coventry. 🚶 300,000. 🚆 🚌 ℹ
Bayley Lane (024 7622 7264). 🛒 Mon–Sat. 🌐 www.visitcoventry.co.uk

AS AN ARMAMENTS centre, Coventry was a prime target for German bombing raids in World War II, and in 1940 the **cathedral** in the city centre was hit. After the war the first totally modern cathedral by Sir Basil Spence (1907–76) was built alongside the ruins. It includes

Epstein's *St Michael Subduing the Devil*, on Coventry Cathedral

sculptures by Sir Jacob Epstein (1880–1959) and a tapestry by Graham Sutherland (1903–80).

The **Herbert Gallery and Museum** has displays on the 11th-century legend of Lady Godiva, who rode naked through the streets. The recently renovated **Museum of British Road Transport** has the largest collection of Britain's road transport in the world, including cars, cycles and models, and features the fastest car in the world as well as interactive displays.

🏛 **Herbert Gallery and Museum**
Jordan Well. ☎ 024 7683 2381.
☐ daily (Sun: pm) 1 Jan. 🖥 🛍
🏛 **Museum of British Road Transport**
Hales St. ☎ 024 7683 2425. ☐ daily.
♿ 🖥 🛍 🌐 www.mbrt.co.uk

Midlands Garden Tour ⑮

Plum tree
in blossom

THE CHARMING COTSWOLD stone buildings perfectly complement the lush gardens for which the region is famous. This picturesque route from Warwick to Cheltenham is designed to show every type of garden, from tiny cottage plots, brimming with bell-shaped flowers and hollyhocks, to the deer-filled, landscaped parks of stately homes. The route follows the escarpment of the Cotswold Hills, taking in spectacular scenery and some of the prettiest Midlands villages on the way.

TIPS FOR DRIVERS

Tour length: 35 miles (50 km).
Stopping-off points: Hidcote Manor has excellent lunches and teas; there are refreshments at Kiftsgate Court and Sudeley Castle. Travellers will find a good choice in Broadway, from traditional pubs and tea shops to the de luxe Lygon Arms. (See also pp636–7.)

Cheltenham Imperial Gardens ⑨
These colourful public gardens on the Promenade were laid out in 1817–18 to encourage people to walk from the town to the spa *(see p316)*.

Sudeley Castle ⑧
The restored castle is complemented by box hedges, topiary and an Elizabethan knot garden *(see p22)*. Catherine Parr, Henry VIII's widow, died here in 1548.

Broadway ⑤
Wisteria and cordoned fruit trees cover 17th-century cottages, fronted by immaculate gardens.

Stanway House ⑦
This Jacobean manor has many lovely trees in its grounds and a pyramid above a cascade of water.

Snowshill Manor ⑥
This Cotswold stone manor contains an extraordinary collection, from bicycles to Japanese armour. There are walled gardens and terraces full of *objets d'art* such as the clock (left). The colour blue is a recurrent theme.

Warwick Castle ①
The castle's gardens
(see pp310–11) include
the Mound, planted in
medieval style, with
grass, oaks, yew trees
and box hedges.

Anne Hathaway's Cottage ②
This has a pretty, informal 19th-
century-style garden *(see p315).*

**Hidcote Manor
Gardens** ③
Started in the
early years of this century,
these beautiful gardens
pioneered the idea of a
garden as a series of
outdoor "rooms",
enclosed by high yew
hedges and planted
according to themes.

Kiftsgate Court Garden ④
This charmingly naturalistic garden
lies opposite Hidcote Manor. It has
many rare and unusual plants on a
series of hillside terraces, including
the enormous "Kiftsgate" Rose, nearly
30 m (100 ft) high.

KEY

▰▰▰	Motorway
▬▬	Tour route
══	Other roads
☆	Viewpoint

0 kilometres   5

0 miles   5

Warwick ⑯

Warwickshire. 🏠 28,000. 🚌 🚉
🛈 The Courthouse, Jury St (01926
492212). 🎪 Sat. 🅦 www.warwick-
uk.co.uk

THOUGH WARWICK suffered a
major fire in 1694, some
spectacular medieval buildings survived. The **Warwick
Doll Museum** in Castle Street
(1573) displays rare toys and
dolls from all over the world.
At the west end of the High
Street, a row of medieval guild
buildings were transformed in
1571 by the Earl of Leicester
(1532–88), who founded the
Lord Leycester Hospital as
a refuge for his old soldiers.

The arcaded **Market Hall**
(1670) is part of the Warwickshire Museum, renowned for
its unusual tapestry map of
the county, woven in 1558.

In Church Street, to the
south of St Mary's Church, is
the **Beauchamp Chapel**
(1443–64). It is a superb example of Perpendicular architecture and has tombs of the Earls
of Warwick. There is a view of
Warwick Castle *(see pp310–
11)* from St Mary's tower.

🏛 **Warwick Doll Museum**
Castle St. 📞 01926 495546.
⬤ Easter–Oct: daily (Sun: pm):
(Nov–Easter: Sat). 🎫 🚻 🅦 www.
warwickshire.gov.uk/museum
🏨 **Lord Leycester Hospital**
High St. 📞 01926 491422. ⬤ Tue–
Sun & public hols. ⬤ 25 Dec, Good
Fri. **Gardens** ⬤ same as house but
Easter–Sep only. 🎫 🚻 ♿ limited.
🏛 **Market Hall** Market Place.
📞 01926 412500. ⬤ Mon–Sat
(May–Sep: daily).
♿ limited. 🚻

**The Lord Leycester Hospital,
now a home for ex-servicemen**

Warwick Castle

WARWICK'S MAGNIFICENT CASTLE is a splendid medieval fortress which is also one of the country's finest stately homes. The original Norman castle was rebuilt in the 14th century, when huge outer walls and towers were added, mainly to display the power of the great feudal magnates, the Beauchamps and the Nevilles, the Earls of Warwick. The castle passed in 1604 to the Greville family who, in the 17th and 18th centuries, transformed it into a great country house. In 1978 the owners of Madame Tussaud's *(see p106)* bought the castle and set up tableaux of wax figures to illustrate its history.

Neville family at prayer (c.1460)

The Ghost Tower is where the ghost of Sir Fulke Greville, murdered by a servant in 1628, is said to walk.

The Mound has remains the motte and bailey ca *(see p472)* and the 1 century keep

Royal Weekend Party
The waxwork valet is part of the award-winning exhibition of the Prince of Wales's visit in 1898.

The Mill and Engine House

Kingmaker Attraction
Dramatic displays recreate medieval life as "Warwick the Kingmaker", Richard Neville, prepared for battle in the Wars of the Roses .

★ Great Hall and State Rooms
Medieval apartments were transformed into the Great Hall and State Rooms. A mark of conspicuous wealth, they display a collection of family treasures from around the world.

View of Warwick Castle, south front, by Antonio Canaletto (1697–1768)

Guy's Tower (1393) had lodgings for guests and members of the Earl of Warwick's retinue.

Ramparts and towers, of local grey sandstone, were added in the 14th century to fortify the castle.

★ **Death or Glory, the Armoury**
The exhibits include Oliver Cromwell's helmet and a massive 14th-century two-handed sword.

Entrance

STAR SIGHTS

★ **Great Hall and State Rooms**

★ **Death or Glory**

The underground dungeon and torture chamber contain a grisly collection of torture instruments.

The Gatehouse is defended by portcullises and "murder holes" through which boiling pitch was dropped onto attackers beneath.

Caesar's Tower

TIMELINE

Shield (1745), Death or Glory

1068 Norman motte and bailey castle built	1264 Simon de Montfort, champion of Parliament against Henry III, sacks Warwick Castle		1478 Castle reverts to Crown after murder of Richard Neville's son-in-law	1893–1910 Visits from future Edward VII

1000	1200	1400	1600	1800

Richard Neville

1356–1401 Present castle built by the Beauchamp family, Earls of Warwick

1449–1471 Richard Neville, Earl of Warwick, plays leading role in Wars of the Roses

1604 James I gives castle to Sir Fulke Greville

1600–1800 Interiors remodelled and gardens landscaped

1642 Royalists imprisoned in the castle

1871 Anthony Salvin (1799–1881) restores Great Hall and State Rooms after fire

Street-by-Street: Stratford-upon-Avon ⑰

A 1930s jester

SITUATED ON THE WEST BANK of the River Avon, in the heart of the Midlands, is one of the most famous towns in England. Stratford-upon-Avon dates back to at least Roman times but its appearance today is that of a small Tudor market town, with mellow, half-timbered architecture and tranquil walks beside the tree-fringed Avon. This image belies its popularity as the most visited tourist attraction outside London, with eager hordes flocking to see buildings connected to William Shakespeare or his descendants.

Bancroft Gardens
There is an attractive boat-filled canal basin here and a 15th-century causeway.

Tourist information

★ Shakespeare's Birthplace
This building was almost entirely reconstructed in the 19th century, but in the style of the Tudor original.

| 0 metres | 100 |
| 0 yards | 100 |

Shakespeare Centre

UNION STREET

BRIDGE STREET

WATE

HIGH STREET

HENLEY STREET

MEER STREET

WOOD STREET

ELY STREET

To train station

P

Harvard House
The novelist Marie Corelli (1855–1924) had this house restored. Next door is the 16th-century Garrick Inn.

STAR SIGHTS

★ Shakespeare's Birthplace

★ Hall's Croft

★ Holy Trinity Church

Town Hall
Built in 1767, there are traces of 18th-century graffiti on the front of the building saying God Save the King.

Royal Shakespeare Theatre

The highly acclaimed resident theatre company, the RSC, has staged all of Shakespeare's plays since it began in 1961.

VISITORS' CHECKLIST

Warwickshire. 22,000. 20 miles (32 km) NW of Stratford-upon-Avon. Alcester Rd. Bridge St. Bridge Foot (01789 293127); Shakespeare Centre, Henley St (01789 204016). Fri. Shakespeare's Birthday: Apr; Stratford Festival: Jul. www.shakespeare-country.co.uk

★ Hall's Croft

John Hall, Shakespeare's son-in-law, was a doctor. This delightful house has one room fitted out as a dispensary, with original Jacobean furniture.

★ Holy Trinity Church

Shakespeare's grave and copies of the parish register entries recording his birth and death are here.

AVON

SOUTHERN LANE

CHAPEL LANE

OLD TOWN

CHURCH STREET

OLD TOWN

Edward VI Grammar School

Nash's House

The foundations of New Place, where Shakespeare died, form the garden beside this house.

Guild Chapel

KEY

- - - Suggested route

...way's ...e

Exploring Stratford-upon-Avon

WILLIAM SHAKESPEARE was born in Stratford-upon-Avon on St George's Day, 23 April 1564. Admirers of his work have been coming to the town since his death in 1616. In 1847 a public appeal successfully raised the money to buy the house in which he was born. As a result Stratford has become a literary shrine to Britain's greatest dramatist. It also has a thriving cultural reputation as the provincial home of the prestigious Royal Shakespeare Company, whose dramas are usually performed in Stratford before playing a second season in London *(see pp126–7)*.

Mosaic of Shakespeare on the beautiful Old Bank (1810)

Anne Hathaway's Cottage, home of Shakespeare's wife

Around Stratford

The centre of Stratford-upon-Avon has many buildings that are connected with William Shakespeare and his descendants. On the High Street corner is the **Cage**, a 15th-century prison. It was converted into a house where Shakespeare's daughter Judith lived, and is now a shop. At the end of the High Street, the **Town Hall** has a statue of Shakespeare on the façade given by David Garrick (1717–79), the actor who in 1769 organized the first Shakespeare festival.

The High Street leads into Chapel Street where the half-timbered **Nash's House** is a museum of local history. It is also the site of **New Place**, where Shakespeare died in 1616, and which is now a herb and knot garden *(see p22)*. In Church Street opposite, the **Guild Chapel** (1496) has a *Last Judgement* painting (c.1500) on the chancel wall. Shakespeare is thought to have attended the **Edward VI Grammar School** (above the former Guildhall) next door.

A left turn into Old Town leads to **Hall's Croft**, home of Shakespeare's daughter Susanna, which displays 16th- and 17th-century medical artefacts. An avenue of lime trees leads to **Holy Trinity Church**, where Shakespeare is buried. A walk along the river follows the Avon to **Bancroft Gardens**, which lies at the junction of the River Avon and the Stratford Canal.

♛ Shakespeare's Birthplace

Henley St. 📞 *01789 204016.* 🕐 *daily.* ⬛ *23–26 Dec.* 📷 ♿ *limited.* 📷 🌐 *www.shakespeare.org.uk*
Bought for the nation in 1847, when it was a public house, Shakespeare's Birthplace was converted back to Elizabethan style. Objects associated with Shakespeare's father, John, a glovemaker and wool merchant, are on display. There is a birth room, in which Shakespeare was supposedly born, and another room has a window etched with visitors' autographs, including that of Sir Walter Scott *(see p498).*

Holy Trinity Church, seen across the River Avon

⛪ Harvard House

High St. 【 *01789 204016.* ◯ *May–Sep: Fri–Sun, bank hol Mon.* 🅖 ♿ *limited.* Ⓦ *www.shakespeare.org.uk*

Built in 1596, this ornate house was the home of Katherine Rogers, whose son, John Harvard, emigrated to America and in 1638 left his estate to a new college, later renamed Harvard University. The house contains a Museum of British Pewter and displays relating to John Harvard.

ENVIRONS: No tour of Stratford would be complete without a visit to **Anne Hathaway's Cottage**. Before her marriage to William Shakespeare she lived at Shottery, 1 mile (1.5 km) west of Stratford. Despite fire damage in 1969, the cottage is still impressive, with some original 16th-century furniture. The Hathaway descendants lived here until the early 20th century *(see p309)*.

⛪ Anne Hathaway's Cottage

Cottage Lane. 【 *01789 292100.* ◯ *daily.* ● *23–26 Dec.* 🅖 🅟 Ⓦ *www.shakespeare.org.uk*

Kenneth Branagh in *Hamlet*

THE ROYAL SHAKESPEARE COMPANY

The Royal Shakespeare Company is renowned for its new interpretations of Shakespeare's work. The company performs at the 1932 Royal Shakespeare Theatre, a windowless brick building adjacent to the Swan Theatre, built in 1986 to a design based on an Elizabethan playhouse. Next to it is a building displaying sets, props and costumes. The RSC also performs at the 150-seat theatre, known as the Other Place, and in London *(see pp126–7)*.

Grevel House, the oldest house in Chipping Campden

Chipping Campden ⓲

Gloucestershire. 👥 *2,500.* 🅗 *Hollis House, Stow-on-the-Wold (01451 831082).* Ⓦ *www.cotswold.gov.uk*

THIS PERFECT Cotswold town is kept in pristine condition by the Campden Trust. Set up in 1929, the Trust has kept alive the traditional skills of stonecarving and repair that make Chipping Campden such a unified picture of golden-coloured and lichen-patched stone. Visitors travelling from the northwest along the B4035 first see a group of ruins: the remains of **Campden Manor**, begun around 1613 by Sir Baptist Hicks, 1st Viscount Campden. The manor was burned by Royalist troops to stop it being sequestered by Parliament at the end of the Civil War *(see pp52–3)*, but the almshouses opposite the gateway were spared. They were designed in the form of the letter "I" (which is Latin for "J"), a symbol of the owner's loyalty to King James I.

The town's **Church of St James**, one of the finest in the Cotswolds, was built in the 15th century, financed by merchants who bought wool from Cotswold farmers and exported it at a high profit. Inside the church there are many elaborate tombs, and a magnificent brass dedicated to William Grevel, describing him as "the flower of the wool merchants of England". He built **Grevel House** (c.1380) in the High Street, the oldest in a fine row of buildings, which is distinguished by a double-storey bay window.

Viscount Campden donated the **Market Hall** in 1627. His contemporary, Robert Dover, founded in 1612 the "Cotswold Olimpicks", long before the modern Olympic Games had been established. The 1612 version included such painful events as the shin-kicking contest. It still takes place on the first Friday after each Spring Bank Holiday, followed by a torchlit procession into town ready for the Scuttlebrook Wake Fair on the next day. The setting for the games is a spectacular natural hollow on **Dover's Hill** above the town, worth climbing on a clear day for the marvellous views over the Vale of Evesham.

The 17th-century Market Hall in Chipping Campden

Tewkesbury's abbey church overlooks the town, crowded onto the bank of the River Severn

Tewkesbury ⑲

Gloucestershire. 🏠 11,000.
ℹ️ Barton St (01684 295027).
🗓️ Wed, Sat. W www.
visitcotswoldsandsevernvale.gov.uk

THIS LOVELY TOWN sits on the confluence of the rivers Severn and Avon. It has one of England's finest Norman abbey churches, **St Mary the Virgin**, which locals saved during the Dissolution of the Monasteries (see p50) by paying Henry VIII £453. Around the church, with its bulky tower and Norman façade, timbered buildings are crammed within the bend of the river. Warehouses are a reminder of past wealth, and Borough Mill on Quay Street, the only mill left harnessed to the river's energy, still grinds corn.

Pump Room detail, Cheltenham

ENVIRONS: Boat trips can be taken from the river to **Upton-on-Severn**'s riverside pubs, 6 miles (10 km) north.

Cheltenham ⑳

Gloucestershire. 🏠 107,000. 🚃 🚌
ℹ️ 77 Promenade (01242 522878).
🗓️ Sun. W www.visitcheltenham.info

CHELTENHAM'S REPUTATION for elegance was first gained in the late 18th century, when high society flocked to the spa town to "take the waters", following the example set by George III (see pp54–5). Many gracious terraced houses were built, in a Neo-Classical style, along broad avenues. These survive around the Queen's Hotel, near **Montpellier**, a lovely Regency arcade lined with craft and antique shops, and in the **Promenade**, with its smart department stores and couturiers. A more modern atmosphere prevails in the newly built Regency Arcade, where the star attraction is the 1987 **clock** by Kit Williams: visit on the hour to see fish blowing bubbles over the onlookers' heads. The **Museum and Art Gallery** is worth a visit to see its unusual collection of furniture and other crafts made by members of the influential Arts and Crafts Movement (see p25), whose strict principles of utilitarian design were laid down by William Morris (see p208).

The **Pitville Pump Room** (1825–30), modelled on the Greek Temple of Ilissos in Athens, is frequently used for performances during the town's renowned annual festivals of music (July) and literature (October).

The event that really attracts the crowds is the Cheltenham Gold Cup – the premier event of the National Hunt season – held in March (see p66).

🏛 **Museum and Art Gallery**
Clarence St. 📞 01242 237431.
⭕ daily. ⬤ 25 Dec, 1 Jan & public hols. ♿ 📷 by arrangement. 🅿️
W www.
cheltenham.artgallery.museum

♨️ **Pitville Pump Room**
Pitville Park. 📞 01242 523852.
⭕ Wed–Mon. ⬤ 25, 26 Dec, 1 Jan, public hols & frequently for functions: call to check. 📷

Fantasy clock, by Kit Williams, in Cheltenham's Regency Arcade

Gloucester Cathedral's nave

Gloucester ㉑

Gloucestershire. 🚶 110,000. 🚆 🚌
🛈 28 Southgate St (01452 421188).
🗓 Wed, Sat. 🌐
www.gloucester.gov.uk/tourism

GLOUCESTER has played a prominent role in the history of England. It was here that William the Conqueror ordered a vast survey of all the land in his kingdom, that was to be recorded in the *Domesday Book* of 1086 *(see p48)*.

The city was popular with the Norman monarchs and in 1216 Henry III was crowned in its magnificent **cathedral**. The solid, dignified nave was begun in 1089. Edward II *(see p425)*, who was murdered in 1327 at Berkeley Castle, 14 miles (22 km) to the southwest, is buried in a tomb near the high altar. Many pilgrims came to honour Edward's tomb, leaving behind generous donations, and Abbot Thoky was able to begin rebuilding in 1331. The result was the wonderful east window and the cloisters, where the fan vault was developed and then copied in other churches all over the country.

The impressive buildings around the cathedral include College Court, with its **House of the Tailor of Gloucester** museum, in the house that the children's author Beatrix Potter used as the setting *(see p355)* for her illustrations of that story. A museum complex has been created in the **Gloucester Docks**, part of which is still a port, linked to the Bristol Channel by the

Gloucester and Sharpness Canal (opened in 1827). In the old port, and housed in a Victorian warehouse, the **National Waterways Museum** incorporates hands-on displays to relate the history of canals.

🏛 **House of the Tailor of Gloucester**
College Court. ▐ 01452 422856.
◯ Mon–Sat. ● public hols.
🅿 🖼

🏛 **National Waterways Museum**
Llanthony Warehouse, Gloucester Docks.
▐ 01452 318054. ◯ daily. ● 25 Dec. 🅿 🖼 ♿ 🔲 🖵
🌐 www.nwm.org.uk

Cirencester ㉒

Gloucestershire. 🚶 20,000.
🚌 🛈 Market Place (01285 654180). 🗓 Mon, Tue (cattle) & Fri.
🌐 www.cotswold.gov.uk

KNOWN AS THE CAPITAL of the Cotswolds, Cirencester has as its focus a market place, where there is a market every Monday and Friday. Overlooking the market is the **Church of St John Baptist**, whose "wineglass" pulpit (1515) is one of the few pre-Reformation pulpits to survive in England. To the west, **Cirencester Park** was laid out by the 1st Earl of Bathurst from 1714, with help from the poet Alexander Pope *(see*

p305). The mansion is surrounded by a massive yew hedge, claimed to be the tallest in the world. Clustering round the park entrance are the 17th- and 18th-century wool merchants' houses of Cecily Hill, built in grand Italianate style. Much humbler Cotswold houses are to be found in Coxwell Street, and underlying this is a Roman town, evidence of which emerges whenever the ground is dug.

The **Corinium Museum** (*Corinium* was the Latin name) features excavated objects in a series of tableaux illustrating life in a Roman household.

♣ **Cirencester Park**
Cirencester Park. ▐ 01285 653135.
◯ daily. ♿
🌐 www.cirencesterpark.co.uk

🏛 **Corinium Museum**
Park St. ▐ 01285 655611. ● until 2004; call for details. 🖼 ♿ 🔲 🅿

Cirencester's fine parish church, one of the largest in England

---

ART AND NATURE IN THE ROMAN WORLD

Cirencester was an important centre of mosaic production in Roman days. Fine examples of the local style are shown in the Corinium Museum and mosaics range from Classical subjects, such as Orpheus taming lions and tigers with the music of his lyre, to the naturalistic depiction of a hare. At

Chedworth Roman Villa, 8 miles (13 km) north, mosaics are inspired by real life. In the *Four Seasons* mosaic, *Winter* shows a peasant, dressed in a woollen hood and a wind-blown cloak, clutching a recently caught hare in one hand and a branch for fuel in the other.

Hare mosaic, Corinium Museum

EAST MIDLANDS

···

DERBYSHIRE · LEICESTERSHIRE · LINCOLNSHIRE
NORTHAMPTONSHIRE · NOTTINGHAMSHIRE

THREE VERY DIFFERENT KINDS OF LANDSCAPE *greet visitors to the East Midlands. In the west, wild moors rise to the craggy heights of the Peak District. These give way to the low-lying plain and the massive industrial towns at the region's heart. In the east, hills and limestone villages stretch to a long, flat seaboard.*

The East Midlands owes much of its character to a conjunction of the pastoral with the urban. The spa resorts, historical villages and stately homes coexist within a landscape shaped by industrialization. Throughout the region there are swathes of scenic countryside – and grimy industrial cities.

The area has been settled since prehistoric times. The Romans mined lead and salt, and they built a large network of roads and fortresses. Anglo-Saxon and Viking influence is found in many of the place names. During the Middle Ages profits from the wool industry enabled the development of towns such as Lincoln, which still has many fine old buildings. The East Midlands was the scene of ferocious battles during the Wars of the Roses and the Civil War, and insurgents in the Jacobite Rebellion reached as far as Derby.

In the west of the region is the Peak District, Britain's first national park. Created in 1951, it draws crowds in search of the wild beauty of the heather-covered moors, or the wooded dales of the River Dove. The peaks are very popular with rock climbers and hikers.

The eastern edge of the Peaks descends through stone-walled meadows to sheltered valleys. The Roman spa of Buxton adds a final note of elegance before the flatlands of Derbyshire, Leicestershire and Nottinghamshire are reached. An area of coal mines and factories since the late 18th century, the landscape is set to be transformed over the next century into a new national forest.

Well-dressing dance, an ancient custom at Stoney Middleton in the Peak District

◁ **West front of Chatsworth House, a superb Baroque stately home in the Peak District**

Exploring the East Midlands

THE EAST MIDLANDS is a popular tourist destination, easily accessible by road, but best explored on foot. Numerous well-marked trails pass through the Peak District National Park. There are superb country houses at Chatsworth and Burghley and the impressive historic towns of Lincoln and Stamford to discover.

SIGHTS AT A GLANCE

Burghley pp330–31 **8**
Buxton **1**
Chatsworth pp322–3 **2**
Lincoln pp328–9 **7**
Matlock Bath **3**
Northampton **10**
Nottingham **6**
Stamford **9**

Walks and Tours
Peak District Tour **5**
Tissington Trail **4**

GETTING AROUND

The M6, M1 and A1 are the principal road routes to the East Midlands, but they are subject to frequent delays because of the volume of traffic they carry. It can be faster and more interesting to find cross-country routes to the region, for example through the attractive countryside and villages around Stamford and Northampton. Roads in the Peak District become very congested during the summer and an early start to the day is advisable. Lincoln and Stamford are well served by fast mainline trains from London. Rail services in the Peak District are far more limited, but local lines run as far as Matlock and Buxton.

KEY

▭	Motorway
▭	Major road
▭	Scenic route
▭	Scenic path
▭	River
☀	Viewpoint

View of Burghley House from the north courtyard

SEE ALSO

- **Where to Stay** pp558–59
- **Where to Eat** pp593–95

Peak District countryside seen from the Tissington Trail

Lincoln Cathedral towering over half-timbered buildings

0 kilometres 15

0 miles 15

Buxton Opera House, a late 19th-century building restored in 1979

Buxton ❶

Derbyshire. 🏛 *20,000.* ✈ 🚉
ℹ️ *The Crescent (01298 25106).*
🗓 *Tue, Sat.* 🅦 www.highpeak.gov.uk

Buxton was developed as a spa town by the 5th Duke of Devonshire during the late 18th century. It has many fine Neo-Classical buildings, including the **Devonshire Royal Hospital** (1790), originally stables, at the entrance to the town. The **Crescent** was built (1780–90) to rival Bath's Royal Crescent *(see p246).*

At its southwest end, the tourist information office is housed in the former town baths. Here, a spring where water surges from the ground at a rate of 7,000 litres (1,540 gallons) an hour can be seen. Buxton water is bottled and sold but there is a public fountain at **St Ann's Well**, opposite.

Steep gardens known as the Slopes lead from the Crescent to the small, award-winning **Museum and Art Gallery**, with geological and archaeological displays. Behind the Crescent, overlooking the Pavilion Gardens, is the striking 19th-century iron and glass **Pavilion**, and the splendidly restored **Opera House**, where a Music and Arts Festival is held in summer.

🏛 **Buxton Museum and Art Gallery**
Terrace Rd. 📞 *01298 24658.* ⭕
Easter–Sep: Tue–Sun; Oct–Easter: Tue–Sat. ⬤ *25 Dec–2 Jan.* ♿ 🚻
🅦 www.derbyshire.gov.uk
🚻 **Pavilion and Gardens**
St John's Rd. 📞 *01298 23114.*
⭕ *daily.* ⬤ *25 Dec.* ♿ 🍽 🖥 🚻

Chatsworth House and Gardens ❷

Chatsworth is one of Britain's most impressive stately homes. Between 1687 and 1707, the 4th Earl of Devonshire replaced the old Tudor mansion with this Baroque palace. The house has beautiful gardens, landscaped in the 1760s by Capability Brown *(see p22)* and developed by the head gardener, Joseph Paxton *(see pp56–7),* in the mid-19th century.

First house built in 1552 by Bess of Hardwick

Summerhouse

Round ponds, known as the Spectacles

★ **Cascade**
Water tumbles down the steps of the Cascade, built in 1696 to a French design.

STAR SIGHTS
★ Cascade
★ Chapel

Paxton's "Conservative" Wall
This iron-and-glass conservatory wall was designed in 1848 by Joseph Paxton, the creator of Chatsworth's Great Conservatory (now demolished).

Garden entrance

House entrance

South front and canal pond with Emperor fountain

Maze: site of
Paxton's Great
Conservatory

Rhododendron Walk

Grotto

★ **Chapel**
*The chapel (1693) is
resplendent with
art and marble.*

War Horse
*This sculpture
(1991) is by
Elisabeth Frink.*

Canal pond

Sea-horse
fountain

State Rooms
*The rooms have
fine interiors and
superb art, such as
this* trompe l'oeil *by Jan
van der Vaart (1651–1727).*

Matlock ❸

Derbyshire. 👥 *23,000.* 🚆
ℹ️ *Crown Square (01629 583388).*
🌐 *www.derbyshiredales.gov.uk*

MATLOCK WAS DEVELOPED as a spa from the 1780s. Interesting buildings include the massive structure (1853) on the hill above the town, built as a hydrotherapy centre but now council offices. On the hill opposite is the mock-Gothic **Riber Castle**.

From Matlock, the A6 winds through the outstandingly beautiful **Derwent Gorge** to **Matlock Bath**. Here, cable cars ascend to the **Heights of Abraham** pleasure park, with caves, nature trail and extensive views. Lead-mining is the subject of the **Peak District Mining Museum**, and visitors can inspect the old **Temple Mine** nearby. **Sir Richard Arkwright's Cromford Mill** (1771), a world heritage site and the first ever water-powered cotton spinning mill, lies at the southern end of the gorge *(see p327)*.

🌟 **Heights of Abraham** On A6.
📞 *01629 582365.* ⬜ *Feb–Mar: Sat, Sun; Easter–Nov: daily.* 🅿️ ♿ *limited.*
🏛️ **Peak District Mining Museum** The Pavilion, off A6. 📞 *01629 583834.* ⬜ *daily.* 🅿️ ♿ 🗄️ 🌐 *www.peakmines.co.uk*
⛏️ **Temple Mine**
Temple Rd, off A6. 📞 *01629 583834.* ⬜ *call for details.* ● *25 Dec.* 🅿️
⛏️ **Cromford Mill**
Mill Lane, Cromford. 📞 *01629 824297.* ⬜ *daily.* ● *25 Dec.* ♿
🌐 *www.cromfordmill.co.uk*

Cable cars taking visitors to the Heights of Abraham

Tissington Trail ❹

See p325.

Peak District Tour ❺

See pp326–7.

Nottingham ❻

Nottinghamshire. 👥 *269,000.*
🚆 🚌 ℹ️ *Smithy Row (0115 9155330).* 🍴 *daily.*
🌐 *www.profilenottingham.co.uk*

THE NAME OF NOTTINGHAM often conjures up the image of the evil Sheriff, adversary of Robin Hood. **Nottingham Castle** stands on a rock riddled with underground passages. The castle houses a museum, with displays on the city's history, and what was Britain's first municipal art gallery, featuring works by Sir Stanley Spencer (1891–1959) and Dante Gabriel Rossetti (1828–82). At the foot of the castle, Britain's oldest tavern, the **Trip to Jerusalem** (1189), is still in business. Its name may refer to the 12th- and 13th-century crusades, but much of it is 17th-century.

There are several museums near the castle, ranging from the **Tales of Robin Hood**, which tells the story of the outlaw, to the **Museum of Costume and Textiles**, explaining Nottingham's role as a leading centre for embroidery, lace-making, tapestries and knitted textiles.

ENVIRONS: Stately homes within a few miles of Nottingham include the Neo-Classical **Kedleston Hall** *(see pp24–5)*. "Bess of Hardwick", Countess of Shrewbury *(see p322)*, built the spectacular **Hardwick Hall** *(see p290)*.

♠ **Nottingham Castle and Museum**
Castle Rd. 📞 *0115 9153700.*
⬜ *daily.* ● *24–27 Dec, 1 Jan.* 🅿️
Sat, Sun & public hols. 📷 🗄️ ♿
🏛️ **Tales of Robin Hood**
30–38 Maid Marion Way. 📞 *0115 9483284.* ⬜ *daily.* ● *24–26 Dec.*
🅿️ ♿ 🗄️ 📷
🏛️ **Museum of Costume and Textiles**
51 Castle Gate. 📞 *0115 9153500.*
⬜ *Wed–Mon, public hols.* ● *24 Dec–1 Jan.* 📷
🏰 **Kedleston Hall**
(NT) off A38. 📞 *01332 842191.*
⬜ *Apr–Oct: Sat–Wed (pm).* 🅿️ 📷
🍴 ♿
🏰 **Hardwick Hall**
(NT) off A617. 📞 *01246 850430.*
⬜ *Apr–Oct: Wed, Thu, Sat, Sun & public hols.* 🅿️ ♿ *limited.* 🍴 📷

ROBIN HOOD OF SHERWOOD FOREST

England's most colourful folk hero was a legendary swordsman, whose adventures are depicted in numerous films and stories. He lived in Sherwood Forest, near Nottingham, with a band of "merry men", robbing the rich to give to the poor. As part of an ancient oral tradition, Robin Hood figured mainly in ballads; the first written records of his exploits date from the 15th century. Today historians think that he was not one person, but a composite of many outlaws who refused to conform to medieval feudal constraints.

Victorian depiction of Friar Tuck and Robin Hood

Tissington Trail ❹

THE FULL-LENGTH Tissington Trail runs for 13 miles (22 km), from the village of Ashbourne to Parsley Hay, where it meets the High Peak Trail. This is a short version, taking an easy route along a dismantled railway line around Tissington village and providing good views of the beautiful White Peak countryside. The Derbyshire custom of well-dressing is thought to have originated in pre-Christian times. It was revived in the early 17th century, when the Tissington village wells were decorated in thanksgiving for deliverance from the plague, in the belief that the fresh water had had a medicinal effect. Well-dressing is still an important event in the Peakland calendar, and can be seen in other villages where the water supplies were prone to dry up.

Crakelow Cutting ③
The view to the north is of open farmland, dotted with small stands of trees.

Crakelow Farm

Railway Cutting ②
The old railway's limestone cuttings are now home to wild flowers, lizards and butterflies.

Downhill Track ④
The track runs along an 18th-century dry-stone wall, built as a result of land enclosure.

KEY

- **– –** Route
- **=** Minor road
- **P** Parking
- **i** Information
- **⌂** Church
- **🚻** Toilets

A515

Town Head Farm

Tissington

Old Station ①
Tissington's old railway station has a refreshment hatch.

A515

B5056

Tissington Hall Well ⑤
This and the other four wells in Tissington are decorated on Ascension Day (the 40th day after Easter). Framed boards have a layer of clay into which rice, seeds and flower petals are pressed.

TIPS FOR WALKERS

Starting point: Old Station. **i** Ashbourne Tourist Information (01335 343666). **Getting there:** Car from Buxton, Matlock or Ashbourne. **Length:** 3 miles (5 km). **Difficulty:** Mostly flat trail along unused railway track and path. **W** www.derbyshiredales.gov.uk

0 metres 500

0 yards 500

Peak District Tour ❺

T HE PEAK DISTRICT'S natural beauty and sheep-grazed crags contrast with the factories of nearby valley towns. Designated Britain's first National Park in 1951, the area has two distinct types of landscape. In the south are the gently rolling hills of the limestone White Peak. To the north, west and east are the wild, heather-clad moorlands of the Dark Peak peat bogs, superimposed on millstone grit.

Detail, Buxton Opera House

Edale ⑤
The high plateau of scenic Edale mark the starting point of the 256 mile (412 km) Pennine Way footpath *(see p32)*.

Buxton ⑥
This lovely spa town's opera house *(see p322)* is known as the "theatre in the hills" because of its magnificent setting.

TIPS FOR DRIVERS

Tour length: 40 miles (60 km).
Stopping-off points: There are refreshments at Crich Tramway Village and Arkwright's Mill in Cromford. Eyam has good old-fashioned tea shops. The Nag's Head in Edale is a charming Tudor inn. Buxton has many pubs and cafés. (See also pp636–7.)

Arbor Low ⑦
This stone circle, known as the "Stonehenge of the North", dates from around 2000 BC and consists of 46 recumbent stones enclosed by a ditch.

KEY

▬▬ Tour route

═══ Other roads

☀ Viewpoint

Dovedale ⑧
Popular Dovedale is one of the prettiest of the Peak District's river valleys, with its stepping stones, thickly wooded slopes and wind-sculpted rocks. Izaac Walton (1593–1683), author of *The Compleat Angler*, used to fish here.

Hathersage ④
There are spectacular panoramic views over the moors above Hathersage, which is thought to be "Morton" in Charlotte Brontë's *(see p398)* Jane Eyre.

Eyam ③
This is famous for the villagers' self-imposed quarantine to contain the plague of 1665–6. There is a fine Saxon cross in the churchyard.

Crich Tramway Village ②
This unique museum is in a disused quarry. Visitors can take rides on old trams from all over the world, along reconstructed Victorian streets.

Cromford ①
Arkwright's Mill *(see p324)* was the world's first water-powered cotton mill. It stands next to the Cromford Canal, part of which can be toured by horse-drawn narrowboats in the summer.

0 kilometres   3

0 miles   2

Street-by-Street: Lincoln ⑦

Carving in Angel Choir

Surrounded by the flat landscape of the Fens, Lincoln rises dramatically on a cliff above the River Witham, the three towers of its massive cathedral visible from afar. The Romans *(see pp44–5)* founded the first fortress here in AD 50. By the time of the Norman Conquest *(see p47)*, Lincoln was one of the most important cities in England (after London, Winchester and York). The city's wealth was due to its strategic importance for the export of wool from the Lincolnshire Wolds to Europe. Lincoln has managed to retain much of its historic character. Many remarkable medieval buildings have survived, most of which are along the aptly named Steep Hill, leading to the cathedral.

3rd-century Newport Arch

Museum of Lincolnshire Life

WESTGATE

BAILGATE

CASTLE HILL

DRURY LANE

STEEP HILL

MICHAELGATE

Norman House (1180)

★ **Lincoln Castle**
The early Norman castle, rebuilt at intervals, acted as the city prison from 1787 to 1878. The chapel's coffin-like pews served to remind felons of their fate.

KEY

‒ ‒ ‒ Suggested route

Jew's House
Lincoln had a large medieval Jewish community. This mid-12th-century stone house, one of the oldest of its kind, was owned by a Jewish merchant.

15th-century Stonebow Gate and railway station

0 metres		100
0 yards		100

STAR SIGHTS

★ Lincoln Castle

★ Lincoln Cathedral

VISITORS' CHECKLIST

Lincolnshire. 85,000.
Humberside, 30 miles (48 km);
E Midlands, 51 miles (82 km).
St Mary St. Melville St.
Castle Hill (01522 873214).
W www.lincoln.gov.uk

★ Lincoln Cathedral
The west front is a harmonious mix of Norman and Gothic styles. Inside, the best features include the Angel Choir, with the figure of the Lincoln Imp.

Alfred, Lord Tennyson
A statue of the Lincolnshire-born poet (1809–92) stands in the grounds.

The 14th-century **Pottergate Arch**

Arboretum

Ruins of Bishop's Palace

EASTGATE

MINISTER YARD

GREENSTONE PLACE

POTTERGATE

DANESGATE

TERRACE

LINDUM ROAD

Coach station

Usher Art Gallery
This is packed with clocks, ceramics, and silver. There are paintings by Peter de Wint (1784–1849) and J M W Turner (see p93).

MISERICORDS

Misericords are ledges that project from the underside of the hinged seat of a choir stall, which provide support while standing.

St Francis of Assisi

Lincoln Cathedral's misericords in the early Perpendicular-style canopied choir stalls are some of the best in England. The wide variety of subjects includes parables, fables, myths, biblical scenes and irreverent images from daily life.

One of a pair of lions

Burghley House ❽

WILLIAM CECIL, 1ST LORD BURGHLEY (1520–98) was Queen Elizabeth I's adviser and confidant for 40 years. He built the wonderfully dramatic Burghley House in 1555– 87, probably designing it himself. The roof line bristles with stone pyramids, chimneys disguised as Classical columns and towers shaped like pepper pots. The busy skyline only resolves itself into a symmetrical pattern

Portrait of Sir Isaac Newton, Billiard Room

when viewed from the west, where a lime tree stands, one of many planted by Capability Brown *(see p22)* when the surrounding deer park was landscaped in 1760. Burghley's interior is lavishly decorated with Italian paintings of Greek gods enacting their dramas across the walls and ceiling.

★ Old Kitchen
Gleaming copper pans hang from the walls of the fan-vaulted kitchen, little altered since the Tudor period.

North Gate
Intricate examples of 19th-century wrought-iron work adorn the principal entrances.

The Billiard Room
has many fine portraits inset in oak panelling.

Cupolas were very fashionable details, inspired by European Renaissance architecture.

A chimney has been disguised as a Classical column.

Mullioned windows were added in 1683 when glass became less expensive.

The Gatehouse, with its side turrets, is a typical feature of the "prodigy" houses of the Tudor era *(see p290)*.

West Front
Featuring the Burghley crest, the West Front was finished in 1577 and formed the original main entrance.

STAR SIGHTS

★ Old Kitchen

★ Heaven Room

★ Hell Staircase

★ Heaven Room
Gods tumble from the sky, and satyrs and nymphs play on the walls and ceiling in this masterpiece by Antonio Verrio (1639–1707).

Obelisk and clock (1585)

The Great Hall has a double hammer-beam roof and was a banqueting hall in Elizabethan days.

The wine cooler (1710) is thought to be the largest in existence.

The Fourth George Room, one of a suite, is panelled in oak stained with ale.

★ Hell Staircase
Verrio painted the ceiling to show Hell as the mouth of a cat crammed with tormented sinners. The staircase, of local stone, was installed in 1786.

Stamford ❾

Lincolnshire. 🏠 18,000. ≥ 🏪 🛈
27 St Mary's St (01780 755611). 🛒
Fri. W www.stamfordonline.co.uk

STAMFORD is a showpiece town, famous for its many churches and its Georgian townhouses. Stamford retains a medieval street plan, with a warren of winding streets and cobbled alleys.

The spires of the medieval churches (five survive of the original eleven) give Stamford the air of a miniature Oxford.

Barn Hill, leading up from All Saints Church, is the best place for a view of Stamford's Georgian architecture in all its variety. Below it is Broad Street, where the **Stamford Museum** covers the history of the town. By far the most popular exhibit is a waxwork of Britain's fattest man, Daniel Lambert, who was 336 kg (53 stone) and died while attending Stamford Races in 1809.

🏛 **Stamford Museum**
Broad St. 📞 01780 766317. ○
Apr–Sep: daily (Sun: pm); Oct–Mar:
Mon–Sat. ♿ limited. 🏪 W www.
lincolnshire.gov.uk/stamfordmuseum

Northampton ❿

Northamptonshire. 🏠 187,000.
≥ 🏪 🛈 Guildhall Rd (01604
838800). 🛒 Tue–Sat (Thu: antiques).
W www.northampton.gov.uk

THIS MARKET TOWN was once a centre for shoe-making, and the **Central Muscum and Art Gallery** holds the world's largest collection of footwear. One of many fine old buildings is the Victorian Gothic **Guildhall**. Six miles west of the town is **Althorp House**, family home of Diana Princess of Wales. Visitors can tour the house, grounds, see an exhibition on Diana and her island resting place.

🏛 **Central Museum and Art Gallery**
Guildhall Rd. 📞 01604 238548. ○
daily (Sun: pm). ● 25, 26 Dec. ♿ 🏪
🏛 **Althorp House**
Great Brington (off A428). 📞 01604
770107. ○ Jul–Sep daily. ● 31 Aug.
🎫 🖥 ♿ 🏪 W www.althorp.com

THE NORTH COUNTRY

The North Country at a Glance

RUGGED COASTLINES, spectacular walks and climbs, magnificent stately homes and breathtaking cathedrals all have their place in the north of England, with its dramatic history of Roman rule, Saxon invasion, Viking attacks and border skirmishes. Reminders of the industrial revolution are found in towns such as Halifax, Liverpool and Manchester, and peace and inspiration in the dramatic scenery of the Lake District, with its awe-inspiring mountains and waters.

Hadrian's Wall (see pp408–9), *built around 120 to protect Roman Britain from the Picts to the north, cuts through rugged Northumberland National Park scenery.*

NORTHUMB
(see pp400–4

Northumber

Durh

The Lake District (see pp342–57) *is a combination of superb peaks, tumbling rivers and falls and shimmering lakes such as Wast Water.*

Cumbria

Yorkshire Dales National Park (see pp370–72) *creates a delightful environment for walking and touring the farming landscape, scattered with attractive villages such as Thwaite, in Swaledale.*

Lancashire

LANCASHIRE AND THE LAKES
(see pp342–365)

Manchester

The Walker Art Gallery (see pp364–5) *in Liverpool is one of the jewels in the artistic crown of the north, with an internationally renowned collection ranging from Old Masters to modern art. Sculpture includes John Gibson's* Tinted Venus *(c.1851–6).*

Liverpool

◁ **The 11th-century Alnwick Castle, Alnwick, Northumberland, from across the River Aln**

Durham Cathedral (see pp414–5), *a striking Norman structure with an innovative southern choir aisle and fine stained glass, has towered over the city of Durham since 995.*

Fountains Abbey (see pp376–7), *one of the finest religious buildings in the north, was founded in the 12th century by monks who desired simplicity and austerity. Later the abbey became extremely wealthy.*

Castle Howard (see pp384–5), *a triumph of Baroque architecture, offers many magnificent settings, including this Museum Room (1805–10), designed by CH Tatham.*

York (see pp390–95) *is a city of historical treasures, ranging from the medieval to Georgian. Its magnificent minster has a large collection of stained glass and the medieval city walls are well preserved. Other sights include churches, narrow alleyways and notable museums.*

Cleveland

North Yorkshire

YORKSHIRE
AND THE
HUMBER
REGION
(e pp366–399)

East Riding of Yorkshire

Leeds

0 kilometres   25

0 miles   25

The Industrial Revolution in the North

THE FACE OF NORTHERN ENGLAND in the 19th century was dramatically altered by the development of the coal mining, textile and shipbuilding industries. Lancashire, Northumberland and the West Riding (*see p367*) of Yorkshire all experienced population growth and migration to cities. The hardships of urban life were partly relieved by the actions of several wealthy industrial philanthropists, but many people lived in extremely deprived conditions. Although most traditional industries have now declined sharply or disappeared as demand has moved elsewhere, a growing tourist industry has developed in many of the former industrial centres.

Back-to-backs *or colliers' rows, such as these houses at Easington, were provided by colliery owners from the 1800s onwards. They comprised two small rooms for cooking and sleeping, and an outside toilet.*

1815 Sir Humphrey Davy invented a safety oil lamp for miners. Light shone through a cylindrical gauze sheet which prevented the heat of the flame igniting methane gas in the mine. Thousands of miners benefited from this device.

Coal mining *was a family industry in the North of England with women and children working alongside the men.*

1750	1800
PRE-STEAM	STEAM AGE
1750	1800

1781 Leeds–Liverpool Canal opened. The building of canals facilitated the movement of raw materials and finished products, and aided the process of mechanization immeasurably.

1830 Liverpool Manchester rai opened, connecting tw the biggest cities ou London. Within a month railway carried passeng

Halifax's Piece Hall (see p399), *restored in 1976, is the most impressive surviving example of industrial architecture in northern England. It is the only complete 18th-century cloth market building in Yorkshire. Merchants sold measures of cloth known as "pieces" from rooms lining the cloisters inside.*

Hebden Bridge (see p398), *a typical West Riding textile mill town jammed into the narrow Calder Valley, typifies a pattern of workers' houses surrounding a central mill. The town benefited from its position when the Rochdale Canal (1804) and then the railway (1841) took advantage of this relatively low-level route over the Pennines.*

Saltaire (see p397) *was a model village built by the wealthy cloth merchant and mill-owner Sir Titus Salt (1803–76), for the benefit of his workers. Seen here in the 1870s, it included houses and facilities such as shops, gardens and sportsfields, with almshouses, a hospital, school and chapel. A disciplinarian, Salt banned alcohol and pubs from Saltaire.*

George Hudson (1800–71) built the first railway station in York (see p394) in 1840–42. In the 1840s he owned more than a quarter of the railways in Britain and was known as the "railway king".

1842 Coal Mines Act prevented women and children from working in harsh conditions in the mines.

Port Sunlight (see p365) *was founded by William Hesketh Lever (1851–1925) to provide housing for workers at his Sunlight soap factory. Between 1889 and 1914 he built 800 cottages. Amenities included a pool.*

Strikes to improve working conditions were common. Violence flared in July 1893 when colliery owners locked miners out of their pits and stopped their pay after the Miners' Federation resisted a 25 per cent wage cut. Over 300,000 men struggled without pay until November, when work resumed at the old rate.

1850	1900
FULL MECHANIZATION	
1850	1900

Power loom weaving transformed the textile industry while creating unemployment among skilled hand loom weavers. By the 1850s, the West Riding had 30,000 power looms, used in cotton and woollen mills. Of 79,000 workers, over half were to be found in Bradford alone.

Furness dry dock was built in the 1890s when the shipbuilding industry moved north, in search of cheap labour and materials. Barrow-in-Furness, Glasgow (see pp502–5) and Tyne and Wear (see p410) were the new centres.

Joseph Rowntree (1836–1925) founded his chocolate factory in York in 1892, having formerly worked with George Cadbury. As Quakers, the Rowntrees believed in the social welfare of their workers (establishing a model village in 1904), and, with Terry's confectionary (1767), they made a vast contribution to York's prosperity. Today, Nestlé Rowntree is the world's largest chocolate factory and York is Britain's chocolate capital.

North Country Abbeys

NORTHERN ENGLAND has some of the finest and best preserved religious houses in Europe. Centres of prayer, learning and power in the Middle Ages, the larger of these were designated abbeys and were governed by an abbot. Most were located in rural areas, considered appropriate for a spiritual and contemplative life. Viking raiders had destroyed many Anglo-Saxon religious houses in the 8th and 9th centuries *(see pp46–7)* and it was not until William the Conqueror founded the Benedictine Selby Abbey in 1069 that monastic life revived in the north. New orders, Augustinians in particular, arrived from the Continent and by 1500 Yorkshire had 83 monasteries.

Cistercian monk

Ruins of St Mary's Abbey today

The Liberty of St Mary was the name given to the land around the abbey, almost a city within a city. Here, the abbot had his own market, fair, prison and gallows – all exempt from the city authorities.

St Mary's Abbey

Founded in York in 1086, this Benedictine abbey was one of the wealthiest in Britain. Its involvement in the wool trade in York and the granting of royal and papal privileges and land led to a relaxing of standards by the early 12th century. The abbot was even allowed to dress in the same style as a bishop, and was raised by the pope to the status of a "mitred abbot". As a result, 13 monks left in 1132, to found Fountains Abbey *(see pp376–7)*.

Gatehouse and St Olave's church

Interval tower

Water tower

Hospitium or guest house

Monasteries and Local Life

As one of the wealthiest landowning sections of society, the monasteries played a vital role in the local economy. They provided employment, particularly in agriculture, and dominated the wool trade, England's largest export during the Middle Ages. By 1387 two thirds of all wool exported from England passed through St Mary's Abbey, the largest wool trader in York.

Cistercian monks tilling their land

Where to See Abbeys Today

Fountains Abbey *(see pp376–7)*, founded by Benedictine monks and later taken over by Cistercians, is the most famous of the numerous abbeys in the region. Rievaulx *(see p379)*, Byland *(see p378)* and Furness *(see p356)* were all founded by the Cistercians, and Furness became the second wealthiest Cistercian house in England after Fountains. Whitby Abbey *(see p382)*, sacked by the Vikings, was later rebuilt by the Benedictine order. Northumberland is famous for its early Anglo-Saxon monasteries, such as Ripon, Lastingham and Lindisfarne *(see pp404–5)*.

Mount Grace Priory (see p380), *founded in 1398, is the best-preserved Carthusian house in England. The former individual gardens and cells of each monk are still clearly visible.*

THE DISSOLUTION OF THE MONASTERIES (1536–40)

By the early 16th century, the monasteries owned one-sixth of all English land and their annual income was four times that of the Crown. Henry VIII ordered the closure of all religious houses in 1536, acquiring their wealth in the process. His attempt at dissolution provoked a large uprising of Catholic northerners led by Robert Aske later that year. The rebellion failed and Aske and others were executed for conspiracy. The dissolution continued under Thomas Cromwell, who became known as "the hammer of the monks".

Thomas Cromwell (c.1485–1549)

The large Abbot's House testified to the grand lifestyle that late medieval abbots adopted.

The Chapter House, an assembly room, was the most important building after the church.

Lavatory

Kitchen

The Warming House was the only room in the monastery, apart from the kitchen, which had a fire.

Refectory

The Abbey Wall had battlements added in 1318 to protect it against raids by Scottish armies.

Common parlour

Cloister

Kirkham Priory, an Augustinian foundation of the 1120s, enjoys a tranquil setting on the banks of the River Derwent, near Malton. The finest feature of the ruined site is the 13th-century gatehouse which leads into the priory complex.

Kirkstall Abbey was founded in 1152 by monks from Fountains Abbey. The well-preserved ruins of this Cistercian house near Leeds include the church, the late Norman chapter house and the abbot's lodging. This evening view was painted by Thomas Girtin (1775–1802).

...asby Abbey lies beside the River Swale, outside the pretty market town of Richmond. Among the ...mains of this Premonstratensian ...house, founded in 1155, are the ...-century refectory and sleeping ...rters and 14th-century gatehouse.

The Geology of the Lake District

THE LAKE DISTRICT contains some of England's most spectacular scenery. Concentrated in just 900 sq miles (231 sq km) are the highest peaks, deepest valleys and longest lakes in the country. Today's landscape has changed little since the end of the Ice Age 10,000 years ago, the last major event in Britain's geological history. But the glaciated hills which were revealed by the retreating ice were once part of a vast mountain-chain whose remains can also be found in North America. The mountains were first raised by the gradual fusion of two ancient landmasses which, for millions of years, formed a single continent. Eventually the continent broke into two, forming Europe and America, separated by the widening Atlantic Ocean.

Piece of Lake District slate

Honister Pass, with its distinctive U-shape, is an example of a glaciated valley, once completely filled with ice.

GEOLOGICAL HISTORY

The oldest rock formed as sediment under an ocean called Iapetus. Some 450 million years ago, Earth's internal movements made two continents collide, and the ocean disappear.

1 *The collision buckled the former sea bed into a mountain range. Magma rose from Earth's mantle, altered the sediments and cooled into volcanic rock.*

2 *In the Ice Age, glaciers slowly excavated huge rock basins in the mountainsides, dragging debris to the valley floor. Frost sculpted the summits.*

3 *The glaciers retreated 10,000 years ago, their meltwaters forming lakes in valleys dammed by debris. As the climate improved, plants colonized the fells.*

RADIATING LAKES

The diversity of lakeland scenery owes much to its geology: hard volcanic rocks in the central lakes give rise to rugged hills, while soft slates to the north produce a more rounded topography. The lakes form a radial pattern, spreading out from a central volcanic rock zone.

Scafell Pike is the highest peak in England. One of the three Scafell Pikes, its two neighbours are Broad Crag and Ill Crag.

Great Gable

Old Man of Coniston

Coniston Water

Wast Water is the deepest of the lakes. Its southeastern cliffs are streaked with granite scree – the debris formed each year as rock shattered by the winter frost tumbles down during the spring thaw.

MAN ON THE MOUNTAIN

The sheltered valley floors with their benign climate and fertile soils are ideal for settlement. Farmhouses, dry-stone walls, pasture and sheep pens are an integral part of the landscape. Higher up, the absence of trees and bracken are the result of wind and a cooler climate. Old mine workings and tracks are the relics of once-flourishing industries.

Plantations *of coniferous trees are a recent feature of the landscape. Some see them as harming traditional views and disturbing the ecology.*

Summer grazing

Copper and graphite mines

Tracks

Dry-stone walls *(see p293)*

Slate *and other local stone has long been incorporated into buildings: slate roofs, stone walls, lintels and bridges.*

Hedges

400–500 m (130–170 ft)

300–400 m (100–130 ft)

Sheep pens for winter grazing

waite

▲ *Blencathra*

nt Water

▲ *Helvellyn*

Ullswater

▲ *Place Fell*

▲ *High Street*

Windermere

Skiddaw *is composed of slate, formed when the muddy sediment of the ancient ocean floor was altered by extreme pressure.*

Striding Edge *is a long, twisting ridge which leads to the summit of Helvellyn. It was sharpened by the widening of the valleys on either side caused by the build up of glaciers.*

The Langdale Pikes *are remnants of the volcanic activity which once erupted in the area. They are made of hard igneous rocks, known as Borrowdale Volcanics. Unlike the Skiddaw Slates, they have not eroded smoothly, so they leave a craggy skyline.*

LANCASHIRE AND THE LAKES

CUMBRIA · LANCASHIRE

THE LANDSCAPE PAINTER *John Constable (1776–1837) declared that the Lake District, now visited by 18 million people annually, had "the finest scenery that ever was". The Normans built many religious houses here, and William II created estates for English barons. Today, the National Trust is its most important landowner.*

Within the 30 mile (45 km) radius of the Lake District lies an astonishing number of fells and lakes. Today, all looks peaceful, but from the Roman occupation to the Middle Ages, the northwest was a turbulent area, as successive kings and rulers fought over the territory. Historians can revel in the various Celtic monuments, Roman remains, stately homes and monastic ruins. Although the scenery is paramount, there are many outdoor activities as well as spectator sports, such as Cumbrian wrestling, and wildlife to observe.

Lancashire's portfolio of tourist attractions includes the fine county town of Lancaster, bright Blackpool with its autumn illuminations and fairground attractions, and the peaceful seaside beaches to the south. Inland, the most appealing regions are the Forest of Bowland, a sparse expanse of heathery grouse moor, and the picturesque Ribble Valley. Further south still are the industrial conurbations of Manchester and Merseyside, where the attractions are more urban.

There are many fine Victorian buildings in Manchester, where the industrial quarter of Castlefield has been revitalized. Liverpool, with its restored Albert Dock, is best known as the seaport city of the Beatles. It has a lively club scene and is increasingly used as a film location. Both cities have good art galleries and museums.

Jetty at Grasmere, one of the most popular regions of the Lake District

◁ Restored Albert Dock, lining the River Mersey in Liverpool

Exploring Lancashire and the Lakes

THE LAKE DISTRICT'S natural scenery outweighs any of its man-made attractions. Its natural features are the result of geological upheavals over millennia *(see pp340–41)*, and four of its peaks are more than 1,000 m (3,300 ft). Human influences have left their mark too: the main activities are quarrying, mining, farming and tourism.

The Lakes are most crowded in summer when activities include lake trips and hill-walking. The best bases are Keswick and Ambleside, while there are also good hotels on the shores of Windermere and Ullswater and in the Cartmel area.

Lancashire's Bowland Forest is an attractive place to explore on foot, with picturesque villages. Further south, Manchester and Liverpool have excellent museums and galleries.

Watersports on Derwentwater in the Northern Fells and Lakes area

GETTING AROUND

For many, the first glimpse of the Lake District is from the M6 near Shap Fell, but the A6 is a more dramatic route. You can reach Windermere by train, but you need to change at Oxenholme, on the mainline route from Euston to Carlisle. Penrith also has rail services and bus links into the Lakes. L'al Ratty, the miniature railway up Eskdale, and the Lakeside & Haverthwaite railway, which connects with the steamers on Windermere,

make for enjoyable outings. Regular buses link all the main centres where excursions are organized. One of the most enterprising is the Mountain Goat minibus, in Windermere and Keswick.

Lancaster, Liverpool and Manchester are on the main rail and bus routes and also have airports. For Blackpool, you need to change trains in Preston. Wherever you go in the area, one of the best means of getting around is on foot.

View over Crummock Water, north of Buttermere,
one of the quieter Western Lakes

KEY

▬ Motorway
▬ Major road
▬ Scenic route
-●- Scenic path
〰 River
🔆 Viewpoint

0 kilometres 20
0 miles 10

Preserved docks and Liver Building, Liverpool

Carlisle ❶

Cumbria. 🏛 *102,000.* ✕ *mainly private.* ≋ 🚌 ℹ *The Old Town Hall, Green Market (01228 625600).* 🌐 *www.historic-carlisle.org.uk*

D UE TO ITS proximity to the Scottish border, this city has long been a defensive site. Known as Luguvalium by the Romans, it was an outpost of Hadrian's Wall *(see pp408–9).* Carlisle was sacked and pillaged repeatedly by the Danes, the Normans and border raiders, and suffered damage as a Royalist stronghold under Cromwell *(see p52).*

Today, Carlisle is the capital of Cumbria. In its centre are the timber-framed Guildhall and market cross, and fortifications still exist around its West Walls, drum-towered gates and its Norman **castle**. The castle tower has a small museum devoted to the King's Own Border Regiment. The cathedral dates from 1122 and features a decorative east window. Carlisle's **Tullie House Museum** recreates the city's past with sections on Roman history and Cumbrian wildlife. Nearby lie the evocative ruins of

Saxon iron sword in the Tullie House Museum

Façade of Hutton-in-the-Forest with medieval tower on the right

Lanercost Priory (c.1166) and the remains of the unique **Birdoswald Roman Fort**.

♣ **Carlisle Castle**
(EH) Castle Way. 📞 *01228 591922.* ◯ *daily.* ♿ *limited.* 🎫 🏠

🏛 **Tullie House Museum**
Castle St. 📞 *01228 534781.* ◯ *daily (Sun: pm).* ● *1 Jan, 25, 26 Dec.* ♿

♦ **Lanercost Priory**
(EH) Nr Brampton. 📞 *016977 3030.* ◯ *Apr–Oct: daily.* ♿ *limited.*

♣ **Birdoswald Roman Fort**
(EH) Gilsland, Brampton. 📞 *016977 47602.* ◯ *Mar–Oct: daily.* ♿ *limited.* 🏠 🏠
🌐 *www.birdoswaldromanfort.org.uk*

Penrith ❷

Cumbria. 🏛 *15,000.* ℹ *Robinson's School, Middlegate (01768 867466).* 🚉 *Tue, Sat.* 🌐 *www.visiteden.co.uk*

T IMEWARP SHOPFRONTS on the market square and a 14th-century **castle** of sandstone are Penrith's main attractions.

There are some strange hog-back stones in St Andrew's churchyard, allegedly a giant's grave, and the 285 m (937 ft) Beacon provides stunning views of distant fells.

ENVIRONS: Just northeast of Penrith at Little Salkeld is a famous Bronze Age circle (with 66 tall stones) known as **Long Meg and her Daughters.** Six miles (9 km) northwest of Penrith lies **Hutton-in-the-Forest.** The oldest part of this house is the 13th-century tower. Inside is a magnificent Italianate staircase, a sumptuously panelled 17th-century Long Gallery, a delicately stuccoed Cupid Room dating from the 1740s, and several Victorian rooms. Outside, you can walk around the walled garden and topiary terraces, or explore the woods.

♣ **Penrith Castle**
Ullswater Rd. ◯ *daily.* ♿ *in grounds.*

🏰 **Hutton-in-the-Forest**
Off B5305. 📞 *017684 84449.* **House** ◯ *Easter–Sep: Thu, Fri, Sun & public hols (pm).* **Grounds** ◯ *Apr–Oct: Sun–Fri.* ● *25 Dec.* ♿ *limited.* 🏠 🏠

Dalemain ❸

Penrith, Cumbria. 📞 *017684 86450.* ≋ 🚌 *Penrith then taxi.* ◯ *Apr–Sep: Sun–Thu.* ♿ *limited.* 🎫 🏠

A SEEMLY GEORGIAN façade gives this fine house near Ullswater the impression of architectural unity, but hides a greatly altered medieval and Elizabethan structure with a maze of rambling passages. Public rooms include a superb Chinese drawing room with hand-painted wallpaper, and

---

TRADITIONAL CUMBRIAN SPORTS

Cumberland wrestling is one of the most interesting sports to watch in the summer months. The combatants, often clad in longjohns and embroidered velvet pants, clasp one another in an armlock and attempt to topple each other over. Technique and good balance outweigh physical force. Other traditional Lakeland sports include fell-racing, a gruelling test of speed and stamina up and down local peaks at ankle-breaking speed. Hound-trailing is also a popular sport in which specially bred hounds follow an aniseed trail over the hills. Sheep-dog trials, steam fairs, flower shows and gym-khanas take place in summer. The Egremont Crab Fair in September holds events such as greasy-pole climbing.

Cumberland wrestlers

Sheep resting at Glenridding, on the southwest shore of Ullswater

a panelled 18th-century drawing room. Several small museums occupy various outbuildings, and the gardens contain a fine collection of fragrant shrub roses and a huge silver fir.

Sumptuous Chinese drawing room at Dalemain

Ullswater ➍

Cumbria. ➔ *Penrith.* ℹ *Main car park, Glenridding, Penrith (017684 82414).* ⓦ *www.lake-district.gov.uk*

O FTEN CONSIDERED the most beautiful of all Cumbria's lakes, Ullswater stretches from gentle farmland near Penrith to dramatic hills and crags at its southern end. The main western shore road can be very busy. In summer, two restored Victorian steamers ply

regularly from Pooley Bridge to Glenridding. One of the best walks crosses the eastern shore from Glenridding to Hallin Fell and the moorland of Martindale. The western side passes Gowbarrow, where Wordsworth's immortalized "host of golden daffodils" bloom in spring *(see p354).*

Keswick ➎

Cumbria. ⌂ *5,000.* ℹ *Moot Hall, Market Sq (017687 72645).* ⓦ *www.keswick.org*

P OPULAR AS A tourist venue since the advent of the railway in Victorian times, Keswick now has guest houses, a summer repertory theatre, outdoor equipment shops and a serious parking problem in high season. Its most striking central building is the **Moot Hall**, dating from 1813, now used as the tourist office. The town prospered on wool and leather until, in Tudor times, deposits of graphite were discovered. Mining then took over as the main industry and Keswick became an important centre for pencil manufacture. In World War II, hollow pencils were made to hide espionage maps on thin paper. The factory includes the **Pencil**

Museum with interesting audiovisual shows. Among the many fine exhibits at the **Keswick Museum and Art Gallery** are the original manuscripts of Lakeland writers, musical stones and many other curiosities.

To the east of the town lies the ancient stone circle of Castlerigg, thought to be older than Stonehenge.

🏛 **Pencil Museum**
Carding Mill Lane. (*017687 73626.*
◯ *daily.* ● *25, 26 Dec,1 Jan.* 🎦 &
🚻 ⓦ *www.pencil.co.uk*
🏛 **Keswick Museum and Art Gallery**
Fitz Park, Station Rd. (*017687 73263.* ◯ *call for details.* 🎦 & 🚻

Outdoor equipment shop in Keswick

Northern Fells and Lakes ❻

The rare red squirrel, native to the area

MANY VISITORS praise this northern area of the Lake District National Park for its scenery and geological interest *(see pp340–41)*. It is ideal walking country, and nearby Derwentwater, Thirlmere and Bassenthwaite provide endless scenic views, rambles and opportunities for watersports. Large areas surrounding the regional centre of Keswick *(see p347)* are accessible only on foot, particularly the huge mass of hills known as Back of Skiddaw – located between Skiddaw and Caldbeck – or the Helvellyn range, east of Thirlmere.

The Whinlatter Pass is an easy route from Keswick to the forested Lorton Vale. It gives a good view of Bassenthwaite Lake and a glimpse of Grisedale Pike.

Bassenthwaite is best view from the east shore. The road passes through Dodd Wood at the foot of Skidda

CARLISLE

B5291

WORKINGTON

A66

High Lorton

LORTON VALE

WHINLATTER PASS

B5292

B5292

LOWESWATER

Braithwaite

BASSENTHWAITE LAKE

A591

Derwent

Newlands Beck

DERWE

Grange

BUTTERMERE

Lorton Vale

The lush, green farmland south of Cockermouth creates a marked contrast with the more rugged mountain landscapes of the central Lake District. In the village of Low Lorton is the private manor house of Lorton Hall, dating from the 15th century.

Derwentwater

Surrounded by woodland slopes and fells, this attractive oval lake is dotted with tiny islands. One of these was inhabited by St Herbert, a disciple of St Cuthbert (see p405), who lived there as a hermit until 687. A boat from Keswick provides a lake excursion.

THE MAJOR PEAKS

The Lake District hills are the highest in England. Although they seem small by Alpine or world standards, the scale of the surrounding terrain makes them look extremely grand. Some of the most important peaks are shown on the following pages. Each peak is regarded as having its own personality. This section shows the Skiddaw fells, which are north of Keswick.

① Blencathra
▲ Skiddaw
▲ Grisedale Pike
③ ▲ Grasmoor
▲ Knott Rigg
▲ Helvellyn
▲ Great Gable
▲ High Street
Wastwater Screes
▲ Scafell
▲ Hard Knott
▲ The Old Man of Coniston
⑤
⑥
②

KEY

From ① Blencathra to ② Cockermouth *(see opposite)*

From ③ Grisedale Pike to ④ the Old Man of Coniston *(see pp350–51)*

From ⑤ the Old Man of Coniston to ⑥ Windermere and Tarn Crag *(see pp352–3)*

National Park boundary

Skiddaw
At 931 m (3,054 ft) Skiddaw is England's fourth highest peak. Its rounded shape makes it a manageable two-hour walk for anyone reasonably fit.

Blencathra, also known as Saddleback because of its twin peaks (868 m; 2,847 ft), is a challenging climb, especially in winter.

St John's in the Vale
This valley contains Castle Rock for climbers, and its old legends were used by Sir Walter Scott (see p498) in The Bridal of Triermain. *Lakeland poet John Richardson is buried in the churchyard.*

Thirlmere was created as a reservoir to serve Manchester in 1879.

Castlerigg Stone Circle
Described by Keats (see p131) as "a dismal cirque of Druid stones upon a forlorn moor", these ancient stones overlook Skiddaw, Helvellyn and Crag Hill.

KEY

🛈 Information
▬ Major road
▬ Minor road
❋ Viewpoint

0 kilometres 5
0 miles 3

Crummock Water, one of the quieter "western lakes"

Cockermouth 7

Cumbria. 8,000. Workington. Town Hall, Market St (01900 822634).
W www.western-lakedistrict.co.uk

COLOURWASHED TERRACES and restored workers' cottages beside the river are especially attractive in the busy market town of Cockermouth, which dates from the 12th century. The place not to miss is the handsome **Wordsworth House**, in the Main Street, where the poet was born *(see p354)*. This fine Georgian building still contains a few of the family's possessions, and is furnished in the style of the late 18th century. Wordsworth mentions the attractive terraced garden, which overlooks the River Derwent, in his *Prelude*. The local parish church contains a Wordsworth memorial window.

Cockermouth **castle** is partly ruined but still inhabited and closed to the public. The town has small museums of printing, toys and a mineral collection, and an art gallery. The **Jennings Brewery** invites visitors for tours and tastings.

Wordsworth House
(NT) Main St. 01900 824805. for refurbishment. Call for details.
Jennings Brewery
Castle Brewery. 01900 821011. Mon–Sat (Jul, Aug: daily). 1 Jan, 25, 26 Dec.
W www.jenningsbrewery.co.uk

Newlands Valley 8

Cumbria. Workington then bus. Cockermouth. Town Hall, Market St, Cockermouth (01900 822634); Market Sq, Keswick (017687 72645).
W www.western-lakedistrict.co.uk

FROM THE gently wooded shores of Derwentwater, the Newlands Valley runs through a scattering of farms towards rugged heights of 335 m (1,100 ft) at the top of the pass, where steps lead to the waterfall, Moss Force. Grisedale Pike, Grasmoor and Knott Rigg all provide excellent fell walks. Local mineral deposits of copper, graphite, lead and even small amounts of gold and silver were extensively mined here from Elizabethan times onwards. **Little Town** was used as a setting by Beatrix Potter *(see p355)* in *The Tale of Mrs Tiggywinkle*.

Kitchen, with an old range and tiled floor, at Wordsworth House

Blencathra 868 m (2,847 ft) · Grisedale Pike 790 m (2,591 ft) · Grasmoor 850 m (2788 ft) · Wandope · White Pike · Robinson · Great Dodd · Dalehead · Fleetwith Pike · Raise · Looking Stead · Helvellyn 950 m (3,118 ft) · Great G 899 m (2,949 ft) · Knott Rigg · Crummock Water · Ennerdale · Buttermere · Buttermere village · Innominate Tarn and Haystacks · Pillar · Mosedale · Black Sail Pass · Kirk Fell

Buttermere ❾

Cumbria. 🚂 *Penrith*. 🚌 *Cocker-mouth.* 🚌 *Penrith to Keswick; Keswick to Buttermere.* ℹ️ *Town Hall, Market St, Cockermouth (01900 822634).*

INTERLINKING WITH Crummock Water and Loweswater, Buttermere and its surroundings contain some of the most appealing countryside in the region. Often known as the "western lakes", the three are remote enough not to become too crowded. Buttermere is a jewel amid grand fells: High Stile, Red Pike and Haystacks. Here the ashes of the celebrated hill-walker and author of fell-walking books, A W Wainwright, are scattered.

The village of Buttermere, with its handful of houses and inns, is a popular starting point for walks round all three lakes. Loweswater is hardest to reach and therefore the quietest, surrounded by woods and hills. Nearby Scale Force is the highest waterfall in the Lake District, plunging 36 m (120 ft).

Verdant valley of Borrowdale, a favourite with artists

Borrowdale ❿

Cumbria. 🚂 *Workington*. 🚌 *Cocker-mouth.* ℹ️ *Town Hall, Market St, Cockermouth (01900 822634).*

THIS ROMANTIC VALLEY, subject of a myriad sketches and watercolours before photography stole the scene, lies beside the densely wooded shores of Derwentwater under towering crags. It is a popular trip from Keswick and a great variety of walks are possible along the valley.

The tiny hamlet of **Grange** is one of the prettiest spots, where the valley narrows dramatically to form the "Jaws of Borrowdale". Nearby Castle Crag has superb views.

From Grange you can complete the circuit of Derwentwater along the western shore, or move southwards to the more open farmland around Seatoller. As you head south by road, look out for a National Trust sign *(see p25)* to the **Bowder Stone**, a delicately poised block weighing nearly 2,000 tonnes, which may have fallen from the crags above or been deposited by a glacier millions of years ago.

Two attractive hamlets in Borrowdale are **Rosthwaite** and **Stonethwaite**. Also worth a detour, preferably on foot, is Watendlath village, off a side road near the famous beauty spot of **Ashness Bridge**.

WALKING IN THE LAKE DISTRICT

Typical Lake District stile over dry-stone wall

Two long-distance footpaths pass through the Lake District's most spectacular scenery. The 70 mile (110 km) Cumbrian Way runs from Carlisle to Ulverston via Keswick and Coniston. The western section of the Coast-to-Coast Walk *(see pp32–3)* passes through this area. There are hundreds of shorter walks along lake shores, nature trails or following more challenging uphill routes. Walkers should stick to paths to avoid erosion, and check weather conditions at National Park information centres.

④

Scafell Pike (978 m 3,210 ft) — Langdale Pikes — Hard Knott 550 m (1,803 ft) — Hardknott Pass — Carrs — Grey Friar — Swirl How — Dow Crag — Old Man of Coniston 803 m (2,633 ft) — Caw

Wastwater Screes — Crinkle Crags 924 m (2,816 ft) — Blea Tarn — Harter Fell — Eskdale — Ravenglass and Eskdale Railway — Seathwaite Tarn — Seathwaite — River Duddon

Convivial Wasdale Head Inn *(see p561)* at Wasdale Head

Wastwater ⓫

Cumbria. ≥ *Whitehaven.* ℹ *12 Main St, Egremont (01946 820693).*

A SILENT REFLECTION of truly awesome surroundings, black, brooding **Wastwater** is a mysterious, evocative lake. The road from Nether Wasdale continues along its northwest side. Along its eastern flank loom walls of sheer scree over 600 m (2,000 ft) high. Beneath them the water looks inky black, whatever the weather, plunging an icy 80 m (260 ft) from the waterline to the bottom to form England's deepest lake. You can walk along the screes, but it is an uncomfortable and dangerous scramble. Boating on the lake is banned for conservation reasons, but fishing permits are available from the nearby National Trust camp site.

At **Wasdale Head** lies one of Britain's grandest views: the austere pyramid of **Great Gable**, centrepiece of a fine mountain composition, with the huge forms of Scafell and **Scafell Pike**. The scenery is utterly unspoilt, and the only buildings lie at the far end of the lake: an inn and a tiny church commemorating fallen climbers. Here the road ends, and you must turn back or take to your feet, following signs for Black Sail Pass and Ennerdale, or walk up the grand fells ahead. Wasdale's irresistible backdrop was the inspiration of the first serious British mountaineers, who flocked here during the 19th century, insouciantly clad in tweed jackets, carrying little more than a length of rope slung over their shoulders.

Eskdale ⓬

Cumbria. ≥ *Ravenglass then narrow-gauge railway to Eskdale (Easter–Oct: daily; Dec–Feb: Sat, Sun).* ℹ *12 Main St, Egremont (01946 820693).* �W *www.eskdale.info.co.uk*

THE PASTORAL DELIGHTS of Eskdale are best encountered over the gruelling **Hardknott Pass**, which is the most taxing drive in the Lake District, with steep gradients. You can pause at the 393-m (1,291-ft) summit to explore the Roman **Hardknott Fort** or enjoy the lovely view. As you descend into Eskdale, rhododendrons and pines flourish in a landscape of small hamlets, narrow lanes and gentle farmland. The main settlements below are the attractive village of Boot and coastal Ravenglass, both with old corn mills.

Just south of Ravenglass is the impressive **Muncaster Castle**, the richly furnished home of the Pennington family. Another way to enjoy the scenery is to take the miniature railway (La'l Ratty) from Ravenglass to Dalegarth.

🚂 **Eskdale Mill**
Boot. ☎ *019467 23335.* ☐ *Apr– Sep: Tue–Sun, public hols.* 🔲 🔲 🔲

♣ **Muncaster Castle**
Ravenglass. ☎ *01229 717614.* **Castle** ☐ *mid-Mar–mid-Nov: Sun–Fri (pm) & public hols.* **Garden** ☐ *daily.* 🔲 🔲 🔲 *ground floor and garden.* 🔲 �W *www.muncaster.co.uk*

Remains of the Roman Hardknott Fort, Eskdale

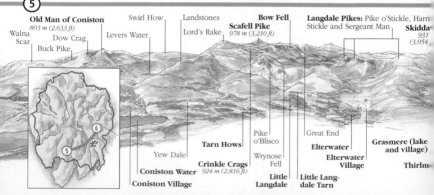

⑤

Old Man of Coniston
803 m (2,633 ft)

Walna Scar

Dow Crag

Buck Pike

Swirl How

Levers Water

Landstones

Lord's Rake

Bow Fell

Scafell Pike
978 m (3,210 ft)

Langdale Pikes: Pike o'Stickle, Harri Stickle and Sergeant Man

Skidda 931 (3,054

Yew Dale

Tarn Hows

Coniston Water 924 m (2,816 ft)

Coniston Village

Crinkle Crags

Pike o'Blisco

Wrynose Fell

Little Langdale

Great End

Little Langdale Tarn

Elterwater

Elterwater Village

Grasmere (lake and village)

Thirlm

Autumnal view of Seathwaite, in the Duddon Valley, a popular centre for walkers and climbers

Duddon Valley ⓭

Cumbria. ☒ Foxfield, Ulverston.
🛈 The Square, Broughton-in-Furness
(01229 716115).
🆆 www.lakelandgateway.info

ALSO KNOWN as Dunnerdale, this picturesque tract of countryside inspired 35 of Wordsworth's sonnets *(see p354)*. The prettiest stretch lies between Ulpha and Cockley Beck. In autumn the colours of heather moors and a light sprinkling of birch trees are particularly beautiful. Stepping stones and bridges span the river at intervals, the most charming being Birk's Bridge, near Seathwaite. At the southern end of the valley, where

the River Duddon meets the sea at Duddon Sands, is the pretty village of Broughton-in-Furness. Note the stone slabs used for fish on market day in the square.

Langdale ⓮

Cumbria. ☒ Windermere. 🛈 Market Cross, Ambleside (015394 32582).
🆆 www.amblesideonline.co.uk

STRETCHING FROM Skelwith Bridge, where the Brathay surges powerfully over waterfalls, to the summits of Great Langdale is the two-pronged Langdale Valley. Walkers and climbers throng here to take on **Pavey Ark, Pike o'Stickle,**

Crinkle Crags and **Bow Fell**. The local mountain rescue teams are the busiest in Britain.

Great Langdale is the more spectacular valley and it is often crowded, but quieter **Little Langdale** has many attractions too. It is worth completing the circuit back to Ambleside via the southern route, stopping at Blea Tarn. Reedy **Elterwater** is a picturesque spot, once a site of the gunpowder industry. Wrynose Pass, west of Little Langdale, climbs to 390 m (1,281 ft), a warm-up for Hardknott Pass further on. At its top is Three Shires Stone, marking the former boundary of the old counties of Cumberland, Westmorland and Lancashire.

⑥

Rydal Water, one of the major attractions of the Lake District

Ambleside ⑯

Cumbria. 🏘 3,400. 🚌 ℹ️ *Central Buildings, Market Cross (015394 32582).* 🛒 *Wed.*
🌐 *www.amblesideonline.co.uk*

AMBLESIDE has good road connections to all parts of the Lakes and is an attractive base, especially for walkers and climbers. Mainly Victorian in character, it has a good range of outdoor clothing, crafts and specialist food shops. An enterprising little cinema and a summer classical music festival add life in the evenings. Sights in town are small-scale: the remnants of the Roman fort of Galava, AD 79, Stock Ghyll Force waterfall and **Bridge House**, now a National Trust information centre.

ENVIRONS: Within easy reach are the wooded Rothay valley and the **Kirkstone Galleries** at Skelwith Bridge, with their contemporary design products. At nearby Troutbeck is the restored farmhouse of **Townend**, dating from 1626,

The tiny Bridge House over Stock Beck in Ambleside

Grasmere and Rydal ⑮

Cumbria. **Grasmere** 🏘 700. **Rydal** 🏘 100. 🚌 *Grasmere.* ℹ️ *Redbank Rd, Grasmere (015394 35245).* 🌐 *www.lake-district.gov.uk*

THE POET William Wordsworth lived in both these pretty villages on the shores of two sparkling lakes. Fairfield, Nab Scar and Loughrigg Fell rise steeply above their reedy shores and offer good opportunities for walking. Grasmere is now a sizable settlement and the famous Grasmere sports *(see p346)* attract large crowds every August.

The Wordsworth family is buried in St Oswald's Church, and crowds flock to the annual ceremony of strewing the church's earth floor with fresh rushes. Most visitors head for **Dove Cottage**, where the poet spent his most creative years. The museum in the barn behind includes such artefacts as the great man's socks. The Wordsworths moved to a larger house, **Rydal Mount**, in

Rydal in 1813 and lived here until 1850. The grounds have waterfalls and a summerhouse. Dora's Field nearby is a blaze of daffodils in spring and Fairfield Horseshoe offers an energetic, challenging walk.

🏛 Dove Cottage and the Wordsworth Museum
Off A591 nr Grasmere. 📞 *015394 35544.* ⏰ *daily.* ⬤ *24–26 Dec, mid-Jan–mid-Feb.* 📷 🎫 🚻 🏠
🌐 *www.wordsworth.org.uk*

🏛 Rydal Mount
Rydal. 📞 *015394 33002.* ⏰ *Mar–Oct: daily; Nov–Feb: Wed–Mon.* ⬤ *25 Dec; Jan.* 📷 ♿ *limited.* 🏠

WILLIAM WORDSWORTH (1770–1850)

Best known of the Romantic poets, Wordsworth was born in the Lake District and spent most of his life there. After school in Hawkshead and a period at Cambridge, a legacy enabled him to pursue his literary career. He settled at Dove Cottage with his sister Dorothy and in 1802 married an old school friend, Mary Hutchinson. They lived simply, walking, bringing up their children and receiving visits from poets such as Coleridge and de Quincey. Wordsworth's prose works include one of the earliest guidebooks to the Lake District.

BEATRIX POTTER AND THE LAKE DISTRICT

Although best known for her children's stories with characters such as Peter Rabbit and Jemima Puddle-duck, which she also illustrated, Beatrix Potter (1866–1943) became a champion of conservation in the Lake District after moving there in 1906. She married William Heelis, devoted herself to farming, and was an expert on Herdwick sheep. To conserve her beloved countryside, she donated land to the National Trust.

Cover illustration of *Jemima Puddleduck* (1908)

whose interior gives an insight into Lakeland domestic life.

🏛 Kirkstone Galleries
Skelwith Bridge. 📞 *015394 34002.* ⬤ *daily.* ⬤ *24–26 Dec.* 🚻 ♿ ☐

🏛 Townend
(NT) Troutbeck, Windermere. 📞 *015394 32628.* ⬤ *Apr–Oct: Tue–Fri, Sun & bank hol Mon; pm.* ▨

Windermere ⑰

Cumbria. 🚆 *Windermere.* 🚌 Victoria St. ℹ *Victoria St (015394 46499)* or *Glebe Rd, Bowness-on-Windermere (015394 42895).* Ⓦ *www.lakelandgateway.info*

A̲t over 10 miles (16 km) long, this dramatic watery expanse is England's largest mere. Industrial magnates built mansions around its shores long before the railway arrived. Stately **Brockhole**, now a national park visitor centre, was one such grand

estate. When the railway reached Windermere in 1847, it enabled crowds of workers to visit the area on day trips.

Today, a year-round car ferry service connects the lake's east and west shores (it runs between Ferry Nab and Ferry House), and summer steamers link Lakeside, Bowness and Ambleside on the north-south axis. Belle Isle, a wooded island on which a unique round house stands, is one of the lake's most attractive features, but landing is not permitted. **Fell Foot Park** is at the south end of the lake, and there are good walks on the northwest shore. A quite stunning viewpoint is Orrest Head 238 m (784 ft) northeast of Windermere town.

Environs: Bowness-on-Windermere, on the east shore, is a hugely popular centre. Many of its buildings display Victorian details, and

St Martin's Church dates back to the 15th century. The **Windermere Steamboat Museum** has a collection of superbly restored craft, and one of these, *Swallow*, makes regular lake trips. The **World of Beatrix Potter** recreates her characters in an exhibition, and a film tells her life story.

Beatrix Potter wrote many of her books at **Hill Top**, the 17th-century farmhouse at Near Sawrey, northwest of Windermere. Hill Top is furnished with many of Potter's possessions, and left as it was in her lifetime. The **Beatrix Potter Gallery** in Hawkshead holds annual exhibitions of her manuscripts and illustrations.

🏚 Brockhole Visitor Centre
On A591. 📞 *015394 46601.* ⬤ *Apr–Oct: daily.* ♿ ☐ 🚻

♣ Fell Foot Park
(NT) Newby Bridge. 📞 *015395 31273.* ⬤ *daily.* ♿ ☐

🏛 Windermere Steamboat Museum
Rayrigg Rd, Windermere. 📞 *015394 45565.* ⬤ *late Mar–Nov: daily.* ▨ ♿ ☐ 🚻 Ⓦ *www.steamboat.co.uk*

🏛 World of Beatrix Potter
The Old Laundry, Crag Brow. 📞 *015394 88444.* ⬤ *daily.* ⬤ *25 Dec, last three wks in Jan.* ▨ ☐ ♿ 🚻 limited. Ⓦ *www.hop-skip-jump.com*

🏚 Hill Top
(NT) Near Sawrey, Ambleside. 📞 *015394 36269.* ⬤ *Apr–Oct: Sat–Wed.* ▨ 🚻

🏛 Beatrix Potter Gallery
(NT) The Square, Hawkshead. 📞 *015394 36355.* ⬤ *Apr–Oct: Sat–Wed.* ▨ 🚻

Boats moored along the shore at Ambleside, the north end of Windermere

Peaceful Coniston Water, the setting of Arthur Ransome's novel, *Swallows and Amazons* (1930)

Coniston Water ⑱

Cumbria. 🚆 *Windermere then bus.* 🚌 *Ambleside then bus.* 🛈 *Coniston car park, Ruskin Ave (015394 41533).* 🆆 www.coniston-net.com

F OR THE FINEST VIEW of this stretch of water just outside the Lake District, you need to climb. The 19th-century art critic, writer and philosopher John Ruskin, had a fine view from his house, **Brantwood**, where his paintings and memorabilia can be seen today. Contemporary art exhibitions and events take place throughout the year.

An enjoyable excursion is the summer lake trip from Coniston Pier on the National Trust steam yacht, *Gondola*, calling at Brantwood. Coniston was also the scene of Donald Campbell's fatal attempt on the world water speed record in 1967. The green slate village of Coniston, once a centre for copper-mining, now caters for local walkers.

Also interesting is the traffic-free village of **Hawkshead** to the northwest, with its quaint alleyways and timber-framed houses. To the south is the vast Grizedale Forest, dotted with woodland sculptures.

Just north of Coniston Water is the man-made **Tarn Hows**, a landscaped tarn surrounded by woods. There is a pleasant climb up the 803 m (2,635 ft) Old Man of Coniston.

🏛 Brantwood
Off B5285, nr Coniston. 📞 015394 41396. ◯ mid-Mar–mid-Nov: daily; mid-Nov–mid-Mar: Wed–Sun. 🖼 🍽 🔲 🛈 🆆 www.brantwood.org.uk

Kendal ⑲

Cumbria. 🏘 26,000. 🚆 🛈 *Town Hall, Highgate (01539 725758).* 🚐 *Mon–Sat.* 🆆 www.kendaltown.org.uk

A BUSY MARKET TOWN, Kendal is the administrative centre of the region and the southern gateway to the Lake District. Built in grey limestone, it has an arts centre, the **Brewery**, and a central area which is best enjoyed on foot. **Abbot Hall**,

Kendal mint cake, the famous lakeland energy-booster for walkers

built in 1759, has paintings by Turner and Romney as well as Gillows furniture. In addition, the hall's stable block contains the **Museum of Lakeland Life**, with occasional lively workshops demonstrating local crafts and trades. There are dioramas of geology and wildlife in the **Museum of Natural History and Archaeology**. About 3 miles (5 km) south of the town is 14th-century

Sizergh Castle, with a fortified tower, carved fireplaces and a lovely garden.

🏛 Abbot Hall Art Gallery & Museum of Lakeland Life
Kendal. 📞 01539 722464. ◯ mid-Feb–20 Dec: Mon–Sat. 🖼 🚹 gallery. 🎟 by arrangement. 🔲 🛈
🆆 www.abbothall.org.uk
🏛 Kendal Museum of Natural History and Archaeology
Station Rd. 📞 01539 721374. ◯ mid-Feb–20 Dec: Mon–Sat. 🖼 🛈
🆆 www.kendalmuseum.org.uk
🏰 Sizergh Castle
(NT) off A591 & A590. 📞 015395 60070. ◯ Apr–Oct: Sun–Thu. 🖼 🚹 ground floor & grounds. 🔲 🛈

Furness Peninsula ⑳

Cumbria. 🚆 🚌 *Barrow-in-Furness.* 🛈 *28 Duke St, Barrow-in-Furness (01229 894784).*

B ARROW-IN-FURNESS *(see p337)* is the peninsula's main town. Its **Dock Museum**, cleverly built over a Victorian dock where ships were repaired, traces the history of Barrow using interactive computer displays.

Ruins of the red sandstone walls of **Furness Abbey** remain in the wooded Vale of Deadly Nightshade, with a small exhibition of monastic life. The historic town of Ulverston received its charter in 1280. **Ulverston Heritage**

Centre charts its development from market town to port. Stan Laurel, of Laurel and Hardy fame, was born here in 1890. His memorabilia **museum** has a cinema.

🏛 Dock Museum
North Rd, Barrow-in-Furness. 📞 01229 894444. ⏰ Easter–Oct: Tue–Sun; Nov–Easter: Wed–Sun (Sat, Sun: pm); public hols. ♿ 🅿 🏪
Ⓦ www.dockmuseum.org.uk

🏰 Furness Abbey
Vale of Deadly Nightshade. 📞 01229 823420. ⏰ Easter–Sep: daily; Oct–Easter: Wed–Sun. 🔴 24–26 Dec, 1 Jan. 🅿 📷 ♿ limited.

🏛 Ulverston Heritage Centre
Lower Brook St. 📞 01229 580820. ⏰ Apr–Dec: Mon–Sat; Jan–Mar: Mon, Tue, Thu–Sat. 🔴 25, 26 Dec, 1 Jan. 🅿 📷 ♿ limited.

🏛 Laurel and Hardy Museum
Upper Brook St, Ulverston. 📞 01229 582292. ⏰ daily. 🔴 25 Dec; Jan. 📷 ♿

Staircase at Holker Hall

Cartmel ㉑

Cumbria. 🚶 700. 🚉 Main St, Grange-over-Sands (015395 34026). Ⓦ www.grangetic@southlakeland.gov.uk

THE HIGHLIGHT of this pretty village is its 12th-century **priory**, one of the finest Cumbrian churches. Little remains of the original priory except the gatehouse in the village centre. The restored church has an attractive east window, a stone-carved 14th-century tomb, and beautiful misericords.

Cartmel also boasts a small racecourse. The village has given its name to its surroundings, a hilly district of green farmland with mixed woodland and limestone scars.

A major local attraction is **Holker Hall**, former residence of the Dukes of Devonshire. Inside are lavishly furnished rooms, with fine marble fireplaces, and a superb oak staircase. Outside are stunning gardens and a deer park.

🏰 Holker Hall
Cark-in-Cartmel. 📞 015395 58328. ⏰ Apr–Nov: Sun–Fri. 📷 ♿ limited. 🎥 by arrangement. 🅿 🏪
Ⓦ www.holker-hall.co.uk

Levens Hall ㉒

Nr Kendal, Cumbria. 📞 015395 60321. 🚌 from Kendal or Lancaster. ⏰ Apr–mid-Oct: Sun–Thu. 🅿 📷 ♿ gardens only. 🏪
Ⓦ www.levenshall.co.uk

THE OUTSTANDING attraction of this Elizabethan mansion is its topiary, but the house itself has much to offer. Built around a 13th-century tower, it contains a fine collection of Jacobean furniture and watercolours by Peter de Wint (1784–1849). Also of note are the ornate ceilings, Charles II dining chairs, the earliest example of English patchwork and the gilded hearts on the drainpipes.

The yew and box topiary was designed in 1694 by French horticulturist Guillaume Beaumont.

The 18th-century Turret Clock has a single hand, a common design of the period.

Main entrance

Box hedges were a common component of geometrically designed gardens of this period.

Over 300 years old, the garden's box-edged beds are filled with colourful herbaceous displays.

The complex topiary, shaped into cones, spirals and pyramids, is kept in shape by gardeners. Some specimens are 6 m (20 ft) high.

Morecambe Bay, looking northwest towards Barrow-in-Furness

Morecambe Bay ㉓

Lancashire. ⊠ *Morecambe.*
🚢 *Heysham (to Isle of Man).*
🛈 *Marine Rd. (01524 582808).*
W www.lancaster.gov.uk

THE BEST WAY to explore Morecambe Bay is by train from Ulverston to Arnside. The track follows a series of low viaducts across a huge expanse of glistening tidal flats where thousands of wading birds feed and breed. The bay is one of the most important bird reservations in the country. On the Cumbrian side of the bay, retirement homes have expanded the sedate Victorian resort of Grange-over-Sands, which grew up after the arrival of the railway in 1857. Its best feature is its natural setting. Nearby, **Hampsfield Fell** and **Humphrey Head Point** give fine views along the bay.

Leighton Hall ㉔

Carnforth, Lancashire. 📞 *01524 734474.* 🚌 *to Yealand Conyers (from Lancaster).* ◯ *by appointment.* ♿ *ground floor only.* 🅿 *pm only.* ❑ ❑ W www.leightonhall.com

LEIGHTON HALL'S estate dates back to the 13th century, but most of the building is 19th-century, including its Neo-Gothic façade. It is owned by the Gillow family, of the Lancastrian furniture business, whose products are now prized antiques. Excellent pieces can be seen here, including a ladies' work-box inlaid with biblical scenes. In the afternoon, weather permitting, the hall's large collection of birds of prey display their aerial prowess.

Lancaster ㉕

Lancashire. 👥 *50,000.* ⊠
🅿 🛈 *Castle Hill (01524 32878).* ◷ *Mon–Sat.*
W www.lancaster.gov.uk

THIS COUNTY TOWN of Lancashire is tiny compared to Liverpool or Manchester (now counties in their own right), but it has a long history. The Romans named it after their camp over the River Lune. Originally a defensive site, it developed into a prosperous port largely on the proceeds of the slave trade. Today, its university and cultural life still thrive. The Norman **Lancaster Castle** was expanded in the 14th and 16th centuries. It has been a crown court and a prison since the 13th century. The Shire Hall is decorated with 600 heraldic shields. Some fragments from Hadrian's Tower (which has a collection of torture instruments) are 2,000 years old.

The nearby priory church of **St Mary** is on Castle Hill. Its main features include a Saxon doorway and carved 14th-century choir stalls. There is an outstanding museum of furniture in the 17th-century **Judge's Lodgings**, while the **Maritime Museum**, in the Georgian custom house on St George's Quay, contains displays on the port's history. The **City Museum**, based in the old town hall, concentrates on the history of Lancaster.

The splendid **Lune Aqueduct** carries the canal over the River Lune on five wide arches. Other attractions are found in **Williamson Park**, site of the 1907 Ashton Memorial. This folly was built by the local linoleum magnate and politician, Lord Ashton.

Tawny eagle at Leighton Hall

CROSSING THE SANDS

Morecambe Bay sands are very dangerous. Travellers used to cut across the bay at low tide to shorten the long trail around the Kent estuary. Many perished as they were caught by rising tides or quicksand, and sea fogs hid the paths. Locals who knew the bay became guides, and today you can travel with a guide from Kents Bank to Hest Bank near Arnside.

The High Sheriff of Lancaster Crossing Morecambe Sands (anon)

There are fine views from the top of this 67 m (220 ft) domed structure. Opposite is the tropical butterfly house and the pavilion café.

♠ **Lancaster Castle**
Castle Parade. [01524 64998. ◯ daily. ● 1 Jan, 25 Dec. ⬛ ✦ only (limited when court is in session). ▯
W www. lancastercastle.com

🏛 **Judge's Lodgings**
Church St. [01524 32808. ◯ Apr–Jun, Oct: daily (Sat, Sun: pm only); Jul–Sep: daily. ● Nov–Good Fri. ⬛ ▯

🏛 **Maritime Museum**
Custom House, St George's Quay. [01524 64637. ◯ daily (Nov–Easter: pm). ● 24–26, 31 Dec, 1 Jan. ⬛ ♿
⬛ ▯ W www.nettingthebay.org.uk

🏛 **City Museum**
Market Sq. [01524 64637. ◯ Mon–Sat. ● 24 Dec–2 Jan. ♿ ▯

🌿 **Williamson Park**
Wyresdale Rd. [01524 33318.
◯ daily. ⬛ ♿ limited. ⬛ ▯
W www.williamsonpark.u-net.com

Ribble Valley ㉖

Lancashire. 🚆 Clitheroe. 🛈 Market Place, Clitheroe (01200 425566).
🍴 Tue, Thu, Sat.
W www.ribblevalley.gov.uk

CLITHEROE, A SMALL market town with a hilltop castle, is a good centre for exploring the Ribble Valley's rivers and old villages, such as Slaidburn. Ribchester has a **Roman Museum**, and there is a ruined **Cistercian abbey** at Whalley. To the east is 560 m (1,830 ft) Pendle Hill, with a Bronze Age burial mound at its peak.

🏛 **Roman Museum**
Ribchester. [01254 878261. ◯ daily. ⬛ ♿ ✦ by arrangement. ▯

⛪ **Whalley Abbey**
Whalley. [01254 828400. ◯ daily.
● 24 Dec–2 Jan. ⬛ ♿ ⬛ ▯
W www.whalleyabbey.org

Blackpool ㉗

Lancashire. 🏘 150,000. ✈ 🚆 🚌
🛈 Clifton St (01253 478222).
W www.blackpooltourism.com

BRITISH HOLIDAY patterns have changed in the past few decades, and Blackpool is no longer the apogee of seaside entertainment, but it remains a

Coming from the Mill (1930) by L S Lowry

unique experience. A wall of amusement arcades, piers, bingo halls and fast-food stalls stretch behind the sands. At night, entertainers strut their stuff under the bright lights. The town attracts thousands of visitors in September and October when the Illumina-tions trace the skeleton of the 158 m (518 ft) Blackpool Tower. Blackpool's resort life dates back to the 18th century, but it burst into prominence when the railway first arrived in 1840, bringing Lancastrian workers to their holiday resort.

Blackpool Tower, painted gold for its centenary in 1994

Salford Quays ㉘

Salford. 🚉 Harbour City (from Manchester). 🛈 City Council (0161 848 8601). W www.salford.gov.uk

THE QUAYS, to the west of Manchester city centre, were once the terminal docks for the **Manchester Ship Canal**. However, after the docks closed in 1982 the area became sadly run down. Since the 1990s all this has changed dramatically, with the creation of new residential and leisure facilities. In 2000 **The Lowry** opened, a spectacular new arts complex with theatres and galleries, including one dedicated to the world's largest collection of works by Salford-born artist L S Lowry. Across the footbridge over the canal is Trafford (Manchester United Football Club's ground at Old Trafford is nearby), where you will find the **Imperial War Museum North**, which opened in 2002. Sited in a striking building by architect Daniel Libeskind, its collection emphasizes war as seen from the point of view of the people caught up in it.

🏛 **The Lowry**
Pier 8, Salford Quays. [0161 876 2000. ◯ daily. ● 25 Dec. ♿ 🍴
⬛ ▯ W www.thelowry.com

🏛 **Imperial War Museum North**
Trafford Wharf. [0870 220 3435.
◯ daily. ● 25, 26 Dec. ♿ 🍴 ⬛
▯ W www.iwm.org.uk/north

Manchester ㉙

Sign for the John Rylands Library

Manchester's history dates back to Roman times, when, in AD 79, Agricola's legions set up a base camp called Mancunium on the site of the present city. It rose to prominence in the late 18th century, when Richard Arkwright's steam-powered spinning machines introduced the brave new world of cotton processing. By 1830, the first railway linked Manchester and Liverpool, and in 1894 the Manchester Ship Canal *(see p359)* opened, allowing cargo vessels 36 miles (55 km) inland. Confident civic buildings sprang up from the proceeds of cotton wealth, but these were in stark contrast to the overcrowded slums of the millworkers. Social discontent led writers, politicians and reformers to espouse liberal or radical causes. One result was the foundation in 1821 of the forthright local newspaper, the *Manchester Guardian*, a forerunner of today's national paper, the *Guardian*. The city was the first to introduce massive slum clearance and smokeless zones during the 1950s.

Exploring Manchester

Manchester is a fine, compact city with much to see in its central areas. It has a lively club scene, one of the largest Chinatowns in the world outside China and a wide range of restaurants. The restoration of the tram system has helped ease the pressures of urban transport, and the car-bombing of the city centre in 1996 has been seized as an opportunity to redevelop the main shopping areas and rationalize some of the street layouts. The mills and docks have left a huge architectural heritage, much of which is providing sites for imaginative development, including, on the west side of the city, **Salford Quays** *(see p359)*. Among the fine 19th-century buildings

Urbis, a new interactive museum on life in cities

MANCHESTER CITY CENTRE

Castlefield ②
Free Trade Hall ④
G-Mex Centre ③
John Rylands Library ⑤
Manchester Art Gallery ⑧
Museum of Science and
    Industry in Manchester ①
Royal Exchange ⑥
Town Hall ⑦

KEY

🚌 Bus station
🚏 Coach station
🚋 Tram
— Tramline
🚆 Train station
🅿 Parking
ℹ Tourist information
✝ Church

0 metres 250
0 yards 250

The Neo-Gothic Town Hall by Alfred Waterhouse, opened 1877

are the **John Rylands Library** founded over a hundred years ago by the widow of a local cotton millionaire, the **Town Hall**, the **Royal Exchange**, now a theatre and restaurant, and the **Free Trade Hall**. Behind the **cathedral** is **Chetham's Library**, housed in part of a well-preserved group of late-medieval buildings. The former central railway station, closed in 1969, is now the **G-Mex Centre**, a huge exhibition and conference complex. The once derelict industrial site of **Castlefield** has come back to life as a thriving office, residential and leisure area, offering museums, narrowboat trips and the worlds' first ever passenger railway station, now home to the Museum of Science and Industry *(below).*

🏛 Museum of Science and Industry in Manchester
Liverpool Rd. 📞 0161 832 2244.
⭕ daily. ⬤ 24–26 Dec. 💷 ♿ 🖵
W www.msim.org.uk
One of the largest science museums in the world, the spirit of scientific enterprise and industrial might of Manchester's heyday is conveyed here. Among the best sections are the Power Hall, a collection of working steam engines, the Electricity Gallery, tracing the history of domestic power, and an exhibition on the Liverpool and Manchester Railway. A collection of planes that made flying history are displayed in the Air and Space Gallery.

🏛 Manchester Art Gallery
Mosley St & Princess St. 📞 0161 235 8888. ⭕ Tue–Sun. ⬤ Mondays except Bank Holidays, 24–26, 31 Dec, 1 Jan, Good Fri. ♿ 🍴 🖵
W www.manchestergalleries.org
The gallery reopened in summer 2002, doubling its display space after a £35 million makeover and a brand new extension by architect Sir Michael Hopkins. The original building was designed by Sir Charles Barry (1795–1860) in 1824, and contains an excellent collection of British art, notably Pre-Raphaelites such as Holman Hunt and Dante Gabriel Rossetti. Early Italian, Flemish and French Schools are also represented. The gallery has a fine collection of decorative arts, from the Greeks to Picasso to contemporary craftworkers, in the Gallery of Craft & Design.

🏛 Urbis
Cathedral Gdns. 📞 0161 605 8200.
⭕ daily. ⬤ 25 Dec. 💷 ♿ 🍴 0161 605 8282. 🖵 🖵
W www.urbis.org.uk
The Urbis museum, opened in 2002, is set in a dramatic high-rise glass building, and explores life in different cities around the world through interactive exhibits. The visit begins with a one-minute sky glide in a glass elevator, then proceeds through four cascading floors of themed exhibitions.

🏛 Whitworth Art Gallery
University of Manchester, Oxford Rd. 📞 0161 275 7450. ⭕ daily (Sun: pm). ⬤ 24 Dec–2 Jan, Good Fri. 🍴 🖵 ♿
W www.whitworth.man.ac.uk
The Manchester machine tool manufacturer and engineer Sir Joseph Whitworth bequeathed money for this gallery, originally intended to be a museum of industrial art and design that would inspire the city's textile trade. The fine red-brick building is Edwardian, while the modern interior dates from the 1960s. It houses a superb collection of contemporary art, textiles and prints. Jacob Epstein's *Genesis* nude occupies the entrance, and there is an important collection of British watercolours by Turner *(see p93),* Girtin and others. Look out for the Japanese woodcuts and a collection of historic and modern wallpapers.

Jacob Epstein's *Genesis* (1930–1) in the Whitworth Art Gallery

---

THE PETERLOO MASSACRE

In 1819, the working conditions of Manchester's factory workers were so bad that social tensions reached breaking point. On 16 August, 50,000 people assembled in St Peter's Field to protest at the oppressive Corn Laws. Initially peaceful, the mood darkened and the poorly trained mounted troops panicked, charging the crowd with their sabres. Eleven were killed and many wounded. The incident was called Peterloo (the Battle of Waterloo had taken place in 1815). Reforms such as the Factory Act came in that year.

G Cruikshank's *Peterloo Massacre* cartoon

Liverpool ③

Traces of settlement on Merseyside date back to the 1st century. In 1207 "Livpul", a fishing village, was granted a charter by King John. The population was only 1,000 in Stuart times, but during the 17th and 18th centuries Liverpool's westerly seaboard gave it a leading edge in the lucrative Caribbean slave trade. The first docks opened in 1715 and eventually stretched 7 miles (11 km) along the Mersey. Liverpool's first ocean steamer set out from here in 1840, and would-be emigrants to the New World poured into the city from Europe, including a flood of Irish refugees from the potato famine. Many settled permanently in Liverpool and a large, mixed community developed. Today, the port handles even greater volumes of cargoes than in the 1950s and 1960s, but container ships use Bootle docks. Despite economic and social problems, the irrepressible "Scouse" or Liverpudlian spirit re-emerged in the Swinging Sixties, when four local lads stormed the pop scene. Many people still visit Liverpool to pay homage to the Beatles, but the city is also known for its orchestra, the Liverpool Philharmonic, its sport (football and the Grand National steeplechase) and its universities.

Liver Bird on the Royal Liver Building

Victorian ironwork, restored and polished, at Albert Dock

Exploring Liverpool

Liverpool's waterfront by the Pier Head, guarded by the mythical Liver Birds (a pair of cormorants with seaweed in their beaks) on the **Royal Liver Building**, is one of the most easily recognized in Britain. Nearby are the famous ferry terminal across the River Mersey and the revitalized

LIVERPOOL CITY CENTRE

Beatles Story ⑥
Cavern Quarter ①
Liverpool Museum ②
Merseyside Maritime
  Museum ⑧
Metropolitan Cathedral ⑤
Museum of Liverpool Life ⑨

Royal Liver Building ⑩
St George's Hall ④
Tate Liverpool ⑦
Town Hall ⑪
The Walker pp364–5 ③

KEY

🚌 Bus station

🚆 British Rail station

⛴ Ferry terminal

🅿 Parking

ℹ Tourist information

✝ Church

0 metres   250
0 yards   250

docklands. Other attractions include top-class museums and fine galleries, such as the **Walker** *(see pp364–5)*. Its wealth of interesting architecture includes some fine Neo-Classical buildings in the city centre, such as the gargantuan **St George's Hall**, and two cathedrals.

Albert Dock

📋 *0151 708 7334.* ⭕ *daily.* ⚫ *25 Dec, 1 Jan.* 💷 *some attractions.* ♿ ⓦ www.albertdock.com

There are five warehouses surrounding Albert Dock, all designed by Jesse Hartley in 1846. The docks were closed by 1972. After a decade of dereliction, these Grade I listed buildings were restored in a development that includes museums, galleries, shops, restaurants, bars and businesses.

Albert Dock quay beside the River Mersey

🏛 Merseyside Maritime Museum

Albert Dock. 📋 *0151 478 4499.* ⭕ *daily.* ♿ *limited.* 📱 📷 ⓦ www.merseysidemaritimemuseum.org.uk

Devoted to the history of the Port of Liverpool, this large complex has good sections on shipbuilding and the Cunard and White Star liners as well as a Transatlantic Slavery gallery. The area on the Battle of the Atlantic in World War II includes models and charts. Another gallery deals with emigration to the New World. The **HM Customs and Excise National Museum** is also located here, and examines the history of the subject, including smuggling, as well as customs and excise today. Across the quayside is the rebuilt Piermaster's House and the Cooperage.

Ship's bell in the Maritime Museum

🏛 Museum of Liverpool Life

Pier Head, Albert Dock. 📋 *0151 478 4499.* ⭕ *daily.* ♿ 📷 ⓦ www.museumofliverpoollife.org.uk

Many aspects of Liverpool culture converge here. Exhibits cover the history of Liverpool, its people and their contribution to international life. The *City Soldier's* gallery explores life in the King's Regiment in times of war and peace. Other interactive exhibits and accounts of daily life tell stories of sporting and political events since the 1800s.

🏛 Beatles Story

Britannia Vaults. 📋 *0151 709 1963.* ⭕ *daily.* ⚫ *25, 26 Dec.* 💷 ♿ 📷 ⓦ www.beatlesstory.com

In a walk-through exhibition, this museum records the history of The Beatles' meteoric rise to fame, from their first record, *Love Me Do,* through Beatlemania to their last live appearance together in 1969, and their eventual break-up. The hits that mesmerized a generation can be heard.

🏛 Tate Liverpool

Albert Dock. 📋 *0151 702 7400.* ⭕ *Tue–Sun, public hols.* ⚫ *Mon; Good Fri, 24–26 Dec, 1 Jan.* 💷 *some exhibitions.* ♿ 📷 *by arrangement.* 📱 📷 ⓦ www.tate.org.uk/liverpool

Tate Liverpool has one of the best contemporary art collections outside London. Marked by bright blue and orange panels and arranged over three floors, the gallery was converted from an old warehouse by architect James Stirling. It opened in 1988 as Tate Britain's *(see p93)* first outstation.

THE BEATLES

Liverpool has produced many good bands and a host of singers, comedians and entertainers before and since the 1960s. But the Beatles – John Lennon, Paul McCartney, George Harrison and Ringo Starr – were the most sensational, and locations associated with the band, however tenuous, are revered as shrines in Liverpool. Bus and walking tours trace the hallowed ground of the Salvation Army home at *Strawberry Fields* and *Penny Lane* (both outside the city centre), as well as the boys' old homes. The most visited site is Mathew Street, near Moorfields Station, where the Cavern Club first throbbed to the Mersey Beat. The original site is now a shopping arcade, but the bricks have been used to create a replica. Nearby are statues of the Beatles and *Eleanor Rigby*.

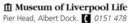

Liverpool: The Walker

FOUNDED IN 1873 by Sir Andrew Barclay Walker, a local brewer and Mayor of Liverpool, this gallery houses one of the finest art collections in the North. Paintings range from early Italian and Flemish works to Rubens, Rembrandt, Poussin, and French Impressionists such as Degas's *Woman Ironing* (c.1892–5). Among the strong collection of British artists from the 18th century onward are works by Millais and Turner and Gainsborough's *Countess of Sefton* (1769). There is 20th-century art by Hockney and Sickert, and the sculpture collection includes works by Henry Moore.

Italian dish (c.1500)

Seashells *(1874)* *Albert Moore painted female figures based on antique statues. Influenced by Whistler (see p505), he adopted subtle shading.*

Interior at Paddington *(1951) Lucian Freud's friend Harry Diamond posed for six months for this picture, intended by the artist to "make the human being uncomfortable".*

15

14

13

12

5

8

9

10

11

Ground floor

First fl

Façade was designed by H H Vale and Cornelius Sherlock.

Main entrance

GALLERY GUIDE

All the picture galleries are on the first floor. Rooms 1–2 house medieval and Renaissance paintings; Rooms 3 and 4 have 17th-century Dutch, French, Italian and Spanish art. British 18th- and 19th-century works are in Rooms 5–9. Rooms 11–15 have 20th-century and contemporary British art, and Room 10 has Impressionists and Post-Impressionists.

The Sleeping Shepherd Boy *(c.1835) The great Neo-Classical sculptor of the mid-19th century, John Gibson (1790–1866), used traditional colours to give his statuary a smooth appearance.*

The 7th-century Kingston Brooch in Liverpool Museum

🏛 Liverpool Museum

William Brown St. ☎ 0151 478 4399. ● closed for renovation until spring 2005. & ☐ ✓ W www.liverpoolmuseum.org.uk

Five floors of exhibits in this excellent museum include collections of Egyptian, Greek and Roman pieces, natural history, archaeology, space and time. Highlights include hands-on Exploration Zones, a Planetarium and a Discovery Centre. The museum is being extensively renovated to create a new aquarium, gallery of world cultures and Bug House.

🏛 Anglican Cathedral

St James' Mount. ☎ 0151 709 6271. ☐ daily. & ☐ ✓ W www.liverpoolcathedral.org.uk

Although Gothic in style, this building was only completed in 1978. The largest Anglican cathedral in the world is a fine red sandstone edifice designed by Sir Giles Gilbert Scott. The foundation stone was laid in 1904 by Edward VII but, dogged by two world wars, building work dragged on to modified designs.

🏛 Metropolitan Cathedral of Christ the King

Mount Pleasant. ☎ 0151 709 9222. ☐ daily. Donation. & ✓ W www. liverpoolmetrocathedral.org.uk

Liverpool's Roman Catholic cathedral rejected traditional forms in favour of a striking modern design. Early plans, drawn up by Pugin and later by Lutyens (see p25) in the 1930s, proved too expensive. The final version, brainchild of Sir Frederick Gibberd and built from 1962–7, is a circular building surmounted by a stylized crown of thorns 88 m (290 ft) high. It is irreverently known as "Paddy's Wigwam" by non-Catholics (a reference to Liverpool's large Irish population). Inside, the stained glass lantern, designed by John Piper and Patrick Reyntiens, floods the circular nave with diffused blueish light. There is a fine bronze of Christ by Elisabeth Frink (1930–94).

ENVIRONS: A spectacular richly timbered building dating from 1490, **Speke Hall** lies 6 miles (10 km) east of Liverpool's centre, surrounded by lovely grounds. The oldest parts of the hall enclose a cobbled courtyard dominated by two yew trees, Adam and Eve.

Birkenhead on the Wirral peninsula has been linked to Liverpool by ferry for over 800 years. Now, road and rail tunnels supplement access. The Norman Priory is still in use on Sundays, and stately Hamilton Square was designed from 1825–44 by J Gillespie Graham, one of the architects of Edinburgh's New Town.

On the Wirral side is **Port Sunlight Village** (see p337), a Victorian garden village built by enlightened soap manufacturer William Hesketh Lever for his factory workers. He also founded the **Lady Lever Art Gallery** here for his collection of works of art, including Pre-Raphaelite paintings.

🏫 Speke Hall

(NT) The Walk, Speke. ☎ 0151 427 7231. ☐ Apr–Oct: Wed–Sun (pm); Nov–mid-Dec: Sat, Sun (pm); public hols. 🅿 & limited. ☐ ✓

🏫 Port Sunlight Village & Heritage Centre

95 Greendale Rd, Port Sunlight, Wirral. ☎ 0151 644 6466. ☐ Apr–Oct: 10am–4pm; Nov–Mar: 11am–4pm daily. ● Christmas wk. 🅿 ✓ & ✓ W www.portsunlightvillage.com

Entrance to the half-timbered manor house of Speke Hall

Christ Discovered in the Temple (1342) Simone Martini's Holy Family conveys emotional tension through highly expressive body language.

KEY TO FLOORPLAN

- ☐ 13th–17th-century European
- ☐ 18th–19th-century British, Pre-Raphaelites and Victorian
- ☐ Impressionist/Post-Impressionist
- ☐ 20th-century and contemporary British
- ☐ Sculpture gallery
- ☐ Craft and design gallery
- ☐ Special exhibitions
- ☐ Non-exhibition space

YORKSHIRE AND THE HUMBER REGION

NORTH YORKSHIRE · EAST RIDING OF YORKSHIRE

WITH THE HISTORIC CITY *of York at its heart, this is an area of picturesque moorland and valleys. To the north lie the Yorkshire Dales and the North York Moors; eastwards, a coastline of beaches; and southwards, a landscape of lush meadows.*

Yorkshire was originally made up of three separate counties, formerly known as "Ridings". Today it covers over 5,000 sq miles (12,950 sq km). The northeast section has dramatic limestone scenery that was carved by glaciers in the Ice Age. Farming was the original livelihood, and the dry-stone walls weaving up precipitous scars and fells were used to divide the land. Imposed on this were the industries of the 19th century; blackened mill chimneys and crumbling viaducts are as much a part of the scenery as the grand houses of those who profited from them.

Close to the Humber, the landscape is very different, dominated historically by the now flagging fishing industry, and geographically by lush, sprawling meadows. Its coastline is exceptional, and further north are the attractions of wide, sandy beaches and bustling harbour towns. Yet it is the contrasting landscapes that make the area so appealing, ranging from the bleak moorland of the Brontë novels to the ragged cliff coast around Whitby, and the flat expanse of Sunk Island.

The city of York, where Roman and Viking relics exist side by side, is second only to London in the number of visitors that tread its streets. Indeed the historical centre of York is the region's foremost attraction. Those in search of a real taste of Yorkshire, however, should head for the countryside. In addition to excellent touring routes, a network of rewarding walking paths range from mellow ambles along the Cleveland Way to rocky scrambles over the Pennine Way at Pen-y-Ghent.

Lobster pots on the quayside at the picturesque fishing port of Whitby

◁ **The peaceful valley of Rosedale, North York Moors**

Exploring Yorkshire and the Humber Region

Yorkshire covers a wide area, once made up of three counties or "Ridings". Until the arrival of railways, mining and the wool industry in the 19th century, the county was a farming area. Dry-stone walls dividing fields still pepper the northern part of the county, alongside 19th-century mill chimneys and country houses. Among the many abbeys are Rievaulx and the magnificent Fountains. The medieval city of York is a major attraction, as are Yorkshire's beaches. The Humber region is character-ized by the softer, rolling countryside of the Wolds, and its nature reserves attract enormous quantities of birds.

Rosedale village in the North York Moors

SIGHTS AT A GLANCE

Bempton and Flamborough
  Head **26**
Beverley **27**
Bradford **35**
Burton Agnes **25**
Burton Constable **28**
Byland Abbey **10**
Castle Howard pp384–5 **22**
Coxwold **11**
Eden Camp **23**
Fountains Abbey pp376–7 **7**
Grimsby **31**
Halifax **38**
Harewood House **33**
Harrogate **3**
Haworth **36**
Hebden Bridge **37**
Helmsley **13**
Holderness and Spurn
  Head **30**
Hutton-le-Hole **16**
Kingston upon Hull **29**
Knaresborough **4**

Leeds **34**
Magna **41**
Mount Grace Priory **15**
National Coal Mining
  Museum **39**
Newby Hall **6**
North York Moors **17**
North York Moors Railway **18**
Nunnington Hall **12**
Rievaulx Abbey **14**
Ripley **5**
Ripon **8**
Robin Hood's Bay **20**
Scarborough **21**
Sutton Bank **9**
Whitby **19**
Wharram Percy **24**
York pp390–95 **32**
Yorkshire Dales National
  Park **1**
Yorkshire Sculpture Park **40**

Walks
Malham Walk **2**

(map labels) Darlington, RICHMOND, Swale, Pennine Way, Kendal, A684, Ribble, YORKSHIRE DALES NATIONAL PARK, B6160, Ure, Nidd, FOUNTAINS ABBEY, Wharfe, MALHAM WALK, RIPL HAR, A59, SKIPTON, Clitheroe, Aire, Pennine Way, A629, Aire, A650, HAREWOOD H, HAWORTH, BRADFORD, HEBDEN BRIDGE, A6033, A6036, LE, M62, Calder, HALIFAX, NATIONAL COAL MINING MUSEUM, M62, HUDDERSFIELD, A64, Manchester, A616, YORKSHIR SCULPTUR PAR, A6024, A628, Manchester, PEAK DISTRICT NATIONAL PA, SHE, Chest

Section of Lendal Bridge (1863)
crossing the Ouse in York

Middlesbrough

WHITBY 19 ROBIN HOOD'S BAY 20

MOUNT GRACE PRIORY 15

NORTH YORK MOORS NATIONAL PARK

Cleveland Way

Esk

A684

A169

A171

NORTH YORK MOORS 17

18

NORTH YORK MOORS RAILWAY

HUTTON-LE-HOLE 16

Seven

A170

RIEVAULX ABBEY 14

13 HELMSLEY

Derwent

21

SCARBOROUGH

HTON BANK 9

10 BYLAND ABBEY

12 NUNNINGTON HALL

A170

Hertford

COXWOLD 11

CASTLE HOWARD 22

Rye

23 EDEN CAMP

A64

A165

BEMPTON & FLAMBOROUGH HEAD 26

BY HALL

Ouse

A19

A64

Derwent

24

WHARRAM PERCY

BURTON AGNES 25

ARESBOROUGH

Nidd

A59

A166

A166

NORTH SEA

32 YORK

A164

A165

A1079

A63

BEVERLEY 27

Hull

28 BURTON CONSTABLE

Aire

M62

A63

KINGSTON UPON HULL 29

B1238

M62

A15

SUNK ISLAND

Don

Trent

Humber

A180

HOLDERNESS & SPURN HEAD 30

A1

DONCASTER ●

M180

A15

GRIMSBY 31

A16

M18

NA 41

A1(M)

Newark-on-Trent

M1

Nottingham

0 kilometres   15

0 miles   10

GETTING AROUND
The area is served by the A1, the M1, the M62 and the A59. Trains run to major cities such as York and Leeds, and there are train or coach (bus) links between many towns and hamlets. The Yorkshire Dales and North York Moors national parks are good for walkers, and cyclists can enjoy rides around York and the river Humber.

KEY

▬ Motorway

▬ Major road

▬ Minor road

▬ Scenic route

-- Scenic path

▬ River

☀ Viewpoint

Yorkshire Dales National Park ❶

THE YORKSHIRE DALES is a farming landscape, formed from three principle dales, Swaledale, Wharfedale and Wensleydale, and a number of small ones, such as Deepdale. Glaciation in the Ice Age helped carve out these steep-sided valleys, and this scenery contrasts with the high moorlands. However, 12 centuries of settlement have altered the landscape in the form of cottages, castles and villages which create a delightful environment for walking. A national park since 1954, the area provides recreation while serving local community needs.

Monk's Wynd – one of Richmond's narrow, winding streets

Malham Walk
(see p373)

KEY

▬▬	Major road
▬▬	Minor road
▭▭	Other roads
▬▬	National Park boundary

0 kilometres   20

0 miles   15

The green, rolling landscape of Deepdale, near Dent

Exploring Swaledale

Swaledale's prosperity was founded largely on wool, and it is famous for its herd of sheep that graze on the wild higher slopes in the harshest weather. The fast-moving river Swale that gives the northern-most dale its name travels from bleak moorland down magni-ficent waterfalls into the richly wooded lower slopes, passing through the village of Reeth and the town of Richmond.

♠ Richmond Castle
(EH) Tower Street. ☎ *01748 822493.* ☐ *daily.* 🅿️ 🚻 limited. 📷

Swaledale's main point of entry is the medieval market town of Richmond, which has the largest cobbled marketplace in England. Alan Rufus, the Norman 1st Earl of Richmond, began building the castle in 1071, and some of the masonry on the curtain walls probably dates from that time. It has a fine Norman keep, 30 m (100 ft) high with walls 3.3 m (11 ft) thick. An 11th-century arch leads into a courtyard containing Scolland's Hall (1080), one of England's oldest buildings.

Richmond's marketplace was once the castle's outer bailey. Its quaint, narrow streets gave rise to the song, *The Lass of Richmond Hill* (1787), written by Leonard McNally for his wife, Frances I'Anson, who was brought up in Hill House, on Richmond Hill. Turner (see *p93)* depicted the town many times. The Georgian Theatre (1788), which was restored in 1962, is the only one of its age still surviving.

🏛 Swaledale Folk Museum
Reeth Green. **[** *01748 884373.* ☐ *Easter–Oct: daily.* ☒
Reeth, a town that became known as the centre of the lead-mining industry and helped bring prosperity to the region, houses this museum in a former Methodist Sunday school (1830). Included in it are mining and wool-making artifacts (wool from the hardy Swaledale sheep was another mainstay of the economy) and brass band memorabilia.

🦌 Buttertubs
Near Thwaite, on the B6270 Hawes road, are a series of potholes that streams fall into. These became known as the Buttertubs when farmers going to market lowered their butter into the holes to keep it cool.

Buttertubs, near Thwaite

Exploring Wensleydale
The largest of the Yorkshire dales, Wensleydale is famous for its cheese and more recently for James Herriot's books and the television series, *All Creatures Great and Small*. It is easy walking country for anyone seeking an alternative to major moorland hikes.

🏛 Dales Countryside Museum
Station Yard, Hawes. **[** *01969 667450.* ☐ *daily.* ☒ ♿
In a former railway goods warehouse in Hawes, capital of Upper Wensleydale, is a

Barrels at the Theakston Brewery

fascinating museum, filled with items from life and industry in the 18th- and 19th-century Upper Dales. This includes cheese- and butter-making equipment. Wensleydale cheese was created by monks at nearby Jervaulx Abbey. There is also a rope-making works a short walk away.

Hawes itself is the highest market town in England, at 259 m (850 ft) above sea level. It is a thriving centre where thousands of sheep and cattle are auctioned each summer.

🦌 Hardraw Force
☒ *at Green Dragon Inn, Hardraw.*
At the tiny village of Hardraw, nearby, is England's tallest single-drop waterfall, with no outcrops to interrupt its 29 m (96 ft) fall. It became famous in Victorian times when the daredevil Blondin walked across it on a tightrope. Today, you can walk right under this fine waterfall, against the rock face, and look through the stream without getting wet.

🦌 Aysgarth Waterfalls
ℹ *National Pk Centre (01969 663424)* ☐ *Fri–Sun.*
An old packhorse bridge gives a clear view of the point at which the previously placid River Ure suddenly begins to plunge in foaming torrents over wide limestone shelves. Turner painted the impressive lower falls in 1817.

🏛 Theakston Brewery
Masham. **[** *01765 680000.* ☐ *Apr–Nov: call for details.* ☒ 🎦 🅿
w www.theakstons.co.uk
The pretty town of Masham is the home of Theakston brewery, creator of the potent ale Old Peculier. The history

VISITORS' CHECKLIST

N Yorkshire. ☒ *Skipton.* **ℹ** *01756 752748 (Wed, Fri–Mon).* **w** www.destinationdales.org

of this local family brewery from its origin in 1827 is on display in the visitors' centre. Masham village itself has an attractive square once used for sheep fairs, surrounded by 17th- and 18th-century houses. There is a medieval church.

♠ Bolton Castle
Castle Bolton, nr Leyburn. **[** *01969 623981.* ☐ *daily.* ☒ 🅿 🅿
w www.boltoncastle.co.uk
Situated in the village of Castle Bolton, this castle was built in 1379 by the 1st Lord Scrope, Chancellor of England. It was used as a fortress from 1568 to 1569 when Mary, Queen of Scots *(see p497)* was held prisoner here by Elizabeth I *(see pp50–51).*

♠ Middleham Castle
Middleham, nr Leyburn. **[** *01969 623899.* ☐ *Jan–Mar: 10am–4pm Wed–Sun; Apr–Sep: 10am–6pm daily; Oct: 10am–5pm daily; Nov–Dec: 10am–4pm daily.* ● *24–26 Dec.* 🅿 ☒ ♿
Owned by Richard Neville, Earl of Warwick, it was built in 1170. The castle is better known as home to Richard III *(see p49)* when he was made Lord of the North. It was once one of the strongest fortresses in the north but became uninhabited during the 15th century, when many of its stones were used for nearby buildings. The keep provides a fine view of the landscape.

Remains of Middleham Castle, once residence of Richard III

Extensive ruins of Bolton Priory, dating from 1154

Exploring Wharfedale

This dale is characterized by gritstone moorland, contrasting with quiet market towns along meandering sections of river. Many consider Grassington a central point for exploring Wharfedale, but the showpiece villages of Burnsall, overlooked by a 506 m (1,661 ft) fell, and Buckden, 701 m (2,302 ft), near Buckden Pike, also make excellent bases.

Nearby are the Three Peaks of Whernside, 736 m (2,416 ft), Ingleborough, 724 m (2,376 ft) and Pen-y-Ghent 694 m (2,278 ft). They are known for their potholes and tough terrain, but this does not deter keen walkers from attempting to climb them all in one day. If you sign in at the Pen-y-Ghent café at Horton-in-Ribblesdale, at the centre of the Three Peaks, and complete the 20 mile (32 km) course, reaching the summit of all three peaks in less than 12 hours, you can qualify for membership of the Three Peaks of Yorkshire Club.

🛈 Burnsall

St Wilfrid's, Burnsall. 🛈 01756 720331. ◯ Apr–Oct: daily to dusk. ♿
Preserved in St Wilfrid's church graveyard are the original village stocks, gravestones from Viking times and a headstone carved in memory of the Dawson family by sculptor Eric Gill (1882–1940). The village has a five-arched bridge and hosts Britain's oldest fell race every August.

🏛 Upper Wharfedale Museum

The Square, Grassington. ◯ Mar–Oct: daily (pm). 📷 ♿ limited.
This folk museum is set in two 18th-century lead miners' cottages. Its exhibits illustrate the domestic and working history of the area, including farming and lead mining.

🛈 Bolton Priory

Bolton Abbey, Skipton. 🛈 01756 718009. ◯ daily. ♿
One of the most beautiful areas of Wharfedale is around the village of Bolton Abbey, set in an estate owned by the Dukes of Devonshire. While preserving its astounding beauty, its managers have incorporated over 30 miles (46 km) of footpaths, many suitable for the disabled and young families.

The ruins of Bolton Priory, established by Augustinian canons in 1154 on the site of a Saxon manor, are extensive. They include a church, chapter house, cloister and prior's lodging. These all demonstrate the wealth accumulated by the canons from the sale of wool from their flocks of sheep. The priory nave is still used as a parish church. Another attraction of the estate is the "Strid", a point where the River Wharfe surges spectacularly through a gorge, foaming yellow and gouging holes out of the rocks.

🐾 Stump Cross Caverns

Greenhow Hill, Pateley Bridge. 🛈 01756 752780 or 01423 711282. ◯ Apr–Oct: daily; Nov–Mar: Sat, Sun & public hols (call for details). 📷 ▣ 🛈 W www.stumpcrosscaverns.co.uk
These caves were formed over a period of half a million years: trickles of underground water formed intertwining passages and carved them into fantastic shapes and sizes. Sealed off in the last Ice Age, the caves were only discovered in the 1850s when lead miners sank a mine shaft into the caverns.

⚓ Skipton Castle

High St. 🛈 01756 792442. ◯ daily (Sun: pm). ● 25 Dec. 📷 ▣ 🛈 W www.skiptoncastle.co.uk
The market town of Skipton is still one of the largest auctioning and stockraising centres in the north. Its 11th-century castle was almost entirely rebuilt by Robert de Clifford in the 14th century. Beautiful Conduit Court was added by Henry, Lord Clifford, in Henry VIII's reign. The central yew tree was planted by Lady Anne Clifford in 1659 to mark restoration work to the castle after Civil War damage.

Conduit Court (1495) and yew tree at Skipton Castle

Malham Walk ❷

THE MALHAM AREA, shaped by glacial erosion 10,000 years ago, has one of Great Britain's most dramatic limestone landscapes. The walk from Malham village can take over four hours if you pause to enjoy the viewpoints and take a detour to Gordale Scar. Those who are short of time tend to go only as far as Malham Cove. This vast natural amphitheatre, formed

Sandpiper at Malham Tarn

by a huge geological tear, is like a giant boot-heel mark in the landscape. Above lie the deep crevices of Malham Lings, where rare flora such as hart's-tongue flourishes. Unusual plants grow in the lime-rich Malham Tarn, said to have provided inspiration for Charles Kingsley's *The Water Babies* (1863). Coot and mallard visit the tarn in summer and tufted duck in winter.

Where the path meets the road ⑤
From here, you can catch a bus back to Malham village.

Malham Tarn ④
Yorkshire's second-largest lake lies 305 m (1,000 ft) above sea level in a designated nature reserve.

Malham Lings ③
This fine limestone pavement was formed when Ice Age meltwater seeped into cracks in the rock, then froze and expanded.

Gordale Scar ⑥
Guarded by steep limestone cliffs, this deep gorge was created by meltwater from Ice Age glaciers.

Malham Cove ②
The black streak in the centre of this 76 m (250 ft) cove is the site of a former waterfall.

Malham ①
An attractive riverside village, it has an information centre with details of drives and walks.

KEY

▬ ▬ Walk route

═══ Minor road

☆ Viewpoint

🅿 Parking

ℹ Tourist information

🚻 Toilets

0 kilometres   1
0 miles   ½

TIPS FOR WALKERS

Starting point: *Malham.* **Getting there:** *Leave M65 at Junction 14 and take A56 to Skipton, then follow signs to Malham which is off A65.* **Length:** *7 miles (11 km).* **Difficulty:** *Malham Cove is steep but the Tarn area is flatter.*
ℹ *01729 830363.*

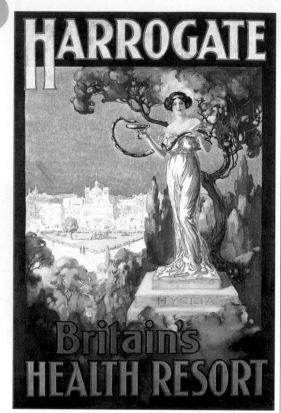

A 1920s poster advertising the spa town of Harrogate

Harrogate ❸

North Yorkshire. 🚶 69,000. 🚆 🚌
ℹ️ Assembly Rooms, Crescent Rd
(01423 537300).
[W] www.harrogate.gov.uk

B ETWEEN 1880 and World War I, Harrogate was the north's leading spa town, with nearly 90 medicinal springs. It was ideal for aristocrats who, after a tiring London season, were able to stop for a health cure before journeying on to grouse-shooting in Scotland.

Today, Harrogate's main attractions are its spa town atmosphere, fine architecture, public gardens and its conven-ience as a centre for visiting North Yorkshire and the Dales.

The naturally welling spa waters may not currently be in use, but you can still go for a Turkish bath in one of the country's most attractive steam rooms. The entrance at the side of the Royal Bath Assembly Rooms (1897) is unassuming, but once inside, the century-old **Harrogate Turkish Baths** are a visual feast of tiled Victoriana.

The town's spa history is recorded in the **Royal Pump Room Museum**. At the turn of the century, the waters were thought to be rich in iron early in the day. So, between 7am and 9am the 1842 octagonal building would have been filled with rich and fashionable people drinking glasses of water. Poorer people could take water from the pump outside. Today you can sample the waters and enjoy the museum's exhibits, including a Penny Farthing bicycle.

Harrogate is also known for the rainbow-coloured flower-beds in **The Stray**, a common space to the south of the town centre, and for the ornamental **Harlow Car Gardens**, owned by the Royal Horticultural Society. Visitors can enjoy the delicious cakes at **Betty's Café Tea Rooms** (see p598).

🛁 **Harrogate Turkish Baths**
Assembly Rooms, Crescent Rd.
📞 01423 556746. ⭕ **Men**: Mon,
Wed & Fri: (pm); Sat. **Women**: Mon
(am); Tue & Thu: (pm); Fri (am); Sun.
Mixed (in bathing suits): Tue (am);
(couples only in bathing suits): Fri
(eve); Sun (eve). 🖼️

🏛️ **Royal Pump Room Museum**
Crown Pl. 📞 01423 556188. ⭕
daily. ⚫ 24–26 Dec, 1 Jan. 🖼️ 🦽 🚻

🛁 **Betty's Café Tea Rooms**
1 Parliament St. 📞 01423 502746.
⭕ daily. ⚫ 25–26 Dec, 1 Jan.
[W] www.bettysandtaylors.co.uk

🌷 **Harlow Car Gardens**
Crag Lane. 📞 01423 565418. ⭕ daily.
🖼️ 🦽 🍴 🛍️ [W] www.rhs.org.uk

Knaresborough ❹

North Yorkshire. 🚶 14,000. 🚆
🚌 from Harrogate. ℹ️ 9 Castle
Courtyard, Market Place (01423
866896). 🛍️ Wed.

P ERCHED PRECIPITOUSLY above the River Nidd is one of England's oldest towns, mentioned in the Domesday Book of 1086 (see p48). Its historic streets – which link the church, John of Gaunt's ruined castle, and the market place with the river – are now lined with fine 18th-century houses.

Nearby is **Mother Shipton's Cave**, reputedly England's oldest tourist attraction. It first went on show in 1630 as the birthplace of Ursula Sontheil,

Mother Shipton's cave, with objects encased in limestone

The south front of Newby Hall

a famous local prophetess. Today, people can view the effect the well near her cave has on objects hung below the dripping surface. Almost any item, from umbrellas to soft toys, will become encased in limestone within a few weeks.

🏕 Mother Shipton's Cave
Prophesy House, High Bridge. 📞 01423 864600. ⭕ Easter–Oct: daily; Nov, Feb–Easter: Sat, Sun. ⭕ Dec, Jan. 🅿🔁🔁🖥🚻

Ripley ❺

North Yorkshire. 🏘 150. 🚌 from Harrogate or Ripon. 🚉 01423 537300. 🆆 www.harrogate.gov.uk

SINCE THE 1320s, when the first generation of the Ingilby family lived in an early incarnation of **Ripley Castle**, the village has been made up almost exclusively of castle employees. The influence of one 19th-century Ingilby had the most visual impact. In the 1820s, Sir William Amcotts Ingilby was so entranced by a village in Alsace Lorraine that he created a similar one in French Gothic style, complete with an *Hotel de Ville*. Present-day Ripley has a cobbled market square, and quaint cottages line the streets.

Ripley Castle, with its 15th-century gatehouse, was where Oliver Cromwell *(see p52)* stayed following the Battle of Marston Moor. The 28th generation of Ingilbys live here, and it is open for tours. The attractive grounds contain two lakes and a deer park, as well as more formal gardens.

⚜ Ripley Castle
Ripley. 📞 01423 770152. ⭕ Sep–May: Tue, Thu, Sat, Sun; Jun–Aug: daily. ⭕ 25 Dec. 🅿🔁🔁🖥🚻

Newby Hall ❻

Nr Ripon, North Yorkshire. 📞 01423 322583. ⭕ Apr–Sep: Tue–Sun and Bank Holiday Mondays. 🅿🔁🍴🚻 🆆 www.newbyhall.com

NEWBY HALL stands on land once occupied by the de Nubie family in the 13th century, and has been in the hands of the current family since 1748. The central part of the present house was built in the late 17th century in the style of Sir Christopher Wren.

Visitors will find 25 acres of gardens to explore. Laid out in a series of compartmented areas off a main axis, each garden is planted to come into flower during a different season. There is also a Woodland Discovery Walk, where contemporary sculpture is displayed.

For children, there is an adventure garden with activities and a miniature railway that runs through the gardens alongside the river Ure. River boat rides are also available. Each year a number of special events are staged, including Plant Fairs, a Historic Vehicle Rally and two Craft Fairs.

Fountains Abbey ❼

See pp376–7.

Ripon ❽

North Yorkshire. 🏘 14,000. 🚌 from Harrogate. 🚉 Minster Rd (01765 604625). 🛍 Thu. 🆆 www.riponcity.info

RIPON, A CHARMING small city, is best known for the cathedral and "the watch", which has been announced since the Middle Ages by the Wakeman. In return for protecting Ripon citizens, he would charge an annual toll of two pence per household. Today, a man still blows a horn in the Market Square each evening at 9pm, and every Thursday a handbell is rung to open the market.

The **Cathedral of St Peter and St Wilfrid** is built above a 7th-century Saxon crypt. At less than 3 m (10 ft) high and just over 2 m (7 ft) wide, it is held to be the oldest complete crypt in England. The cathedral is known for its collection of misericords *(see p329)*, which include both pagan and Old Testament examples. The architectural historian Sir Nikolaus Pevsner (1902–83) considered the cathedral's West Front the finest in England.

Ripon's **Prison and Police Museum**, housed in the 1686 "House of Correction", looks at police history and the conditions in Victorian prisons.

🏛 Prison and Police Museum
St Marygate. 📞 01765 690799. ⭕ Apr–Oct: daily. ⭕ Nov–Mar. 🅿🔁 🚻 🆆 www.riponmuseums.co.uk

Ripon's Wakeman, blowing his horn in the Market Square

Fountains Abbey ●

Nestling in the wooded valley of the River Skell are the extensive sandstone ruins of Fountains Abbey and the outstanding water garden of Studley Royal. Fountains Abbey was founded by Benedictine monks in 1132 and taken over by Cistercians three years later. By the mid-12th century it had become the wealthiest abbey in Britain, though it fell into ruin during the Dissolution (see p50). In 1720, John Aislabie, the MP for Ripon and Chancellor of the Exchequer, developed the land and forest of the abbey ruins. He began work, continued by his son William, on the famous water garden, the statuary and Classical temples in the grounds. This makes a dramatic contrast to the simplicity of the abbey.

Fountains Hall
Built by Sir Stephen Proctor around 1611, with stones from the abbey ruins, its design is attributed to architect Robert Smythson. It included a great hall with a minstrels' gallery and an entrance flanked by Classical columns.

THE ABBEY

The abbey buildings were designed to reflect the Cistercians' desire for simplicity and austerity. The abbey frequently dispensed charity to the poor and the sick, as well as travellers.

The Chapel of Nine Altars *at the east end of the church was built from 1203 to 1247. It is ornate, compared to the rest of the abbey, with an 18-m (60-ft) high window complemented by another at the western end of the nave.*

Chapter house

Cloister

Cellarium (storehouse)

Kitchen

Abbot's house

Monks' infirmary hall

Refectory

Lay brothers' infirmary

Lay brothers' refectory

The undercroft, *supported by 19 pillars, with vaulting 90 m (300 ft) long, was used for storing fleeces which the abbey monks sold to Venetian and Florentine merchants.*

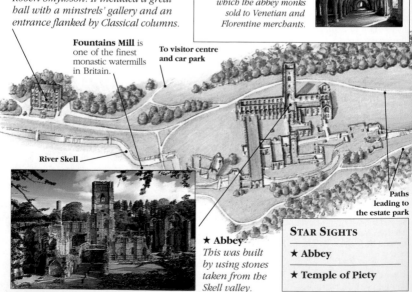

Fountains Mill is one of the finest monastic watermills in Britain.

To visitor centre and car park

River Skell

Paths leading to the estate park

★ **Abbey**
This was built by using stones taken from the Skell valley.

STAR SIGHTS

★ **Abbey**

★ **Temple of Piety**

St Mary's Church
This sumptuous Victorian Gothic church was built by architect William Burges in 1871–8. Inside, the choir stalls are decorated with multi-coloured carved parrots.

Octagon Tower

Footpath to St Mary's Church

Lake

Banqueting House

Moon Pond

Cascade

Canal

Anne Boleyn's Seat
This Gothic alcove, with a fine view of the abbey, was built in the late 18th century to replace her statue.

Temple of Fame
The columns of this domed building are made of hollow timber but look like sandstone.

★ Temple of Piety
This garden house was originally dedicated to Hercules. It was renamed as a symbol of filial piety by William Aislabie after his father's death in 1742.

The 19th-century white horse, seen on one of the walks around Sutton Bank

Sutton Bank ⑨

North Yorkshire. ☒ *Thirsk.* ℹ *Sutton Bank (01845 597426).*

Notorious among motorists for its 1 in 4 gradient, which climbs for about 107 m (350 ft), Sutton Bank itself is well known for its panoramic views. On a clear day you can see from the Vale of York to the Peak District *(see pp326–7).* William and his sister Dorothy Wordsworth stopped here to admire the vista in 1802, on their way to visit his future wife, Mary Hutchinson, at

Brompton. Apart from Sutton Bank, where you can walk round the white horse, the area is less wild than the coastal side, and suitable for children.

Byland Abbey ⑩

(EH) Coxwold, York. ☎ *01347 868614.* 🚌 *from York or Helmsley.* ☒ *Thirsk.* ☐ *Apr–Jul, Sep: Thu–Mon; Aug: daily.* 🅿 🅱 *limited.*

This cistercian monastery was founded in 1177 by monks from Furness Abbey in Cumbria. It featured what was

then the largest Cistercian church in Britain, 100 m (328 ft) long and 41 m (135 ft) wide across the transepts. The lay-out of the entire monastery, including extensive cloisters and the west front of the church, is still visible, as is the green and yellow glazed tile floor. Fine workmanship is shown in carved stone details and in the capitals, kept in the small museum.

In 1322 the Battle of Byland was fought nearby, and King Edward II *(see p40)* narrowly escaped capture when the invading Scottish army learned that he was dining with the Abbot. In his hurry to escape, the king had to leave many treasures behind, which were looted by the invading soldiers.

Coxwold ⑪

North Yorkshire. 🏘 *160.* ℹ *49 Market Place, Thirsk (01845 522755).* 🅦 *www.herriotcountry.com*

Situated just inside the bounds of the North York Moors National Park *(see p381),* this charming village nestles at the foot of the Howardian Hills. Its pretty houses are built from local stone, and the 15th-century church has some fine Georgian

Shandy Hall, home of author Laurence Sterne, now a museum

box pews and an impressive octagonal tower. But Coxwold is best known as the home of the author Laurence Sterne (1713–68), whose writings include *Tristram Shandy* and *A Sentimental Journey*.

Sterne moved here in 1760 as the church curate. He rented a rambling house that he named **Shandy Hall** after a Yorkshire expression meaning eccentric. Originally built as a timber-framed, open-halled house in the 15th century, it was modernized in the 17th century and Sterne later added a façade. His grave lies beside the porch at Coxwold's church.

♁ Shandy Hall
Coxwold. **☎** 01347 868465. **◯**
May–Sep: Wed & Sun (pm). **▨ ♿**
limited. **Gardens ◯** *Sun–Fri.* **□**

Nunnington Hall ⓬

(NT) Nunnington, York. **☎** *01439 748283.* **≋** *Malton, then bus or taxi.*
◯ *Apr–May, Sep–Oct: Wed–Sun (pm); Jun–Aug: Tue–Sun, public hols (pm).*
□ ▨ ♿ *ground floor.* **▣**

SET IN ALLURING surroundings, this 17th-century manor house is a combination of architectural styles, including features from the Elizabethan and Stuart periods. Both inside and outside, a notable architectural feature is the use of the broken pediment (the upper arch is left unjoined).

Nunnington Hall was a family home until 1952, when Mrs Ronald Fife donated it to the National Trust. A striking

The miniature Queen Anne drawing room at Nunnington Hall

feature is the panelling in the Oak Hall. Formerly painted, it extends over the three-arched screen to the Great Staircase. Nunnington's collection of 22 miniature furnished period rooms is popular with visitors.

A mid-16th-century tenant Dr Robert Huickes, physician to Henry VIII *(see p50–51)*, is best known for advising Elizabeth I that she should not, at the age of 32, consider having any children.

Helmsley ⓭

North Yorkshire. **⚐** *2,000.* **≋** *from Malton or Scarborough.* **ℹ** *Town Hall, Market Place (01439 770173).* **⌂** *Fri.* **ⓦ** *www.ryedale.gov.uk/tourism*

THIS PRETTY MARKET TOWN is noted for its **castle**, now an imposing ruin. Built from 1186 to 1227, its main function and strength as a fortress is illustrated by the remaining keep, tower and curtain walls. The original D-shaped keep had one part blasted away in the Civil War *(see p52)*, but remains the

dominant feature. The castle was so impregnable that there were few attempts to force entry. However, in 1644, after holding out for a three-month seige against Sir Thomas Fairfax, the Parliamentary general, the castle was finally taken.

Helmsley church tower

Rievaulx Abbey ⓮

(EH) Nr Helmsley, North Yorkshire. **☎** *01439 798228.* **≋** *Thirsk or Scarborough, then bus or taxi.* **◯** *Apr–Sep: daily; Oct–Mar: Thu–Mon.* **▨ ♿** *limited.* **▣ □**

RIEVAULX IS PERHAPS the finest abbey in the area, due to both its dramatic setting in the steep wooded valley of the River Rye and its extensive remains. It is surrounded by steep banks that form natural barriers from the outside world. Monks of the French Cistercian order from Clairvaux founded this, their first major monastery in Britain, in 1132. The main buildings were finished before 1200. The layout of the chapel, kitchens and infirmary give an idea of monastic life.

Rievaulx Abbey, painted by Thomas Girtin (1775–1802)

Mount Grace Priory ruins, with farm and mansion in foreground

Mount Grace Priory ⓯

(EH/NT) On A19, NE of Northallerton,
North Yorks. **[** *01609 883494.* **⤢**
Northallerton then bus. **◯** *Apr–Sep:*
daily; Oct–Mar: Thu–Mon. **🖻 ♿**
ground floor, shop & grounds. **⬛**

Fᴏᴜɴᴅᴇᴅ ʙʏ Thomas Holland,
Duke of Surrey, and in use
from 1398 until 1539, this is
the best-preserved Carthusian
or charterhouse monastery *(see
pp338–9)* in England. The
monks, just 20 of them at the
beginning, took a vow of
silence and lived in solitary
cells, each with his own garden and an angled
hatch so that he would
not even see the per-
son serving his food.
They only met at
matins, vespers and
feast-day services.
Attempts at escape by
those who could not
endure the rigour of
the rules were pun-
ished by imprisonment.
   The ruins of the
priory include the for-
mer prison, gatehouse
and outer court, barns,
guesthouses, cells and
the church. The 14th-
century church, the
best-preserved section
of the site, is particu-
larly small, as it was
only rarely used by
the community. A cell
has been reconstructed
to give an impression
of monastic life.

Hutton-le-Hole ⓰

North Yorkshire. **👥** *400.* **⤢** *Malton*
then bus. **🛏** *The Ropery, Pickering*
(01751 473791).
w *www.ryedale.gov.uk*

Tʜɪꜱ ᴘɪᴄᴛᴜʀᴇꜱqᴜᴇ ᴠɪʟʟᴀɢᴇ is
characterized by a spacious
green, grazed by roaming
sheep, and surrounded by
houses, an inn and shops.
Lengths of white wood,
replacing stone bridges, span
the moorland stream. Its
cottages, some with date
panels over the doors, are
made from limestone, with red
pantiled roofs. In the village
centre is the excellent

Wheelwright's workshop at Ryedale Folk Museum

Ryedale Folk Museum,
which records the lifestyle
of an agricultural community
using Romano-British artifacts
and reconstructed buildings.

🏛 Ryedale Folk Museum
Hutton-le-Hole. **[** *01751 417367.* **◯**
mid-Mar–mid-Nov: daily. **⬛ 🖻 ♿**

North York Moors Tour ⓱

See p381.

North Yorkshire Moors Railway ⓲

Pickering & Grosmont, North Yorkshire.
[*01751 472580.* **◯** *Apr–Oct: daily;*
Nov–Mar: some weekends (call for
details). **🖻 ▢ ♿ ⬛ w** www.
northyorkshiremoorsrailway.com

Dᴇꜱɪɢɴᴇᴅ in 1831 by George
Stephenson as a route
along the North York Moors
and links with the Esk Valley,
Pickering and Whitby *(see
p382)*, this railway was considered an engineering miracle.
Due to budget constraints,
Stephenson was not able to
build a tunnel, so had to lay
the route down the mile-long
(1.5 km) incline between Beck
Hole and Goathland. The area
around Fen Bog had to be
stabilized using timber, heather,
brushwood and fleeces
so that a causeway
could be built over it.
A horse was used to
pull a coach along the
track at 10 miles (16
km) per hour. After
horsepower came
steam, and for almost
130 years the railway
linked Whitby to the
rest of the country. In
the early 1960s the line
was closed but in
1967, a group of locals
began a campaign to
relaunch it, and in
1973 it was officially
reopened. Today, the
18 mile (29 km) line
runs from Pickering via
Levisham, Newtondale
Halt and Goathland
before stopping at
Grosmont, through the
scenic heart of the
North York Moors.

North York Moors ⑰

The area between Cleveland, the Vale of York and the Vale of Pickering is known as the North York Moors National Park. The landscape consists of bleakly beautiful moors interspersed with lush green valleys. Agriculture is still the main source of income here as it has been for centuries, and until the advent of coal, the communities' local source of fuel was turf. In the 19th century, the geology of the area created extractive industries which included ironstone, lime, coal and building stone.

Mallyan Spout
A footpath leads to this waterfall from Goathland.

Farndale
During springtime, this area is famous for the beauty and profusion of its daffodils.

"Fat Betty" White Cross Crosses and standing stones are a feature of the Moors.

THE MOORS CENTRE, DANBY

Egton Bridge

LEAEHOLM

Wheeldale Gill

Goathland
A centre for forest and moorland walks, it has 19th-century houses and good accommodation.

WHITBY

West Beck

Thorgill

Seven

Dove

Hartoft Beck

Ruimoor Beck

Blawarth Beck

Rosedale Abbey
Named after the priory that has long since gone, this beautiful village still has some remains of the kilns from its 19th-century ironstone mining industry.

Hutton-le-Hole
This lovely village has the excellent Ryedale Folk Museum.

Spaunton

Wade's Causeway
Often called the Roman Road, its origins and destination are unknown. Long considered Roman in date, this is now less certain, although it may date from towards the end of the Roman occupation.

Lastingham
Lastingham's church, dating from 1078, has a Norman crypt with stone carving.

0 kilometres   2

0 miles   2

Whitby ⑲

WHITBY'S KNOWN HISTORY dates back to the 7th century, when a Saxon monastery was founded on the site of today's famous 13th-century abbey ruins. In the 18th and early 19th centuries it became an industrial port and shipbuilding town, as well as a whaling centre. In the Victorian era, the red-roofed cottages at the foot of the east cliff were filled with workshops crafting jet into jewellery and ornaments. Today, the tourist shops that have replaced them sell antique-crafted examples of the distinctive black gem.

Jet comb (c.1870)

VISITORS' CHECKLIST

North Yorkshire. 🏠 13,500. ✈ Teeside, 50 miles (80 km) NW Whitby. 🚃 Station Sq. ℹ Langborne Rd (01947 602674). 🚌 Tue, Sat. 🎉 Whitby Festival: Jun; Angling Festival: Jul; Lifeboat Day: Jul or Aug; Folk Week: 17–23 Aug; Whitby Regatta: Aug. 🌐 www.discoveryorkshirecoast.com

Exploring Whitby

Whitby is divided into two by the estuary of the River Esk. The Old Town, with its pretty cobbled streets and pastel-hued houses, huddles round the harbour. High above it is St Mary's Church with a wood interior reputedly fitted by ships' carpenters. The ruins of the 13th-century Whitby Abbey, nearby, are still used as a landmark by mariners. From them you get a fine view over the still-busy harbour, strewn with colourful nets. A pleasant place for a stroll, the harbour is overlooked by an imposing bronze clifftop statue of the explorer Captain James Cook (1728–79), who was apprenticed as a teenager to a Whitby shipping firm.

Lobster pots lining the quayside of Whitby's quaint harbour

Medieval arches above the nave of Whitby Abbey

⛪ Whitby Abbey

(EH) Abbey Lane. 📞 01947 603568. 🕐 Apr–Sep: daily; Oct–Mar: Thu–Mon. 📷 ♿ 🏠

The monastery founded in 657 was sacked by Vikings in 870. In the 11th century it was rebuilt as a Benedictine Abbey. The ruins date mainly from the 13th century. A visitor centre has recently been added.

⛪ St Mary's Parish Church

East Cliff. 📞 01947 603421. 🕐 daily.

Stuart and Georgian alterations to this Norman church have left a mixture of twisted wood columns and maze-like 18th-century box pews. The 1778 triple-decker pulpit has rather avant-garde decor – ear-trumpets used by a Victorian rector's deaf wife.

🏛 Captain Cook Memorial Museum

Grape Lane. 📞 01947 601900. 🕐 Mar: Sat & Sun; Apr–Oct: daily. 📷 🏠 🌐 www.cookmuseumwhitby.co.uk

The young James Cook slept in the attic of this 17th-century harbourside house when he was apprenticed nearby. The museum has displays of period furniture in the style described in the inventories of the house, and watercolours by artists who travelled on his voyages.

🏛 Whitby Museum and Pannett Art Gallery

Pannett Park. 📞 01947 602908. 🕐 May–Sep: daily (Sun: pm); Oct–Apr: Tue–Sun (Sun: pm); 🌑 Sun: am; 24 Dec–2 Jan. 📷 museum. ♿ limited. 🏠

The Pannett park grounds, museum and gallery were a gift of Whitby solicitor, Robert Pannett (1834–1920), to house his art collection. Among the museum's treasures are objects illustrating local history, such as jet jewellery, and Captain Cook artifacts.

🏛 Museum of Victorian Whitby

Entrance through Venus Trading shop, Sandgate. 📞 01947 601221. 🕐 daily. 📷

Among the exhibits on Victorian life in Whitby is the animated wheel-house of a whaling ship.

⛪ Caedmon's Cross

East Cliff.

On the path side of the abbey's clifftop graveyard is the cross of Caedmon, an illiterate labourer who worked at the abbey in the 7th century. He had a vision that inspired him to compose cantos of Anglo-Saxon religious verse still sung today.

Cross of Caedmon (1898)

Robin Hood's Bay ⑳

North Yorkshire. 🕍 *1,400*. 🚆 🚌 *Whitby*. 🚻 *Langbourne Rd, Whitby (01947 602674).*
W *www.discoveryorkshirecoast.com*

LEGEND HAS IT that Robin Hood (*see p324*) kept his boats here in case he needed to make a quick getaway. The village has a history as a smugglers' haven, and many houses have ingenious hiding places for contraband. The cobbled main street is so steep that visitors need to leave their vehicles in the car park. In the village centre, attractive, narrow streets full of colour-washed stone cottages huddle around a quaint quay. There is a rocky beach with rock pools for children to play in. At low tide, the pleasant walk south to Boggle Hole takes 15 minutes, but you need to keep an eye on the tides.

Cobbled alley in the Bay Town area of Robin Hood's Bay

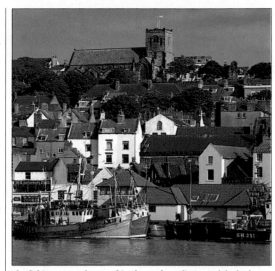

The fishing port and town of Scarborough nestling round the harbour

Scarborough ㉑

North Yorkshire. 🕍 *54,000*. 🚆 🚌 🚻 *Pavilion House, Valley Bridge Rd (01723 373333).* 🛒 *Mon–Sat.*
W *www.discoveryorkshirecoast.com*

THE HISTORY OF Scarborough as a resort can be traced back to 1626, when it became known as a spa. In the Industrial Revolution (*see pp336–7*) it was nicknamed "the Queen of the Watering Places", but the post-World War II trend for holidays abroad has meant fewer visitors. The town has two beaches; the South Bay amusement arcades contrast with the quieter North Bay.

Playwright Alan Ayckbourn premiers his work at the Stephen Joseph theatre, and Anne Brontë (*see p398*) is buried in St Mary's Church.

Bronze and Iron Age relics have been found on the site of **Scarborough Castle**, and **Wood End Museum** exhibits local geology and history. The **Rotunda** (1828–9) was one of Britain's first purpose-built museums. Works by local artist Atkinson Grimshaw (1836–93) hang in **Scarborough Art Gallery**. The **Sea-Life and Marine Sanctuary**'s baby seals are its main attraction.

♣ **Scarborough Castle**
(EH) Castle Rd. 📞 *01723 372451.* ◯ *Apr–Sep: daily; Oct–Mar: Thu–Mon.* 🎫 🛒 🚻

🏛 **Wood End Museum**
The Crescent. 📞 *01723 367326.* ◯ *Jun–Sep: Tue–Sun; Oct–May: Wed, Sat, Sun & public hols.* 🚻 🎫

🏛 **Rotunda Museum**
Vernon Rd. 📞 *01723 374839.* ◯ *Jun–Sep: daily; Oct–May: Tue, Sat, Sun & public hols.* ● *25 & 26 Dec, 1 Jan.* 🚻 🎫

🏛 **Scarborough Art Gallery**
The Crescent. 📞 *01723 374753.* ◯ *Jun–Sep: Tue–Sun; Oct–May: Thu, Fri, Sat & public hols.* ● *25 & 26 Dec, 1 Jan.* 🚻 🎫 🛒

🐟 **Sea-Life and Marine Sanctuary**
Scalby Mills Rd. 📞 *01723 376125.* ◯ *daily.* ● *25 Dec.* 🎫 🛒 🛒 🚻
W *www.sealife.co.uk*

THE GROWING POPULARITY OF SWIMMING

During the 18th century, sea-bathing came to be regarded as a healthy pastime, and from 1735 onwards men and women, on separate stretches of the coast, could be taken out into the sea in bathing huts, or "machines". In the 18th century, bathing was segregated although nudity was permitted. The Victorians brought in fully clothed bathing, and 19th-century workers from Britain's industrial heartlands used the new steam trains to visit the coast for their holidays. At this time, British seaside resorts such as Blackpool (*see p359*) and Scarborough expanded to meet the new demand.

A Victorian bathing hut on wheels

Castle Howard ❷

Pillar detail in the Great Hall, carved by Samuel Carpenter

Still owned and lived in by the Howard family, Castle Howard was created by Charles, 3rd Earl of Carlisle. In 1699, he commissioned Sir John Vanbrugh, a man of dramatic ideas but with no previous architectural experience, to design a palace for him. Vanbrugh's grand designs of 1699 were put into practice by architect Nicholas Hawksmoor *(see p24)* and the main body of the house was completed by 1712. The West Wing was built in 1753–9, using a design by Thomas Robinson, son-in-law of the 3rd Earl. Castle Howard was used as the location for the television version of Evelyn Waugh's novel *Brideshead Revisited* (1945).

Temple of the Four Winds
Vanbrugh's last work, designed in 1724, has a dome and four Ionic porticoes. Situated in the grounds at the end of the terrace, it is typical of an 18th-century "landscape building".

East Wing

The front façade boldly faces north, which is unusual for the 17th century, while all the state rooms have a southerly aspect, with superb views over the gardens.

North Front

★ Great Hall
Rising 20 m (66 ft), from its 515 sq m (5,500 sq ft) floor to the dome, the Great Hall has columns by Samuel Carpenter (1660–1713), wall paintings by Pellegrini and a circular gallery.

SIR JOHN VANBRUGH

Vanbrugh (1664–1726) trained as a soldier, but became better known as a playwright, architect and member of the Whig nobility. He collaborated with Hawksmoor over the design of Blenheim Palace, but his bold architectural vision, later greatly admired, was mocked by the establishment. He died while working on the garden buildings and grounds of Castle Howard.

Chapel Stained Glass
*Admiral Edward Howard
tered the chapel in 1870–75.
be windows were designed by
Edward Burne-Jones and
nade by William Morris & Co.*

VISITORS' CHECKLIST

A64 from York. 📞 *01653 648
333.* 🚌 *York then bus, or Malton
then taxi.* **House** ⬜ *mid-Feb–Oct:
11am–4pm daily.* **Grounds** ⬜
10am–4:30pm daily. 🅿️ ♿ 🚻
⬜ W www.castlehoward.co.uk

Bust of the 7th Earl
*J H Foley sculpted this portrait
bust, which stands at the top of
the Grand Staircase in the West
Wing, in 1870.*

★ Long Gallery
*The Howard lineage is
illustrated here by a large
number of portraits,
including works by
Reynolds and Pannini.*

West Wing

Tourist entrance

Antique Passage
*Antiquities collected in the
18th and 19th centuries by
the various earls of Carlisle
are on display here. The
plethora of mythical
figures and gods reflects
contemporary interest in
Classical civilizations.*

STAR SIGHTS

★ **Great Hall**

★ **Long Gallery**

Museum Room
*Furniture here includes
Regency chairs, Persian
rugs and this 17th-
century cabinet.*

Eden Camp 🟢

Malton, North Yorkshire. 🔵 *01653 697777.* 🚂 *Malton then taxi.* 🔵 *mid-Jan–late Dec: daily.* 🔵 📷 🔵 💻 🔵 www.edencamp.co.uk

THIS IS AN UNUSUAL, award-winning theme museum which pays tribute to the British people during World War II. Italian and German prisoners of war were kept at Eden Camp between 1939 and 1948. Today, some original huts built by Italian prisoners in 1942 are used as a museum, with period tableaux and a soundtrack. Each hut adopts a theme to take the visitor through civilian life in war-time, from Chamberlain's radio announcement of the outbreak of hostilities to the coming of peace. Visitors, including schoolchildren and nostalgic veterans, can see the Doodle-bug V-1 bomb which crashed outside the Officers' Mess, take tea in the canteen or experience a night in the Blitz. A tour can last for several hours.

British and American flags by the sign for Eden Camp

Wharram Percy 🟢

(EH) North Yorkshire. 🔵 *01904 601901 (English Heritage).* 🚂 *Malton, then taxi.* 🔵 *daily.*

THIS IS ONE of England's most important medieval village sites. Recent excavations have unearthed evidence of a 30-household community, with two manors, and the remains of a medieval church. There is also a millpond which has beautiful wild flowers in late spring. Wharram Percy is set in a pretty valley, sign-posted off the B1248 from Burdale, in the heart of the green, rolling Wolds. It is about 20 minutes' walk from the car park, and makes an ideal picnic stop.

Alabaster carving on the chimney-piece at Burton Agnes

Burton Agnes 🟢

On A614, nr Driffield, East Yorks. 🔵 *01262 490324.* 🚂 *Driffield, then bus.* 🔵 *Apr–Oct: daily.* 📷 🔵 *limited.* 🔵 🔵 🔵 www.burton-agnes.com

OF ALL the grand houses in this area, Burton Agnes Hall is a firm favourite. This is partly because the attractive, red-brick Elizabethan mansion has such a homely atmosphere. One of the first portraits you see in the Small Hall is of Anne Griffith, whose father, Sir Henry, built the house. There is a monument to him in the local church.

Burton Agnes has remained in the hands of the original family and has changed little since it was built, between 1598 and 1610. You enter it by the turreted gatehouse, and the entrance hall has a fine Elizabethan alabaster chimney piece. The massive oak stair-case is an impressive example of Elizabethan woodcarving.

In the library is a collection of Impressionist and Post-Impressionist art, pleasantly out of character with the rest of the house, including works by André Derain, Renoir and Augustus John. The extensive grounds include a purpose-built play area for children.

Bempton and Flamborough Head 🟢

East Yorkshire. 👥 *4,300.* 🚂 *Bempton.* 🔵 *Bridlington.* 🔵 *25 Prince St, Bridlington (01262 673474).* 🔵 www.eastriding.gov.uk

BEMPTON, which consists of 5 miles (8 km) of steep chalk cliffs between Speeton and Flamborough Head, is the largest seabird-breeding colony in England, and is famous for its puffins. The ledges and fissures provide ideal nest-sites for more

Nesting gannet on the chalk cliffs at Bempton

than 100,000 pairs of birds. Today, eight different species, including skinny black shags and kittiwakes, thrive on the Grade 1 listed *(see p617)* Bempton cliffs. Bempton is the only mainland site for goose-sized gannets, well known for their dramatic fishing techniques. May, June and July are the best bird-watching months.

The spectacular cliffs are best seen from the north side of the Flamborough Head peninsula.

Beverley ㉗

East Riding of Yorkshire. 🚶 *30,000.*
ℹ️ *34 Butcher Row (01482 867430).*
📅 *Sat.* 🅦 *www.inbeverley.co.uk*

THE HISTORY of Beverley dates back to the 8th century, when Old Beverley served as a retreat for John, later Bishop of York, who was canonized for his healing powers. Over the centuries Beverley grew as a medieval sanctuary town. Like York, it is an attractive combination of both medieval and Georgian buildings.

Minstrel Pillar in St Mary's Church

The best way to enter Beverley is through the last of five medieval town gates, the castellated North Bar (rebuilt 1409–10). The bars were constructed so that market goods had to pass through them and a toll (levy) paid.

The skyline is dominated by the twin towers of the magnificent **minster**. This was co-founded in 937 by Athelstan, King of Wessex, in place of the church that John of Beverley had chosen as his final resting place in 721. The decorated nave is the earliest surviving building work which dates back to the early 1300s. It is particularly famous for its 16th-century choir stalls and 68 misericords *(see p329).*

The minster contains many early detailed stone carvings, including a set of four from about 1308 that illustrate figures with ailments such as toothache and lumbago. On the north side of the altar is the richly carved 14th-century Gothic Percy tomb, thought to be that of Lady Idoine Percy. Also on the north side is the Fridstol, or Peace Chair, said to date from 924-39, the time of Athelstan. Anyone who sat on it would be granted 30 days' sanctuary.

Within the North Bar, **St Mary's Church** has a 13th-century chancel and houses Britain's largest number of medieval

The inspiration for Lewis Carroll's White Rabbit, St Mary's Church

stone carvings of musical instruments. The brightly painted 16th-century Minstrel Pillar is particularly notable. Painted on the panelled chancel ceiling are portraits of monarchs after 1445. On the richly sculpted doorway of St Michael's Chapel is the grinning pilgrim rabbit said to have inspired Lewis Carroll's White Rabbit in *Alice in Wonderland.*

Southeast of the minster, the **Museum of Army Transport** contains over 100 exhibits of army vehicles. A Saturday market takes place near here.

🏛 **Museum of Army Transport**
Flemingate. 📞 *01482 860445.*
🔲 *daily.* 🈲 ♿ 🔲 🚻 🅦 *www. museum-of-army-transport.co.uk*

Beverley Minster, one of Europe's finest examples of Gothic architecture

Burton Constable ㉘

Nr Hull, East Yorkshire. ☎ 01964 562400. ≋ Hull then taxi. ○ Easter–Oct: Sat–Thu. 🗺 ♿ 📷 ☐ ☐
W www.burtonconstable.com

THE CONSTABLE FAMILY have been leading landowners since the 13th century, and have lived at Burton Constable since work began on it in 1570. It is an Elizabethan house, altered in the 18th century by Thomas Lightholer, Thomas Atkinson and James Wyatt. Today, its 30 rooms include Georgian and Victorian interiors. It has a fine collection of Chippendale furniture and family portraits dating from the 16th century. Most of the collections of prints, textiles and drawings belong to Leeds City Art Galleries. The family still lives in the south wing.

Painting of Burton Constable (c.1690) by an anonymous artist

The Princes' Dock in Kingston upon Hull's restored docks area

Kingston upon Hull ㉙

Kingston upon Hull. 🏙 270,000. ≋ 🚌 ⛴ ❚ Paragon St. (01482 223559). ▲ Tue, Fri, Sat.
W www.hullcc.gov.uk

THERE IS A LOT MORE to Hull than the heritage of a thriving fishing industry. The restored town centre docks are attractive, and Hull's Old Town, laid out in medieval times, is all cobbled, winding streets and quaintly askew red-brick houses. You can follow the "Seven Seas" Fish Trail, a path of inlaid metal fishes on the city's pavements that illustrates the many different varieties that have been landed in Hull, from anchovy to shark.

In Victoria Square is the **Maritime Museum**. Built in 1871 as the offices of the Hull Dock Company, it traces the city's maritime history. Among its exhibits are an ornate whalebone and vertebrae bench and a display of complicated rope knots such as the Eye Splice and the Midshipman's Hitch.

An imposing Elizabethan building, **Hands on History**, explores Hull's story through a collection of some of its families' artifacts.

In the heart of the Old Town, the **William Wilberforce House** is one of the surviving examples of the High Street's brick merchants' dwellings. Its first-floor oak-panelled rooms date from the 17th century, but most of the house is dedicated to the Wilberforce family, whose connection began in 1732 with the grandfather of the abolitionist.

Nearby is the **Streetlife Transport Museum**, Hull's most popular and noisiest museum, loved by children. It features Britain's oldest tramcar. New to Hull, at the mouth of the River Hull, **The Deep** is the world's only submarium, in a stunning building and dramatic setting. With lots of exciting sea life and state-of-the-art technology, it is ideal for families.

🏛 **Maritime Museum**
Queen Victoria Sq. ☎ 01482 613903. ○ daily (Sun: pm). ♿ 📷
W www.hullcc.gov.uk/museums

🏛 **Hands on History**
South Churchside. ☎ 01482 613952. ○ daily (Sun: pm). ● 23–27 Dec, 1 Jan, Good Fri. 📷 ♿

WILLIAM WILBERFORCE (1758–1833)

William Wilberforce, born in Hull to a merchant family, was a natural orator. After studying Classics at Cambridge, he entered politics and in 1784 gave one of his first public addresses in York. The audience was captivated, and Wilberforce realized the potential of his powers of persuasion. From 1785 onwards, adopted by the Pitt government as spokesman for the abolition of slavery, he conducted a determined and conscientious campaign. But his speeches won him enemies, and in 1792, threats from a slave-importer meant that he needed a constant armed guard. In 1807 his bill to abolish the lucrative slave trade became law.

A 19th-century engraving of Wilberforce by J Jenkins

🏛 **William Wilberforce Hse**
High St, Hull. 📞 01482 613921. ⭕ daily (Sun: pm). 🚻 ♿ limited.

🏛 **Streetlife Transport Museum**
High St, Hull. 📞 01482 613902. ⭕ Mon–Sat, Sun pm. ♿ 🚻

🍴 **The Deep**
Hull (via Citadel Way). 📞 01482 381000. ⭕ daily. ♿ 🖥 🚻 🅿
🌐 www.thedeep.co.uk

Holderness and Spurn Head ➌⓪

East Riding of Yorkshire. 🚆 Hull (Paragon St) then bus. 🛈 120 Newbegin, Hornsea (01964 536404).

T HIS CURIOUS FLAT AREA east of Hull, with straight roads and delicately waving fields of oats and barley, in many ways resembles Holland, except that its mills are derelict. Beaches stretch for 30 miles (46 km) along the coastline. The main resort towns are **Withernsea** and **Hornsea**.

The Holderness landscape only exists because of erosion higher up the coast. The sea continues to wash down tiny bits of rock which accumulate. Around 1560, this began to form a sandbank, and by 1669 it had became large enough to be colonized as Sonke Sand. The last bits of silting mud and debris joined the island to the mainland as recently as the 1830s. Today, you can drive through the eerie, lush wilderness of Sunk Island on the way east to Spurn Head. This is located at the tip of the Spurn Peninsula,

a 3.5 mile (6 km) spit of land that has also built up as the result of coastal erosion elsewhere. Flora, fauna and birdlife have been protected here by the Yorkshire Wildlife Trust since 1960. Walking here gives the eerie feeling that the land could be eroded from under your feet at any time. A surprise discovery at the end of Spurn Head is a tiny community of pilots and lifeboat crew, constantly on call to guide ships into Hull harbour, or help cope with disasters.

Fishing boat at Grimsby's National Fishing Heritage Centre

Grimsby ➌➊

NE Lincs. 👥 92,000. 🚆 🚌 🛈 42–43 Alexandra Rd, Cleethorpes (01472 323111). 🌐 www.nelincs.gov.uk

P ERCHED at the mouth of the River Humber, Grimsby was founded in the Middle Ages by a Danish fisherman

by the name of Grim, and rose to prominence in the 19th century as one of the world's largest fishing ports. Its first dock was opened in 1800 and, with the arrival of the railways, the town secured the means of transporting its catch all over the country. Even though the traditional fishing industry had declined by the 1970s, dock area redevelopment has ensured that Grimsby's unique heritage is retained.

This is best demonstrated by the award-winning **National Fishing Heritage Centre**, a museum that recreates the industry in its 1950s heyday, capturing the atmosphere of the period. Visitors sign on as crew members on a trawler and, by means of a variety of vivid interactive displays, travel from the back streets of Grimsby to the Arctic fishing grounds. On the way, they can experience the roll of the ship, the smell of the fish and the heat of the engine. The tour can be finished off with a guided viewing of the restored 1950s trawler, the *Ross Tiger*.

Other attractions in Grimsby include an International Jazz Festival every September, a restored Victorian shopping street called Abbeygate, a market, a wide selection of restaurants, and the nearby seaside resorts of Cleethorpes, Mablethorpe and Skegness.

🏛 **National Fishing Heritage Centre**
Heritage Sq, Alexandra Dock. 📞 01472 323345. ⭕ Easter–Oct: daily. 🎥 ♿ 🖥 🖥

Isolated lighthouse at Spurn Head, at the tip of Spurn Peninsula

Street-by-Street: York 🔢

THE CITY OF YORK has retained so much of its medieval structure that walking into its centre is like entering a living museum. Many of the ancient timbered houses, perched on narrow, winding streets, such as the Shambles, are protected by a Conservation order. Cars are banned from the centre, so there are always student bikes bouncing over cobbled streets. Its strategic position led to its development as a railway centre in the 19th century.

Monk Bar coat of arms

★ York Minster
England's largest medieval church was begun in 1220 (see pp392–

Stonegate
The medieval red devil is a feature of this street, built over a Roman road.

Thirsk ←

Helmsley

HIGH PETERGATE

LOW PETE

DEANGATE

ST LEONARDS PLACE

DUNCOMBE PLACE

STONEGATE

BLAKE STREET

DAVYGATE

York City Art Gallery

St Mary's Abbey

Yorkshire Museum
contains a fine collection of fossils, discovered at Whitby in the 19th century.

MUSEUM STREET

LENDAL STREET

CONEY STRE

Lendal Bridge

OUSE

Railway station, coach station, National Railway Museum, and Leeds

Ye Old Starre Inne is one of the oldest pubs in York.

St Olave's Church
The 11th-century church, next to the gatehouse of St Mary's Abbey (see p338), was founded by the Earl of Northumbria in memory of St Olaf, King of Norway. To the left is the Chapel of St Mary on the Walls.

Guildhall
This two-headed medieval roof boss is on the 15th-century Guildhall, situated beside the River Ouse and restored after bomb damage during World War II.

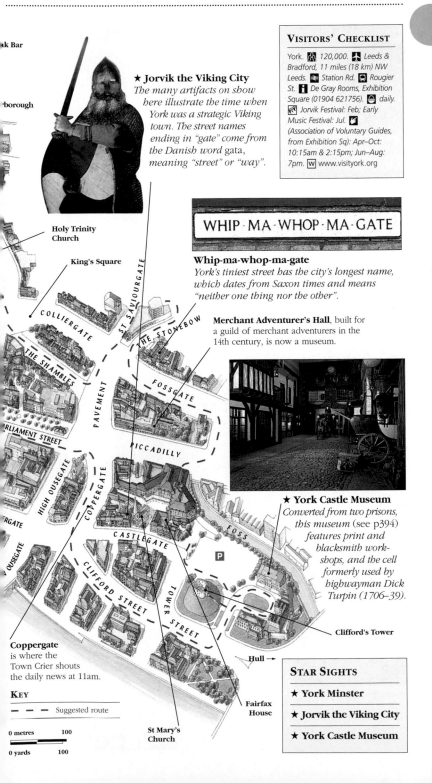

k Bar

-borough

★ Jorvik the Viking City
The many artifacts on show here illustrate the time when York was a strategic Viking town. The street names ending in "gate" come from the Danish word gata, *meaning "street" or "way".*

VISITORS' CHECKLIST

York. 👥 120,000. ✈ Leeds & Bradford, 11 miles (18 km) NW Leeds. 🚉 Station Rd. 🚌 Rougier St. ℹ De Gray Rooms, Exhibition Square (01904 621756). 🛒 daily. 🎭 Jorvik Festival: Feb; Early Music Festival: Jul. 🎫 (Association of Voluntary Guides, from Exhibition Sq): Apr–Oct: 10:15am & 2:15pm; Jun–Aug: 7pm. 🌐 www.visityork.org

WHIP · MA · WHOP · MA · GATE

Whip-ma-whop-ma-gate
York's tiniest street has the city's longest name, which dates from Saxon times and means "neither one thing nor the other".

Merchant Adventurer's Hall, built for a guild of merchant adventurers in the 14th century, is now a museum.

Holy Trinity Church

King's Square

ST SAVIOURGATE

COLLIERGATE

THE STONEBOW

THE SHAMBLES

FOSSGATE

PAVEMENT

RLIAMENT STREET

PICCADILLY

HIGH OUSEGATE

COPPERGATE

FOSS

CASTLEGATE

P

CLIFFORD STREET

TOWER STREET

★ York Castle Museum
Converted from two prisons, this museum (see p394) features print and blacksmith work-shops, and the cell formerly used by highwayman Dick Turpin (1706–39).

Clifford's Tower

Hull →

Coppergate
is where the Town Crier shouts the daily news at 11am.

KEY

– – – Suggested route

| 0 metres | 100 |
| 0 yards | 100 |

St Mary's Church

Fairfax House

STAR SIGHTS

★ York Minster

★ Jorvik the Viking City

★ York Castle Museum

York Minster

Central sunflower in rose window

T HE LARGEST Gothic cathedral north of the Alps, York Minster is 158 m (519 ft) long and 76 m (249 ft) wide across the transepts, and houses the largest collection of medieval stained glass in Britain *(see p395)*. The word "minster" usually means a church served by monks, but priests always served at York. The first minster began as a wooden chapel used to baptize King Edwin of Northumbria in 627. There have been several cathedrals on or near the site, including an 11th-century Norman structure. The present minster was begun in 1220 and completed 250 years later. In July 1984, the south transept roof was destroyed by fire. Restoration cost £2.25 million.

Central Tower
Reconstructed in 1420–65 (after partial collapse in 1407) from a design by the master stonemason William Colchester, its geometrical roof design has a central lantern.

Great East Window *(p395)*

The Choir has a vaulted entrance with a 15th-century boss of the Assumption of the Virgin.

Exit in south transept

The 16th-century rose window

★ **Choir Screen**
Sited between the choir and the nave, this 15th-century stone screen depicts kings of England from William I to Henry VI, and has a canopy of angels.

★ **Chapter House**
A Latin inscription near the entrance of the wooden-vaulted Chapter House (1260–85) reads: "As the rose is the flower of flowers, so this is the house of houses".

The Nave, built in 1291, was severely damaged by fire in 1840. Rebuilding costs were heavy but it was re-opened with a new peal of bells in 1840.

The western towers, with their
15th-century decorative panelling
and elaborate pinnacles, contrast
with the simpler design of the
north transept. The southwest
tower is the minster belfry.

Great West Door

West Window

Timbered interior of the Merchant Adventurers' Hall

Monk Bar

This is one of York's finest
original medieval gates,
situated at the end of
Goodramgate. It is vaulted on
three floors, and the portcullis
still works. In the Middle
Ages, the rooms above it
were rented out, and it was a
prison in the 16th century. Its
decorative details include
men holding stones ready to
drop on intruders.

York City Art Gallery

Exhibition Sq. 01904 697979.
daily. 24–26 Dec, 1 Jan.
W www.york.art.museum
This Italianate building of
1879 holds a wide-ranging
collection of paintings from
western Europe dating from
the early 14th century. There
is also a collection of British
and foreign studio pottery,
including work by Bernard
Leach, William Staite Murray
and Shoji Hamada.

A 15th-century French portrait of St
Anthony in York City Art Gallery

Clifford's Tower

(EH) Clifford's St. 01904 646940.
daily. 24–26 Dec, 1 Jan.
W www.english-heritage.org.uk
Sited on top of a mound that
William the Conqueror built
for his original wooden castle,
destroyed by fire during anti-
Jewish riots in 1190, Clifford's
Tower dates from the 13th
century. Built by Henry III,
it was named after the de
Clifford family, who were
constables of the castle.

ARC

St Saviourgate. 01904 654324.
Mon–Fri. mid-Dec–5 Jan,
Good Fri.
Housed in a restored medieval
church off the Shambles, the
ARC is a centre for exploring
archaeology. Visitors become
archaeological detectives
and can discover how
archaeologists have pieced
together clues from the past
to unravel the history of the
Viking age in York.

Merchant Adventurers' Hall

Fossgate. 01904 654818.
Easter–Sep: daily; Oct–Easter: Mon–Sat.
24 Dec–3 Jan.
Built by the York Merchants'
Guild, which controlled the
northern cloth trade in the
15th–17th centuries, this building has fine timberwork. The
Great Hall is probably the best
example of its kind in Europe.
Among its paintings is an un-
attributed 17th-century copy of
Van Dyck's portrait of Charles
I's queen, Henrietta Maria.
Below the Great Hall is the
hospital, which was used by
the guild until 1900, and a
private chapel.

Exploring York

THE APPEAL OF YORK is its many layers of history. A medieval city constructed on top of a Roman one, it was first built in AD 71, when it became capital of the northern province and was known as Eboracum. It was here that Constantine the Great was made emperor in 306, and reorganized Britain into four provinces. A hundred years later, the Roman army had withdrawn. Eboracum was renamed Eoforwic, under the Saxons, and then became a Christian stronghold. The Danish street names are the reminder that it was a Viking centre from 867, and one of Europe's chief trading bases. Between 1100 and 1500 it was England's second city. The glory of York is the minster (see pp392–3). The city also boasts 18 medieval churches, 3 mile long (4.8 km) medieval city walls, elegant Jacobean and Georgian architecture and fine museums.

Grand staircase and fine plaster ceiling at Fairfax House

The Middleham Jewel, Yorkshire Museum

🏛 York Castle Museum

The Eye of York. 🛈 01904 650333. ⏰ daily. 🖼 🚻 ground floor only. 🚻 🛈 🅦 www.york.castle.museum

Housed in two 18th-century prisons, the museum has a fine folk collection, started by Dr John Kirk of the market town of Pickering. Opened in 1938, its period displays include a Jacobean dining room, a moorland cottage, and a 1950s front room. It also contains an exhibition on the traditions of birth, marriages and death in Britain from 1700 to 2000.

The most famous exhibits include the reconstructed Victorian street of Kirkgate, complete with shopfronts, and the Anglo Saxon York Helmet, discovered in 1982.

🔒 York Minster

See pp392–3.

🏛 Jorvik, The Viking City

Coppergate. 🛈 01904 643211. ⏰ daily. 🖼 🚻 ring first. 🚻 🅦 www.vikingjorvik.com

This popular centre is built on the site of the original Viking settlement which archaeologists uncovered at Coppergate. It is most famous for recreating the smells of Viking York. A dynamic vision of 10th-century York combines with new technology to transform archaeological evidence and bring the hub of the Viking world to life.

🏛 Yorkshire Museum and St Mary's Abbey

Museum Gardens. 🛈 01904 551800. ⏰ daily. 🖼 🚻 🚻 🛈

Yorkshire Museum was in the news when it purchased the 15th-century Middleham Jewel for £2.5 million, one of the finest pieces of English Gothic jewellery found this century. Other exhibits include 2nd-century Roman mosaics and an Anglo-Saxon silver gilt bowl.

St Mary's Abbey (see p338) in the riverside grounds is where the medieval York Mystery Plays are set every few years.

🏛 Fairfax House

Castlegate. 🛈 01904 655543. ⏰ daily (Sun: pm, Fri: booked tour only 11am, 2pm). ● 6 Jan–20 Feb. 🖼 🚻 🚻 limited. 🛈 🅦 www.fairfaxhouse.co.uk

From 1755 to 1762 Viscount Fairfax built this fine Georgian town house for his daughter, Anne. The house was designed by John Carr (see p24), and restored in the 1980s. Between 1920 and 1965 it was a cinema and dancehall. Today, visitors can see the bedroom of Anne Fairfax (1725– 93), and a fine collection of 18th-century furniture, porcelain and clocks.

🏛 National Railway Museum

Leeman Rd. 🛈 01904 621261. ⏰ daily. 🚻 🚻 🛈 🅦 www.nrm.org.uk

The world's largest railway museum and the 2001 European Museum of the Year, covers nearly 200 years of history using a variety of visual aids. Visitors can try wheel-tapping and shunting in the interactive gallery, or find out what made Stephenson's Rocket so successful. Exhibits include uniforms, rolling stock from 1797 onward and Queen Victoria's Royal Train carriage, as well as the very latest rail innovations.

Reproduction of Stephenson's Rocket (right) and 1830s first-class carriage in York's National Railway Museum

The Stained Glass of York Minster

YORK MINSTER houses the largest collection of medieval stained glass in Britain, some of it dating from the late 12th century. The glass was generally coloured during production, using metal oxides to produce the desired colour, then worked on by craftsmen on site. When a design had been produced, the glass was first cut, then trimmed to shape. Details were painted on, using iron oxide-based paint which was fused to the glass by firing in a kiln. Individual pieces were then leaded together to form the finished window.

Part of the fascination of the minster glass is its variety of subject matter. Some windows were paid for by lay donors who specified a particular subject, others reflect ecclesiastical patronage.

Window detail

Miracle of St Nicholas (late 12th century) was put in the nave over 100 years after it was made. It shows a Jew's conversion.

The Five Sisters in the north transept are the largest examples of grisaille glass in Britain. This popular 13th-century technique involved creating fine patterning on clear glass and decorating it with black enamel.

St John the Evangelist, in part of the Great West Window (c.1338), is holding an eagle, itself an example of stickwork, where paint is scraped off to reveal clear glass.

Noah's Ark with its distinct boat-like shape is easily identified in the Great East Window.

Edward III is a fine example of the 14th-century "soft" style of painting, achieved by stippling the paint.

The Great East Window (1405-8), the size of a tennis court, is the largest area of medieval painted glass in the world. The Dean and Chapter paid master glazier John Thornton four shillings a week for this celebration of the Creation.

Walter Skirlaw, whose bishopric was revoked in favour of Richard Scrope, donated this window on its completion in 1408.

Harewood House 33

Leeds. 0113 2181010. *Leeds then bus.* Mar–Nov: daily. by arrangement. www.harewood.org

DESIGNED BY John Carr in 1759, Harewood House is the Yorkshire home of the Earl and Countess of Harewood.

The grand Palladian exterior is impressive, with interiors created by Robert Adam and an unrivalled collection of 18th-century furniture made specifically for Harewood by Yorkshire-born Thomas Chippendale (1711–79). There is a collection of paintings by Italian and English artists, including Reynolds and Gainsborough, and two watercolour rooms. The grounds by Capability Brown *(see p22)* include the **Harewood Bird Garden**, which has exotic species and a breeding programme of certain endangered varieties.

Bali starling, one of Harewood's rare birds

Leeds 34

Leeds. 750,000. *Leeds City Station (0113 2425242).* Mon–Sat. www.leeds.gov.uk

THE THIRD LARGEST of Britain's provincial cities, Leeds was at its most prosperous during the Victorian period. The most impressive legacy from this era is a series of ornate, covered shopping arcades. Also of note is the **Town Hall**, designed by Cuthbert Brodrick and opened by Queen Victoria in 1858.

Today, although Leeds is primarily an industrial city, it also offers a thriving cultural scene. Productions at **The Grand** by Opera North, one of Britain's top operatic companies, are of a high quality.

The **City Art Gallery** has an impressive collection of British 20th-century art and fine examples of Victorian paintings including works by local artist Atkinson Grimshaw (1836–93). Among the late 19th-century

French art are works by Signac, Courbet and Sisley. The Henry Moore Institute, added in 1993, is devoted to the research, study and display of sculpture of all periods. It comprises a reading room, study centre, library and video gallery, as well as galleries and an archive of material on and by Moore and other sculptural pioneers.

The **Armley Mills Museum**, in a 19th-century woollen mill, explores the industrial heritage of Leeds. Filled with original equipment, recorded sounds and models in 19th-century workers' clothes, it traces the history of the ready-to-wear industry.

A striking waterfront development by the River Aire has attracted two museums. The **Royal Armouries Museum**, from the Tower of London, tells the story of arms and armour around the world in battle, sport, self-defence and fashion, using live demonstrations, film, music and poetry. The **Thackray Medical Museum**, the largest of its kind in Europe, is a fascinating interactive display of medical advances, from a re-created vision of Victorian slum life to modern-day medical challenges.

Leeds has two sights that are especially suitable for children. **Tropical World**

The County Arcade, one of Leeds' restored shopping arcades

features crystal pools, a rainforest house, butterflies and tropical fish. There is also a farm and a Rare Breeds centre in the grounds of the Tudor-Jacobean **Temple Newsam House**, which has major art and furniture collections including Chippendale pieces.

City Art Gallery
The Headrow. 0113 2478248. daily (Sun: pm).
Armley Mills Museum
Canal Rd, Armley. 0113 2637861. Tue–Sun (Sun: pm), public hols. 25, 26 Dec, 1 Jan.
Royal Armouries
Armouries Drive. 0113 2201999. daily. 24, 25 Dec.
Thackray Medical Museum
Beckett St. 0113 2457084. daily. 24–26, 31 Dec, 1 Jan.
Tropical World
Canal Gdns, Princes Ave. 0113 266 1850. daily. 25, 26 Dec.
Temple Newsam House
Off A63. 0113 2647321. Tue–Sun. 25, 26 Dec, Jan.

Working loom at the Armley Mills Museum in Leeds

The Other Side (1990–93) by David Hockney at Bradford's 1853 Gallery in Saltaire

Bradford ⑤

Bradford. 🏠 *492,000.* ✈
🚉 🚌 🛈 *City Hall, Centenary Square*
(01274 753678). 🏪 *Mon–Sat.*
🌐 *www.visitbradford.com*

IN THE 16TH CENTURY, Bradford was a thriving market town, and the opening of its canal in 1774 boosted trade. By 1850, it was the world's capital for worsted (fabric made from closely twisted wool). Many of the city's well-preserved civic and industrial buildings date from this period, such as the Wool Exchange on Market Street. In the 1800s a number of German textile manufacturers settled in what is now called Little Germany. Their houses are characterized by decora-tive stone carvings that illustrated the wealth and standing of the occupants.

The **National Museum of Photography, Film and Television**, founded in 1983, explores the technology and art of these media. There is a television section called TV Heaven, where visitors can ask to watch their favourite programme. They are also encouraged to see themselves read the news on TV. The giant IMAX screen uses the world's largest film format. Film subjects include journeys

Daguerreotype camera by Giroux (1839)

into space, the ocean and the natural world.

The **Colour Museum** traces dyeing and textile printing from ancient Egypt to the present day with an emphasis on hands-on elements. **Bradford Industrial Museum** is housed in an original spinning mill. As well as seeing and hearing all the mill machinery, you can ride on a horse-drawn tram. Saltaire, a Victorian industrial village *(see p337)*, is on the outskirts of the city. Built by Sir Titus Salt for his Salts Mill workers, it was completed in 1873. The **1853**

Gallery has the world's largest collection of works by David Hockney, born in Bradford.

🏛 **National Museum of Photography, Film and Television**
Pictureville. 📞 *01274 202030.* ⬜ *daily (school hols); Tue–Sun (school terms); public holidays.* ⬛ *24–26 Dec.*
🅿 ♿ 🍴 🌐 *www.nmpft.org.uk*

🏛 **Colour Museum**
1 Providence St. 📞 *01274 390955.* .
⬜ *Tue–Sat.* ⬛ *24 Dec–2 Jan.* 🅿 🖼
♿ 🌐 *www.sdc.org.uk*

🏛 **Bradford Industrial Museum**
Moorside Mills, Moorside Rd. 📞
01274 435900. ⬜ *Tue–Sat, Sun (pm), public hols.* ⬛ *25, 26 Dec.* 🅿 ♿ 🚻

🏛 **1853 Gallery**
Salts Mill, Victoria Rd. 📞 *01274 531163.* ⬜ *daily.* ⬛ *25–26 Dec, 1 Jan.* ♿ 🍴 🚻 🅿
🌐 *www.saltsmill.org.uk*

BRADFORD'S INDIAN COMMUNITY

Immigrants from the Indian subcontinent originally came to Bradford in the 1950s to work in the mills, but with the decline of the textile industry many began small businesses. By the mid-1970s there were 1,400 such enterprises in the area. Almost one fifth were in the food sector, born out of simple cafés catering for mill-workers whose families were far away. As Indian food became more popular, these restaurants thrived, and today there are over 200 serving the highly spiced dishes of the Indian subcontinent.

Balti in a Bradford restaurant

Haworth Parsonage, home to the Brontë family, now a museum

Haworth 36

Bradford. 🏠 5,000. 🚇 Keighley.
ℹ️ 2–4 West Lane (01535 642329).
🌐 www.yorkshirevisitor.com

THE SETTING OF HAWORTH, in bleak Pennine moorland dotted with farmsteads, has changed little since it was home to the Brontë family. The village boomed in the 1840s, when there were more than 1,200 hand-looms in operation, but it is more famous today for the Brontë connection.

You can visit the **Brontë Parsonage Museum**, home from 1820–61 to novelists Charlotte, Emily and Anne, their brother Branwell and their father, the Revd Patrick Brontë. Built in 1778–9, the house remains decorated as it was during the 1850s. Eleven rooms, including the children's study and Charlotte's room, display letters, manuscripts, furniture and personal objects.

The nostalgic Victorian **Keighley and Worth Valley Railway** runs through Haworth. It stops at Oakworth station, where parts of *The Railway Children* were filmed. At the end of the line is the Railway Museum at Oxenhope.

🏛 Brontë Parsonage Museum
Church St. 📞 01535 642323.
⭕ daily. ⬤ 24–27 Dec; Jan. 🈺 📷
♿ limited. 🌐 www.bronte.info

Charlotte Brontë's childhood story book, for her sister, Anne

THE BRONTË SISTERS

Charlotte Brontë (1816–55)

During a harsh, motherless childhood, Charlotte, Emily and Anne retreated into fictional worlds of their own, writing poems and stories. As adults, they had to work as governesses, but still published a poetry collection in 1846. Only two copies were sold, but in the following year Charlotte's *Jane Eyre*, became a bestseller, arousing interest in Emily's *Wuthering Heights* and Anne's *Agnes Grey*. After her siblings' deaths in 1848–9, Charlotte published her last novel, *Villette*, in 1852. She married the Revd Nicholls, her father's curate, in 1854, but died shortly afterwards.

Hebden Bridge 37

Calderdale. 🏠 12,500. 🚇 ℹ️
1 Bridgegate (01422 845266). 🛒 Thu.
🌐 www.hebdenbridge.co.uk

HEBDEN BRIDGE is a delightful South Pennines former mill town, surrounded by steep hills and former 19th-century mills. The houses seem to defy gravity as they cling to the valley sides. Due to the gradient, one house is made from two bottom floors, and the top two floors form another unit. To separate ownership of these "flying freeholds", an Act of Parliament was devised.

There is a superb view of Hebden Bridge from nearby **Heptonstall**, where the poet Sylvia Plath (1932–63) is buried. The village contains a Wesleyan chapel (1764).

Halifax 38

Calderdale. 🏠 88,000. 🚇 🚉
ℹ️ Piece Hall (01422 368725).
🛒 Thu–Sat.
🌐 www.calderdale.gov.uk

HALIFAX'S HISTORY has been influenced by textiles since the Middle Ages, but today's visual reminders date mainly from the 19th century. The town inspired William Blake's vision of "dark Satanic mills" in his poem *Jerusalem* (1820). The wool trade helped to make the Pennines into Britain's industrial backbone.

Until the mid-15th century cloth production was modest, but vital enough to inspire the 11th-century Gibbet Law, which stated that anyone caught stealing cloth could be hanged. There is a replica of the gibbet used for decapitation at the bottom of Gibbet Street. Many of Halifax's 18th- and 19th-century buildings owe their existence to wealthy cloth traders. Sir Charles Barry (1795–1860), architect of the Houses of Parliament, was commissioned by the Crossley family to design the Town Hall. They also paid for the landscaping of the People's Park by the creator of the Crystal Palace, Sir Joseph Paxton (1801–65). Thomas Bradley's

Large Two Forms (1966–9) by Henry Moore in Bretton Country Park

18th-century **Piece Hall** was where wool merchants once sold their cloth, trading in one of the 315 "Merchants' Rooms". It has a massive Italianate courtyard, now beautifully restored. Today, Halifax's market takes place here.

Eureka! is a hands-on children's museum, with exhibits such as the Giant Mouth Machine. **Shibden Hall Museum** is a fine period house, parts of which date to the 15th century.

ENVIRONS: The nearby village of **Sowerby Bridge** was an important textile centre from the Middle Ages to the 1960s. Today visitors come to enjoy the scenic canals.

🏛 **Eureka!**
Discovery Rd. ☎ 01422 330069.
◯ daily. ● 24–26 Dec. ☒ & ▢
W www.eureka.org.uk

🏛 **Shibden Hall Museum**
Listers Rd. ☎ 01422 352246.
◯ daily (Sun: pm). ● 24 Dec–
2 Jan. ▢ ☒ ▢

National Coal Mining Museum ㊴

Wakefield. ☎ 01924 848806.
🚋 Wakefield then bus. ◯ daily.
● 24–26 Dec, 1 Jan. & ▢ ▢ ▢
W www.ncm.org.uk

HOUSED IN THE old Caphouse Colliery, this museum gives visitors the chance to go into a real mine shaft: warm clothing is advised. An underground tour takes you 137 m (450 ft) down, equipped with a hat and a miner's lamp. You can enter some of the narrow seams and see exhibits such as life-size working models. Other displays depict mining methods and conditions from 1820 to the present day.

Yorkshire Sculpture Park ㊵

Wakefield. ☎ 01924 830302.
🚋 Wakefield then bus. ◯ daily.
● 24, 25, 29–31 Dec. & ▢ ▢
W www.ysp.co.uk

THIS IS ONE of Europe's leading open-air galleries, situated in 45 ha (110 acres) of 18th-century parkland. Each year a series of large exhibitions of sculpture by international artists is organized alongside the main collection, which includes work by Barbara Hepworth and Sol LeWitt. Bretton Country Park, next to the sculpture park, has the largest collection of Henry Moore sculptures in Europe.

Magna ㊶

Rotherham. ☎ 01709 720002.
🚋 Rotherham Central or Sheffield then bus (No. 69). ◯ daily.
● 24–25 Dec. ☒ & ▮▮
▢ ▢
W www.magnatrust.org.uk

A FORMER STEEL WORKS has been imaginatively converted into a huge science adventure centre, with an emphasis on interactive exhibits, noise and spectacle designed to appeal to 4–15-year-olds. In the Air, Fire, Water and Earth Pavilions visitors can get close to a tornado, operate real diggers or discover what it's like to detonate a rock face. There are also multimedia displays on the lives of steelworkers and on how a giant furnace operated, as well as a show that features robots with artificial intelligence that evolve and learn as they hunt each other down.

The Face of Steel display at Magna

NORTHUMBRIA

NORTHUMBERLAND · COUNTY DURHAM

E NGLAND'S NORTHEAST *extremity is a tapestry of moorland, ruins, castles, cathedrals and huddled villages. With Northumberland National Park and Kielder Water reservoir to the north, a rugged eastern coastline, and the cities of Newcastle and Durham to the south, the area combines a dramatic history with abundant natural beauty.*

The empty peaceful hills, elusive wildlife and panoramic vistas of Northumberland National Park belie the area's turbulent past. Warring Scots and English, skirmishing tribes, cattle drovers and whisky smugglers have all left traces on ancient routes through the Cheviot Hills. Slicing through the southern edge of the park is the famous reminder of the Romans' 400-year occupation of Britain, Hadrian's Wall, the northern boundary of their empire.

Conflict between Scots and English continued for 1,000 years after the Romans departed, and even after the 1603 union between the two crowns. A chain of massive crenellated medieval castles punctuates the coastline, while other forts that once defended the northern flank of England along the River Tweed lie mostly in ruins. Seventh-century Northumbria was the cradle of Christianity under St Aidan, but this was sharply countered by Viking violence from 793 onward, as the Scandinavian invaders raided the monasteries. But a reverence for Northumbrian saints is in the local psyche, and St Cuthbert and the Venerable Bede are both buried in Durham Cathedral. The influence of the Industrial Revolution, concentrated around the mouths of the rivers Tyne, Wear and Tees, made Newcastle upon Tyne the north's main centre for coal mining and shipbuilding. Today, the city is famous for its "industrial heritage" attractions and urban regeneration schemes.

Section of Hadrian's Wall, built by the Romans in about 120, looking east from Cawfields

◁ **The towers of Durham Cathedral, rising above the River Wear**

Eyemouth

BERWICK-UPON-TWEE

Exploring Northumbria

Hᴵꜱᴛᴏʀɪᴄ ꜱɪᴛᴇꜱ ᴀʀᴇ ᴘʟᴇɴᴛɪꜰᴜʟ along Northumbria's coast. South of Berwick-upon-Tweed, a causeway leads to the ruined priory and castle on Lindisfarne, and there are major castles at Bamburgh, Alnwick and Warkworth. The hinterland is a region of wide open spaces, with wilderness in the Northumberland National Park, and fascinating Roman remains of Hadrian's Wall at Housesteads and elsewhere. The glorious city of Durham is dominated by its castle and cathedral, and Newcastle upon Tyne has a lively nightlife.

SIGHTS AT A GLANCE

Alnwick Castle **5**
Bamburgh **4**
Barnard Castle **17**
Beamish Open Air Museum **13**
Berwick-upon-Tweed **1**
Cheviot Hills **8**
Corbridge **10**
Durham pp414–15 **14**
Farne Islands **3**
Hadrian's Wall pp408–409 **11**
Hexham **9**
Kielder Water **7**
Lindisfarne **2**
Middleton-in-Teesdale **16**
Newcastle upon Tyne **12**
Warkworth Castle **6**

Walks and Tours
North Pennines Tour **15**

SEE ALSO

- *Where to Stay* pp563–4
- *Where to Eat* pp599–601

The wilderness of Upper Coquetdale in the sparsely populated Cheviot Hills

Kelso

Pennine Way

CHEVIOT HILLS

8

A68

Rede

NORTHUMBERLAND

NATIONAL PARK

7

KIELDER WATER

B6320

North Tyne

OTTE

A696

CORR

Carlisle

A69

Tyne

HEXHAM

9

Pennine Way

15 NORTH PENNINES TOUR

B6295

A689

Penrith

MIDDLETON-IN-TEESDALE

0 kilometres   10

0 miles   10

Penrith
A66

Gret

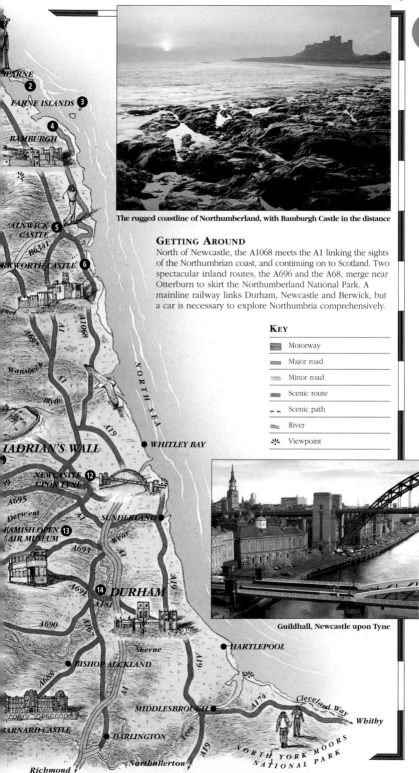

The rugged coastline of Northumberland, with Bamburgh Castle in the distance

GETTING AROUND

North of Newcastle, the A1068 meets the A1 linking the sights of the Northumbrian coast, and continuing on to Scotland. Two spectacular inland routes, the A696 and the A68, merge near Otterburn to skirt the Northumberland National Park. A mainline railway links Durham, Newcastle and Berwick, but a car is necessary to explore Northumbria comprehensively.

KEY

	Motorway
	Major road
	Minor road
	Scenic route
- -	Scenic path
	River
☆	Viewpoint

Guildhall, Newcastle upon Tyne

View over Berwick-upon-Tweed's three bridges

Berwick-upon-Tweed ❶

Northumberland. 🚶 13,000.
🚉 🚌 106 Mary Gate (01289
330733). 🛒 Wed, Sat.
🔲 www.berwickonline.org.uk

BETWEEN THE 12th and 15th
centuries Berwick-upon-
Tweed changed hands 14
times in the wars between the
Scots and English. Its position,
at the mouth of the river which
divides the two nations, made
the town strategically vital.

The English finally gained
permanent control in 1482
and maintained Berwick as a
fortified garrison. Ramparts
dating from 1555, 1.5 miles
(2.5 km) long and 7 m (23 ft)
thick, offer superb views over
the Tweed. Within the 18th-
century barracks are the **King's
Own Scottish Borderers
Regimental Museum**, an **art
gallery**, and **By Beat of
Drum**, charting the history of
British infantrymen.

🏛 King's Own Scottish Borderers Regimental Museum

The Barracks. 📞 01289 307427.
🕐 Mon–Sat. ⬤ 22 Dec–3 Jan,
public hols. 📷 🚹

Lindisfarne ❷

Northumberland. 🚌 Berwick-upon-
Tweed then bus. 🚹 106 Mary Gate,
Berwick-upon-Tweed (01289
330733). 🔲 www.lindisfarne.co.uk

TWICE DAILY a long, narrow
neck of land sinks under
the North Sea tide for five
hours, separating Lindisfarne,
or Holy Island, from the coast.
At low tide, visitors stream over
the causeway to the island
made famous by St Aidan, St
Cuthbert and the Lindisfarne
gospels. Nothing remains of
the Celtic monks' monastery,
finally abandoned in 875 after
successive Viking attacks, but
the magnificent arches of the
11th-century **Lindisfarne
Priory** are still visible.

After 1540, stones from the
priory were used to build
Lindisfarne Castle, which
was restored and made into
a private home by Sir Edwin
Lutyens *(see p25)* in 1903. It
includes an attractive walled
garden created by Gertrude
Jekyll *(see p23)*.

⚓ Lindisfarne Castle

(NT) Holy Island. 📞 01289 389244.
🕐 Mar–Nov: Sat–Thu & Good Fri
(pm). 📷

Farne Islands ❸

(NT) Northumberland. 🚢 from Seahouses (Apr–Oct). 🚹 106 Mary Gate,
Berwick-upon-Tweed (01289 330733).

THERE ARE BETWEEN 15 and
28 Farne Islands off the
coast from Bamburgh, some
of them periodically covered
by sea. Nature wardens and
lighthouse keepers share
them with seals, puffins and
other seabirds. Boat tours
depart from **Seahouses**
harbour and can land on
Staple and Inner Farne, site
of St Cuthbert's 14th-century
chapel, or Longstone,
where Grace Darling's
lighthouse is located.

Lindisfarne Castle (1540), the main landmark on the island of Lindisfarne

Celtic Christianity

St Cuthbert on a sea voyage

THE IRISH MONK St Aidan arrived in Northumbria in 635 from the island of Iona, off western Scotland, to evangelize the north of England. He founded the monastery on the island of Lindisfarne, and it became one of the most important centres for Christianity in England. This and other monastic communities thrived in Northumbria, becoming rich in scholarship, although the monks lived simply. It also emerged as a place of pilgrimage after miracles were reported at the shrine of St Cuthbert, Lindisfarne's most famous bishop. But the monks' pacifism made them defenceless against 9th-century Viking raids.

St Aidan's Monastery *was added to over the centuries to become Lindisfarne Priory. This 8th-century relic with interlaced animal decorations is from a cross at the site.*

The Venerable Bede *(673–735), the most brilliant early medieval scholar, was a monk at the monastery of St Paul in Jarrow. He wrote* The Ecclesiastical History of the English People *in 731.*

St Aidan *(600–651), an Irish missionary, founded a monastery at Lindisfarne and became Bishop of Northumbria in 635. This 1960 sculpture of him, by Kathleen Parbury, is in Lindisfarne Priory grounds.*

St Cuthbert *(635–87) was the monk and miracle worker most revered of all. He lived as a hermit on Inner Farne (a chapel was built there in his memory) and later became Bishop of Lindisfarne.*

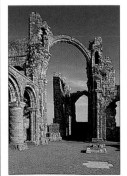

Lindisfarne Priory *was built by Benedictines in the 11th century, on the site of St Aidan's earlier monastery.*

THE LINDISFARNE GOSPELS

This book of richly illustrated portrayals of Gospel stories is one of the masterpieces of the "Northumbrian Renaissance" which left a permanent mark on Christian art and history-writing. The work was carried out by monks at Lindisfarne under the direction of Bishop Eadfrith, around 700. Monks managed to save the book and carried it with them when they fled from Lindisfarne in 875 after suffering repeated Viking raids. Other treasures were plundered.

Elaborately decorated initial to the *Gospel of St Matthew* **(c.725)**

Illustration of Grace Darling from the 1881 edition of *Sunday at Home*

Bamburgh ④

Northumberland. 🏛 *1,100.* 🚂 *Berwick.* ℹ️ *Seahouses (01665 720884; Apr–Oct); 106 Mary Gate, Berwick-upon-Tweed (01289 330733).*

D
UE TO NORTHUMBRIA's history of hostility against the Scots, there are more strongholds and castles here than in any other part of England. Most were built from the 11th to the 15th centuries by local warlords, as was Bamburgh's red sandstone **castle**. Its coastal position had been fortified since prehistoric times, but the first major stronghold was built in 550 by a Saxon chieftain, Ida the Flamebearer.

In its heyday between 1095 and 1464, Bamburgh was the royal castle that was used by the Northumbrian kings for coronations. By the end of the Middle Ages it had fallen into obscurity, then in 1894 it was bought by Newcastle arms tycoon Lord Armstrong, who restored it. Works of art are exhibited in the cavernous Great Hall, and there are suits of armour and medieval artifacts in the basement.

Bamburgh's other main attraction is the tiny **Grace Darling Museum** which celebrates the bravery of the 23-year-old, who, in 1838, rowed through tempestuous seas with her father, the keeper of the Longstone lighthouse, to rescue nine people from the wrecked *Forfarshire* steamboat.

⚓ **Bamburgh Castle**
Bamburgh. 🗲 *01668 214515.* ◯ *Mar–Nov: daily.* 🗁 🚻 🖥 🛇
🔲 www.bamburghcastle.com
🏛 **Grace Darling Museum**
Radcliffe Rd. ◯ *Easter–Oct: daily.* 🚻

Alnwick Castle ⑤

Alnwick, Northumberland. 🗲 *01665 510777.* 🚂 🚍 *Alnmouth.* ◯ *April–Oct: daily.* 🗁 🚻 *limited.* 🖥 🛇
🔲 www.alnwickcastle.com

D
OMINATING THE MARKET town on the River Aln is another great fortress, Alnwick Castle. Described by the Victorians as the "Windsor of the north", it is the main seat of the Duke of Northumberland, whose family, the Percys, have lived here since 1309. This border stronghold has survived many battles, but now peacefully dominates the pretty market town of Alnwick, overlooking landscape designed by Capability Brown. The stern medieval exterior belies the treasure house within, furnished in palatial Renaissance style with a collection of Meissen china and paintings by Titian, Van Dyck and Canaletto. The Postern Tower contains early British and Roman relics. The **Regimental Museum of Royal Northumberland Fusiliers** is in the Abbot's Tower. Other attractions are the Percy State coach, the dungeon and superb countryside views.

Carrara marble fireplace (1840) at Alnwick Castle

Warkworth Castle ⑥

(EH) Warkworth, nr Amble. 🗲 *01665 711423.* ◯ *daily.* ● *24–26 Dec, 1 Jan.* 🛇 🗁 🚻 *limited.*

W
ARKWORTH CASTLE sits on a green hill overlooking the River Coquet. It was one of the Percy family homes. Shakespeare's *Henry IV* features the castle in the scenes between the Earl of Northumberland and his son, Harry Hotspur.

Much of the present-day castle remains date from the 14th century. The unusual turreted, cross-shaped keep, which was also added in the 14th century, is a central feature of the castle tour.

Warkworth Castle reflected in the River Coquet

Kielder Water ⑦

Yarrow Moor, Falstone, Hexham. 🗲 *0870 2403549.* ◯ *daily.* 🚻
🔲 www.kielder.org

O
NE OF THE top attractions of Northumberland, Kielder Water lies close to the Scottish border, surrounded by spectacular scenery. With a perimeter of 27 miles (44 km), it is Europe's largest man-made lake, and offers facilities for sailing, windsurfing, canoeing, water-skiing and fishing. In summer, the cruiser *Osprey* departs from Leaplish on trips around the lake. The Kielder Water Exhibition, next to the Tower Knowe Visitor Centre, depicts the history of the valley from the Ice Age to the present day.

Cheviot Hills 🄏

THESE BARE, LONELY MOORS, smoothed into rounded humps by Ice Age glaciers, form a natural border with Scotland. Walkers and outdoor enthusiasts find a near-wilderness unmatched anywhere else in England. This remotest extremity of the Northumberland National Park nevertheless has a long and vivid history. Roman legions, warring Scots and English border raiders, cattle drovers and whisky smugglers have all left traces along the ancient routes and tracks they carved out here.

VISITORS' CHECKLIST

Northumberland. 🚋 *Hexham.* ℹ️ *Wooler (01668 282123), Eastburn, South Park.* ☎ *01434 605555.*

The Cheviots' isolated burns and streams are among the last habitats in England for the shy, elusive otter.

Chew Green Camp, which to the Romans was ad fines, or, "towards the last place", has fine views from the remaining fortified earthworks.

The Pennine Way starts in Derbyshire and ends at Kirk Yetholm in Scotland. The final stage (shown here) goes past Byrness, crosses the Cheviots and traces the Scottish border.

Uswayford Farm track

Uswayford Farm, is perhaps the most remote farm in England, and one of the hardest to reach. It is set in deserted moorland.

KEY

▰▰▰ A roads

▰▰▰ B roads

▰▰▰ Minor roads

--- Pennine Way

🔆 Viewpoint

0 kilometres 5

0 miles 5

Alwinton, a tiny village built mainly from grey stone, is situated beside the River Coquet. It is an access point for many fine walks in the area, and the wild landscape is deserted except for sheep.

Hexham ⑨

Northumberland. 🏠 14,000. 🚆
🚗 🚻 Wentworth Car Park
(01434 652220). 🚌 Tue.
W www.hadrianswallcountry.org

THE BUSY MARKET TOWN of Hexham was established in the 7th century, growing up around the church and monastery built by St Wilfrid, but the Vikings sacked and looted it in 876. In 1114, Augustinians began work on a priory and abbey on the original church ruins to create **Hexham Abbey**, which still towers over the market square. The Saxon crypt, built partly with stones from the former Roman fort at Corbridge, is all

Ancient stone carvings at Hexham Abbey

that remains of St Wilfrid's Church. The south transept has a 12th-century night stair: stone steps leading from the dormitory. In the chancel is the Frith Stool, a Saxon throne in the centre of a circle which protected fugitives.

Medieval streets, many with Georgian and Victorian shopfronts, spread out from the market square, The 15th-century Moot Hall was once a council chamber and the old gaol (jail) contains a **museum** of border history.

Hadrian's Wall ⑪

ON THE ORDERS of Emperor Hadrian, work began in AD 120 on a 73 mile (117 km) wall to be erected across northern England, to mark and defend the northern limits of the British province and the northwest border of the Roman Empire. Troops were stationed at milecastles along the wall, and large turrets, later forts, were built at 5 mile (8 km) intervals. The wall, now the responsibility of English Heritage, was abandoned in 383 as the Empire crumbled, but much of it remains.

Location of Hadrian's Wall

Carvoran Fort is probably pre-Hadrianic. Little of the fort survives, but the Roman Army museum nearby covers the wall's history.

Great Chesters Fort was built facing east to guard Caw Gap, but there are few remains today. To the south and east of the fort are traces of a civil settlement and a bathhouse.

Vindolanda is the site of several forts. The first timber fort dated from AD 90 and a stone fort was not built until the 2nd century. The museum has a collection of Roman writing tablets providing details of food, clothes and work.

Emperor Hadrian (76–138) came to Britain in 120 to order a stronger defence system. Coins were often cast to record emperors' visits, such as this bronze sestertius. Until 1971, the penny was abbreviated to d, short for denarius, a Roman coin.

Housesteads Settlement includes the remains of terraced shops or taverns.

Cawfields, 2 m (3 km) north of Haltwhistle, is the access point to one of the highest and most rugged sections of the wall. To the east, the remains of a milecastle sit on Whin Sill crag.

⛪ Hexham Abbey
Market Place. 📞 01434 602031.
🕐 daily. ♿ 🚻
🏛 Border History Museum
Old Gaol, nr Hallgate. 📞 01434
652349. ⬤ for renovation until mid-
2004: call for details. 🖼 📷

Corbridge 🔟

Northumberland. 👥 4,000. 🚉
ℹ️ Hill St (01434 632815).

THIS QUIET TOWN conceals a
few historic buildings
constructed with stones from
the Roman garrison town of

**The parson's 14th-century forti-
fied tower house at Corbridge**

nearby Corstopitum. Among
these are the thickset Saxon
tower of St Andrew's Church
and the 14th-century fortified
tower house built to protect
the local clergyman. Excavations of Corstopitum, now
known as **Corbridge Roman
Site and Museum**, have
exposed earlier forts, a well-
preserved granary, temples,
fountains and an aqueduct.

🏛 Corbridge Roman Site
and Museum
(EH) 📞 01434 632349. 🕐 Apr–Oct:
daily; Nov–Mar: Wed–Sun. ⬤ 24–26
Dec, 1 Jan. 📷 🖼 ♿ limited. 🖼

THE WALL COAST-TO-COAST

The wall runs eastward from Bowness on the
Solway Firth to the mouth of the Tyne at Wallsend.
The B6318 and A69 provide access to major sites.

KEY

〰️〰️ Route of the wall

0 kilometres   20

0 miles   20

Carrawburgh Fort, a 500-man
garrison, guarded the Newbrough
Burn and North Tyndale approaches.

Limestone Corner Milecastle is
sited at the northernmost part of
the wall and has magnificent views
of the Cheviot Hills *(see p407)*.

*Sewingshields Milecastle, with
magnificent views west to Housesteads,
is one of the best places for walking.
This reconstruction shows the layout
of a Roman milecastle on the wall.*

Chesters Fort was a
bridgehead over the
North Tyne. In the
museum are altars, sculp-
tures and inscriptions.

Chesters Bridge crossed the
Tyne. The original Hadrianic
bridge was rebuilt in 207. The
remains of this second bridge
abutment can still be seen.

*Housesteads Fort is the best-
preserved site on the wall, with
fine views over the countryside.
The excavated remains include
the commanding officer's house
and a Roman hospital.*

0 metres   500

0 yards   500

Newcastle upon Tyne ⑫

Newcastle upon Tyne. 🏙 *273,000.*
🚶 🚆 🚇 ⚓ 🛈 *Railway station;*
132 Granger St (0191 2610610). ⚓
Sun. 🅆 *www.newcastle.gov.uk*

NEWCASTLE OWES ITS NAME TO
its Norman **castle**
which was founded in
1080 by Robert Curt-
hose, the eldest son of
William the Conqueror
(see p47). The Romans
had bridged the Tyne
and built a fort on the
site 1,000 years earlier.
During the Middle Ages
it was used as a base
for English campaigns
against the Scots. From
the Middle Ages, the
city flourished as a coal
mining and exporting
centre. It was known in
the 19th century for
engineering, steel
production and later

as the world's foremost ship-
yard. The city's industrial base
has recently declined, but
"Geordies", as inhabitants of
the city are known, have re-
focused their civic pride on the
ultra-modern Metro Centre
shopping mall at Gateshead,
southwest of the city, and

Newcastle United soccer team.
The city's lively night scene
includes clubs, pubs and ethnic restaurants. The visible
trappings of its past are reflected in the magnificent **Tyne
Bridge** and in **Earl Grey's
Monument**, as well as the
grand façades in the city centre
thoroughfares, such as
Grey Street. On the
quayside there are
some dramatic new
features, notably
Baltic, the contempo-
rary art centre, **The
Sage Gateshead**, the
international centre
for music, and the
tilting **Gateshead
Millennium Bridge**.

Bridges crossing the Tyne at Newcastle

♣ **The Castle**
St Nicholas St. ☎ *0191 232
7938.* ☐ *daily.* 🎦 🛈
Curthose's original
wooden "new castle"
was rebuilt in stone in
the 12th century. Only

Beamish Open Air Museum ⑬

**Tram
symbol**

THIS GIANT OPEN AIR MUSEUM, spread over
120 ha (300 acres) of County Durham, recreates an authentic picture of family, working
and community life in the northeast in the 19th
and early 20th centuries.
It has a High Street, a
colliery village, a
disused mine, a
school, chapel and farm, all
with guides in period costume. A
restored tramline serves the different
parts of the museum, which carefully avoids romanticizing the past.

The station, which dates
back to 1913, has a
platform, a signal box, a
wrought-iron footbridge and
a goods yard.

***Home Farm** recreates the atmo-
sphere of an old-fashioned farmyard.
Rare breeds of cattle and sheep,
more common before the advent
of mass breeding, can be seen.*

School

Miners' houses were tiny, oil-lit
dwellings, backing onto vegetable
plots and owned by the colliery.

Chapel

the thickset, crenellated keep remains intact with two suites of royal apartments. A series of staircases spiral up to the renovated battlements, from which there are fine views over the city and the Tyne.

🏰 St Nicholas Cathedral

St Nicholas Sq. **📞** *0191 2321939.* **◯** *daily.* **♿**
This is one of Britain's tiniest cathedrals. There are remnants inside of the original 11th-century Norman church on which the present 14th- and 15th-century structure was founded. Its most striking feature is its ornate "lantern tower" – half tower, half spire – of which there are only three others in Britain.

🏛 Bessie Surtees' House

41–44 Sandhill. **📞** *0191 2611585.* **◯** *Mon–Fri.* **●** *25 Dec–2 Jan, public hols.* **♿** *limited.* **📷**
The story of beautiful, wealthy Bessie, who lived here before

Reredos of the Northumbrian saints in St Nicholas Cathedral

eloping with penniless John Scott, later Lord Chancellor of England, is the romantic tale behind these half-timbered 16th- and 17th-century houses. The window through which Bessie escaped now has a blue glass pane.

🌉 Tyne Bridge

Newcastle–Gateshead. **◯** *daily.* **♿**
Opened in 1928, this steel arch was the longest of its type in Britain with a span of 162 m (531 ft). Designed by Mott, Hay and Anderson, it soon became the city's most potent symbol.

🌉 Earl Grey's Monument

Grey St.
Benjamin Green created this memorial to the 2nd Earl Grey, Liberal Prime Minister from 1830 to 1834.

🏛 Baltic

The Centre for Contemporary Art Gateshead. **📞** *0191 478 1810.* **◯** *daily.* **📷** **🍴** **🛒** **w** *www.balticmill.com*
This former grain warehouse has been converted by architect Dominic Williams into a major new international centre for contemporary art, one of the biggest in Europe, with amazing views of Tyneside from its rooftop restaurant.

♿📷 *The Town has a sweet shop, newspaper office, solicitor, dentist and music teacher. There is also a pub.*

VISITORS' CHECKLIST

Beamish, Co. Durham. **📞** *0191 370 4000.* **🚆 🚌** *Durham, then bus.* **◯** *Apr–Oct: 10am–5pm daily (last adm 3pm); Nov–Mar: High Street only 10am–4pm Tue–Thu, Sat & Sun.* **📷 📷** **w** *www.beamish.org.uk*

The Co-op stocked everything a family needed at the turn of the century. A full range of foods available in 1913 is displayed.

Pockerley Manor farm

The 1825 Railway

Steam Winding Engine

Entrance
♿📷🛒ℹ️
P

Mahogany Drift mine, *a tunnel driven into coal seams near the surface, was here long before the museum and was worked from the 1850s to 1958. Visitors are given guided tours to underground pits.*

Houses built by the London Lead Company in Middleton-in-Teesdale

Durham 🄔

See pp414–5.

North Pennines Tour 🄕

See p413.

Cotherstone cheese, a speciality of the Middleton-in-Teesdale area

Middleton-in-Teesdale 🄖

County Durham. 🄯 1,100. 🄯 Darlington. 🄯 10 Market Place (01833 641001).

C LINGING TO A HILLSIDE amid wild Pennine scenery on the River Tees is this old lead mining town. Many of its rows of grey stone cottages were built by the London Lead Company, a paternalistic, Quaker-run organization who influenced every corner of its employees' daily lives.

The company began mining in 1753, and soon it virtually owned the town. Workers were expected to observe strict temperance, send their children to Sunday school and conform to the many company maxims. Today, mining has all but ceased in Teesdale, with Middleton standing as a monument to the 18th-century idea of the "company town". The offices of the London Lead Company can still be seen, as well as Nonconformist chapels from the era and a memorial fountain made of iron.

The crumbly Cotherstone cow's milk cheese, a speciality of the surrounding dales, is available in the shops.

Barnard Castle 🄗

County Durham. 🄯 5,000. 🄯 Darlington. 🄯 Woodleigh, Flatts Rd (01833 690909). 🄯 Wed.

B ARNARD CASTLE, known in the area as "Barney", is a little town full of character, with old shopfronts and a cobbled market overlooked by the ruins of the Norman castle from which it takes its name. The original Barnard Castle was built around 1125–40 by Bernard Balliol, ancestor of the founder of Balliol College, Oxford (see p210), to guard a river crossing point. Later, the market town grew up around the fortification.

Today, Barnard Castle is known for the extraordinary French-style château to the east of the town, surrounded by acres of formal gardens. Started in 1860 by the local aristocrat John Bowes and his French wife Josephine, an artist and actress, it was never a private residence, but always intended as a museum and public monument. The château finally opened in 1892, by which time the couple were both dead. Nevertheless, the **Bowes Museum** stands as a monument to his wealth and her extravagance.

The museum houses a strong collection of Spanish art which includes El Greco's *The Tears of St Peter*, dating from the 1580s, and Goya's *Don Juan Meléndez Váldez*, painted in 1797. Clocks, porcelain, furniture, musical instruments, toys and tapestries are among its treasures, with a mechanical silver swan as a showpiece.

🏛 **Bowes Museum**
Barnard Castle. 🄯 01833 690606. 🄯 daily. 🄯 🄯 🄯 (summer). 🄯 🄯 W www.bowesmuseum.org.uk

The Bowes Museum, a French-style château near Barnard Castle

North Pennines Tour ⑮

S TARTING JUST TO THE SOUTH of Hadrian's Wall, this tour explores the South Tyne Valley, and Upper Weardale. It crosses one of England's wildest and most remote tracts of moorland, then heads north again. The high ground is mainly blanketed with heather, dotted with sheep or criss-crossed with dry-stone

Sheep grazing on the moors

walls, a feature of this region. Harriers and other birds hover above, and streams tumble into valleys of tightly huddled villages.

Celts, Romans and other settlers have left imprints on the North Pennines. The wealth of the area was based on lead mining and stone quarrying which has long co-existed with farming.

Haltwhistle ①
In the Church of the Holy Cross is the tombstone of John Ridley, brother of Protestant martyr, Nicholas Ridley, burnt at the stake in 1555 *(see p210)*.

Haydon Bridge ③
There are some delightful walks near this spa town where the painter John Martin was born in 1789. Nearby Langley Castle is worth a visit.

Hexham ④
A pretty old town *(see p408)*, Hexham has a fine abbey.

Blanchland ⑤
Some houses in this lead-mining village are built on the site of a 12th-century abbey, using the original stone.

Bardon Mill ②
To the north is the Roman fort and civilian settlement of Vindolanda *(see p408)*.

Allendale ⑦
With its capital at Allendale Town, this is an area of spectacular scenery, with many walking and trout fishing opportunities.

Stanhope ⑥
An 18th-century castle overlooks the market square. The giant stump of a fossilized tree, said to be 250 million years old, guards the graveyard.

KEY

▬▬ Tour route

══ Other roads

☆ Viewpoint

TIPS FOR DRIVERS

Length: 50 miles (80 km)
Stopping-off points: Several pubs in Stanhope serve bar meals, and the Durham Dales Centre provides teas all year round. Horsley Hall Hotel at Eastgate serves meals all day. (See also pp636–7.)

0 kilometres   5

0 miles   5

Durham ⑭

Cathedral Sanctuary knocker

THE CITY OF DURHAM was built on Island Hill or "Dunholm" in 995. This rocky peninsula, which defies the course of the River Wear's route to the sea, was chosen as the last resting place for the remains of St Cuthbert. The relics of the Venerable Bede were brought to the site 27 years later, adding to its attraction for pilgrims. Durham Cathedral was treated by architects as an experiment for geometric patterning, while the Castle served as the Episcopal Palace until 1832, when Bishop William van Mildert gave it up and surrendered part of his income to found Britain's third university. The 23 ha (57 acre) peninsula has many footpaths, views and fine buildings.

★ Cathedral
Built from 1093 to 1274, it is a striking Norman structure.

Old Fulling Mill, a largely 18th-century building, houses a museum of archaeology.

Prebend's footbridge was built in 1777. A sculpture by Colin Winbourne is situated at the "island" end.

College Green

Monastic kitchen

Church of St Mary the Less

College gatehouse

South Bailey

St Cuthbert's Tomb

"Our Daily Bread" Window
This modern stained glass window in the north nave aisle was donated in 1984 by a local department store.

Galilee Chapel
Architects began work on the exotic Galilee Chapel in 1170, drawing inspiration from the Great Mosque of Cordoba in Andalusia. It was altered by Bishop Langley (d.1437) whose tomb is by the west door.

STAR SIGHTS

★ Cathedral

★ Castle

★ Castle

Begun in 1072, the castle is a fine Norman fortress. The keep, sited on a mound, is now part of the university.

Town Hall
(1851)

St Nicholas'
Church
(1857)

alace
reen

Tunstal's Chapel

Situated at the end of the Tunstal's Gallery, the castle chapel was built c.1542. Its fine woodwork includes this unicorn misericord (see p329).

Castle Gatehouse

Traces of Norman stonework can be seen in the outer arch, while the sturdy walls and upper floors are 18th century, rebuilt in a style dubbed "gothick" by detractors.

University
buildings
were built by
Bishop John Cosin
in the 17th century.

rch of St
y le Bow

Kingsgate
ootbridge,
built from
2–3, leads
to North
Bailey.

CATHEDRAL ARCHITECTURE

The vast dimensions of the 900-year-old columns, piers and vaults, and the inventive giant lozenge and chevron, trellis and dogtooth patterns carved into the stone columns, are the main innovative features of Durham Cathedral. It is believed that 11th- and 12th-century architects such as Bishop Ranulph Flambard tried to unify all parts of the structure. This can be seen in the south aisle of the nave below.

Ribbed vaults,
criss-crossing
above the nave,
are now common
in church ceilings.
One of the major
achievements of
Gothic architecture,
they were first
built at Durham.

The lozenge shape
is a pattern from
prehistoric carving,
but never before
seen in a cathedral.

Chevron patterns
on some of the piers
in the nave are
evidence of
Moorish influence.

WALES

Wales at a Glance

WALES IS A COUNTRY of outstanding natural beauty with varied landscapes. Visitors come to climb dramatic mountain peaks, go walking in the forests, fish in the broad rivers and enjoy the miles of unspoilt coastline. The country's many seaside resorts have long been popular with English holidaymakers. As well as outdoor pursuits there is the vibrancy of Welsh culture, with its strong Celtic roots, to be experienced. Finally there are many fine castles, ruined abbeys, mansions and cities full of magnificent architecture.

Beaumaris Castle *was intended to be a key part of Edward I's "iron ring" to contain the rebellious Welsh (see p422). Begun in 1295 but never completed, the castle (see p424) has a sophisticated defence structure that is unparalleled in Wales.*

Anglesey

Caernarfonshire & Merionethshire

Portmeirion *(see pp440–41) is a private village whose astonishing buildings seem rather incongruous in the Welsh landscape. The village was created by the architect Sir Clough Williams-Ellis to fulfill a personal ambition. Some of the buildings are assembled from pieces of architecture taken from sites around the country.*

Cardi

Carmarthensh

Pembrokeshire

St David *is the smallest city in Britain. The cathedral (see pp450–51) is the largest in Wales, and its nave is noted for its carved oak roof and beautiful rood screen. Next to the cathedral is the medieval Bishop's Palace, now a ruin.*

◁ **Caernarfon's colourful quayside marina**

Llanberis and Snowdon
(see p437) *is an area
famous for dangerous, high
peaks, long popular with
climbers. Mount Snowdon's
summit is most easily
reached from Llanberis. Its
Welsh name,* Yr Wyddfa
Fawr, *means "great tomb"
and it is the legendary
burial place of a giant slain
by King Arthur (see p273).*

Conwy Castle *guards one of the
best-preserved medieval fortified
towns in Britain (see pp432–3).
Built by Edward I, the castle
was besieged and came close
to surrender in 1294. It was
taken by Owain Glyndŵr's
supporters in 1401.*

Flintshire

erconwy
Colwyn

Denbighshire

NORTH WALES
(see pp426–41)

Wrexham

Powys

SOUTH AND MID-WALES
(see pp442–61)

The Brecon Beacons *(see pp454–5) is a national park,
a lovely area of mountains, forest and moorland in South
Wales, which is a favourite with walkers and naturalists.
Pen-y-Fan is one of the principal summits.*

Cardiff Castle's
*(see pp458–9) Clock
Tower is just one of
many 19th-century
additions by the
eccentric but gifted
architect William
Burges. His flamboy-
ant style still delights
and amazes visitors.*

Monmouthshire

rdiff, Swansea & Environs

0 kilometres   25

0 miles   25

A PORTRAIT OF WALES

L ONG POPULAR WITH BRITISH HOLIDAYMAKERS, *the many charms of Wales are now becoming better known internationally. They include spectacular scenery and a vibrant culture specializing in male-voice choirs, poetry and a passionate love of team sports. Governed from Westminster since 1536, Wales has its own distinct Celtic identity and in 1999 finally gained partial devolution.*

Much of the Welsh landmass is covered by the Cambrian Mountain range, which effectively acts as a barrier from England. Wales is warmed by the Gulf Stream and has a mild climate, with more rain than most of Britain. The land is unsuitable for arable farming, but sheep and cattle thrive; the drove roads, along which sheep used to be driven across the hills to England, are now popular walking trails. It is partly because of the rugged terrain that the Welsh have managed to maintain their separate identity and their ancient language.

One of Wales's splendid National Parks

Welsh is an expansive, musical language, spoken by only one-fifth of the 2.7 million inhabitants, but in parts of North Wales it is still the main language of conversation. There is an official bilingual policy: road signs are in Welsh and English, even in areas where Welsh is little spoken. Welsh place names intrigue visitors, being made up of native words that describe features of the landscape or ancient buildings. Examples include *Aber* (river mouth), *Afon* (river), *Fach* (little), *Llan* (church) *Llyn* (lake) and *Nant* (valley).

Wales was conquered by the Romans, but not by the Saxons. The land and the people therefore retained Celtic patterns of settlement and husbandry for six centuries before the Norman Conquest in 1066. This allowed time for the development of a distinctive Welsh nation whose homogeneity continues to this day.

The early Norman kings subjugated the Welsh by appointing "Marcher Lords" to control areas bordering England. A string

Rugby: the popular Welsh sport

of massive castles provides evidence of the turbulent years when Welsh insurrection was a constant threat. It was not until 1535 that Wales formally became part of Britain, and it would take nearly 500 years before the people of Wales regained partial autonomy.

Religious non-conformism and radical politics are deeply rooted in Welsh consciousness. Saint David converted the country to Christianity in the 6th century. Methodism, chapel and teetotalism became firmly entrenched in

Mountain sheep: a familiar sight in rural Wales

A *gorsedd* (assembly) of bards at the eisteddfod

of music derives from the ancient bards: minstrels and poets, who may have been associated with the Druids. Bardic tales of quasi-historical figures and magic were part of the oral tradition of the Dark Ages. They were first written down in the 14th century as the *Mabinogion,* which has inspired Welsh poets up to the 20th century's Dylan Thomas. The male-voice choirs found in many towns, villages and factories, particularly in the industrial south, express the Welsh musical heritage. Choirs compete in eisteddfods: festivals that celebrate Welsh culture.

the Welsh psyche during the 19th century. Even today some pubs stay closed on Sundays (alcohol is not sold at all in the Llŷn Peninsula). A long-standing oral tradition in Wales has produced many outstanding public speakers, politicians and actors. Welsh labour leaders have played important roles in the British trade union movement and the development of socialism.

Welsh heritage is steeped in song, music, poetry and legend rather than handicrafts, although one notable exception is the carved Welsh lovespoon – a craft recently revived. The well-known Welsh love

Welsh lovespoon

In the 19th century, the opening of the South Wales coalfield in Mid-Glamorgan – for a time the biggest in the world – led to an industrial boom, with mass migration from the countryside to the iron and steelworks. This prosperity was not to last: apart from a brief respite in World War II, the coal industry has been in terminal decline for decades, causing severe economic hardship. Today tourism is being promoted in the hope that the wealth generated, by outdoor activities in particular, will be able to take "King Coal's" place.

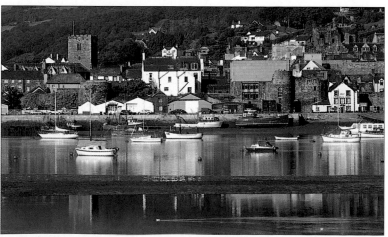

Conwy's picturesque, medieval walled town, fronted by a colourful harbour

The History of Wales

St David, patron saint of Wales

WALES HAS BEEN SETTLED since prehistoric times, its history shaped by many factors, from invasion to industrialization. The Romans set up bases in the mountainous terrain, but it was effectively a separate Celtic nation when Offa's Dyke was built as the border with England in 770. Centuries of cross-border raids and military campaigns followed before England and Wales were formally united by the Act of Union in 1535. The rugged northwest, the former stronghold of the Welsh princes, remains the heartland of Welsh language and culture.

Owain Glyndwr, heroic leader of Welsh opposition to English rule

THE CELTIC NATION

Ornamental Iron Age bronze plaque from Anglesey

WALES WAS SETTLED by waves of migrants in prehistoric times. By the Iron Age *(see pp42–3)*, Celtic farmers had established hillforts and their religion, Druidism. From the 1st century AD until the legions withdrew around 400, the Romans built fortresses and roads, and mined lead, silver and gold. During the next 200 years, Wales was converted to Christianity by missionaries from Europe. St David *(see pp450–51)*, the Welsh patron saint, is said to have turned the leek into a national symbol. He persuaded soldiers to wear leeks in their hats to distinguish themselves from Saxons during a 6th-century skirmish.

The Saxons *(see pp46–7)* failed to conquer Wales, and in 770 the Saxon King Offa built a defensive earthwork along the unconquered territory *(see p447)*. Beyond Offa's Dyke the people called

themselves *Y Cymry* (fellow countrymen) and the land *Cymru*. The Saxons called the land "Wales" from the Old English *wealas*, meaning foreigners. It was divided into kingdoms of which the main ones were Gwynedd in the north, Powys in the centre and Dyfed in the south. There were strong trade, cultural and linguistic links between each.

MARCHER LORDS

THE NORMAN INVASION of 1066 *(see p47)* did not reach Wales, but the border territory ("the Marches") was given by William the Conqueror to three powerful barons based at Shrewsbury, Hereford and Chester. These Marcher Lords made many incursions into Wales and controlled most of the lowlands. But the Welsh

Edward I designating his son Prince of Wales in 1301

princes held the mountainous northwest and exploited English weaknesses. Under Llywelyn the Great (d.1240), North Wales was almost completely independent; in 1267 his grandson, Llywelyn the Last, was acknowledged as Prince of Wales by Henry III.

In 1272 Edward I came to the English throne. He built fortresses and embarked on a military campaign to conquer Wales. In 1283 Llywelyn was killed in a skirmish, a shattering blow for the Welsh. Edward introduced English law and proclaimed his son Prince of Wales *(see p430)*.

OWAIN GLYNDŴR'S REBELLION

WELSH RESENTMENT against the Marcher Lords led to rebellion. In 1400 Owain Glyndŵr (c.1350–1416), a descendant of the Welsh princes, laid waste to English-dominated towns and castles. Declaring himself Prince of Wales, he found Celtic allies in Scotland, Ireland, France and Northumbria. In 1404 Glyndŵr captured Harlech and Cardiff, and formed a parliament in Machynlleth *(see p448)*. In 1408 the French made a truce with the English king, Henry IV. The rebellion then failed and Glyndŵr went into hiding until his death.

Union with England

Wales suffered greatly during the Wars of the Roses *(see p49)* as Yorkists and Lancastrians tried to gain control of the strategically important Welsh castles. The wars ended in 1485, and the Welshman Henry Tudor, born in Pembroke, became Henry VII. The Act of Union in 1535 and other laws abolished the Marcher Lordships, giving Wales parliamentary representation in London instead. English practices replaced inheritance customs and English became the language of the courts and administration. The Welsh language survived, partly helped by the church and by Dr William Morgan's translation of the Bible in 1588.

Vernacular Bible, which helped to keep the Welsh language alive

Industry and Radical Politics

The industrialization of south and east Wales began with the development of open-cast coal mining near Wrexham and Merthyr Tydfil in the 1760s. Convenient ports and the arrival of the railways helped the process. By the second half of the 19th century open-cast mines had been superseded by deep pits in the Rhondda Valley.

Living and working conditions were poor for industrial and agricultural workers. A series of "Rebecca Riots" in

Miners from South Wales pictured in 1910

South Wales between 1839 and 1843, involving tenant farmers (dressed as women) protesting about tithes and rents, was forcibly suppressed. The Chartists, trade unions and the Liberal Party had much Welsh support.

The rise of Methodism *(see p267)* roughly paralleled the growth of industry: 80 per cent of the population was Methodist by 1851. The Welsh language persisted, despite attempts by the British government to discourage its use, which included punishing children caught speaking it.

Wales Today

In the 20th century the Welsh, for the first time, became a power in British politics. David Lloyd George, although not born in Wales, grew up there and was the first British Prime Minister to come from a Welsh family. Aneurin Bevan, a miner's son who became a Labour Cabinet Minister, helped create the National Health Service *(see p59)*.

Welsh nationalism continued to grow: in 1926 Plaid Cymru, the Welsh Nationalist Party, was formed. In 1955 Cardiff

was recognized as the capital of Wales *(see p456)* and four years later the ancient symbol of the red dragon became the emblem on Wales' new flag. Plaid Cymru won two parliamentary seats at Westminster in 1974, and in a 1998 referendum the Welsh espoused limited home rule.

The Welsh language has declined: whereas half the population could speak it in 1901, the figure was down to 21 per cent 70 years later. The 1967 Welsh Language Act gave it protection by making Welsh compulsory in schools and the television channel S4C (Sianel 4 Cymru), formed in 1982, broadcasts many programmes in Welsh.

From the 1960s the steel and coal industries declined, creating mass unemployment. This has been only partly alleviated by the emergence of new, high-tech industries, and by the recent growth in tourism and higher education.

The logo of S4C, Wales's own television station

Castles of Wales

A French 15th-century painting of Conwy Castle

WALES IS RICH in romantic medieval castles. Soon after the Battle of Hastings, in 1066 *(see p47)*, the Normans turned their attentions to Wales. They built earth and timber fortifications, later replaced by stone castles, initiating a building programme that was pursued by the Welsh princes and invading forces. Construction reached its peak during the reign of Edward I *(see p422)*. As the need for security lessened in the later Middle Ages, some castles became stately homes.

The north gatehouse was planned to be 18 m (60 ft) high, providing lavish royal accommodation, but its top storey was never built.

The inner ward was lined with a hall, granary, kitchens and stables.

Rounded towers, with fewer blind spots than square ones, gave better protection.

Arrow slit

BEAUMARIS CASTLE

The last of Edward I's Welsh castles *(see p430)*, this perfectly symmetrical, concentric design was intended to combine impregnable defence with comfort. Invaders would face many obstacles before reaching the inner ward.

Moat

Curtain wall

WHERE TO SEE WELSH CASTLES

In addition to Beaumaris, in North Wales there are medieval forts at Caernarfon *(see p430)*, Conwy *(see p432)* and Harlech *(see p440)*. Edward I also built Denbigh, Flint (near Chester) and Rhuddlan (near Rhyll). In South and mid-Wales, Caerphilly (near Cardiff), Kidwelly (near Carmarthen) and Pembroke were built between the 11th and 13th centuries. Spectacular sites are occupied by Cilgerran (near Cardigan), Criccieth (near Porthmadog) and Carreg Cennen *(see p454)*. Chirk Castle, near Llangollen, is a good example of a fortress that has since become a stately home.

Caerphilly, 6 miles (10 km) north of Cardiff, is a huge castle with concentric stone and water defences that cover 12 ha (30 acres).

Harlech Castle (see p440) is noted for its massive gatehouse, twin towers and the fortified stairway to the sea. It was the headquarters of the Welsh resistance leader Owain Glyndŵr (see p422) from 1404–8.

CASTELL-Ŷ-BERE

This native Welsh castle at the foot of Cader Idris (see p440) was founded by Llywelyn the Great in 1221 (see p422), to secure internal borders rather than to resist the English.

Entrance

The D-shaped, elongated tower is a typical feature of Welsh castles.

The castle's construction follows the shape of the rock. The curtain walls are too low and insubstantial to be of much practical use.

Drawbridge

The Chapel Tower has a beautiful medieval chapel.

The protected dock, on a channel that originally led to the sea, received supplies during sieges.

The inner wall, with an inner passage, was higher than the curtain wall to permit simultaneous firing.

Twin-towered gatehouse

EDWARD I AND MASTER JAMES OF ST GEORGE

In 1278 Edward I brought over from Savoy a master stonemason who became a great military architect, James of St George. Responsible for planning and building at least 12 of Edward's fine Welsh castles, James was paid well and liberally pensioned off, indicating the esteem in which he was held by the king.

Edward I (see p422) was the warrior king whose castles played a key role in the subjugation of the Welsh people.

A plan of Caernarfon Castle illustrates how its position, on a promontory surrounded by water, has determined the building's shape and defence.

Caernarfon Castle (see p430), birthplace of the ill-fated Edward II (see p315), was intended to be the official royal residence in North Wales, and has palatial private apartments.

Castell Coch was restored in Neo-Gothic style by Lord Bute and William Burges (see p458). Mock-castles were built by many Victorian industrialists.

Conwy Castle (see p433), like many other castles, required forced labour on a massive scale for its construction.

NORTH WALES

·····························

ABERCONWY & COLWYN · ANGLESEY · CAERNARFONSHIRE &
MERIONETHSHIRE · DENBIGHSHIRE · FLINTSHIRE · WREXHAM

THE NORTH WALES LANDSCAPE *has a dramatic quality reflected in its history. In prehistoric times, Anglesey was a stronghold of the religious elite known as the Druids. Roman and Norman invasions concentrated on the coast, leaving the mountains to the Welsh. These wild areas are the centre of Welsh language and culture.*

Defence and conquest have been constant themes in Welsh history. North Wales was the scene of ferocious battles between the Welsh princes and Anglo-Norman monarchs determined to establish English rule. The string of formidable castles which still stand in North Wales are as much a testament to Welsh resistance as to the wealth and strength of the invaders. Several massive fortresses, including Beaumaris, Caernarfon and Harlech, almost surround the rugged high country of Snowdonia, an area that even today maintains an untamed quality.

Sheep and cattle farming are the basis of the rural economy here, though there are also large areas of forestry. Along the coast, tourism is a major activity. Llandudno, a purpose-built Victorian resort, popularized the sandy northern coastline in the 19th century. The area continues to attract large numbers of visitors, though major development is confined to the narrow coastal strip that lies between Prestatyn and Llandudno, leaving the island of Anglesey and the remote Llŷn Peninsula largely untouched. The Llŷn Peninsula remains one of the strongholds of the Welsh language, along with rather isolated inland communities, such as Dolgellau and Bala.

No part of North Wales can truly be called industrial, though there are still remnants of the once-prosperous slate industry in Snowdonia, where the stark, grey quarries provide a striking contrast to the natural beauty of the surrounding mountains. At the foot of Snowdon (the highest mountain in Wales), the villages of Beddgelert, Betws-y-Coed and Llanberis are popular bases for walkers who come to enjoy the spectacular views and striking beauty of this remote region.

Caernarfon Castle, one of the forbidding fortresses built by Edward I

◁ **The River Dee at Llangollen, still an area of unspoilt natural beauty**

Exploring North Wales

THE DOMINANT FEATURE of North Wales is Snowdon, the highest mountain in Wales. Snowdonia National Park extends dramatically from the Snowdon massif south beyond Dolgellau, with thickly wooded valleys, mountain lakes, moors and estuaries. To the east are the softer Clwydian Hills, and unspoilt coastlines can be enjoyed on Anglesey and the beautiful Llŷn Peninsula.

A lighthouse perched on the sea cliffs of Anglesey

KEY

- ▬ Major road
- ▬ Minor road
- ▬ Scenic route
- ➤ Scenic path
- ～ River
- ☼ Viewpoint

The peaks and moorland of Snowdonia

GETTING AROUND

The main route into North Wales from the northwest of England is the A55, a good dual carriageway which bypasses several places that used to be traffic bottlenecks, including Conwy. The other main route through the region is the A5 Shrewsbury to Holyhead road, which follows a trail through the mountains pioneered by the 19th-century engineer Thomas Telford *(see p433)*. Rail services run along the coast to Holyhead, connecting with ferries across the Irish Sea to Dublin and Dun Laoghaire. Scenic branch lines travel from Llandudno Junction to Blaenau Ffestiniog (via Betws-y-Coed) and along the southern Llŷn Peninsula.

SIGHTS AT A GLANCE

Aberdyfi **16**
Bala **7**
Beaumaris **2**
Beddgelert **11**
Betws-y-Coed **8**
Blaenau Ffestiniog **9**
Caernarfon **1**
Conwy pp432–3 **3**
Dolgellau **15**
Harlech **14**
Llanberis and Snowdon **10**
LLandudno **4**
LLangollen **6**
Llŷn Peninsula **12**
Portmeirion pp440–41 **13**
Ruthin **5**

RHYL

COLWYN BAY
A55

A55

A548

A525

A55

Gwyd

Offa's Dyke Path

DENBIGH
A544
A543
A525

A494

A55

Liverpool

Chester

5 RUTHIN

WS-Y-COED
A5

A525

A494

A483

WREXHAM

Dee

A5
Dee

6 LLANGOLLEN

A525

A4212
A494

7 BALA

0 kilometres   10

0 miles   10

A458 Shrewsbury

The imposing castle built at Conwy by Edward I in the 13th century

Caernarfon Castle, built by Edward I as a symbol of his power over the conquered Welsh

Caernarfon ❶

Caernarfonshire & Merionethshire (Gwynedd). 🚶 10,000. 🚌
ℹ️ Castle St (01286 672232). 🚆 Sat.
🌐 www.gwynedd.gov.uk

ONE OF THE MOST FAMOUS castles in Wales looms over this busy town. Both were created after Edward I's defeat of the last native Welsh prince, Llywelyn ap Gruffydd (Llywelyn the Last) in 1283 (see p422). The town walls merge with modern streets that spread beyond the medieval centre to a market square.

Overlooking the town and its harbour, **Caernarfon**

THE INVESTITURE

In 1301 the future Edward II became the first English Prince of Wales (see p422), a title since held by the British monarch's eldest son. In 1969 the invest-iture in Caernarfon Castle of Prince Charles (above) as Prince of Wales drew 500 million TV viewers.

Castle (see p425), with its polygonal towers, was built as a seat of government for North Wales. Caernarfon was a thriving port in the 19th century, and during this period the castle ruins were restored by the architect Anthony Salvin. Displays in the castle include the Royal Welch Fusiliers Museum, and exhibitions tracing the history of the Princes of Wales and exploring the theme "Chief-tains and Princes".

On the hill above the town are the ruins of **Segontium**, a Roman fort built in about AD 78. Local legend claims that the first Christian Emperor of Rome, Constantine the Great, was born here in 280.

♣ Caernarfon Castle
Y Maes. 📞 01286 677617. ◯ daily.
🅿️ 🎫 call for details. 🚻
🌐 www.cadw.wales.gov.uk

⋔ Segontium
Beddgelert Rd. 📞 01286 675625. ◯ daily (Sun: pm). ● 24, 26 Dec, 1 Jan.
♿ limited. 🌐 www.nmgw.ac.uk

Beaumaris ❷

Anglesey (Gwynedd). 🚶 2,000. 🚌
ℹ️ Llanfair PG, Station Site, Holyhead Rd, Anglesey (01248 713177).
🌐 www.anglesey.gov.uk

HANDSOME GEORGIAN and Victorian architecture gives Beaumaris the air of a resort on England's southern coast. The buildings reflect this sailing centre's past role as Anglesey's chief port, before the island was linked to the mainland by the road and

railway bridges built across the Menai Strait in the 19th century. This was the site of Edward I's last, and possibly greatest, **castle** (see p424), which was built to command this important ferrying point to the mainland of Wales.

Ye Olde Bull's Head inn, on Castle Street, was built in 1617. Its celebrated literary patrons have included Dr Samuel Johnson (1709–84) and Victorian novelist Charles Dickens (see p177).

The town's **Courthouse**, was built in 1614 and the recently restored 1829 **Gaol** preserves its soundproofed punishment room and a huge treadmill for prisoners. Two public hangings took place here. Richard Rowlands, the last victim, protested his inno-cence and cursed the church clock as he was led to the gallows, declaring that its four faces would never show the same times again. It failed to show consistent times until it had an overhaul in 1980.

Beaumaris's award-winning **Museum of Childhood** con-tains a collection of toys from the 19th and 20th centuries.

♣ Beaumaris Castle
Castle St. 📞 01248 810361. ◯ daily.
🅿️ ♿ 🌐 www.cadw.wales.gov.uk

⚖️ Courthouse
Castle. 📞 01248 810921. ◯ Apr–Sep: daily. 🅿️ ♿ 🚻

⚖️ Gaol
Bunkers Hill. 📞 01248 810921. ◯ Apr–Sep: daily. 🅿️ ♿ limited. 🚻

⛫ Museum of Childhood
Castle St. 📞 01248 712498. ◯ 2 wks before Easter–Nov: daily (Sun: pm).
🅿️ 🚻 🌐 www.cadw.wales.gov.uk

ALICE IN WONDERLAND

The Gogarth Abbey Hotel, Llandudno, was the summer home of the Liddells. Their friend, Charles Dodgson (1832–98), would entertain young Alice Liddell with stories of characters such as the White Rabbit and the Mad Hatter. As Lewis Carroll, Dodgson wrote his magical tales in *Alice's Adventures in Wonderland* (1865) and *Through the Looking-Glass* (1871).

Arthur Rackham's illustration (1907) of *Alice in Wonderland*

🏛 **The Alice in Wonderland Centre**
Trinity Sq. 📞 *01492 860082.* ⬜ *Easter–Oct: daily; Nov–Easter: Mon–Sat.* ⬤ *1 Jan, 2 wks in Nov, 25–26 Dec.* 🏷 ⬛ 📷 ⬛
🆆 *www.wonderland.co.uk*

🔺 **Great Orme Copper Mines**
Off A55. 📞 *01492 870447.* ⬜ *Feb–Oct: daily.* 🏷 ⬛ *limited.* ⬛ ⬛

Ruthin 🖱

Denbighshire (Clwyd). 🏠 *5,000.* 🚌 ℹ️ *Craft Centre, Park Rd (01824 703992).* ⬤ *1st Tue of every month; Thu (indoor).*
🆆 *www.borderlands.co.uk*

RUTHIN'S LONG-STANDING prosperity as a market town is reflected in its fine half-timbered medieval buildings. These include the National Westminster and Barclays banks in St Peter's Square. The former was a 15th-century courthouse and prison, the latter the home of Thomas Exmewe, Lord Mayor of London in 1517–18. **Maen Huail** ("Huail's stone"), a boulder outside Barclays, is said to be where King Arthur *(see p273)* beheaded Huail, his rival in a love affair.

St Peter's Church, on the edge of St Peter's Square, was founded in 1310 and has a Tudor oak roof in the north aisle, with 500 carved panels. Next to the Castle Hotel is the 17th-century **Myddleton Arms** pub, whose seven unusual, Dutch-style, dormer windows are known locally as the "eyes of Ruthin".

Conwy 🖱

See pp432–3.

Llandudno 🖱

Gwynedd. 🏠 *19,000.* 🚉 🚌 ℹ️ *1–2 Chapel St (01492 876413).*
🆆 *www.llandudno-tourism.co.uk*

Llandudno's crescent-shaped bay

LLANDUDNO retains much of the holiday spirit of the 19th century, when the new railways brought crowds to the coast. Its **pier**, more than 700 m (2,295 ft) long, and its canopied walkways recall the heyday of seaside holidays. The town is proud of its association with the author Lewis Carroll. **The Alice in Wonderland Centre** is a grotto decorated with life-sized scenes from his books.

Llandudno's cheerful seaside atmosphere owes much to a strong sense of its Victorian roots – unlike many British seaside towns, which embraced the flashing lights and funfairs of the 20th century. To take full advantage of its sweeping beach, Llandudno was laid out between its two headlands, Great Orme's Head and Little Orme's Head.

Great Orme's Head, now a Country Park and Nature Reserve, rises to 207 m (670 ft) and has a long history. In the Bronze Age copper was mined here; the **copper mines** and their excavations are open to the public. The **church** on the headland was built from timber in the 6th century by St Tudno, rebuilt in stone in the 13th century, restored in 1855 and is still in use. Local history and wildlife can be traced in an information centre on the summit.

There are two effortless ways to reach the summit: on the **Great Orme Tramway**, one of only three cable-hauled street tramways in the world (the others are in San Francisco and Lisbon), or by the **Llandudno Cable Car**. Both operate only in summer.

The "eyes of Ruthin", an unusual feature in Welsh architecture

Street-by-Street: Conwy ❸

CONWY IS ONE OF BRITAIN'S most underrated historic towns. Until the early 1990s it was famous as a traffic bottleneck, but thanks to a town bypass, its concentration of architectural riches – unparalleled in Wales – can now be appreciated. The castle dominates: a brooding, intimidating monument built by Edward I (see p424). But Conwy is set apart from other medieval towns by its amazingly well-preserved town walls. Fortified with 21 towers and three gateways, the walls form an almost unbroken shield around the old town.

Smallest House
This fisherman's cottage on the quayside, just over 3 m (10 ft) high, is said to be the smallest house in Britain.

St Mary's Church
This medieval church, on the site of a 12th-century Cistercian abbey, is set in peaceful grounds.

Plas Mawr, the "Great Mansion", was built by a nobleman, Robert Wynne, in 1576.

BERRY STREET

CHAPEL STREET

HIGH STREET

Bangor

LANCASTER SQUARE

CHURCH STREET

UPPER GATE STREET

ROSEMARY LANE

Upper Gate

Llywelyn's Statue
Llywelyn the Great (see p422) was arguably Wales's most successful medieval leader.

Aberconwy House
This restored 14th-century house was once the home of a wealthy merchant.

THOMAS TELFORD

Thomas Telford (1757–1834) was the gifted Scottish engineer responsible for many of Britain's roads, bridges and canals. The Menai Bridge (*see p430*), the Pontcysyllte Aqueduct (*see p436*) and Conwy Bridge are his outstanding works in Wales. Telford's graceful bridge at Conwy has aesthetic as well as practical qualities. Completed in 1826 across the mouth of the Conwy estuary, it was designed in a castellated style to blend with the castle. Before the bridge's construction the estuary could only be crossed by ferry.

VISITORS' CHECKLIST

Conwy. 🏘 8,000. 🚆 Conwy. ℹ️ 01492 592248. **Aberconwy House (NT)** ☎️ 01492 592246. ⭕ Wed–Mon. ⚫ Nov–Mar. ♿ **Conwy Castle** ☎️ 01492 592358. ⭕ daily. ♿ 🎫 **Smallest House** ☎️ 01492 593484. ⭕ Apr–Oct: daily. ♿ 🌐 www.stayinnorthwales.com

★ Town Walls
These remarkably well-preserved medieval walls are 1,280 m (4,200 ft) long and over 9 m (30 ft) high.

Chester

NEW BRIDGE

CASTLE STREET

CASTLE STREET

STREET

Telford's bridge

Railway bridge

0 metres 50
0 yards 50

Entrance to castle

KEY

– – – Suggested route

STAR SIGHTS

★ Town Walls

★ Conwy Castle

★ Conwy Castle
This atmospheric watercolour, Conwy Castle *(c.1770), is by the Nottingham artist Paul Sandby.*

Pontcysyllte Aqueduct, built in 1795–1805, carrying the Llangollen Canal

Llangollen ❻

Denbighshire. 🏯 5,000. 🚌 ❘ℹ️
Town Hall, Castle St (01978 860828).
🚢 Tue. 🆆 www.llangollen.org.uk

BEST KNOWN for its annual Eisteddfod (festival), this pretty town sits on the River Dee, which is spanned by a 14th-century bridge. The town became notorious in the 18th century, when two eccentric Irishwomen, Lady Eleanor Butler and Sarah Ponsonby, the "Ladies of Llangollen", set up house together in the half-timbered **Plas Newydd**. Their unconventional dress and literary enthusiasms attracted such celebrities as the Duke of Wellington (see p150) and William Wordsworth (see p354). The ruins of a 13th-century castle, **Castell Dinas Brân**, occupy the summit of a hill overlooking the house.

ENVIRONS: Boats on the **Llangollen Canal** sail from Wharf Hill in summer and cross the spectacular 300 m (1,000 ft) long Pontcysyllte Aqueduct, built by Thomas Telford (see p433).

🏛 Plas Newydd
Hill St. ☎ 01978 861314.
◑ Easter–Oct: daily. 🈂️ ♿ limited.

Bala ❼

Gwynedd. 🏯 2,000. 🚃 from Llangollen. ❘ℹ️ Penllyn, Pensarn Rd (01678 521021). 🆆 www.bala.co.uk

BALA LAKE, Wales's largest natural lake, lies between the Aran and Arenig mountains at the fringes of Snowdonia National Park. It is popular for water-sports and boasts a unique fish called a *gwyniad*, which is related to the salmon.

The little grey-stone town of Bala is a Welsh-speaking community, its houses strung out along a single street at the eastern end of the lake. Thomas Charles (1755–1814), a Methodist church leader, once lived here. A plaque on his former home recalls Mary Jones who walked 28 miles (42 km) barefoot from Abergynolwyn to buy a Bible. This led to Charles establishing the Bible Society, providing cheap bibles to the working classes.

The narrow-gauge **Bala Lake Railway** follows the lake shore from Llanuwchllyn, 4 miles (6 km) southwest.

Betws-y-Coed ❽

Conwy. 🏯 600. 🚉 ❘ℹ️ The Old Stables (01690 710426).
🆆 www.betws.org.uk

THIS VILLAGE near the peaks of Snowdonia has been a hill-walking centre since the 19th century. To the west are the **Swallow Falls**, where the River Llugwy flows through a wooded glen. The bizarre **Tŷ Hyll** ("Ugly House"), is a *tŷ unnos* ("one-night house"); traditionally, houses erected between dusk and dawn on common land were entitled to freehold rights, and the owner could enclose land as far as he could throw an axe from the door. To the east is **Waterloo Bridge**, built by Thomas Telford to celebrate the victory against Napoleon.

🏛 Tŷ Hyll
Capel Curig. ☎ 01690 720287.
House ◑ Easter–Sep: daily. **Grounds** ◑ Easter–Sep: daily; Oct–Easter: Mon–Fri. 🈂️ ♿ limited.

WORLD CULTURES IN LLANGOLLEN

Llangollen's International Eisteddfod (see p63) in the first half of July draws musicians, singers and dancers from around the world. First held in 1947 as a gesture of post-war international unity, it now attracts over 12,000 performers from nearly 50 countries to the six-day-long competition-cum-fair.

Choristers at the Eisteddfod, a popular Welsh festival

The ornate Waterloo Bridge, built in 1815 after the famous battle

◁ The picturesque village of Beddgelert in Snowdonia National Park

A view of the Snowdonia countryside from Llanberis Pass, the most popular route to Snowdon's peak

Blaenau Ffestiniog 🟢

Gwynedd. 🔼 5,500. �È 🔢 Betws-y-Coed (01690 710426); Jun–Sep: 01766 830360. 🔼 Tue (Jun–Sep).

BLAENAU FFESTINIOG, once the slate capital of North Wales, sits among mountains riddled with quarries. The **Llechwedd Slate Caverns**, overlooking Blaenau, opened to visitors in the early 1970s, marking a new role for the declining industrial town. The electric Miners' Tramway takes passengers on a tour into the original caverns.

On the Deep Mine tour, visitors descend on Britain's steepest passenger incline railway to the underground chambers, while sound effects recreate the atmosphere of a working quarry. The dangers included landfalls and floods, as well as the more gradual threat of slate dust breathed into the lungs.

There are slate-splitting demonstrations on the surface, a quarryman's cottage and a re-creation of a Victorian village to illustrate the cramped and basic living conditions endured by workers between the 1880s and 1945.

The popular narrow-gauge **Ffestiniog Railway** (see pp438–9) runs from Blaenau to Porthmadog.

🏛 Llechwedd Slate Caverns

Off A470. 🔲 01766 830306. 🔘 daily. 🌀 🔩 except the Deep Mine. 🔲 🔲 W www.llechwedd.co.uk

Llanberis and Snowdon 🟢

Gwynedd. 🔼 2,100. 🔢 High St, Llanberis (01286 870765). W www.gwynedd.gov.uk

SNOWDON, which at 1,085 m (3,560 ft) is the highest peak in Wales, is the main focus of the vast Snowdonia National Park, whose scenery ranges from this rugged mountain country to moors and sandy beaches.

The easiest route to Snowdon's summit begins in Llanberis: the 5 mile (8 km) **Llanberis Track**. From Llanberis Pass, the Miners' Track (once used by copper miners) and the Pyg Track are alternative paths. Walkers should beware of sudden weather changes and dress accordingly. The narrow-gauge **Snowdon Mountain Railway**, which opened in 1896, is an easier option.

Llanberis was a major 19th-century slate town, with grey terraces hewn into the hills. Other attractions are the 13th-century shell of **Dolbadarn Castle**, and, above Lake Peris, the **Electric Mountain**, which has tours of Europe's biggest hydro-electric pumped storage station.

🏰 Dolbadarn Castle

Off A4086 nr Llanberis. 🔲 01286 870765. 🔘 Jul–Sep: daily; Oct–Jun: call for details.

🔢 Electric Mountain

Llanberis. 🔲 01286 870636. 🔘 Feb–Mar: Thu–Sun; Easter–20 Dec: daily. 🌀 🔩 🔲 🔲

BRITAIN'S CENTRE OF SLATE

Welsh slates provided roofing material for Britain's new towns in the 19th century. In 1898, the slate industry employed nearly 17,000 men, a quarter of whom worked at Blaenau Ffestiniog. Foreign competition and new materials later took their toll. Quarries such as Dinorwig in Llanberis and Llechwedd in Blaenau Ffestiniog now survive on the tourist trade.

The dying art of slate-splitting

The village of Beddgelert, set among the mountains of Snowdonia

Beddgelert ⑪

Gwynedd. 🏘 *500.* 🛈 *High St,*
Porthmadog (01766 512981);
Jun–Aug: 01766 890615.
W *www.gwynedd.gov.uk*

BEDDGELERT enjoys a spectacular location in Snowdonia. The village sits on the confluence of the Glaslyn and Colwyn rivers at the approach to two mountain passes: the beautiful Nant Gwynant Pass, which leads to Snowdonia's highest reaches, and the Aberglaslyn Pass, a narrow wooded gorge which acts as a gateway to the sea.

Business was given a boost by Dafydd Pritchard, the landlord of the Royal Goat Hotel, who in the early 19th century adapted an old Welsh legend to associate it with Beddgelert. Llywelyn the Great *(see p422)* is said to have left his faithful hound Gelert to guard his infant son while he went hunting. He returned to find the cradle overturned and Gelert covered in blood. Thinking the dog had savaged his son, Llywellyn slaughtered Gelert, but then discovered the boy, unharmed, under the cradle. Nearby was the corpse of a wolf, which Gelert had killed to protect the child. To support the tale, Pritchard created **Gelert's Grave** (*bedd Gelert* in Welsh) by the River Glaslyn, a mound of stones a short walk south of the village.

ENVIRONS: There are many fine walks in the area: one leads south to the Aberglaslyn Pass and along a disused part of the Welsh Highland Railway. The **Sygun Copper Mine**, 1 mile (1.5 km) northeast of Beddgelert, offers self-guided tours of caverns recreating the life of Victorian miners.

🔦 Sygun Copper Mine
On A498. 📞 *01766 890595/510100.*
🕐 *Mar–Nov: daily; Oct–Feb: call for*
opening hours. 💷 🚫 *limited.* 📷
W *www.syguncoppermine.co.uk*

Ffestiniog Railway

Engine
plaque

THE FFESTINIOG narrow-gauge railway takes a scenic 14 mile (22 km) route from Porthmadog Harbour to the mountains and the slate town of Blaenau Ffestiniog *(see p437)*. Designed to carry slate from the quarries to the quay, the railway replaced a horse-drawn tramway constructed in 1836, operating on a 60 cm (2 ft) gauge. After closure in 1946, it was reconstructed by volunteers and re-opened in sections from 1955–82.

Steam traction *trains were first used on the Ffestiniog Railway in 1863. There are some diesel engines but most trains on the route are still steam-hauled.*

Llŷn Peninsula ⑫

Gwynedd. 🚃 🚌 *Pwllheli.*
🚢 *Aberdaron to Bardsey Island.*
ℹ️ *Min-y-don, Station Sq, Pwllheli
(01758 613000).*
🌐 *www.nwt.co.uk*

THIS 24 MILE (38 km) finger of land points southwest from Snowdonia into the Irish Sea. Although it has popular beaches, notably at Pwllheli, Criccieth, Abersoch and Nefyn, the coast's overriding feature is its untamed beauty. Views are at their most dramatic in the far west and along the mountain-backed northern shores.

The windy headland of **Braich-y-Pwll**, to the west of Aberdaron, looks out towards Bardsey Island, the "Isle of 20,000 Saints". This became a place of pilgrimage in the 6th century, when a monastery was founded here. Some of the saints are said to be buried in the churchyard of the ruined 13th-century **St Mary's Abbey**. Close by is **Porth Oer**, a small bay also known as "Whistling Sands" (the sand is meant to squeak, or whistle, underfoot).

East of Aberdaron is the 4 mile (6.5 km) bay of **Porth Neigwl**, known in English as Hell's Mouth, the scene of many shipwrecks due to the bay's treacherous currents. Hidden in sheltered grounds above Porth Neigwl bay, 1 mile (1.5 km) northeast of Aberdaron, is **Plas-yn-Rhiw**, a small, medieval manor house with Tudor and Georgian additions and lovely gardens.

The former quarrying village and "ghost town" of **Llithfaen**, tucked away below the sheer cliffs of the mountainous north coast, is now a centre for Welsh language studies.

🏛️ **Plas-yn-Rhiw**
(NT) off B4413. 📞 *01758 780219.*
⬜ *Apr–mid-May: Thu–Mon; mid-May–Sep: Wed–Mon.* 🎫 ♿ *limited.*

Llithfaen village, now a language centre, on the Llŷn Peninsula

Tan-y-Bwlch station is part of a National Park by the same name set in the heart of Snowdonia. Nature trails lead from this stop to the park's lakes and forests.

BETWYS-Y-COED

A470

P

Blaenau Ffestiniog

ℹ️

ℹ️ Tan-y-Grisiau

A496

Moelwyn Tunnel

Campbell's Platform

Dduallt

Tan-y-Bwlch

P

Plas Halt

A496

A487

DOLGELLAU, BALA

A496

Tan-y-Grisiau is a request stop for a power station visitor centre, and is near a waterfall and a lake.

VISITORS' CHECKLIST

🏛️ *01766 516073.* 📞 *bookings 01766 516024.* 🚃 *Porthmadog.* ⬜ *Mar–Nov: daily; Dec–Feb: phone to check.* ⬛ *25 Dec.* 🚻
🎫 ♿ 🅿️ 🌐 *www.festrail.co.uk*

KEY

▭▭	Ffestiniog Railway
○	Station
—	British Rail
≡≡	Major roads

Portmeirion ⓭

Gwynedd. 📞 *01766 770000.*
🚊 *Minffordd.* ⭕ *daily.* ⬤ *25 Dec.*
📷 ♿ *limited.* 🎫 🍴 🛍 🏠
🅦 *www.portmeirion-village.com*

T HIS BIZARRE ITALIANATE village
on a private peninsula at
the top of Cardigan Bay was
created by Welsh architect Sir
Clough Williams-Ellis (1883–
1978). He fulfilled a childhood
dream by building a village
"to my own fancy on my own
chosen site". About 50 buildings surround a central
piazza, in styles from
Oriental to Gothic.
Visitors can stay
at the luxurious
hotel or in one
of the charming
village cottages.
Portmeirion has
been an atmo-
spheric location
for many films
and television
programmes,
including the
popular 1960s
television series
The Prisoner.

**Sir Clough
Williams-Ellis at
Portmeirion**

Hercules *is a life-size 19th-
century copper statue near
the Town Hall, where a 17th-
century ceiling, rescued from
a demolished mansion,
depicts his legend.*

Fountain Cottage is
where Noel Coward
(1899–1973) wrote
Blithe Spirit.

**The *Amis
Reunis*** is a
stone replica
of a boat that
sank in the bay

**Swimming
pool**

The Portmeirion Hotel
*has many exotic interiors: the
furniture in the Jaipur Bar
comes from Rajasthan, India.*

Harlech ⓮

Gwynedd. 🏘 *1,300.* 🚊 ℹ️ *High St
(01766 780658).* 🛒 *Sun (summer).*
🅦 *www.gwynedd.gov.uk*

T HIS SMALL TOWN with fine
beaches is dominated by
Harlech Castle, a medieval
fortress *(see p424)* built by
Edward I between 1283 and
1289. The castle sits on a precipitous crag, with superb
views of Tremadog Bay and

the Llŷn Peninsula to the west,
and Snowdonia to the north.
When the castle was built, the
sea reached a fortified stairway
cut into the cliff, so that supplies could arrive by ship, but
now the sea has receded. A
towering gatehouse protects
the inner ward, enclosed by
walls and four round towers.
Despite its defences, Harlech
Castle fell to Owain Glyndŵr
(see p422) in 1404, and served
as his court until its recapture

four years later. The song *Men
of Harlech* is thought to have
been inspired by the castle's
heroic resistance during an
eight-year siege in the Wars
of the Roses *(see p49).*

♟ **Harlech Castle**
Castle Sq. 📞 *01766 780552.* ⭕ *daily.*
📷 🏠 🅦 *www.cadw.wales.gov.uk*

Dolgellau ⓯

Gwynedd. 🏘 *2,650.* ℹ️ *Eldon Sq
(01341 422888).* 🛒 *Fri (livestock).*
🅦 *www.gwynedd.gov.uk*

T HE DARK LOCAL STONE gives
a stern, solid look to this
market town, where the Welsh
language and customs are still
very strong. It lies in the long
shadow of the 892 m (2,927 ft)
mountain of Cader Idris where,
according to legend, anyone
who spends a night on its
summit will awake a poet or
a madman – or not at all.
Dolgellau was gripped by
gold fever in the 19th century,
when high-quality gold was

Harlech Castle's strategic site overlooking mountains and sea

The Triumphal Arch is the main entrance to Portmeirion village.

Central Piazza

Lodge

Campanile

Royal Dolphin Cottage

Bristol Colonnade

Viewing platform

The Ship Shop sells Portmeirion's famous flowered pottery.

The Pantheon was built in 1958, but lack of funds meant that the dome was originally made from plywood instead of copper and painted green. The Pantheon's unusual façade is formed by the upper half of a music room fireplace by Norman Shaw (see p25).

Dolgellau's grey-stone buildings, dwarfed by the mountain scenery

discovered in the Mawddach Valley nearby. The deposits were not large enough to sustain an intensive mining industry for long. Nevertheless, up until 1999, small amounts were mined and crafted locally into fine jewellery.

Dolgellau is a good centre for walking, whether you wish to take gentle strolls through beautiful leafy countryside or strenuous hikes across extreme terrain with dramatic mountain views. The lovely **Cregennen lakes** are set high in the hills above the thickly wooded **Mawddach Estuary** to the northwest; north are the harsh, bleak **Rhinog moors**, one of Wales's last true wildernesses.

Aberdyfi 16

Gwynedd. 🏠 900. 🚉 🚌 ℹ️ *Wharf Gardens (01654 767321).*
🌐 www.gwynedd.gov.uk

PERCHED ON THE MOUTH of the Dyfi Estuary, this little harbour resort and sailing centre makes the most of its splendid but rather confined location, its houses occupying every yard of a narrow strip of land between mountain and sea. In the 19th century, local slate was exported from here, and between the 1830s and the 1860s about 100 ships were built in the port. *The Bells of Aberdovey*, a song by Charles Dibdin for his opera *Liberty Hall* (1785), tells the legend of Cantref-y-Gwaelod, thought to have been located here, which was protected from the sea by dykes. One stormy night, the sluice gates were left open by Prince Seithenyn, when he was drunk, and the land was lost beneath the waves. The submerged church bells are said to peal under the water to this day.

Neat Georgian houses by the sea, Aberdyfi

SOUTH AND MID-WALES

CARDIFF, SWANSEA & ENVIRONS · CARDIGANSHIRE
CARMARTHENSHIRE · MONMOUTHSHIRE · POWYS · PEMBROKESHIRE

S*OUTH AND MID-WALES are less homogeneous regions than North Wales. Most of the population lives in the southeast corner. To the west is Pembrokeshire, the loveliest stretch of Welsh coastline. To the north the industrial valleys give way to the wide hills of the Brecon Beacons and the rural heartlands of central Wales.*

South Wales's coastal strip has been settled for many centuries. There are prehistoric sites in the Vale of Glamorgan and Pembrokeshire. The Romans established a major base at Caerleon, and the Normans built castles all the way from Chepstow to Pembroke. In the 18th and 19th centuries, coal mines and ironworks opened in the valleys of South Wales, attracting immigrants from all over Europe. Close communities developed here, focused on the coal trade, which turned Cardiff from a sleepy coastal town into the world's busiest coal-exporting port.

The declining coal industry has again changed the face of this area: slag heaps have become green hills, and the valley towns struggle to find alternative forms of employment. Coal mines such as Blaenafon's Big Pit are now tourist attractions; today, many of the tour guides taking visitors underground are ex-miners, who can offer a first-hand glimpse of the hard life found in mining communities before the pits closed.

The southern boundary of the Brecon Beacons National Park marks the beginning of rural Wales. With a population sparser than anywhere in England, this is an area of small country towns, hill-sheep farms, forestry plantations and spectacular man-made lakes.

The number of Welsh-speakers increases and the sense of Welsh culture becomes stronger as you travel further from the border with England, with the exception of an English enclave in south Pembrokeshire.

The changing face of the coal industry: former miners take visitors down the Big Pit in Blaenafon

◁ **Magnificent coastal scenery near St David's, Pembrokeshire**

Exploring South and Mid-Wales

MAGNIFICENT COASTAL SCENERY marks the Pembrokeshire Coast National Park and cliff-backed Gower Peninsula, while Cardigan Bay and Carmarthen Bay offer quieter beaches. Walkers can enjoy grassy uplands in the Brecon Beacons and gentler country in the leafy Wye Valley. Urban life is concentrated in the southeast of Wales, where old mining towns line the valleys north of Cardiff, the capital.

Cliffs of the Pembrokeshire Coast National Park

GETTING AROUND

The M4 motorway is the major route into Wales from the south of England, and there are good road links west of Swansea running to the coast. The A483 and A488 give access to mid-Wales from the Midlands. Frequent rail services connect London with Swansea, Cardiff and the ferry port of Fishguard.

SIGHTS AT A GLANCE

SEE ALSO

• *Where to Stay* pp566–8
• *Where to Eat* pp602–4

Wrexham

A458

Vyrnwy

POWIS CASTLE ● **WELSHPOOL**
❶

A483

gellau

A470

● **NEWTOWN**

Severn

● **LLANIDLOES**

44

518

ELAN VALLEY

Shrewsbury

KNIGHTON ❷

The rolling hills near Knighton, on the borderlands between Wales and England

A483

A488

LLANDRINDOD
❹ **WELLS**

A470

Wye

● **BUILTH WELLS**

A483

Leominster

35

MYNYDD EPYNT

A470

A438

HAY-ON-WYE ❸

KEY

▬	Motorway
▬	Major road
▬	Minor road
▬	Scenic route
- ● -	Scenic path
▬	River
☙	Viewpoint

OVERY
O WALES *Usk*
R

A40

A479

Hereford

A465

Olla's Dyke Path

❶₃ **BRECON**
BEACONS

A470

A40

A40

463

BLAENAFON ❶₆

A4043

A4042

MONMOUTH
❶₇

A449

A40

A466

❶₈ **TINTERN**
ABBEY

A470

● **RHONDDA**

CAERLEON ❶₅

M4

Bristol

M4

CARDIFF
❶₄

0 kilometres 15

0 miles 10

A detail of Cardiff Castle's clocktower, part of the ornate embellishments added in the 19th century

Italianate terraces and formal gardens at Powis Castle, adding a Mediterranean air to the Welsh borderlands

Powis Castle ❶

(NT) Welshpool, Powys. 📞 01938
551944. 🚆 Welshpool then bus.
🕐 Apr–Jun & Sep–Oct: Wed–Sun;
Jul–Aug: Tue–Sun & public hols. 🎫
♿ limited. ⬛ 🚻
🌐 www.castlewales.com/powis

POWIS CASTLE – the spelling
is an archaic version of
"Powys" – has outgrown its
military roots. Despite its sham
battlements and dominant
site, 1 mile (1.6 km) to the
southwest of the town of
Welshpool, this red-stone
building has served as a
country mansion for
centuries. It began life
in the 13th century as
a fortress, built by the
princes of Powys to
control the border
with England.

The castle is entered
through one of few
surviving medieval
features: a gateway,
built in 1283 by Owain
de la Pole. The gate is
flanked by two towers.

The castle's lavish
interiors soon banish
all thoughts of war.
A **Dining Room**,
decorated with fine
17th-century panelling
and family portraits,
was originally designed
as the castle's Great

Hall. The **Great Staircase**,
added in the late 17th century
and elaborately decorated
with carved fruit and flowers,
leads to the main apartments:
an early 19th-century library,
the panelled **Oak Drawing
Room** and the Elizabethan
Long Gallery, where ornate
plasterwork on the fireplace
and ceiling date from the
1590s. In the **Blue Drawing
Room** there are three 18th-
century Brussels tapestries.

The Herbert family bought
the property in 1587 and
were proud of their Royalist
connections; the panelling in

The richly carved 17th-century Great Staircase

the **State Bedroom** bears the
royal monogram. Powis Castle
was defended for Charles I in
the Civil War *(see pp52–3)*, but
fell to Parliament in 1644. The
3rd Baron Powis, a supporter
of James II, had to flee the
country when William and
Mary took the throne in 1688
(see pp52–3).

The castle's **Clive Museum**
has an exhibition concerning
"Clive of India" (1725–74), the
general and statesman who
helped strengthen British
control in India in the mid-
18th century. The family's
link with Powis Castle was
established by the 2nd
Lord Clive, who mar-
ried into the Herbert
family and became the
Earl of Powis in 1804.

The gardens at Powis
are among the best-
known in Britain, with
their series of elegant
Italianate terraces,
adorned with statues,
niches, balustrades
and hanging gardens,
all stepped into the
steep hillside beneath
the castle walls. Created
between 1688 and
1722, these are the
only formal gardens
of this period in
Britain that are still
kept in their original
form *(see pp22–3)*.

Knighton ❷

Powys. 🏠 *3,500.* 🚆 🅸 *West St (01547 528753).* 🅰 *Thu.*
🆆 www.offasdyke.demon.co.uk

KNIGHTON'S WELSH NAME, Tref y Clawdd ("The Town on the Dyke"), reflects its status as the only original settlement on **Offa's Dyke**. In the 8th century, King Offa of Mercia (central and southern England) constructed a ditch and bank to mark out his territory, and to enable the enforcement of a Saxon law: "Neither shall a Welshman cross into English land without the appointed man from the other side, who should meet him at the bank and bring him back again without any offence being committed." Some of the best-preserved sections of the 6 m (20 ft) high earthwork lie in the hills around Knighton. The Offa's Dyke Footpath runs for 177 miles (285 km) along the border between England and Wales.

Knighton is set on a steep hill, sloping upwards from **St Edward's Church** (1877) with its medieval tower, to the summit, where a castle once stood. The main street leads via the market square, marked by a 19th-century clock tower, along **The Narrows**, a Tudor street with little shops. **The Old House** on Broad Street is a medieval "cruck" house (curved timbers form a frame to support the roof), with a hole in the ceiling instead of a chimney.

Knighton's clock

Hay-on-Wye ❸

Powys. 🏠 *1,300.* 🅸 *Oxford Rd (01497 820144).* 🅰 *Thu.*
🆆 www.hay-on-wye.co.uk

BOOK-LOVERS from all over the world come to this quiet border town in the Black Mountains. Hay-on-Wye has over 30 second-hand book-shops stocking millions of titles, and in early summer hosts a prestigious Festival of Literature. The town's love affair with books began when a bookshop was opened in the 1960s by Richard Booth, who claims the (fictitious) title of King of Independent Hay and lives in **Hay Castle**, a 17th-century mansion in the grounds of the original 13th-century castle. Hay's oldest inn, the 16th-century **Three Tuns** on Bridge Street, is still functioning and has an attractive half-timbered façade.

ENVIRONS: Hay sits on the approach to the Black Mountains and is surrounded by rolling hills. To the south are the heights of Hay Bluff and the Vale of Ewyas, where the 12th-century ruins of **Llanthony Priory** *(see p455)* retain fine pointed arches.

One of Hay-on-Wye's bookshops

🔺 Hay Castle
🅲 *01497 820503.* ⬜ *daily.* ⬛ *25 Dec.* 🅶 *grounds only.* 🅷

Llandrindod Wells ❹

Powys. 🏠 *5,000.* 🚆 🅸 *Memorial Gardens (01597 822600).* 🅰 *Fri.*
🆆 www.visitllandrindod.co.uk

LLANDRINDOD is a perfect example of a Victorian town, with canopied streets, delicate wrought ironwork, gabled villas and ornamental parklands. This purpose-built spa town became Wales's premier inland resort of the 19th century. Its sulphur and magnesium spring waters were taken to treat skin complaints and a range of other ailments.

The town now makes every effort to preserve its Victorian character, with a lake and the well-tended **Rock Park Gardens**. The **Heritage Centre** houses a heritage exhibition and a restored 19th-century **Pump Room** is now a restaurant and is the focus of the summer Victorian Festival, when residents don period costume and cars are banned from the town centre.

The **Radnorshire Museum** traces the town's past as one of a string of 19th-century Welsh spas which included Builth, Llangammarch and **Llanwrtyd** (now a pony trekking centre).

🏢 Heritage Centre
Rock Park. 🅲 *01597 829267.* ⬜ *Tue–Sat.* ⬛ *Christmas week.* 🅶 🅷 🅳
🏛 Radnorshire Museum
Memorial Gardens. 🅲 *01597 824513.* ⬜ *Tue–Sat & public hols (& Sun pm Apr–Oct).* ⬛ *25, 26 Dec, 1 Jan.* 🅶 🅷 *limited.*

Victorian architecture on Spa Road, Llandrindod Wells

Craig Goch, one of the original chain of Elan Valley reservoirs

Elan Valley 5

Powys. ☲ *Llandrindod.*
ℹ *Rhayader (01597 810898).*
W *www.elanvalley.org.uk*

A STRING OF SPECTACULAR
reservoirs, the first of the
country's man-made lakes,
has made this one of Wales's
most famous valleys. **Caban
Coch, Garreg Ddu, Pen-y-
Garreg** and **Craig Goch**,
were created between 1892
and 1903 to supply water to
Birmingham, 73 miles (117
km) away. They form a chain
of lakes about 9 miles (14 km)
long, holding 50 billion litres
(13 billion gallons) of water.
Victorian engineers selected
these high moorlands on the
Cambrian Mountains, for their
high annual rainfall of 1,780
mm (70 inches). The choice
created bitter controversy
and resentment: more than
100 people had to move from
the valley that was flooded in
order to create Caban Coch.

Unlike their more utilitarian
modern counterparts, these
dams were built during an era
when decoration was seen as
an integral part of any design.
Finished in dressed stone,
they have an air of grandeur
which is lacking in the huge
Claerwen reservoir, a stark
addition built during the early
1950s to double the lakes' cap-
acity. Contained by a 355 m
(1,165 ft) dam, it lies 4 miles
(6 km) along the B4518 that
runs through Elan Valley and
offers magnificent views.

The remote moorlands and
woodlands surrounding the
lakes are an important habitat

for wildlife; the red kite can
often be seen here. The **Elan
Valley Visitors' Centre**,
beside the Caban Coch dam,
describes the construction of
the lakes, as well as the
valley's own natural
history. **Elan Village**,
set beside the centre,
is an unusual ex-
ample of a model
workers' village, built
during the 1900s to
house the water-
works staff. Outside
the centre is a statue
of the poet Percy
Bysshe Shelley
(see p210), who
stayed in the valley at
the mansion of
Nantgwyllt in 1810
with his wife, Harriet. The
house now lies underneath
the waters of Caban Coch,
along with the rest of the old
village. Among the buildings
submerged were the village
school and a church.

The trail from Machynlleth to
Devil's Bridge, near Aberystwyth

Machynlleth 6

Powys. 🏘 *2,200.* ☲ **ℹ** *Canolfan
Owain Glyndŵr (01654 702401).*
🅰 *Wed.*

HALF-TIMBERED BUILDINGS
and Georgian façades
appear among the grey-stone
houses in Machynlleth. It was
here that Owain Glyndŵr,
Wales's last native leader *(see
p422)*, held a parliament in
1404. The restored **Parliament
House** has displays on his life
and a brass-rubbing centre.

The ornate **Clock Tower**,
in the middle of Maengwyn
Street, was erected in 1874 by
the Marquess of Londonderry
to mark the coming of age of
his heir, Lord Castlereagh.
The Marquess lived in **Plas
Machynlleth**, a 17th-century
house in parkland off the main
street, which is now
a centre of Celtic
heritage and culture.

**Senedd-dy
Owain Glyndŵr
Tywysog Cymru
Arddangosfa**

Parliament House
sign, Machynlleth

ENVIRONS: In an old
slate quarry 2.5 miles
(4 km) to the north,
a "village of the
future" is run by the
**Centre for Alter-
native Technology**.
A water-balanced
cliff railway takes
summer visitors to
view low-energy
houses and organic
gardens, to see how to make
the best of Earth's resources.

🏛 **Parliament House**
Maengwyn St. **【** *01654 702827.*
◯ *Easter–Oct: Mon–Sat.* 🚻 ♿
🏛 **Centre for Alternative
Technology** On A487. **【** *01654
702400.* ◯ *daily.* ● *early Jan.* 📷
✓ ♿ 🍴 🚻 **W** *www.cat.org.uk*

Aberystwyth 7

Ceredigion. 🏘 *11,000.* ☲ 🚌 **ℹ**
Terrace Rd (01970 612125).
W *www.ceredigion.gov.uk*

THIS SEASIDE AND UNIVERSITY
town claims to be the
cultural capital of mid-Wales.
By the standards of this rural
area, "Aber" is a big place, its
population increased for
much of the year by students.

To Victorian travellers,
Aberystwyth was the "Biarritz

of Wales". There have been no great changes along the promenade, with its gabled hotels, since the 19th century. **Constitution Hill**, a steep outcrop at the northern end, can be scaled in summer on the electric **Cliff Railway**, built in 1896. At the top, in a *camera obscura*, a lens

Buskers on Aberystwyth's seafront

projects views of the town. The ruined **Aberystwyth Castle** (1277) is located south of the promenade. In the town centre, the **Ceredigion Museum**, set in a former music hall, traces the history of the town.

To the northeast of the town centre, **The National Library of Wales**, next to Aberystwyth University, has a valuable collection of ancient Welsh manuscripts.

SAVIN'S HOTEL

When the Cambrian Railway opened in 1864, businessman Thomas Savin put £80,000 into building a new hotel in Aberystwyth for package tourists. The scheme made him bankrupt, but the seafront building, complete with mock-Gothic tower, was bought by campaigners attempting to establish a Welsh university. The "college by the sea" opened in 1872, and is now the Theological College.

Mosaics on the college tower

ENVIRONS: During the summer the narrow-gauge Vale of Rheidol Railway runs 12 miles (19 km) to **Devil's Bridge**, where a dramatic series of waterfalls plunges through a wooded ravine and a steep trail leads to the valley floor.

🏛 **Ceredigion Museum**
Terrace Rd. 🅒 01970 633088.
⬜ Mon–Sat. ⬤ 25 Dec–2 Jan, Good Fri. 🅱 🅶

Aberaeron ❽

Ceredigion. 👥 1,500.
🚉 Aberystwyth, then bus. 🛈 The Quay (01545 570602).
🆆 www.ceredigion.gov.uk

ABERAERON'S HARBOUR, lined with Georgian houses, became a trading port and shipbuilding centre in the early 19th century. Its orderly streets were laid out in pre-railway days, when the ports along Cardigan Bay enjoyed considerable wealth. The last boat was built here in 1994 and its harbour is now full of holiday sailors. The harbour can be crossed via a wooden footbridge.

On the quayside, the popular Honey Bee Ice Cream Parlour serves world-renowned ice creams to a loyal clientele. There is also a centre of local crafts in the town, Clos Pengarreg.

Rows of brightly painted Georgian houses lining the purpose-built harbour at Aberaeron

St Davids ❾

S⟨T⟩ DAVID, the patron saint of Wales, founded a monastic settlement in this remote corner of southwest Wales in about 550, which became one of the most important Christian shrines. The present cathedral, built in the 12th century, and the Bishop's Palace, added a century later, are set in a grassy hollow below St Davids town, officially Britain's smallest city. The date of St David's death, 1 March, is commemorated throughout Wales.

Icon of Elijah, south transept

St David's Cathedral, the largest in Wales

★ Great Hall
The open arcade and decorated parapet were added by Bishop Gower (1328–47) to unify different sections of the palace.

The Private Chapel
was a late 14th-century addition, built, like the rest of the palace, over a series of vaults.

Entrance

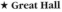

BISHOP'S PALACE
The bishop's residence, built between 1280 and 1350 and now in ruins, had lavish private apartments.

Palace latrines

Typical medieval window

Rose window

The Bishop's Hall,
smaller than the Great Hall, may have been reserved for private use.

GREAT HALL
This reconstruction shows the hall before the lead was stripped from the roof. Bishop Barlow, St David's first Protestant bishop (1536–48), is thought to have been responsible for the lead's removal.

Wooden screen

Vault

STAR SIGHTS
★ Great Hall
★ Nave Ceiling
★ St David's Statue

★ Nave Ceiling
The roof of the nave is lowered and hidden by an early 16th-century oak ceiling. A beautiful 14th-century rood screen divides the nave from the choir.

VISITORS' CHECKLIST

Cathedral Close, St Davids.
📞 01437 720199. ⇄
Haverfordwest then bus.
○ 9am–6pm daily (Sat & Sun: pm). 🚻 📷 🆆 www.
stdavidscathedral.org.uk

Stained Glass Window
In the nave's west end, eight panels, produced in the 1950s, radiate from a central window showing the dove of peace.

CATHEDRAL
St David was one of the founders of the 6th-century monastic movement, so this was an important site of pilgrimage. Three visits here equalled one to Jerusalem.

St Mary's College Chapel

Bishop Vaughan's Chapel has a fine fan-vaulted early Tudor roof.

Entrance

Tower Lantern Ceiling
The medieval roof was decorated with episcopal insignia when restored in the 1870s by Sir George Gilbert Scott.

Sixteenth-Century Choir Stalls
The royal coat of arms on one of the carved choir stalls shows that the sovereign is a member of St David's Chapter. There are some interesting misericords (see p329) in these stalls.

★ St David's Statue
A statue of the saint is placed near the shrine. Thought to symbolize the Holy Spirit, a dove is said to have landed on David's shoulder as he spoke to a gathering of bishops.

Tenby ❿

Pembrokeshire (Dyfed). ⌖ *5,000.*
🚂 🚌 🅿 ℹ *The Croft (01834 842402).* 🅆 *www.tenbywales.co.uk*

Tenby has successfully trodden the fine line between over-commercialization and popularity, refusing to submit its historic character to the garish excesses of some seaside towns. Georgian houses overlook its handsome harbour, which is backed by a well-preserved medieval clifftop town of narrow streets and passages. The old town was defended by a headland fortress, now ruined, flanked by two wide beaches and a ring of 13th-century walls. These survive to their full height in places, along with a fortified gateway, the **Five Arches**.

The three-storeyed **Tudor Merchant's House** is a 15th-century relic of Tenby's highly prosperous seafaring days, with original fireplaces and chimneys. There are regular boat trips from the harbour to **Caldey Island**, 3 miles (5 km) offshore, home of a perfume-making monastic community.

🏛 **Tudor Merchant's House**
(NT) Quay Hill. ☎ *01834 842279.*
◐ *Apr–Sep: Thu–Tue; Oct: Thu, Fri, Sun–Tue (Sun: pm).* ● *Nov–Mar.* 🎟
🎫 *for pre-booked parties.*

A partly medieval restaurant next to the Tudor Merchant's House

Swansea and the Gower Peninsula ⓫

Swansea. ⌖ *230,000.* 🚂 🚌 🅿 ℹ
Plymouth St (01792 468321). 🛒 *Mon–Sat.* 🅆 *www.swansea.gov.uk*

Swansea, Wales's second city, is set along a wide, curving bay. The city centre was rebuilt after heavy bombing in World War II but, despite the modern buildings, a traditional Welsh atmosphere prevails. This is particularly noticeable in the excellent food market, full of Welsh delicacies such as laverbread *(see p36)* and locally caught cockles.

The award-winning **Maritime Quarter** redevelopment has transformed the old docklands, and is worth a visit.

A statue of copper magnate John Henry Vivian (1779–1855) overlooks the marina. The Vivians, a leading Swansea

Swansea's most celebrated son, the poet Dylan Thomas

family, founded the **Glynn Vivian Art Gallery**, which has exquisite Swansea pottery and porcelain. Archaeology and Welsh history feature at the **Swansea Museum**, the oldest museum in Wales.

The life and work of local poet Dylan Thomas (1914–53) is celebrated in the recently opened **Dylan Thomas Centre**. A permanent exhibition, Man and Myth, includes the original drafts of his poems, letters and memorabilia. His statue overlooks the Maritime Quarter. Thomas spent his childhood in the city's suburbs. **Cwmdonkin Park** was the scene of an early poem, *The Hunchback in the Park*, and its water garden has a memorial stone quoting from his *Fern Hill*.

Swansea's austere **Guildhall** (1934) has a surprisingly rich interior. The huge panels, by Sir Frank Brangwyn (1867–1956), on the theme of the British Empire, were originally

Picturesque fishermen's cottages at the Mumbles seaside resort

painted for the House of Lords.

Swansea Bay leads to the **Mumbles**, a popular water-sports centre at the gateway to the 19 mile long (30 km) Gower Peninsula, which in 1956 was the first part of Britain to be declared an Area of Outstanding Natural Beauty. A string of sheltered, south-facing bays leads to Oxwich and Port-Eynon beaches.

Rhossili's enormous beach leads to north Gower and a coastline of low-lying burrows, salt marshlands and cockle beds. The peninsula is littered with ancient sites such as **Parc Le Breose**, a prehistoric burial chamber.

Near Camarthen is the **National Botanic Garden of Wales**, with formal gardens centred on The Great Glasshouse which contains a Mediterranean ecosystem.

🏛 **Glynn Vivian Art Gallery**
Alexandra Rd. ☎ *01792 516900.*
◐ *Tue–Sun & public hols.* ● *23–26 Dec, 1 Jan.* ♿ *limited.* 🏛 🎫 *by arrangement.*

🏛 **Swansea Museum**
Victoria Rd. ☎ *01792 653763.*
◐ *Tue–Sun & public hols.* ● *25, 26 Dec, 1 Jan.* 🏛 ♿ *limited.*

🏛 **Dylan Thomas Centre**
Somerset Pl. ☎ *01792 463980.*
◐ *Tue–Sun, bank hols.* ♿ 🎫 *by arrangement.* 🍴 🛍 🅿
🅆 *www.dylanthomas.com*

🏛 **Guildhall**
St Helen's Rd. ☎ *01792 635489.*
◐ *Mon–Fri.* ● *public hols.* ♿
🌷 **National Botanic Garden of Wales**
Middleton Hall, Llanarthne. ☎ *01558 668768.* ◐ *daily.* 🎟 ♿ 🍴 🛍 🅿
🅆 *www.gardenofwales.org.uk*

Wild Wales Tour ⑫

THIS TOUR WEAVES ACROSS the Cambrian Mountains' windswept moors, green hills and high, deserted plateaux. New roads have been laid to the massive Llyn Brianne Reservoir, north of Llandovery, and the old drover's road across to Tregaron has a tarmac surface. But the area is still essentially a "wild Wales" of hidden hamlets, isolated farmsteads, brooding highlands and traditional, quiet market towns.

Llanidloes ⑥
The town was a centre of religious and social unrest in the 17th and 18th centuries (*see p423*). There is a rare example of a free-standing Tudor market hall. The medieval church was restored in the late 19th century.

Devil's Bridge ④
This is a popular, romantic beauty spot with waterfalls, rocks, wooded glades and an ancient stone bridge – built by the Devil, according to legend.

Strata Florida ③
This famous ruined abbey was an important political, religious and educational centre during the Middle Ages.

Elan Valley ⑤
This is an area of lakes and important wildlife habitats (*see p448*).

TIPS FOR DRIVERS

Length: *87 miles (140 km), including the scenic Claerwen Reservoir detour.*
Stopping-off points: *There are many good tea shops and restaurants in the market towns of Llandovery and Llanidloes. (See also pp636–7.)*

Llandovery ①
At the confluence of two rivers, this pretty town has a ruined castle, a cobbled market square and charming Georgian façades.

Twm Siôn Cati's Cave ②
This illustration shows the retreat of a 16th-century poet, Tom John, a Welsh outlaw who subsequently achieved respectability by marrying an heiress

KEY

▬▬ Tour route
══ Other roads
🔆 Viewpoint

0 kilometres   5

0 miles   5

Brecon Beacons ⑬

Trekking in the Beacons

THE BRECON BEACONS National Park covers 520 sq miles (1,345 sq km) from the Wales–England border almost all the way to Swansea. There are four mountain ranges within the park: the Black Mountain (to the west), Fforest Fawr, the Brecon Beacons and the Black Mountains (to the east). Much of the area consists of high, open country with smooth, grassy slopes on a bedrock of red sandstone. The park's southern rim has limestone crags, wooded gorges, waterfalls and caves. Visitors can enjoy many outdoor pursuits, from fishing in the numerous reservoirs to pony trekking, caving and walking.

Llyn y Fan Fach
This remote, myth-laden glacial lake is a 4 mile (6.5 km) walk from Llanddeusant.

The Black Mountain, a largely unexplored wilderness of knife-edged ridges and high, empty moorland, fills the western corner of the National Park.

0 kilometres 10

0 miles 5

Fforest Fawr ("Great Forest") is named after an area that was a medieval royal hunting ground.

Dan-yr-Ogof Caves
A labyrinth of caves runs through the Brecon Beacons. Guided tours of two large caves are offered here.

Carreg Cennen Castle
Spectacularly sited, the ruined medieval fortress of Carreg Cennen (see p424) stands on a sheer limestone cliff near the village of Trapp.

KEY

▬▬	A road
═══	B road
━━	Minor road
– –	Footpath
☼	Viewpoint

Hay Bluff
At 677 m (2,221 ft), Hay Bluff looks out across border country. A narrow mountain road climbs from Hay-on-Wye to the Gospel Pass before dropping to Llanthony.

Brecon is an old market town with handsome Georgian buildings.

The Black Mountains form part of the border with England.

Llanthony Priory
This 12th-century ruin has simply carved but elegant stonework. In the 19th century a small hotel (still open) was built in part of the priory.

Tretower Castle and Court comprise a ruined Norman keep and a late-medieval manor house.

Pen y Fan
At 886 m (2,907 ft), Pen y Fan is the highest point in South Wales. Its distinctive, flat-topped summit, once a Bronze Age burial ground (see pp42–3), can be reached by footpaths from Storey Arms on the A470.

Monmouthshire and Brecon Canal
This peaceful waterway, completed in 1812, was once used to transport raw materials between Brecon and Newport. It is now popular with leisure boats.

Cardiff ⑭

CARDIFF WAS FIRST OCCUPIED by the Romans, who built a fort here in AD 75 *(see pp44–5)*. Little is known of its subsequent history until Robert FitzHamon *(see p458)*, a knight in the service of William the Conqueror, was given land here in 1093. By the 13th century, the settlement was substantial enough to be granted a royal charter, but it remained a quiet country town until the 1830s when the Bute family, who inherited land in the area, began to develop it as a port. By 1913 this was the world's busiest coal-exporting port, profiting from rail links with the South Wales mines. Its wealth paid for grandiose architecture, while the docklands became a raucous boom-town. Cardiff was confirmed as the first Welsh capital in 1955, by which time demand for coal was falling and the docks were in decline. The city is now dedicated to commerce and administration, and is being transformed by urban renewal programmes.

Fireplace detail in the Banqueting Hall, Cardiff Castle *(see pp458–9)*

City Hall's dome, adorned with a dragon, the emblem of Wales

Exploring Cardiff

Cardiff is a city with two focal points. The centre, laid out with Victorian and Edwardian streets and gardens, is the first of these. There is a Neo-Gothic castle and Neo-Classical civic buildings, as well as indoor shopping malls and a 19th-century **covered market**. Canopied arcades, lined with shops, lead off the main streets, the oldest being the **Royal Arcade** of 1856. The **Millennium Stadium** (on the site of Cardiff Arms Park, the first home of Welsh rugby) opened in 1999 with the Rugby World Cup, and is open for tours every day.

To the south of the centre, the docklands are now being transformed into the second focal point by the creation of a marina and waterfront. A new Cardiff is taking shape, especially around the Inner Harbour area. The **Pier Head Building**, constructed on

Cardiff Bay in 1896 for the Cardiff Railway Company, is a reminder of the city's heyday. Its intricate decoration and terracotta detail was partly influenced by the red Mogul buildings of India. Another attraction in the area is **Techniquest**, a hands-on science museum.

The wooden **Norwegian Church** on Waterfront Park was first erected in 1868 for Norwegian sailors bringing wooden props for use in the coal pits of the South Wales valleys. Once surrounded by warehouses, it was taken apart and rebuilt during the dockland development. The **Cardiff Bay Visitor Centre**, near the Pier Head Building, has displays on the various building projects that are uniting the civic centre with the maritime district.

♜ Cardiff Castle
See pp458–9.

🏛 City Hall and Civic Centre
Cathays Park. ☎ 029-2087 1727.
🕐 Mon–Fri. 🔴 public hols. 🔓 ✔

Cardiff's civic centre of Neo-Classical buildings in white Portland stone is set among parks and avenues around Alexandra Gardens. The City Hall (1905), one of its first buildings, is dominated by its 60 m (200 ft) dome and clock tower. Members of the public can visit the first-floor Marble Hall, which is furnished with Siena marble columns and statues of Welsh heroes, among them St David, Wales's patron saint *(see pp450–51)*. The Crown Building, at the northern end of the complex,

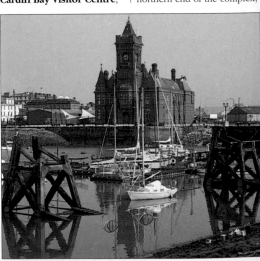

The Pier Head Building overlooking the redeveloped area of Cardiff Bay

now houses the Welsh Office, which is responsible for all Welsh government affairs.

🏛 National Museum and Gallery of Wales

Cathays Park. **☎** 029-2039 7951. ◯ Tue–Sun, public hols. ⬤ 24, 25 Dec. ♿ ✉ by arrangement. 🖼 📷 ☖ www.nmgw.ac.uk

Opened in 1927, the museum occupies an impressive civic building with a colonnaded portico, guarded by a statue of David Lloyd George *(see p423)*. Displays include a fine collection of Impressionist art by Renoir, Monet and Van Gogh, donated by two local sisters Gwendoline and Margaret Davies.

🏛 Crafts in the Bay

The Flourish, Lloyd George Ave., Cardiff Bay. **☎** 029-2048 4611. ◯ daily. ♿ 📧

An extensive new crafts gallery, organized by the Makers' Guild in Wales, opened here in March 1996.

Statue of Welsh politician David Lloyd George

The building now houses a wide variety of craft displays and demonstrations, including textile weaving and ceramic making.

As well as the permanent displays, there are frequently changing exhibitions on crafts-related themes. Visitors are free to browse around the centre or to book up for one of the workshops (www.makersguildinwales.org.uk).

ENVIRONS: Established during the 1940s at St Fagans, on the western edge of the city, the open-air **Museum of Welsh Life** was one of the first of its kind. Buildings from all over Wales, including workers' terraced cottages, farmhouses, a tollhouse, a row of shops, a chapel and an old schoolhouse have been carefully reconstructed within the 40 ha (100 acre) parklands, along with a recreated Celtic village. There is also a Tudor mansion

which can be visited, boasting its own beautiful gardens in the grounds.

Llandaff Cathedral lies in a deep, grassy hollow beside the River Taf at Llandaff – a pretty "village suburb" which is 2 miles (3 km) northwest of the city centre. The cathedral was first a medieval building, occupying the site of a 6th-century monastic community.

Restored after suffering severe bomb damage during World War II, it was eventually reopened in 1957 with the addition of Sir Jacob Epstein's huge, stark statue, *Christus*, which is mounted on a concrete arch.

🏛 Museum of Welsh Life

St Fagans. **☎** 029-2057 3500. ◯ daily. ♿ 🍴 ☖ www.nmgw.ac.uk

CARDIFF TOWN CENTRE

0 metres   500
0 yards   500

KEY

🚌 Coach station
🚉 Railway station
🅿 Parking
🛈 Tourist information
✝ Church

Cardiff Castle

Cardiff castle began life as a Roman fort, whose remains are separated from later work by a band of red stone. A keep was built within the Roman ruins in the 12th century. Over the following 700 years, the castle passed to several powerful families and eventually to John Stuart, son of the Earl of Bute, in 1776. His great-grandson, the 3rd Marquess of Bute, employed the "eccentric genius", architect William Burges, who created an ornate mansion between 1869 and 1881, rich in medieval images and romantic detail.

Arab Room
The gilded ceiling, with Islamic marble and lapis lazuli decorations, was built in 1881.

Animal Wall
A lion and other creatures guard the wall to the west of the castle. They were added between 1885 and 1930.

Herbert Tower

★ **Summer Smoking Room**
This was part of a complete bachelor suite in the Clock Tower, that also included a Winter Smoking Room.

Clock Tower

Main entrance to apartments

TIMELINE

AD 75 Roman fort constructed	**1107** Castle inherited by Mabel FitzHamon, whose husband is made Lord of Glamorgan	**1423–49** Beauchamp family adds the Octagon Tower and Great Hall ceiling	**1869** 3rd Marquess of Bute begins reconstruction
	1183 Castle damaged during Welsh uprising	**1445–1776** Castle passes in turn to Nevilles, Tudors and Herberts	

1000	1200	1400	1600	1800

1093 First Norman fort built by Robert FitzHamon of Gloucester	**1308–1414** Despenser family holds castle		**1776** Bute family acquires the castle
		Chaucer Room wall detail	**1947** The castle is given in trust to the city of Cardiff

VISITORS' CHECKLIST

Castle St, Cardiff. 📞 029-2087
8100. ⬜ Mar–Oct: 9:30am–
6pm daily; Nov–Feb: 9:30am–
4:30pm daily. 🚻 ♿ 🚹 🏪
Ⓦ www.cardiffcastle.com

★ Banqueting Hall
*The design and decoration of
this room depicts the castle's
history, making impressively
ingenious use of the murals
and castellated fireplace.*

The Octagon Tower, also
called the Beauchamp
Tower, is the setting for
Burges's Chaucer Room,
decorated with themes
from the *Canterbury
Tales* (see p174).

★ Roof Garden
*Using tiles, shrubs and
a central fountain,
Burges aimed to create
a Mediterranean feel
in this indoor garden,
turning it into the
crowning glory of the
castle's apartments.*

**The Bute
Tower** had
a suite of
private rooms
added in 1873,
including a
dining room,
bedroom and
sitting room.

★ Library
*Carved figures representing ancient characters
of Greek, Assyrian, Hebrew and Egyptian
alphabets decorate the library's chimneypiece.*

STAR SIGHTS

★ Banqueting Hall

★ Library

★ Summer Smoking
Room

★ Roof Garden

Remains of Caerleon's amphitheatre, built in the 2nd century

Caerleon ⑮

Newport (Gwent). ⚒ *11,000.*
ℹ *5 High St (01633 422656).*
ⓦ *www.caerleon.net*

TOGETHER WITH YORK *(see pp390–91)* and Chester *(see pp298–9)*, Caerleon was one of only three fortress settlements in Britain built for the Romans' elite legionary troops. From AD 74 Caerleon *(Isca* to the Romans, after the River Usk, which flows beside the town) was home to the 2nd Augustan Legion, which had been sent to Wales to crush the native Silures tribe. The remains of their base now lie between the modern town and the river.

The excavations at Caerleon are of great social and military significance. The Romans built not just a fortress for their crack 5,500-strong infantry division but a complete town to service their needs, including a stone amphitheatre. Judging by the results of the excavation work carried out since the archaeologist Sir Mortimer Wheeler unearthed the amphitheatre in 1926, Caerleon is one of the largest and most important Roman military sites in Europe. The defences enclosed an area of 20 ha (50 acres), with 64 rows of barracks, arranged in pairs, a hospital, and a bath-house complex.

Outside the settlement, the amphitheatre's large stone foundations have survived in an excellent state of preserva-

An altar at Caerleon's Legionary Museum

tion. Six thousand spectators could enjoy the blood sports and gladiators' combat.

More impressive still is the fortress baths complex, which opened to the public in the mid-1980s. The baths were designed to bring all the home comforts to an army posted to barbaric Britain. The Roman troops could take a dip in the open-air swimming pool, play sports in the exercise yard or covered hall, or enjoy a series of hot and cold baths.

Nearby are the foundations of the only Roman legionary barracks on view in Europe. The many excavated artifacts, including a collection of engraved gemstones, are displayed at the **Roman Legionary Museum**.

🏛 Roman Legionary Museum
High St. 【 *01633 423134.* ◯
Mon–Sat, Sun (pm). ◯ *24–26 Dec,
1 Jan.* ♿ 🛈 ⓦ *www.nmgw.ac.uk*

**Big Pit Mining Museum, reminder
of a vanished industrial society**

Blaenafon ⑯

Torfaen. ⚒ *6,000.* ℹ *Blaenafon
Ironworks, North St.* 【 *01495
792615.* ⓦ *www.blaenafontic.com*

COMMERCIAL COAL-MINING has now all but ceased in the South Wales valleys – an area which only 100 years ago was gripped by the search for its "black gold". Though coal is no longer produced at **Big Pit** in Blaenafon, the **Mining Museum** provides a vivid reminder of this tough industry. The Big Pit closed as a working mine in 1980, and opened three years later as a museum. Visitors follow a marked-out route around the mine's surface workings to the miners' baths, the blacksmith's forge, the workshops and the engine house. There is also a replica of an underground gallery, where mining methods are explained. But the climax of any visit to Big Pit is beneath the ground. Kitted out with helmets, lamps and safety batteries, visitors descend by cage 90 m (300 ft) down the mineshaft and then are guided by ex-miners on a tour of the underground workings and pit ponies' stables.

Blaenafon also has remains of the iron-smelting industry. Across the valley from Big Pit stand the 18th-century smelting furnaces and workers' cottages that were once part of the **Blaenafon Ironworks**, and which are now a museum.

🏛 Big Pit Mining Museum
Blaenafon. 【 *01495 790311.* ◯
mid-Feb–Nov: daily. ♿ *phone first.*
🅿 🛈 🛈 ⓦ *www.nmgw.ac.uk*
🏛 Blaenafon Ironworks
North St. 【 *01495 792615.*
◯ *Apr–Oct: daily.* 🅿 🛈

Monmouth ⑰

Monmouthshire (Gwent). ⚒ *12,000.*
🚌 ℹ *Shire Hall (01600 713899).*
🅰 *Fri, Sat.* ⓦ *www.visitwyevalley.com*

THIS MARKET TOWN, which sits at the confluence of the Wye and Monnow rivers, has many historical associations. The 11th-century castle, behind Agincourt Square, is in ruins but the **Regimental Museum**,

Monnow Bridge in Monmouth, once a watchtower and jail

beside it, remains open to the public. The castle was the birthplace of Henry V *(see p49)* in 1387. Statues of Henry V (on the façade of Shire Hall) and Charles Stewart Rolls stand in the Square. Rolls, born at nearby Hendre, co-founded Rolls-Royce cars, and died in a flying accident in 1910.

Lord Horatio Nelson *(see p54)*, the famous admiral, visited Monmouth in 1802. An excellent collection of Nelson memorabilia, gathered by Lady Llangattock, mother of Charles Rolls, is displayed at the **Nelson Museum**.

Monmouth was the county town of the old Monmouthshire. The wealth of elegant Georgian buildings, including the elaborate **Shire Hall**,

which dominates Agincourt Square, reflect its former status. The most famous architectural feature in Monmouth is **Monnow Bridge**, a narrow 13th-century gateway on its western approach, thought to be the only surviving fortified bridge gate in Britain.

For a lovely view over the town, climb the Kymin, a 256 m (840 ft) hill crowned by a **Naval Temple** built in 1801.

⋔ Monmouth Castle and Regimental Museum
The Castle. 📞 01600 772175. ◯ Apr–Oct: daily (pm); Nov–Mar: Sat & Sun (pm). ⬤ 25 Dec. ⓚ ⓦ www. monmouthcastlemuseum.org.uk

🏛 Nelson Museum
Priory St. 📞 01600 710630. ◯ daily (Sun: pm). 🗺 ⓚ 🚻

Tintern Abbey ⑱

Monmouthshire (Gwent). 📞 01291 689251. 🚌 Chepstow then bus. ◯ daily. ⬤ 24–26 Dec, 1 Jan. 🚻 🗺 ⓚ
ⓦ www.cadw.wales.gov.uk

EVER SINCE THE 18th century, travellers have been enchanted by Tintern's setting in the steep and wooded Wye Valley and by the majestic ruins of its abbey. Poets were often inspired by the scene. Wordsworth's sonnet, *Lines composed a few miles above Tintern Abbey*, embodied his romantic view of landscape:

> *once again*
> *Do I behold these steep and*
> *   lofty cliffs,*
> *That on a wild, secluded*
> *   scene impress*
> *Thoughts of more deep*
> *   seclusion*

The abbey was founded in 1131 by Cistercian monks, who cultivated the surrounding lands (now forest), and developed it as an influential religious centre. By the 14th century this was the richest abbey in Wales, but along with other monasteries it was dissolved in 1536. Its skeletal ruins are now roofless and exposed, the soaring arches and windows giving them a poignant grace and beauty.

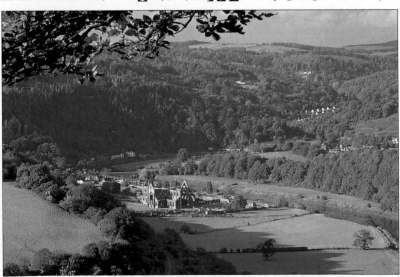

Tintern Abbey in the Wye Valley, in the past a thriving centre of religion and learning, now a romantic ruin

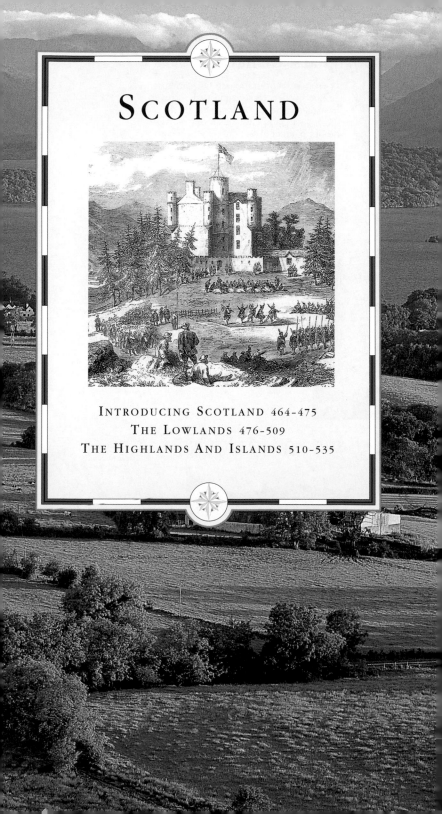

SCOTLAND

Scotland at a Glance

Sᴛʀᴇᴛᴄʜɪɴɢ from the rich farmlands of the Borders to a chain of isles only a few degrees south of the Arctic Circle, the Scottish landscape has a diversity without parallel in Britain. As you travel northwest from Edinburgh, the land becomes more mountainous and its archaeological treasures more numerous. In the far northwest, Scotland's earliest relics stand upon the oldest rock on Earth.

Western Isles

Skye (see pp520–21), *renowned for its dramatic scenery, has one of Scotland's most striking coast-lines. On the east coast, a stream plunges over Kilt Rock, a cliff of hexagonal basalt columns named after its likeness to an item of Scottish national dress.*

THE HIGHLANDS
AND ISLANDS
(see pp510–35)

Argyll and Bute

Clyde Valley

Ayrshire

The Trossachs (see pp480–81) *are a beautiful range of hills straddling the border between the Highlands and the Lowlands. At their heart, the forested slopes of Ben Venue rise above the still waters of Loch Achray.*

Culzean Castle (see pp508–9) *stands on a cliff's edge on the Firth of Clyde, amid an extensive country park. One of the jewels of the Lowlands, Culzean is a magnificent showcase of work by the Scottish-born architect, Robert Adam (see p24).*

◁ **Loch Lomond, the Lowlands**

Shetland

Orkney

Highland

The Cairngorms (see pp530–31) *cover an area prized for its beauty and diversity of wildlife, though there are also many historical relics to be found, such as this early 18th-century arch at Carrbridge.*

Moray

Aberdeenshire

Royal Deeside (see pp526–7) *in the Grampians has been associated with British royalty since Queen Victoria bought Balmoral Castle in 1852.*

Perthshire & Tayside

tral

Fife

The Lothians

THE LOWLANDS
(see pp476–509)

The Borders

Edinburgh (see pp490–97) *is the capital of Scotland. Between its medieval castle and the Palace of Holyroodhouse stretches the Royal Mile – a concentration of historic sights, ranging from the old Scottish Parliament buildings to the house of John Knox. Georgian terraces predominate in the New Town.*

umfries
&
alloway

The Burrell Collection (see pp506–7), *on the southern outskirts of Glasgow, is a museum of some of the city's greatest art treasures. It is housed in a spacious, glass building opened in 1983.*

0 kilometres	50
0 miles	50

A PORTRAIT OF SCOTLAND

F ROM THE GRASSY HILLS *of the Borders to the desolate Cuillin Ridge of Skye, the landscape of Scotland is breathtaking in its variety. Lonely glens, sparkling lochs and ever-changing skies give the land a challenging character, which is reflected in the qualities of the Scottish people. Tough and self-reliant, they have made some of Britain's finest soldiers, its boldest explorers and most astute industrialists.*

The Scots are proud of their separate identity and their own systems of law and education and, in 1998, voted overwhelmingly for their own parliament. Many Scots welcomed this as a long-awaited reversal of the Act of Union that united the English and Scottish parliaments in 1707. But despite their national pride, they are not a homogeneous people, the main division is between traditionally Gaelic-speaking Highlanders, and the Lowlanders who spoke Scots, a form of Middle English which is now extinct. Today, though Gaelic survives (chiefly in the Western Isles), most people speak regional dialects or richly accented English. Many Scottish surnames derive from Gaelic: the prefix "mac" means "son of". A Norse heritage can be found in the far north, where Shetlanders welcome the annual return of the sun during the Viking fire festival, Up Helly Aa.

A hammer-thrower at the Braemar Games

In the 16th century, a suspicion of authority and dislike of excessive flamboyance attracted many Scots to the Presbyterian church with its absence of bishops and its stress on simple worship. The Presbyterian Church of Scotland was established in 1689, though a substantial Catholic minority remained which today predominates in the crofting (small-scale farming) communities of the Western Isles. Now sparsely populated, the Isles preserve a rural culture that once dominated the Highlands, a region that is the source of much that is distinctively Scottish. The clan system originated there, along with the tartans, the bagpipes and such unique sports as tossing the caber – a large tree trunk. Highland sports, along with traditional dances, are still performed at annual games *(see p64)*.

Edinburgh bagpiper

Resourcefulness has always been a prominent Scottish virtue, and Scotland has produced a disproportionately high number of Britain's geniuses. James Watt designed the first effective steam engine to power the Industrial Revolution, while Adam Smith became the 18th century's most influential economist. In the 19th century, James Simpson discovered the anaesthetic qualities of

The Viking festival, Up Helly Aa, in Lerwick, Shetland

With some of the harshest weather conditions in Europe it is perhaps less surprising that Scotland has bred numerous great explorers, the most famous being Robert Scott (of the Antarctic) and African missionary David Livingstone. There is also a strong intellectual and literary tradition, from the 18th-century philosopher David Hume, through novelists Sir Walter Scott and Robert Louis Stevenson, to the poetry of Robert Burns. Today Scotland hosts a variety of arts festivals, such as Edinburgh's.

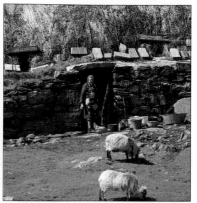

A traditional stone croft on the Isle of Lewis

chloroform, James Young developed the world's first oil refinery and Alexander Bell revolutionized communications by inventing the telephone. The 20th century saw one of the greatest advances in medicine with the discovery of penicillin by Alexander Fleming.

The Scots are also known for being shrewd businessmen, and have always been prominent in finance: both the Bank of England and the Royal Bank of France were founded by Scots, while Andrew Carnegie created one of 19th century-America's biggest business empires.

Detail of Edinburgh's Festival Fringe office

With a population density only one-fifth of England and Wales, Scotland has vast tracts of untenanted land which offer numerous outdoor pleasures. It is richly stocked with game, and the opening of the grouse season on 12 August is a highlight on the social calendar. Fishing and hill-walking are popular and in winter thousands flock to the Cairngorms and Glencoe for skiing. Though the weather may be harsher than elsewhere, the Scots will claim that the air is purer – and that enjoying rugged conditions is what distinguishes them from their soft southern neighbours.

The blue waters of Loch Achray in the heart of the Trossachs, north of Glasgow

The History of Scotland

Bonnie Prince Charlie, by G Dupré

SINCE THE ROMAN INVASION of Britain, Scotland's history has been characterized by its resistance to foreign domination. The Romans never conquered the area, and when the Scots extended their kingdom to its present boundary in 1018, a long era of conflict began with England. After many wars, the Scots finally accepted union with the "auld enemy": first with the union of crowns, and then with the Union of Parliament in 1707. In 1999 the inauguration of the Scottish Parliament was a dramatic change.

An elaborately carved Pictish stone at Aberlemno, Angus

EARLY HISTORY

THERE IS MUCH EVIDENCE in Scotland of important prehistoric population centres, particularly in the Western Isles, which were peopled mostly by Picts who originally came from the Continent. By the time Roman Governor Julius Agricola invaded in AD 81, there were at least 17 independent tribes, including the Britons in the southwest, for him to contend with.

The Romans reached north to the Forth and Clyde valleys, but the Highlands deterred them from going further. By 120, they had retreated to the line where the Emperor Hadrian had built his wall to keep the Picts at bay (not far from today's border). By 163 the Romans had retreated south for the last time. The Celtic influence began when

"Scots" arrived from Ireland in the 6th century, bringing the Gaelic language with them.

The Picts and Scots united under Kenneth McAlpin in 843, but the Britons remained separate until 1018, when they became part of the Scottish kingdom.

THE ENGLISH CLAIM

THE NORMAN KINGS regarded Scotland as part of their territory but seldom pursued the claim. William the Lion of Scotland recognized English sovereignty by the Treaty of Falaise (1174), though English control never spread to the northwest. In 1296 William Wallace, supported by the French (the start of the Auld Alliance, which lasted two centuries), began the long war of independence. During this bitter conflict, Edward I seized the sacred Stone of Destiny from Scone (see p484), and took it to Westminster Abbey. The war lasted for more than 100 years. Its great hero was Robert the Bruce, who defeated the English in 1314 at Bannockburn. The English held the upper hand after that, even though the Scots would not accept their rule.

John Knox statue, Edinburgh

THE ROAD TO UNION

THE SEEDS OF UNION between the crowns were sown in 1503 when James IV of Scotland married Margaret Tudor, daughter of Henry VII. When her brother, Henry VIII, came to the throne, James sought to assert independence but was defeated and killed at Flodden Field in 1513. His granddaughter, Mary, Queen of Scots (see p497), married the French Dauphin in order to cement the Auld Alliance and gain assistance in her claim to

Bruce in Single Combat at Bannockburn (1906) by John Hassall

the throne of her English cousin, Elizabeth I. She had support from the Catholics wanting to see an end to Protestantism in England and Scotland. However, fiery preacher John Knox won support for the Protestants and established the Presbyterian Church in 1560. Mary's Catholicism led to the loss of her Scottish throne in 1568, and her subsequent flight to England, following defeat at Langside. Finally, after nearly 20 years of imprisonment she was executed for treason by Elizabeth in 1587.

The factories on Clydeside, once creators of the world's greatest ships

UNION AND REBELLION

ON ELIZABETH I's death in 1603, Mary's son, James VI of Scotland, succeeded to the English throne and became James I, king of both countries. Thus the crowns were united, though it was 100 years before the formal Union of Parliaments in 1707. During that time, religious differences within the country

Articles of Union between England and Scotland, 1707

reached boiling point. There were riots when the Catholic-influenced Charles I restored bishops to the Church of Scotland and authorized the printing of a new prayer book. This culminated in the signing, in Edinburgh in 1638, of the National Covenant, a document that condemned all Catholic doctrines. Though the Covenanters were suppressed, the Protestant William of Orange took over the English throne in 1688 and the crown passed out of Scottish hands.

In 1745, Bonnie Prince Charlie *(see p521)*, descended from the Stuart kings, tried to seize the throne from the Hanoverian George II. He marched far into England, but was driven back and defeated at Culloden field *(see p523)* in 1746.

INDUSTRIALIZATION AND SOCIAL CHANGE

IN THE LATE 18TH AND 19th centuries, technological progress transformed Scotland from a nation of crofters to an industrial powerhouse. In the notorious Highland Clearances *(see p517)*, from the 1780s on, landowners ejected tenants from their smallholdings and gave the land over to sheep and other livestock. The first ironworks was established in 1760 and was soon followed by coal mining, steel production and shipbuilding on the Clyde. Canals were cut, railways and bridges built.

A strong socialist movement developed as workers sought to improve their conditions. Keir Hardie, an Ayrshire coal miner, in 1892 became the first socialist elected to parliament, and in 1893 founded the Independent Labour Party. The most enduring symbol of this time is the spectacular Forth rail bridge *(see p488)*.

SCOTLAND TODAY

ALTHOUGH THE STATUS of the country appeared to have been settled in 1707, a strong nationalist sentiment remained and was heightened by the Depression of the 1920s and '30s which had severe effects on the heavily industrialized Clydeside. This was when the Scottish National Party formed, advocating self-rule. The Nationalists asserted themselves in 1950 by stealing the Stone of Scone from Westminister Abbey.

The discovery of North Sea oil in 1970 encouraged a nationalist revival and, in 1979, the Government promised to establish a separate assembly if 40 per cent of the Scottish electorate endorsed the plan in a referendum. This figure was finally surpassed in 1998, and the Scottish Parliament was duly inaugurated in 1999.

A North Sea oil rig, helping to provide prosperity in the 1970s

Clans and Tartans

THE CLAN SYSTEM, by which Highland society was divided into tribal groups led by autocratic chiefs, can be traced to the 12th century, when clans were already known to wear the chequered wool cloth later called tartan. All members of the clan bore the name of their chief, but not all were related by blood. Though they had noble codes of hospitality, the clansmen had to be warriors to protect their herds, as can be seen from their mottoes. After the Battle of Culloden *(see p523)*, all the clan lands were forfeited to the Crown, and the wearing of tartan was banned for nearly 100 years.

***The Mackays**, also known as the Clan Morgan, won lasting renown during the Thirty Years War.*

***The MacLeods** are of Norse heritage. The clan chief still lives in Dunvegan Castle, Skye (see p520).*

***The MacDonalds** were the most powerful of all the clans, holding the title of Lords of the Isles.*

***The Mackenzies** received much of the lands of Kintail (see p516) from David II in 1362.*

CLAN CHIEF

The chief was the clan's patriarch, judge and leader in war, commanding absolute loyalty from his clansmen who gave military service in return for his protection. The chief summoned his clan to do battle by sending a runner across his land bearing a burning cross.

Bonnet with eagle feathers, clan crest and plant badge.

Dirk

Sporran, or pouch, made of badger's skin.

Feileadh-mor, or "great plaid" (the early kilt), wrapped around waist and shoulder.

Basket-hilted sword

***The Campbells** were a widely feared clan who fought the Jacobites in 1746 (see p523).*

***The Black Watch**, raised in 1729 to keep peace in the Highlands, was one of the Highland regiments in which the wearing of tartan survived. After 1746, civilians were punished by exile for up to seven years for wearing tartan.*

The Sinclairs came from France in the 11th century and became Earls of Caithness in 1455.

The Frasers came to Britain from France with William the Conqueror (see p47) in 1066.

George IV, dressed as a Highlander, visited Edinburgh in 1822, the year of the tartan revival. Many tartan "sets" (patterns) date from this time, as the original ones were lost.

The Gordons were famously good soldiers; the clan motto is "by courage, not by craft".

The Stuarts were Scotland's royal dynasty. Their motto was "no one harms me with impunity".

CLAN TERRITORIES

The territories of 10 prominent clans are marked here with their clan crests. Dress tartans tend to be colourful, while hunting tartans are darker.

The Douglas clan were prominent in Scottish history, though their origin is unknown.

PLANT BADGES

Each clan had a plant associated with its territory. It was worn on the bonnet, especially on the day of battle.

Scots pine was worn by the MacGregors of Argyll.

Rowan berries were worn by the Clan Malcolm.

Ivy was worn by the Clan Gordon of Aberdeenshire.

Spear thistle, now a national symbol, was a Stuart badge.

Cotton grass was worn by the Clan Henderson.

HIGHLAND CLANS TODAY

Once the daily dress of the clansmen, the kilt is now largely reserved for formal occasions. The one-piece *feileadh-mor* has been replaced by the *feileadh-beag*, or "small plaid", made from approximately 7 m (23 ft) of material with a double apron fastened at the front with a silver pin. Though they exist now only in name, the clans are still a strong source of pride for Scots, and many still live in areas traditionally belonging to their clans. Many visitors to Britain can trace their Scots ancestry *(see p27)* to the Highlands.

Modern Highland formal dress

Evolution of the Scottish Castle

T HERE ARE FEW more romantic sights in the British Isles than a Scottish castle on an island or at a lochside. These formidable retreats, often in remote settings, were essential all over the Highlands, where incursions and strife between the clans were common. From the earliest Pictish *brochs (see p43)* and Norman-influenced motte and bailey castles, the distinctively Scottish tower-house evolved, first appearing in the 14th century. By the mid-17th century fashion had become more important than defence, and there followed a period in which numerous huge Scottish palaces were built.

Detail of the Baroque façade, Drumlanrig

MOTTE AND BAILEY

These castles first appeared in the 12th century. They stood atop two adjacent mounds enclosed by a wall, or palisade, and defensive ditches. The higher mound, or motte, was the most strongly defended as it held the keep and chief's house. The lower bailey was where the people lived. Of these castles little more than earthworks remain today.

Keep, with chief's house, lookout and main defence

All that remains today of Duffus Castle, Morayshire

Duffus Castle, (c.1150), was atypically made of stone rather than wood. Its fine defensive position dominates the surrounding flatlands north of Elgin.

Bailey enclosing dwellings and storehouses

Motte of earth or rock, sometimes partially man-made

EARLY TOWER-HOUSE

Designed to deter local attacks rather than a major assault, the first tower-houses appeared in the 13th century, though their design lived on for 400 years. They were built initially on a rectangular plan, with a single tower divided into three or four floors. The walls were unadorned, with few windows. Defensive structures were on top, and extra space was made by building adjoining towers. Extensions were made as vertically as possible, to minimize the area open to attack.

Crenellated parapet for sentries

Featureless, straight walls with arrow slits for windows

Claypotts Castle (c.1570) with uniquely projecting garrets above its towers

Braemar Castle (c.1630), a conglomeration of extended towers

Neidpath Castle, standing upon a steep rocky crag above the River Tweed, is an L-shaped tower-house dating from the late 14th century. Once a stronghold for Charles II, its walls still bear damage from a siege conducted by Oliver Cromwell (see p52).

Small, inconspicuous doorway

LATER TOWER-HOUSE

Though the requirements of defence were being replaced
by those of comfort, the style of the early tower-house
remained popular. By the 17th century, wings for accommodation were being added around the original tower
(often creating a courtyard). The battlements and turrets
were kept more for decorative than defensive reasons.

Drum Castle *(see p527)*, a 13th-
century keep with a mansion
house extension from 1619

Priest's room with
secret access

The original 15th-
century tower-house

Round angle tower,
containing stairway

A 16th-century horizon-
tal extension

Traquair House (see p499), *by the Tweed,
is reputedly the oldest continuously inhabited
house in Scotland. The largely unadorned,
roughcast exterior dates to the 16th century,
when a series of extensions were built around
the original 15th-century tower-house.*

Decorative,
corbelled turret

Blair Castle *(see p529)*, incorporating a medieval tower

CLASSICAL PALACE

By the 18th century, the defensive imperative had
passed and castles were built in the manner of country
houses, rejecting the vertical tower-house in favour
of a horizontal plan (though the building of imitation
fortified buildings continued into the 19th century with
the mock-Baronial trend). Outside influences came
from all over Europe, including Renaissance and
Gothic revivals, and echoes of French châteaux.

Dunrobin Castle (c.1840), Sutherland

Larger windows due to a
lesser need for defence

Balustrades instead of
battlements

Decorative cupola

Drumlanrig Castle (see p500) *was built in
the 17th century. There are many traditional
Scots aspects as well as such Renaissance
features as the decorated stairway and façade.*

Renaissance-style colonnade

Baroque horseshoe stairway

Scottish Food and Drink

The SCOTTISH LARDER is generous in meat and fish, which are usually served simply, without heavy sauces. Grouse and deer range the hills, Aberdeen Angus beef is world famous, and the rivers are renowned for their salmon and trout. With Scotland's cold, wet climate and shallow soil, wheat was grown less than oats, which are still present in traditional Scottish foods, such as porridge and oatcakes (rather than bread) and, of course, haggis.

Porridge *is a breakfast of oats, boiled in water and milk, with salt or sugar.*

Kippers*, eaten at breakfast, are fresh herring split down the back, salted and cured by smoking over a fire.*

Poached salmon *tastes best when cooked whole in a bouillon of water, wine and vegetables, during which its deep red flesh turns a delicate pink. Salmon are caught in all Scotland's rivers.*

Scotch broth *is a light, thin soup based on neck of mutton, to which pearl barley and vegetables are added.*

Venison *is allowed to hang for ten days before being seasoned with mixed spices, wine and vinegar, and then roasted.*

Haggis*, served boiled with swedes, or "neeps", and potatoes, is spiced sheep's innards, here mixed with oatmeal.*

MARMALADE

Marmalade was created in Dundee *(see p485)* in the 1700s after a rash purchase left grocer James Keiller with a large cargo of bitter Seville oranges. He was unable to re-sell them, so his wife Janet added them to a preserve. Word soon spread about her delicious creation which now appears on breakfast tables throughout the world.

Dundee cake *is a rich, sweet cake made of dried fruits and spices topped with almonds.*

Shortbread   Bonchester

Bonnet

Traditional orange

Grapefruit and ginger

Scottish oatcakes *are flat biscuits of fine oatmeal which accompany sweets or savouries. Hard Bonnet and soft Bonchester are popular among the Scottish cheeses.*

HOW WHISKY IS MADE

Traditionally made from just barley, yeast and stream water, Scottish whisky (from the Gaelic *usquebaugh*, or the "water of life") takes a little over three weeks to produce, though it must be given at least three years to mature. Maturation usually takes place in oak casks, often in barrels previously used for sherry. The art of blending was pioneered in Edinburgh in the 1860s.

Barley grass

1 Malting is the first stage. Barley grain is soaked in water and spread on the malting floor. With regular turning the grain germinates, producing a "green malt". Germination stimulates the production of enzymes which turn the starches into fermentable sugars.

2 Drying of the barley halts germination after 12 days of malting. This is done over a peat fire in a pagoda-shaped malt-kiln. The peat-smoke gives flavour to the malt and eventually to the mature whisky. The malt is gleaned of germinated roots and then milled.

3 Mashing of the ground malt, or "grist", occurs in a large vat, or "mash tun", which holds a vast quantity of hot water. The malt is soaked and begins to dissolve, producing a sugary solution called "wort", which is then extracted for fermentation.

4 Fermentation occurs when yeast is added to the cooled wort in wooden vats, or "washbacks". The mixture is stirred for hours as the yeast turns the sugar into alcohol, producing a clear liquid called "wash".

5 Distillation involves boiling the wash twice so that the alcohol vaporizes and condenses. In copper "pot stills", the wash is distilled – first in the "wash still", then in the "spirit still". Now purified, with an alcohol content of 57 per cent, the result is young whisky.

6 Maturation is the final process. The whisky mellows in oak casks for a legal minimum of three years. Premium brands give the whisky a 10- to 15-year maturation, though some are given up to 50 years.

Traditional drinking vessels, or *quaichs*, made of silver

Blended whiskies are made from a mixture of up to 50 different single malts.

Single malts vary according to regional differences in the peat and stream water used.

THE LOWLANDS

CLYDE VALLEY · CENTRAL SCOTLAND · FIFE · THE LOTHIANS
AYRSHIRE · DUMFRIES AND GALLOWAY · THE BORDERS

*S*OUTHEAST *of the Highland boundary fault line lies a part of Scotland very different in character from its northern neighbour. If the Highlands embody the romance of Scotland, the Lowlands have traditionally been her powerhouse. Lowlanders have always prospered in agriculture and, more recently, in industry and commerce.*

Being the region of Scotland closest to the English border, the Lowlands inevitably became the crucible of Scottish history. For centuries after the Romans built the Antonine Wall *(see p44)* across the Forth–Clyde isthmus, the area was engulfed in conflict. The Borders are scattered with the castles of a territory in uneasy proximity to rapacious neighbours, and the ramparts of Stirling Castle overlook no fewer than seven different battlefields fought over in the cause of independence.

The ruins of medieval abbeys, such as Melrose, also bear witness to the dangers of living on the invasion route from England, though the woollen trade founded by their monks still flourishes in Peebles and Hawick.

North of the Borders lies Edinburgh, the cultural and administrative capital of Scotland. With its Georgian squares dominated by a medieval castle, it is one of Europe's most elegant cities. While the 18th and 19th centuries saw a great flowering of the arts in Edinburgh, the city of Glasgow became a merchant city second only to London.

Fuelled by James Watt's development of the steam engine in the 1840s, Glasgow became the cradle of Scotland's Industrial Revolution, which created a prosperous cotton industry and launched the world's greatest ships.

Both cities retain this dynamism today: Edinburgh annually hosts the world's largest arts festival, and Glasgow is acclaimed as a model of industrial renaissance.

A juggler performing at the annual arts extravaganza, the Edinburgh Festival

◁ Glamis Castle, 12 miles (19 km) north of Dundee, with its typically Scottish turreted exterior

Exploring the Lowlands

THE LOWLANDS are traditionally all the land south of the fault line stretching northeast from Loch Lomond to Stonehaven. Confusingly, they include plenty of wild upland country. The region illustrates the diversity of Scotland's scenery. The wooded valleys and winding rivers of the borders give way to the stern hills of the Cheviots and Lammermuirs. Fishing villages cling to the rocky east coast, while the Clyde coast and its islands are dotted with holiday towns. Inland lies the Trossachs, a romantic area of mountain, loch and woodland east of Loch Lomond that is a magnet for walkers *(see pp32–3)* and well within reach of Glasgow.

Loch Katrine seen from the Trossachs

SEE ALSO

- **Where to Stay** pp568-70
- **Where to Eat** pp604-6

SIGHTS AT A GLANCE

Walks and Tours
Tour of the Borders **18**

Aberdeen
STONEHAVEN

A94

A92

KEY

Motorway

Major road

Scenic route

Long-distance footpath

River

Viewpoint

GETTING AROUND

Access to the Lowlands is made easy from the south by the M74 to Glasgow or A702 to Edinburgh which connect the region to the M6 in England. Other motorways lead to Edinburgh, Glasgow, Stirling and Perth, north of which A roads lead to the Highlands. Glasgow, Edinburgh and Prestwick have international airports. Ferries from Ardrossan provide access to the Isle of Arran.

GLAMIS CASTLE **5**

A94

A85

4 PERTH

Firth of Tay

6 DUNDEE

A914

7 ST ANDREWS

A91

FALKLAND PALACE **9**

A915

8 EAST NEUK

DUNFERMLINE

10

Firth of Forth

A1

THGOW PALACE

4 15 FORTH BRIDGES

16 EDINBURGH

ST ABB'S HEAD

17

A1

B6438

23

A702

A6112

A68

Berwick-upon-Tweed, Newcastle upon Tyne

A7

A6089

A698

TRAQUAIR HOUSE

MELROSE ABBEY

19

TOUR OF THE BORDERS

18

2 BIGGAR

21

20

ABBOTSFORD HOUSE

A72

A701

A68

Tweed

A708

Teviot

A7

Southern Upland Way

HAWICK

A68

OFEAT

CHEVIOT HILLS

0 kilometres   20

0 miles   20

09

MFRIES

M74

ay Firth

Carlisle

Edinburgh Castle viewed from Princes Street

The Trossachs ❶

COMBINING THE RUGGEDNESS of the Grampians with the pastoral tranquillity of the Borders, this beautiful region of craggy hills and sparkling lochs is the colourful meeting place of the Lowlands and Highlands. Home to a wide variety of wildlife, including the golden eagle, peregrine falcon, red deer and the wildcat, the Trossachs have inspired numerous writers, including Sir Walter Scott (*see p498*) who made the area the setting for several of his novels. It was the home of Scotland's folk hero, Rob Roy, who was so well known that, in his own lifetime, he was fictionalized in *The Highland Rogue* (1723), a novel attributed to Daniel Defoe.

Golden eagle

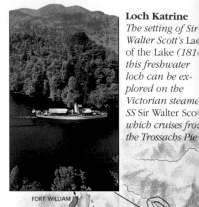

Loch Katrine
The setting of Sir Walter Scott's Lady of the Lake (181... this freshwater loch can be explored on the Victorian steame... SS Sir Walter Sco... which cruises fro... the Trossachs Pie...

Loch Lomond
Britain's largest freshwater lake was immortalized in a ballad composed by a local Jacobite soldier, dying far from home. He laments that though he will return home before his companions who travel on the high road, he will be doing so on the low road (of death).

Luss
With its exceptionally picturesque cottages, Luss is one of the prettiest villages in the Lowlands. Surrounded by grassy hills, it occupies one of the most scenic parts of Loch Lomond's western shore.

The West Highland Way provides a good footpath through the area.

*Map labels:*

FORT WILLIAM

Inveruglas

LOCH ARKLET

Tarbe...

BEN LOMOND
▲
974 m
3,196 ft

Kinloch...

BEN UIRD
▲
596 m
1,955 ft

Luss

Balma...

LOCH LOMOND

Balloch

GLASGOW

A82 · A811 · B829 · B837

KEY

🅷	Tourist information
▬▬	A road
▭▭	B road
═══	Minor road
- -	Footpath
⚶	Viewpoint

0 kilometres   5

0 miles   5

Inchmahome Priory

Mary, Queen of Scots (see p497) was hidden in this island priory to escape the armies of Henry VIII (see p498).

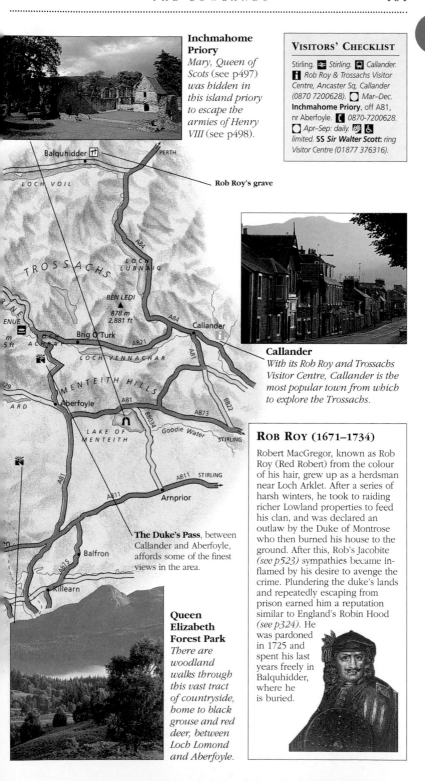

Callander
With its Rob Roy and Trossachs Visitor Centre, Callander is the most popular town from which to explore the Trossachs.

The Duke's Pass, between Callander and Aberfoyle, affords some of the finest views in the area.

Queen Elizabeth Forest Park
There are woodland walks through this vast tract of countryside, home to black grouse and red deer, between Loch Lomond and Aberfoyle.

ROB ROY (1671–1734)

Robert MacGregor, known as Rob Roy (Red Robert) from the colour of his hair, grew up as a herdsman near Loch Arklet. After a series of harsh winters, he took to raiding richer Lowland properties to feed his clan, and was declared an outlaw by the Duke of Montrose who then burned his house to the ground. After this, Rob's Jacobite *(see p523)* sympathies became inflamed by his desire to avenge the crime. Plundering the duke's lands and repeatedly escaping from prison earned him a reputation similar to England's Robin Hood *(see p324).* He was pardoned in 1725 and spent his last years freely in Balquhidder, where he is buried.

The 17th-century town house of the Dukes of Argyll, Stirling

Stirling **2**

Stirling. 🏚 28,000. 🚌 📍
ℹ 41 Dunbarton Rd (0870 7200620).
ⓦ www.visitscottishheartlands.org

SITUATED BETWEEN the Ochil Hills and the Campsie Fells, Stirling grew up around its castle, historically one of Scotland's most important fortresses. Below the castle the Old Town is still protected by the original 16th-century walls, built to keep Mary Queen of Scots safe from Henry VIII. The medieval **Church of the Holy Rude**, on Castle Wynd, where the infant James VI was crowned in 1567, has one of Scotland's few surviving hammerbeam oak roofs. The ornate façade of **Mar's Wark** is all that remains of a grand palace which, though never completed, was commissioned in 1570 by the 1st Earl of Mar. It was destroyed by the Jacobites *(see p523)* in 1746. Opposite stands the beautiful 17th-century town house of the Dukes of Argyll.

ENVIRONS: Two miles (3 km) south, the **Bannockburn Heritage Centre** stands by the field where Robert the Bruce defeated the English *(see p468)*. After the battle, he dismantled the castle so it would not fall back into English hands. A bronze equestrian statue commemorates the man who is an icon of Scottish independence.

🏛 **Bannockburn Heritage Centre**
(NTS) Glasgow Rd. 📞 01786 812664. 🕐 Apr–Sep: 10am–5:30pm daily; Oct–Mar: 11am–4:30pm daily. 🌑 24 Dec–Feb. 🈷 🚻

Stirling Castle

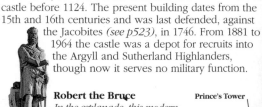

Gargoyle on castle wall

RISING HIGH on a rocky crag, this magnificent castle, which dominated Scottish history for centuries, now remains one of the finest examples of Renaissance architecture in Scotland. Legend says that King Arthur *(see p273)* wrested the original castle from the Saxons, but there is no evidence of a castle before 1124. The present building dates from the 15th and 16th centuries and was last defended, against the Jacobites *(see p523)*, in 1746. From 1881 to 1964 the castle was a depot for recruits into the Argyll and Sutherland Highlanders, though now it serves no military function.

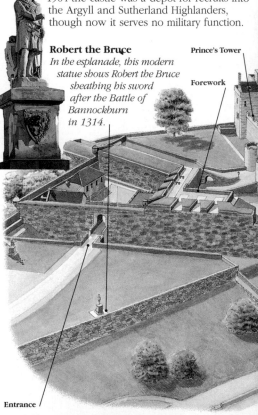

Robert the Bruce
In the esplanade, this modern statue shows Robert the Bruce sheathing his sword after the Battle of Bannockburn in 1314.

Prince's Tower

Forework

Entrance

Stirling Castle in the Time of the Stuarts, painted by Johannes Vorsterman (1643–99)

★ **Palace**
The otherwise sparse interiors of the royal apartments contain the Stirling Heads. These Renaissance roundels depict 38 figures, thought to be contemporary members of the royal court.

VISITORS' CHECKLIST

Castle Wynd, Stirling. **C** 01786 450000. ○ Apr–Sep: 9:30am–6pm daily; Oct–Mar: 9:30am–5pm daily (last adm: 45 mins before closing). ● 25–26 Dec, 1–2 Jan. 📷 ○ except museum. 🛗 limited. 🎫 🍴 🛍 🛒
W www.historic-scotland.gov.uk

The King's Old Building houses the Regimental Museum of the Argyll and Sutherland Highlanders.

★ **Chapel Royal**
Seventeenth-century frescoes by Valentine Jenkins adorn the chapel, reconstructed in 1594.

Nether Bailey

The Great Hall, built in 1500, has been restored to its former splendour.

STAR SIGHTS

★ **Palace**

★ **Chapel Royal**

The Elphinstone Tower was made into a gun platform in 1714.

Grand Battery
Seven guns stand on this parapet, built in 1708 during a strengthening of defences following the revolution of 1688 (see p53).

STIRLING BATTLES

At the highest navigable point of the Forth and holding the pass to the Highlands, Stirling occupied a key position in Scotland's struggles for independence. Seven battlefields can be seen from the castle; the 67 m (220 ft) Wallace Monument at Abbey Craig recalls William Wallace's defeat of the English at Stirling Bridge in 1297, foreshadowing Bruce's victory in 1314 *(see p468)*.

The Victorian Wallace Monument

Perth seen from the east across the Tay

Doune Castle ❸

Doune, Stirling. ☎ 01786 841742.
�æ 🔲 Stirling then bus. 🔲
Apr–Sep: 9:30am–6:30pm, daily;
Oct–Mar: 9:30am–4pm, Sat–Wed.
🔴 21 Dec–8 Jan. 🖂 🔥 limited.

Built as the residence of Robert, Duke of Albany, in the 14th century, **Doune Castle** was a Stuart stronghold until it fell into ruin in the 18th century. Now fully restored, it is one of the most complete castles of its time and offers a unique insight into the medieval royal household.

The Gatehouse, once a self-sufficient residence, leads through to the central courtyard from which the Great Hall can be entered. Complete with its reconstructed open-timber roof, minstrels' gallery and central fireplace, the Hall adjoins the Lord's Hall and Private Room with its original privy and well-hatch. A number of private stairs and narrow passages illustrate the ingenious means by which the royal family tried to protect itself during times of danger.

Perth ❹

Perthshire. 🏠 45,000. 🚆 🔲
🛈 West Mill St (01738 450600).
W www.perthshire.co.uk

Once the capital of medieval Scotland, Perth's rich heritage is reflected in many of its buildings. It was in the **Church of Saint John**, founded in 1126, that John Knox *(see p469)* delivered many of his fiery sermons. The Victorianized **Fair Maid's House**, on North Port, is one of the oldest houses in town (c.1600) and was the fictional home of the heroine of Sir Walter Scott's *(see p498) The Fair Maid of Perth* (1828).

In **Balhousie Castle**, the Museum of the Black Watch commemorates the first Highland regiment, while the **Art Gallery and Museum** has displays on local industry and exhibitions of Scottish painting.

Environs: Two miles (3 km) north of Perth, the Gothic mansion of **Scone Palace** stands on the site of an abbey destroyed in 1559. Between the 9th and 13th centuries, Scone guarded the sacred Stone of Destiny *(see pp468–9)*, now kept in Edinburgh Castle *(see pp492–3)*. Some of Mary, Queen of Scots' *(see p497)* embroideries are on display within.

⚜ **Balhousie Castle**
RHQ Black Watch, Hay St. ☎ 0131 310 8530. 🔲 May–Sep: Mon–Sat; Oct–Apr: Mon–Fri. 🔴 23 Dec–6 Jan. W www.theblackwatch.co.uk
🏛 **Art Gallery and Museum**
78 George St. ☎ 01738 632488. 🔲 10am–5pm Mon–Sat. 🔥
⚜ **Scone Palace**
A93 to Braemar. ☎ 01738 552300. 🔲 Easter–Oct: 9:30am–5pm daily; Nov–Easter: Fri (grounds only). 🖂 🔥 W www.scone-palace.co.uk

Glamis Castle ❺

Forfar, Angus. ☎ 01307 840242. 🚆 🔲 Dundee then bus. 🔲 Apr–Oct: 10:30am–5:30pm daily. 🖂 🔥
W www.glamis-castle.co.uk

With the pinnacled fairy-tale outline of a Loire chateau, the imposing medieval tower-house of **Glamis**

Glamis Castle with statues of James VI (left) and Charles I (right)

Castle began as a royal hunting lodge in the 11th-century but underwent extensive reconstruction in the 17th century. It was the childhood home of Queen Elizabeth the Queen Mother, and her former bedroom can be seen with a youthful portrait by Henri de Laszlo (1878–1956).

Many rooms are open to the public, including Duncan's Hall, the oldest in the castle and Shakespeare's setting for the king's murder in *Macbeth*. Together, the rooms present an array of china, paintings, tapestries and furniture spanning five centuries. In the grounds stand a pair of wrought-iron gates made for the Queen Mother on her 80th birthday in 1980.

Dundee ❻

Dundee City. 🏘 150,000. ✈ ☒
🚌 🚆 21 Castle Street (01382 527527). ♟ Tue, Fri–Sun.
ⓦ www.angusanddundee.co.uk

FAMOUS FOR ITS CAKE, marmalade and the DC Thomson publishing empire (creators of children's magazines *Beano* and *Dandy*), **Dundee** was also a major ship-building centre in the 18th and 19th centuries, a period which can be atmospherically recreated by a trip to the Victoria Docks.

HMS Unicorn, built in 1824, is the oldest British-built warship still afloat and is still fitted as it was on its last voyage. Berthed at Riverside is the royal research ship *Discovery*, built here in 1901 for Captain Scott's first voyage to the Antarctic. Housed in a Victorian Gothic building, the **McManus Galleries** provide a glimpse of Dundee's industrial heritage, as well as exhibitions on archaeology and Victorian art. The **Howff Burial Ground**, near City Square, has intriguing Victorian tombstones.

🏛 **HMS *Unicorn***
Victoria Docks, City Quay. 📞 01382 200900. ⬭ Apr–Oct: daily; Nov–Mar: Sat & Sun, pm only Wed–Fri. ⬤ late Dec–early Jan. 🎫 ♿ limited.
🏛 ***Discovery***
Discovery Point.
📞 01382 201245.
⬭ daily (Sun pm). 🎫 ♿
ⓦ www.rrsdiscovery.com
🏛 **McManus Galleries**
Albert Sq. 📞 01382 432084.
⬭ daily (to 7pm Thu, Sun pm only). ⬤ 25 & 26 Dec, 1–3 Jan. ♿
ⓦ www.dundeecity.gov.uk

View of **St Andrews** over the ruins of the cathedral

St Mary's College insignia, St Andrews University

St Andrews ❼

Fife. 🏘 14,000. 🚆 Leuchars.
🚌 Dundee. 🚆 70 Market St (01334 472021). ⓦ www.standrews.co.uk

SCOTLAND'S OLDEST UNIVERSITY town and one-time ecclesiastical capital, **St Andrews** is now a shrine to golfers from all over the world (*see below*). Its three main streets and numerous cobbled alleys, full of crooked housefronts, dignified university buildings and medieval churches, converge on the venerable ruins of the 12th-century **cathedral**. Once the largest in Scotland, the cathedral was later pillaged for stones to build the town. **St Andrew's Castle** was built for the bishops of the town in 1200. The dungeon can still be seen. The city's golf courses to the west are each open for a modest fee. The **British Golf Museum** tells how the city's Royal and Ancient Golf Club became the ruling arbiter of the game.

♟ **St Andrew's Castle**
The Scores. 📞 01334 477196.
⬭ Apr–Sep: 9:30–6:30pm; Oct–Mar: 9:30–4:30pm daily. ⬤ 25 & 26 Dec, 1 & 2 Jan. 🎫 ♿
🏛 **British Golf Museum**
Bruce Embankment. 📞 01334 460046. ⬭ Easter–mid-Oct: 9:30am–5:30pm daily; mid-Oct–Easter: 11am–3pm daily. 🎫 ♿

THE ANCIENT GAME OF GOLF

Scotland's national game was pioneered on the sandy links around St Andrews. The earliest record dates from 1457, when golf was banned by James II on the grounds that it was interfering with his subjects' archery practice.

Mary, Queen of Scots (*see p497*) enjoyed the game and was berated in 1568 for playing straight after the murder of her husband Darnley.

Mary, Queen of Scots at St Andrews in 1563

The central courtyard of Falkland Palace, bordered by rose bushes

East Neuk ❽

Fife. ⇆ *Leuchars.* 🚌 *Glenrothes & Leuchars.* ℹ *70 Market Street, St Andrews (01334 472021).*

A STRING of pretty fishing villages scatters the shoreline of the **East Neuk** (the eastern "corner") of Fife, stretching from Earlsferry to Fife Ness. Much of Scotland's medieval trade with Europe passed through these ports, a connection reflected in the Flemish-inspired crow-stepped gables of many of the cottages. Although the herring industry has declined and the area is now a peaceful holiday centre, the sea still dominates village life. Until the 1980s, fishing boats were built at St Monans, a charming town of narrow twisting streets, while Pittenweem is the base for the East Neuk fishing fleet.

The town is also known for **St Fillan's Cave**, the retreat of a 9th-century hermit whose relic was used to bless the army of Robert the Bruce *(see p468)* before the Battle of Bannockburn. A church stands among the cobbled lanes and colourful cottages of Crail; the stone by the church gate is said to have been hurled to the mainland from the Isle of May by the Devil.

Several 16th- to 19th-century buildings in the village of Anstruther contain the **Scottish Fisheries Museum** which tells the area's history with the aid of interiors, boats and displays on whaling. From the village you can also embark for the nature reserve on the **Isle of May** which teems with seabirds and grey seals. The statue of Alexander Selkirk in Lower Largo recalls the local boy whose adventures inspired Daniel Defoe's *Robinson Crusoe* (1719). Disagreeing with his captain, he was dumped on a desert island for four years.

🏛 Scottish Fisheries Museum
Harbour Head, St Ayles, Anstruther. 📞 *01333 310628.* 🕐 *10am–5:30pm daily.* ⬤ *25, 26 Dec, 1, 2 Jan.* 🦽 ♿ w *www.scottish-fisheries-museum.org*

THE PALACE KEEPER

Due to the size of the royal household and the necessity for the king to be itinerant, the office of Keeper was created by the medieval kings who required custodians to maintain and replenish the resources of their many palaces while they were away. Now redundant, it was a hereditary title and gave the custodian permanent and often luxurious lodgings.

James VI's bed in the Keeper's Bedroom, Falkland Palace

Falkland Palace ❾

(NTS) Falkland, Fife. 📞 *01337 857397.* ⇆ 🚌 *Ladybank, Kirkcaldy, then bus.* 🕐 *Mar–Oct:10am-6pm daily (Sun: pm).* 🎫 🦽 ♿ w *www.nts.org*

T HIS STUNNING Renaissance palace was designed as a hunting lodge of the Stuart kings. Although its construction was begun by James IV in 1500, most of the work was carried out by his son, James V *(see p496)*, in the 1530s. Under the influence of his two French wives he employed French workmen to redecorate the façade of the East Range with dormers, buttresses and medallions, and to build the beautifully proportioned South Range. The palace fell into ruin during the years of the Commonwealth *(see p52)* and was occupied briefly by Rob Roy *(see p481)* in 1715.

After buying the estates in 1887, the 3rd Marquess of Bute became the Palace Keeper and restored it. The richly panelled interiors are filled with superb furniture and portraits of the Stuart monarchs. The royal tennis court, the oldest in Britain, was built in 1539 for James V.

Dunfermline ❿

Fife. 🏘 *45,000.* ⇆ 🚌 ℹ *1 High St (01383 720999).* w *www.standrews.com/fife*

S COTLAND'S CAPITAL until 1603, Dunfermline is dominated by the ruins of the 12th-century abbey and palace which recall its royal past. In the 11th century, the town was the seat of King Malcolm III, who founded a priory on the present site of the **Abbey Church**. With its Norman nave and 19th-century choir, the church contains the tombs of 22 Scottish kings and queens, including Robert the Bruce *(see p468)*.

The ruins of King Malcolm's **palace** soar over the beautiful gardens of Pittencrieff Park. Dunfermline's most famous son, philanthropist Andrew Carnegie (1835–1919), had been forbidden entrance to the park as a boy. After making his fortune, he bought the entire Pittencrieff estate and gave it to the people of Dunfermline. He was born in the town, though moved to Pennsylvania in his teens. There he made a vast fortune in the iron and steel industry. The **Carnegie Birthplace Museum** is still furnished as it was when he lived there, and tells the story of his meteoric career.

🏛 Carnegie Birthplace Museum

Moodie St. 📞 *01383 724302*. 🅿
Apr–Oct: daily (Sun: pm). 📱 🖼 ♿

The 12th-century Norman nave of Dunfermline Abbey Church

Culross ⑪

(NTS) Fife. 🏠 *450*. 🚆 *Dunfermline.* 🚌 *Dunfermline.* ℹ *NTS, The Palace (01383 880359).* 🅿 *Easter–Sep: noon–5pm daily; Oct–Dec: noon–4pm Sat & Sun.* **Garden** 🅿 *10am–dusk all year.* 🖼 ♿ *limited.* 🎦 📱

A N IMPORTANT religious centre in the 6th century, the town of Culross is said to have been the birthplace of St Mungo in 514. Now a beautifully preserved 16th- and 17th-century village, Culross prospered in the 16th century with the growth of its coal and salt industries, most notably under Sir George Bruce. He took charge of the Culross colliery in 1575 and created a drainage system called the "Egyptian Wheel" which cleared a mile-long (1.5 km) mine beneath the River Forth.

During its subsequent decline Culross stood unchanged for over 150 years. The National Trust for Scotland began restoring the town in 1932 and now provides a guided tour, which starts at the **Visitors' Centre**.

Built in 1577, Bruce's **palace** has the crow-stepped gables, decorated windows and red pantiles typical of the period. The interior retains its original early 17th-century painted ceilings. Crossing the Square, past the **Oldest House**, dating from 1577, head for the **Town House** to the west. Behind it, a cobbled street known as the Back Causeway (with its raised section for nobility) leads to the turreted **Study**, built in 1610 as a house for the Bishop of Dunblane. The main room is open to visitors and should be seen for its original Norwegian ceiling. Continuing northwards to the ruined abbey, fine church and Abbey House, don't miss the Dutch-gabled **House with the Evil Eyes**.

The 16th-century palace of industrialist George Bruce, Culross

Linlithgow Palace ⑫

Linlithgow, West Lothian. 📞 *01506 842896.* 🚆 🚌 🅿 *Apr–Sep: 9:30am–6:30pm daily; Oct–Mar: 9:30am–4:30pm Mon–Sat, 2–4:30pm Sun.* 🅿 *25, 26 Dec, 1, 2 Jan.* 🖼 ♿ *limited.* 🌐 *www.historic-scotland.gov.uk*

O N THE EDGE of Linlithgow Loch stands the former royal palace of **Linlithgow**. Today's remains are mostly of the palace of James I in 1425. The scale of the building is demonstrated by the 28 m (94 ft) long Great Hall, with its huge fireplace and windows. Mary, Queen of Scots *(see p497)*, was born here in 1542.

Falkirk Wheel ⑬

Lime Rd, Tamfourhill, Falkirk. 📞 *01324 619888; booking line: 08700 500208.* 🚆 *Falkirk.* 🅿 *Feb–Nov:* **Boat trips** *9am–5pm daily* **Visitor Centre** *9am–6pm daily.* 🖼 *boat trip.* 📱 📷 🌐 *www.thefalkirkwheel.co.uk*

T HIS IMPRESSIVE boat lift is the first ever to revolve, and the centrepiece of Scotland's ambitious canal regeneration scheme. Once important for commercial transport, the Union and the Forth and Clyde canals were blocked by several roads in the 1960s. Now the Falkirk Wheel gently swings boats between the two waterways creating an uninterrupted link between Glasgow and Edinburgh. Visitors can ride the wheel on boats that leave the visitor's centre every half hour.

The rotating Falkirk Wheel boat lift

Hopetoun House ⑭

West Lothian. 📞 *0131 331 2451.* 🚆
Dalmeny then taxi. ⏰ *mid-Apr–Sep:*
10am-5:30pm daily. 🅿️ 🏛️ ♿ *limited.*
🎫 🛍️ Ⓦ *www.hopetounhouse.com*

AN EXTENSIVE PARKLAND by the Firth of Forth, designed in the style of Versailles, is the setting for one of Scotland's finest stately homes. The original house was built by 1707; it was later absorbed into William Adam's grand extension. The dignified, horseshoe-shaped plan and lavish interior plasterwork represent Neo-Classical 18th-century architecture at its finest. The red and yellow drawing rooms, with their Rococo plasterwork and highly ornate mantelpieces, are particularly impressive. The Marquess of Linlithgow, whose family still occupies part of the house, is a descendant of the 1st Earl of Hopetoun, for whom the house was built.

A wooden panel above the main stair, depicting Hopetoun House

Forth Bridges ⑮

Edinburgh. 🚆 🚌 *Dalmeny, Inver-*
keithing. 🏨 *Queensferry Lodge Hotel,*
N Queensferry (01383 417759).

THE SMALL TOWN of South Queensferry is dominated by the two great bridges that span the mile (1.6 km) across the River Forth to North Queensferry. The spectacular rail bridge, the first major steel-built bridge in the world, was opened in 1890 and remains

The shattered crags and cliffs of St Abb's Head

one of the greatest engineering achievements of the late Victorian era. Its massive cantilevered sections are held together by more than 6.5 million rivets, and the painted area adds up to some 55 ha (135 acres). The saying "it's like painting the Forth Bridge" has become a byword for non-stop, repetitive endeavour. It also inspired *The Bridge* (1986) by the writer Iain Banks.

The neighbouring road bridge was the largest suspension bridge outside the USA when it was opened in 1964, a distinction now held by the Humber Bridge in England. The two bridges make an impressive contrast, best seen from South Queensferry promenade. The town received its name from the 11th-century Queen Margaret *(see p493)*, who used the ferry here on her journeys between Edinburgh and the royal palace at Dunfermline *(see p487)*.

Edinburgh ⑯

See pp490–97.

St Abb's Head ⑰

(NTS) Scottish Borders. 🚆 *Berwick-*
upon-Tweed. 🚌 *from Edinburgh.*

THE JAGGED CLIFFS of St Abb's Head, rising 91 m (300 ft) from the North Sea near the southeastern tip of Scotland, offer a spectacular view of thousands of seabirds wheeling and diving below. This 80 ha (200 acre) nature reserve is an important site for cliff-nesting sea birds and becomes, during the May to June breeding season, the home of more than 50,000 birds, including fulmars, guillemots, kittiwakes and puffins that throng the headland near the fishing village of St Abbs. The village has one of the few unspoiled working harbours on Britain's east coast. A clifftop trail begins at the **Visitors' Centre**, where displays include identification boards and a touch table where young visitors can get to grips with wings and feathers.

🏛️ **Visitors' Centre**
St Abb's Head. 📞 *018907 71443.*
⏰ *Easter–Oct: 10am-5pm daily.* 🎫

The huge, cantilevered Forth Rail Bridge, seen from South Queensferry

A Tour of the Borders ⑱

BECAUSE OF THEIR PROXIMITY to England, the Scottish Borders are scattered with the ruins of many ancient buildings destroyed in the conflicts between the two nations. Most poignant of all are the Border abbeys, whose magnificent architecture bears witness to their former spiritual and political power. Founded during the 12th-century reign of David I, the abbeys were destroyed by Henry VIII *(see p498)*.

Kelso Abbey ②
The largest of the Border Abbeys, Kelso was once the most powerful ecclesiastical establishment in Scotland.

Melrose Abbey ⑥
Once one of the richest abbeys in Scotland, it is here that Robert the Bruce's heart is buried *(see p498)*.

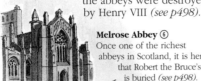

Floors Castle ①
Open in summer, the Duke of Roxburgh's ancestral home was built in the 18th century by William Adam.

Scott's View ⑤
This was Sir Walter Scott's favourite view of the Borders. During his funeral, the hearse stopped here briefly as Scott had done so often in life.

Dryburgh Abbey ④
Set on the banks of the Tweed, Dryburgh is considered the most evocative monastic ruin in Scotland. Sir Walter Scott is buried here.

KEY

▬	Tour route
═	Other roads
☀	Viewpoint

TIPS FOR DRIVERS

Length: 32 miles (50 km).
Stopping-off points: There is a delightful walk northwards from Dryburgh Abbey to the footbridge over the River Tweed.

0 kilometres   5

0 miles   3

Jedburgh Abbey ③
Though established in 1138, fragments of 9th-century Celtic stonework survive from an earlier structure. A Visitors' Centre illustrates the lives of the Augustinian monks who once lived here.

Edinburgh ⑯

WITH ITS STRIKING medieval and Georgian districts, overlooked by the extinct volcano of Arthur's Seat and, to the north-east, Calton Hill, Edinburgh is widely regarded as one of Europe's most handsome capitals. The city is famous for the arts (it was once known as "the Athens of the North"), a pre-eminence reflected in its hosting every year of Britain's largest arts extravaganza, the Edinburgh Festival (*see p495*). Its museums and galleries display the riches of many cultures.

Royal Scots soldiers from the castle

Exploring Edinburgh

Edinburgh falls into two main sightseeing areas, divided by Princes Street, the city's most famous thoroughfare and commercial centre. The Old Town straddles the ridge between the castle and the Palace of Holyroodhouse, with most of the city's medieval history clustered in the alleys of the Grassmarket and Royal Mile areas. The New Town, to the north, evolved after 1767 when wealthy merchants expanded the city beyond its medieval walls. This district contains Britain's finest concentration of Georgian architecture.

🏛 National Gallery of Scotland

The Mound. 📞 0131 624 6200. 🕐 10am–5pm Fri–Wed, 10am–7pm Thu. 🚻 📷 by appointment. 🆆 www.nationalgalleries.org
One of Scotland's finest art galleries, the National Gallery of Scotland is worth visiting for its 15th- to 19th-century British and European paintings alone, though plenty more can

be found to delight the art-lover. Ranks of paintings hang on deep red walls behind a profusion of statues and other works. Highlights among the Scottish works include portraits by Allan Ramsay and Henry Raeburn, such as his *Reverend Robert Walker Skating on Duddingston Loch* (c.1800). The Early German collection includes Gerard David's almost comic-strip treatment of the *Three Legends of Saint Nicholas* (c.1500). Works by Raphael, Titian and Tintoretto accompany southern European paintings such as Velázquez's *An Old Woman Cooking Eggs* (1620) and the entire room devoted to *The Seven Sacraments* (c.1640) by Nicholas Poussin. Flemish painters represented include Rembrandt, Van Dyck and Rubens while, among the British, important works by Reynolds, Ramsay and Gainsborough can be seen.

Raeburn's *Rev. Robert Walker Skating on Duddingston Loch*

The doorway of the Georgian House, 7 Charlotte Square

🚻 Georgian House

(NTS) 7 Charlotte Sq. 📞 0131 226 3318. 🕐 daily. ● mid-Dec–mid-Jan. 📷 🚻 limited. 🆆 www.nts.org.uk
In the heart of the New Town, Charlotte Square is a superb example of Georgian architecture, its north side, built in the 1790s, being a masterwork by the architect Robert Adam (*see pp24–5*). The Georgian House at No. 7 has been furnished and re-painted in its original 18th-century colours which provide a memorable introduction to the elegance of wealthy New Town life. The dining room table is arranged with Sheffield plate, Wedgwood china and mid-18th-century glasses, while the chairs are mainly Edinburgh "brander backs". The formal drawing room is in stately contrast to the intimacy of the parlour with its Staffordshire and Spode china services.

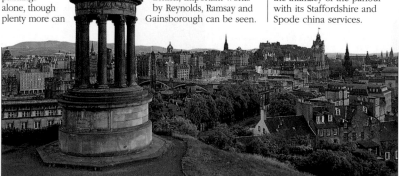

The view from Duncan's Monument on Calton Hill, looking west towards the castle

🏛 Scottish National Gallery of Modern Art & Dean Gallery

Belford Rd. 📞 0131 624 6200. ◯ 10am–5pm Mon–Sat, noon–5pm Sun. 🔲 🔲 www. nationalgalleries.org

Situated in extensive grounds to the northwest of the

Medieval chessmen, Museum of Scotland

city centre, a classical 19th-century school is home to this gallery. Most European and American 20th-century greats are represented here, from Vuillard and Picasso, to Magritte and Lichtenstein. Work by John Bellany can be found among the Scottish painters. Sculpture by Henry Moore is on display in the garden.

Lichtenstein's *In the Car*, National Gallery of Modern Art

🏛 Museum of Scotland

Chambers St. 📞 0131 225 7534. ◯ 10am–5pm Mon–Sat, noon–5pm Sun. ⬤ 25 Dec. 🔲 🔲 🔲 www.nms.ac.uk

This purpose-built museum houses the Scottish Collections of the National Museums of Scotland. Exhibitions tell the story of Scotland, the land and its people, dating from its geological beginnings right up to the constitutionally exciting events of today.

Key exhibits include the famous medieval *Lewis Chessmen*; *Pictish Chains*, known as Scotland's earliest crown jewels; the *Ellesmere* railway locomotive and icons of the 20th century selected both by famous Scots and the public. Children's guidebooks and activities are available.

🏛 Scottish National Portrait Gallery

1 Queen St. 📞 0131 556 8921. ◯ 10am–5pm Mon–Sat, noon–5pm Sun. 🔲 🔲 by appointment. 🔲 www.nationalgalleries.org

The National Portrait Gallery contains a rich and informative exhibition on the royal house of Stuart, explaining the turbulent history of 12 generations of Scottish monarchs from Robert the Bruce *(see p468)* to Queen Anne. Memorabilia from many reigns include Mary, Queen of Scots' *(see p497)* jewellery and a silver travelling canteen abandoned by Bonnie Prince Charlie *(see p521)* at Culloden *(see p523)*. The upper gallery has portraits of famous Scots, including Robert Burns *(see p501)* by Alexander Nasmyth.

EDINBURGH CITY CENTRE

Edinburgh Castle pp492–3 ②
Georgian House ①
Gladstone's Land ⑤
Greyfriars Bobby ⑥
Museum of Antiquities & Scottish National Portrait Gallery ③
Museum of Childhood ⑩

National Gallery of Scotland ④
Palace of Holyroodhouse ⑪
Parliament House ⑧
Royal Museum of Scotland ⑨
St Giles Cathedral ⑦

KEY

🚌 Long-distance bus station
🚆 Railway station
🅿 Parking
ℹ Tourist information
✝ Church

0 kilometres 1
0 miles 0.5
🔲 Royal Mile

Edinburgh Castle

Beam support in the Great Hall

S TANDING UPON the basalt core of an extinct volcano, Edinburgh Castle is an assemblage of buildings dating from the 12th to the 20th centuries, reflecting its changing role as fortress, royal palace, military garrison and state prison. Though there is evidence of Bronze Age occupation of the site, the original fortress was built by the 6th-century Northumbrian King Edwin, from whom the city takes its name. The castle was a favourite royal residence until the Union of Crowns *(see p469)* in 1603, after which the king resided in England. After the Union of Parliaments in 1707, the Scottish regalia were walled up in the Palace for over a hundred years. The castle is now the zealous possessor of the so-called Stone of Destiny, a relic of ancient Scottish kings which was seized by the English and not returned until 1996.

Scottish Crown
Now on display in the palace, the Crown was restyled by James V of Scotland in 1540.

Military Prison

Old Back Parade

Governor's House
Complete with Flemish-style crow-stepped gables, this building was constructed for the governor in 1742 and now serves as the Officers' Mess for the castle garrison.

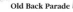

Vaults
This French graffiti, dating from 1780, recalls the many prisoners who were held in the vaults during the wars with France in the 18th and 19th centuries.

MONS MEG

Positioned outside St Margaret's Chapel, the siege gun (or *bombard*) Mons Meg was made in Belgium in 1449 for the Duke of Burgundy, who gave it to his nephew, James II of Scotland. It was used by James against the Douglas family in their stronghold of Threave Castle *(see p501)* in 1455, and later by James IV against Norham Castle in England. After exploding during a salute to the Duke of York in 1682, it was kept in the Tower of London until it was returned to Edinburgh in 1829, at Sir Walter Scott's request.

STAR SIGHTS

★ **Great Hall**

★ **Palace**

Argyle Battery
This fortified wall commands a spectacular view to the north beyond the city's Georgian district of New Town.

VISITORS' CHECKLIST

Castle Hill. ☎ *0131 225 9846*.
◯ *Apr–Oct: 9:30am–6pm daily;*
Nov–Mar: 9:30am–5pm daily (last
adm: 45 mins before closing).
● *25, 26 Dec.* ♿ 🅿
🎫 🍴 🛍 🛍
ⓦ *www.historic-scotland.gov.uk*

★ **Palace**
Mary, Queen of Scots (see p497) gave birth to James VI in this 15th-century palace, where the Scottish regalia are on display.

Entrance

Royal Mile →

The Esplanade is the location of the Military Tattoo *(see p495).*

The Half Moon Battery was built in the 1570s as a platform for the artillery defending the northeastern wing of the castle.

St Margaret's Chapel
This stained glass window depicts Malcolm III's saintly queen, to whom the chapel is dedicated. Probably built by her son, David I, in the early 12th century, the chapel is the castle's oldest existing building.

★ **Great Hall**
With its restored open-timber roof, the Hall dates from the 15th century and was the meeting place of the Scottish parliament until 1639.

Exploring the Royal Mile: Castlehill to High Street

Eagle sign outside Gladstone's Land

THE ROYAL MILE is a stretch of four ancient streets (from Castlehill to Canongate) which formed the main thoroughfare of medieval Edinburgh, linking the castle to the Palace of Holyroodhouse. Confined by the city wall, the "Old Town" grew upwards, with some tenements climbing to 20 storeys. It is still possible, among the 66 alleys and closes off the main street, to sense the city's medieval past.

Locator map

The Scotch Whisky Centre introduces visitors to Scotland's national drink.

The Camera Obscura contains an observatory from which to view the city.

Gladstone's Land is a preserved 17th-century merchant's house.

← Edinburgh Castle

CASTLE HILL

LAWNMARKET

The **"Hub"** (c.1840) has the city's highest spire.

Lady Stair's House
This 17th-century house is now a museum of the lives and works of Burns, Scott (see p498) and Stevenson.

🏛 Gladstone's Land

(NTS) 477B Lawnmarket. ☎ 0131 2265856. 🕐 Apr–Oct: 10am–5pm Mon–Sat, 2–5pm Sun 🖼

This 17th-century merchant's house, recently restored, provides a window on life in a typical Old Town house before overcrowding drove the rich to the Georgian New Town. "Lands", as they were known, were tall, narrow buildings erected on small plots of land. The six-storey Gladstone's Land was named after Thomas Gledstanes, the merchant who built it in 1617. The house still has the original arcade booths on the street front and a painted ceiling with fine Scandinavian floral designs. Though extravagantly furnished, it also contains items which are a reminder of the less salubrious side of the old city, such as wooden overshoes which had to be worn in the dirty streets. A chest in the beautiful Painted Chamber is said to have been given by a Dutch sea captain to a Scottish merchant who saved him from a shipwreck. A similar house, Morocco Land, can be found on Canongate *(see p497)*.

The bedroom of Gladstone's Land

🏛 Parliament House

Parliament Sq, High St. ☎ 0131 2252595. 🕐 9am–5pm Mon–Fri. ● public hols. ♿ limited.

This majestic, Italianate building was constructed in the 1630s for the Scottish parliament. Parliament House has been home to the Court of Session and the Supreme Court since the Union of Parliaments *(see p469)* in 1707. It is worth seeing, as much for the spectacle of its gowned and wigged advocates as for the stained-glass window in its Great Hall, commemorating the inauguration of the Court of Session by James V, in 1532.

The Signet Library has one of the city's most lavish interiors. Visits can be made after a written application.

St Giles Cathedral *A bagpiping angel can be found on the arched entrance to the Chapel of the Thistle.*

The City Chambers were designed by John Adam in the 1750s.

BANK STREET

HIGH STREET

GEORGE IV BRIDGE

Charles II Statue

The Heart of Midlothian is an arrangement of granite cobblestones on the former site of the city jail.

Parliament House was built in 1639. The Scottish parliament convened here from 1640 until 1707.

Rib-vaulting in the Thistle Chapel, St Giles Cathedral

🔒 St Giles Cathedral

Royal Mile. 📞 0131 2259442. ⏱ Oct–Apr: 9am–5pm Mon–Sat (Sun pm); May–Sep: 9am–7pm Mon–Fri, 9am–5pm Sat (Sun: pm). 🚫 25, 26 Dec, 1 Jan. 📷 Ⓦ www.stgiles.net

Properly known as the High Kirk (church) of Edinburgh, it is ironic that St Giles is popularly known as a cathedral. Though it was twice the seat of a bishop in the 17th century, it was from here that John Knox *(see p469)* directed the Scottish Reformation with its emphasis on individual worship freed from the authority of bishops. A tablet marks the place where Jenny Geddes, a stallholder from a local market, scored a victory for the Covenanters *(see p469)* by hurling her stool at a preacher reading from an English prayer book in 1637.

The Gothic exterior is dominated by a 15th-century tower.

Inside, the impressive Thistle Chapel can be seen, with its elaborate rib-vaulted roof and carved heraldic canopies. The chapel honours the knights, past and present, of the Order of the Thistle. The carved royal pew in the Preston Aisle is used by the Queen when she stays in Edinburgh.

EDINBURGH FESTIVAL

Every year, for three weeks in late summer *(see p63)*, Edinburgh hosts one of the world's most important arts festivals, with every available space (from theatres to street corners) overflowing with international artists and performers. It has been held in Edinburgh since 1947 and brings together the best in contemporary theatre, music, dance and opera. The alternative Festival Fringe, with some 600 companies involved, balances the classic productions with a host of innovative performances. The most popular event is the Edinburgh Tattoo, held on the Castle Esplanade – a spectacle of Scottish infantry battalions marching to pipe bands from all over the world.

Street performer from the Edinburgh Festival Fringe

Exploring the Royal Mile: High Street to Canongate

THE SECOND SECTION of the Royal Mile passes two monuments to the Reformation: John Knox's House and the Tron Kirk. The latter is named after a medieval *tron* (weighing beam) that stood nearby. The Canongate was once an independent district, owned by the canons of the Abbey of Holyrood, and sections of its south side have been restored. Beyond Morocco's Land, the road stretches for the final half-mile (800 m) to the Palace of Holyroodhouse.

Locator map

HIGH STREET

SOUTH BRIDGE STREET

The Mercat Cross marks the city centre. It was here that Bonnie Prince Charlie *(see p521)* was proclaimed king in 1745.

The Tron Kirk was built in 1630 for the Presbyterians who left St Giles Cathedral when it came under the Bishop of Edinburgh's control.

🏛 Museum of Childhood

42 High St. **📞** *0131 529 4142.* **◌** *10am–5pm Mon–Sat (& Sun pm during Festival).* **⬤** *25–27 Dec.* **♿** *limited.*

This lovely museum is not merely a toy collection but a magical insight into childhood, with all its joys and trials. Founded in 1955 by a city councillor, Patrick Murray (who claimed to enjoy eating children for breakfast), it was the first museum in the world to be devoted to the history and theme of childhood. The collection includes medicines, school books and prams as well as galleries full of old-fashioned toys. With its nickel-odeon, antique slot machines

An 1880 automaton of the Man on the Moon, Museum of Childhood

The entrance to the Palace of Holyroodhouse, seen from the west

and the general enthusiasm of visitors, this has been called the world's noisiest museum.

🏛 Palace of Holyroodhouse

East end of Royal Mile. **📞** *0131 524 1120.* **◌** *Apr–Oct: 9:30am–6pm; Nov–Mar: 9:30am–4:30pm; daily.* **♿** *limited.* **W** *www.royal.gov.uk*

Now the Queen's official Scottish residence, the Palace of Holyroodhouse is named after the "rood", or cross, which King David I is said to have seen between the antlers of a stag he was hunting here in 1128. The present palace was built in 1529 to accommodate James V *(see p487)* and his French wife, Mary of Guise, though it was remodelled in

the 1670s for Charles II. The Royal Apartments (including the Throne Room and Royal Dining Room) are used for investitures and banquets whenever the Queen visits the palace, though they are otherwise open to the public. A chamber in the James V tower is associated with the unhappy reign of Mary, Queen of Scots. It was here, in 1566, that she saw the murder of her trusted Italian secretary, David Rizzio, by her jealous husband, Lord Darnley. She had married Darnley a year earlier in Holyroodhouse chapel.

Bonnie Prince Charlie held court here in 1745 in the Jacobite *(see p523)* rising.

John Knox's House

Dating from 1490, the oldest house in the city was the home of John Knox (see p469) in the 1560s. It is due to re-open in 2005 after refurbishment.

Morocco Land is a reproduction of a 17th-century tenement house. It takes its name from the statue of a Moor which adorns the entrance.

CANONGATE

→ **The Palace of Holyroodhouse**

Museum of Childhood

Though created as a museum for adults by a city councillor who was known to dislike children, this lively musem now attracts flocks of young visitors.

MUSEUM OF CHILDHOOD

Moubray House was to be the signing place of the Treaty of Union in 1707 *(see p469)*, until a mob forced the authorities to retreat to another venue.

🏛 Royal Museum of Scotland

Chambers St. **🛈** *0131 247 4219.*
◯ *10am–5pm Mon–Sat, noon–5pm Sun.* **◉** *25 Dec.* **🛈 ♿ 📷 🍴**
W www.nms.ac.uk

This elegant museum, purpose-built in 1866, houses the National Museum of Scotland's international collections. Exhibits include examples from the applied arts and sciences. The Main Hall's fine collection of Asian sculpture includes a beautiful 13th-century statue of the Hindu goddess Parvati. European Art from 1200 to 1800 is on the first floor, while the second floor exhibits rare scientific instruments.

Parvati, at the Royal Museum of Scotland

Geological specimens and Eastern decorative arts are on the top floor.

🐕 Greyfriars Bobby

On an old drinking fountain near the gateway to Greyfriars Church stands the statue of a little Skye terrier. This com-memorates the dog who, for 14 years, guarded the grave of his master, John Gray, who died in 1858. The people of Edinburgh fed him until his death in 1872. He was also granted citizenship to prevent him being destroyed as a stray.

MARY, QUEEN OF SCOTS (1542–87)

Born only days before the death of her father, James V, the young Queen Mary spent her childhood in France, after escaping Henry VIII's invasion of Scotland *(see p498)*. A devout Catholic, she married the French Dauphin, and made claims on the English throne. This alarmed Protestants through-out England and Scotland, and when she returned as a widow to Holyroodhouse, aged 18, she was harangued for her faith by John Knox *(see p469)*. In 1567 she was accused of murdering her second husband, Lord Darnley. Two months later, when she married the Earl of Bothwell (also implicated in the murder), rebellion ensued. She lost her crown and fled to England where she was held prisoner for 20 years, before being charged with treason and beheaded at Fotheringhay.

The ruins of Melrose Abbey, viewed from the southwest

Melrose Abbey ⑲

Abbey Street, Melrose, Scottish
Borders. ☎ 01896 822562.
◯ Oct–Mar: 9:30am–4:30pm
Mon–Sat, 2–4:30pm Sun; Apr–Sep:
9:30am–6:30pm daily. ● 25, 26
Dec, 1, 2 Jan. 🅰 🔶 limited.

T HE ROSE-PINK RUINS of one
of the most beautiful of
the border abbeys (see p489)
bear testimony to the hazards
of standing in the path of successive English invasions.
Built by David I in 1136 for
Cistercian monks from Yorkshire, and also to replace a
7th-century monastery, Melrose
was repeatedly ransacked by
English armies, notably in 1322
and 1385. The final blow, from
which none of the abbeys

recovered, came in 1545 during Henry VIII's destructive
Scottish policy known as the
"Rough Wooing". This resulted
from the failure of the Scots to
ratify a marriage treaty between
Henry VIII's son and the infant
Mary, Queen of Scots (see
p497). What remains of the
abbey are the outlines of cloisters, the kitchen and other
monastic buildings and the
shell of the abbey church with
its soaring east window and
profusion of medieval carvings. The rich decorations of
the south exterior wall include
a gargoyle shaped like a pig
playing the bagpipes.

An embalmed heart, found
here in 1920, is probably that
of Robert the Bruce (see
p468), who had decreed that

his heart be taken on a crusade to the Holy Land. It was
returned to Melrose after its
bearer, Sir James Douglas (see
p501), was killed in Spain.

Abbotsford House ⑳

Galashiels, Scottish Borders. ☎ 01896
752043. 🚌 from Galashiels. ◯
mid-Mar–May & Oct: 9:30am–5pm
daily (Sun: 2–5pm); Jun–Sep: daily. 🅰
🔶 limited. 🅰 🔳 www.melrose.
bordernet.co.uk/abbotsford

F EW HOUSES bear the stamp
of their creator so intimately
as Abbotsford House, the
home of Sir Walter Scott for
the last 20 years of his life.
He bought a farm here in 1811,
known as Clarteyhole ("dirty
hole" in Scots), though he
soon renamed it Abbotsford,
after the monks of Melrose
Abbey who used to cross the
River Tweed nearby. He later
demolished the house to
make way for the turreted
building we see today, funded
by the sales of his novels.

Scott's library contains more
than 9,000 rare books and his
collections of historic relics
reflect his passion for the
heroic past. An extensive
collection of arms and armour
includes Rob Roy's broad-
sword (see p481). Stuart
mementoes include a crucifix
that belonged to Mary, Queen
of Scots and a lock of Bonnie
Prince Charlie's (see p521)
hair. The small study in which
he wrote his Waverley novels
can be visited as can the
room, overlooking the river,
in which he died in 1832.

SIR WALTER SCOTT

Sir Walter Scott (1771–1832)
was born in Edinburgh and
trained as a lawyer. He is best
remembered as a major champion and literary figure of
Scotland, whose poems and
novels (most famously his
Waverley series) created
enduring images of a heroic
wilderness filled with the
romance of the clans. His
orchestration, in 1822, of the
state visit of George IV to
Edinburgh (see p471) was an
extravaganza of Highland culture that helped re-establish
tartan as the national dress of Scotland. He served as Clerk of
the Court in Edinburgh's Parliament House (see p494) and for
30 years was Sheriff of Selkirk in the Scottish Borders, which
he loved. He put the Trossachs (see pp480–81) firmly on the
map with the publication of the Lady of the Lake (1810). His
final years were spent writing to pay off a £114,000 debt
following the failure of his publisher in 1827. He died with his
debts paid, and was buried at Dryburgh Abbey (see p489).

The Great Hall at Abbotsford,
adorned with arms and armour

Traquair House ㉑

Peebles, Scottish Borders. 📞 *01896
830 323.* 🚌 *from Peebles.* ⏰
*Easter–Jun, Sep, Oct: noon–5:30pm;
Jul–Aug: 10:30am–5:30pm; daily.* 🅿️
♿ *limited.* 🆆 *www.traquair.co.uk*

AS SCOTLAND'S OLDEST continuously inhabited house,
Traquair has deep roots in
Scottish religious and political
history, stretching back over
900 years. Evolving from a
fortified tower to a stout-
walled 17th-century
mansion *(see
p473)*, the house
was a Catholic
Stuart stronghold for
500 years. Mary,
Queen of Scots *(see
p497)* was among the
many monarchs to have
stayed here and her bed
is covered by a counter-
pane which she made.
Family letters and
engraved Jacobite
(see p523) drinking
glasses are among
relics recalling the
period of the
Highland rebellions.

**Mary, Queen of
Scots' crucifix,
Traquair House**

After a vow made
by the 5th Earl, Traquair's
Bear Gates (the "Steekit
Yetts"), which closed after
Bonnie Prince Charlie's *(see
p521)* visit in 1745, will not
reopen until a Stuart reas-
cends the throne. A secret
stairway leads to the Priest's
Room which attests to the
problems faced by Catholic
families until Catholicism was
legalized in 1829. Traquair
House Ale is still produced in
the 18th-century brewhouse.

Biggar ㉒

Clyde Valley. 👥 *2,000.* ℹ️ *High St
(01899 221066).*

THIS TYPICAL Lowland market town has a number of
museums worth visiting.
The **Gladstone Court
Museum** boasts a recon-
structed Victorian street
complete with a milliner's,
printer's and a village library,
while the grimy days of the
town's industrial past are
recalled at the **Gasworks
Museum**, with its collection
of engines, gaslights and
appliances. Established in
1839 and preserved in
the 1970s, the Biggar
Gasworks is the only
remaining rural gas-
works in Scotland.

🏛 **Gladstone Court
Museum**
Northbank Rd. 📞 *01899 221050.*
⏰ *Apr–Oct: 11am–4:30pm Mon–Sat,
2–4:30pm Sun.* 🅿️ ♿
🏛 **Gasworks Museum**
Gasworks Rd. 📞 *01899 221070.*
⏰ *Jun–Sep: 2–5pm daily.*

Pentland Hills ㉓

The Lothians. 🚆 *Edinburgh, then
bus.* ℹ️ *Regional Park Headquarters,
Biggar Rd, Edinburgh (0131 4453383).*

THE PENTLAND HILLS, stretching for 16 miles (26 km)
southwest of Edinburgh, offer
some of the best hill-walking
country in the Lowlands.
Leisurely walkers can saunter
along the many signposted
footpaths, while the more
adventurous can take the
chairlift at the Hillend dry ski
slope to reach the higher
ground leading to the 493 m
(1,617 ft) hill of Allermuir. Even
more ambitious is the classic
scenic route along the ridge
from Caerketton to West Kip.

To the east of the A703,
in the lee of the Pentlands,
stands the exquisite and
ornate 15th-century **Rosslyn
Chapel**. It was originally
intended as a church, but
after the death of its founder,
William Sinclair, it was also
used as a burial ground for
his descendants. The delicately
wreathed Apprentice Pillar
recalls the legend of the
apprentice carver who was
killed by the master stonemason in a fit of jealousy at
his pupil's superior skill.

⛪ **Rosslyn Chapel**
Roslin. 📞 *0131 4402159.* ⏰ *10am–
5pm daily (Sun: pm only).* 🅿️ ♿

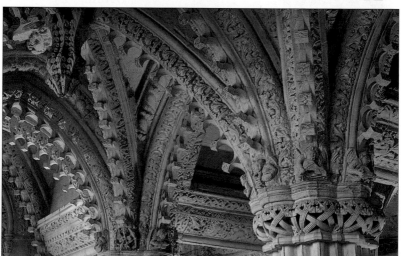

Details of the decorated vaulting in Rosslyn Chapel

The Classical 18th-century tenements of New Lanark on the banks of the Clyde

New Lanark ㉔

Clyde Valley. 🏘 *150.* ⚡ 🚌 *Lanark.*
ℹ️ *Horsemarket, Ladyacre Rd
(01555 661661).* 🚌 *Mon.*
ⓦ *www.newlanark.org*

S ITUATED BY THE falls of the
River Clyde, the village of
New Lanark was founded in
1785 by the industrial entre-
preneur David Dale. Ideally

DAVID LIVINGSTONE

Scotland's great missionary
doctor and explorer was
born in Blantyre where he
began working life as a
mill boy at the age of ten.
Livingstone (1813–73)
made three epic journeys
across Africa, from 1840,
promoting "commerce and
Christianity". He became
the first European to see
Victoria Falls and died in
1873 while searching for
the source of the Nile. He
is buried in Westminster
Abbey *(see pp94–5).*

located for the working of its
water-driven mills, the village
had become Britain's largest
cotton producer by 1800.
Dale and his successor, Robert
Owen, were philanthropists
whose reforms proved that
commercial success need not
undermine the wellbeing of
the workforce. Now a museum,
New Lanark is a window on to
working life in the early 19th
century. The **New Millennium
Experience** provides a
special-effects ride through
time, from the life of a mill girl
in 1820 to the 23rd century.

ENVIRONS: 15 miles (24 km)
north, Blantyre has a memorial to the famous Scottish
explorer David Livingstone.

🏛 New Millennium Experience
New Lanark Visitor Centre. 📞 *01555
661345.* ⏰ *11am–5pm daily.* ⬤ *25
Dec, 1 Jan.* 🅿️ 🅳 ☑️ *by appt.*

Glasgow ㉕

See pp502–7.

Sanquhar ㉖

Dumfries & Galloway. 🏘 *2,500.* ⚡
🚌 ℹ️ *64 Whitesands, Dumfries
(01387 253862).*

N OW OF CHIEFLY historic
interest, the town of
Sanquhar was famous in the
history of the Covenanters

(see p469). In the 1680s, two
declarations opposing the rule
of bishops were pinned to the
Mercat Cross, the site of which
is now marked by a granite
obelisk. The first protest was
led by a local teacher, Richard
Cameron, whose followers
became the Cameronian regiment. The Georgian **Tolbooth**
was designed by William
Adam *(see p534)* in 1735 and
houses a local interest museum
and tourist centre. The Post
Office, opened in 1763, is the
oldest in Britain, predating
the mail coach service.

Drumlanrig Castle ㉗

Thornhill, Dumfries & Galloway. 📞
01848 330248. ⚡ 🚌 *Dumfries, then
bus.* ⭘ *Easter, May–Sep: 11am–4pm
Mon–Sat, noon–4pm Sun.* 🅿️ 🅳

R ISING SQUARELY from a
grassy platform, the
massive fortress-palace of
Drumlanrig *(see p473)* was
built from pink sandstone
between 1679 and 1691 on the
site of a 15th-century Douglas

**The Baroque front steps and
doorway of Drumlanrig Castle**

stronghold. A formidable multi-turreted exterior contains a priceless collection of art treasures as well as such Jacobite relics as Bonnie Prince Charlie's camp kettle and sash. Hanging within oak-panelled rooms are paintings by Holbein and Rembrandt. The emblem of a crowned and winged heart, shown throughout the castle, recalls Sir James, the "Black Douglas", who bore Robert the Bruce's *(see p468)* heart while on crusade to fulfil a vow made by the king. After being mortally wounded he threw the heart at his enemies with the words "forward brave heart!"

The sturdy island fortress of Threave Castle on the Dee

Threave Castle ㉘

Castle Douglas, Dumfries & Galloway. (07711 223101 or 01556 502611. Dumfries. ○ Apr–Sep: 9:30am–6:30pm daily (last boat leaves island 6pm); Oct: phone to check.

THIS MENACING GIANT of a tower, a 14th-century Black Douglas *(see above)* stronghold standing on an island in the Dee, commands the most complete medieval riverside harbour in Scotland. Douglas's struggles against the early Stewart kings culminated in his surrender here after a two-month siege in 1455 – but only after James II had brought the cannon Mons Meg *(see p492)* to batter the castle. Threave was dismantled after Protestant Covenanters *(see p469)* defeated its Catholic de-fenders in 1640. Inside the

tower, only the shell of the kitchen, great hall and domestic levels remains. Over the 15th-century doorway is the "gallows knob", a reminder of when the owners are said to have boasted that it never lacked its noose. Access to the castle is by small boat.

Whithorn ㉙

Dumfries & Galloway. 1,000. Stranraer. Dashwood Sq, Newton Stewart (01671 402431). www.dumfriesandgalloway.co.uk

THE EARLIEST SITE of continuous Christian worship in Scotland, Whithorn (meaning white house) takes its name from the white chapel built here by St Ninian in 397. Though nothing remains of his chapel, a guided tour of the archaeological dig reveals evidence of Northumbrian, Viking and Scottish settlements ranging from the 5th to the 19th centuries. A visitors' centre, **The Whithorn Story**, provides information on the excavations and contains a collection of carved stones. One, dedicated to Latinus, dates to 450, making it Scotland's earliest Christian monument.

🏛 **The Whithorn Story**
The Whithorn Trust, 45–47 George St. (01988 500508. ○ Apr–Oct: 10:30am–5pm daily. www.whithorn.com

Culzean Castle ㉚

See pp508–9.

Robert Burns surrounded by his creations, by an unknown artist

Burns Cottage ㉛

Burns National Heritage Park, Alloway, South Ayrshire. (01292 443700. Ayr, then bus. ○ Oct–Mar: 10am–5pm; Apr–Sep: 9:30am–5:30pm; daily. 25 & 26 Dec, 1 & 2 Jan. www.burnsheritagepark.com

ROBERT BURNS (1759–96), Scotland's favourite poet, was born and spent his first seven years in this small thatched cottage in Alloway. Built by his father, the cottage still contains much of its original furniture. There is also a small museum next door displaying many of Burns's manuscripts along with early editions of his works. Much of his poem *Tam o' Shanter* (1790) is set in Alloway, which commemorates him with a huge monument on the outskirts of the village.

Burns became a celebrity following the publication in 1786 of the Kilmarnock Edition of his poems. Scots everywhere gather to celebrate Burns Night *(see p65)* on his birthday, 25 January.

SCOTTISH TEXTILES

Weaving in the Scottish Borders goes back to the Middle Ages, when monks from Flanders established a thriving woollen trade with the Continent. Cotton became an important source of wealth in the Clyde Valley during the 19th century, when handloom weaving was overtaken by power-driven mills. The popular Paisley patterns were based on Indian designs.

A colourful pattern from Paisley

Glasgow ㉕

The coat of arms of Glasgow city

THOUGH ITS CELTIC NAME, *Glas cu*, means "dear green place", Glasgow is more often associated with its industrial past, and once enjoyed the title of Second City of the Empire (after London). Glasgow's architectural standing, as Scotland's finest Victorian city, reflects its era of prosperity, when ironworks, cotton mills and ship-building were fuelled by Lanarkshire coal. The Science Centre now sits on the Clyde's revitalized south bank. Glasgow rivals Edinburgh *(see pp490–97)* in the arts, with galleries such as the Kelvingrove and the Burrell Collection *(see pp506–7).*

Glasgow's medieval cathedral viewed from the southwest

Exploring Glasgow

With some relics of its grimy industrial past and glossy new image, modern Glasgow is a city of contrasts. The deprived area of the East End, with its busy weekend market, the "Barras", stands by the restored 18th-century Merchant City and Victorian George Square. The more affluent West End prospered in the 19th century as a retreat for wealthy merchants escaping the heavily industrialized Clydeside, and it is here that Glasgow's chief galleries and museums can be found.

South of the river, the Govan and Gorbals districts give way to the Pollok Country Park, site of the Burrell Collection. An underground network provides easy travel around the city.

🏛 Glasgow Cathedral

Cathedral Square. **(** *0141 5526891.* ☐ *Apr–Sep: 9:30am–6pm Mon–Sat, 1–5pm Sun; Oct–Mar: 9:30am–4pm Mon–Sat, 1–4pm Sun.* 👤 As one of the only cathedrals to escape destruction during the Scottish Reformation *(see pp468–9)* – by adapting itself to Protestant worship – this is

a rare example of an almost complete 13th-century church. It was built on the site of a chapel founded by the city's patron saint, St Mungo, a 6th-century bishop of Strathclyde. According to legend, Mungo placed the body of a holy man named Fergus on a cart yoked to two wild bulls, telling them to take it to the place ordained by God. In the "dear green place" at which the bulls stopped he built his church. Because of its sloping site, the cathedral is on two levels.

GLASGOW CITY CENTRE

Art Gallery and Museum ③
Glasgow Cathedral ⑧
Glasgow School of Art ⑤
Hunterian Art Gallery ①
Museum of Transport ②
Provand's Lordship ⑦

People's Palace ⑩
St Mungo Museum of Religious Art ⑨
Tenement House ④
Willow Tea Room ⑥

0 kilometres   1

0 miles   0.5

KEY

🚌 Bus station

🚍 Long-distance bus station

🚆 Railway station

Ⓤ Underground station

🅿 Parking

ℹ Tourist information

✝ Church

Dalí's *Christ of St John of the Cross* at the
St Mungo Museum of Religious Life and Art

Situated in the cathedral precinct, this new museum is a world first. The main exhibition illustrates religious themes with superb artifacts, including a 19th-century dancing Shiva and an Islamic painting entitled the *Attributes of Divine Perfection* (1986) by Ahmed Moustafa. An exhibition on religion in Glasgow throws light on the life of the missionary David Livingstone *(see p500)*. Recently moved from the Kelvingrove Art Gallery and Museum *(see p505)*, Salvador Dalí's powerful work *Christ of St John of the Cross* (1951) is now here. Outside you can visit Britain's only permanent Zen Buddhist garden.

The crypt contains the tomb of St Mungo, surrounded by an intricate forest of columns springing up to end in delicately carved rib-vaulting. The Blackadder Aisle, reputed to have been built over a cemetery blessed by St Ninian *(see p501)*, has a ceiling thick with decorative bosses.

🏛 St Mungo Museum of Religious Life and Art

2 Castle St. 📞 0141 5532557. ⭘ 10am–5pm daily (11am Fri & Sat). ♿ 🎥 by appointment. 🖥 🛈

🚇 Tenement House

(NTS) 145 Buccleuch St.
📞 0141 3330183. ⭘ *Mar–Oct: 2–5pm daily.* 🎥 🎟 *by appointment.*
Less a museum than a time capsule, the Tenement House is an almost undisturbed record of life in a modest Glasgow flat in a tenement estate during the early 20th century. Glasgow owed much of its vitality and neighbourliness to tenement life, though many of these Victorian and Edwardian apartments were to earn a bad name for poverty

The preserved Edwardian kitchen of the Tenement House

and overcrowding, and many have now been pulled down. The Tenement House was first owned by Miss Agnes Toward who lived here from 1911 until 1965. It remained largely unaltered and, since Agnes threw very little away, it is now a treasure-trove of social history. The parlour, previously used only on formal occasions, has afternoon tea laid out on a white lace cloth. The kitchen, with its coal-fired range and box bed, is filled with the tools of a vanished era such as a goffering iron for crisping waffles, a washboard and a stone hot-water bottle.

Agnes's lavender water and medicines are still in the bathroom, as though she had stepped out for a minute 70 years ago, and forgotten to return home.

The Kelvingrove Art Gallery and the Glasgow University buildings, viewed from the south

Glasgow's medieval house, Provand's Lordship

🏛 Provand's Lordship

3 Castle St. 📞 0141 5528819.
🕐 10am–5pm daily (11am Fri & Sun).
Now a museum, Provand's Lordship was built as a canon's house in 1471, and is the city's oldest surviving house. Its low ceilings and austere wooden furnishings create a vivid impression of life in a wealthy 15th-century household. It is thought that Mary, Queen of Scots (see p497)

Mackintosh's interior of the Willow Tea Room

may have stayed here when she made a visit to Glasgow in 1566 to see her cousin and husband, Lord Darnley.

🏛 Willow Tea Room

217 Sauchiehall St. 📞 0141 332 0521.
🕐 9am–4:30pm Mon–Sun. 🗎
🌐 www.willowtearooms.co.uk
This is the sole survivor of a series of delightful tea rooms created by Charles Rennie Mackintosh in 1904 for the celebrated restaurateur Miss Kate Cranston.
Everything from the high-backed chairs to the tables and cutlery was his design. In particular, the 1904 Room de Luxe sparkles with silver furniture and flamboyant leaded glass work. Another Willow Tea Room opened in 1997 at No. 97 Buchanan Street, which recreates Cranston's original Ingram Street Tea Rooms.

🏛 Museum of Transport

1 Bunhouse Rd. 📞 0141 2872000.
🕐 10am–5pm Mon–Thu, Sat, 11am–5pm Fri, Sun. 🚻 📷 🗎
🌐 www.glasgowmuseums.com
Housed in Kelvin Hall, this imaginative museum conveys the optimism and vigour of the city's industrial heyday. Model ships and ranks of gleaming Scottish-built steam engines, cars and motorcycles recall the 19th and early 20th centuries, when Glasgow's supremacy in shipbuilding, trade and manufacturing made her the "second city" of the British Empire. Old Glasgow can be seen through fascinating footage of the town in the cinema and through a reconstruction of a 1938 street, with Art Deco shop fronts, a cinema and an Underground station.

The Museum of Transport's reconstructed 1938 street, with Underground station

⛪ Glasgow Necropolis

Cathedral Sq. 📞 0141 2873961.
🕐 daily. 🗎 🚻 limited.
Behind the cathedral, the reformer John Knox (see p469) surveys the city from his Doric pillar overlooking a Victorian cemetery. It is filled with crumbling monuments to the dead of Glasgow's wealthy merchant families.

CHARLES RENNIE MACKINTOSH

A Mackintosh floral design

Glasgow's most celebrated designer, Charles Rennie Mackintosh (1868–1928), entered Glasgow School of Art at 16. After his first big break with the Willow Tea Room, he became a leading figure in the Art Nouveau movement, developing a unique style that borrowed from Gothic and Scottish Baronial designs. He believed a building should be a fully integrated work of art, creating furniture and fittings that complemented the overall construction. Nowhere is this total design better seen than in the Glasgow School of Art, which he designed in 1896. Unrecognized in his lifetime, Mackintosh's work is now widely imitated. Its characteristic straight lines and flowing detail are the hallmark of early 20th-century Glasgow style, in all fields of design from textiles to architecture.

🏛 People's Palace

Glasgow Green. 📞 0141 5540223.
🕐 10am–5pm Mon–Thu, Sat,
11am–5pm Fri & Sun. 🚻 🖳 📷
🅆 www.glasgow.gov.uk

This Victorian sandstone structure was built in 1898 as a cultural museum for the people of Glasgow's East End. It houses everything from temperance tracts to trade-union banners, suffragette posters to comedian Billy Connolly's banana-shaped boots, providing a social history of the city from the 12th century. A conservatory at the back contains an exotic winter garden.

🏛 Glasgow School of Art

167 Renfrew St. 📞 0141 3534526.
🕐 by appointment only. 📷
🎞 🚻 limited. 🅆 www.gsa.ac.uk

Widely considered to be Charles Rennie Mackintosh's greatest architectural work, the Glasgow School of Art was built between 1897 and 1909 to a design he submitted in a competition. It was built in two periods due to financial constraints. The later, western wing displays a softer design than the more severe eastern half, built only a few years earlier and compared by a contemporary critic to a prison.

A student guide takes you through the building to the Furniture Gallery, Board Room and the Library, the latter a masterpiece of spatial composition. Each room is an exercise in contrasts between height, light and shade with innovative details echoing the architectural themes of the structure. How much of the school can be viewed depends on curricular requirements at the time of visiting.

🏛 Hunterian Art Gallery

82 Hillhead St. 📞 0141 3305431.
🕐 9:30am–5pm Mon–Sat. 🌑 24
Dec–5 Jan & public hols. 📷 🚻
limited. 🅆 www.hunterian.gla.ac.uk

Built to house a number of paintings bequeathed to Glasgow University by ex-student and physician Dr William Hunter (1718–83), the Hunterian Art Gallery contains Scotland's largest print collection and works by major European artists stretching back to the 16th century. A collection of work by Charles

George Henry's *Japanese Lady with a Fan* (1894), Art Gallery and Museum

Mackintosh is supplemented by a complete reconstruction of No. 6 Florentine Terrace, where he lived from 1906 to 1914. A major collection of 19th- and 20th-century Scottish art includes work by William McTaggart (1835–1910), but the gallery's most famous collection is of work by the painter James McNeill Whistler (1834–1903).

Whistler's *Sketch for Annabel Lee* (c.1869), Hunterian Art Gallery

🏛 Kelvingrove Art Gallery and Museum

Argyle St, Kelvingrove. 📞 0141 287
2699. 🌑 until mid–2006. **McLellan**
Galleries 270 Sauchiehall St. 📞
0141 565 4100. 🕐 10am–5pm
Mon–Sat, 11am–5pm Fri & Sun.
🅆 www.glasgow.gov.uk

An imposing red sandstone building, Scotland's most popular gallery houses a magnificent art collection. The gallery is currently closed for refurbishment, but more than 200 exhibits can be viewed at the McLellan Galleries. Kelvingrove's 17th-century Dutch and Flemish masters including Rembrandt can be seen, as well as 19th-century British artists such as Turner and Constable. Scottish art and design is well represented with rooms dedicated to the Scottish Colourists and the Glasgow Style. Also included here are two recently acquired works by Charles Rennie Mackintosh: a fine gesso panel and a 1904 writing cabinet.

The Georgian Pollok House, viewed from the south

⚜ Pollok House

(NTS) 2060 Pollokshaws Rd. [ ]
(0141) 616 6410. ⬤ *10am–5pm
daily.* ⬤ *25, 26 Dec, 1, 2 Jan.* 🅿
Apr–Oct only. [W] *www.nts.org.uk*

Pollok House is Glasgow's
finest 18th-century domestic
building and contains one of
Britain's best collections of
Spanish paintings. The Neo-
Classical central block was
finished in 1750, the sobriety
of its exterior contrasting with
the exuberant plasterwork
within. The Maxwells have
lived at Pollok since the mid-
13th century, but the male
line ended with Sir John
Maxwell, who added the
grand entrance hall in the
1890s and designed most of
the terraced gardens and
parkland beyond.

    Hanging above the family
silver, porcelain, hand-painted
Chinese wallpaper and Jaco-
bean glass, the Stirling Maxwell
collection is strong on British
and Dutch schools, including
William Blake's *Sir Geoffrey
Chaucer and the Nine and
Twenty Pilgrims* (1745) and
William Hogarth's portrait of
James Thomson, who wrote
the words to *Rule Britannia*.

    Spanish 16th- to 19th-
century art predominates: El
Greco's *Lady in a Fur Wrap*
(1541) hangs in the library,
while the drawing room contains works by Francisco de
Goya and Esteban Murillo. In
1966 Anne Maxwell
Macdonald gave the house
and 146 ha (361 acres) of
parkland to the City of
Glasgow. The park provides
the site for the city's
fascinating Burrell Collection.

Glasgow: The Burrell Collection

GIVEN TO THE CITY in 1944 by Sir
William Burrell (1861–1958), a
wealthy shipping owner, this internationally acclaimed collection is the
star of Glasgow's renaissance, with
objects of major importance in numerous fields of interest. The building
was purpose-built in 1983. In the sun,
the stained glass blazes with colour,
while the shaded tapestries seem a
part of the surrounding woodland.

Hutton Castle Drawing Room
*This is a reconstruction of the Drawing
Room at Burrell's own home – the
16th-century Hutton Castle, near
Berwick-upon-Tweed. The Hall and
Dining Room can also be seen nearby.*

Bull's Head
*Dating from
the 7th
century BC,
this bronze
head from
Turkey was
once part of a
cauldron handle.*

Figure of a Lohan
*This sculpture of
Buddha's disciple
dates from the Ming
Dynasty (1484).*

**Hornby
Portal**
*This detail
shows the
arch's heraldic
display. The
14th-century
portal comes from
Hornby Castle in
Yorkshire.*

Main entrance

STAR EXHIBITS

★ **Stained Glass**

★ **Tapestries**

Rembrandt van Rijn
This self-portrait, signed and dated 1632, has pride of place among the Dutch paintings hanging in the 17th- and 18th-century room.

Mezzanine floor

VISITORS' CHECKLIST

2060 Pollokshaws Rd, Glasgow.
📞 (0141) 287 2550. 🚆 Pollokshaws West. 🚌 45, 47, 48, 57 from Glasgow. 🕐 10am–5pm Mon–Thu, Sat, 11am–5pm Fri, Sun. 🍴 🖥 📷 📹 ♿ 🏛 ⛺

GALLERY GUIDE
Except for a mezzanine-floor display of paintings, the exhibitions are on the ground floor. Right of the entrance hall, rooms are devoted to tapestries, stained glass and sculpture, while ancient civilizations, Oriental art and the period galleries are ahead.

KEY TO FLOORPLAN

☐ Ancient civilizations

☐ Oriental art

☐ Medieval and post-medieval European art, stained glass and tapestries

☐ Period galleries

■ Hutton Castle Rooms

☐ Paintings and drawings

☐ Temporary exhibition area

Matthijs Maris
This popular Dutch painter's ethereal style appealed to late 19th-century tastes. The Sisters (1875) is one of over 50 Maris works acquired by Burrell.

Ground floor

Lecture theatre

★ **Stained Glass**
This 15th-century Norwich School panel, depicting a youth snaring birds, is one of many secular themes illustrated in the stained-glass display.

★ **Tapestries**
Scenes from the Life of Christ and of the Virgin *(c.1450), a Swiss work in wool, is one of many tapestries on show.*

Culzean Castle ⑳

Robert Adam by George Willison

S TANDING ON A CLIFF'S EDGE in an extensive parkland estate, the 16th-century keep of Culzean (pronounced Cullayn), home of the Earls of Cassillis, was remodelled between 1777 and 1792 by the Neo-Classical architect Robert Adam *(see p24)*. Restored in the 1970s, it is now a major showcase of his later work. The grounds became Scotland's first public country park in 1969 and, with farming flourishing alongside ornamental gardens, they reflect both the leisure and everyday activities of a great country estate.

View of Culzean Castle (c.1815), by Nasmyth

Lord Cassillis' Rooms contain typical mid-18th-century furnishings, including a gentleman's wardrobe of the 1740s.

The clock tower, fronted by the circular carriageway, was originally the coach house and stables. The clock was added in the 19th century, and today the buildings are used for residential and educational purposes and a shop.

A PLAN OF CULZEAN CASTLE

FIRST FLOOR

- Blue Drawing Room
- Picture Room
- State Bedroom
- Lord Cassillis' Rooms
- Saloon Ante Room
- Saloon
- Dressing Room
- Eisenhower Presentation
- Front Hall
- Entrance
- Library
- Kitchen
- Dining Room
- Scullery
- Armoury
- Ailsa Exhibition
- Oval Staircase

GROUND FLOOR

STAR SIGHTS

★ Saloon

★ Oval Staircase

Armoury
Displayed on the walls is the world's most important collection of flintlock pistols, used by the British Army and Militia between the 1730s and 1830s

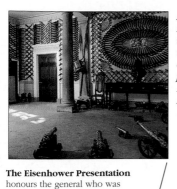

VISITORS' CHECKLIST

(NTS) 4 miles (6 km) West of Maybole. 📞 *01655 884400.*
🚌 *Ayr, then bus.* **Castle** ⬜ *Apr–Oct: 10am–5:30pm daily (last adm: 5pm).* **Grounds** ⬜ *dawn until dusk daily.* 🅿 ♿ 🚻

Fountain Court
This sunken garden is a good place to begin a tour of the grounds to the east.

The Eisenhower Presentation honours the general who was given the top floor of Culzean in gratitude for his role in World War II.

Carriageway

★ Saloon
With its restored 18th-century colour scheme and Louis XVI chairs, this elegant saloon perches on the cliff's edge 46 m (150 ft) above the Firth of Clyde. The carpet is a copy of the one designed by Adam.

★ Oval Staircase
Illuminated by an overarching skylight, the staircase, with its Ionic and Corinthian pillars, is considered one of Adam's finest achievements.

THE HIGHLANDS AND ISLANDS

ABERDEENSHIRE · MORAY · ARGYLL & BUTE · PERTH & KINROSS
SHETLAND · ORKNEY · WESTERN ISLES · HIGHLANDS · ANGUS

MOST OF THE STOCK IMAGES *of Scottishness– clans and tartans, whisky and porridge, bagpipes and heather– originate in the Highlands and enrich the popular picture of Scotland as a whole. But for many centuries the Gaelic-speaking, cattle-raising Highlanders had little in common with their southern neighbours.*

Clues to the non-Celtic ancestors of the Highlanders lie scattered across the Highlands and Islands in the form of stone circles, brochs and cairns some over 5,000 years old. By the end of the 6th century, the Gaelic-speaking Celts had arrived from Ireland, along with St Columba who taught Christianity. Its fusion with Viking culture in the 8th and 9th centuries produced St Magnus Cathedral in the Orkney Isles.

For over 1,000 years, Celtic Highland society was founded on a clan system, built on family ties to create loyal groups dependent on a feudal chief.

However, the clans were systematically broken up by England after 1746, following the defeat of the Jacobite attempt on the British crown, led by Bonnie Prince Charlie (*see p521*). A more romantic vision of the Highlands started in the early 19th century. Its creation was largely due to Sir Walter Scott, whose novels and poetry depicted the majesty and grandeur of a country previously considered merely poverty-stricken and barbaric. Another great popularizer was Queen Victoria, whose passion for Balmoral helped to establish the trend for acquiring Highland sporting estates. But behind the sentimentality lay harsh economic realities that drove generations of Highlanders to seek a new life overseas.

Today, over half the inhabitants of the Highlands and Islands still live in communities of less than 1,000. Oil and tourism have supplemented fishing and whisky as the main businesses and population figures are rising.

A wintry dawn over the Cairngorms, the home of Britain's only herd of reindeer

◁ The stunningly sited castle of Eilean Donan, Loch Duich in Glen Shiel

Exploring the Highlands and Islands

To the north and west of Stirling (the historic gateway to the Highlands) lie the magnificent mountains and glens, fretted coastlines and lonely isles that are the epitome of Scottish scenery. Inverness, the Highland capital, makes a good starting point for exploring Loch Ness and the Cairngorms, while Fort William holds the key to Ben Nevis. Inland from Aberdeen lie Royal Deeside and the Spey Valley whisky heartland. The romantic Hebrides can be reached by ferry from Oban or Ullapool.

0 kilometres 25

0 miles 25

Highland cattle grazing on the Isle of Skye

SEE ALSO

GETTING AROUND

There are no motorways in the region, though travel by car is made easy by a good system of A roads. Single-track roads predominate on the isles, which are served by a ferry network and a new bridge to Skye. The rail link ends to the west at Kyle of Lochalsh and to the north at Wick and Thurso. There are regular flights from London to Inverness, Aberdeen and Wick.

SHETLAND **1**

LERWICK

ORKNEY **2**

KIRKWALL

JOHN O' GROATS **3**

0 kilometres   50

0 miles   25

JOHN O'GROATS **3**

A836

WICK

A9

Thurso

Naver

Halladale

Helmsdale

A9

8 DORNOCH

A836

Moray Firth

STRATHPEFFER

10 BLACK ISLE A96 ELGIN **16**

14 FORT GEORGE

15 CAWDOR CASTLE

13 CULLODEN

12

INVERNESS

1 LOCH NESS

A95

A96

Spey

23

CAIRNGORMS

MOUNTAINS

Dee

A93

Don

17 ABERDEEN

18 ROYAL DEESIDE TOUR

A93

BLAIR CASTLE **22**

L. Rannoch

21 KILLIECRANKIE WALK

20 PITLOCHRY

South Esk

A9

19 DUNKELD

Loch Tay

A82

Dundee

Perth

Stirling

KEY

▬▬	Major road
▬▬	Scenic route
▬ ▬	Scenic path
▬▬	River
☆	Viewpoint

Colour-washed houses at the harbour of Tobermory, Mull

SIGHTS AT A GLANCE

Shetland ❶

Shetland. 🏃 23,000. ⊠ 🛳 from
Aberdeen and Stromness on mainland
Orkney. 🛈 Lerwick (01595 693434).
ⓦ www.visitshetland.com

LYING SIX DEGREES SOUTH of
the Arctic Circle, the rugged Shetland islands are
Britain's most northerly region
and were, with Orkney, part
of the kingdom of Norway
until 1469. In the main town
of Lerwick, this Norse heritage
is remembered during the
ancient midwinter festival Up
Helly Aa *(see p466)*, in which
costumed revellers set fire to
a replica Viking longship. Also
in the town, the **Shetland
Museum** tells the story of a
people dependent on the sea,
right up to modern times with
the discovery of North Sea oil
and gas in the 1970s.

One of Shetland's greatest
treasures is the Iron Age
tower, **Mousa Broch**, which
can be visited on its isle by
boat from Sandwick. There is
more ancient history at Jarlshof
where a museum explains the
sprawling sea-front ruins which
span 3,000 years.

A boat from Lerwick sails to
the isle of Noss where grey
seals bask beneath sandstone
cliffs crowded with Shetland's
seabirds – a spectacle best
seen between May and June.

🏛 Shetland Museum
The Hillhead, Lerwick. ▐ 01595
695057. ◯ 10am–5pm Wed–
Sat. ♿

Orkney ❷

Orkney. 🏃 19,800. ⊠ 🛳 from Gills
Bay, Caithness; John o'Groats (May–
Sep); Scrabster, Aberdeen. 🛈 Broad
St, Kirkwall (01856 872856).
ⓦ www.visitorkney.com

THE FERTILE ISLES of Orkney
are remarkable for the
wealth of prehistoric monuments which place them
among Europe's most trea-
sured archaeological sites. In the
town of Kirkwall, the sandstone **St Magnus Cathedral**
stands amid a charming core of
narrow streets. Its many interesting tombs include that of
its 12th-century patron saint.

THE SHETLAND SEABIRD ISLES

As seabirds spend most of their time away
from land, nesting is a vulnerable period in
their lives. The security provided by the
inaccessible cliffs at such sites as Noss and
Hermaness on Unst finds favour with thousands of migrant and local birds.

Puffin

Great Skua

Fulmar

Black Guillemot

Razorbills

Herring Gull

Nearby, the early 17th-century
Earl's Palace is widely held
to be one of Scotland's finest
Renaissance buildings. To the
west of Kirkwall lies Britain's
most impressive chambered
tomb, the cairn of **Maes Howe**.
Dating from 2000 BC, the
tomb has runic graffiti on its
walls believed to have been
left by Norsemen returning
from the crusades in 1150.

Nearby, the great **Standing
Stones of Stenness** may have
been associated with Maes
Howe rituals, though these still
remain a mystery. Further west,
on a bleak heath, stands the
Bronze Age **Ring of Brodgar**.

Another archaeological treasure can be found in the Bay
of Skail – the complete Stone
Age village of **Skara Brae**. It
was unearthed by a storm in
1850, after lying buried for
4,500 years. Further south, the

**The Norman façade of the
St Magnus Cathedral, Orkney**

---

town of Stromness was a vital
centre of Scotland's herring
industry in the 18th century. Its
story is told in the local museum, while the **Pier Arts
Centre** displays British and
international art.

🏛 Earl's Palace
Palace Rd, Kirkwall. ▐ 0131 668
8800. ◯ Apr–Sep: 9:30am–6:30pm
daily. 🎟 ♿ limited.
ⓦ www.historic-scotland.gov.uk
🏛 Pier Arts Centre
Victoria St, Stromness. ▐ 01856
850209. ◯ 10:30am–5pm Tue–Sat.

John o'Groats ❸

Highland. 🏃 500. ⊠ 🚌 🚉 Wick
🛳 John o'Groats to Burwick, Orkney
(May–Sep). 🛈 John o'Groats (01955
611373).

SOME 876 miles (1,409 km)
north from Land's End,
Britain's most northeasterly
mainland village faces Orkney,
8 miles (13 km) across the
turbulent Pentland Firth. The
village takes its name from a
15th-century Dutchman John
de Groot, who, to avoid accu-
sations of favouritism, is said
to have built an octagonal
house here with one door for
each of his eight heirs. The
spectacular cliffs and rock
stacks of Duncansby Head lie
a few miles further east.

Western Isles **4**

WESTERN SCOTLAND ENDS with this remote chain of islands, made of some of the oldest rock on Earth. Almost treeless landscapes are divided by countless waterways, the western, windward coasts edged by miles of white sandy beaches. For centuries, the eastern shores, composed largely of peat bogs, have provided the islanders with fuel. Man has been here for 6,000 years, living off the sea and the thin turf, though such monuments as an abandoned Norwegian whaling station on Harris attest to the difficulties in commercializing the islanders' traditional skills. Gaelic, part of an enduring culture, is widely spoken.

The Black House Museum, a traditional croft on Lewis

The monumental Standing Stones of Callanish in northern Lewis

Lewis and Harris

Western Isles. ☒ 22,000. ✈ Stornoway. ⛴ Uig (Skye), Ullapool, Kyle of Lochalsh. ⓘ Stornoway, Lewis (01851 703088); Tarbert, Harris (01859 502011). ⓦ www.visithebrides.com **Black House Museum** ⓘ 01851 710395. ◯ Mon–Sat. ⬛ ♿ ◧ ⬛

Forming the largest landmass of the Western Isles, Lewis and Harris are a single island, though Gaelic dialects differ between the two areas. From **Stornoway**, with its bustling harbour and colourful house fronts, the ancient **Standing Stones of Callanish** are only 16 miles (26 km) to the west. Just off the road on the way to Callanish are the ruins of **Carloway Broch**, a Pictish *(see p468)* tower over 2,000 years old. The more recent past can be explored at Arnol's **Black House Museum** – a showcase of crofting life as it was until only 50 years ago.

South of the rolling peat moors of Lewis, a range of mountains marks the border with Harris, which one enters as one passes Aline Lodge at the head of Loch Seaforth. Only a little less spectacular than the "Munros" (peaks over 914 m; 3,000 ft) of the mainland and the Isle of Skye

(see pp520–21), the mountains of Harris are a paradise for the hillwalker and, from their summits on a clear day, the distant Isle of St Kilda can be seen 50 miles (80 km) to the west.

The ferry port of Tarbert stands on a slim isthmus separating North and South Harris. The tourist office provides addresses for local weavers of the tough Harris Tweed. Some still use plants to make their dyes.

From the port of Leverburgh, close to the southern tip of Harris, a ferry can be taken to the isle of North Uist, where a causeway has been built to Berneray.

The Uists, Benbecula and Barra

Western Isles. ☒ 7,200. ✈ Barra, Benbecula. ⛴ Uig (Skye), Ullapool, Oban, Mallaig. ◧ ⟷ Oban, Mallaig, Kyle of Lochalsh. ⓘ Lochmaddy, North Uist (01876 500321); Lochboisdale, South Uist (01878 700286); Castlebay, Barra (01871 810336). ⓦ www.visithebrides.com

After the dramatic scenery of Harris, the lower-lying, largely waterlogged southern isles may seem an anticlimax, though they nurture secrets well worth discovering. Long, white, sandy beaches fringe the Atlantic coast, edged with one of Scotland's natural treasures: the lime-rich soil known as *machair*. During the summer months, the soil is covered with wild flowers.

From **Lochmaddy**, North Uist's main village, the A867 crosses 3 miles (5 km) of causeway to Benbecula, the isle from which Flora MacDonald smuggled Bonnie Prince Charlie *(see p521)* to Skye. Another causeway leads to South Uist, with its golden beaches renowned as a National Scenic Area. From Lochboisdale, a ferry sails to the tiny isle of Barra. The ferry docks in Castlebay, affording an unforgettable view of **Kisimul Castle**, the ancestral stronghold of the MacNeils of Barra.

The remote and sandy shores of South Uist

The western side of the Five Sisters of Kintail, seen from above Loch Duich

Skye **⑤**

See pp520–21.

The Five Sisters **⑥**

Skye & Lochalsh. ⇄ *Kyle of Lochalsh.* 🚌 *Glenshiel.* 🛈 *Bayfield Lane, Portree, Isle of Skye (01478 612137).* 🖳 *www.visithighlands.com*

DOMINATING one of Scotland's most haunting regions, the awesome summits of the Five Sisters of Kintail rear into view at the northern end of Loch Cluanie as the A87 enters Glen Shiel. The **Visitor Centre** at Morvich offers ranger-led excursions in the summer. Further west, the road passes **Eilean Donan Castle**, connected by a bridge. A Jacobite *(see p523)* stronghold, it was destroyed in 1719 by English warships. In the 19th century it was restored and now contains Jacobite relics.

♟ Eilean Donan Castle
Off A87, nr Dornie. **(** *01599 555202.* ☐ *Apr–Sep: 10am–5pm; Oct, Nov: 11am–4pm; daily.* 🖼

Wester Ross **⑦**

Ross & Cromarty. ⇄ *Achnasheen, Strathcarron.* 🛈 *Gairloch (01445 712130).*

LEAVING LOCH CARRON to the south, the A890 suddenly enters the northern Highlands and the great wilderness of Wester Ross. The Torridon

Estate includes some of the oldest mountains on Earth (Torridonian rock is over 600 million years old), and is home to red deer, wild cats and wild goats. Peregrine falcons and golden eagles nest in the towering sandstone mass of Liathach, above the village of Torridon with its breathtaking views over Applecross to Skye. The **Torridon Countryside Centre** provides guided walks in season and essential information on the natural history of the region.

To the north, the A832 cuts through the Beinn Eighe National Nature Reserve in which remnants of the ancient Caledonian pine forest still stand on the banks and isles of Loch Maree.

Along the coast, exotic gardens thrive in the warming currents of the Gulf Stream, most impressive being **Inverewe Garden** created in 1862 by Osgood Mackenzie (1842–1922). May and June are the months to see the display of

Typical Torridonian mountian scenery in the Wester Ross

rhododendrons and azaleas; July and August for the herbaceous borders.

🏛 Torridon Countryside Centre
(NTS) Torridon. **(** *01445 791221.* ☐ *May–Sep: 10am–6pm Mon–Sat, 2–5pm Sun.* 🖼 🚻 🖳 *www.nts.org.uk*

♣ Inverewe Garden
(NTS) off A832, nr Poolewe. **(** *01445 781200.* ☐ *mid-Mar–Oct: 9:30am–dusk daily.* 🖼 🚻

Dornoch **⑧**

Sutherland. 🏘 *2,200.* ⇄ *Golspie, Tain.* 🛈 *The Square, Dornoch (01862 810916).* 🖳 *www.visitdornoch.com*

WITH ITS FIRST-CLASS golf course and extensive sandy beaches, **Dornoch** is a popular holiday resort, though it has retained a peaceful atmosphere. Now the parish church, the medieval cathedral was all but destroyed in a clan dispute in 1570; it was finally restored in the 1920s for its 700th anniversary. A stone at the beach end of River Street marks the place where Janet Horne, the last woman to be tried in Scotland for witchcraft, was executed in 1722.

ENVIRONS: Twelve miles (19 km) northeast of Dornoch is the stately Victorianized pile of **Dunrobin Castle**, magnificently situated in a great park with formal gardens overlooking the sea. Since the 13th century, this has been the seat of the Earls of Sutherland.

Many of its rooms are open to visitors. A steam-powered fire engine is among the miscellany of objects on display.

South of Dornoch stands the town of **Tain**. Though patronized by medieval kings as a place of pilgrimage, it became an administrative centre of the Highland Clearances. All is explained in the heritage centre, **Tain Through Time**.

♣ **Dunrobin Castle**
Nr Golspie. (*01408 633177.*
◯ *Apr–mid-Oct: 10:30am–4:30pm Mon–Sat, noon–4:30pm Sun.* 🏛
🅦 *www.highlandescape.com*
🏛 **Tain Through Time**
Tower St. (*01862 894089.* ◯ *Apr–Oct: 10am–6pm Mon–Sat; Nov–Mar: by arrangement.* 🏛 🅖 🏛

The serene cathedral precinct in the town of Dornoch

Strathpeffer ❾

Ross & Cromarty. 🏠 *1,400.*
🚌 *Dingwall, Inverness.* 🚏 *Inverness.*
ℹ *North Kessock (01463 731505; Easter–Oct).*

STANDING 5 miles (8 km) from the Falls of Rogie and to the east of the Northwest Highlands, the popular town of Strathpeffer still has the refined charm for which it was well known in Victorian times, when it flourished as a spa and health resort. The grand hotels and gracious layout of Strathpeffer recall the days when royalty from all over Europe used to flock to the chalybeate- and sulphur-laden springs, which were believed to help in the cure of tuberculosis.

The shores of the Black Isle in the Moray Firth

The Black Isle ❿

Ross & Cromarty. 🚌 🚏 *Inverness.*
ℹ *North Kessock (01463 731505; Easter–Oct).*

THOUGH THE DRILLING platforms in the Cromarty Firth are reminders of how oil has changed the local economy, the peninsula of the Black Isle is still largely composed of farmland and fishing villages. The town of **Cromarty** was an important port in the 18th century, with thriving rope and lace industries. Many of its merchant houses still stand; the museum in the **Cromarty Courthouse** provides heritage tours of the town. **In the Steps of Hugh Miller** is a museum to the theologian and geologist Hugh Miller (1802–56), who was born in the cottage; adjacent is the newly opened Miller House, which has exhibitions on three floors. **Fortrose** boasts a ruined 14th-century cathedral, while a stone on Chanonry Point commemorates the Brahan Seer, a 17th-century prophet burnt alive in a tar barrel by the Countess of Seaforth after he foresaw her husband's infidelity. For local archaeology, visit **Groam House Museum** in Rosemarkie.

🏛 **Cromarty Courthouse**
Church St, Cromarty. (*01381 600 418.* ◯ *Apr–Oct: 10am–5pm daily.* 🏛
🏛 **In the Steps of Hugh Miller**
(NTS) Church St, Cromarty. (*01381 600245.* ◯ *Apr–Oct: noon–5pm daily.* 🏛 🅖 *limited.*
🏛 **Groam House Museum**
High St, Rosemarkie. (*01381 620 961.* ◯ *May–Sep: 10am–5pm daily (Sun pm); Oct–Apr: Sat & Sun (pm).*

THE HIGHLAND CLEARANCES

During the heyday of the clan system *(see p470),* tenants paid their clan chiefs rent for their land in the form of military service. However, with the decline of the clan system after the Battle of Culloden *(see p523)* and the coming of sheep from the borders, landowners were able to command a financial rent their tenants were unable to afford and the land was bought up by Lowland and English farmers. In what became known as "the year of the sheep" (1792), thousands of tenants were evicted to make way for sheep. Many emigrated to Australia, America and Canada. Ruins of their crofts can still be seen in Sutherland and Wester Ross.

The Last of the Clan (1865) by Thomas Faed

Isle of Skye ☷

Otter by the coast at Kylerhea

THE LARGEST of the Inner Hebrides, Skye can be reached by the bridge linking Kyle of Lochalsh and Kyleakin. A turbulent geological history has given the island some of Britain's most varied and dramatic scenery. From the rugged volcanic plateau of northern Skye to the ice-sculpted peaks of the Cuillins, the island is divided by numerous sea lochs, leaving the traveller never more than 8 km (5 miles) from the sea. Limestone grasslands predominate in the south, where the hillsides, home of sheep and cattle, are scattered with the ruins of crofts abandoned during the Clearances *(see p517)*. Historically, Skye is best known for its association with Bonnie Prince Charlie.

Skeabost has the ruins of a chapel which is associated with St Columba. Medieval tombstones can be found in the graveyard.

Grave of Flora MacDonald

Kilm

WESTERN ISLES

Uic

LOCH SNIZORT

• Lusta

B886

•Milovaig

A850

B884

Dunvegan

Ske

A863

Dunvegan Castle

For over seven centuries, Dunvegan Castle has been the seat of the chiefs of the Clan MacLeod. It contains the Fairy Flag, a fabled piece of magical silk treasured for its protection.

0 kilometres   10

0 miles   5

Portnalong

B8009

Talisker   Carbost

The Talisker Distillery produces one of the best Highland malts, often described as "the lava of the Cuillins".

C
S
AL
S
(3.

Cuillins

Britain's finest mountain range is within walking distance of Sligachan, and in summer a boat sails from Elgol to the desolate inner sanctuary of Loch Coruisk. As he fled across the surrounding moorland, Bonnie Prince Charlie is said to have claimed: "even the Devil shall not follow me here!"

KEY

ⓘ	Tourist information
▰▰▰	Major road
▭▭▭	Minor road
══	Narrow lane
☆	Viewpoint

◁ **Dawn over the desolate tablelands of northern Skye, viewed from the Quiraing**

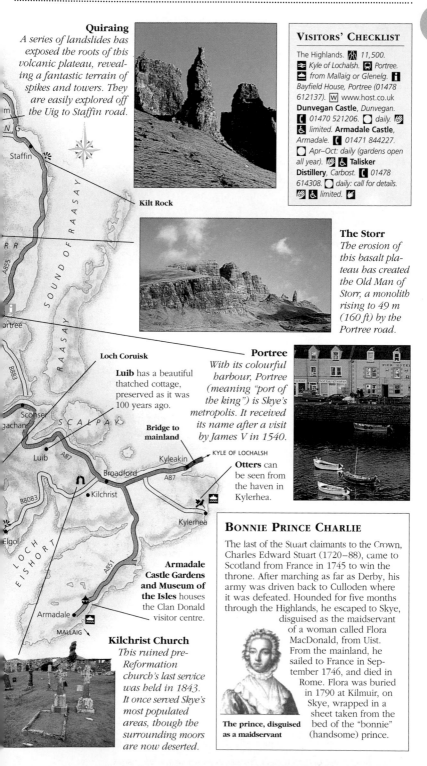

Quiraing

A series of landslides has exposed the roots of this volcanic plateau, revealing a fantastic terrain of spikes and towers. They are easily explored off the Uig to Staffin road.

Kilt Rock

The Storr

The erosion of this basalt plateau has created the Old Man of Storr, a monolith rising to 49 m (160 ft) by the Portree road.

Loch Coruisk

Luib has a beautiful thatched cottage, preserved as it was 100 years ago.

Bridge to mainland

Portree

With its colourful harbour, Portree (meaning "port of the king") is Skye's metropolis. It received its name after a visit by James V in 1540.

KYLE OF LOCHALSH

Otters can be seen from the haven in Kylerhea.

Armadale Castle Gardens and Museum of the Isles houses the Clan Donald visitor centre.

Kilchrist Church

This ruined pre-Reformation church's last service was held in 1843. It once served Skye's most populated areas, though the surrounding moors are now deserted.

BONNIE PRINCE CHARLIE

The last of the Stuart claimants to the Crown, Charles Edward Stuart (1720–88), came to Scotland from France in 1745 to win the throne. After marching as far as Derby, his army was driven back to Culloden where it was defeated. Hounded for five months through the Highlands, he escaped to Skye, disguised as the maidservant of a woman called Flora MacDonald, from Uist. From the mainland, he sailed to France in September 1746, and died in Rome. Flora was buried in 1790 at Kilmuir, on Skye, wrapped in a sheet taken from the bed of the "bonnie" (handsome) prince.

The prince, disguised as a maidservant

The ruins of Urquhart Castle on the western shore of Loch Ness

Loch Ness ⑪

Inverness. 🚋 🚌 *Inverness.* ℹ️ *Castle Wynd, Inverness (01463 234353).* 🌐 www.loch-ness-scotland.com

AT 24 MILES (39 km) long, one mile (1.5 km) at its widest and up to 305 m (1,000 ft) deep, **Loch Ness** fills the northern half of the Great Glen fault from Fort William to Inverness. It is joined to lochs Oich and Lochy by the 22 mile (35 km) Caledonian

THE LOCH NESS MONSTER

First sighted by St Columba in the 6th century, "Nessie" has attracted increasing attention since ambiguous photographs were taken in the 1930s. Though serious investigation is often undermined by hoaxers, sonar techniques continue to yield enigmatic results: plesiosaurs, giant eels and too much whisky are the most popular explanations. Nessie appears to have a close relative in the waters of Loch Morar (*see p532*).

Canal, designed by Thomas Telford (*see p433*). On the western shore, the A82 passes the ruins of the 16th-century **Urquhart Castle**, which was blown up by government supporters in 1692 to prevent it falling into Jacobite hands. A short distance to the west, **Loch Ness 2000 Exhibition Centre** provides a wealth of audio-visual information.

⚓ Urquhart Castle
Nr Drumnadrochit. 📞 *01456 450551.* ⏰ *Easter–Sep: 9:30am–6:30pm; Oct–Easter: 9:30am–4:30pm; daily.* 📷 🚻 🅿️

🏛 Loch Ness 2000 Exhibition Centre
Drumnadrochit. 📞 *01456 450573.* ⏰ *Apr–May, Sep: 9:30am–6:30pm daily; Jul & Aug: 9am–8pm daily; Oct–Mar: 9:30am–4:30pm daily.* 📷 ♿ 🖥 🅿️

Inverness ⑫

Highland. 🏛 *60,000.* 🚋 🚌 ℹ️ *Castle Wynd (01463 234353).* 🌐 www.highlandfreedom.com

AS THE HIGHLAND capital, Inverness makes an ideal base from which to explore the surrounding countryside. The Victorian castle dominates the town centre, the oldest buildings of which are found in nearby Church Street. Today

Kilt maker with royal Stuart tartan

the castle is used as law courts. The **Inverness Museum and Art Gallery** provides a good introduction to the history of the Highlands with exhibits including a lock of Bonnie Prince Charlie's (*see p521*) hair and a fine collection of Inverness silver. The **Scottish Kiltmaker Visitor Centre** explores the history and tradition of Scottish kilts as well as workshops, while those in search of tartans and knitwear should visit the **James Pringle Weavers of Inverness**. **Jacobite Cruises** runs regular summer cruises along the Caledonian Canal and on to Loch Ness. The unfolding scenery makes this a most pleasant and tranquil way to spend a sunny afternoon.

🏛 Museum and Art Gallery
Castle Wynd. 📞 *01463 237114.* ⏰ *9am–5pm Mon–Sat.* ♿ 🌐 www.invernessmuseum.com

🏠 James Pringle Weavers of Inverness
Holm Woollen Mill, Dores Rd. 📞 *01463 223311.* ⏰ *9am–5pm Mon–Sat, 11am–5pm Sun.* ♿

🏛 Scottish Kiltmaker Visitor Centre
Huntly St. 📞 *01463 222781.* ⏰ *9am–5pm daily.* ⏰ *25 Dec, 1 Jan.* 📷

Jacobite Cruises
Glenurquhart Road. 📞 *01463 233999.* ⏰ *Easter–Oct: daily; Nov–Mar: limited.* 📷 ♿ 🌐 www.jacobite.co.uk

Culloden ⓭

(NTS) Inverness. 🚆 🚌 *Inverness.*
ⓦ www.nts.org.uk

A DESOLATE STRETCH of moorland, Culloden looks much as it did on 16 April 1746, the date of the last battle to be fought on British soil *(see p469)*. Here the Jacobite cause, with Bonnie Prince Charlie's *(see p521)* leadership, finally perished under the onslaught of Hanoverian troops led by the Duke of Cumberland. All is explained in the excellent **NTS Visitor Centre**.

ENVIRONS: Signposted for a mile (1.5 km) or so east are the outstanding Neolithic burial sites, the **Clava Cairns**.

🛈 **NTS Visitor Centre**
On the B9006 east of Inverness.
📞 *01463 790607.* ⏰ *Apr–Oct: 9am–6pm; Nov–Mar: 10am–4pm daily.* ⚫ *Jan.* ♿ ⚫

Fort George ⓮

Inverness. 📞 *01667 462777.*
🚆 🚌 *Inverness, Nairn.* ⏰ *9:30am–6:30pm Mon–Sat, 2–5pm Sun.*
⚫ *25, 26 Dec.* ♿ ⚫ ⚫
ⓦ www.historicscotland.co.uk

O NE OF THE FINEST works of European military architecture, Fort George stands on a windswept promontory jutting into the Moray Firth, ideally located to suppress the Highlanders. Completed in 1769, the fort was built after the Jacobite risings to discourage further rebellion in the Highlands and has remained a military garrison

THE JACOBITE MOVEMENT

The first Jacobites (mainly Catholic Highlanders) were the supporters of James II of England (James VII of Scotland) who was deposed by the "Glorious Revolution" of 1688 *(see p53)*. With the Protestant William of Orange on the throne, the Jacobites' desire to restore the Stuart monarchy led to the uprisings of 1715 and 1745. The first, in support of James VIII, the "Old Pretender", ended at the Battle of

James II, by Samuel Cooper (1609–72)

Sheriffmuir (1715). The failure of the second uprising, with the defeat at Culloden, saw the end of Jacobite hopes and led to the end of the clan system and the suppression of Highland culture for over a century *(see p471)*.

The drawbridge on the eastern side of Cawdor Castle

ever since. The Fort houses the **Regimental Museum** of the Queen's Own Highlanders, and some of its barrack rooms reconstruct the conditions of the common soldiers stationed here more than 200 years ago. The **Grand Magazine** contains an outstanding collection of arms and military equipment. The battlements also make an excellent place from which to watch dolphins in the Moray Firth.

A contemporary picture, *The Battle of Culloden* (1746), by D Campbell

Cawdor Castle ⓯

On B9090 (off A96). 📞 *01667 404615.* 🚆 *Nairn, then bus.* 🚌 *from Inverness.* ⏰ *May–mid-Oct: 10am–5pm daily.* ♿ gardens & ground floor only. 🍴
ⓦ www.cawdorcastle.com

W ITH ITS TURRETED central tower, moat and drawbridge, Cawdor Castle is one of the most romantic stately homes in the Highlands. Though the castle is famed for being the 11th-century home of Shakespeare's *(see p310)* Macbeth and the scene of his murder of King Duncan, it is not historically proven that either came here.

An ancient holly tree preserved in the vaults is said to be the one under which, in 1372, Thane William's donkey, laden with gold, stopped for a rest during its master's search for a place to build a fortress. According to legend, this was how the site for the castle was chosen. Now, after 600 years of continuous occupation (it is still the home of the Thanes of Cawdor) the house is a treasury of family history, containing a number of rare tapestries and portraits by the 18th-century painters Joshua Reynolds (1723–92) and George Romney (1734–1802). Furniture in the Pink Bedroom and Woodcock Room includes work by Chippendale and Sheraton. In the Old Kitchen, the huge Victorian cooking range stands as a shrine to below-stairs drudgery. The grounds provide nature trails and a nine-hole golf course.

Elgin 🔟

Moray. 🏛 25,000. 🚉 🏢
🛈 17 High St, Moray (01343 542666).

WITH ITS COBBLED market-place and crooked lanes, the popular holiday centre of Elgin still retains much of its medieval layout. The 13th-century **cathedral** ruins next to King Street are all that remain of one of Scotland's architectural triumphs, the design of its tiered windows reminiscent of the cathedral at St Andrews (see p485). Once known as the Lantern of the North, the cathedral was severely damaged in 1390 by the Wolf of Badenoch (the son of Robert II) in revenge for his excommunication by the Bishop of Moray. Even worse damage came in 1576 when the Regent Moray ordered the stripping of its lead roofing. Among its outstanding remains is a Pictish cross-slab in the nave, and a basin in a

Details of the central tower of Elgin Cathedral

corner where one of Elgin's benefactors, Andrew Anderson, was kept as a baby by his homeless mother. As well as local history, the **Elgin Museum** has anthropological, geological displays, while the **Moray Motor Museum** has over 40 vehicles.

🏛 **Elgin Museum**
1 High St. 📞 01343 543675. 🕐 Apr–Oct: 10am–5pm daily (Sun: pm). Phone to check times. 🛈 🅿 🅱 limited.
🏛 **Moray Motor Museum**
Bridge St, Bishopmill. 📞 01343 544933. 🕐 Easter–Oct: 11am–5pm daily. 🅿 🅱

Aberdeen 🔟

S COTLAND'S THIRD LARGEST CITY and Europe's offshore oil capital, Aberdeen has prospered since the discovery of petroleum in the North Sea in 1970. The sea bed has now yielded 50 oilfields. Widely known as the Granite City, its rugged outlines are softened by sumptuous year-round floral displays in its public parks and gardens, the Duthie Park Winter Gardens being the largest indoor garden in Europe. The picturesque village of Footdee, which sits at the end of the city's 2 mile (3 km) beach, has good views back to the busy harbour.

The spires of Aberdeen, rising behind the city harbour

Exploring Aberdeen
The city centre flanks the mile-long (1.5 km) Union Street ending to the east at the Mercat Cross. The cross stands in Castlegate, the one-time site of the city castle. From here the cobbled Shiprow winds southwest and passes Provost Ross's House (see p526) on its way to the harbour with its fish market. A bus can be taken a mile (1.5 km) north of the centre to Old Aberdeen which, with its medieval streets and wynds, has the peaceful character of a separate village. Driving is restricted in some streets.

🏛 **King's College**
College Bounds, Old Aberdeen. 📞 01224 272000. **Chapel** 🕐 Opening times vary – phone to check. 🅱
Kings College was founded in 1495 as the city's first university. The inter-denominational chapel (the only part of the college open to the public), in the past consecutively Catholic and Protestant, has a lantern tower rebuilt after a storm in 1633. Stained-glass windows by Douglas Strachan add a contemporary touch to the interior which contains a 1540 pulpit, later carved with heads of Stuart monarchs.

🔒 **St Andrew's Cathedral**
King St. 📞 01224 640290. 🕐 May–Sep: 11am–4pm Tue–Fri. 🅱 🅿 by appointment.
The Mother Church of the Episcopal Communion in America, St Andrew's has a memorial to Samuel Seabury, the first Episcopalian bishop in the United States, who was consecrated in Aberdeen in 1784. Coats of arms adorn the ceiling above the north and south aisles, contrasting colourfully with the white walls and pillars. They represent the American States and local Jacobite (see p523) families.

The elegant lantern tower of the chapel at King's College

PROVOST SKENE'S HOUSE

Guestrow. ☎ 01224 641086. ◷ 10am–5pm Mon–Sat, 1–4pm Sun.
● 25, 26, 31 Dec–2 Jan. �W www.aagm.co.uk

Once the home of Sir George Skene, a 17th-century provost (mayor) of Aberdeen, the house was built in 1545. Inside, period rooms span 200 years of design. The Duke of Cumberland stayed here before the Battle of Culloden *(see p523)*.

(see p523)

VISITORS' CHECKLIST

City of Aberdeen. 🏠 212,000.
✈ ⊯ 🚌 Guild St. ℹ Union
St (01224 288828).
W www.aberdeen-grampian.com

The 18th-century Parlour, with its walnut harpsichord and covered chairs by the fire, was the informal room in which the family would have tea.

The Regency Room typifies early 19th-century elegance. A harp dating from 1820 stands by a Grecian-style sofa and a French writing table.

The Painted Gallery has one of Scotland's most important cycles of religious art. The panels are early 17th century, though the artist is unknown.

The 17th-century Great Hall contains heavy oak dining furniture. Provost Skene's wood-carved coat of arms hangs above the fireplace.

The Georgian Dining Room, with its Classical design, was the main formal room in the 16th century and still has its original flagstone floor.

Entrance

ABERDEEN CITY CENTRE

Aberdeen Art Gallery ①
St Andrew's Cathedral ⑤
Marischal College ④
Maritime Museum ⑦
Mercat Cross ⑥
Provost Skene's
House ③
St Nicholas
Kirk ②

KEY

🚌 Long-distance bus station
⊯ Railway station
⚓ Ferry service
P Parking
ℹ Tourist information
✝ Church

0 metres 200
0 yards 200

🏛 Art Gallery

Schoolhill. [01224 523700. ◯ 10am–5pm Mon–Sat, 2–5pm Sun. ● 25 Dec–2 Jan. 🅰 🆆 www.aagm.co.uk

Housed in a Neo-Classical building, purpose-built in 1884, the Art Gallery has a wide range of exhibitions, with an emphasis on contemporary work. A fine collection of Aberdonian silver can be found among the decorative arts on the ground floor, and is the subject of a video presentation. A permanent collection of 18th–20th-century fine art features such names as Toulouse-Lautrec, Reynolds and Zoffany. Several of the works were bequeathed in 1900 by a local granite merchant, Alex Macdonald. He commissioned many of the paintings in the Macdonald

Aberdonian silver in the Art Gallery

Room, which displays 92 self-portraits by British artists. Occasional poetry-readings, music recitals and films are on offer.

🛉 St Nicholas Kirk

Union St. [01224 643494. ◯ May–Sep: 10am–4pm daily; Oct–Apr: Mon–Fri (am). 🅰

Founded in the 12th century, St Nicholas is Scotland's largest parish church. Though the present structure dates from 1752, many relics of earlier times can be seen inside.

After being damaged during the Reformation, the interior was divided into two. A chapel in the East Church contains iron rings used to secure witches in the 17th century, while in the West Church there are some embroidered panels attributed to one Mary Jameson (1597–1644).

🏛 Maritime Museum

Shiprow. [01224 337700. ◯ 10am–5pm Mon–Sat, noon–3pm Sun. 🅰 🖵 🖻

Overlooking the harbour is Provost Ross's House, which dates back to 1593 and is one of the oldest residential buildings in the town. This museum traces the history of Aberdeen's seafaring tradition. Exhibitions include ship-wrecks, rescues, shipbuilding and the oil installations off Scotland's east coast.

🛉 St Machar's Cathedral

The Chanonry. [01224 485988. ◯ 9am–5pm daily. 🅰

Dominating Old Aberdeen, the 15th-century edifice of St Machar's is the oldest granite building in the city. The stonework of one arch even dates as far back as the 14th century. The impressive nave now serves as a parish church and its magnificent oak ceiling is adorned with the coats of arms of 48 popes, emperors and princes of Christendom.

Royal Deeside Tour ⓲

Since Queen Victoria's purchase of the Balmoral estate in 1852, Deeside has been best known as the summer home of the British Royal Family, though it has been associated with royalty since the time of Robert the Bruce *(see p468)*. The route follows the Dee, formerly a prolific salmon river, through some magnificent Grampian scenery.

Muir of Dinnet Nature Reserve ④

An information centre on the A97 provides an excellent place from which to explore this beautiful mixed woodland area, formed by the retreating glaciers of the last Ice Age.

Balmoral ⑥

Bought by Queen Victoria for 30,000 guineas in 1852, after its owner choked to death on a fishbone, the castle was rebuilt in the Scottish Baronial style at Prince Albert's request.

Ballater ⑤

The old railway town of Ballater has royal warrants on many of its shop fronts. It grew as a 19th-century spa town, its waters reputedly providing a cure for tuberculosis.

Dunkeld ⑲

Perth & Kinross. 🏠 *2,500.* 🚆 *Birnam.*
🚌 ℹ️ *The Cross (01350 727688).*
🌐 *www.perthshire.co.uk*

Sɪᴛᴜᴀᴛᴇᴅ ʙʏ the River Tay,
this ancient and charming
village was all but destroyed
in the Battle of Dunkeld, a
Jacobite *(see p523)* defeat, in
1689. The **Little Houses**
lining Cathedral Street were
the first to be rebuilt, and are
fine examples of imaginative
restoration. The ruins of the
14th-century **cathedral** enjoy
an idyllic setting on shady
lawns beside the Tay, against
a backdrop of steep and
wooded hills. The choir is used
as the parish church and its
north wall contains a Leper's
Squint: a hole through which
lepers could see the altar
during mass. It was while on
holiday in the Dunkeld countryside that Beatrix Potter *(see
p355)* found the location for
her Peter Rabbit stories.

The ruins of Dunkeld Cathedral

Pitlochry ⑳

Perth & Kinross. 🏠 *2,500.* 🚆 🚌
ℹ️ *22 Atholl Rd (01796 472215).*
🌐 *www.pitlochry.org.uk*

Sᴜʀʀᴏᴜɴᴅᴇᴅ ʙʏ the pine-
forested hills, Pitlochry
became famous after Queen
Victoria *(see p56)* described it
as one of the finest resorts in
Europe. In early summer,
salmon swim up the ladder
built into the Power Station
Dam, on their way to spawning
grounds upriver. The **Power
Station Visitor Centre** outlines the hydro-electric scheme
which harnesses the waters
of the River Tummel. The
home of Bell's whisky, the
Blair Athol Distillery, gives
an insight into whisky making
(see p475) and is open for
tours. The **Festival Theatre**,
one of Scotland's most famous,
puts on a summer season when
the programme changes daily.

ℹ️ **Power Station Visitor
Centre**
Pitlochry. 📞 *01796 473152.*
🕐 *late Mar–Oct: 10am–5:30pm
Mon–Fri (Jul & Aug: daily).* 💳 ☑️
🎭 **Festival Theatre**
Port-na-Craig. 📞 *01796 472680.*
🕐 *May–Oct: daily.* 💳 ♿ ☑️
🏭 **Blair Athol Distillery**
Perth Rd. 📞 *01796 482003.* 🕐 *Apr–
Sep: Mon–Sat (& Sun pm Jun–Sep); Oct:
Mon–Fri; Nov–Mar: Mon–Fri pm.* ●
22 Dec–3 Jan. 🎫 💳 ♿ *limited.* ☑️

TIPS FOR DRIVERS

Length: 69 miles (111 km).
*Stopping-off points: Crathes
Castle café (May–Sep: daily);
Station Restaurant, Ballater (food
served all day). (See also pp636–7).*

Drum Castle ①
This impressive 13th-century keep
was granted by Robert the Bruce to
his standard bearer in 1323, in
gratitude for his services.

PETERHEAD
A96
ABERDEEN
A93
A956
Peterculter
A980
Dee
A93
Crathes
B9077
STONEHAVEN
A90
B974

Banchory ③
Local lavender is a popular
attraction here. From the 18th-
century Brig o' Feugh, salmon
can be seen.

**Crathes Castle
and Gardens** ②
This is the family home of
the Burnetts, who were
made Royal Foresters of
Drum by Robert the Bruce.
Along with the title, he
gave Alexander Burnett
the ivory Horn of Leys
which is still on display.

0 kilometres   5
0 miles   4

KEY

━━━ Tour route
═══ Other roads
🔆 Viewpoint

Killiecrankie Walk ㉑

I N AN AREA famous for its scenery and historical connections, this circular walk offers typical Highland views. The route is fairly flat, though ringed by mountains, and follows the River Garry south to Loch Faskally, meandering through a wooded gorge, passing the Soldier's Leap and a Victorian viaduct. There are several ideal picnic spots along the way. Returning along the River Tummel, the walk crosses one of Queen Victoria's favourite Highland areas, before doubling back along the rivers to complete the circuit.

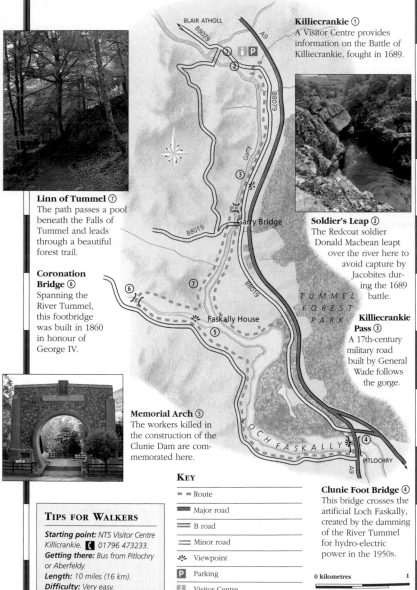

BLAIR ATHOLL

Killiecrankie ①
A Visitor Centre provides information on the Battle of Killiecrankie, fought in 1689.

Linn of Tummel ⑦
The path passes a pool beneath the Falls of Tummel and leads through a beautiful forest trail.

Coronation Bridge ⑥
Spanning the River Tummel, this footbridge was built in 1860 in honour of George IV.

Garry Bridge

Soldier's Leap ②
The Redcoat soldier Donald Macbean leapt over the river here to avoid capture by Jacobites during the 1689 battle.

Faskally House

TUMMEL FOREST PARK

Killiecrankie Pass ③
A 17th-century military road built by General Wade follows the gorge.

Memorial Arch ⑤
The workers killed in the construction of the Clunie Dam are commemorated here.

LOCH FASKALLY

PITLOCHRY

Clunie Foot Bridge ④
This bridge crosses the artificial Loch Faskally, created by the damming of the River Tummel for hydro-electric power in the 1950s.

KEY

- ▪▪ Route
- ▬ Major road
- ═ B road
- ═ Minor road
- ✷ Viewpoint
- 🅿 Parking
- ℹ Visitor Centre

0 kilometres   1

0 miles   0.5

TIPS FOR WALKERS

Starting point: *NTS Visitor Centre Killiecrankie.* 📞 *01796 473233.*
Getting there: *Bus from Pitlochry or Aberfeldy.*
Length: *10 miles (16 km).*
Difficulty: *Very easy.*

The Three Sisters, Glencoe, in late autumn

Blair Castle ㉒

Blair Atholl, Perthshire. ☎ 01796 481207. ☲ Blair Atholl. ○ Apr–Oct: 10am–6pm daily; Nov–Mar: 9:30am–12.30pm Tue. ⌨ ♿ limited. ⟦W⟧ www.blair-castle.co.uk

THIS RAMBLING, turreted castle has been altered so often in its 700-year history that it provides a unique insight into the history of Highland aristocratic life. The 18th-century wing, with its draughty Victorian passages hung with antlers, has a display containing the gloves and pipe of Bonnie Prince Charlie (see p521) who spent two days here gathering Jacobite (see p523) support. Family portraits cover 300 years and include paintings by such masters as Johann Zoffany and Sir Peter Lely. Sir Edwin Landseer's *Death of a Stag in Glen Tilt* (1850) was painted nearby. In 1844 Queen Victoria visited the castle and conferred on its owners, the Dukes of Atholl, the distinction of being allowed to maintain a private army. The Atholl Highlanders still flourish.

THE MASSACRE OF GLENCOE

In 1692, the chief of the Glencoe MacDonalds was five days late in registering an oath of submission to William III, giving the government an excuse to root out a nest of Jacobite (p523) supporters. For ten days 130 soldiers, captained by Robert Campbell, were hospitably entertained by the unsuspecting MacDonalds. At dawn on 13 February, in a terrible breach of trust, the soldiers fell on their hosts, killing some 38 MacDonalds. Many more died in their wintry mountain hideouts. The massacre, unsurprisingly, became a political scandal, though there were to be no official reprimands for three years.

Detail of The Massacre of Glencoe by James Hamilton

The Cairngorms ㉓

See pp530–31.

Glencoe ㉔

Highland. ☲ Fort William. ▣ Glencoe. ⓘ Cameron Sq, Fort William (01397 703781).

RENOWNED for its awesome scenery and savage history, Glencoe was compared by Dickens to "a burial ground of a race of giants". The precipitous cliffs of Buachaille Etive Mor and the knife-edged ridge of Aonach Eagach (both over 900 m; 3,000 ft) present a formidable challenge even to experienced mountaineers.

Against a dark backdrop of craggy peaks and the tumbling River Coe, the Glen offers superb hill-walking in the summer. Stout footwear, waterproofs and attention to safety warnings are essential. Details of routes, ranging from the easy half-hour between the **NTS Visitor Centre** and Signal Rock (from which the signal was given to commence the massacre) to a stiff 6 mile (10 km) haul up the Devil's Staircase can be had from the Visitor Centre. Guided walks are offered in summer by the NTS Ranger service.

ⓘ **NTS Visitor Centre**
Ballachulish. ☎ 01855 811307. ○ Mar–Oct: 10am–5pm daily. ⌨ ♿

The Cairngorms ㉒

Rising to a height of 1,309 m (4,296 ft), the Cairngorm mountains form the highest landmass in Britain. Cairn Gorm itself is the site of one of Britain's first ski centres. A weather station at the mountain's summit provides regular reports, essential in an area known for sudden changes of weather. Walkers should be sure to follow the mountain code without fail. The funicular railway that climbs Cairn Gorm affords superb views over the Spey Valley. Many estates in the valley have centres which introduce the visitor to Highland land use.

Wild goat

Strathspey Steam Railway
This track between Aviemore and Broomhill dates from 1863.

Aviemore, the commercial centre of the Cairngorms, provides buses to the ski area 13 km (9 miles) away.

Kincraig Highland Wildlife Park
Driving through this park, the visitor can see bison alongside wolves and wild boar. All of these animals were once common in the Highlands.

INVERNESS
Carrbridge
Boat of Garten
Aviemore
Coylum
LOCH AN EILEIN
Kincraig
LOCH INSH
Kingussie
NEWTONMORE
Tolvah
PERTH
Feshie
BRAERIACH
1,295 m (4,248 ft)
LOCH EINICH

0 kilometres   5
0 miles   5

The Cairngorms by Aviemore

Rothiemurchus Estate
Highland cattle can be seen among many other creatures at Rothiemurchus. A visitor centre provides guided walks and illustrates life on a Highland estate.

Loch Garten Nature Reserve

Ospreys now thrive in this reserve in Abernethy Forest, which was established in 1959 to protect the first pair seen in Britain for 50 years.

GRANTOWN-ON-SPEY

Broomhill

A 95

B970

Nethy Bridge

E N

The **Cairngorm Reindeer Centre** provides walks in the hills among Britain's only herd of reindeer.

Skiing

From the Coire Cas car park, a funicular railway can be taken to the restaurant at the summit. There are 28 ski runs in all.

Nethy

C H

P

CAIRN GORM
▲
1,245 m
(4,084 ft)

BEN MACDHUI
▲
1,309 m
(4,296 ft)

CAIRNGORM

MOUNTAINS

Ben MacDhui is Britain's second highest peak, after Ben Nevis.

KEY

🛈	Tourist information
▬	Major road
▭	Minor road
▭	Narrow lane
- -	Footpath
⚞	Viewpoint

FLORA OF THE CAIRNGORMS

With mixed woodland at their base and the summits forming a sub-polar platcau, the Cairngorms present a huge variety of flora. Ancient Caledonian pines (once common in the area) survive in Abernethy Forest, while arctic flowers flourish in the heights.

The Cairngorm plateau holds little life except lichen (Britain's oldest plant), wood rush and cushions of moss campion, which is often completely covered with pink flowers.

Shady corries are important areas for alpine plants such as arctic mouse-ear, hare's foot sedge, mountain rock-cress and alpine speedwell.

Pinewoods occupy the higher slopes, revealing purple heather as they become sparser.

Mixed woodland covers the lower ground which is carpeted with heather and deergrass.

1,200 m (3,950 ft)

1,000 m (3,300 ft)

800 m (2,650 ft)

600 m (2,000 ft)

400 m (1,300 ft)

200 m (650 ft)

0 m (0 ft)

An idealized section of the Cairngorm plateau

Road to the Isles Tour ㉕

THIS SCENIC ROUTE goes past vast mountain-corridors, breathtaking beaches of white sand and tiny villages, to the town of Mallaig, one of the ferry ports for the isles of Skye, Rum and Eigg. As well as the stunning scenery, the area is steeped in Jacobite history *(see p523)*.

TIPS FOR DRIVERS

Tour length: 45 miles (72 km).
Stopping-off points: Glenfinnan NTS Visitors' Centre (01397 722 250) explains the Jacobite risings and serves refreshments; the Old Library Lodge, Arisaig, has good Scottish food. (See also pp636–7.)

Mallaig ⑦
The Road to the Isles ends at Mallaig, an active little fishing port with a very good harbour and one of the ferry links to Skye *(see pp520-21)*.

Morar ⑥
The road continues through Morar, an area renowned for its white sands, and Loch Morar, rumoured to be the home of a 12 m (40 ft) monster known as Morag.

Prince's Cairn ⑤
Crossing the Ardnish Peninsula to Loch Nan Uamh, a cairn marks the spot from which Bonnie Prince Charlie finally left Scotland for France in 1746.

Oban ㉖

Argyll & Bute. 🏠 *8,500.* 🚢 🚉 🚌
ℹ️ *Argyll Sq (01631 563122).*
🌐 *www.scottishheartlands.org*

LOCATED ON the Firth of Lorne and commanding a magnificent view of the Argyll coast, the bustling port of Oban is a popular destination for travellers on their way to Mull and the Western Isles *(see p515)*.

Dominating the skyline is McCaig's Tower, an unfinished Victorian imitation of the Colosseum in Rome. It is worth making the 10-minute climb from the town centre for the sea views alone. Attractions in the town include working centres for glass, pottery and whisky; the Oban distillery produces one of the country's finest malt whiskies *(see p475)*. The **Scottish Sealife Sanctuary** rescues injured and orphaned seals and has displays of underwater life. A busy harbour shelters car ferries going to Barra and South Uist, Mull, Tiree and Colonsay islands.

🏛 **Scottish Sealife Sanctuary**
Barcaldine. 📞 *01631 720386.* ⭘ *daily (winter: phone to check).* 🅿️ 🖼
♿ 🍴 🌐 *www.sealsanctuary.co.uk*

Mull ㉗

Argyll & Bute. 🏠 *2,800.* 🚢 *from Oban, Kilchoan, Lochaline.* ℹ️ *Main Street, Tobermory (01688 302182).*

MOST ROADS on this easily accessible Hebridean island follow the sharply indented rocky coastline, affording wonderful sea views. From Craignure, the Mull and West Highland Railway serves the baronial **Torosay Castle**. A pathway through its gardens is lined with statues, while inside, 19th-century furniture and paintings can be found. On a promontory to the east lies **Duart Castle**, home of the chief of Clan Maclean. Visitors can see the Banqueting Hall and State Rooms in the 13th-century keep. Its dungeons once held prisoners from a Spanish Armada galleon sunk by a Donald Maclean in 1588.

Looking out to sea across Tobermory Bay, Mull

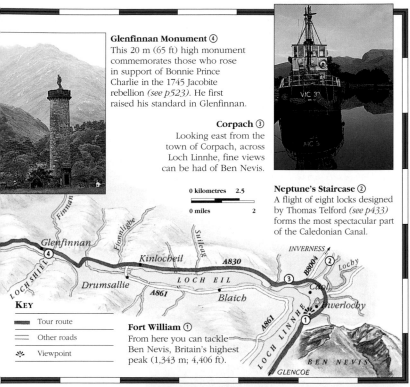

Glenfinnan Monument ④
This 20 m (65 ft) high monument commemorates those who rose in support of Bonnie Prince Charlie in the 1745 Jacobite rebellion *(see p523)*. He first raised his standard in Glenfinnan.

Corpach ③
Looking east from the town of Corpach, across Loch Linnhe, fine views can be had of Ben Nevis.

Neptune's Staircase ②
A flight of eight locks designed by Thomas Telford *(see p433)* forms the most spectacular part of the Caledonian Canal.

0 kilometres   2.5

0 miles   2

KEY

━━━ Tour route

═══ Other roads

🔆 Viewpoint

Fort William ①
From here you can tackle Ben Nevis, Britain's highest peak (1,343 m; 4,406 ft).

ENVIRONS: From Fionnphort, a ferry goes to **Iona**, where St Columba *(see p511)* began his mission in Scotland in 563. North of Iona, the Isle of Staffa should be visited for its magnificent **Fingal's Cave**.

♠ Torosay Castle
Off A849, Nr Craignure. [01680 812421. **Castle** ⬜ Apr–Oct: 10:30am–5pm daily. **Gardens** ⬜ Apr Sep: 9am 7pm; Oct Mar: dawn dusk; daily. 🖼 🔆 📷 for groups.

♠ Duart Castle
Off A849, nr Craignure. [01680 812309. ⬜ Apr–Oct: 10:30am–5:30pm daily. 🖼

Loch Awe ㉘

Argyll & Bute. 🚆 🚌 Dalmally.
🅘 Inveraray (01499 302063).

ONE OF the longest of Scotland's freshwater lochs, Loch Awe fills a 25 mile (40 km) glen in the south-western Highlands. A short drive east of the village of Lochawe leads to the lochside

The ruins of Kilchurn Castle on the shore of Loch Awe

remains of **Kilchurn Castle**, which was abandoned after being struck by lightning in the 18th century. Dwarfing the castle is the huge bulk of Ben Cruachan, whose summit can be reached by the narrow Pass of Brander, in which Robert the Bruce *(see p468)* fought the Clan MacDougal in 1308. From the A85, a tunnel leads to the cavernous Cruachan Power Station.

Near the village of Taynuilt the preserved Lorn Furnace at Bonawe is a reminder of the iron-smelting industry that caused the destruction of much of the area's woodland in the 18th and 19th centuries.

Marked prehistoric cairns are found off the A816 between Kilmartin and Dunadd. The latter boasts a 6th-century hill fort from which the Stone of Destiny *(see p468)* originated.

Inveraray Castle 29

Inveraray, Argyll & Bute. 🚂 *Arrochar, then bus.* 📞 *01499 302203.* ⬤ *Jun–Sep: daily; Apr & May, Oct: Sat–Thu; 10am–5.45pm (Sun: 1:30–5:45pm).* 🎦 ♿ *limited.* 📷
W www.inveraray-castle.com

THIS MULTI-TURRETED mock Gothic palace is the family home of the powerful Clan Campbell who have been the Dukes of Argyll since 1701. The castle was built in 1745 by architects Roger Morris and William Adam on the ruins of a 15th-century castle, and the conical towers added later, after a fire in 1877. Magnificent interiors, designed by Robert Mylne in the 1770s, form a backdrop to a huge collection of Oriental and European porcelain and Regency furniture and portraits by Ramsay, Gainsborough and Raeburn. The Armoury Hall features a display of weaponry collected by the Campbells to fight the Jacobites (*see p523*).

Auchindrain Museum 30

Inveraray, Argyll & Bute. 📞 *01499 500235.* 🚌 *Inveraray, then bus.* ⬤ *Apr–Sep: 10am–5pm daily.* 🅿 🎦 ♿ *limited.*

THE FIRST OPEN-AIR museum in Scotland, Auchindrain illuminates the working lives of the kind of farming community that was typical of the Highlands until the late 19th century. Originally a township of some 20 thatched buildings, the site was communally farmed by its tenants until the last one retired in 1962. Visitors can wander through the buildings, many of which combine

The pinnacled, Gothic exterior of Inveraray Castle

living space, kitchen and cattle shed under one roof. Some of them are furnished with box beds and old rush lamps. The homes of Auchindrain are a quite fascinating memorial to the time before the transition from subsistence to commercial farming.

An old hay turner at the Auchindrain Museum

Crarae Gardens 31

Crarae, Argyll & Bute. 📞 *01546 886614 or NTS (0131 243 9300).* 🚌 *Inveraray, then bus.* ⬤ *Easter–Oct: 9am–6pm; Nov–Easter: 10am–dusk; daily.* **Visitor Centre** ⬤ *Apr–Oct: 10am–5pm daily.* 🎦 ♿ *limited.*
W www.crarae-gardens.org

CONSIDERED the most beguiling of the gardens of the West Highlands, the **Crarae Gardens** were created in the 1920s by Lady Grace Campbell. She was the aunt of explorer Reginald Farrer, whose specimens from Tibet were the beginnings of a collection of exotic plants.

The gardens are nourished by the warmth of the Gulf Stream and the high rainfall. Although there are many unusual Himalayan rhododendrons flourishing here, the gardens are also home to exotic plants from Tasmania, New Zealand and the USA. Plant collectors still contribute to the gardens, which are best seen in spring and early summer against the blue waters of Loch Fyne.

Jura 32

Argyll & Bute. 👣 *200.* ⛴ *from Kennacraig to Islay, then Islay to Jura.* ℹ *Bowmore (01496 810254).*

BARREN, MOUNTAINOUS and overrun by red deer, the isle of Jura has only one road which connects the single village of Craighouse to the Islay ferry. Though walking is restricted during the stalking (deer hunting) season between August and October, the island offers superb hill-walking, especially on the slopes of the three main peaks, known as the Paps of Jura. The tallest of these is Beinn An Oir at 784 m (2571 ft). Beyond the northern tip of the isle are the notorious whirlpools of Corryvreckan. The novelist George Orwell (who came to the island to write his final novel, *1984*) nearly lost his life here in 1946 when he fell into the water. A legend tells

Lagavulin distillery, producer of one Scotland's finest malts, on Islay

Mist crowning the Paps of Jura, seen at sunset across the Sound of Islay

of Prince Breackan who, to win the hand of a princess, tried to keep his boat anchored in the whirlpool for three days, held by ropes made of hemp, wool and maidens' hair. The Prince drowned when a single rope, containing the hair of a girl who had been untrue, finally broke.

Islay ㉝

Argyll & Bute. 🏔 3,500. ⛴ from Kennacraig. 🛈 The Square, Bowmore (0870-7200617). 🆆 www.isle-of-islay.com

THE MOST SOUTHERLY of the Western Isles, Islay (pronounced 'Eyeluh') is the home of respected Highland single malt whiskies Lagavulin and Laphroaig. Most of the island's distilleries produce heavily peated malts with a distinctive tang of the sea. The Georgian village of Bowmore has the island's oldest distillery and a circular church designed to minimize the Devil's possible lurking-places. The **Museum of Islay Life** in Port Charlotte contains fascinating information on social and natural history. Seven miles (11 km) east of Port Ellen stands the Kildalton Cross. A block of local green stone adorned with Old Testament scenes, it is one of the most impressive 8th-

century Celtic crosses in Britain. Worth a visit for its archaeological and historical interest is the medieval stronghold of the Lords of the Isles, **Finlaggan**. Islay's beaches support a variety of bird life, some of which can be observed at the RSPB reserve at Gruinart.

🏛 Museum of Islay Life
Port Charlotte. 📞 01496 850358. ⭕ Easter–Oct: 10am–5pm Mon–Sat, 2–5pm Sun. 🈵 ♿

Kintyre ㉞

Argyll & Bute. 🏔 6,000. ✈ Oban. 🚌 Campbeltown. 🛈 MacKinnon House, The Pier, Campbeltown (01586 552056).

A LONG, NARROW PENINSULA stretching far south of Glasgow, Kintyre has superb views across to the islands of Gigha, Islay and Jura. The 9 mile (14 km) Crinan Canal,

opened in 1801, is a delightful inland waterway, its 15 locks bustling with pleasure craft in the summer. The town of Tarbert (meaning "isthmus" in Gaelic) takes its name from the neck on which it stands, which is narrow enough to drag a boat across between Loch Fyne and West Loch Tarbert. This feat was first achieved by the Viking King Magnus Barfud who, in 1198, was granted by treaty as much land as he could sail around. Travelling south past Campbeltown, the B842 ends at the headland known as the Mull of Kintyre, which was made famous when former Beatle Paul McCartney commercialized a traditional pipe tune of the same name. Westward lies the isle of Rathlin, where Robert the Bruce *(see p468)* learned patience in his struggles against the English by watching a spider weaving a web in a cave.

Fishing boats and yachts moored at Tarbert harbour, Kintyre

TRAVELLERS'
NEEDS

WHERE TO STAY

Whatever your budget or accommodation preferences, you should be able to find somewhere to suit you from the large choice given in the hotel listings section that follows *(see pp542–73)*. The listings include over 370 suggestions, ranging from palatial five-star establishments to humble guest-houses. The common factor in this selection is that they are all, we believe, good of their kind, offering distinctive character or exceptional

Hilton doorman,
London

qualities of hospitality, facilities or value for money. Location is another prime consideration for inclusion. All the hotels and guesthouses listed make convenient touring bases for one or more of the destinations featured in this book, or have attractive or interesting settings enjoyable in their own right. On the next few pages we outline some of the types of accommodation available in Britain, along with various aspects of choosing, booking and paying for somewhere to stay.

COUNTRY-HOUSE HOTELS

The quintessentially british country-house hotel has proliferated in the last few decades. Many indifferent hotels try and claim the title with a cursory decorative makeover, but the genuine article stands head and shoulders above them. Individual examples vary widely, but the best country-house hotels are usually set in buildings of architectural or historic interest filled with antiques or high-quality traditional furnishings. They generally have extensive grounds, but are not always in deeply rural locations. Comfort, even luxury, is assured, along with good food and service – frequently with a high price tag. Many such hotels are still owned and personally managed by resident proprietors; others belong to groups or chains.

BOUTIQUE AND DESIGNER HOTELS

There is a new breed of sophisticated, contemporary hotel that has been making waves in Britain for some years now. These ultra-cool temples of style revel in innovative architecture, funky décor and hip high-tech gadgetry. Most exude an air of uncluttered minimalism, and some have outstanding restaurants. The best-known examples are perhaps in London (the Hempel, *p542*, for instance, or the Sanderson, *p544*), but they can be found elsewhere too, usually in city centres. Trend-setting, upmarket micro-chains like Malmaison or **Hotel du Vin** could perhaps be included in this category. Most of these hotels are expensive, but facilities, furnishings, service and privacy justify the cost.

Atholl Palace Hotel *(see p572)*

HOTEL GROUPS

New hotel groups have taken the place of many of the long-established names, providing reliably standardized accommodation at all price levels in most parts of Britain. The majority of chain hotels (operated by the same company under identical corporate branding) lie in accessible, convenient locations. Though lacking in much individuality, they are practical and efficiently run, and usually represent good value for money.

Budget chains offering no-frills, motel-lodge-style accommodation include **Ibis**, Travelodge and Premier Lodge; further up the scale are mid-market chains like Holiday Inn or **Novotel.** Chain-hotel rates generally don't include breakfast, but look out for inclusive leisure-

Buckland Manor *(see p555),* Worcestershire

◁ **The 11th-century ruins of Corfe Castle, Dorset**

The Swan at Lavenham, Suffolk *(see p548)*, a converted coaching inn

break rates at pricier chains like De Vere or Moat House.

Hotel consortiums – groups of similar but individually owned hotels which market themselves under the same umbrella – include **Best Western** and **Pride of Britain.** There's also **Wolsey Lodges**, a group of private houses, many beautifully furnished and often sited in buildings of notable architectural or historic interest.

INNS AND PUBS WITH ROOMS

THE COACHING INN is a familiar concept in Britain. Many of these fine old hostelries date from the 18th century, though some are even older, such as The George of Stamford *(see p559)*, and often provide reliable restaurants, traditional décor and a warm and friendly atmosphere.

Other types of pub or inn now offer accommodation and reputable food, and many have become much more welcoming to families. Britain's best inns are very comfortable and stylish and bear comparison with any good hotel. Some budget hotel chains, such as Travel Inn or Innkeeper's Lodge, specialize in adding purpose-built accommodation blocks to existing branded dining pubs like Beefeater or Vintage Inns.

BED-AND-BREAKFASTS AND GUEST HOUSES

THE B*B is probably the best-known and certainly the most widely used type of budget accommodation in Britain. These establishments are generally family-owned private homes or farmhouses. Accommodation and facilities tend to be simple (bedrooms may not have TV, telephones, or en-suite bathrooms, for instance), but the best can be quite sophisticated. Prices include breakfast (generally a traditional British fry-up, but other options are usually available as well).

Many B&Bs are reluctant to accept credit cards or travellers' cheques, or may charge a premium for doing so. It's advisable to have some alternative method of payment, preferably cash or, for British nationals, a personal cheque backed by a cheque guarantee card. Any regional tourist office should be able to supply a list of local registered B&Bs on request, though they cannot make specific recommendations, and may charge a fee or a commission for making bookings on your behalf.

HOTEL GRADINGS

RECENT BUT ONLY partially successful attempts have been made to harmonize the confusing and often conflicting systems of accommodation classification used by the various tourist boards and motoring organizations, such as the AA and RAC. In England, hotel gradings are now based on a system of one to five stars awarded for facilities and service (the more stars, the more luxurious you can expect your hotel to be). Guesthouses and B&Bs are graded with one to five diamonds, a quality score which is based on various aspects of the accommodation, including cleanliness and hospitality. Special awards (gold and silver, ribbons, rosettes, eggcups, etc) are given for excellence in certain categories, such as an exceptional breakfast or a warm welcome. Scotland and Wales have their own quality-based gradings.

Hintlesham Hall, Suffolk *(see p548)*

PRICES AND BOOKINGS

MAKE SURE you understand clearly what terms you are being offered when you book. Some hotels just quote room rates, others quote a B&B or half board (dinner, bed and breakfast) rate per person. Rates are generally inclusive of VAT and service but some top-range hotels make additional charges; most charge hefty single-person supplements.

Prices in London start at around £80 per night for a standard en-suite double room, including breakfast, but could be well over £200 (without breakfast) at the top end of the scale. Outside London, expect to pay upward of around £60 for facilities of a similar standard.

The elegant hallway of the Gore Hotel in London (see p542)

Bed-and-breakfast accommodation outside London starts from around £35 per person per night (though prices vary seasonally and regionally). Farm guesthouses (which often include dinner) can be very good value, at around £30 for half board per person.

Most hotels request confirmation in writing and a deposit in advance (a credit card number will generally do). E-mail bookings are now commonplace, and some hotels have an on-line booking facility. Websites are usually updated more often than hotel brochures and tariffs. Business or chain hotels often give big discounts; contact central reservations as well as the

The folly of Doyden Castle, Cornwall, now a National Trust holiday cottage

hotel itself to see which one will give you the best deal.

A hotel booking, whether made by telephone or in writing, is a legally binding contract. If you don't show up, the full cost of your stay may be charged. Most hotels will refund your deposit if they are able to relet the room, but some will charge a penalty, depending how close to your stay you cancel. Most annual travel insurance policies cover cancellation charges for pre-booked UK hotel stays of more than two days, provided you have a satisfactory reason.

Watch out for those hidden extras. Telephone charges from hotel rooms are a very common cause of complaint; most hotels charge a high mark-up, and rates quoted per unit do not always indicate too clearly how much time you get for your money. Consider using a lobby payphone instead. Certain chains have a regrettable policy of charging meals or other extras to your credit card weeks after you have left the hotel; check your card statement carefully.

There is no need to tip staff unless they go out of their way to perform some very exceptional duty, such as booking theatre tickets or restaurants for you.

Roadside signboard for bed-and-breakfast

SELF CATERING

SELF CATERING has many attractions, especially for families on a budget and with young children. Tourist boards give accommodation a one to five star rating for quality and facilities, much the same as for hotels. The range of places to let for holiday rentals is huge, from luxury apartments to log cabins or converted farm buildings. Character properties are available from conservation organizations such as the **Landmark Trust**, which restores buildings of historic or architectural interest and makes them available for short-term lets, or the **National Trust** (see p25), which has a number of holiday cottages on its estates. They tend to be very popular, so book well ahead.

Annually updated self-catering guides are a useful source of listings. Also try specialist agencies, tour operators and the small ads in newspapers. Tourist offices can supply up-to-date regional lists and can also offer a booking service.

Confirm what is included in the price (cleaning, electricity, etc.) and check whether any extra fees, deposits or insurance charg will be added to the bill.

CARAVANNING, CAMPING AND MOTOR HOMES

MOST OF BRITAIN'S campsites and caravan (trailer) parks open only for about six months of the year (typically from Easter to October), but you will need to make reservations in advance. Helpful organizations in Britain include the **Camping and Caravanning Club** and the Caravan Club, which publish lists of their member parks and operate their own grading systems. Camping or caravanning pitches typically cost between £6 and £10 per night. The **Forestry Commission** operates a number of sites in scenic woodland locations throughout the UK.

Motor homes give greater freedom to explore at your own pace and a wider choice of places to stay – including most campsites and caravan parks. Some operators will let you pick up your vehicle directly from an airport or ferry terminal. The **Motor Caravanners' Club** produces a useful monthly magazine.

Campsite, Ogwen Valley, Snowdonia

DISABLED TRAVELLERS

ALL THE UK'S TOURIST boards now provide detailed information about disabled access in their accommodation and sight-seeing guides, and can send further information on request. National Accessible Scheme gradings are awarded to properties inspected and approved under the Tourism for All initiative for various categories of disability.

For more information on these gradings, or other advice on accommodation and travel for disabled visitors, contact **Holiday Care**. Another useful organization is **RADAR** (the Royal Association for Disability and Rehabilitation), which publishes a yearly *Holidays in the British Isles: A Guide for Disabled People.* The listings on pp542–73 indicate which hotels have wheelchair access, but you are strongly advised to check when booking that it matches your needs. The same is true of camping and caravan sites.

DIRECTORY

For useful information on all types of accommodation, see
W www.visitbritain.com

HOTELS

Accor Hotels
(Ibis, Novotel)
C 020-8237 7474.
W www.accorhotels.com

Best Western
Amy Johnson Way,
Clifton Moor,
York, YO30 4GP.
C 08457 747474.
(central reservations).
W www.bestwestern.co.uk

Hilton International
Hilton Reservations
Worldwide, 4 Cadogan Sq.,
Cadogan St
Glasgow G2 7PH.
C 00800 888 44 888.
W www.hilton.co.uk

Hotel du Vin
12 Southgate Street,
Winchester, Hants, SO23
9EF. C 01962 850676.
W www.hotelduvin.com

Pride of Britain
Cowage Farm, Foxley
Wiltshire, SN16 0JH.
C 0870-609 3012.
W www.
prideofbritainhotels.com

Wolsey Lodges
9 Market Place, Hadleigh,
Ipswich, Suffolk, IP7 5DL.
C 01473 822058.
W www.wolsey-
lodges.co.uk

CARAVANNING, CAMPING AND MOTOR HOMES

Camping and Caravanning Club
Westwood Way, Coventry,
West Midlands, CV4 8JH.
C 0247 669 4995.
W www.campingand
caravanningclub.co.uk

Forestry Commission
231 Corstorphine Road,
Edinburgh, EH12 7AT.
C 0131 334 0303.
W www.forestry.gov.uk

Motor Caravanners' Club
Freepost, TK1292
Twickenham TW2 5BR.
C 020-8893 3883.
W www.motorcaravanners.
org.uk

SELF-CATERING

Landmark Trust
Shottesbrooke, Maiden-
head, Berkshire SL6 3SW.
C 01628 825925.
W www.
landmarktrust.co.uk

National Trust
PO Box 39, Bromley, Kent
BR1 3XL.
C 0870 458 4000.
W www.
nationaltrust.org.uk

National Trust for Scotland
Wemyss Hse, 28 Charlotte
Square, Edinburgh EH2 4ET.
C 0131 243 9300.
W www.nts.org.uk

Snowdonia Tourist Services
High Street, Porthmadog,
Gwynedd LL49 9PG.
C 01766 513829.
W www.sts-holidays.com

DISABLED TRAVELLERS

Holiday Care
7th flr, Sunley Hse, 4
Bedford Pk, Croydon CR0
2AP.
C 0845 124 9971.
W www.holidaycare.org.uk

RADAR
Unit 12, City Forum,
250 City Road,
London, EC1V 8AF.
C 020-7250 3222.
W www.radar.org.uk

Choosing a Hotel

THE HOTELS in this guide have been selected across a wide price range for their excellent facilities and locations. Many also have a recommended restaurant. The chart lists the hotels by region, starting with London; colour-coded thumb tabs indicate the regions covered on each page. For restaurant listings, see pp574–607.

	Credit Cards	Restaurant	Children Welcome	Garden/Terrace	Number of Rooms
LONDON					
PADDINGTON: *Delmere*. **Map** 2 E1. w www.delmerehotels.com £££ 130 Sussex Gardens W2. (020 7706 3344. FAX 020 7262 1863. A well-managed welcoming hotel that stands out in a street packed with budget accommodation. Bedrooms are small but tidy. ⊟ TV ⌂ & ⚡ P	AE DC MC V	■			36
PADDINGTON: *Mornington*. **Map** 2 E1. w www.mornington.com £££ 12 Lancaster Gate, W2. (020 7262 7361. FAX 020 7706 1028. Cool bedrooms contrast with the masculine clubbiness of the bar at this Swedish hotel which offers *Smorgasbord* buffet breakfasts. ⊟ TV ⌂ ⚡	AE DC MC V		●		66
PADDINGTON: *Hempel*. **Map** 2 E1. w www.the-hempel.co.uk £££££ 31 Craven Hill Gardens, W2. (020 7298 9000. FAX 020 7402 4666. Anouska Hempel's ultra-chic design statement combines innovative decor, superb service and state-of-the-art technology. ⊟ TV ⌂ &	AE DC	■	●		46
NOTTING HILL: *Abbey Court*. **Map** 1 B2. w www.abbeycourthotel.co.uk £££ 20 Pembridge Gardens, W2. (020 7221 7518. FAX 020 7720 0858. Quiet rooms furnished with books and personal touches mark this Victorian townhouse near Notting Hill Gate. ⊟ TV	AE DC MC V		●	■	24
NOTTING HILL: *Pembridge Court*. **Map** 1 B2. w www.pemct.co.uk ££££ 34 Pembridge Gardens, W2. (020 7229 9977. FAX 020 7727 4982. A family-run hotel full of framed Victoriana. A ginger cat, Churchill, welcomes visitors. ⊟ ⌂	AE DC MC V		●		20
NOTTING HILL: *Portobello*. **Map** 1 A2. w www.portobello-hotel.co.uk ££££ 22 Stanley Gardens, W11. (020 7727 2777. FAX 020 7792 9641. Eccentric place that has an exotic, sophisticated decor – a mix of Victorian and Edwardian periods. Rooms range from tiny to lavish. ● 23 Dec–1 Jan. ⊟ TV ⌂	AE MC V	■	●		24
KENSINGTON: *Abbey House*. **Map** 1 C3. w www.abbeyhousekensington.com £ 11 Vicarage Gate, W8. (020 7727 1873. FAX 020 7727 1873. Once a Victorian family home, now a no-frills bed-and-breakfast. Rooms though spacious are simply furnished without *en suite* bathrooms. TV ⚡			●		16
KENSINGTON: *Kensington House*. **Map** 2 D5. w www.kenhouse.com £££ 15–16 Prince of Wales Terrace, W8. (020 7937 2345. FAX 020 7368 6700. This smart, newly opened townhouse hotel combines period interest with understated contemporary style. ⊟ TV ⌂ ⚡	AE DC MC V	■	●		41
KENSINGTON: *The Gore*. **Map** 2 D5. w www.gorehotel.com £££££ 189 Queen's Gate, SW7. (020 7584 6601. FAX 020 7589 8127. This idiosyncratic Victorian hotel is over a chic restaurant. Bedrooms vary from tiny singles to Tudor fantasies with their own minstrels' galleries. Charming service. ⊟ TV ⌂ & ⚡	AE DC MC V	■	●		53
KNIGHTSBRIDGE: *Basil Street*. **Map** 5 A3. w www.thebasil.com £££££ 8 Basil St, SW3. (020 7581 3311. FAX 020 7581 3693. An enduringly popular hotel just off Sloane Street. It has a long history and lots of personality. Its brasserie-wine bar is superb and very good value for this expensive area. ⊟ TV ⌂ & ⚡ P	AE DC MC V	■	●		80
KNIGHTSBRIDGE: *Beaufort*. **Map** 5 A3. w www.thebeaufort.co.uk £££££ 33 Beaufort Gardens, SW3. (020 7584 5252. FAX 020 7589 2834. An aristocratic hideaway in a quiet square with beautifully decorated rooms. Room service available. ⊟ TV ⌂ & ⚡	AE DC MC V		●		29
KNIGHTSBRIDGE: *Halkin*. **Map** 5 A3. w www.halkin.co.uk £££££ 5 Halkin St, SW1. (020 7333 1000. FAX 020 7333 1100. Sophisticated Italian design with Oriental touches makes this hotel a startling experience. The Thai restaurant overlooks a courtyard. ⊟ TV ⌂ ⚡	AE DC MC V	■	●	■	41

Price categories for a standard double room per night, inclusive of breakfast, service charges and any additional taxes such as VAT: ⓔ under £65 ⓔⓔ £65–£100 ⓔⓔⓔ £100–£150 ⓔⓔⓔⓔ £150–£200 ⓔⓔⓔⓔⓔ £200 plus	**RESTAURANT** Hotel restaurant or dining room serving more than just breakfast; often open to non-residents. **CHILDREN WELCOME** Especially welcoming to families. May have children's facilities such as cots, babysitting, family rooms, etc. **GARDEN/TERRACE** Hotels with a garden, courtyard or terrace, often providing tables for eating outside. **CREDIT CARDS** Indicates which credit cards are accepted: *AE* American Express; *DC* Diners Club; *MC* Master Card/Access; *V* Visa.			

	CREDIT CARDS	RESTAURANT	CHILDREN WELCOME	GARDEN/TERRACE	NUMBER OF ROOMS
SOUTH KENSINGTON: *Five Sumner Place.* **Map** 2 E5. ⓔⓔⓔ 5 Sumner Place, SW7. ☎ 020 7584 7586. 🖵 www.sumnerplace.com A small, award-winning hotel with a quiet, courteous welcome and good facilities. Breakfast is served with complimentary newspapers. 🔳 📺 🔆 ♿ ✉	AE MC V		●		13
SOUTH KENSINGTON: *Blakes.* **Map** 2 E5. 🖵 www.blakeshotels.com ⓔⓔⓔⓔⓔ 33 Roland Gardens, SW7. ☎ 020 7370 6701. **FAX** 020 7373 0442. Opulent hotel, each room a fantasy of natural materials and antiques. Secluded gardens and an Oriental-style restaurant. 🔳 📺 🔆 ♿ ✉	AE MC V	■	●	■	49
VICTORIA: *Morgan House.* **Map** 5 B4. 🖵 www.morganhouse.co.uk ⓔ 120 Ebury St, SW1. ☎ 020 7730 2384. **FAX** 020 7730 8442. This stylish budget B&B in a Georgian terrace has light, modern decor; just four rooms have private bathrooms. 🔳 📺 ✉	MC V		●		11
VICTORIA: *Tophams Belgravia.* **Map** 5 B4. 🖵 www.tophams.co.uk ⓔⓔⓔ 28 Ebury St, SW1. ☎ 020 7730 8147. **FAX** 020 7823 5966. Several adjacent townhouses make up this classy hotel. Family heirlooms deck cosy public rooms. 🔳 📺 ♿ ✉	AE DC MC V	■	●		39
VICTORIA: *Windermere.* **Map** 5 C4. 🖵 www.windermere-hotel.co.uk ⓔⓔⓔ 142–144 Warwick Way, SW1. ☎ 020 7834 5163. **FAX** 020 7630 8831. Inexpensive, friendly hotel, ten minutes' walk from Victoria Station. Lovely breakfast room which doubles as a dining room. Light, clean bedrooms. Helpful service. 🔳 📺	AE MC V	■	●		22
VICTORIA: *Goring.* **Map** 5 B4. 🖵 www.goringhotel.co.uk ⓔⓔⓔⓔⓔ 15 Beeston Place, SW1. ☎ 020 7396 9000. **FAX** 020 7834 4393. Fine Belgravia hotel with elegant furnishings and a warm welcome. Immaculate gardens make a pleasant backdrop. 🔳 📺 🔆 ♿ ✉ P	AE DC MC V	■		■	74
WESTMINSTER: *Dolphin Square.* **Map** 6 D5. ⓔⓔⓔⓔ Chichester St, SW1. ☎ 020 7834 3800. 🖵 www.dolphinsquarehotel.co.uk In a tranquil garden located by the Thames and near Tate Britain, this luxurious hotel also houses the new restaurant Allium. 🔳 📺 🔆 ♿ ✉ P	AE DC	■	●	■	148
ST JAMES'S: *22 Jermyn Street.* **Map** 6 D1. 🖵 www.22jermyn.com ⓔⓔⓔⓔⓔ 22 Jermyn St, SW1. ☎ 020 7734 2353. **FAX** 020 7734 0750. A luxurious complex of suites and studios with round-the-clock service, a video library and use of the nearby health club. 🔳 📺 🔆 ♿ ✉	AE DC MC V		●		18
MAYFAIR: *Chesterfield.* **Map** 6 D1. 🖵 www.redcarnationhotels.com ⓔⓔⓔⓔ 35 Charles St, W1. ☎ 020 7491 2622. **FAX** 020 7491 4793. This quiet, well-kept place near Berkeley Square is decked with fruit and flowers; bedrooms are deluxe and staff welcoming. 🔳 📺 🔆 ♿ ✉ P	AE DC MC V	■	●		110
MAYFAIR: *Brown's.* **Map** 6 D1. 🖵 www.roccofortehotels.com ⓔⓔⓔⓔⓔ Albemarle St, W1. ☎ 020 7493 6020. **FAX** 020 7493 9381. This long-established and stylish hotel now forms part of the luxurious Rocco Forte hotels collection. 🔳 📺 🔆 ✉	AE DC MC V	■	●		118
OXFORD STREET & SOHO: *Edward Lear.* **Map** 3 5A. 🖵 www.edlear.com ⓔⓔ 28–30 Seymour St, W1. ☎ 020 7402 5401. **FAX** 020 7706 3766. Clean, simple bed-and-breakfast, once the home of the author Edward Lear. Single travellers and families are made very welcome. 📺 ✉	AE MC V		●		31
OXFORD STREET & SOHO: *Durrants.* **Map** 3 A4. ⓔⓔⓔ George St, W1. ☎ 020 7935 8131. **FAX** 020 7487 3510. 🖵 www.durrantshotel.co.uk Georgian hotel that still has the feel of the old coaching inn it once was. The look is of old leather and wood. Bedrooms are unfussy. 🔳 📺 🔆 ♿	AE MC V	■	●		92

Price categories for a standard double room per night, inclusive of breakfast, service charges and any additional taxes such as VAT:
£ under £65
££ £65–£100
£££ £100–£150
££££ £150–£200
£££££ £200 plus

RESTAURANT
Hotel restaurant or dining room serving more than just breakfast; often open to non-residents.

CHILDREN WELCOME
Especially welcoming to families. May have children's facilities such as cots, babysitting, family rooms, etc.

GARDEN/TERRACE
Hotels with a garden, courtyard or terrace, often providing tables for eating outside.

CREDIT CARDS
Indicates which credit cards are accepted: *AE* American Express; *DC* Diners Club; *MC* Master Card/Access; *V* Visa.

	CREDIT CARDS	RESTAURANT	CHILDREN WELCOME	GARDEN/TERRACE	NUMBER OF ROOMS
OXFORD STREET & SOHO: *Hazlitt's*. Map 3 A4. £££££ 6 Frith St, W1. 020 7434 1771. FAX 020 7439 1524. W www.hazlittshotel.com Three 18th-century houses in the heart of Soho make a peaceful bolthole, for artistic temperaments of many kinds. The interior is furnished with Victorian antiques with mod cons unobtrusively incorporated.	AE DC MC V				23
OXFORD STREET & SOHO: *Sanderson*. Map 3 A4. ££££££ 50 Berners St, W1. 020 7300 1400. FAX 020 7300 1401. W www.lanschragerhotels.com One of London's sleekest hotels. Decor is truly eye-catching with courtyard, fountains and voguish bedrooms.	AE DC MC V	■	●	■	150
BLOOMSBURY: *Generator*. Map 4 D3. W www.the-generator.co.uk £ 37 Tavistock Place, WC1. 020 7388 7666. FAX 020 7388 7644. Somewhere between sci-fi and industrial chic, this recently refurbished hostel provides budget solutions for impecunious travellers.	MC V	■	●		200
BLOOMSBURY: *Academy*. Map 4 D3. W www.theetoncollection.com ££ 21 Gower St, WC1. 020 7631 4115. FAX 020 7636 3442. Five Georgian townhouses with courtyard gardens near the heart of London University. Inside, the ambience is sophisticated without excess.	AE DC MC V		●		49
BLOOMSBURY: *Charlotte Street*. Map 4 E4. £££££ 15 Charlotte St, W1. 020 7806 2000. W www.firmdale.com The "Bloomsbury" theme incorporates original period art in the spacious, public areas, while bedrooms run to mini-TV screens in the granite bathrooms and exemplary high-tech facilities.	AE DC MC V	■	●	■	52
COVENT GARDEN & STRAND: *Fielding*. Map 4 F5. ££ 4 Broad Court, Bow St, WC2. 020 7836 8305. W www.the-fielding-hotel.co.uk A good-value hotel near the Royal Opera House with limited but clean facilities. No meals served; no children under 12.	AE DC MC V				24
COVENT GARDEN & STRAND: *Covent Garden*. Map 4 E5. £££££ 10 Monmouth St, WC2. 020 7806 1000. FAX 020 7806 1100. W www.firmdale.com A discreet but theatrical hotel on one of Covent Garden's most interesting streets. A tour-de-force of dramatic interior design.	AE MC V	■	●		58
COVENT GARDEN & STRAND: *One Aldwych*. Map 4 F5. ££££££ Aldwych, WC2. 020 7300 1000. FAX 020 7300 1001. W www.onealdwych.com Filled with contemporary works of art, every inch of this hotel is imaginative, with well-thought out rooms. Underwater classical music plays in the swimming pool.	AE DC MC V	■	●		105
COVENT GARDEN & STRAND: *Savoy*. Map 4 F5. ££££££ Strand, WC2. 020 7836 4343. FAX 020 7240 6040. W www.the-savoy.com Flamboyant Art Deco hotel with glorious waterfront views, combining period character with modern comforts.	AE DC MC V	■	●	■	263
REGENTS PARK & MARYLEBONE: *Dorset Square*. Map 3 A3. £££££ 39–40 Dorset Sq, NW1. 020 7723 7874. FAX 020 7724 3328. W www.firmdale.com Beautifully restored Regency building with antiques, overlooking an 18th-century square. Rooms have character; service is friendly.	AE MC V	■	●		38
WATERLOO & SOUTHWARK: *Travel Inn County Hall*. Map 6 F3. £ Belvedere Rd, SE1. 0870 238 3300. FAX 020 7902 1619. W www.travelinn.co.uk Excellent value in the old GLC building next to the London Eye. Practical and spacious rooms (breakfast not included). Book in advance.	AE MC V	■	●		313
WATERLOO & SOUTHWARK: *Novotel London Waterloo*. Map 6 F3. £££ 113 Lambeth Rd, SE1. 0870 850 4520. FAX 020 7793 0202. W www.novotel.com A bland but convenient chain hotel with spacious rooms ideal for business visitors and families. Front rooms have views of Westminster.	AE DC MC V	■	●		187

CITY: *Novotel Tower Bridge.* **Map** 8 E3. W www.novotel.com £££££ | AE DC MC V | ◼ ● ◼ | 203
10 Pepys St, EC3. ▐ 020 7265 6000. FAX 020 7265 6060.
This recently opened chain hotel in a fascinating part of London has well-equipped pleasing bedrooms. Good value for families. 🛏 TV ⌂ ⅍ ⚞

CITY: *Great Eastern.* **Map** 8 E2. W www.great-eastern-hotel.co.uk £££££ | AE DC MC | ◼ ● | 267
Liverpool St, EC2. ▐ 020 7618 5000. FAX 020 7618 5001.
A restoration of Liverpool Street's grand railway hotel with smart restaurants and elegant bedrooms. 🛏 TV ⌂ ⅍ ⚞

CITY: *Rookery.* **Map** 8 E2. W www.rookeryhotel.com £££££ | AE DC MC V | ● | 33
Peter's Lane, Cowcross St, EC1. ▐ 020 7336 0931. FAX 020 7336 0932.
Lovingly restored B&B in several 18th-century town houses near Smithfield market. All rooms have handsome period furnishings. 🛏 TV ⚞

CANARY WHARF: *Four Seasons Canary Wharf* £££££ | AE DC MC V | ◼ ● | 142
46 Westferry Circus, E14. ▐ 020 7510 1999. W www.fourseasons.com
A stunning complex with superb waterfront views and facilities. The Holmes Place leisure centre is just next door. 🛏 TV ⌂ ⅍ ⚞ P

HAMPSTEAD: *La Gaffe* W www.lagaffe.co.uk ££ | AE MC V | ◼ | 18
107–111 Heath St, NW3. ▐ 020 7435 8965. FAX 020 7794 7592.
A cheerful, family-run Italian restaurant-with-rooms, in the heart of Hampstead village. Bedrooms are simple but pretty. 🛏 TV

THE DOWNS AND CHANNEL COAST

BATTLE: *Fox Hole Farm* £ | MC V | ◼ | 3
Kane Hythe Rd, Battle, E Sussex TN33 9QU. ▐ & FAX 01424 772053.
Deep in the Sussex countryside, this delightful farmhouse offers a bucolic but stylish B&B experience, with light evening meals by arrangement. Self-catering cottages available. ● *Christmas.* 🛏 TV ⚞ P

BEAULIEU: *Master Builder's House* W www.themasterbuilders.co.uk £££££ | AE MC V | ◼ | 25
Buckler's Hard, Beaulieu, Hampshire SO42 7XB. ▐ 01590 616253. FAX 01590 616297.
The former home of a ship builder enjoys a stunning waterfront location. Recently refurbished, it is comfortable and charming inside. Bedrooms in the main building have most character. 🛏 TV ⚞ P

BILLINGSHURST: *Old Wharf* @ david.mitchell@farming.co.uk ££ | ◼ | 3
Newbridge, Wisborough Green, Billingshurst, W Sussex RH14 0HG. ▐ & FAX 01403 784096.
A fascinating canal-side warehouse imaginatively converted into a B&B. Tasteful decor, immaculate bedrooms and restful views. Swimming pool, tennis, fishing. Cash and cheques only. ● *Christmas & New Year.* 🛏 TV ⚞ P

BRIGHTON: *Dove Waldorf* £ | AE MC V | ● | 9
18 Regency Sq, Brighton, E Sussex BN1 2FG. ▐ 01273 779222. FAX 01273 746912.
A bright and friendly guesthouse in an elegant square near the seafront. Bedrooms vary; best are at the front. 🛏 TV ⚞

BRIGHTON: *Pelirocco* W www.hotelpelirocco.co.uk £££ | AE DC MC V | | 19
10 Regency Sq, Brighton, E Sussex BN1 2 FG. ▐ 01273 327055. FAX 01273 733845.
Funkily themed bedrooms and hip young staff attract a trendy clientele to this unconventional interpretation of a Georgian townhouse. 🛏 TV ⌂ ⚞

CANTERBURY: *Magnolia House* W treespace.virgin.net/magnolia.canterbury ££ | AE DC MC V | ◼ | 7
36 St Dunstans Terrace, Canterbury, Kent CT2 8AX. ▐ & FAX 01227 765121.
High standards are constantly maintained in this trim B&B. Dinner by arrangement in winter. 🛏 TV ⚞ P

CANTERBURY: *The Falstaff* W www.corushotels.com/thefalstaff £££ | AE DC MC V | ◼ | 47
8–10 St Dunstan's St, Canterbury, Kent CT2 8AF. ▐ 01227 462138. FAX 01227 463525.
This 15th-century coaching inn by the West Gate barbican has been efficiently but sympathetically modernized with contemporary colour-schemes and business facilities. 🛏 TV ⚞ P

EASTBOURNE: *Grand* W www.grandeastbourne.com £££££ | AE DC MC V | ◼ ● ◼ | 152
King Edwards Parade, Eastbourne, E Sussex BN21 4EQ. ▐ 01323 412345. FAX 01323 412233.
This splendid institution, after recent renovation, maintains the same dignity and high standards as always. It now has indoor and outdoor pools and a spa. Acclaimed restaurant, and welcoming staff. 🛏 TV ⌂ P ⅍

Price categories for a standard double room per night, inclusive of breakfast, service charges and any additional taxes such as VAT: £ under £65 ££ £65–£100 £££ £100–£150 ££££ £150–£200 £££££ £200 plus	**RESTAURANT** Hotel restaurant or dining room serving more than just breakfast; often open to non-residents. **CHILDREN WELCOME** Especially welcoming to families. May have children's facilities such as cots, babysitting, family rooms, etc. **GARDEN/TERRACE** Hotels with a garden, courtyard or terrace, often providing tables for eating outside. **CREDIT CARDS** Indicates which credit cards are accepted: *AE* American Express; *DC* Diners Club; *MC* Master Card/Access; *V* Visa.	CREDIT CARDS	RESTAURANT	CHILDREN WELCOME	GARDEN/TERRACE	NUMBER OF ROOMS

Hotel	CREDIT CARDS	RESTAURANT	CHILDREN WELCOME	GARDEN/TERRACE	NUMBER OF ROOMS
EAST GRINSTEAD: *Gravetye Manor* W www.gravetyemanor.co.uk £££££ Vowels Lane, East Grinstead, W Sussex RH19 4LJ. 01342 810567. FAX 01342 810080. A truly splendid country house, tastefully furnished and surrounded by glorious gardens. Save this one for a real treat – you'll remember it for more than the bill, especially its superb cooking *(see also p583).*	MC V	■	●	■	18
GUILDFORD: *Angel Posting House & Livery* W www.slh.com/angel ££££ 91 High St, Guildford, Surrey GU1 3DP. 01483 564555. FAX 01483 533770. A historic hostelry on the London–Portsmouth coaching route. The interior is traditional, atmospheric, handsome. Vaulted cellar restaurant.	AE DC MC V		●		21
LEWES: *Millers* W www.hometown.aol.com/millers134 ££ 134 High St, Lewes, E Sussex BN7 1XS. 01273 475631. With just two rooms, it's advisable to book ahead for this idiosyncratic bed-and-breakfast in the town centre. The house dates from the 16th century.			●	■	2
LEWES: *Shelleys* W www.shelleys-hotel.com ££££ 137 High St, Lewes, E Sussex BN7 1XS. 01273 472361. FAX 01273 483152. Once an aristocratic manor house, Shelleys has more than a touch of class, especially during the Glyndebourne opera season.	AE DC MC V	■	●	■	19
NEW MILTON: *Chewton Glen* W www.chewtonglen.com ££££££ Christchurch Rd, New Milton, Hampshire BH25 6QS. 01425 275341. FAX 01425 272310. Everything is geared towards pampering at this luxury establishment deep in the forest. For energetic activity, wonderful food or sybaritic relaxation, this hotel is hard to match. Indoor and outdoor pools *(see also p583).*	AE DC MC V	■	●	■	59
RINGLESTONE: *Ringlestone Inn* W www.ringlestone.com £££ Ringlestone, Maidstone, Kent ME17 1NX. 01622 859900. FAX 01622 859966. A cosy village inn, popular with non-residents for its food and old-world charm. Bedrooms are in separate annexes. Extensive, attractively landscaped grounds. Handy for exploring North Kent and the Medway Valley.	AE DC MC V	■	●	■	3
RINGWOOD: *Moortown Lodge* W www.moortownlodge.co.uk ££ 244 Christchurch Rd, Ringwood, Hampshire BH24 3AS. 01425 471404. FAX 01425 476527. This attractively decorated restaurant-with-rooms in an early Georgian building makes a convenient base for Bournemouth and the New Forest. Rear rooms are quieter. ● 24 Dec–mid-Jan; 1 week in July.	AE MC V	■	●		7
ROYAL TUNBRIDGE WELLS: *Hotel du Vin* W www.hotelduvin.com ££ Crescent Rd, Tunbridge Wells, Kent TN1 2LY. 01892 526455. FAX 01892 512044. This vivacious, stylish place belies the town's staid, conservative image. The interior is voguishly contemporary, and the atmosphere constantly buzzing. Brilliant food and wine.	AE DC MC V			■	36
RYE: *Jeake's House* W www.jeakeshouse.com ££ Mermaid St, Rye, E Sussex TN31 7ET. 01797 222828. FAX 01797 222623. A delightful B&B in one of the town's quaintest streets, occupying what was once a 17th-century Quaker meeting house. Bedrooms are full of character. A wood-panelled parlour provides space to relax in the evenings.	MC V				11
RYE: *Old Vicarage* W www.oldvicaragerye.co.uk ££ 66 Church Sq, Rye, E Sussex TN31 7HF. 01797 222119. FAX 01797 227466. A friendly place by the church in a charming Georgian cottage filled with antiques and fresh country furnishings. Delicious breakfasts; sherry in the evenings. ● Christmas.				■	4
SANDGATE: *Sandgate* W www.sandgatehotel.com ££ The Esplanade, Sandgate, Folkestone, Kent CT20 3DY. 01303 220444. FAX 01303 220496. A charming family-owned seafront hotel ten minutes' drive from the Channel Tunnel. The rooms are immaculate and the service exemplary. It includes a restaurant and bar, and serves all-day breakfast at weekends.	AE DC MC V	■	●	■	15

SEAVIEW: *Seaview* W www.seaviewhotel.co.uk £££ — AE DC MC V — 16
High St, Seaview, Isle of Wight PO34 5EX. 01983 612711. FAX 01983 613729.
This long-established hotel combines warm and well-practised hospitality with superb seafood, in a modest Victorian villa close to the sea near Ryde. ● *Christmas.* 🚕 TV 🏊 P

SWAY: *Nurse's Cottage* W www.nursescottage.co.uk £££ — AE MC V — 3
Station Rd, Sway, Lymington, Hampshire SO41 6BA. & FAX 01590 683402.
An unassuming bungalow in a quiet New Forest village, now firmly established as a dazzling restaurant-with-rooms. Bedroom facilities run to CD and video players. ● *3 weeks in Nov, 2 in Mar.* 🚕 TV 🏊 P &

WINCHESTER: *Wykeham Arms* ££ — AE DC MC V — 14
75 Kingsgate St, Winchester, Hamphire SO23 9PE. 01962 853834. FAX 01962 854411.
A successful blend of historic inn, stylish bar-restaurant and smart central hotel, just behind the cathedral. Full of character and memorabilia; always popular with locals and visitors *(see also p608).* ● *25 Dec.* 🚕 TV 🏊 P

YARMOUTH: *George* W www.thegeorge.co.uk ££££ — AE MC V — 17
Quay St, Yarmouth, Isle of Wight PO41 0PE. 01983 760331. FAX 01983 760425.
Next to the Lymington ferry terminal on the old town square, this smart historic inn dates from the 17th century. Accomplished restaurant and a simpler brasserie. Parking can be tricky. 🚕 TV 🏊

EAST ANGLIA

ALDEBURGH: *Wentworth* W www.wentworth-aldeburgh.com £££ — AE DC MC V — 37
Wentworth Rd, Aldeburgh, Suffolk IP15 5BD. 01728 452312. FAX 01728 454343.
A solid Victorian seaside hotel with well-decorated bedrooms and tasty dinners. Sea views are worth the extra charge. ● *27 Dec–5 Jan.* 🚕 TV 🏊 P &

BLAKENEY: *White Horse* W www.blakeneywhitehorse.co.uk ££ — AE MC V — 10
4 High St, Blakeney, Holt, Norfolk NR25 7Al. 01263 740574. FAX 01263 741303.
A friendly, down-to-earth pub offering distinctly above-average food in an upmarket coastal village. Recently refurbished. ● *1 Jan.* 🚕 TV P

BUCKDEN: *Lion* W www.lionhotel.co.uk ££ — AE MC V — 15
High Street, Buckden, Cambridgeshire PE19 5XA. 01480 810313. FAX 01480 811070.
A fine old building full of oak timbers and panelling, just off the A1. Well-furnished bedrooms, some in an annexe. ● *1 Jan.* 🚕 TV P &

BURNHAM MARKET: *Hoste Arms* W www.hostearms.co.uk £££ — MC V — 43
The Green, Burnham Market, King's Lynn, Norfolk PE31 8HD. 01328 738777.
An important part of the social fabric of a pretty Norfolk village, this excellent Georgian inn provides a splendid array of bistro-style food and tastefully furnished rooms – some in an annexe. 🚕 TV P

BURY ST EDMUNDS: *Ounce House* W www.ouncehouse.co.uk ££ — AE DC MC V — 3
Northgate St, Bury St Edmunds, Suffolk IP33 1HP. 01284 761779. FAX 01284 768315.
A thoroughly civilized, family-run B&B within easy walking distance of the historic centre. Classy furnishings; friendly welcome. 🚕 TV 🏊 P

CAMBRIDGE: *Meadowcroft* W www.meadowcrofthotel.co.uk £££ — AE MC V — 18
Trumpington Rd, Cambridge CB2 2EX. 01223 346120. FAX 01223 346138.
This smartly furnished Victorian hotel lies about a mile from the centre. Decor enhances its handsome period features. ● *Christmas & New Year.* 🚕 TV 🏊 P &

CAMPSEA ASHE: *Old Rectory* ££ — DC MC V — 7
Campsea Ashe, Woodbridge, Suffolk IP13 0PU. & FAX 01728 746524.
This comfortable, antique-and-print-filled house offers tranquil Wolsey Lodge hospitality, and some excellent cooking. Bedrooms are light and pleasing. Lovely big gardens. ● *Christmas.* 🚕 🏊 P

COGGESHALL: *White Hart* W www.oldenglish.co.uk ££ — AE DC MC V — 18
Market End, Coggeshall, Essex CO6 1NH. 01376 561654. FAX 01376 561789.
This fine 15th-century guildhall-cum-coaching inn is a local landmark. The interior is furnished with antiques. Good Italian food. 🚕 TV P

DEDHAM: *Dedham Hall* W www.dedhamhall.demon.co.uk ££ — MC V — 6
Brook St, Dedham, Colchester, Essex CO7 6AD. 01206 323027. FAX 01206 323293.
An idyllic base for Constable Country. Partly 15th-century, this friendly place offers residential art courses as well as very cosy accommodation and elegant fixed-price dinners. Large gardens. ● *Christmas.* 🚕 TV P &

Price categories for a standard double room per night, inclusive of breakfast, service charges and any additional taxes such as VAT: £ under £65 ££ £65–£100 £££ £100–£150 ££££ £150–£200 £££££ £200 plus	**RESTAURANT** Hotel restaurant or dining room serving more than just breakfast; often open to non-residents. **CHILDREN WELCOME** Especially welcoming to families. May have children's facilities such as cots, babysitting, family rooms, etc. **GARDEN/TERRACE** Hotels with a garden, courtyard or terrace, often providing tables for eating outside. **CREDIT CARDS** Indicates which credit cards are accepted: *AE* American Express; *DC* Diners Club; *MC* Master Card/Access; *V* Visa.	CREDIT CARDS	RESTAURANT	CHILDREN WELCOME	GARDEN/TERRACE	NUMBER OF ROOMS

Listing	Credit Cards	Restaurant	Children Welcome	Garden/Terrace	Number of Rooms
DEDHAM: *Maison Talbooth* �〉 www.talbooth.com ££££ Stratford Rd, Dedham, Colchester, Essex CO7 6HN. 〖 01206 322367. FAX 01206 322752. The Victorian accommodation wing of Dedham's top-flight restaurant (Le Talbooth is a short walk – *see p584*). Lavish country-house decor. 🛏 TV P	AE DC MC V	■	●	■	10
DUNWICH: *Ship Inn* W www.shipinndunwich.co.uk ££ St James St, Dunwich, Suffolk IP 17 3DT. 〖 01728 648219. FAX 01728 648675. A popular brick-built village pub with cosy bars and a conservatory. Pretty, rustic bedrooms, some with sea views. Super breakfasts. ● 25 Dec. 🛏 TV P	MC V	■		■	3
GREAT DUNMOW: *The Starr* W www.the-starr.co.uk £££ Market Place, Great Dunmow, Essex CM6 1AX. 〖 01371 874321. FAX 01371 876337. The food's the thing at this historic 16th-century inn, but there are some ritzy bedrooms in the adjacent converted stable-block. Ask for the four-poster Oak Room. ● first week Jan. 🛏 TV 🍽 P &	AE DC MC V	■	●		8
GRIMSTON: *Congham Hall* W www.conghamhallhotel.co.uk ££££ Lynn Rd, Grimston, King's Lynn, Norfolk PE32 1AH. 〖 01485 600250. FAX 01485 601191. Though grand, this Georgian country house surrounded by parkland is unpretentious and relaxing. 🛏 TV 🍽 P	AE DC MC V	■	●	■	14
HINTLESHAM: *Hintlesham Hall* W www.hintleshamhall.com £££££ George St, Hintlesham, Ipswich, Suffolk IP8 3NS. 〖 01473 652268. FAX 01473 652463. A blend of Tudor and Georgian architecture set in 175 acres of grounds. Decor and food are unashamedly lavish, as are the posher suites. Loads of leisure facilities. *(See also p585.)* 🛏 TV	AE DC MC V	■	●	■	33
HUNTINGDON: *Old Bridge* W www.huntsbridge.com £££££ 1 High St, Huntingdon, Cambridgeshire PE29 3TQ. 〖 01480 424300. FAX 01480 411017. It's difficult to miss this handsome 18th-century building on its eponymous bridge over the Ouse. Spacious and smartly furnished, its attractive gardens shield it from passing traffic. *(See also p585.)* 🛏 TV 🍽 P &	AE DC MC V	■	●	■	24
IPSWICH: *Marlborough* W www.themarlborough.co.uk ££ Henley Rd, Ipswich, Suffolk IP1 3SP. 〖 01473 257677. FAX 01473 226927. A Victorian town house in a residential area near a park, with a solid reputation for high standards of service, food and furnishings. 🛏 TV P &	AE DC MC V	■	●	■	22
LAVENHAM: *Lavenham Priory* W www.lavenhampriory.co.uk ££ Water St, Lavenham, Suffolk CO10 9RW. 〖 01787 247404. FAX 01747 248472. One of picturesque Lavenham's less pricy options, this delightful listed B&B has beautifully furnished rooms with character. ● Christmas, New Year. 🛏 TV 🍽 P	MC V			■	6
LAVENHAM: *Swan* W www.macdonaldhotels.co.uk £££ High St, Lavenham, Suffolk CO10 9QA. 〖 01787 247477. FAX 01787 248286. This well-known hostelry was built on the proceeds of the wool trade. The recently refurbished bedrooms are stylish and comfortable. 🛏 TV 🍽 P	AE DC MC V	■	●	■	51
LOWESTOFT: *Ivy House Farm* W www.ivyhousefarm.co.uk ££ Ivy Lane, Oulton Broad, Lowestoft, Suffolk NR33 8HY. 〖 01502 501353. FAX 01502 501539. Located in a quiet backwater, these converted farm buildings house rustic but sophisticated units. Super food; lovely gardens. 🛏 TV 🍽 P &	AE DC MC V	■	●	■	19
NORTH WALSHAM: *Beechwood* W www.beechwood-hotel.co.uk £££ 20 Cromer Rd, North Walsham, Norfolk NR28 0HD. 〖 01692 403231. FAX 01692 407284. A stylish small hotel with enthusiastic, attentive hosts. A handy base for exploring north-west Norfolk and the Broads. 🛏 TV 🍽 P	MC V	■		■	10
NORWICH: *By Appointment* ££ 25–29 St George's St, Norwich, Norfolk NR3 1AB. 〖 & FAX 01603 630730. The food is irresistible at this delightfully eccentric restaurant-with-rooms. Bedrooms are designed to pamper; lots of personal touches. 🛏 TV 🍽 P	MC V	■			4

NORWICH: *Catton Old Hall* [W] www.catton-hall.co.uk ££ — AE DC MC V — 7
Lodge Lane, Catton, Norwich, Norfolk NR6 7HG. [01603 419379. [FAX] 01603 400339.
North-east of the centre, this welcoming 17th-century farmhouse is full of
character and family mementoes. Fine dinners by arrangement. 🚗 TV ☀ P

PETERBOROUGH: *Express by Holiday Inn* [W] www.hiexpress.co.uk ££ — AE DC MC V — 80
East of England Way, Alwalton, Peterborough PE2 6HE. [01733 284450. [FAX] 01733 284451.
An unusually appealing chain hotel beside the East of England Showground.
Excellent value, especially for families sharing a room. 🚗 TV ☀ P ♿

SOUTHWOLD: *Swan* [W] www.adnams.co.uk ££££ — MC V — 43
Market Place, Southwold, Suffolk IP18 6EG. [01502 722186. [FAX] 01502 724800.
This elegant and comfortable hotel stands near Adnams' brewery, a focal
point for centuries. Some bedrooms in garden annexe. 🚗 TV 🔆 P ♿

SWAFFHAM: *Strattons* [W] www.strattons-hotel.co.uk £££ — AE MC V — 7
4 Ash Close, Swaffham, Norfolk PE37 7NH. [01760 723845. [FAX] 01760 720458.
An eco-friendly, award-winning venture in a neo-classical villa near the
town centre. The interior is dashingly decorated; regional produce is on the
menu. *(See also p585.)* ● *Christmas.* 🚗 TV ☀ P

WELLINGHAM: *Manor House Farm* ££ — 4
Wellingham, nr Fakenham, Norfolk PE32 2IH. [01328 838227. [FAX] 01328 838348.
This bed and breakfast is an 18th-century farmhouse with good views over
the countryside. Two rooms are in a converted stable block with a kitchenette
and large sitting room. Food includes farm produce. Horse-riding available
nearby. Family room; children over 12 preferred. 🚗 TV ☀ P ♿

WOODBRIDGE: *Seckford Hall* [W] www.seckford.co.uk £££ — AE DC MC V — 32
Woodbridge, Suffolk IP13 6NU. [01394 385678. [FAX] 01394 380610.
Off the A12 in peaceful grounds, this Elizabethan house is crammed with
historic interest, as well as every modern comfort. ● *25 Dec.* 🚗 TV ☀ P

THAMES VALLEY

AYLESBURY: *Hartwell House* [W] www.hartwell-house.com £££££ — AE MC V — 46
Oxford Rd, Aylesbury, Oxfordshire HP17 8NL. [01296 747444. [FAX] 01296 747450.
Impeccably restored, this palatial country house's unabashed luxury is tastefully
restrained. Superb Capability Brown grounds *(see p22)*, spa, indoor pool, tennis
courts. 🚗 TV 🔆 ☀ P

BURFORD: *Burford House* [W] www.burfordhouse.co.uk £££ — AE MC V — 8
99 High St, Burford, Oxfordshire OX18 4QA. [01993 823151. [FAX] 01993 823240.
Classic gold-stone and timbered building with a smart interior. Light lunches
and traditional teas are available, but no evening meals. ● *25–26 Dec, 2 weeks
Jan.* 🚗 TV P

CHIPPERFIELD: *Two Brewers* ££ — AE DC MC V — 20
The Common, Chipperfield, King's Langley, Hertfordshire WD4 9BS. [01923 265266.
A huddle of cottages on the edge of the village cricket pitch presents a timeless
English scene. Inside, the bucolic idyll continues in firelit, low-ceilinged bars.
Bedrooms are in outbuildings away from the noise. ● *25 & 26 Dec.* 🚗 TV P ♿

CLANFIELD: *Plough at Clanfield* [W] www.theplough.tablesir.com £££ — AE DC MC V — 12
Bourton Rd, Clanfield, Bampton, Oxfordshire OX18 2RB. [01367 810222.
Striking Elizabethan manor with traditional country furnishings, beams and
creaky floorboards. Well known for its food. ● *Christmas.* 🚗 TV ☀ P ♿

GREAT TEW: *Falkland Arms* [W] www.falklandarms.org.uk ££ — AE MC V — 5
Great Tew, Chipping Norton, Oxfordshire OX7 4DB. [01608 683653. [FAX] 01608 683656.
Stone-built, creeper-covered pub full of old-world charm. Snug bedrooms and
good home cooking. *(See also p609.)* ● *24–27 Dec, 31 Dec–1 Jan.* 🚗 TV ☀ P

HARPENDEN: *Harpenden House* ££££ — AE DC MC V — 76
18 Southdown Rd, Harpenden, Hertfordshire AL5 1PE. [01582 449955.
[FAX] 01582 769858. [W] www.corushotels.com/harpendenhouse
This handsome Georgian house is an efficient business hotel with easy access to
the North London motorway network. 🚗 TV ☀ P ♿

HENLEY-ON-THAMES: *Red Lion* [W] www.redlionhenley.co.uk £££ — AE MC V — 26
Hart St, Henley-on-Thames, Oxfordshire RG9 2AR. [01491 572161. [FAX] 01491 410039.
Overlooking the Thames, this fine old building is one of Henley's dominant
features. Plenty of antiques and rowing memorabilia scattered about. 🚗 TV P

Price categories for a standard double room per night, inclusive of breakfast, service charges and any additional taxes such as VAT: £ under £65 ££ £65–£100 £££ £100–£150 ££££ £150–£200 £££££ £200 plus	**RESTAURANT** Hotel restaurant or dining room serving more than just breakfast; often open to non-residents. **CHILDREN WELCOME** Especially welcoming to families. May have children's facilities such as cots, babysitting, family rooms, etc. **GARDEN/TERRACE** Hotels with a garden, courtyard or terrace, often providing tables for eating outside. **CREDIT CARDS** Indicates which credit cards are accepted: *AE* American Express; *DC* Diners Club; *MC* Master Card/Access; *V* Visa.	CREDIT CARDS	RESTAURANT	CHILDREN WELCOME	GARDEN/TERRACE	NUMBER OF ROOMS

KINGSTON BAGPUIZE: *Fallowfields* W www.fallowfields.com £££
Farringdon Rd, Southmoor, Kingston Bagpuize, Abingdon, Oxfordshire OX13 5BH.
(01865 820416. FAX 01865 821275.
Family-run country house in a sensitively updated historic building. Home-grown produce features on the menu. Most rooms have jacuzzis. 🚗 TV ≈ P
Credit Cards: AE MC V — Restaurant ■, Children ●, Garden ■, Rooms 10

LONG CRENDON: *Angel* W www.angelsrestaurant.co.uk ££
47 Bicester Rd, Long Crendon, Aylesbury, Buckinghamshire HP18 9EE.
(01844 208268. FAX 01844 202497.
The food's the thing at this chic 16th-century inn, but there are quaint bedrooms with uneven floors upstairs (often booked). *(See also p586.)* 🚗 TV ≈ P
Credit Cards: MC V — Restaurant ■, Children ●, Garden ■, Rooms 3

MARLOW: *Compleat Angler* W www.compleatangler-hotel.co.uk £££££
Marlow Bridge, Marlow, Buckinghamshire SL17 1RG. (0870 400 8100. FAX 01628 486388.
A spectacular riverbank setting overlooking Marlow Weir draws the crowds to this traditional hostelry. Good-value leisure breaks. 🚗 TV ⌂ ≈ P
Credit Cards: AE DC MC V — Restaurant ■, Children ●, Garden ■, Rooms 64

MOULSFORD: *Beetle & Wedge* W www.beetle&wedgehotel.co.uk £££££
Ferry Lane, Moulsford on Thames, Wallingford, Oxfordshire OX10 9JF. (01491 651381.
Jerome K Jerome used to live in this idyllic waterfront hideaway. Today visitors beat a path to its door for sophisticated food and smartly furnished rooms. Best river views are from the main building. *(See also p587.)* 🚗 TV ≈ P ♿
Credit Cards: AE DC MC V — Restaurant ■, Children ●, Garden ■, Rooms 10

OXFORD: *Burlington House* W www.burlington-house.co.uk ££
374 Banbury Rd, Oxford OX2 7PP. (01865 513513. FAX 01865 311785.
This upmarket guesthouse in north Oxford is acquiring a loyal following for its great breakfasts and reasonable prices. ● *Christmas.* 🚗 TV ≈ P ♿
Credit Cards: AE MC V — Garden ■, Rooms 11

OXFORD: *Old Bank* W www.oldbank-hotel.co.uk ££££
92–94 High St, Oxford OX1 4BN. (01865 799599. FAX 01865 799598.
Located in a former bank, this hotels's contemporary interior is sleek and stylish, with lots of modern gadgetry. ● *25–26 Dec.* 🚗 TV ⌂ ≈ P ♿
Credit Cards: AE DC MC V — Restaurant ■, Children ●, Garden ■, Rooms 44

OXFORD: *Old Parsonage* W www.oldparsonage-hotel.co.uk ££££
1 Banbury Rd, Oxford OX2 6NN. (01865 310210. FAX 01865 311262.
This ancient creeper-clad building, with its central location and steepish tariffs, is smartly decked out and hard to resist. ● *25–26 Dec.* 🚗 TV P
Credit Cards: AE DC MC V — Restaurant ■, Children ●, Garden ■, Rooms 30

ST ALBANS: *Comfort* W www.choicehotels.com ££
Ryder House, Holywell Hill, St Albans, Hertfordshire AL1 1HG. (01727 848849.
This central hotel occupies an attractive historic building. It retains some character inside as well. Simple meals; helpful staff. 🚗 TV ⌂ ≈ P ♿
Credit Cards: AE DC MC V — Restaurant ■, Children ●, Rooms 60

SHEFFORD WOODLANDS: *Fishers Farm* W www.fishersfarm.co.uk £
Shefford Woodlands, Hungerford, Berkshire RG17 7AB. (01488 648466. FAX 01488 648706.
Welcoming B&B on a family farm. From the open-plan kitchen (meals prepared on request) views extend over the fields. Indoor swimming pool. 🚗 ≈ P
Credit Cards: — Children ●, Garden ■, Rooms 3

STADHAMPTON: *Crazy Bear* W www.crazybearhotel.co.uk £££
Bear Lane, Stadhampton, nr Oxford OX44 7UR. (01865 890714. FAX 01865 400481.
Wacky country pub with outré decor and a choice of Thai or modern British cooking. The zany bedrooms cater for sophisticates. 🚗 TV P
Credit Cards: AE MC V — Restaurant ■, Children ●, Garden ■, Rooms 12

WINDSOR: *Sir Christopher Wren's House* W www.wrensgroup.com ££££
Thames St, Windsor, Berkshire SL4 1PX. (01753 861354. FAX 01753 860172.
A riverside location near Eton Bridge and Windsor Castle. A genuine Wren pedigree (1676) with streamlined facilities. 🚗 TV ≈ P *charge; book ahead.*
Credit Cards: AE DC MC V — Restaurant ■, Children ●, Garden ■, Rooms 92

WOODSTOCK: *Feathers* W www.feathers.co.uk £££
Market St, Woodstock, Oxfordshire OX20 1SX. (01993 812291. FAX 01993 813158.
Smart central hotel in 17th-century premises. Interior decor is dashing and upbeat; the cooking is accomplished modern British. 🚗 TV
Credit Cards: AE DC MC V — Restaurant ■, Children ●, Garden ■, Rooms 20

YATTENDON: *Royal Oak* W www.corushotels.com/royaloak £££ AE DC MC V ■ ■ 5
The Square, Yattendon, Thatcham, Berkshire RG18 0UG. (01635 201325.
A great country pub in a pretty village, with a sophisticated but informal
atmosphere and immaculate bedrooms. Award-winning food. ■ TV ⚡ P

WESSEX

ABBOTSBURY: *Abbey House* W www.theabbeyhouse.co.uk £ ■ ● 5
Church St, Abbotsbury, Dorset DT3 4JJ. (01305 871330. FAX 01305 871088.
This charming guesthouse was once the infirmary for the Benedictine abbey
nearby. Lunch only served (Apr–Oct). Occasional concerts. ■ TV ⚡ P

BATH: *Villa Magdala* W www.villamagdala.co.uk ££ AE MC V ■ 18
Henrietta Rd, Bath BA2 6LX. (01225 466329. FAX 01225 483207.
A Victorian villa overlooking Bath's delightful Henrietta Park make a quiet,
relaxing stay. ● Christmas week. ■ TV ⚡ P

BATH: *Royal Crescent* W www.royalcrescent.co.uk £££££ AE DC MC V ■ ● ■ 45
16 Royal Crescent, Bath BA1 2LS. (01225 823333. FAX 01225 339401.
For the ultimate Regency experience, this ultra-discreet establishment is truly
sumptuous inside (see p246). Staff are friendly; luxury spa. ■ TV ⬆ & ⚡ P

BATHFORD: *Eagle House* W www.eaglehouse.co.uk ££ MC V ● ■ 8
Church St, Bathford, Bath BA1 7RS. (01225 859946. FAX 01225 859430.
Understated Georgian elegance just outside Bath. Family-friendly and a
sociable Labrador. Cooked breakfast extra. ● 20 Dec–3 Jan. ■ TV & ⚡ P

BOURNEMOUTH: *Miramar* W www.miramar-bournemouth.com £££ AE MC V ■ ● ■ 43
East Overcliff Dr, Bournemouth, Dorset BH1 3AL. (01202 556581. FAX 01202 291242.
Views from the clifftops are the main appeal of this smart, traditionally
furnished Edwardian hotel. Ask for a sea-view room. ■ TV ⬆ & ⚡ P

BRADFORD-ON-AVON: *Bradford Old Windmill* ££ MC V ■ ■ 3
4 Masons Lane, Bradford-on-Avon, Wiltshire BA15 1QN.
(01225 866842. FAX 01225 866648. W www.bradfordoldwindmill.co.uk
B&B in a stone-built, 19th-century windmill with quirky bedrooms – the circular
tower room has a round bed. Vegetarian cooking. ● Jan–Feb. ■ TV ⚡ P

BRISTOL: *Hotel du Vin* W www.hotelduvin.com £££ AE DC MC V ■ ● 40
The Sugar House, Narrow Lewins Mead, Bristol BS1 2NU. (0117 925 5577.
Several converted warehouses create an interesting setting for this trendy hotel-
restaurant. Dynamic decor, exemplary facilities and bistro food. ■ TV ⬆ & P

CALNE: *Chilvester Hill House* W www.chilvesterhillhouse.co.uk ££ AE DC MC V ■ 3
Calne, Wiltshire SN11 0LP. (01249 813981. FAX 01249 814217.
A civilized welcome is guaranteed at this quiet Victorian country home (a
long-established Wolsey Lodge) just off the A4. Good cooking. ■ TV ⚡ P

DORCHESTER: *Casterbridge* W www.casterbridgehotel.co.uk ££ AE DC MC V ● ■ 14
49 High St, Dorchester, Dorset DT1 1HU. (01305 264043. FAX 01305 260884.
Family-run B&B in a Georgian townhouse, offering a smart but unpretentious
stay. Breakfast served in the conservatory. ● 25–26 Dec. ■ TV & ⚡ P

DULVERTON: *Ashwick House* W www.ashwickhouse.co.uk ££ ■ ■ 6
Dulverton, Somerset TA22 9QD. (& FAX 01398 323868.
Tranquil Edwardian house in the heart of Exmoor. The terrace makes a
splendid vantage point for summertime breakfasts. ■ TV ⚡ P

EVERSHOT: *Summer Lodge* W www.summerlodgehotel.com £££££ AE DC MC V ■ ● 18
Evershot, Dorchester, Dorset DT2 0JR. (01935 83424. FAX 01935 83005.
This gorgeous Georgian dower house in deepest Wessex countryside is perfect
for a peaceful, pampered stay. Wonderful food and caring service. ■ TV & P

GILLINGHAM: *Stock Hill House* W www.stockhillhouse.co.uk £££££ MC V ■ 8
Stock Hill, Gillingham, Dorset SP8 5NR. (01747 823626. FAX 01747 825628.
A flamboyant interior stuffed with antiques makes this 19th-century gentleman's
residence an entertaining stay. Superb cooking and fine wines. ■ TV ⚡ P

GLASTONBURY: *Number 3* W www.numberthree.co.uk ££ AE DC MC V ● ■ 5
3 Magdalene St, Glastonbury, Somerset BA6 9EW. (01458 832129. FAX 01458 834227.
An ideal B&B base in central Glastonbury, this elegant Georgian house was
once home to Winston Churchill's mother. ● Dec–Jan. ■ TV ⚡ P

For key to symbols see back flap

Price categories for a standard double room per night, inclusive of breakfast, service charges and any additional taxes such as VAT:
ⓔ under £65
ⓔⓔ £65–£100
ⓔⓔⓔ £100–£150
ⓔⓔⓔⓔ £150–£200
ⓔⓔⓔⓔⓔ £200 plus

RESTAURANT
Hotel restaurant or dining room serving more than just breakfast; often open to non-residents.
CHILDREN WELCOME
Especially welcoming to families. May have children's facilities such as cots, babysitting, family rooms, etc.
GARDEN/TERRACE
Hotels with a garden, courtyard or terrace, often providing tables for eating outside.
CREDIT CARDS
Indicates which credit cards are accepted: *AE* American Express; *DC* Diners Club; *MC* Master Card/Access; *V* Visa.

		CREDIT CARDS	RESTAURANT	CHILDREN WELCOME	GARDEN/TERRACE	NUMBER OF ROOMS
KIMMERIDGE: *Kimmeridge Farmhouse* @ kimmeridgefarmhouse@hotmail.com ⓔ Kimmeridge, Wareham, Dorset BH20 5PE. ☎ 01929 480990. FAX 01929 481503. Super B&B on a working farm, perfect for exploring Purbeck and the Coastal Path. Parts of the house date from the 14th century. ● *Christmas.* 🛏 TV 💈 P					■	3
LACOCK: *At the Sign of the Angel* w www.lacock.co.uk ⓔⓔⓔ 6 Church St, Lacock, Wiltshire SN15 2LB. ☎ 01249 730230. FAX 01249 730527. Antique, half-timbered inn (a former wool-merchant's house) in a showcase Wiltshire village. The restaurant is a focal point *(see also p588)*, but the quaint bedrooms are full of character. ● *23–31 Dec.* 🛏 TV 👦 P	AE DC MC V	■	●		10
MIDDLE WINTERSLOW: *The Beadles* w www.guestaccom.co.uk/754.htm ⓔ Middleton, Middle Winterslow, Salisbury, Wiltshire SP5 1QS. ☎ 01980 862922. A friendly guesthouse near Salisbury. The house is modern neo-Georgian, skilfully decorated in period style. Dinners by arrangement. 🛏 TV 💈 P	MC V			■	3
MONTACUTE: *Milk House* ⓔ The Borough, Montacute, Somerset TA15 6XB. ☎ 01935 823823. A captivating 15th-century B&B with country furnishings – a real home-from-home. Appetizing dinners by arrangement. ● *Nov–Mar.* 🛏 💈			●	■	3
PORLOCK WEIR: *Andrews on the Weir* ⓔⓔ Porlock Weir, Minehead, Somerset TA24 8PB. ☎ 01643 863300. w www.andrewsontheweir.co.uk In a picturesque hamlet where Exmoor meets the sea, this stylish restaurant-with-rooms has immaculate bedrooms. ● *2nd–3rd weeks of Jan.* 🛏 TV 💈 P	AE DC MC V	■		■	5
SHEPTON MALLET: *Charlton House* w www.charltonhouse.com ⓔⓔⓔⓔ Charlton Rd, Shepton Mallet, Somerset BA4 4PR. ☎ 01749 342008. FAX 01749 346362. Interior design is the watchword at this 17th-century manor. A showcase of luscious fabrics and daring colour-schemes. Top-quality cooking. 🛏 TV P	AE DC MC V	■	●		25
SHIPTON GORGE: *Innsacre Farmhouse* w www.innsacre.com ⓔⓔ Shipton Lane, Shipton Gorge, Bridport, Dorset DT6 4LJ. ☎ & FAX 01308 456137. This delightful farm guesthouse has inglenook fires and plenty of imaginative home cooking. Recently refurbished bedrooms have dashing rustic decor (duvets and dark oak beds). No showers. ● *24 Dec–3 Jan.* 🛏 TV 💈 P	MC V	■		■	4
TEFFONT EVIAS: *Howard's House* w www.howardshousehotel.co.uk ⓔⓔⓔ Teffont Evias, Salisbury, Wiltshire SP3 5RJ. ☎ 01722 716392. FAX 01722 716820. This relaxing hideaway west of Salisbury is a 17th-century dower house in pretty gardens. Dinners are memorably excellent. ● *Christmas.* 🛏 TV P	AE DC MC V	■	●	■	9
WAREHAM: *Priory* w www.theprioryhotel.co.uk ⓔⓔⓔⓔ Church Green, Wareham, Dorset BH20 4ND. ☎ 01929 551666. FAX 01929 554519. Beautiful old priory in gorgeous riverside gardens. Ambitious cooking in an atmospheric cellar restaurant. 🛏 TV 💈 P	DC MC V	■		■	18
WEYMOUTH: *Seaham Guesthouse* w www.theseaham.co.uk ⓔ 3 Waterloo Place, Weymouth, Dorset DT4 7NU. ☎ 01305 782010. Impeccable B&B with friendly, informal owners. Bedrooms are cosy, some with sea views. Early-bird breakfasts for ferry travellers. ● *Christmas week.* 🛏 TV 💈	AE MC V				5
WIMBORNE MINSTER: *Beechleas* w www.beechleas.com ⓔⓔ 17 Poole Rd, Wimborne Minster, Dorset BH21 1QA. ☎ 01202 841684. FAX 01202 849344. The dining room is the focal point at this welcoming place – a Georgian townhouse with a graciously furnished interior. Some bedrooms are in a quieter coach-house annexe. ● *24 Dec–12 Jan.* 🛏 TV 👦 💈 P	AE DC MC V	■	●	■	9
WOOKEY HOLE: *Glencot House* w www.glencothouse.co.uk ⓔⓔ Glencot Lane, Wookey Hole, Wells, Somerset BA5 1BH. ☎ 01749 677160. FAX 01749 670210. A Victorian mansion in Jacobean style, set in parkland. Ornate panelling, antique furnishings and curios make it a fascinating stay. 🛏 TV 💈 P	AE DC MC V	■	●	■	13

DEVON AND CORNWALL

ASHBURTON: *Tugela* @ paul@tugelahotel.freeserve.co.uk   £   MC V   7
68 East St, Ashburton, Devon TQ13 7AX. [01364 652206. FAX 01364 652 477.
A positive welcome for families with children is a major attraction of this Georgian townhouse, but it also offers tasty home cooking, stylish decor and lots of toys and games. ● *Christmas & 3 weeks in Jan.* 🛏 TV 🍴 P

BELSTONE: *Tor Down House* W www.tordownhouse.co.uk   ££   MC V   2
Belstone, Okehampton, Devon EX20 1QY. [& FAX 01837 840731.
Idyllic B&B in a thatched longhouse on the edge of Dartmoor. Super gardens, welcoming hosts and loads of character. ● *Nov–Mar.* 🛏 TV 🍴 P

BIGBURY-ON-SEA: *Burgh Island* W www.burghisland.com   £££££   MC V   15
Bigbury-on-Sea, Kingsbridge, Devon TQ7 4BG. [01548 810514. FAX 01548 810243.
Romantic Art Deco-themed hotel on a tidal island. Visitors arrive by sea tractor to find themselves in a glamorous 1930s time warp. Rates include extravagant suites and a lavish dinner. *(See also p277.)* ● *first 3 weeks Jan.* 🛏 TV P

BISHOP'S TAWTON: *Halmpstone Manor* W www.halmpstonemanor.co.uk   £££   AE DC MC V   5
Bishop's Tawton, Barnstaple, Devon EX32 0EA. [01271 830321. FAX 01271 830826.
This manor house is an elegant country-house hotel with charming, professional staff. ● *Christmas, New Year & Feb.* 🛏 TV 🍴 P

BOSCASTLE: *The Old Rectory* W www.stjuliot.com   ££   MC   4
St Juliot, Boscastle, Cornwall PL35 0BT. [01840 250 225.
Thomas Hardy stayed in this Victorian rectory, which has large gardens and is near the beach. Breakfasts with home produce. 🛏 TV 🍴 P

BOTALLACK: *Botallack Manor*   £   3
Botallack, St Just, Penzance, Cornwall TR19 7QG. [01736 788525.
Joyce Cargeeg has been offering her hospitable style of B&B in this granite house near Land's End for more than 50 years. ● *Christmas.* 🛏 TV 🍴 P

CHILLATON: *Quither Mill* W www.quithermill.co.uk   ££   MC V   4
Quither, Tavistock, Devon PL19 0PZ. [& FAX 01822 860160.
A converted mill is the setting for this relaxed Wolsey Lodge. Mouthwatering dinners served house-party style at a single table. 🛏 TV ♿ 🍴 P

CRACKINGTON HAVEN: *Manor Farm*   ££   5
Crackington Haven, Bude, Cornwall EX23 0JW. [01840 230 304.
An historic farmhouse close to a dramatic stretch of Heritage Coast. Beautifully furnished interior and delicious dinners. ● *Christmas & New Year.* 🛏 TV P

EXETER: *Barcelona* W www.hotelbarcelona-uk.com   ££   AE DC MC V   46
Magdalen St, Exeter, Devon EX2 4HY. [01392 281000. FAX 01392 281001.
Voguish conversion of a former eye hospital, the bistro buzzes with a trendy crowd, and bedrooms are fitted with electronic extras. 🛏 TV 📺 ♿ P

FOWEY: *Marina* W www.themarinahotel.co.uk   £££   AE MC V   13
17 The Esplanade, Fowey, Cornwall PL23 1HY. [01726 833315. FAX 01726 832779.
Dazzling estuary views from a former bishop's residence with considerable style and good food. 🛏 TV ♿ P

GALMPTON: *Maypool Park* W www.maypoolpark.co.uk   ££   MC V   10
Maypool, Galmpton, Devon TQ5 0ET. [01803 842442. FAX 01803 845782.
This tranquil retreat stands high above the River Dart, next to Agatha Christie's former home, and within easy reach of Torbay. 🛏 TV 🍴 P

GITTISHAM: *Combe House* W www.thishotel.com   £££   AE DC MC V   15
Gittisham, Nr Honiton, Devon EX14 3AD. [01404 540400. FAX 01404 46004.
This fascinating country house set amid parklands has been restored with antiques and period fittings. Friendly hosts, ambitious cooking. 🛏 TV 🍴 P

HELSTON: *Nansloe Manor* W www.nansloe-manor.co.uk   £££   AE MC V   8
Meneage Rd, Helston, Cornwall TR13 0SB. [01326 574691. FAX 01326 564680.
A friendly family welcome and good cooking make this quietly grand Georgian building special. The atmosphere is relaxing. 🛏 TV P

KINGSWEAR: *Nonsuch House* W www.nonsuch-house.co.uk   ££   MC V   3
Church Hill, Kingswear, Devon TQ6 0BX. [01803 752829. FAX 01803 752357.
Breathtaking views towards Dartmouth from this superior Edwardian guest-house. Elegant decor and welcoming family hosts. 🛏 TV 🍴

For key to symbols see back flap

Price categories for a standard double room per night, inclusive of breakfast, service charges and any additional taxes such as VAT:
£ under £65
££ £65–£100
£££ £100–£150
££££ £150–£200
£££££ £200 plus

RESTAURANT
Hotel restaurant or dining room serving more than just breakfast; often open to non-residents.

CHILDREN WELCOME
Especially welcoming to families. May have children's facilities such as cots, babysitting, family rooms, etc.

GARDEN/TERRACE
Hotels with a garden, courtyard or terrace, often providing tables for eating outside.

CREDIT CARDS
Indicates which credit cards are accepted: AE American Express; DC Diners Club; MC Master Card/Access; V Visa.

	CREDIT CARDS	RESTAURANT	CHILDREN WELCOME	GARDEN/TERRACE	NUMBER OF ROOMS
LANDEWEDNACK: *Landewednack House* ££ Church Cove, Landewednack, The Lizard, Cornwall TR12 7PQ. 01326 290909. FAX 01326 290192. @ landewednackhouse@amserve.com Beautiful gardens and elegantly furnished rooms in a quiet Georgian rectory. Heated outdoor pool; close to the sea. Meals to order. ● Christmas. ▬ TV ✎ P	MC V	■		■	3
MAWNAN SMITH: *Meudon* W www.meudon.co.uk ££££ Mawnan Smith, Falmouth, Cornwall TR11 5HT. 01326 250541. FAX 01326 250543. Traditional hospitality at this long-established, family-run hotel. Sub-tropical gardens running down to the sea provide a stunning backdrop. Excellent value for lone travellers. ● 3 Jan–early Feb. ▬ TV ⬆ ♿ P	AE DC MC V	■	●	■	29
MEMBURY: *Lea Hill* W www.leahill.co.uk £££ Membury, Axminster, Devon EX13 7AQ. 01404 881881. FAX 01404 881890. Idyllic complex of thatched buildings in rolling countryside. Immaculate; bold but tasteful decor. Super breakfasts. ▬ TV P	AE MC V			■	11
MORTEHOE: *Cleeve House* W www.cleevehouse.co.uk £ North Morte Rd, Mortehoe, Woolacombe, Devon EX34 7ED. 01271 870719. A civilized welcome in an extended modern house on a stunning bit of coastline. Afternoon teas and home-laid breakfast eggs. ● Nov–Mar. ▬ TV ♿ ✎ P	MC V	■			7
NEWQUAY: *Sands* W www.sandsresort.co.uk £££ Watergate Rd, Porth, Newquay, Cornwall TR7 3LX. 01637 872864. FAX 01637 876365. A large, well-equipped family resort near North Cornwall's wonderful surfing beaches. Bedrooms are light and spacious. ● end Nov–Feb. ▬ TV ♿ ✎ P	MC V	■	●	■	70
NORTH BOVEY: *Blackaller* W www.blackaller.co.uk ££ North Bovey, Moretonhampstead, Devon TQ13 8QY. 01647 440322. FAX 01647 441131. A 17th-century woollen mill in a wooded Dartmoor valley run on relaxed, unassuming, eco-friendly lines. Decor is tastefully rustic. ● Jan–Feb. ▬ TV ✎ P		■		■	3
PELYNT: *Jubilee Inn* W www.jubileeinn.com ££ Jubilee Hill, Pelynt, Nr Looe, Cornwall PL13 2JZ. 01503 220312. FAX 01503 220920. A cheerful, unpretentious pub-with-rooms. A wide range of meals is served, sometimes in the sheltered beer gardens. Bedrooms are cottagey. ▬ TV P	MC V	■		■	11
PENZANCE: *Summer House* W www.summerhouse-cornwall.com ££ Cornwall Terrace, Penzance, Cornwall TR18 4HL. 01736 363744. FAX 01736 360959. Mediterranean cooking and chic bedrooms make a winning combination in this charming venture just behind the promenade. ● Nov–Feb. ▬ TV ✎ P	MC V	■		■	5
PERRANUTHNOE: *Ednovean Farm* W www.ednoveanfarm.co.u ££ Perranuthnoe, Nr Penzance, Cornwall TR20 9LZ. 01736 711883. FAX 01736 710480. A flair for interior decor and sumptuous breakfasts distinguish this converted farmhouse B&B with vistas of St Michael's Mount. ● Christmas. ▬ TV ✎ P	AE MC V			■	3
PLYMOUTH: *Athenaeum Lodge* W www.athenaeumlodge.co.uk £ 4 Athenaeum St, The Hoe, Plymouth, Devon PL1 2RQ. & FAX 01752 665005. This well-kept townhouse B&B, with pink-and-pretty bedrooms, stands near Drake's famous bowling green (see p278). ● Christmas & New Year. ▬ TV ✎ P	MC V				9
ROCK: *St Enodoc* W www.enodoc-hotel.co.uk ££££ Rock, Nr Wadebridge, Cornwall PL27 6LA. 01208 863394. FAX 01208 863970. This breezily designed place overlooks the Camel estuary. It's cheerful, well-managed and very stylish. New World cooking. ● Jan–mid-Feb. ▬ TV ✎ P	AE MC V	■	●	■	20
ST BLAZEY: *Nanscawen Manor* W www.nanscawen.com ££ Prideaux Rd, Luxulyan Valley, St Blazey, Cornwall PL24 2SR. 01726 814488. A secluded B&B in gardens lush enough to evoke the nearby Eden Project (see pp270–71). The cottagey façade is deceptive; it's smartly spacious. ▬ TV ✎ P	MC V			■	3

ST HILARY: *Ennys* w www.ennys.co.uk ££ MC V ■ 5
Trewhella Lane, St Hilary, Penzance, Cornwall TR20 9BZ. 01736 740262. FAX 01736 740055.
The perfect rustic B&B: a 17th-century farmhouse with delightful gardens
and a pool. Family suites in converted barn. ● Nov–Mar. 🛏 TV ⚡ P

ST KEYNE: *Well House* w www.wellhouse.co.uk £££ MC V ■ ● ■ 9
St Keyne, Liskeard, Cornwall PL14 4RN. 01579 342001. FAX 01579 343891.
In the tranquil Looe Valley, this Victorian tea-planter's home makes a sophis-
ticated retreat. Good food and fine wines; tennis and swimming. 🛏 TV P

ST MAWES: *Rising Sun* w www.innsofcornwall.co.uk £££ MC V ■ ● ■ 8
The Square, St Mawes, Truro, Cornwall TR2 5DJ. 01326 270233. FAX 01326 270198.
This classy harbourfront pub makes a valuable contribution to St Mawes'
upmarket image. The bedrooms exude an air of casual chic. 🛏 TV P

ST MAWES: *Hotel Tresanton* w www.tresanton.com £££££ AE MC V ■ ● ■ 29
St Mawes, Truro, Cornwall TR2 5DR. 01326 270055. FAX 01326 270053.
This exceptional hotel, redesigned in 1997 by its present owner, was
originally a cluster of old houses overlooking the sea. Beautiful views, an
elegant and casual atmosphere and an excellent restaurant. 🛏 TV P

SALCOMBE: *Soar Mill Cove* w www.makepeacehotels.co.uk £££££ AE MC V ■ ● ■ 20
Soar Mill Cove, Salcombe, Devon TQ7 3DS. 01548 561566. FAX 01548 561223.
It's hard to imagine a more peaceful coastal hideaway. This family-run hotel
provides excellent cooking and supreme comfort. ● Jan. 🛏 TV ⚡ P

TEIGNMOUTH: *Thomas Luny House* w www.thomas-luny-house.co.uk ££ MC V ■ 4
Teign St, Teignmouth, Devon TQ14 8EG. 01626 772976.
A quiet, upmarket B&B in a charming Regency house, beautifully kept and
full of personality. Summer breakfasts in the walled garden. 🛏 TV ⚡ P

VERYAN: *Nare* w www.narehotel.co.uk £££££ MC V ■ ● ■ 39
Carne Beach, Veryan, Truro, Cornwall TR2 5PF. 01872 501111. FAX 01872 501856.
This gloriously located hotel keeps visitors of all ages satisfied. Lots to do, plus
space to relax. Two heated swimming pools; lovely gardens. 🛏 TV P

WIDEGATES: *Coombe Farm* w www.coombefarmhotel.co.uk ££ AE MC V ● ● 3
Widegates, Looe, Cornwall PL13 1QN. 01503 240223. FAX 01503 240895.
A rural guesthouse offering a great welcome to families. Large grounds and
plenty of animals and activities. ● Nov–Feb. 🛏 TV ⚡ P

HEART OF ENGLAND

ARMSCOTE: *Fox & Goose* w www.aboveaverage.co.uk ££ AE MC V ■ 4
Armscote, Stratford-upon-Avon, Warwickshire CV37 8DD. & FAX 01608 682293.
This charming village pub-with-rooms is catching on fast since a new owner
took it several rungs upmarket. Now it fizzes with life. ● 25–26 Dec. 🛏 TV P

BIBURY: *Swan* w www.swanhotel.co.uk ££££ AE DC MC V ■ 20
Bibury, Cirencester, Gloucestershire GL7 5NW. 01285 740695. FAX 01285 740473.
This riverside coaching inn is extremely photogenic; inside, the Swan is
comfortably smart with well-equipped bedrooms. 🛏 TV ⚡ P

BIRMINGHAM: *Hotel du Vin & Bistro* w www.hotelduvin.com £££ AE DC MC V ■ ● 66
25 Church St, Birmingham B3 2NR. 0121-200 0600. FAX 0121-236 0889.
A temple of style in a redundant eye hospital. This witty, glamorous,
centrally placed hotel-brasserie oozes casual chic. 🛏 TV ⚡

BLACKWELL: *Blackwell Grange* w www.blackwellgrange.co.uk ££ AE MC V ■ 4
Blackwell, Shipston-on-Stour, Warwickshire CV36 4PF. 01608 682357. FAX 01608 682856.
Historic working farm in tranquil Cotswold surroundings. A beautifully
furnished and personal family home. ● Christmas & New Year. 🛏 TV ⚡ P

BLOCKLEY: *Old Bakery* w ££££ AE MC V ■ 3
High St, Blockley, Moreton-in-Marsh, Gloucestershire GL56 9EU. & FAX 01386 700408.
Award-winning, sociable hotel in converted Victorian cottage. Lovely Cotswold
surroundings. Room rates include dinner. ● Dec–Jan, 2 weeks Jun. 🛏 TV ⚡ P

BROAD CAMPDEN: *Malt House* w www.malt-house.co.uk £££ AE MC V ■ ● ■ 7
Broad Campden, Chipping Campden, Gloucestershire GL55 6UU. 01386 840295.
Idyllic Cotswold guesthouse with charming gardens. Generous breakfasts make
use of home-grown produce. Elegant bedrooms. ● 23–27 Dec. 🛏 TV ⚡ P

Price categories for a standard double room per night, inclusive of breakfast, service charges and any additional taxes such as VAT:
£ under £65
££ £65–£100
£££ £100–£150
££££ £150–£200
£££££ £200 plus

RESTAURANT
Hotel restaurant or dining room serving more than just breakfast; often open to non-residents.
CHILDREN WELCOME
Especially welcoming to families. May have children's facilities such as cots, babysitting, family rooms, etc.
GARDEN/TERRACE
Hotels with a garden, courtyard or terrace, often providing tables for eating outside.
CREDIT CARDS
Indicates which credit cards are accepted: *AE* American Express; *DC* Diners Club; *MC* Master Card/Access; *V* Visa.

	CREDIT CARDS	RESTAURANT	CHILDREN WELCOME	GARDEN/TERRACE	NUMBER OF ROOMS
BROADWAY: *Barn House* @ barnhouse@btinternet.com £ 152 High St, Broadway, Worcestershire WR12 7AJ. & FAX 01386 858633. Quiet B&B in large, beautiful grounds on the edge of a popular Cotswold village. Simple, cottagey bedrooms. Swimming pool. TV P			●	■	4
BUCKLAND: *Buckland Manor* W www.bucklandmanor.com £££££ Buckland, Broadway, Gloucestershire WR12 7LY. 01386 852626. FAX 01386 853557. Archetypal Cotswold manor dating back to Domesday times. Glorious gardens. Exquisitely furnished in country-house style. TV P	AE DC MC V	■		■	13
CHELTENHAM: *Georgian House* W www.georgianhouse.net ££ 77 Montpellier Terrace, Cheltenham, Gloucestershire GL50 1XA. 01242 515577. A classic sandstone terrace gives an authentic air of Georgian living to this reasonably priced B&B. Hearty breakfasts. ● *Christmas–New Year.* TV P	AE DC MC V				3
CHELTENHAM: *Kandinsky* W www.hotelkandisky.com ££ Bayshill Rd, Cheltenham, Gloucestershire GL50 3AS. 01242 527788. FAX 01242 226412. The exterior is conventional Regency, but inside this is a delightfully funky place with eccentricities galore. Unobtrusive service and a pizzeria. TV P	AE DC MC V	■	●	■	48
CHIPPING CAMPDEN: *Cotswold House* W www.cotswoldhouse.co ££££ The Square, Chipping Campden, Gloucestershire GL55 6AN. 01386 840330. Townhouse architecture and attractive decor in a Cotswold location. The restaurant attracts many non-residents. Charming rear garden. TV P	AE MC V	■	●	■	20
EVESHAM: *Evesham* W www.eveshamhotel.com £££ Cooper's Lane, off Waterside, Evesham, Worcestershire WR11 6DA. 01386 765566. This entertaining, unconventional place is family-friendly, with themed bedrooms and loads to do in the grounds. Indoor swimming pool. Very popular at weekends – book well ahead. ● *25–26 Dec.* TV P	AE DC MC V	■	●	■	40
GLEWSTONE: *Glewstone Court* W www.glewstonecourt.com ££ Glewstone, Ross-on-Wye, Herefordshire HR9 6AW. 01989 770367. FAX 01989 770282. A relaxed air pervades this rambling country house overlooking the Wye Valley. Good cooking (regional and organic produce). ● *25–27 Dec.* TV P	AE MC V	■	●	■	8
HEREFORD: *Castle House* W www.castlehse.co.uk ££££ Castle St, Hereford HR1 2NW. 01432 356321. FAX 01432 365909. This dynamic venture utilizes two secluded Georgian villas in the city centre. The interior is extravagantly luxurious. Local specialities feature. TV P	AE MC V	■	●	■	15
HOPWAS: *Oak Tree Farm* ££ Hints Rd, Hopwas, Tamworth, Staffordshire B78 3AA. & FAX 01827 56807. Just off the M42, these converted farm buildings enjoy views of open countryside. This high-quality B&B offers immaculate bedrooms, excellent breakfasts and an indoor swimming pool. ● *Christmas & New Year.* TV P	AE MC V			■	7
ILMINGTON: *Howard Arms* W www.howardarms.com ££ Lower Green, Ilmington, Shipston-on-Stour, Warwickshire CV36 4LT. & FAX 01608 682226. A classy dining pub in a charming Cotswold village. The building is ancient, the interior furnished with taste. Real ales and fine wines. TV P	MC V			■	3
IRONBRIDGE: *Library House* W www.libraryhouse.com £ Severn Bank, Ironbridge, Shropshire TF8 7AN. 01952 432299. FAX 01952 433967. A charming Georgian B&B cottage (formerly the local library) by the famous iron bridge. Crammed with books. Pretty garden. ● *Jan.* TV				■	4
LEDBURY: *Feathers* W www.feathers-ledbury.co.uk ££ High St, Ledbury, Herefordshire HR8 1DS. 01531 635266. FAX 01531 638955. This striking timbered coaching inn offers a comfortably furnished, traditional interior. Streetside bedrooms may be noisy. Gym; indoor pool. TV P	AE DC MC V	■	●	■	19

LEYSTERS: *Hills Farm* W www.thehillsfarm.co.uk £
Leysters, Leominster, Herefordshire HR6 0HP. (01568 750205. FAX 01568 750306.
This farmhouse B&B is a delightful place to unwind. Several rooms are in
converted outbuildings. Masses of books, boardgames and magazines.
Dinner if pre-booked. ● *Nov–Feb & 2 weeks in June.* ▮ TV & ✂ P

LITTLE MALVERN: *Holdfast Cottage* W www.holdfast-cottage.co.uk ££
Marlbank Rd, Little Malvern, Worcestershire WR13 6NA. (01684 310288. FAX 01684 311117.
Quintessential country cottage in rural location overlooking the Malvern
Hills. Cosy bedrooms full of thoughtful extras. ▮ TV & ✂ P

LUDLOW: *Mr Underhill's* W www.mr-underhills.co.uk £££
Dinham Weir, Ludlow, Shropshire SY8 1EH. (01584 874431.
Acclaimed restaurant-with-rooms in a beautifully located mill on the River
Teme. All the crisp, simple bedrooms enjoy good views. Brilliant modern
European cooking. ● *Christmas week & 1 week Jan.* ▮ TV ✂ P

MALVERN WELLS: *Cottage in the Wood* W www.cottageinthewood.co.uk ££
Holywell Rd, Malvern Wells, Worcestershire WR14 4LG. (01684 575859. FAX 01684 560662.
Surrounded by rolling, wooded countryside, this family-run Georgian dower
house is an ideal Malvern touring base. ▮ TV P

NORTON: *Hundred House* W www.hundredhouse.co.uk £££
Bridgnorth Rd, Norton, Shropshire TF11 9EE. (01952 730353. FAX 01952 730355.
Effortlessly decorated, family-run inn with a cosy, homespun feel. The
brasserie features wide-ranging menus and home-brewed ales. ▮ TV ✂ P

OAKAMOOR: *Bank House* W www.smoothhound.co.uk/hotels/bank.html ££
Farley Lane, Oakamoor, Stoke-on-Trent, Staffordshire ST10 3BD. (& FAX 01538 702810.
Outstanding B&B accommodation in the quiet Churnet Valley near Alton
Towers Theme Park. Large lovely garden ● *Christmas week.* ▮ TV ✂ P

PAINSWICK: *Painswick* W www.painswickhotel.com £££
Kemps Lane, Painswick, Gloucestershire GL6 6YB. (01452 812160. FAX 01452 814059.
A grandly elegant Palladian-style rectory in a charming village near
Gloucester. Despite its splendour, it is entirely unstuffy and informal. ▮ TV P

PRESTBURY: *White House Manor* W www.thewhitehouse.uk.com £££
New Rd, Prestbury, Macclesfield, Cheshire SK10 4HP. (01625 829376. FAX 01625 828627.
Romantic bedrooms team up with some talented cooking in this picturesque
village. A useful base for Quarry Bank Mill. ● *25–26 Dec.* ▮ TV & ✂ P

SHREWSBURY: *Albright Hussey* W www.albrighthussey.co.uk £££
Ellesmere Rd, Shrewsbury, Shropshire SY4 3AF. (01939 290571. FAX 01939 291143.
Historic moated-and-mullioned manor house, with wide-ranging international
menus. Characterful bedrooms in the original house. ▮ TV & ✂ P

STRATFORD-UPON-AVON: *Victoria Spa Lodge* ££
Bishopton Lane, Stratford-upon-Avon, Warwickshire CV37 9QY. (01789 267985.
FAX 01789 204728. W www.stratford-upon-avon.co.uk/victoriaspa.htm
A friendly canalside B&B just outside Stratford, set in a grand, gabled
building with tall chimneys (the former pump-room of a spa). Light, fresh
bedrooms and plenty of period features. ▮ TV ✂ P

SUTTON COLDFIELD: *New Hall* W www.newhallhotel.net £££££
Walmley Rd, Sutton Coldfield, West Midlands B76 1QX. (0121 378 2442. FAX 0121 378 4637.
Romantic escapism on the northern fringes of the Black Country. This ancient
moated manor in gorgeous grounds has fine period features. ▮ TV & ✂ P

TEWKESBURY: *Abbey Antiques* @ brazdys@amserve.net £
61 Church St, Tewkesbury, Gloucestershire GL20 5RZ. (& FAX 01684 298145.
An antique shop B&B, with plenty of interesting bits and bobs. The abbey
bells peal out across the road, and hens scuffle round the garden. ▮ TV ✂ P

ULLINGSWICK: *The Steppes* W www.steppeshotel.co.uk ££
Ullingswick, Hereford HR1 3JG. (01432 820424. FAX 01432 820042.
Rustic charm and superb home cooking in skilfully converted farm buildings
of great character and antiquity. A delightfully peaceful base for exploring
rural Herefordshire. ● *Nov–mid-Feb.* ▮ TV & ✂ P

WILMCOTE: *Pear Tree Cottage* W www.peartreecot.co.uk £
Church Rd, Wilmcote, Stratford-upon-Avon, Warwickshire CV37 9UX. (01789 205889.
B&B in a gorgeous timbered cottage with Shakespearean associations. Good
breakfasts; super gardens; self-catering apartment. ● *23 Dec–10 Jan.* ▮ TV ✂ P

Establishment	Credit cards					Number of rooms
Leysters: Hills Farm	MC V			■		5
Little Malvern: Holdfast Cottage	MC V	■	●	■		8
Ludlow: Mr Underhill's	MC V	■	●	■		6
Malvern Wells: Cottage in the Wood	AE MC V	■	●	■		31
Norton: Hundred House	MC V	■	●	■		10
Oakamoor: Bank House	DC MC V		●	■		3
Painswick: Painswick	AE MC V	■	●	■		19
Prestbury: White House Manor	AE MC V	■		■		11
Shrewsbury: Albright Hussey	AE DC MC V	■	●	■		26
Stratford-upon-Avon: Victoria Spa Lodge	MC V		●	■		7
Sutton Coldfield: New Hall	AE DC MC V	■	●	■		60
Tewkesbury: Abbey Antiques				■		3
Ullingswick: The Steppes	MC V	■		■		6
Wilmcote: Pear Tree Cottage				■		5

<table>
<tr><td colspan="2">

Price categories for a standard double room per night, inclusive of breakfast, service charges and any additional taxes such as VAT:
£ under £65
££ £65–£100
£££ £100–£150
££££ £150–£200
£££££ £200 plus

</td></tr>
</table>

RESTAURANT
Hotel restaurant or dining room serving more than just breakfast; often open to non-residents.

CHILDREN WELCOME
Especially welcoming to families. May have children's facilities such as cots, babysitting, family rooms, etc.

GARDEN/TERRACE
Hotels with a garden, courtyard or terrace, often providing tables for eating outside.

CREDIT CARDS
Indicates which credit cards are accepted: *AE* American Express; *DC* Diners Club; *MC* Master Card/Access; *V* Visa.

	CREDIT CARDS	RESTAURANT	CHILDREN WELCOME	GARDEN/TERRACE	NUMBER OF ROOMS
WINCHCOMBE: *Wesley House* W www.wesleyhouse.co.uk **££** High St, Winchcombe, Gloucestershire GL54 5LJ. **(** 01242 602366. **FAX** 01242 609046. A historic restaurant-with-rooms in a fine Cotswold wool town. Bedrooms are shoehorned into improbably small spaces, but very classy and cosy. ⊟ TV ⩢	AE MC V	■	●	■	6

EAST MIDLANDS

	CREDIT CARDS	RESTAURANT	CHILDREN WELCOME	GARDEN/TERRACE	NUMBER OF ROOMS
ASWARBY: *Tally Ho Inn* **£** Aswarby, Sleaford, Lincolnshire NG34 8SA. **(** 01529 455205. **FAX** 01529 455773. Unassuming roadside inn offering quiet bedrooms in a barn conversion. Good bar meals; pretty gardens. A useful base for the Lincolnshire fens. ⊟ TV P	MC V	■	●	■	6
BABWORTH: *The Barns* W www.thebarns.co.uk **£** Morton Fram, Babworth, Retford, Nottinghamshire DN22 8HA. **(** 01777 706336. Good-value, welcoming B&B in appealing farm conversion near the A1. Fresh, stylish rooms; immaculate gardens; rural setting. ⊟ TV ⩢ P	AE DC MC V		●	■	6
BASLOW: *Cavendish* W www.cavendish-hotel.net **£££** Baslow, Bakewell, Derbyshire DE45 1SP. **(** 01246 582311. **FAX** 01246 582312. A graciously furnished hotel on the Chatsworth estate where antiques mingle with works of modern art. Gorgeous views; super cooking. ⊟ TV ⩢ P	AE DC MC V	■	●	■	24
BIGGIN-BY-HARTINGTON: *Biggin Hall* W www.bigginhall.co.uk **££** Biggin, Buxton, Derbyshire SK17 0DH. **(** 01298 84451. **FAX** 01298 84681. A 17th-century stone house of great character in the Peak District National Park. Light, calm interior, with open views and open fires. ⊟ TV ⩧ ⩢ P	AE MC V	■			19
BUXTON: *Buxton's Victorian Guesthouse* W www.buxtonvictorian.co.uk **£** 3A Broad Walk, Buxton, Derbyshire SK17 6JE. **(** 01298 78759. **FAX** 0101298 74732. An elegant B&B overlooking the Pavilion Gardens, a short stroll from the town centre. Interior decor is themed on Gilbert & Sullivan operas. ⊟ TV ⩢ P	MC V		●		9
CASTLE ASHBY: *Falcon* W www.english-inns.co.uk/falconhotel **£££** Castle Ashby, Northamptonshire NN7 1LF. **(** 01604 696200. **FAX** 01604 696673. An ancient estate village provides an attractive backdrop for this inn. Smartly furnished, cottagey bedrooms and large gardens. ⊟ TV ⩧ P	AE MC V	■	●	■	16
EAST BARKWITH: *Bodkin Lodge* **£** Grange Farm, Torrington Lane, East Barkwith, Lincolnshire LN8 5RY. **(** & **FAX** 01673 858249. This outstandingly hospitable B&B has views of the Lincolnshire Wolds. If it's full, try The Grange farmhouse nearby (same family) – children accepted; no wheelchair access. Light supper available. ● *Christmas & New Year.* ⊟ TV ⩧ ⩢ P		■		■	2
GLOSSOP: *Wind in the Willows* W www.windinthewillows.co.uk **£££** Derbyshire Level, Glossop, Derbyshire SK13 7PT. **(** 01457 868001. **FAX** 01457 853354. Spacious, welcoming hotel in large gardens, with views of the Snake Pass. Handsome antique beds in some rooms. Traditional English cooking. ⊟ TV P	AE DC MC V	■		■	12
HOPE: *Underleigh House* W www.underleighhouse.co.uk **££** Off Edale Road, Hope, Derbyshire S33 6RF. **(** 01433 621272. **FAX** 01433 621324. Set high above Edale, this welcoming B&B enjoys peaceful panoramas. Ideal walking base; light, floral bedrooms. ● *Christmas & New Year.* ⊟ TV ⩢ P	MC V			■	6
LANGAR: *Langar Hall* W www.langarhall.com **££££** Langar, Nottingham NG13 9HG. **(** 01949 860559. **FAX** 01949 861045. Gracious hospitality in a charming Regency-style house in a rural village setting. Stylish, individual bedrooms; top-notch cooking. ⊟ TV ⩧ ⩢ P	AE DC MC V	■	●	■	12
LINCOLN: *D'Isney Place* W www.disneyplacehotel.co.uk **££** Eastgate, Lincoln LN2 4AA. **(** 01522 538881. **FAX** 01522 511321. Superior B&B in a fine 18th-century house close to the cathedral. No public rooms; breakfast is served in the well-equipped, comfortable bedrooms. Welcoming, unobtrusive service; secluded garden. ⊟ TV ⩢ P	AE DC MC V		●	■	17

MATLOCK BATH: *Hodgkinson's* [W] www.hodgkinsons-hotel.co.uk ££
150 South Parade, Matlock Bath, Derbyshire DE4 3NR. [C] 01629 582170. FAX 01629 584891.
Idiosyncratic, well-placed hotel attractively furnished in Victorian style.
Italian chef-patron. Interesting gardens. ● 24–26 Dec. [TV] [P]
AE MC V — 7

NOTTINGHAM: *Greenwood Lodge* [W] www.greenwoodlodgecityguesthouse.co.uk £
Third Ave, Sherwood Rise, Nottingham NG7 6JH. [C] & FAX 0115-962 1206.
A mile north of the city centre, this secluded 19th-century guesthouse is
flamboyantly decked with period antiques. Welcoming owners. [TV]
MC V — 6

NOTTINGHAM: *Lace Market* [W] www.lacemarkethotel.co.uk £££
29–31 High Pavement, The Lace Market, Nottingham NG1 1HE. [C] 0115-852 3232.
A contemporary hotel in the city's fascinating lace-making district. Trendy
restaurant; bedrooms full of bold colours and gadgetry. [TV] [&] *limited.*
AE DC MC V — 42

OAKHAM: *Barnsdale Lodge* [W] www.barnsdalelodge.co.uk ££
The Avenue, Rutland Water North Shore, Rutland LE15 8AH. [C] 01572 724678.
A handy base for Rutland Water and Burghley, this attractively extended stone
farmhouse is now a cheerful, thriving hotel with good facilities. [TV] [&]
AE DC MC V — 45

OAKHAM: *Lord Nelson's House* [W] www.nelsons-house.com ££
11 Market Place, Oakham, Rutland LE15 6DT. [C] & FAX 01572 723199.
Classy but informal restaurant-with-rooms in the centre of Rutland's historic
county town. Quaint, half-timbered building. Attentive service. ● 24 Dec–
9 Jan, 10 days Easter, 2 weeks late July. [TV]
MC V — 4

PAULERSPURY: *Vine House* [W] www.vinehouse-hotel.com ££
100 High St, Paulerspury, Northamptonshire NN12 7NA. [C] 01327 811267. FAX 01327 811309.
The restaurant reigns supreme *(see also p595)*, but bedrooms are charming
and elegantly personalized too. Just off the A5, this welcoming place makes
a convenient touring base near Northampton. ● 24 Dec–7 Jan. [TV] [P]
MC V — 6

SARACEN'S HEAD: *Pipwell Manor* [W] www.smoothhound.co.uk/hotels/pipwell £
Washway Rd, Saracen's Head, Holbeach, Lincolnshire PE12 8AL. [C] & FAX 01406 423119.
A great B&B in an early Georgian house, furnished with style and care.
Bedrooms are simple but charming. Excellent breakfasts; gorgeous gardens.
A perfect base for exploring the Fens. ● Christmas & New Year. [P]
£ — 4

STAMFORD: *George of Stamford* [W] www.georgehotelofstamford.com £££
71 St Martins, Stamford, Lincolnshire PE9 2LB. [C] 01780 750750. FAX 01780 750701.
This ancient coaching inn has beckoned travellers off the Great North Road
since medieval times. Its handsome, rambling interior contains extensive bar-
dining space, and lavishly individual bedrooms. *(See also p610.)* [TV] [&] [P]
AE DC MC V — 47

UPPER HAMBLETON: *Finch's Arms* [W] www.finchsarms.co.uk ££
Oakham Rd, Upper Hambleton, Oakham, Rutland LE15 TL. [C] 01572 756575.
This upmarket pub-with-rooms is set in a charming village surrounded by
Rutland Water. Interesting cooking. [TV] [P]
AE DC MC V — 6

UPPINGHAM: *Lake Isle* [W] www.lakeisle.com ££
16 High St East, Uppingham, Rutland LE15 9PZ. [C] & FAX 01572 822951.
Friendly restaurant-with-rooms in Georgian townhouse on historic
Uppingham's classy main street. Some rooms in annexe cottages. [TV] [P]
AE DC MC V — 12

LANCASHIRE AND THE LAKES

AMBLESIDE: *Drunken Duck* [W] www.drunkenduckinn.co.uk ££
Barngates, Ambleside, Cumbria LA22 0NG. [C] 015394 36347 FAX 015394 36781.
A lively, dining-pub-with-rooms in a South Lakeland setting. Bedrooms are
stylish and inviting. Room rates include afternoon tea. ● 25 Dec. [TV] [P]
AE MC V — 16

AMBLESIDE: *Rowanfield* [W] www.rowanfield.com ££
Kirkstone Rd, Ambleside, Cumbria LA22 9ET. [C] 015394 33686. FAX 015394 31569.
Superior farmhouse accommodation with spectacular views near the
Kirkstone Pass. Beautifully decorated rooms. ● end Nov–mid-Mar. [TV] [P]
MC V — 8

AMBLESIDE: *Wateredge Inn* [W] www.wateredgeinn.co.uk ££
Waterhead Bay, Ambleside, Cumbria LA22 0EP. [C] 015394 32332. FAX 015394 31878.
Inn-with-rooms with a glamorous waterfront setting at the northern tip of Lake
Windermere. Stylish dining; bright, neat bedrooms in all sizes. [TV] [&] [P]
AE DC MC V — 21

BASSENTHWAITE: *Pheasant* [W] www.the-pheasant.co.uk £££
Bassenthwaite Lake, Cockermouth, Cumbria CA13 9YE. [C] 017687 76234. FAX 017687 76002.
The snug bar is a focal point at this well-loved hostelry. Plenty of lounge space;
great cooking. Refurbished bedrooms are bright and sleek. ● 25 Dec. [&] [P]
MC V — 13

<table>
<tr><td>

Price categories for a standard double room per night, inclusive of breakfast, service charges and any additional taxes such as VAT:
£ under £65
££ £65–£100
£££ £100–£150
££££ £150–£200
£££££ £200 plus

</td><td>

RESTAURANT
Hotel restaurant or dining room serving more than just breakfast; often open to non-residents.

CHILDREN WELCOME
Especially welcoming to families. May have children's facilities such as cots, babysitting, family rooms, etc.

GARDEN/TERRACE
Hotels with a garden, courtyard or terrace, often providing tables for eating outside.

CREDIT CARDS
Indicates which credit cards are accepted: *AE* American Express; *DC* Diners Club; *MC* Master Card/Access; *V* Visa.

</td></tr>
</table>

		CREDIT CARDS	RESTAURANT	CHILDREN WELCOME	GARDEN/TERRACE	NUMBER OF ROOMS

BLACKPOOL: *Raffles* W www.raffleshotelblackpool.co.uk   £ — AE MC V — ■ — ● — — — 17
73–76 Hornby Rd, Blackpool, Lancashire FY1 4QJ. (01253 294713. FAX 01253 294240.
Near the Tower, this flower-decked, blue-and-white B&B is easy to spot. It's very neat, with refurbished bedrooms. Traditional dinners; tearooms.

BOWNESS-ON-WINDERMERE: *Lindeth Fell* W www.lindethfell.co.uk   £££ — MC V — ■ — ● — ■ — 14
Lyth Valley Rd, Bowness-on-Windermere, Cumbria LA23 3JP. (015394 43286.
A relaxing country-house hotel with glorious lakeland views and beautiful gardens. Fresh, tasteful decor and lots of personality.

BOWNESS-ON-WINDERMERE: *Linthwaite House* W www.linthwaite.com   £££ — AE DC MC V — ■ — ● — ■ — 26
Crook Rd, Bowness-on-Windermere, Cumbria LA23 3JA. (015394 88600.
Dazzling Windermere views grace the beautiful grounds of this smart country-house hotel. Sophisticated menus; fishing and croquet.

BUTTERMERE: *Wood House* W www.wdhse.co.uk   ££ — — — ■ — — — ■ — 3
Buttermere, Cockermouth, Cumbria CA13 9XA. (017687 70208. FAX 017687 70241.
Tranquil National Trust property on the shores of Crummock Water. Beautifully furnished and decorated. Splendid home cooked dinners served house-party style. ● *mid-Nov–mid-Feb.*

CARLISLE: *Number Thirty-One* W www.number31.freeservers.com   ££ — AE MC V — ■ — — — — — 3
31 Howard Place, Carlisle, Cumbria CA1 1HR. (& FAX 01228 597080.
Outstanding Victorian townhouse run with enthusiasm. Decor is bold and full of panache. Carefully considered, soundproofed bedrooms. ● *Nov–Feb.*

CARTMEL FELL: *Lightwood* W www.lightwoodguesthouse.co.uk   £ — MC V — ■ — ● — ■ — 6
Cartmel Fell, Grange-over-Sands, Cumbria LA11 6NP. (& FAX 015395 31454.
17th-century farmhouse of great character with charming cottagey bedrooms, attractive gardens and good home cooking. ● *Christmas.*

COCKERMOUTH: *The Trout* W www.trouthotel.co.uk   £££ — AE MC V — ■ — ● — ■ — 43
Crown St, Cockermouth, Cumbria CA13 0EJ. (01900 823591. FAX 01900 827514.
17th-century building in a unique setting on the banks of the River Derwent. Short walk to Cockermouth. Lovely, extensive gardens. *limited.*

CONISTON: *Bankground* W www.bankground.com   ££ — MC V — — — ● — ■ — 15
East of Lake Rd, Coniston, Cumbria LA21 8AA. (015394 41264. FAX 015394 41900.
15th-century farmhouse across the lake from Coniston village and adjoining Grizedale Forest. Family-run B&B that is a good base for walking trips.

COWAN BRIDGE: *Hipping Hall* W www.kirby-lonsdale.com   ££ — AE MC V — ■ — ● — ■ — 7
Cowan Bridge, Kirkby Lonsdale, Carnforth, Lancashire LA6 2JJ. (015242 71187.
An elegant, rambling country house in lovely grounds. Beautifully furnished. Cooking makes ambitious use of local produce. ● *Christmas.*

GRANGE-IN-BORROWDALE: *Borrowdale Gates*   £££ — AE MC V — ■ — ● — ■ — 31
Grange-in-Borrowdale, Keswick, Cumbria CA12 5UQ. (01768 777204.
FAX 017687 77254. W www.borrowdale-gates.com
This award-winning, well-managed hotel enjoys glorious views. Spacious and smart. Tariffs include an excellent, satisfying dinner. ● *Jan.*

GRASMERE: *Howfoot Lodge* W www.howfoot.co.uk   ££ — MC V — ■ — ● — ■ — 6
Town End, Grasmere, Cumbria LA22 9SH. (015394 35366. FAX 015394 35268.
This Victorian villa, owned by the Wordsworth Trust, is furnished with period features, and set in landscaped gardens. Excellent base for walkers.

KESWICK: *The Grange* W www.grangekeswick.com   ££ — MC V — — — — — ■ — 10
Manor Brow, Keswick, Cumbria CA12 4BA. (& FAX 017687 72500.
This well-established B&B on the outskirts of town has lovely views and gardens. ● *Mid-Nov–mid-Mar.*

LORTON: *New House Farm* w www.newhouse-farm.co.uk　££　MC V　■　■　5
Lorton, nr Cockermouth, Cumbria CA13 9UU. & FAX 01900 85404.
A lovely Vale of Lorton location makes this characterful farm guesthouse a
winner. Organized teas in the barn and superb suppers.

MANCHESTER: *Eleven Didsbury Park* w www.elevendidsburypark.com　£££　AE DC MC V　●　■　17
11 Didsbury Park, Didsbury Village, Manchester M20 5LH. 0161 448 7711.
Stylish Victorian townhouse in a smart conservation suburb. Contemporary
decor and high-quality gadgetry. Hot-tub in the garden. No restaurant, but
evening deli service in rooms.

MANCHESTER: *Crowne Plaza Midland*　££££　AE DC MC V　■　●　303
Peter St, Manchester M60 2DS. 0161 236 3333. FAX 0161 932 4100.
w www.manchester-themidland.crowneplaza.com
This sumptuous, palatial hotel harkens back to the golden era of railway
travel. Neoclassical, Louis XIII and art nouveau styles.

MANCHESTER: *The Lowry* w www.thelowryhotel.com　£££££　AE DC MC V　■　●　165
50 Dearmans Pl, Chapel Wharf, Salford, Manchester M3 5LH. 0161 827 4000.
Located in the heart of the city, this luxury contemporary hotel is in a quiet
riverside location. Restaurant run by Marco Pierre White.

MELLOR: *Millstone* w www.shirehotels.co.uk　££　AE DC MC V　■　●　24
3 Church Lane, Mellor, Blackburn, Lancashire BB2 7JR. 01254 813333. FAX 01254 812628.
This former coaching inn makes a good base for rural Lancashire. Bedrooms
are neat and practical. Beamed and panelled public areas.

MUNGRISDALE: *Mill Hotel* w www.themillhotel.com　£££　■　■　8
Mungrisdale, Penrith, Cumbria CA11 0XR. 017687 79659. FAX 017687 79155.
Not to be confused with the neighbouring Mill Inn, this small hotel makes a
delightful stay. Good restaurant. ● Nov–Feb.

NEWLANDS: *Swinside Lodge* w www.swinsidelodge-hotel.co.uk　£££　MC V　■　■　7
Grange Rd, Newlands, Keswick, Cumbria CA12 5UE. & FAX 017687 72948.
A gorgeous, isolated setting near Cat Bells. Smart decor; lots of books and
maps, and excellent cooking (rates include dinner).

PENRITH: *North Lakes* w www.shireinns.co.uk　£££　AE DC MC V　■　●　■　84
Ullswater Rd, Penrith, Cumbria CA11 8QT. 01768 868111. FAX 01768 868291.
Unimpressive setting, but this modern block beside the M6 has an attractive
chalet-style interior. Indoor pool and fitness centre.

SEATOLLER: *Seatoller House* w www.seatollerhouse.co.uk　££　MC V　■　●　■　10
Seatoller, Borrowdale, Keswick, Cumbria CA12 5XN. 017687 77218. FAX 017687 77189.
This delightfully laid-back walking base near the Honister Pass is a place to
mix and mingle. Communal meals. ● Dec–Feb.

SELSIDE: *Low Jock Scar* @ ljs@avmail.co.uk　£　MC V　■　■　5
Selside, Kendal, Cumbria LA8 9LE. & FAX 01539 823259.
An utterly secluded but easily accessible location north of Kendal makes this
delightful guesthouse an ideal springboard for the southern Lakes. Super
gardens; tasty suppers. Simple, cosy bedrooms. ● Nov–mid-Mar.

ULLSWATER: *Sharrow Bay* w www.sharrow-bay.com　£££££　AE MC V　■　■　26
Ullswater, Penrith, Cumbria CA10 2LZ. 017684 86301. FAX 017684 86349.
Britain's first proper country-house hotel is still a Lakeland legend. An
incomparable lakeshore setting, exquisite decor, perfect service and
wonderful cooking. (See also p597.) ● Dec–Feb.

ULVERSTON: *Bay Horse* w www.furness.co.uk/bayhorse　££££　AE MC V　■　9
Canal Foot, Ulverston, Cumbria LA12 9EL. 01229 583972. FAX 01229 580502.
At the edge of Morecambe Bay, this smartly comfortable inn provides bedroom
binoculars for birdwatching. Splendid food (rates include dinner).

WASDALE HEAD: *Wasdale Head* w www.wasdale.com　££　AE MC V　■　●　■　14
Wasdale Head, nr Gosforth, Seascale, Cumbria CA20 1X. 019467 26229.
This famous climbing inn occupies a remote, spectacular setting near Wast
Water. Microbrewery on site; loads of character.

WHITEWELL: *Inn at Whitewell*　££　MC V　■　●　■　20
Whitewell, Forest of Bowland, Clitheroe, Lancashire BB7 3AT 01200 448222. FAX 01200 448298.
This wittily sophisticated riverside inn makes a splendid base for exploring
the Ribble Valley. The building has enormous character. Stylishly spectacular
bedrooms. Wonderful food and wines. (See also p597.)

Price categories for a standard double room per night, inclusive of breakfast, service charges and any additional taxes such as VAT: **£** under £65 **£££** £65–£100 **££££** £100–£150 **£££££** £150–£200 **££££££** £200 plus	**RESTAURANT** Hotel restaurant or dining room serving more than just breakfast; often open to non-residents. **CHILDREN WELCOME** Especially welcoming to families. May have children's facilities such as cots, babysitting, family rooms, etc. **GARDEN/TERRACE** Hotels with a garden, courtyard or terrace, often providing tables for eating outside. **CREDIT CARDS** Indicates which credit cards are accepted: *AE* American Express; *DC* Diners Club; *MC* Master Card/Access; *V* Visa.	CREDIT CARDS	RESTAURANT	CHILDREN WELCOME	GARDEN/TERRACE	NUMBER OF ROOMS

	Credit Cards	Restaurant	Children Welcome	Garden/Terrace	Number of Rooms
WINDERMERE: *Gilpin Lodge* w www.gilpinlodge.com **£££££** Crook Rd, Windermere, Cumbria LA23 3NE. (015394 88818. FAX 015394 88058. An elegant and comfortable hotel, both spacious and beautifully furnished. Some split-level suites with jacuzzi baths. Extensive grounds. TV P	DC MC V	■		■	14

YORKSHIRE AND THE HUMBER REGION

	Credit Cards	Restaurant	Children Welcome	Garden/Terrace	Number of Rooms
AMPLEFORTH: *Shallowdale House* w www.shallowdalehouse.demon.co.uk **££** Ampleforth, nr York YO62 4DY. (01439 788325. FAX 01439 788885. Refined guesthouse within easy reach of Rievaulx and Byland abbeys. Simple but stylish rooms with lovely views. ● *Christmas & New Year.* TV P	MC V	■		■	3
BRADFORD: *Beeties* w www.beeties.co.uk **£** 7 Victoria Rd, Saltaire Village, Shipley, Bradford, W Yorkshire BD18 3LA. (01274 581718. Located in a converted fish shop, this restaurant-with-rooms is well placed for visiting the arty village of Saltaire. Tastefully furnished bedrooms. TV	AE MC V	■			5
EAST WITTON: *Blue Lion* w www.thebluelion.co.uk **££** East Witton, Leyburn, N Yorkshire DL8 4SN. (01969 624273. FAX 01969 624189. Classy coaching inn near the ruins of Jervaulx Abbey. Smart food attracts non-residents; it gets busy at weekends and front bedrooms may be noisy. TV P	MC V	■	●	■	12
FLAMBOROUGH: *Manor House* w www.flamboroughmanor.co.uk **££** Flamborough, Bridlington, E Yorkshire YO15 1PD. (& FAX 01262 850943. This elegant Georgian house is a private home and a Wolsey Lodge. Book ahead; dinners feature local seafood. ● *Christmas.* TV P	MC V	■		■	2
GRASSINGTON: *Ashfield House* w www.ashfieldhouse.co.uk **££** Summers Fold, Grassington, N Yorkshire BD23 5AE. (& FAX 01756 752584. This cluster of 17th-century cottages makes a good base for neighbouring Malhamdale. Stylish interiors with simple bedrooms. ● *Jan.* TV P	MC V	■		■	7
HALIFAX: *Holdsworth House* w www.holdsworthhouse.co.uk **£££** Holdsworth Rd, Holmfield, Halifax, W Yorkshire HX2 9TG. (01422 240024. FAX 01422 245174. Period features survive intact in this rambling Jacobean manor in the Calder Valley near Halifax. Bedrooms, in a modern wing, are as attractive as the main house. Elaborate menus. ● *Christmas & New Year.* TV P	AE DC MC V	■	●	■	40
HARROGATE: *Balmoral* w www.balmoralhotel.co.uk **£££** Franklin Mount, Harrogate, N Yorkshire HG1 5EJ. (01423 508208. FAX 01423 530652. Eccentric memorabilia gives this mock-Tudor hotel edge over its rivals. Straightforward business facilities and some ornate bedrooms. TV P	AE MC V	■	●		21
HELM: *Helm* w www.helmyorkshire.com **££** Helm, nr Askrigg, Leyburn, N Yorkshire DL8 3JF. (& FAX 01969 650443. This guesthouse occupies a handsome stone building in one of Wensleydale's best-known villages. Beautifully kept bedrooms. ● *mid-Nov–Dec.* TV P	MC V	■		■	3
HELMSLEY: *Feversham Arms* @ reception@feversham-helmsley.fsnet.co.uk **££££** 178 High St, Helmsley, Yorks YO62 5AG. (01439 770766. Comfortable refurbished coaching inn in small historic market town near Castle Howard *(pp384–5)*. Pool and gym. Room rate includes dinner. TV P	AE MC V	■	●	■	22
INGLEBY GREENHOW: *Manor House Farm* @ mbloom@globalnet.co.uk **££** Ingleby Greenhow, nr Great Ayton, N Yorkshire TS9 6RB. (01642 722384. Remote, charming farmhouse on the edge of the North York Moors. Cottagey bedrooms with views. Rates include a five-course dinner. ● *Dec.* P	MC V	■		■	3
LEEDS: *Malmaison Leeds* w www.malmaison.com **£££** Sovereign Quay, Leeds LS1 1DQ. (0113 398 1000. FAX 0113 398 1002. This ultra-contemporary hotel occupying an old tram-shed offers themed bedrooms and brasserie food. Views of the city skyline. TV	DC MC V	■	●		100

MYTHOLMROYD: *Redacre Mill* [w] www.redacremill.freeserve.co.uk (£) MC V ● ■ 5
Mytholmroyd, Hebden Bridge, W Yorkshire HX7 5DQ. [C] & [FAX] 01422 885563.
A friendly English guesthouse in a converted canalside cotton mill, with
South Indian cuisine. Meals by arrangement [🛏] [TV] [⚡] [P]

OSMOTHERLY: *Three Tuns* (£)(£) AE MC V ■ ■ 7
9 South End, Osmotherley, N Yorkshire DL6 3BN. [C] 01609 883301.
Recently transformed into a quirkily inviting restaurant-with-rooms, this
long-established hostelry lies near Mount Grace Priory. [🛏] [TV] [⚡] [P]

PICKERING: *White Swan* [w] www.white-swan.co.uk (£)(£)(£) AE MC V ■ ■ 12
Market Place, Pickering, N Yorkshire YO18 7AA. [C] 01751 472288. [FAX] 01751 475554.
Central Georgian inn with a breezy modern interior. Bedrooms are plain and
practical. A useful base for the North York Moors Railway. [🛏] [TV] [⚡] [P]

RAMSGILL: *Yorke Arms* [w] www.yorke-arms.co.uk (£)(£)(£)(£) AE DC MC V ■ 14
Ramsgill-in-Nidderdale, N Yorkshire HG3 5RL. [C] 01423 755243. [FAX] 01423 755330.
Top cooking in this restaurant-with-rooms. A former shooting lodge, the
building is ancient and full of character. Bedrooms are elegant. [🛏] [⚡] [P]

REETH: *Arkleside* [w] www.arklesidehotel.co.uk (£)(£) MC V ■ 10
Reeth, nr Richmond, N Yorkshire DL11 6SG. [C] & [FAX] 01748 884200.
Set in a village amid dazzling Swaledale scenery, this guesthouse is a popular
walking base. Bedrooms are smart but variable. ● *24–25 Dec, Jan.* [🛏] [TV] [⚡] [P]

ROYDHOUSE: *Three Acres Inn* [@] 3acres@globalnet.co.uk (£)(£) AE MC V ■ ● ■ 20
Roydhouse, Shelley, Huddersfield, W Yorkshire HD8 8LR. [C] 01484 602606. [FAX] 01484 608411.
Moorland views grace this inn near the Yorkshire Sculpture Park and National
Coal Mining Museum *(see p399)*. The bar-restaurant evokes turn-of-the-century
style. Bedrooms have period character too. ● *25, 31 Dec, 1 Jan.* [🛏] [TV] [⚡] [P]

SCARBOROUGH: *Interludes* [w] www.interludeshotel.co.uk (£) MC V ■ 5
32 Princess St, Scarborough, N Yorkshire YO11 1QR. [C] 01723 360513. [FAX] 01723 368597.
A refined guesthouse in the old town with sea views from some rooms.
Simple dinners and theatre packages available. Tricky parking. [🛏] [TV] [⚡]

WHITBY: *White Horse & Griffin* [w] www.whitehorseandgriffin.co.uk (£)(£) MC V ■ ● 17
Church St, Whitby, N Yorkshire YO22 4BH. [C] & [FAX] 01947 604857.
A quaint old inn on the cobbled main street, furnished with antiques. Local fish
on the menu. Quieter rooms in self-contained annexe cottages. [🛏] [TV] [⚡]

WINTERINGHAM: *Winteringham Fields* [w] www.winteringhamfields.com (£)(£)(£) AE MC V ■ ■ 10
Winteringham, Scunthorpe, Lincolnshire DN15 9PF. [C] 01724 733096. [FAX] 01724 733898.
A superb restaurant-with-rooms and the most elegant touring base near the
Humber Bridge. Worth the journey for its cooking; excellent bedrooms too. *(See
also p599.)* ● *last week Mar & Oct, first week Aug, 2 weeks Christmas.* [🛏] [TV] [⚡] [P]

YORK: *The Hazelwood* [w] www.thehazelwoodyork.com (£)(£) MC V ■ 12
24–25 Portland St, York YO21 7EH. [C] 01904 626548. [FAX] 01904 628032.
Central but secluded townhouse B&B providing unobtrusive service and
opulent, spacious bedrooms. Small rear garden. [🛏] [TV] [⚡] [P]

YORK: *Middlethorpe Hall* [w] www.middlethorpe.com (£)(£)(£)(£) MC V ■ ■ 30
Bishopthorpe Rd, York YO23 2GB. [C] 01904 641241. [FAX] 01904 620176.
Grand historic house-hotel near the racecourse. Period features blend with
luxurious furnishings. Gourmet restaurant; health spa; croquet. [🛏] [TV] [🐾] [P]

NORTHUMBRIA

BERWICK-UPON-TWEED: *Number One Sallyport* [C] & [FAX] 01289 308827. (£) AE MC V ■ ● ■ 3
Off Bridge St, Berwick-upon-Tweed TD15 1EZ. [w] www.1sallyport-bedandbreakfast.com
Charming 17th-century B&B in central Berwick. The owner is an ex-
restaurateur, and serves delicious French Provençal suppers. [🛏] [TV] [⚡] [P]

CHESTER-LE-STREET: *Lumley Castle* [w] www.lumleycastle.com (£)(£)(£) AE DC MC V ■ ● ■ 59
Chester-le-Street, Durham DH3 4NX. [C] 0191 389 1111. [FAX] 0191 387 1437.
With a Norman pedigree, this flamboyantly turreted building is predictably
grand. Elizabethan banquets attract many visitors. Beamish Museum lies
nearby *(see pp410–11).* ● *24–26 Dec, 1 Jan.* [🛏] [TV] [P]

CROOKHAM: *Coach House* [w] www.coachhousecrookham.com (£)(£) MC V ■ ● ■ 9
Crookham, Cornhill-on-Tweed, Northumberland TD12 4TD. [C] 01890 820293. [FAX] 01890 820284.
Close to the Borders, this welcoming guesthouse offers peace, unpretentious
comfort and hearty home cooking. ● *Nov–Easter.* [🛏] [TV] [⚡] [P]

For key to symbols see back flap

Price categories for a standard double room per night, inclusive of breakfast, service charges and any additional taxes such as VAT:

£ under £65
££ £65–£100
£££ £100–£150
££££ £150–£200
£££££ £200 plus

RESTAURANT
Hotel restaurant or dining room serving more than just breakfast; often open to non-residents.

CHILDREN WELCOME
Especially welcoming to families. May have children's facilities such as cots, babysitting, family rooms, etc.

GARDEN/TERRACE
Hotels with a garden, courtyard or terrace, often providing tables for eating outside.

CREDIT CARDS
Indicates which credit cards are accepted: *AE* American Express; *DC* Diners Club; *MC* Master Card/Access; *V* Visa.

	Credit Cards	Restaurant	Children Welcome	Garden/Terrace	Number of Rooms
DURHAM: *Georgian Town House* W www.thegeorgiantownhouse.co.uk **££** 10–11 Crossgate, Durham DH1 4PS. & FAX 0191 386 8070. A friendly, family-run B&B in the heart of the city. Cathedral views from some rooms. Pancake house and café downstairs. Christmas & New Year.				■	8
HALTWHISTLE: *Centre of Britain* W www.centre-of-britain.org.uk **££** Main St, Haltwhistle, Northumberland NE49 0BH. 01434 322422. FAX 01434 322655. A stylish conversion of a 15th-century defensive tower near Hadrian's Wall. Exposed stonework and beams. Bedrooms are light and tasteful.	AE DC MC V	■	●		9
HAMSTERLEY FOREST: *Grove House* W www.grovehouse.biz **££** Hamsterley Forest, Bishop Auckland, Durham DL13 3NL. 01388 488203. FAX 01388 488174. Once a Georgian hunting lodge, portraits and objets d'art decorate this much-loved private home set in protected woodlands. mid-Dec–mid-Jan.		■		■	3
HEXHAM: *Langley Castle* W www.langleycastle.com **£££** Langley on Tyne, Hexham, Northumberland NE47 5LU. 01434 688888. FAX 01434 684019. A Medieval castellated stronghold with baronial interiors. Coach house rooms are cheaper, but just as comfortable.	AE DC MC V	■	●	■	18
HIGH BUSTON: *High Buston Hall* W www.highbuston.com **££** High Buston, Alnmouth, Alnwick, Northumberland NE66 3QH. 01665 830606. This fine Georgian villa surveys sweeping countryside near Warkworth Castle. Warm, unobtrusive welcome. Christmas & New Year.				■	3
NEWCASTLE UPON TYNE: *Malmaison Newcastle* W www.malmaison.com **£££** 104 Quayside, Newcastle upon Tyne NE1 3DX. 0191 245 5000. FAX 0191 245 4545. Sophisticated warehouse conversion on the central waterfront next to the Millennium Bridge and opposite Baltic *(see pp410–11).*	AE DC MC V	■	●		116
ROMALDKIRK: *Rose & Crown* W www.rose-and-crown.co.uk **£** Romaldkirk, Barnard Castle, Durham DL12 9EB. 01833 650213. FAX 01833 650828. The village green makes a quintessentially English backdrop for this delightful inn on the fringes of Teesdale. Inside, it's exceptionally smart but reassuringly traditional. Accomplished cooking. *(See also p600.)* Christmas.	MC V	■	●		12
SEAHOUSES: *Olde Ship* W www.seahouses.co.uk **££** 7–9 Main St, Seahouses, Northumberland NE68 7RD. 01665 720200. FAX 01665 721383. This inn overlooks the harbour, departure point for the Farne Islands *(see p404).* Best rooms are in the annexe. *(See also p611.)* Dec–Jan.	JCB MC V	■		■	18
STANNERSBURN: *Pheasant* W www.thepheasantinn.com **££** Stannersburn, Kielder Water, Northumberland NE48 1DD. 01434 240382. FAX 01434 240382. Creeper-covered inn near Kielder Water's visitor centre *(see p406).* A friendly place, full of character, with unassuming, cosy bedrooms in an adjoining barn conversion. Good food (regional produce). 25 Dec.	MC V	■	●	■	8

NORTH WALES

	Credit Cards	Restaurant	Children Welcome	Garden/Terrace	Number of Rooms
ABERDYFI: *Penhelig Arms* W www.penheligarms.com **££** Aberdyfi, Gwynedd LL35 0LT. 01654 767215. FAX 01654 767690. A whitewashed inn on the seafront. Most rooms have estuary views; those in the annexe have private terraces. *(See also p601.)* 25–26 Dec.	MC V	■	●	■	14
ABERDYFI: *Trefeddian* W www.trefwales.com **£££** Tywyn Rd, Aberdyfi, Gwynedd LL35 0SB. 01654 767213. FAX 01654 767777. This large, friendly hotel enjoys coastal views. Long owned by the same family, it's an energetic place with lots to do. 3 weeks Nov–Dec.	MC V	■	●	■	59
ABERSOCH: *Porth Tocyn* W www.porth-tocyn-hotel.co.uk **£££** Bwlch Tocyn, Abersoch, Gwynedd LL53 7BU. 01758 713303. FAX 01758 713538. A comfortable country-house hotel with family hospitality and traditional cooking. Heated pool; tennis court. *(See also p601.)* mid-Nov–Mar.	MC V	■	●	■	17

BEAUMARIS: *Olde Bull's Head* 〔W〕 www.bullsheadinn.co.uk   £££
Castle St, Beaumaris, Anglesey LL58 8AP. 〔C〕 *01248 810329.* FAX *01248 811294.*
This ancient inn near the castle makes an ideal base for exploring Anglesey.
Furnishings evoke the Victorian era (Dickens stayed here in 1859). Inventive
cooking. *(See also p601 and p611.)* ● *25–26 Dec, 1 Jan.* 〔symbols〕

| | AE MC V | ■ | ● | | 13 |

BEDDGELERT: *Sygun Fawr* 〔W〕 www.sygunfawr.co.uk   ££
Beddgelert, Caernarfon, Gwynedd LL55 4NE. 〔C〕 & FAX *01766 890258.*
Tremendous views at this friendly 17th-century manor. Lots of beams and
stonework. Good cooking and cosy bedrooms. ● *Jan.* 〔symbols〕

| | | ■ | ● | ■ | 9 |

CAPEL GARMON: *Tan-y-Foel* 〔W〕 www.tyfhotel.co.uk   £££
Capel Garmon, Betws-y-Coed, Conwy LL26 0RE. 〔C〕 *01690 710507.* FAX *01690 710681.*
A quiet country retreat set in woodland with fine views along the Conwy
Valley. Stylish contemporary decor. ● *mid-Dec–mid-Feb.* 〔symbols〕

| | AE DC MC V | ■ | | | 7 |

CRICCIETH: *Mynydd Ednyfed* 〔W〕 www.criccieth.net   ££
Caernarfon Rd, Criccieth, Gwynedd LL52 0PH. 〔C〕 *01766 523269.* FAX *01766 522929.*
A secluded, 400-year-old country house in grounds near the sea. Rustic decor
and cottagey bedrooms. Gym and tennis court. ● *23 Dec–4 Jan.* 〔symbols〕

| | MC V | ■ | | | 9 |

GANLLWYD: *Plas Dolmelynllyn* 〔W〕 www.dolly-hotel.co.uk   ££
Ganllwyd, Dolgellau, Gwynedd LL40 2HP. 〔C〕 *01341 440273.* FAX *01341 440273.*
The respectable comfort of the Victorian era is evoked at this historic
country house in quiet countryside near Dolgellau. ● *Nov–Feb.* 〔symbols〕

| | AE DC MC V | ■ | | ■ | 10 |

HARLECH: *Castle Cottage* 〔W〕 www.castlecottageharlech.co.uk   ££
Pen Llech, Harlech, Gwynedd LL46 2YL. 〔C〕 & FAX *01766 780479.*
This quaint old restaurant-with-rooms near the castle has lovely sea and
mountain vistas. Be prepared to share these cosy quarters with a vast array of
ornamental pigs. Talented cooking. *(See also p601.)* ● *3 weeks in Jan.* 〔symbols〕

| | MC V | ■ | ● | | 9 |

LLANABER: *Llwyndu Farmhouse* 〔W〕 www.llwyndu-farmhouse.co.uk   ££
Llanaber, Barmouth, Gwynedd LL42 1RR. 〔C〕 *01341 280144.* FAX *01341 281231.*
This splendidly restored farmhouse dates back several centuries. Antiques and
unusual curios; exposed stonework and timbers. ● *25–26 Dec.* 〔symbols〕

| | MC V | ■ | ● | ■ | 7 |

LLANARMON DYFFRYN CEIRIOG: *West Arms* 〔W〕 www.thewestarms.co.uk   £££
Llanrmon Dyffryn Ceiriog, Llangollen, Wrexham LL20 7LD. 〔C〕 *01691 600665.* FAX *01691 600622.*
This fine hostelry in the tranquil Ceiriog valley has a welcoming ambience and
beamy comfortable bedrooms. 10% service charge. *(See also p601.)* 〔symbols〕

| | MC V | ■ | ● | ■ | 15 |

LLANDRILLO: *Tyddyn Llan* 〔W〕 www.tyddynllan.co.uk   £££
Llandrillo, Corwen, Denbigh LL21 0ST. 〔C〕 *01490 440264.* FAX *01490 440414.*
A rambling Georgian house near Bala Lake. Tastefully furnished and spacious.
Restaurant uses fine local produce. *(See also p602.)* ● *2 weeks Jan.* 〔symbols〕

| | DC MC V | ■ | ● | | 12 |

LLANDDEINIOLEN: *Ty'n Rhos* 〔W〕 www.tynrhos.co.uk   ££
Seion, Llanddeiniolen, Caernarfon LL55 3AE. 〔C〕 *01248 670489.* FAX *01248 670079.*
Gourmet B&B in converted farm buildings, overlooking the quiet countryside
near the Menai Straits. Dinner for residents only. ● *23–30 Dec.* 〔symbols〕

| | AE MC V | | | ■ | 11 |

LLANDUDNO: *St Tudno* 〔W〕 www.st-tudno.co.uk   £££
Promenade, Llandudno, Conwy LL30 2LP. 〔C〕 *01492 874411.* FAX *01492 860407.*
A welcoming seafront hotel in a smart Victorian terrace. Bay windows overlook
the bay. Colourful, spacious rooms; indoor swimming pool. 〔symbols〕

| | AE DC MC V | ■ | ● | ■ | 19 |

LLANDUDNO: *Bodysgallen Hall* 〔W〕 www.bodysgallen.com   ££££
Llandudno, Conwy LL30 1RS. 〔C〕 *01492 584466.* FAX *01492 582519.*
Impressive, historic country-house hotel in a parkland setting with stunning
views. Immaculate and refined inside and out; wonderful food. 〔symbols〕

| | MC V | ■ | | | 34 |

LLANFACHRETH: *Ty Isaf Farmhouse* 〔W〕 www.tyisaf78.freeserve.co.uk   £
Llanfachreth, nr Dolgellau, Gwynedd LL40 1EA. 〔C〕 & FAX *01341 423261.*
This friendly 17th-century longhouse has cosy bedrooms and stacks of
chacter and rural charm. Good Welsh dinners served communally at an oak
table. Resident llamas. ● *mid-Dec–Jan.* 〔symbols〕

| | | ■ | | ■ | 3 |

PENMAENPOOL: *George III* 〔W〕 www.george-3rd.co.uk   ££
Penmaenpool, Dolgellau, Gwynedd LL40 1YD. 〔C〕 *01341 422525.* FAX *01341 423565.*
Unusual waterfront hotel converted from a chandlery, a railway station and
a pub. Atmospheric cellar bar and beamed dining room. 〔symbols〕

| | MC V | ■ | ● | | 11 |

For key to symbols see back flap

Price categories for a standard double room per night, inclusive of breakfast, service charges and any additional taxes such as VAT:

ⓔ under £65
ⓔⓔ £65–£100
ⓔⓔⓔ £100–£150
ⓔⓔⓔⓔ £150–£200
ⓔⓔⓔⓔⓔ £200 plus

RESTAURANT
Hotel restaurant or dining room serving more than just breakfast; often open to non-residents.

CHILDREN WELCOME
Especially welcoming to families. May have children's facilities such as cots, babysitting, family rooms, etc.

GARDEN/TERRACE
Hotels with a garden, courtyard or terrace, often providing tables for eating outside.

CREDIT CARDS
Indicates which credit cards are accepted: *AE* American Express; *DC* Diners Club; *MC* Master Card/Access; *V* Visa.

	CREDIT CARDS	RESTAURANT	CHILDREN WELCOME	GARDEN/TERRACE	NUMBER OF ROOMS
PENMAENPOOL: *Penmaenuchaf Hall* W www.penhall.co.uk ⓔⓔⓔ Penmaenpool, Dolgellau, Gwynedd LL40 1YB. ☎ 01341 422129. FAX 01341 422787. Peace and relaxation are assured at this elegant Victorian mansion, along with ambitious menus and magnificent views of Snowdonia. 🖪 TV 🔥 ☕ P	DC MC V	■		■	14
PORTMEIRION: *Portmeirion* W www.portmeirion-village.com ⓔⓔⓔ Portmeirion, Penrhyndeudraeth, Gwynedd LL48 6ET. ☎ & FAX 01766 770000. A Mediterranean architectural fantasy transported to a wooded estuary above Cardigan Bay. The village-like complex has a sumptuous hotel, self-catering cottage suites and castle accommodation. *(See p440.)* ● 6 Jan–1 Feb. 🖪 TV P	AE DC MC V	■	●	■	68
TALSARNAU: *Maes-y-Neuadd* W www.neuadd.com ⓔⓔⓔⓔ Talsarnau, Gwynedd LL47 6YA. ☎ 01766 780200. FAX 01766 780211. A graciously relaxing and stylish country house in glorious gardens. A 14th-century building with sensitive stone and glass additions. 🖪 TV 🔥 ☕ P	AE DC MC V	■	●	■	16
TYN-Y-GROES: *Groes Inn* W www.groesinn.com ⓔⓔ Tyn-y-Groes, Conwy LL32 8TN. ☎ 01492 650545. FAX 01492 650855. An ancient coaching inn with masses of character and bric-à-brac. Service is pleasantly relaxed but efficient. Good-value bar meals. 🖪 TV ☕ P	AE DC MC V	■	●	■	14

SOUTH AND MID-WALES

	CREDIT CARDS	RESTAURANT	CHILDREN WELCOME	GARDEN/TERRACE	NUMBER OF ROOMS
ABERYSTWYTH: *Conrah Country House* W www.conrah.co.uk ⓔⓔⓔ Chancery, Aberystwyth, Cered SY23 4DF. ☎ 01970 617941. FAX 01970 624546. Traditional country-house hotel with extensive woodland grounds and lovely gardens. Grand views and an indoor pool. ● Christmas. 🖪 TV 🔥 ☕ 🔥 P	AE DC MC V	■		■	17
BRECON: *Cantre Selyf* W www.cantreselyf.co.uk ⓔ 5 Lion St, Brecon, Powys LD3 7AU. ☎ 01874 622904. FAX 01874 622315. Refined but relaxed townhouse in Brecon's attractive old centre. Timbered 17th-century interior. Guests are consulted about dinner menus. ● Dec–Jan. 🖪 🔥 P		■	●	■	3
BROAD HAVEN: *Druidstone* W www.druidstone.co.uk ⓔⓔ Druidston Haven, Broad Haven, Pembrokeshire SA62 3NE. ☎ 01437 781221. Perched high above a quiet beach, this slightly bohemian hotel arouses fierce loyalty. Several en-suite loft rooms and 5 cottages. *(See also p602.)* P	AE MC V	■	●	■	11
CARDIFF: *Big Sleep* W www.thebigsleephotel.com ⓔ Bute Terrace, Cardiff CF10 2FE. ☎ 029-2063 6363. FAX 029-2063 6364. A stylish, imaginative budget venture in a ten-storey office block. The interior is streamlined and contemporary. ● 25–26 Dec. 🖪 TV 🔥 ☕ 🔥 P	AE DC MC V		●		81
CARDIFF: *St David's* W www.thestdavidshotel.com ⓔⓔⓔⓔⓔ Havannah St, Cardiff CF10 5SD. ☎ 029 2045 4045. FAX 029 2031 3075. This luxury spa hotel makes a sleek, contemporary statement on the shores of Cardiff Bay. State-of-the-art health and fitness facilities. 🖪 TV 🔥 ☕ 🔥 P	AE DC MC V	■	●	■	132
CLYTHA: *Clytha Arms* W www.clytha-arms.com ⓔⓔ Clytha, Abergavenny, Monmouth NP7 9BW. ☎ 01873 840206. FAX 01873 840209. Deliciously inventive cooking is the highpoint of this charming country pub near Abergavenny. Several tastefully furnished bedrooms. The Big Pit is an easy drive. Kitchen closed Mondays. *(See also p603.)* ● 25 Dec. 🖪 TV 🔥 P	AE DC MC V	■	●	■	4
CRICKHOWELL: *Gliffaes Country House* W www.gliffaeshotel.com ⓔⓔⓔ Crickhowell, Powys NP8 1RH. ☎ 01874 730371. FAX 01874 730463. Gorgeous gardens and Usk Valley scenery at this creeper-clad, Victorian country house. The spacious, refined interior feels equally serene. 🖪 TV P	AE DC MC V	■	●	■	22
EGLWYSFACH: *Ynyshire Hall* W www.ynyshire-hall.co.uk ⓔⓔⓔⓔ Eglwysfach, Machynlleth, Powys SY20 8TA. ☎ 01654 781209. FAX 01654 781366. This fine Georgian mansion by the mouth of the Dovey was once owned by Queen Victoria. Mature gardens with velvety lawns. 🖪 TV 🔥 P	AE DC MC V	■		■	9

FISHGUARD: *Manor Town House* €€
11 Main St, Fishguard, Pembroke SA65 9HG. & FAX 01348 873260.
This excellent guesthouse stands in the heart of Fishguard's attractive upper town. Splendid harbour views. ● *restricted winter opening.* 🖼 TV ⚡
MC V ■ ● ■ 6

LAKE VYRNWY: *Lake Vyrnwy* W www.lakevyrnwy.com €€€
Lake Vyrnwy, Llanwddyn, Powys SY10 0LY. 01691 870692. FAX 01691 870259.
A lakeshore setting distinguishes this Victorian fishing lodge. Most bedrooms have lake views. Lots of outdoor activities. 🖼 TV ⚡
AE DC MC V ■ ● ■ 35

LLANDEILO: *Cawdor Arms* W www.cawdor-arms.co.uk €
Rhosmaen St, Llandeilo, Carmarthen SA19 6EN. 01558 823500. FAX 01558 822399.
A fine touring base on the west side of the Brecon Beacons, this Georgian inn boasts accomplished food and smart bedrooms. 🖼 TV ⚡ P
MC V ■ ● 17

LLANFIHANGEL-YNG-NGWYNFA: *Cyfie Farm* €€
Llanfihangel, Llanfyllin, Powys SY22 5JE. & FAX 01691 648451.
Top-range B&B in a 17th-century farmhouse, with spectacular views over the Meifod Valley. Roomy suites in converted outbuildings. ● *Jan–Feb.* 🖼 TV ⚡ P
■ ● ■ 3

LLANGAMMARCH WELLS: *Lake Country House* €€€€
Llangammarch Wells, Powys LD4 4BS. 01591 620202. W www.lakecountryhouse.co.uk
This mellow, mainly Edwardian building lies in 52-acre grounds. The interior is grandly tasteful, warm and welcoming. Fishing. 🖼 TV ⚡ P
AE DC MC V ■ ● ■ 19

LLANIGON: *Old Post Office* W www.oldpost-office.co.uk €
Llanigon, Hay-on-Wye, Powys HR3 5QA. 01497 820008.
Delightful cottage B&B in a quiet National Park village just outside Hay. Though small and simple, it is immaculate and stylish inside. 🖼 ⚡ P
● 3

LLANTHONY: *Llanthony Priory* W www.llanthonypriory.supanet.com €€
Llanthony, Abergavenny, Monmouthshire NP7 7NN. 01873 890487. FAX 01873 890844.
A 12th-century Augustinian Priory forms part of this retreat-like hotel in a beautiful quiet location surrounded by hills. Rooms (some with 4-poster beds) are reached by a spiral staircase; real ale and home-cooked food. ⚡
AE DC MC V ■ ■ 5

LLANWRTYD WELLS: *Carlton House* W www.carltonrestaurant.co.uk €€
Dolycoed Rd, Llanwrtyd Wells, Powys LD5 4RA. 01591 610248. FAX 01591 610242.
Food is taken seriously at this restaurant-with-rooms in a Cambrian spa town. A relaxed, cheerful style of budget B&B prevails. ● *10–28 Dec.* 🖼 TV
MC V ■ ● 6

LLYSWEN: *Llangoed Hall* W www.llangoedhall.com €€€€
Llyswen, Brecon, Powys LD3 0YP. 01874 754525. FAX 01874 754545.
A grand, part-Jacobean mansion owned by Sir Bernard Ashley (widower of Laura). Recently refurbished interior and extensive grounds. 🖼 TV P
AE DC MC V ■ ■ 23

MILEBROOK: *Milebrook House* W www.milebrookhouse.co.uk €€
Milebrook, Knighton, Powys LD7 1LT. 01547 528632. FAX 01547 520509.
Poised beside Offa's Dyke and the River Teme, this stone-built Georgian house, in large, attractive gardens, is very close to the English border. 🖼 TV ⚡ P
AE DC MC V ■ ■ 10

THE MUMBLES: *Hillcrest House* W www.hillcresthousehotel.com €€
1 Higher Lane, Langland, The Mumbles, Swansea SA3 4NS. 01792 363700.
This welcoming small hotel has a quiet setting. Tastefully decorated, with strikingly themed bedrooms. Pleasing restaurant. 🖼 TV ⚡
AE MC V ■ ● ■ 6

NANTGAREDIG: *Cwmtwrch Farm* W www.tourlink.co.uk €€
Nantgaredig, Carmarthen SA31 7NY. 01267 290238. FAX 01267 290808.
An ideal country stay is promised in this stylishly renovated farm in twelve acres of grounds. Gym and indoor pool. ● *23–28 Dec.* 🖼 TV ⚡ P
MC V ■ ● ■ 6

NEWPORT: *Cnapan* W www.online-holidays.net cnapan €€
East St, Newport, Pembroke SA42 0SY. 01239 820575.
This Georgian house has a cheerful and welcoming air. Compact, rustic bedrooms with plenty to read. *(See also p603.)* ● *25–26 Dec, Jan–Feb.* 🖼 TV ⚡ P
MC V ■ ● ■ 5

PENALLY: *Penally Abbey* W www.penally-abbey.com €€€
Penally, Tenby, Pembroke SA70 7PY. 01834 843033. FAX 01834 844714.
Neo-Gothic architectural flourishes give this fine country house considerable character. Located on the Pembrokeshire Coast Path near Tenby. 🖼 TV ⚡ P
AE MC V ■ ● ■ 17

PORTHKERRY: *Egerton Grey* W www.egertongrey.co.uk €€€
Porthkerry, Barry, Glamorgan CF62 3BZ. 01446 711666. FAX 01446 711690.
Handy for Cardiff airport, this refined Victorian rectory boasts original plasterwork and mahogany panelling. Traditional menus and service. 🖼 TV ⚡ P
AE MC V ■ ● ■ 10

Price categories for a standard double room per night, inclusive of breakfast, service charges and any additional taxes such as VAT:
£ under £65
££ £65–£100
£££ £100–£150
££££ £150–£200
£££££ £200 plus

RESTAURANT
Hotel restaurant or dining room serving more than just breakfast; often open to non-residents.
CHILDREN WELCOME
Especially welcoming to families. May have children's facilities such as cots, babysitting, family rooms, etc.
GARDEN/TERRACE
Hotels with a garden, courtyard or terrace, often providing tables for eating outside.
CREDIT CARDS
Indicates which credit cards are accepted: *AE* American Express; *DC* Diners Club; *MC* Máster Card/Access; *V* Visa.

	CREDIT CARDS	RESTAURANT	CHILDREN WELCOME	GARDEN/TERRACE	NUMBER OF ROOMS
REYNOLDSTON: *Fairyhill* w www.fairyhill.net (£££) Reynoldston, Swansea SA3 1BS. 01792 390139. FAX 01792 391358. This isolated country house in wooded grounds makes a fine place to unwind. Attentive service and interesting food. ● *Christmas, 1–18 Jan.* TV P	AE MC V	■		■	8
ST BRIDES WENTLOOGE: *Inn at the Elm Tree* w www.the-elm-tree.co.uk (££) St Brides Wentlooge, Newport NP10 8SQ. 01633 680225. FAX 01633 681035. This roadside dining inn, a 19th-century barn conversion, boasts an imaginative contemporary look. Highly regarded food. TV P	AE MC V	■	●	■	10
ST BRIDES WENTLOOGE: *West Usk Lighthouse* (££) Lighthouse Rd, St Brides Wentlooge, Newport NP10 8SF. 01633 810126. FAX 01633 815582. w www.westusklighthouse.co.uk This lighthouse B&B on the salt flats by the Severn boasts a warm welcome. Simple, cosy interior; alternative therapy available. ● *Christmas.* TV P	AE DC MC V		●	■	4
SPITTAL: *Lower Haythog Farm* w www.lowerhaythogfarm.co.uk (£) Spittal, Haverfordwest, Pembroke SA62 5QL. & FAX 01437 731279. B&B on a working farm in central Pembrokeshire offering tremendous value. Good home cooking and cottagey bedrooms. TV P			●	■	6
TINTERN: *Parva Farmhouse* w www.hoteltintern.co.uk (££) Tintern, Chepstow, Monmouth NP16 6SQ. 01291 689411. FAX 01291 689557. An ideal base for exploring Tintern's abbey and the surrounding Wye Valley, this stonebuilt 17th-century building is furnished in rustic style. TV P	AE MC V	■	●	■	9
WHITEBROOK: *Crown at Whitebrook* w www.crownatwhitebrook.co.uk (££) Whitebrook, Monmouth NP25 4TX. 01600 860254. FAX 01600 860607. This restaurant-with-rooms lies in a leafy stretch of Wye Valley. Secluded, but the cooking is popular. The interior is bright and comfortable, with neat, practical bedrooms. *(See also p604.)* ● *Christmas & New Year.* TV P	AE DC MC V	■		■	10
WOLF'S CASTLE: *The Wolfe* w www.the-wolfe.co.uk (££) Wolf's Castle, Haverfordwest, Pembroke SA62 5LS. 01437 741662. FAX 01437 741676. This typical stonebuilt, creeper-clad roadside inn not far from St David's has an Italianate interior, along with the odd wolfish touch. TV P	MC V	■	●	■	3
THE LOWLANDS					
ABERDOUR: *Hawkcraig House* (£) Hawkcraig Point, Aberdour, Fife KY3 0TZ. 01383 860335. An amazing waterfront setting at this charming guesthouse in an old ferryman's house. Book ahead. Excellent dinners. ● *Nov–Mar.* TV P		■	●	■	2
ALLOWAY: *Ivy House* w www.theivyhouse.uk.com (£££) 2 Alloway, Ayrshire KA7 4NL. 01292 442336. FAX 01292 445572. A makeover has given this restaurant-with-rooms near Robbie Burns' cottage an upbeat, contemporary feel. Culzean Castle is an easy drive. TV P	AE MC V	■	●	■	5
AUCHTERARDER: *Gleneagles* w www.gleneagles.com (£££££) Auchterarder, Perth & Kinross. 01764 662231. FAX 01764 662134. Luxury château-style resort hotel with tip-top service, championship golf courses and a health spa. It's surprisingly family-friendly. TV P	AE DC MC V	■	●	■	220
BALQUHIDDER: *Monachyle Mhor* w www.monachylemhor.com (££) Balquhidder, Lochearnhead, Stirling FK19 8PQ. 01877 384622. FAX 01877 384305. A beautiful setting at the end of a remote, lochside glen makes this upbeat, family-run farmhouse memorable. Stylishly rustic bedrooms. TV P	MC V	■		■	10
BLAIRGOWRIE: *Kinloch House* w www.kinlochhouse.com (£££££) By Blairgowrie, Perth & Kinross PH10 6SG 01250 884237. FAX 01250 884333. A traditional country-house hotel in parkland, ideal for a restful break. Heated indoor pool. Room rate includes dinner. ● *18–30 Dec.* TV P	MC V	■	●	■	18

CALLANDER: *Leny House* W www.lenyestate.com   ⓔⓔⓔ
Leny Estate, Callander, Perthshire FK17 8HA. 📞 & 📠 *01877 331078.*
This delightful B&B is a great base for exploring the Trossachs. Originally
16th-century, its present incarnation is largely Victorian. Luxurious and stylish
inside, it retains many period features. ● *Oct–Apr.* 🚗 TV ⚡ P

MC V   3

CLINTMAINS: *Clint Lodge* W www.clintlodge.co.uk   ⓔⓔ
Clintmains, St Boswells, Borders TD6 0DZ. 📞 *01835 822027.* 📠 *01835 822656.*
Views of the Tweed grace this attractive Victorian guesthouse close to Melrose
Abbey. Restful ambience; outstanding breakfasts. ● *25 Dec, 1 Jan.* 🚗 TV P

MC V   5

CUPAR: *Peat Inn* W www.thepeatinn.co.uk   ⓔⓔⓔⓔ
Peat Inn, Cupar, Fife KY15 5LH. 📞 *01334 840206.* 📠 *01334 840530.*
Primarily renowned for its food, the Peat Inn also boasts luxury suites set in
a separate annexe. A romantic base for sightseeing around St Andrews. *(See
also p605.)* ● *25–26 Dec, Sun–Mon.* 🚗 TV 🔧 P

AE MC V   8

DOLLAR: *Castle Campbell* W www.castle-campbell.co.uk   ⓔⓔ
11 Bridge St, Dollar, Clackmannan FK14 7DE. 📞 *01259 742519.* 📠 *01259 743742.*
A simple but dignified Georgian building in the town centre, inoffensively
upholstered in tartan and leather. 🚗 TV ⚡ P

AE DC MC V   8

DUNOON: *Enmore* W www.enmorehotel.co.uk   ⓔⓔ
Marine Parade, Dunoon, Argyll & Bute PA23 8HH. 📞 *01369 702230.* 📠 *01369 702148.*
Modern Scottish cooking in an attractive Georgian house with views over the
Firth of Clyde. Several bedrooms feature jacuzzis. ● *mid-Nov–mid-Feb.* 🚗 TV P

AE MC V   9

EDINBURGH: *7 Danube Street* W www.sevendanubestreet.com   ⓔⓔⓔ
7 Danube St, Edinburgh EH4 1NN. 📞 *0131 332 2755.* 📠 *0131 343 3648.*
A Georgian townhouse award-winning B&B in a quiet location but
centrally located. It offers modern comforts along with antique furniture.
Computer points in rooms; own key and own entrance. ● *25 & 26 Dec.*
🚗 TV ⚡ *throughout.*

MC V   5

EDINBURGH: *The Bonham* W www.thebonham.com   ⓔⓔⓔⓔ
35 Drumsheugh Gardens, Edinburgh EH3 7RN. 📞 *0131 226 6050.* 📠 *0131 226 6080.*
Ultra-smart townhouse boasting rich interior decor with touches of whimsy.
The oak-panelled restaurant serves serious modern European fare. Opulent,
hi-tech bedrooms. 🚗 TV 📺 ♿ ⚡

AE DC MC V   48

EDINBURGH: *The Scotsman* W www.thescotsmanhotel.co.uk   ⓔⓔⓔⓔ
20 North Bridge, Edinburgh EH1 1YT. 📞 *0131 556 5565.* 📠 *0131 652 3652.*
An unusual hotel venture set in the plush Edwardian offices of the eponymous
newspaper. Leisure club and fashionable brasserie dining. 🚗 TV 📺 ♿ P

AE DC MC V   68

EDNAM: *Edenwater House* W www.edenwaterhouse.co.uk   ⓔⓔ
Ednam, Kelso, Borders TD5 7QL. 📞 *01573 224070.* 📠 *01573 226615.*
A quiet stone guesthouse on the edge of the village. Cheviot views from some
rooms. Appetizing dinners served. Good wine list. ● *1–14 Jan.* 🚗 TV ⚡ P

MC V   4

GLASGOW: *Langs* W www.langshotels.com   ⓔⓔⓔ
2 Port Dundas Place, Glasgow G2 3LD. 📞 *0141 333 1500.* 📠 *0141 333 5700.*
A style-conscious glamorous boutique hotel with two trendy restaurants.
Bedrooms are comfortably minimalist. Gym. 🚗 TV 📺 ♿ ⚡ P

AE DC MC V   100

GLASGOW: *One Devonshire Gardens*   ⓔⓔⓔⓔ
1 Devonshire Gardens, Glasgow G12 0UX. 📞 *0141 339 2001.*
📠 *0141 337 1663.* W www.onedevonshiregardens.co.uk
The ultimate luxury townhouse, glamorously refurbished and opulently
decorated, with cooking to match and plenty of hi-tech gadgetry in the
bedrooms. A place for a serious treat. *(See also p605.)* 🚗 TV

AE DC MC V   38

GLENROTHES: *Balbirnie House* W www.balbirnie.co.uk   ⓔⓔⓔⓔ
Balbirnie Park, Markinch, Glenrothes, Fife KY7 6NE. 📞 *01592 610066.* 📠 *01592 610529.*
This elegant Georgian mansion evokes an air of tastefully restrained hedonism.
A certain amount of business and conference trade is tactfully separated
from the main building. Bedrooms are luxuriously individual. 🚗 TV ♿ P

AE DC MC V   30

GULLANE: *Golf Inn*   ⓔⓔ
Main St, Gullane, East Lothian EH31 2AB. 📞 *01620 843259.* 📠 *01620 842066.*
Smartly refurbished village inn with crisp colour schemes and pine furnishings
– even a little trompe l'oeil. Simple, appetizing menus. Good value. 🚗 TV ⚡

AE MC V   14

Price categories for a standard double room per night, inclusive of breakfast, service charges and any additional taxes such as VAT: **£** under £65 **££** £65–£100 **£££** £100–£150 **££££** £150–£200 **£££££** £200 plus	**RESTAURANT** Hotel restaurant or dining room serving more than just breakfast; often open to non-residents. **CHILDREN WELCOME** Especially welcoming to families. May have children's facilities such as cots, babysitting, family rooms, etc. **GARDEN/TERRACE** Hotels with a garden, courtyard or terrace, often providing tables for eating outside. **CREDIT CARDS** Indicates which credit cards are accepted: *AE* American Express; *DC* Diners Club; *MC* Master Card/Access; *V* Visa.			

	CREDIT CARDS	RESTAURANT	CHILDREN WELCOME	GARDEN/TERRACE	NUMBER OF ROOMS
GULLANE: *Greywalls* W www.greywalls.co.uk **£££££** Muirfield, Gullane, E Lothian EH31 2EG. 01620 842144. FAX 01620 842241. Despite its name, this photogenic Lutyens house overlooking the famous golf course is built of warm golden stone. The Jekyll-designed gardens are gorgeous, and the interior suitably refined. ● mid-Oct–mid-Apr. TV P	AE DC MC V	■	●	■	23
HEITON: *Roxburghe* W www.roxburghe.net **££££** Heiton, Kelso, Borders TD5 8JZ. 01573 450331. FAX 01573 450611. This grand Jacobean-style house in extensive parkland makes a supremely comfortable, if highly traditional, Borders base, with lots of on-site outdoor activities. TV P	AE DC MC V	■	●	■	22
INVERSNAID: *Inversnaid Lodge* W www.inversnaidphoto.com **££** Inversnaid, Aberfoyle, Stirling FK8 3TU. 01877 386254. A photogenic setting on the eastern shores of Loch Lomond makes an ideal base for a hotel owned by and geared towards photographers. Simple cottagey bedrooms and straightforward dinners. ● Nov–Mar. P		■		■	9
JEDBURGH: *Hundalee House* W www.accommodation-scotland.org **£** Jedburgh, Borders TD8 6DA. & FAX 01835 863011. Refined B&B in a handsome Georgian manor in 15-acre grounds. Classic interior and a warm welcome. Remarkable value. ● Nov–Mar. TV P			●	■	5
KIRKCUDBRIGHT: *Gladstone House* @ hilarygladstone@aol.com **£** 48 High St, Kirkcudbright, Dumfries & Gall DG6 4JX. & FAX 01557 331734. Charming B&B in an attractive townhouse set back from the Solway water-front. Light, stylish interior. Excellent breakfasts; dinner by request. TV	MC V				3
LINLITHGOW: *Champany Inn* W www.champany.com **£££** Champany, Linlithgow, W Lothian EH49 7LU. 01506 834532. FAX 01506 834302. This restaurant boasts stylish accommodation. Decor and furnishings are classy; bathrooms sparklingly efficient. *(See p605.)* ● 25–26 Dec, 1–2 Jan. TV P	AE DC MC V	■	●	■	16
ST ANDREWS: *Old Course* W www.oldcoursehotel.co.uk **£££££** Old Station Rd, St Andrews, Fife KY16 9SP. 01334 474371. FAX 01334 477668. The legendary seaside links course is effectively the garden of this luxury hotel. Its 1960s exterior wins no beauty contests, but its glamorously stylish interior and exemplary facilities are unsurpassed. ● Christmas. TV P	AE DC MC V	■	●		132
ST BOSWELLS: *Dryburgh Abbey* W www.dryburgh.co.uk **££££** St Boswells, Melrose, Borders TD6 0RQ. 01835 822261. FAX 01835 823945. A ruined abbey beside the River Tweed makes an atmospheric setting for this hotel. Formal restaurant; comfortable, spacious bedrooms. TV P	AE MC V	■	●	■	38
ST FILLANS: *Four Seasons* W www.thefourseasonshotel.co.uk **££** St Fillans, Perthshire PH6 2NF. 01764 685333. FAX 01764 685444. This welcoming hotel has a glorious waterfront location. Comfortable lounge and dining area. Practical bedrooms; 6 chalets. ● Jan & Feb. TV P	AE MC V	■	●	■	18
STRATHKINNESS: *Fossil House* W www.fossil-guest-house.co.uk **£** 12–14 Main St, Strathkinness, St Andrews, Fife KY16 9RU. & FAX 01334 850639. A family-friendly B&B in a converted smallholding (bedrooms are in the court-yard stable-block). Conservatory lounge. TV limited. throughout. P	AE MC V		●	■	4
TROON: *Lochgreen House* W www.costleyhotels.co.uk **£££** Monktonhill Rd, Southwood, Troon, S. Ayrshire KA10 7EN. 01292 313343. FAX 01292 318661. Elegant, antique-filled Edwardian hotel with excellent cooking, served in a baronial-looking modern restaurant. Bedrooms are luxurious. TV P	AE MC V	■		■	40
YARROW: *Tibbie Shiels Inn* W www.tibbieshielsinn.com **£** Yarrow, by Selkirk TD7 5LH. 01750 42231. FAX 01750 42302. Once a hostelry favoured by Sir Walter Scott, this 18th-century inn offers good food and a warm welcome. Beautiful setting on St Mary's Loch. P	MC V	■		■	5

HIGHLANDS AND ISLANDS

ABERDEEN: *Marcliffe at Pitfodels* Ⓦ www.marcliffe.com   £££££
North Deeside Rd, Aberdeen AB15 9YA. 【 01224 861000. FAX 01224 868860.
A smoothly managed, upmarket hotel in large grounds just ten minutes'
drive from the city centre. Beautifully kept inside, it has a warm and
welcoming air. 🛏 TV 🔌 ⚿ ⚡ P
AE DC MC V — 42

ACHILTIBUIE: *Summer Isles* Ⓦ www.summerisleshotel.co.uk   £££
Achiltibuie, Ullapool, Highland IV26 2YG. 【 01854 622282. FAX 01854 622251.
A remote and picturesque setting overlooking the Summer Isles makes this
disarmingly low-key place an idyllic retreat. Quietly sophisticated inside, it
has first class food and lovely bedrooms. ● *Oct–Easter.* 🛏 TV ⚡ P
MC V — 13

ARISAIG: *Old Library Lodge* Ⓦ www.oldlibrary.co.uk   ££
Arisaig, Highland PH39 4NH. 【 01687 450651. FAX 01687 450219.
A modest restaurant-with-rooms on the Road to the Isles, offering five
choices at each course, and much fresh, locally sourced produce. Peaceful,
spacious bedrooms, mostly in a modern rear extension. 🛏 TV ⚡
AE MC V — 6

AULDEARN: *Boath House* Ⓦ www.boath-house.com   ££££
Auldearn, Nairn, Highland IV12 5TW. 【 01667 454896. FAX 01667 455469.
Close to the Moray Firth, this imposing Georgian mansion stands in secluded
20-acre grounds. The strikingly decorated contemporary interior is cool and
spacious. Outstanding food (organic and seasonal). ● *25, 26 Dec.* 🛏 TV ⚿ ⚡ P
AE MC V — 6

BALLATER: *Balgonie Country House* Ⓦ www.balgonie-hotel.co.uk   £££
Braemar Place, Ballater, Aberdeen AB35 5NQ. 【 013397 55482. FAX 013397 55497.
Welcoming hosts play a major role in the success of this secluded Deeside
property, which offers excellent cooking and bright, comfortable rooms. A
good place to unwind. ● *5 Jan–10 Feb.* 🛏 TV P
AE DC MC V — 9

BALLATER: *Darroch Learg* Ⓦ www.darrochlearg.co.uk   £££
Braemar Rd, Ballater, Aberdeen AB35 5UX. 【 013397 55443. FAX 013397 55252.
Two interesting Victorian houses in hilly gardens provide top-notch cooking
and very comfortable rooms. Splendid views towards Lochnagar. Formidable
wine-list. *(See also p606.)* ● *Christmas & 3 weeks in Jan.* 🛏 TV ⚿ ⚡ P
AE DC MC V — 17

CLACHAN-SEIL: *Willowburn* Ⓦ www.willowburn.co.uk   ££££
Clachan-Seil, Isle of Seil, Oban, Argyll & Bute PA34 4TJ. 【 01852 300276. FAX 01852 300597.
Set on a mini-islet connected by bridge to the mainland south of Oban, this
idyllic retreat is a whitewashed cottage with lochside views, and simple,
cheerful decor. Price includes dinner; good seafood. ● *Dec–Feb.* 🛏 TV ⚡ P
MC V — 7

CRINAN: *Crinan* Ⓦ www.crinanhotel.com   £££££
Crinan, Lochgilphead, Argyll & Bute PA31 8SR. 【 01546 830261. FAX 01546 830292.
Vistas over Loch Fyne and the Jura Sound enhance this simple white building.
Seafood is on the menus. Room rate includes dinner. ● *Christmas.* 🛏 TV 🔌 ⚿ P
AE MC V — 20

DUNKELD: *The Pend* Ⓦ www.thepend.com   ££
5 Brae St, Dunkeld, Perth & Kinross PH8 0BA. 【 01350 727586. FAX 01350 727173.
High-quality accommodation in a quiet Georgian townhouse just off the main
street. Beautifully kept interior with antiques and period features. Excellent
breakfasts served at flexible times; imaginative dinners available. TV P
AE DC MC V — 3

DUNKELD: *Kinnaird* Ⓦ www.kinnairdestate.com   £££££
Kinnaird Estate, Dunkeld, Perth & Kinross PH8 0LB. 【 01796 482440. FAX 01796 482289.
Superb country-house accommodation on a huge Tayside sporting estate. Tran-
quil setting; seriously smart but relaxing interior. Highly regarded cooking. *(See
also p607.)* Room rate includes dinner. ● *Mon–Wed in Jan–Feb.* 🛏 TV 🔌 ⚿ P
AE MC V — 9

ERISKA: *Isle of Eriska* Ⓦ www.eriska-hotel.co.uk   £££££
Eriska, Ledaig, Oban, Argyll & Bute PA37 1SD. 【 01631 720371. FAX 01631 720531.
Family-run luxury hideaway in Scots Baronial style with impressive leisure facil-
ities on an island in the Firth of Lorne. Elaborate dinners. ● *Jan.* 🛏 TV ⚿ P
AE MC V — 17

FORT WILLIAM: *Ashburn House* Ⓦ www.highland5star.co.uk   ££
4 Achintore Rd, Fort William, Highland PH33 6RQ. 【 01397 706000. FAX 01397 702024.
Expect a proper Highland welcome and an excellent breakfast at this Victorian
B&B overlooking Loch Linnhe. Bedrooms are well furnished and equipped for
a thoroughly comfortable stay. ● *Dec–Jan.* 🛏 TV ⚡ *throughout.* P
AE MC V — 7

<table>
<tr><td colspan="2">Price categories for a standard double room per night, inclusive of breakfast, service charges and any additional taxes such as VAT:
£ under £65
££ £65–£100
£££ £100–£150
££££ £150–£200
£££££ £200 plus</td><td>RESTAURANT
Hotel restaurant or dining room serving more than just breakfast; often open to non-residents.
CHILDREN WELCOME
Especially welcoming to families. May have children's facilities such as cots, babysitting, family rooms, etc.
GARDEN/TERRACE
Hotels with a garden, courtyard or terrace, often providing tables for eating outside.
CREDIT CARDS
Indicates which credit cards are accepted: AE American Express; DC Diners Club; MC Master Card/Access; V Visa.</td></tr>
</table>

	Credit Cards	Restaurant	Children Welcome	Garden/Terrace	Number of Rooms
FORT WILLIAM: *The Grange* W www.thegrange-scotland.co.uk £££ Grange Rd, Fort William, Highland PH33 6JF. ☎ 01397 705516. FAX 01397 701595. Skillfully restored B&B overlooking the loch. Its beautifully furnished bedrooms are spacious and stylish, with antique beds and luxurious bathrooms. Generous breakfasts. ● Nov–mid-Mar. ▪ TV ▪ throughout. P				■	4
GLENLIVET: *Minmore House* W www.minmorehousehotel.com £££ Glenlivet, Moray AB37 9DB. ☎ 01807 590378. FAX 01807 590472. A tranquil, elegant country house on the Glenlivet estate (former home of the distillery's founder). Glorious Speyside surroundings. Traditionally comfortable bedrooms (some very grand). ● Feb–mid-Mar. ▪ ▪ P	AE MC V	■	●	■	10
GRANTOWN-ON-SPEY: *Culdearn House* W www.culdearn.com £££££ Woodlands Terrace, Grantown-on-Spey, Highland PH26 3JU. ☎ 01479 872106. Exemplary hospitality in a Victorian house on the Speyside whisky trail. Comfortable, well-equipped bedrooms and tasty four-course dinners. Rates include dinner. ● Dec–Jan. ▪ TV ▪ limited. ▪ throughout. P	AE MC V	■		■	7
INVERNESS: *Glenmoriston Town House* W www.glenmoriston.com £££ 20 Ness Bank, Inverness, Highland IV2 4SF. ☎ 01463 223777. FAX 01463 712378. Riverside hotel with tasteful, contemporary decor. Bedrooms attain high standards, with marble bathrooms and lavish furnishings. ▪ TV ▪ P	AE DC MC V	■	●	■	30
INVERNESS: *Millwood House* W www.millwoodhouse.co.uk £££ 36 Old Mill Rd, Inverness, Highland IV2 3HR. ☎ 01463 237254. FAX 0870-4296806. A charming B&B in a private home, quietly set in a lovely residential district. Welcoming and civilized, with attractive, well-equipped bedrooms. Guests may use its beautiful gardens. ● 25 & 26 Dec, 1 & 2 Jan. ▪ TV ▪ P	MC V			■	3
ISLE OF HARRIS: *Leachin House* W www.leachin-house.com £££ Tarbert, Isle of Harris HS3 3AH. ☎ & FAX 01859 502157. Victorian stone building by Norman MacLeod, "father" of the Harris tweed industry, with many period features. On shores of West Loch Tarbert and good base for shooting (arranged by hotel) and fishing. Rates include dinner. ▪ TV P	MC V			■	3
ISLE OF IONA: *Argyll* W www.argyllhoteliona.co.uk £££ Isle of Iona, Argyll & Bute PA76 6SJ. ☎ 01681 700334. FAX 01681 700510. A relaxing retreat with bright simple bedrooms and a sunny conservatory overlooking the sound. Good local cooking. ● Dec & Jan. ▪ P	MC V	■	●	■	16
ISLE OF LEWIS: *Galson Farm* W www.galsonfarm.co.uk £££ South Galson, Isle of Lewis, Western Isles HS2 0SH. ☎ & FAX 01851 850492. Simple, homely accommodation on a working farm. This traditional 18-acre coastal croft dates back to the 18th century. Neat bedrooms and good home cooking (interesting vegetarian options). ▪ TV ▪ P	MC V	■	●	■	4
ISLE OF MULL: *Druimard Country House* W www.druimard.co.uk £££ Dervaig, Tobermory, Isle of Mull PA75 6QW. ☎ 01688 400345. FAX 01688 400345. Stonebuilt Victorian hotel in a quiet glenside setting. Mull's Little Theatre stands in its grounds. Good cooking. Polished service. Rates include dinner. ● Nov–Mar. ▪ TV ▪ ▪ P	MC V	■	●	■	7
ISLE OF SKYE: *Duisdale* W www.duisdale.com £££ Sleat, Isle Ornsay, Isle of Skye IV43 8QW. ☎ 01471 833202. FAX 01471 833404. Friendly Victorian house with magnificent views across the Sound of Sleat. Flamboyantly decorated; stacks of personality. The owner is a Paris-trained chef, so expect some good cooking. Lovely gardens. ● Nov–mid-Mar. ▪ ▪ P	AE MC V	■	●	■	19
ISLE OF SKYE: *Three Chimneys* W www.threechimneys.co.uk £££££ Colbost, Dunvegan, Isle of Skye IV55 8ZT. ☎ 01470 511258. FAX 01470 511358. Spectacular coastal location, superlative cooking and startlingly voguish bedrooms make these converted crofters' cottages the talk of the isles. Perfection without pretension. ● 3 weeks in Jan. ▪ TV ▪ ▪ throughout. P	AE MC V	■	●	■	6

KILLIECRANKIE: *Killiecrankie* ⓦ www.killiecrankiehotel.co.uk   ££££   MC V   10
Killiecrankie, Pitlochry, Perth & Kinross PH16 5LG. ▐ *01796 473220.* **FAX** *01796 472451.*
A relaxing, informal place by the wooded cliffs of the Killiecrankie Pass (an
RSPB bird reserve). Acclaimed cooking – light meals available. Room rates
include dinner. *(See also p607.)* ● *Jan–mid-Feb; Nov & Mar mid-week.* 🛏 TV P

KINGUSSIE: *The Cross* ⓦ www.thecross.co.uk   £££   MC V   8
Tweed Mill Brae, Ardbroilach Road, Kingussie, Highland PH21 1LB. ▐ *01540 661166.*
Acclaimed restaurant-with-rooms in a converted tweed mill near the
Cairngorms. The smartly refurbished interior is light and bright with lots of
modern paintings. Brilliant cooking. ● *23 Dec–Jan.* 🛏 TV 🍴 P

LOCHINVER: *Albannach* ⓦ www.thealbannach.co.uk   ££££   MC V   5
Baddidarroch, Lochinver, Highland IV27 4LP. ▐ *01571 844407.* **FAX** *01571 844285.*
This welcoming house has a wonderful atmosphere and fine views. Home-
grown produce and Lochinver seafood go into its seasonal menus. Rates
include dinner. ● *Mon; mid-Nov–mid-Mar.* 🛏 🍴 *throughout.* P

LOCHRANZA: *Apple Lodge*   ££   4
Lochranza, Isle of Arran KA27 8HJ. ▐ & **FAX** *01770 830229.*
A charming base on the Isle of Arran, handy for the Kintyre ferry, with views
over the nearby castle. Bedrooms are prettily floral; several in a self-contained
cottage annexe. Excellent cooking. ● *Christmas & New Year.* 🛏 TV 🍴 P

MUIR OF ORD: *The Dower House* @ info@thedowerhouse.co.uk   £££   MC V   5
Highfield, Muir of Ord, Ross-shire IV6 7XN. ▐ & **FAX** *01463 870090.*
An extremely agreeable small hotel that is attractively decorated. Pleasing
bedrooms and a first-rate restaurant. 🛏 TV ♿ *limited.* 🍴 P

ORKNEY ISLANDS: *Foveran* ⓦ www.foveranhotel.co.uk   ££   MC V   8
St Ola, Kirkwall, Orkney KW15 1SF. ▐ *01856 872389.* **FAX** *01856 876430.*
A family-run hotel-restaurant with a fine outlook over Scapa Flow.
Recently refurbished under new ownership, it is practical and stylish.
Good home cooking. 🛏 TV 🍴 P

PITLOCHRY: *Atholl Palace* ⓦ www.athollpalace.com   ££££   AE MC V   108
Pitlochry, Perthshire PH16 5LY. ▐ *01796 472400.* **FAX** *01796 473036.*
This grandiose hotel is an excellent example of Scottish Baronial
architecture. Vast rooms. Spa facilities and indoor pool. 🛏 TV 🏊 ♿ 🍴 P

POOLEWE: *Pool House* ⓦ www.poolhousehotel.com   £££££   AE MC V   5
Poolewe, by Achnasheen, Highland IV22 2LD. ▐ *01445 781272.* **FAX** *01445 781403.*
This traditional-looking lochside building has undergone a startling transformation into a series of exotic luxury suites, ideal for a honeymoon or special
occasion. Inverewe Gardens lie just across the bay. ● *Jan.* 🛏 TV 🍴 P

PORT APPIN: *Airds* ⓦ www.airds-hotel.com   £££££   MC V   12
Port Appin, Appin, Argyll & Bute PA38 4DF. ▐ *01631 730236.* **FAX** *01631 730535.*
The views over Loch Linnhe are stunning from this classy old ferry inn.
Country-house furnishings and well-chosen antiques. Accomplished
cooking. *(See also p607.)* ● *6–26 Jan.* 🛏 TV 🍴 P

SPEAN BRIDGE: *Old Pines* ⓦ www.oldpines.co.uk   ££££   MC V   8
Spean Bridge, Fort William, Highland PH34 4EG. ▐ *01397 712324.* **FAX** *01397 712433.*
A Scandinavian house is the setting for this restaurant-with-rooms in a grove
of Scots pines. Bedrooms are neat and pretty; acclaimed home-cooking with
organic local produce. Rates include dinner. 🛏 ♿ 🍴 *throughout.* P

STRONTIAN: *Kilcamb Lodge* ⓦ www.kilcamblodge.com   £££   MC V   11
Strontian, Highland PH36 4HY. ▐ *01967 402257.* **FAX** *01967 402041.*
This comfortable, tastefully furnished country house on the quiet
Ardnamurchan peninsula enjoys a wonderful outlook over a winding sea
loch. A lovely place to relax. Excellent food. 🛏 TV 🍴 P

TORLUNDY: *Inverlochy Castle* ⓦ www.inverlochycastlehotel.com   £££££   AE MC V   17
Torlundy, Fort William, Highland PH33 6SN. ▐ *01397 702177.* **FAX** *01397 702953.*
A grand, luxurious Victorian mansion in palatial parkland. Traditional, classic
interior with very high standards of food, accommodation and service.
Fishing, tennis and croquet in the grounds. ● *Jan–Feb.* 🛏 TV 🍴 P

ULLAPOOL: *Tanglewood House* ⓦ www.tanglewoodhouse.co.uk   ££   MC V   3
Ullapool, Highland IV26 2TB. ▐ & **FAX** *01854 612059.*
This tastefully furnished, highly individual modern house commands
panoramic vistas of Loch Broom from its huge picture windows. Inventive
dinners available on request. ● *Christmas & New Year.* 🛏 TV 🍴 *throughout.* P

For key to symbols see back flap

WHERE TO EAT

RITISH FOOD need strike no terrors to the visiting gourmet's heart; the UK's restaurant scene has moved far from its once dismal reputation. This is partly due to an influx of foreign chefs and cooking styles; you can now sample a wide range of international cuisine throughout Britain, with the greatest choice in London and the other major cities. Home-

Michelin Man at Bibendum, London

grown restaurateurs have risen to the challenge of redeeming British food too, and our indigenous cooking (once thought to consist only of fish and chips, overcooked vegetables, meat pies and lumpy custard) has improved out of all recognition in the last decade. You can now also eat extremely well in Britain whatever your budget – and at most times of day in the towns. Much less elaborate, but well-prepared, affordable food is making a mark in all types of brasseries, restaurants and cafés throughout the country; more modern approaches combine fresh produce and dietary common sense with influences from around the world. The restaurant listings *(see pp578–607)* feature some of the very best places as well as those with a steady track record.

WHAT'S ON THE MENU?

THE CHOICE seems endless in large cities, particularly London. Cuisines from all over the world are represented, as well as their infinite variations – Thai and Tex-Mex, Turkish and Tuscan, Tandoori, Bhel Poori and Balti. There are many more unusual styles of cooking such as Hungarian, Polish, Caribbean and Pacific Rim. French and Italian restaurants are still highly regarded, offering everything from pastries and espresso coffee to the highest standards of *haute cuisine*. Outside the major cities the food scene is more limited, but most towns will have at least a couple of Italian,

Indian and Chinese restaurants. The vague term "modern-international cuisine" adopted by many restaurants disguises a diverse rag-bag of styles. The spectrum ranges from French to Asian recipes, loosely characterized by the imaginative use of fresh, high-quality ingredients, which are cooked simply with imaginative seasonings.

Nostalgic yearnings for British food have produced a revival of hearty traditional dishes such as steak and kidney pie and treacle pudding *(see p37)*, though "Modern British" cooking adopts a lighter, more innovative approach to old-fashioned stodge. The distinctions between this and Modern International food are starting to blur, which is mostly a change for the better as young chefs apply Oriental and Mediterranean flavours to home-grown ingredients.

BREAKFAST

IT USED TO BE SAID that the best way to enjoy British food was to eat breakfast three times a day. Traditional British breakfast starts with cereal and milk followed by bacon, eggs and tomato, perhaps with fried black pudding *(see p36)* in the North and Scotland. It is finished off with toast and marmalade washed down with tea. Or you can just have black coffee and fruit juice, with a croissant or two (known as Continental breakfast in hotels). The price of breakfast is often included in hotel tariffs in Britain.

LUNCH

MANY RESTAURANTS offer light lunches at fixed prices, sometimes of only two courses. The most popular lunchtime foods are sandwiches, salads, baked potatoes with fillings and ploughman's lunches, the latter found mainly in pubs. A traditional Sunday lunch of roast chicken, lamb or beef is served in some pubs and restaurants.

Gay Hussar, London, a top Hungarian restaurant *(see p580)*

AFTERNOON TEA

No visitor should miss the experience of a proper English afternoon tea, which rivals breakfast as the most enjoyable meal of the day (see p36). Some of the most palatial teas are offered by country-house and top London hotels such as the Ritz or Browns. The area that is best known for its classic "cream teas" is the West Country; these always include scones, spread with clotted cream, butter and jam. Wales, Scotland, Yorkshire and the Lake District also offer tasty teas with regional variations; in the North Country a slice of apple pie or fruit cake is served hot with a piece of North Yorkshire Wensleydale cheese on top.

An afternoon tea including sandwiches, cakes and scones

DINNER

At DINNER TIME, the grander restaurants and hotels offer elaborately staged meals, sometimes billed as five or six courses (though one may be simply a sorbet, or coffee with *petits fours*). Dessert is often followed by cheese and crackers. Confusingly, in the North of England and Scotland "lunch" can be called "dinner" and "dinner" may be called "tea".

Generally, you can choose to take your dinner before 6pm or after 9pm only in larger towns, where there is a broad choice of ethnic restaurants, bars and all-day brasseries, which often have long opening hours.

Leith Docks in Edinburgh, a centre of good pubs, bars and restaurants

PLACES TO EAT

Eating venues are extremely varied, with brasseries, bistros, wine bars, tearooms, *tapas* bars and theatre cafés now competing with the more conventional cafés and restaurants. Many pubs also now serve excellent bar food at often reasonable prices (see p608–11).

BRASSERIES, BISTROS AND CAFÉS

French-style café-brasseries are now popular in Britain. Sometimes they stay open all day, serving coffee, snacks and fairly simple dishes along with a selection of beers and wines. Alcoholic drinks, however, may only be available at certain times of day. The atmosphere is usually young and urbane, with decor to match. Drinks such as imported bottled beers, exotic spirits or cocktails may be fairly expensive.

The café at Tate St Ives, Cornwall (see p591)

Wine bars are similar to brasseries, but with a better selection of wines, which may include English varieties (see p148). Some bars have a good range of ciders and real ales as well (see p34). Bistros are another French import, serving full meals at lunch and dinner time with less formality and more moderate prices than you would expect at a restaurant. You should expect to pay anything from £12 to £30 for a standard three-course meal in a bistro.

RESTAURANTS-WITH-ROOMS AND HOTELS

Restaurants-with-rooms are a new breed of small establishments with only a handful of bedrooms and usually excellent food. They tend to be expensive and are usually in a rural location.

Many hotel restaurants happily serve non-residents. They tend to be expensive, but the best can be unparalleled. Hotels serving a high standard of food are also included in the hotel listings.

RESTAURANT ETIQUETTE

As a rule of thumb, the more expensive the restaurant, the more formal the dress code – though few restaurants nowadays will expect men to wear a shirt and tie. If you are not sure, ring first.

Some establishments do not allow smoking at all, while others now have separate sections or tables for people who wish to smoke.

Raymond Blanc's Le Manoir Aux Quat'Saisons *(see p586)*, one of Britain's most acclaimed restaurants-with-rooms

ALCOHOL

BRITAIN'S LAWS concerning the sale of alcohol, the "licensing laws", were once among the most restrictive in Europe. Now they are more relaxed, but some establishments may still only serve alcohol at set times with food. Some unlicensed restaurants operate a "Bring Your Own" policy. A corkage fee is often charged. The Scottish laws are different to the rest of Britain, most apparent in the later closing times of pubs.

VEGETARIAN FOOD

BRITAIN IS AHEAD of many of its European counterparts in providing vegetarian alternatives to meat dishes. A few of our selections serve only vegetarian meals, but most cater for carnivores as well. Vegetarians who want a wider choice should seek out South Indian, Chinese and other ethnic restaurants which have a tradition of vegetarian cuisine.

FAST FOOD

FAST FOOD comes much cheaper, usually well under £10. Apart from the numerous individually owned fish and chip shops, there are many fast food chains in Britain, such as McDonald's, Burger King, Pizza Hut and KFC. Sandwich bars are very popular, and are often good value; some also have seating. Budget cafés, nicknamed "greasy spoons", serve simple, inexpensive food, often in the form of endless variations of the breakfast fry-up (see p36).

Betty's Café in Harrogate *(see p598)*

BOOKING AHEAD

IT IS ALWAYS SAFER to book a table first before making a special journey to a restaurant; city restaurants can be very busy and some of the more renowned establishments can be fully booked a month in advance. If you cannot keep a reservation, you should ring up and cancel. A lot of restaurants operate on knife-edge profit margins, and customers not turning up can threaten their livelihood.

CHECKING THE BILL

ALL RESTAURANTS are required by law to display their current prices outside the door. These amounts include Value Added Tax (VAT), currently at 17.5 per cent. Service and cover charges (if any) are also specified. So you should have a rough idea of what a meal may cost beforehand.

Wine is always pricey in Britain, and extras like coffee or bottled water can be disproportionately expensive.

Service charges (usually between 10 per cent and 15 per cent) are sometimes automatically added to your bill. If you feel that the service has been poor, you are entitled to subtract this service charge. If no service charge has been added, you are expected to add 10 to 15 per cent to the bill, but it is your decision.

Some restaurants may leave the "total" box of credit card slips blank, hoping customers will add something extra to the service charge. Another growing trend is for smart restaurants to boost their sagging profit margins with a "cover charge" for flowers, bread and butter, etc. Live entertainment may also be costed. The majority of restaurants accept credit cards, or cheques with a guarantee card, but pubs and cafés expect cash – do not rely on plastic.

MEALTIMES

BREAKFAST IS A MOVEABLE feast. It may be as early as 6:30am in a city business hotel (most hoteliers will make special arrangements if you have a plane to catch or some other reason for checking out early) or as late as 10:30am in relaxed country house establishments. Few hoteliers relish cooking bacon and eggs that late, however, and some insist you are up and about by 9:00 sharp if you want anything to eat. But you can find breakfast all day long in some urban restaurants. The American concept of Sunday "brunch" (a leisurely halfway house between breakfast and lunch) is becoming increasingly popular in some hotels, restaurants and cafés.

Lunch in pubs and restaurants is usually served between noon and 2:30pm. Try to arrive in time to order the main course before 1:30pm, or you may find choice restricted and service peremptory. Most tourist areas have plenty of cafés, fast-food diners and coffee bars where you can have a snack at any time of day. During peak hours there may be a minimum charge.

If you are lucky enough to be in one of the places where you can get a traditional afternoon tea, it is usually served between 3pm and 5pm.

Dinner is usually served from 6pm until 10pm; some places, especially ethnic restaurants, stay open later. In guest houses or small hotels, dinner may be served at a specific time (sometimes uncomfortably early).

CHILDREN

THE CONTINENTAL NORM of dining out *en famille* is steadily becoming more acceptable in Britain, and visiting a restaurant may no longer entail endless searches for a babysitter. Many places welcome junior diners, and some actively encourage families, at least during the

**L'Artiste Musclé wine bar-bistro
(see p579), London**

day or early evening. Formal restaurants sometimes cultivate a more adult ambience at dinner time, and some impose age limits. If you want to take young children to a restaurant, check when you book. Italian, Spanish, Indian, fast-food restaurants and ice-cream parlours nearly always welcome children, and sometimes provide special menus or high chairs for them. Even traditional English pubs, which were once a strictly adult preserve, are now relaxing their rules to accommodate families and may even provide special rooms or play areas.

Ice-cream parlour sign

The places that welcome children are indicated in the pubs guide *(see pp608–11)*. The restaurant listings also indicate which establishments cater for children's needs.

DISABLED ACCESS

AS IN MOST WALKS of life, restaurant facilities in Britain could be better for disabled visitors, but things are gradually improving. Modern premises usually take account of mobility problems, but it's always best to check first if you have special needs.

PICNICS

EATING OUTSIDE is becoming more popular in Britain, though it is more likely that you will find tables outside pubs in the form of a beer garden, than outside restaurants. One inexpensive option is to make up your own picnic; most towns have good delicatessens and bakeries where you can collect provisions, and in Britain you do not usually have to worry about shops closing at mid-day as they often do on the Continent.

Look out for street markets to pick up fresh fruit and local cheeses at bargain prices. Department stores like Marks & Spencer and supermarkets such as Sainsbury's and Tesco often sell an excellent range of pre-packed sandwiches and snacks; large towns usually have several sandwich bars to choose from. Your hotel or guest house may also be able to provide a packed lunch. Ask for it the night before.

An option for a chillier day is a hot takeaway meal; fish and chips with salt and vinegar all wrapped in paper is not only a British cliché but a national institution.

Eating alfresco at Grasmere in the Lake District

Choosing a Restaurant

THE RESTAURANTS in this guide have been selected across a wide range of price categories for their good value, exceptional food and interesting location. This chart lists the restaurants by region, starting with London. Use the colour-coded thumb tabs, which indicate the regions covered on each page, to guide you to the relevant sections of the chart.

LONDON

	Credit Cards	Children Welcome	Fixed-Price Menu	Vegetarian	Outdoor Tables
BAYSWATER & PADDINGTON: *40 Degrees at Veronicas.* **Map** 1 C2. £€ 3 Hereford Rd, W2. [020 7229 5079. w www.veronicasrestaurant.co.uk Specializing in both classic and modern international cuisine. Choice of dining room includes Victorian style and a modern room with leather tablecloths. 🍷	AE MC V	●	■	●	
NOTTING HILL: *Mandola* **Map** 1 C1. w www.mandolacafe.com £€ 139-143 Westbourne Grove W11. [020-7229 4734. Sudanese cuisine, including a seven salad starter, in a "Khartoum" setting.	MC V	●		●	
NOTTING HILL: *Cortina* **Map** 1 B1. £€€ 33a All Saint's Road, W11. [020-7221 4477. A split-level, cleverly converted terraced house, tastefully decorated. Contemporary modern Italian cuisine, with weekend brunch a highlight. 🍴🍷	AE DC MC V		■	●	■
KENSINGTON: *Sticky Fingers* **Map** 2 D2. £€ 1a Phillimore Gdns, W8. [020-7938 5338. w www.stickyfingers.co.uk American staples like great burgers and plenty of Rolling Stones memorabilia.	AE DC MC V	●		●	
KENSINGTON: *Kensington Place* **Map** 1 C4. £€€ 205 Kensington Church St W8. [020-7727 3184. w www.kensingtonplace.co.uk Minimalist venue attracting a dedicated crowd. Excellent Modern International cuisine includes chicken and goat's cheese mousse with olives. ♿🍷	AE DC MC V	●	■	●	
KENSINGTON: *Wódka* **Map** 1 C4. w www.wodka.co.uk £€€ 12 St Alban's Grove W8. [020-7937 6513. A mixture of classic and modern Polish food (blini with smoked salmon, roast duck), served in a modern but friendly setting. Great range of vodkas. 🍷	AE MC V		■	●	
KENSINGTON: *Bombay Brasserie* **Map** 2 D5. [020-7370 4040 £€€€ Courtfield Close, Courtfield Rd SW7. w www.bombaybrasserielondon.com Acclaimed restaurant with an impressive colonial atmosphere, including conservatory, cocktail bar and pianist. Bombay and regional cuisine. 🍴🍷	AE DC MC V	●		●	
KNIGHTSBRIDGE & VICTORIA: *Oliveto* **Map** 5 B4. £€ 49 Elizabeth St SW1. [020-7730 0074. High-quality Italian food including great pizza, in a delightful street with tempting clothes and food shops; five minutes' walk from Sloane Square. 🍴	AE MC V	●		●	
KNIGHTSBRIDGE & VICTORIA: *Fifth Floor* **Map** 5 A2. £€€ Harvey Nichols, 109-125 Knightsbridge, SW1. [020-7235 5250. w www.harveynichols.com At the top of London's most fashionable department store, Modern British food in a contemporary setting. Also a café, sushi counter and foodmarket. ● 25 & 26 Dec, Easter Sun. 🍴🍷	AE DC MC V	●	■	●	
KNIGHTSBRIDGE & VICTORIA: *Boisdale* **Map** 5 B4. £€€€ 15 Eccleston St, SW1. [020-7730 6922. w www.boisdale.co.uk Traditional and Modern British with Scottish specialities such as haggis and salmon, served in a traditional, clubby atmosphere. 🍷	AE DC MC V	●	■	●	
KNIGHTSBRIDGE & VICTORIA: *L'Incontro* **Map** 5 B4. £€€€ 87 Pimlico Rd, SW1. [020-7730 5062. w www.lincontro-restaurant.com Wonderful Italian dishes with a leaning towards Venetian cuisine – seabass with balsamic vinegar and olive oil – served in an elegant contemporary, Italianate setting.	DC MC V	●	■	●	
KNIGHTSBRIDGE & VICTORIA: *Pétrus* **Map** 5 C4. £€€€€ The Berkeley Hotel, Wilton Place SW1. [020-7930 4272. w www.petrus-restaurant.com Classical French cuisine in this elegant restaurant run by chef Marcus Wareing and co-owned with Gordon Ramsay. Men must wear a tie. ● Sun, public hols. ♿	AE DC MC V	●	■	●	

Price categories include a three-course meal for one, half a bottle of house wine, and all unavoidable extra charges such as cover, service, VAT:
£ under £15
££ £15-£25
£££ £25-£35
££££ £35-£50
£££££ over £50

CHILDREN WELCOME
Restaurants which offer smaller portions and high-chairs for children. Special menus sometimes available.
FIXED-PRICE MENU
A good value fixed-price meal, at lunch, dinner or both, usually of three courses.
VEGETARIAN
Vegetarian specialities served, sometimes for both starters and main courses.
CREDIT CARDS
Indicates which credit cards are accepted: *AE* American Express; *DC* Diners Club; *MC* Master Card/Access; *V* Visa.

	CREDIT CARDS	CHILDREN WELCOME	FIXED-PRICE MENU	VEGETARIAN	OUTDOOR TABLES
KNIGHTSBRIDGE & VICTORIA: *Zafferano* Map 5 B3. £££££ 15 Lowndes St SW1. 020-7235 5800. W www.atoz.com One of London's finest Modern Italian restaurants, with white truffle dishes among the numerous specialities. The wine list includes grappa.	AE DC MC V	●	■	●	
CHELSEA & FULHAM: *Chutney Mary* £££ 535, Kings Rd SW10. 020-7351 3113. W www.realindianfood.com An Indian term for women crossing two cultures, "Chutney Mary" serves a delicious blend of Indian and Western cuisine. Attractive colonial Raj decor. 🌣	AE DC MC V		■	●	
CHELSEA & FULHAM: *Bluebird* ££££ 350 King's Rd SW3. 020-7559 1000. W www.conran.com Inspired conversion of a 1923 garage, which combines Classical, Neo-Georgian and Art Deco elements. Game and crustacea a speciality. ● 25 & 26 Dec, 1 Jan.	AE DC MC V	●	■	●	
CHELSEA & FULHAM: *Aubergine* £££££ 11 Park Walk SW10. 020-7352 3449. Provençale decor, charming service and faultless cuisine: salad of quail, foie gras, sweetbreads and truffle dressing. ● Sun; 23 Dec–1st Mon in Jan. 🍷	AE DC MC V	●	■	●	
CHELSEA & FULHAM: *Bibendum* £££££ 1st Floor, Michelin House, 81 Fulham Rd, SW3. 020-7581 5817. W www.bibendum.co.uk A retro-chic showcase for Modern British cuisine, including bistro dishes, game and offal. The ground floor features an Oyster Bar and separate café. 🌣 🍷	AE DC MC V	●	■		
PICCADILLY & MAYFAIR: *L'Artiste Musclé* Map 5 C1. ££ 1 Shepherd Mkt, W1. 020-7493 6150. French bistro cuisine: boeuf Bourguignon, Toulouse sausage, in a classic bistro setting, with pavement tables overlooking Shepherd Market.	AE MC V			●	■
PICCADILLY & MAYFAIR: *Sofra* Map 2 D2. ££ 18 Shepherd St W1. 020-7493 3320. W www.sofra.co.uk One of London's best-value chains of Turkish restaurants. 🌣	AE MC V	●	■	●	■
PICCADILLY & MAYFAIR: *Carluccio's* Map 3 B5. £££ 3-5 Barrett St, St Christopher's Pl, W1. 020-7935 5927. W www.carluccios.com Authentic Italian dishes available throughout the day, with a shop stocking Carluccio's range of Italian foodstuffs. One of several branches in London. 🔔	AE MC V	●		●	
PICCADILLY & MAYFAIR: *Chor Bizarre* Map 5 C1. £££ 16 Albemarle St W1. 020-7629 9802. W www.chorbizarrerestaurant.com Amid numerous Indian antiques, the menu has a Kashmiri focus, such as *gostaba* (minced lamb with cardamom and yogurt). ● 25 & 26 Dec, 1 Jan. 🌣 🍷	AE DC MC V	●	■	●	
PICCADILLY & MAYFAIR: *Hard Rock Café* Map 5 B1. £££ 150 Old Park Lane W1. 020-7629 0382. W www.hardrock.com No reservations means queues, but the reward is classic American fare (great burgers and a daily special) amid music videos and memorabilia. ● 25 Dec. 🌣	AE DC MC V	●		●	■
PICCADILLY & MAYFAIR: *The Wolseley* Map 6 D1. £££ 160 Piccadilly W1. 020-7499 6996. The art-deco interior, and the star-spotting potential, give this new brasserie and restaurant an air of glamour. Open daily from 7am (9am Sundays). ● 25 Dec.	AE MC V	●		●	
PICCADILLY & MAYFAIR: *Momo* Map 5 C1. ££££ 25 Heddon St, W1. 020-7434 4040. W www.momoresto.com Housed within a wonderful "antique Moroccan palace", the cuisine is North African, balancing tradition with a more modern approach. ● 25 Dec, 1 Jan. 🍷	AE DC MC V		■	●	■
PICCADILLY & MAYFAIR: *Quaglino's* Map 5 C1. ££££ 16 Bury St, SW1. 020-7930 6767. W www.conran.com Modern British brasserie owned by Conran. Classic dishes include calves' liver and bacon, roast guinea fowl with spinach and almonds. ● 25 & 26 Dec, 1 Jan.	AE DC MC V	●	■	●	

For key to symbols see back flap

Price categories include a three-course meal for one, half a bottle of house wine, and all unavoidable extra charges such as cover, service, VAT:
£ under £15
££ £15-£25
£££ £25-£35
££££ £35-£50
£££££ over £50

CHILDREN WELCOME
Restaurants which offer smaller portions and high-chairs for children. Special menus sometimes available.

FIXED-PRICE MENU
A good value fixed-price meal, at lunch, dinner or both, usually of three courses.

VEGETARIAN
Vegetarian specialities served, sometimes for both starters and main courses.

CREDIT CARDS
Indicates which credit cards are accepted: AE American Express; DC Diners Club; MC Master Card/Access; V Visa.

	CREDIT CARDS	CHILDREN WELCOME	FIXED-PRICE MENU	VEGETARIAN	OUTDOOR TABLES
PICCADILLY & MAYFAIR: *The Sugar Club* **Map** 5 C1. ££££ 21 Warwick St W1. 020-7437 7776. www.thesugarclub.co.uk Pacific Rim cuisine, such as spicy kangaroo salad with mint, peanuts and lime chilli dressing, and plenty of New World wines. ● 24 & 25 Dec.	AE DC MC V			●	
PICCADILLY & MAYFAIR: *Veeraswamy* **Map** 3 C5. ££££ Mezzanine Floor, Victory House, 99 Regent St W1. 020-7734 1401. Britain's oldest Indian (established 1927) it is also one of the most modern. Inspiring, original and authentic Indian dishes, with great service.	AE DC MC V	●	■	●	
PICCADILLY & MAYFAIR: *Deca* **Map** 3 C5. £££££ 23 Conduit St W1. 020-7493 7090. A new, elegant setting for superstar chef, Nico Ladenis, to exercise his classical French gastronomic artistry. ● public hols.	AE DC MC V	●	■		
PICCADILLY & MAYFAIR: *Le Gavroche* **Map** 5 C1. £££££ 43 Upper Brook St W1. 020-7408 0881. www.le-gavroche.co.uk Superlative modern and classical French cuisine (lobster mousse with caviar and champagne sauce) in a sophisticated setting. Smart bar for aperitifs and lounge for coffee and cigars. Dress code. ● Christmas.	AE DC MC V		■		
PICCADILLY & MAYFAIR: *Green's Restaurant & Oyster Bar* £££££ **Map** 5 C1. 36 Duke St St James's, SW1. 020-7930 4566. Classic English "gentleman's club" decor, with banquettes and booths, serving a range of British classics, with fish and oysters a feature.	AE DC MC V	●	■	●	
PICCADILLY & MAYFAIR: *The Grill Room* **Map** 2 D2. £££££ The Dorchester Hotel, Park La, W1. 020-7317 6336. www.dorchesterhotel.com Traditional British cuisine (roast Angus beef is the house dish); separate vegetarian menu. Opulent decor.	AE DC MC V	●	■	●	
PICCADILLY & MAYFAIR: *Nobu* **Map** 5 B1. £££££ 19 Old Park Lane, W1. 020-7447 4747. Views over Hyde Park and great staff serve sensational Japanese-South American fusion cuisine, with black cod in miso a signature dish.	AE DC MC V	●	■	●	
REGENT'S PARK & MARYLEBONE: *Blandford St Restaurant* ££££ **Map** 3 B4. 5-7 Blandford St W1. 020-7486 9696. www.blandford-street.co.uk Stylishly modern, streamlined but colourful venue, offering a daily changing menu of Modern British fine dining (marinated loin of Scottish venison). ● Sun.	AE DC MC V	●		●	■
SOHO: *Yo! Sushi* **Map** 4 E5. £ 52-53 Poland St, W1. 020-7287 0443. www.yosushi.co.uk Sushi, sashimi, salads, soups and noodles pass by on a conveyor belt, in this modern setting. Yo! Below bar in the basement. Several branches. ● 25 Dec.	AE MC V	●		●	
SOHO: *Mildred's* **Map** 4 D5. ££ 45 Lexington St W1. 020-7494 1634. Global vegetarian cuisine and an all-organic wine list. ● Sun, bank hols.				●	■
SOHO: *Gay Hussar* **Map** 4 E5. £££ 2 Greek St W1. 020-7437 0973. Bohemian library setting serving various politicians, media and literary figures: chilled wild cherry soup, Transylvanian stuffed cabbage. ● public hols.	AE DC MC V		■	●	
SOHO: *Sri Siam* **Map** 4 E5. £££ 16 Old Compton St W1. 020-7434 3544. This stylish restaurant is the place for your first taste of Thai food; the heat is toned down, but the flavours aren't: seafood dishes, as well as satay and curries.	AE DC MC V				
SOHO: *Alastair Little* **Map** 4 E5. ££££ 49 Frith St W1. 020-7734 5183. Modern International cooking with a distinct Italian accent: Tuscan fish casserole, grilled seabass with flageolet and lemon minestra. ● Sun, public hols.	AE DC MC V	●	■	●	

Soho: *Mezzo* **Map** 4 E5. £££££
100 Wardour St W1. [C] 020-7314 4000. [W] www.conran.com
A Soho landmark, housed in an elegant, mirrored basement, modern European dishes such as bruschetta of goat's cheese. ● 25 & 26 Dec. 🍷
AE DC MC V

Covent Garden & Strand: *Belgo Centraal* **Map** 4 F5. ££
50 Earlham St WC2. [C] 020-7813 2233. [W] www.belgorestaurants.com
An industrial lift takes you down to this modern, monastic basement with benches. Belgian mussel pots and platters a speciality. One of several. ♿
AE DC MC V

Covent Garden & Strand: *Bertorelli's* **Map** 4 F5. £££
44a Floral St WC2. [C] 020-7836 3969.
Modern Italian cuisine with traditional favourites, including pizza, pasta, meat and fish dishes. Relaxed and inviting decor. ● Sun. 🚭 🍷
AE DC MC V

Covent Garden & Strand: *Jo Allen* **Map** 4 F5. £££
13 Exeter St, WC2. [C] 020-7836 0651.
Famous American-owned theatreland basement restaurant; good for quality burgers and chips, Caesar Salad and pecan pie. Pre-theatre menu from 5–6:45pm.
AE MC V

Covent Garden & Strand: *Simpson's-in-the-Strand* **Map** 4 F5. ££££
100 Strand WC2. Map 13 C2. [C] 020-7836 9112.
For a truly traditional English experience, with Victorian interiors, the menu includes a superb traditional breakfast. A smart cocktail bar is ideal for aperitifs.
AE DC MC V

Covent Garden & Strand: *The Ivy* **Map** 4 F5. £££££
1 West St WC2. [C] 020-7836 4751.
An institution of the theatre district, you need to book weeks ahead for this Art Deco style restaurant. Crispy duck salad and fish cakes are classics. 🍷
AE DC MC V

Covent Garden & Strand: *Orso* **Map** 4 F5. ££££
27 Wellington St WC2. [C] 020-7240 5269. [W] www.joeallen.co.uk
A media, theatre-goers rendezvous, with soft terracotta walls, white linen tablecloths and and Italianate pictures, serving Italian regional cuisine. 🚭 🍷
AE MC V

Covent Garden & Strand: *Rules* **Map** 4 F5. ££££
35 Maiden La WC2. [C] 020-7836 5314. [W] www.rules.co.uk
London's oldest surviving restaurant serving traditional British fare since 1798, including Dover sole, rib of beef, amid Edwardian decor. ● 25 & 26 Dec. 🚭
AE DC MC V

Bloomsbury & Fitzrovia: *Wagamama* **Map** 4 E4. £
4 Streatham St WC1. [C] 020-7323 9223. [W] www.wagamama.com
Modern refectory-style, within a spacious, bustling basement, serving various noodle dishes. Queues are fast-moving. Several branches. ● 25 & 26 Dec. 🚭
AE DC MC V

Bloomsbury & Fitzrovia: *Villandry* **Map** 3 C4 £££
170 Great Portland St, W1. [C] 020-7631 3131. [W] www.villandry.com
Chic and thoroughly comprehensive Euro-deli and grocery store with a stylish modern restaurant. The bar has a separate all-day menu. 🚭
AE DC MC V

Bloomsbury & Fitzrovia: *Hakkasan* **Map** 4 D4. ££££
8 Hanway Pl, W1. [C] 020-7907 1888.
Dim sum is served all day, changing to à la carte for dinner, with the lounge bar also serving evening snacks. Modern ethnic decor. ● 24 & 25 Dec. ♿ 🍷
AE MC V

Spitalfields & Clerkenwell: *Quality Chop House* £££
94 Farringdon Road EC1. [C] 020-7837 5093.
Beautiful Victorian diner with its original 1869 fittings. Sausage and mash, and salmon fish cakes are appealing staples. 🚭
AE MC V

Spitalfields & Clerkenwell: *St John Bread and Wine* £££
94–96 Commercial St E1. [C] 020-7247 8724. [W] www.stjohnbreadandwine.com
This recent arrival to Spitalfields has already become a much-loved haunt, serving delicious Modern British food. Open all day. Bread and wine to go, too.
AE MC V

City & Southbank: *Wine Wharf at Vinopolis* **Map** 8 D4. ££
Stoney Street, Borough Market, SE1. [C] 020-7940 8335.
Graze on bar bites, including salads and cheeses, or tackle the fuller menu, in this converted Victorian warehouse. Great wines. ● Sun; 25 & 26 Dec, 1 Jan. 🍷
AE DC MC V

City & Southbank: *Club Gascon* **Map** 7 C2. £££
57 West Smithfield, EC1. [C] 020-796 0699.
Regional cuisine from southwest France, with foie gras, truffle and seafood dishes a speciality. Also served tapas-style in the bar. ● Sun. ♿ 🍷
AE MC V

For key to symbols see back flap

			CREDIT CARDS	CHILDREN WELCOME	FIXED-PRICE MENU	VEGETARIAN	OUTDOOR TABLES
Price categories include a three-course meal for one, half a bottle of house wine, and all unavoidable extra charges such as cover, service, VAT: £ under £15 ££ £15–£25 £££ £25–£35 ££££ £35–£50 £££££ over £50	**CHILDREN WELCOME** Restaurants which offer smaller portions and high-chairs for children. Special menus sometimes available. **FIXED-PRICE MENU** A good value fixed-price meal, at lunch, dinner or both, usually of three courses. **VEGETARIAN** Vegetarian specialities served, sometimes for both starters and main courses. **CREDIT CARDS** Indicates which credit cards are accepted: AE American Express; DC Diners Club; MC Master Card/Access; V Visa.						

CITY & SOUTHBANK: *Anchor & Hope* Map 7 B4. £££ 36 The Cut SE1. 020-7928 9898. This new highly praised gastropub, handy for the South Bank theatres, has seasonal British food like rib of beef and rice pudding. ● Mon lunch, Sun. ♥	MC V			●	
CITY & SOUTHBANK: *Tate Britain Restaurant* Map 7 C3. £££ Tate Britain, Millbank, SE1. 020-7887 8825. w www.tate.org.uk Modern English cuisine, and over 300 wines to choose from. Witty, whimsical murals by Rex Whistler date from 1925 and provide an enchanting setting. ⚡ ♥	AE DC MC V	●	■	●	■
CITY & SOUTHBANK: *The Oxo Tower* Map 7 B3. ££££ Oxo Tower Wharf, Barge House St, SE1. 020-7803 3888. w www.harveynichols.com Set on the eighth floor of this landmark 1930s building, with stunning views along the Thames. Exemplary Modern British cuisine. ● 24–26 Dec. ♥	AE DC MC V	●	■	●	■
CITY & SOUTHBANK: *Le Pont de la Tour* Map 8 F4. £££££ Butlers Wharf SE1. 020-7403 8403. w www.conran.com Riverside marvel with great views, a separate crustacea bar, pianist nightly, and French cuisine. Decor is classic Conran. ♥	AE DC MC V	●	■	●	■
FURTHER AFIELD: *River Café* £££££ Thames Wharf Studios, Rainville Rd W6. 020-7386 4200. w www.rivercafe.co.uk A modern style that also provides river views, serving interpretations of traditional Italian cuisine such as chargrilled squid with chilli and rocket. ♥	AE DC MC V	●			■

THE DOWNS AND CHANNEL COAST

AMBERLEY: *Queen's Room, Amberley Castle* ££££ On B2139, Amberley, W Sussex. 01798 831992. w www.amberleycastle.co.uk A romantic medieval fortress provides a dramatic backdrop for "castle cuisine", a mix of ancient and Modern British recipes. ⚡	AE DC MC V		■	●	
BOUGHTON LEES: *Eastwell Manor* w www.marstonhotels.com ££££ Eastwell Park, Boughton Lees, nr Ashford, Kent. 01233 219955. A grand parkland setting graces this dynamic hotel restaurant where the service is formal but friendly. ♿ ⚡ ♥	AE DC MC V	●	■	●	■
BRIGHTON: *Food for Friends* ££ 17–18 Prince Albert St, Brighton. 01273 202310. w www.foodforfriends.com This vegetarian wholefood café in the Lanes offers friendly service, generous helpings and imaginative cooking amid pine and pot plants. ● 25, 26 Dec. ♿ ⚡	DC MC V	●			
BRIGHTON: *Black Chapati* £££ 12 Circus Parade, New England Rd, Brighton. 01273 699011. Adventurous and eclectic Asian cooking fizzes with original ideas in a stark café setting just outside the town centre. The service is efficient, and the atmosphere friendly and welcoming. ● L; Sun, Mon. ♿	AE MC V			●	
BRIGHTON: *Terre à Terre* £££ 71 East St, Brighton. 01273 729051. Close to the pavilion, pier and the Lanes, this vegetarian retaurant has an imaginative international menu. ● Mon L. ♿ ⚡	AE DC MC V	●		●	
BROCKENHURST: *Simply Poussin* ££ The Courtyard, Brookley Rd, Brockenhurst, Hants. 01590 623063. New Forest produce such as venison and wild pork appears on the menu in robust provincial French-style fare. ● Sun, Mon. ♿ ⚡ ♥	MC V		■		■
CHICHESTER: *Comme Ça* £££ 67 Broyle Rd, Chichester, W Sussex. 01243 788724. This French restaurant is situated close to the Festival Theatre and pre- and post- performance meals are available. Fish specialities such as local seabass. ● Christmas. ⚡ ♥	AE DC MC V	●	■	●	■

CUCKMERE: *Golden Galleon* @ info@goldengalleon.co.uk   £€£
Exceat Bridge, Cuckmere Haven, E Sussex. (01323 892247.
This pub-restaurant has its own brewery and smokery; try the smoked salmon
and duck breast. Conservatory and terrace with sea views. ● *Sun D winter.* & ⇆ ¶

MC
V

EAST GRINSTEAD: *Gravetye Manor*   £€£€£
Vowels Lane, East Grinstead, W Sussex. (01342 810567. W www.gravetyemanor.co.uk
Classic food is served in this plush Elizabethan mansion, a luxury
hotel in gorgeous grounds. ⇆ ¶

MC
V

EDENBRIDGE: *Moulin Blanc*   £€£€
87 High St, Edenbridge, Kent. (01732 866757. W www.honoursmill.co.uk
Mind your head: the beams are low. Well-tried French classics are
daringly adapted in this quiet, friendly restaurant. ● *Sat L, Sun D, Mon.* ¶

MC
V

EMSWORTH: *36 on the Quay*   £€£€£
47 South St, Emsworth, Hants. (01243 375592. W www.36onthequay.co.uk
Restaurant-with-rooms by the waterfront. Food is innovative but disciplined. Local
fish features on the menu. ● *Sat L, Sun, Mon L, bank hols (except Good Fri).* & ⇆ ¶

AE
DC
MC
V

FERNHURST: *King's Arms*   £€£
Midhurst Road, Fernhurst, Surrey. (01428 652005.
The accomplished modern-British cooking always includes fish dishes, the chef's
speciality, at this 17th-century country dining pub. ● *Sun D, 25 Dec, 1 Jan.* & ¶

MC
V

HAMPTON HILL: *Monsieur Max*   £€£€
133 High St, Hampton Hill, Middx. (020-8979 5546. @ monsmax@aol.com
First-class ingredients and proficient cooking are all part of the package of this
Michelin-starred French restaurant. ● *Sat L.* & ¶

AE
DC
MC
V

HASTINGS: *The Coach House Restaurant*   £€£
60a All Saints St, Old Town, Hastings, E Sussex. (01424 428080.
This recently renovated restaurant in the Old Town serves eclectic British food,
including local seafood and meat from Scotland. ● *Mon–Wed* ⇆ ¶

MC
V

HAYWARDS HEATH: *Jeremy's at Borde Hill* (01444 441102.   £€£
Balcombe Rd, Haywards Heath, W. Sussex. W www.houseofgoodfood.co.uk
Vivaciously modern European cooking produces memorable results
in this civilized modern interior overlooking a walled garden. ● *Sun D, Mon.* & ⇆

AE
MC
V

HURSTBOURNE TARRANT: *Esseborne Manor* (01264 736444.   £€£
On A343, N of Hurstbourne Tarrant, Hants. W www.essebornemanor.com
Well-flavoured and sophisticated English country cooking is offered in
this stylish Victorian manor-house hotel. Good-value set lunch. & ⇆ ¶

AE
DC
MC
V

JEVINGTON: *Hungry Monk* W www.hungrymonk.co.uk   £€£
Between Polegate and Alfriston, E Sussex. (01323 482178.
This restaurant's popularity rests partly on its 15th-century setting and on
innovative home produce on the menu. ● *Mon–Sat L.* ⇆ ¶

MC
V

NEW MILTON: *Marryat, Chewton Glen*   £€£€£
Christchurch Rd, New Milton, Hants. (01425 275341. W www.chewtonglen.com
A gastronomic shrine in a tranquil New Forest country-house hotel.
The conservatory restaurant overlooks lovely gardens. & ⇆ ¶

AE
DC
MC
V

RICHMOND: *Nightingales* W www.petershamhotel.co.uk   £€£€
Petersham Hotel, Nightingale Lane, Richmond upon Thames, Surrey. (020 8939 1084.
A superb Thames view adds to the pleasure of mostly traditional
English dining at this Victorian hotel. ● *Sun D.* & ¶

AE
DC
MC
V

RIPLEY: *Drake's*   £€£€£
High St, Ripley, Surrey. (01483 224777.
Ambitious menus change with the seasons. Picturesque setting. In summer
you can have drinks in a walled garden. ● *Sat L, Sun D, Mon.*

AE
MC
V

RYE: *Landgate Bistro*   £€£
5–6 Landgate, Rye, E Sussex. (01797 222829. W www.landgatebistro.co.uk
Local produce like Romney Marsh lamb or freshly caught fish figures
in this pleasant informal restaurant. ● *Sun, Mon; last 2 wks of Apr.* ⇆

MC
V

STORRINGTON: *Fleur de Sel*   £€£€
Manleys Hill, Storrington, W Sussex. (01903 742331.
French cooking at this cottage restaurant where service is calm and efficient.
Seafood is a speciality. ● *Sat L, Sun D, Mon.* & ¶

AE
MC
V

For key to symbols see back flap

Price categories include a three-course meal for one, half a bottle of house wine, and all unavoidable extra charges such as cover, service, VAT:
£ under £15
££ £15–£25
£££ £25–£35
££££ £35–£50
£££££ over £50

CHILDREN WELCOME
Restaurants which offer smaller portions and high-chairs for children. Special menus sometimes available.
FIXED-PRICE MENU
A good value fixed-price meal, at lunch, dinner or both, usually of three courses.
VEGETARIAN
Vegetarian specialities served, sometimes for both starters and main courses.
CREDIT CARDS
Indicates which credit cards are accepted: *AE* American Express; *DC* Diners Club; *MC* Master Card/Access; *V* Visa.

	Credit Cards	Children Welcome	Fixed-Price Menu	Vegetarian	Outdoor Tables
TUNBRIDGE WELLS: *Sankeys* W www.sankeys.co.uk £££ 39 Mount Ephraim, Tunbridge Wells, Kent. (*01892 511422*. A smart wine bar specializing in seafood from all parts of Britain, from Scotland to Cornwall. ● *25, 26 Dec.* & ⊠ ♥	MC V	●		●	■
TUNBRIDGE WELLS: *Thackeray's* ££££ 85 London Rd, Tunbridge Wells, Kent. (*01892 511921*. W www.thackeraysrestaurant.com The novelist's home is now a restaurant and wine bar where local produce is given a Gallic touch. ● *Sun, Mon.* ♥	AE DC MC V	●	■	●	■
WHITSTABLE: *Whitstable Oyster Fishery Co* £££ Royal Native Oyster Stores, Whitstable, Kent. (*01227 276856*. The name suggests what it does best, but other fishy things appear on the menu in this Victorian building on the beach. ● *Sun D (winter), Mon.* &	AE DC MC V	●		●	■
WICKHAM: *Old House* ££££ The Square, Wickham, Hants. (*01329 833049*. @ enq@theoldhousehotel.co.uk British/European-inspired food with exotic touches, served in the timber-framed former stable-block of a Georgian house. ● *Mon L, Sun D.* ⊠	AE MC V	●		●	

EAST ANGLIA

	Credit Cards	Children Welcome	Fixed-Price Menu	Vegetarian	Outdoor Tables
ALDEBURGH: *Regatta* ££ 171–173 High St, Aldeburgh, Suff. (*01728 452011*. W www.regattaaldeburgh.com Seafaring decor reflects the fish specialities which are always cooked with care. Sometimes there's local game on the menu. The ingredients are always top quality, and the service is friendly. ● *Wed.* & ♥	AE MC V	●	■	●	
BURNHAM MARKET: *Fishes'* £££ Market Pl, Burnham Market, Norf. (*01328 738588*. W www.burnhammarket.co.uk Located on the 18th-century village green, this restaurant provides reliable fish specialities: the best of the catch at fair prices. Try the Brancaster oysters, mussels or a seafood platter. ● *Sun D, Mon.* & ♥	DC MC V	●	■		
BURY ST EDMUNDS: *Maison Bleu* ££ 31 Churchgate St, Bury St Edmunds, Suff. (*01284 760623*. W www.maisonbleu.co.uk Straightforward seafood fresh from the market. There's a huge menu and good white wines. Can get very busy. ● *Sun–Mon.* & ⊠	AE MC V	●	■	●	
CAMBRIDGE: *Restaurant Twenty-two* £££ 22 Chesterton Rd, Cambs. (*01223 351880*. W www.restaurant22.co.uk Courteous service complements pleasingly inventive food in Victorian setting. Three-course menus change every month. ● *L; Sun & Mon.* ⊠ ♥	AE DC MC V		■	●	
CAMBRIDGE: *Midsummer House* £££££ Midsummer Common, Cambs. (*01223 369299*. W www.midsummerhouse.co.uk An intimate restaurant serving fixed-price menus of great complexity. Puddings are luscious and elaborate. ● *Sun–Mon.* ⊠ ♥	AE MC V		■	●	■
COLCHESTER: *Warehouse Brasserie* ££ 12A Chapel St North, Colchester, Essex. (*01206 765656*. A popular restaurant with Modern British and Continental home-cooked dishes. Lots of local produce; some light main courses. ● *Sun–Mon.* & ⊠	MC V	●	■	●	
DEDHAM: *Le Talbooth* £££££ Gun Hill, Dedham, nr Colchester, Essex. (*01206 323150*. @ talbooth@talbooth.co.uk Standards stay high at this long-established Tudor restaurant by the River Stour. Creative cooking that is popular with locals and visitors alike. ♥	AE DC MC V	●		●	■
DISS: *Weaver's Wine Bar* ££ Market Hill, Diss, Norf. (*01379 642411*. A charming timbered setting for a cheerful, ad hoc restaurant. ● *Sat L, Sun, Mon L, public hols.* ⊠ ♥	AE DC MC V	●	■	●	

ELY: *Old Fire Engine House* £££ MC V
25 St Mary's St, Ely, Cambs. [01353 662582. W www.theoldfireenginehouse.co.uk
Local produce inspires hearty British cooking in the old fire station
by the cathedral. Friendly, unfussy atmosphere. 🍴 🍷

FRESSINGFIELD: *Fox and Goose* £££ MC V
On B1116, Fressingfield, Suff. [01379 586247. W www.foxandgoose.net
This remote country pub serves a wide range of inventive British and
international dishes. Children are welcomed. 🍴 🍷

HARWICH: *Pier at Harwich* £££ AE DC MC V
The Quay, Harwich, Essex. [01255 241212. W www.milsomhotels.com
A bustling harbourside stop-over with nautical decor and excellent fish.
Comfortable rooms are also available. 🍷

HINTLESHAM: *Hintlesham Hall* ££££ AE DC MC V
On A1071, Hintlesham, Suff. [01473 652268. W www.hintleshamhall.com
Presentation is the key to success at this hotel west of Ipswich.
Excellent cheese-board. (See also p548.) ● Sat L. 🛇 🍴 🍷

HUNTINGDON: *Old Bridge* £££ AE DC MC V
1 High St, Huntingdon, Cambs. [01480 424300. W www.huntsbridge.com
A handsome riverside inn with an airy restaurant proffering British and
Mediterranean fare, and splendid English cheeses. Good teas too. 🛇 🍴 🍷

ICKLINGHAM: *Red Lion* £££ MC V
The Street, Icklingham, Suff. [01638 717802.
Attractive, 16th-century inn with exposed beams and log fires. Choose from the
wide range of seafood, or try game dishes such as wild boar. ● 25 Dec. 🛇 🍷

KELSALE: *Harrison's* £££ MC V
Main Road (A12), Kelsale, Suff. [01728 604444.
This charming thatched restaurant near Aldeburgh uses seasonal local ingredients
in imaginative, Modern British cooking. ● 🍴 Sun & Mon. 🛇 🍴 🍷

NORWICH: *Adlard's* ££££ AE MC V
79 Upper St Giles St, Norwich, Norf. [01603 633522. W www.adlards.co.uk
A deceptively elegant setting belies high-quality cooking of great flair. The
cuisine is Modern British with French overtones. ● Sun, Mon. 🛇 ▶ 🍷

ORFORD: *Butley Orford Oysterage* £££ MC V
Market Hill, The Square, Orford, Woodbridge, Suff. [01394 450277.
Café-restaurant with its own smokehouse and oyster-beds. Enjoy a
snack or meal in a delightful Suffolk village. ● Oct–Mar: Fri & Sat D. 🛇 🍴

SNAPE: *Plough and Snail* W www.snapemaltings.com £££ AE DC MC V
Snape Maltings Riverside Centre, Snape, Suff. [01728 688413.
Sprats and other local fish are the specialities at this popular pub with
restaurant – part of a concert hall/craft shop/art gallery complex. 🛇 🍴

SUDBURY: *Great House Hotel* W www.greathouse.co.uk £££ AE DC MC V
Market Place, Lavenham, Sudbury, Suff. [01787 247431.
This family restaurant combines the finest French and Continental cuisine. Lovely
garden for children outside. Amazing cheese board. Rooms. ● Sun D, Mon. 🛇 🍴 🍷

SWAFFHAM: *Stratton House* ££££ MC V
4 Ash Close, Swaffham, Norf. [01760 723845. W www.strattons-hotel.co.uk
Lady Hamilton once stayed in this 18th-century house, which is now a hotel.
The changing menu includes local organic produce. ● L; 25, 26 Dec. 🍴

THORPE MARKET: *Green Farm Restaurant* [01263 833602. £££ AE DC MC V
North Walsham Road, Thorpe Market, Norf. W www.greenfarmhotel.co.uk
This restaurant in a 16th-century farmhouse has an excellent reputation for top-class
dishes made from fresh local ingredients. Try the crab, sea trout or venison. 🛇 🍴 🍷

WELLS-NEXT-THE-SEA: *The Crown* [01328 710209. ££££ AE DC MC V
The Crown, The Butlands, Wells-Next-The-Sea, Norf. W www.thecrownhotelwells.co.uk
This formal Michelin-star restaurant overlooks the delightful Butlands green, and
uses varied and local produce in a Modern British menu. 🛇 🍴 🍷

WOODBRIDGE: *Captain's Table* ££ MC V
3 Quay Street, Woodbridge, Suff. [01394 383145. W www.captainstable.co.uk
Set in a 16th-century building, this restaurant presents an eclectic British and
European menu cooked with flair. ● Sun D, Mon (except bank hols). 🛇 🍴 🍷

<table>
<tr><td>

Price categories include a three-course meal for one, half a bottle of house wine, and all unavoidable extra charges such as cover, service, VAT:
£ under £15
££ £15-£25
£££ £25-£35
££££ £35-£50
£££££ over £50

</td><td>

CHILDREN WELCOME
Restaurants which offer smaller portions and high-chairs for children. Special menus sometimes available.

FIXED-PRICE MENU
A good value fixed-price meal, at lunch, dinner or both, usually of three courses.

VEGETARIAN
Vegetarian specialities served, sometimes for both starters and main courses.

CREDIT CARDS
Indicates which credit cards are accepted: *AE* American Express; *DC* Diners Club; *MC* Master Card/Access; *V* Visa.

</td></tr>
</table>

	CREDIT CARDS	CHILDREN WELCOME	FIXED-PRICE MENU	VEGETARIAN	OUTDOOR TABLES
THAMES VALLEY					
BRAY: *Waterside Inn* **£££££** Ferry Rd, Bray, Windsor & Maidenhead. 〖 *01628 620691*. Ⓦ www.waterside-inn.co.uk Renowned pillar of French classic cuisine in an idyllic riverside setting. The set lunches are excellent. ● *Mon; Jan; Jun–Aug: Tue L.* ⓰ 🍴	AE DC MC V	●	■	●	
CHINNOR: *Sir Charles Napier* **££££** Spriggs Alley, nr Chinnor, Oxon. 〖 *01494 483011*. Service is informal, but the food is good in this Chiltern pub-restaurant. The garden has eccentric sculptures. ● *Sun D, Mon.* ⓰ 🍴	AE MC V	●	■	●	■
COOKHAM: *Manzano's* **£££** 19–21 Station Hill Parade, Cookham, Windsor & Maidenhead. 〖 *01628 525775*. Intimate, family-run restaurant full of friendly enthusiasm and specialities such as suckling pig and roast lamb. A takeaway tapas menu is also available. ● *Sat L, Sun, bank hols.* ⓰ 🍴 ▶	AE MC V	●	■	●	■
DINTON: *La Chouette* **££££** Westlington Green, Dinton, Bucks. 〖 *01296 747422*. Belgian gastronomic flair in this beautiful 16th-century building. The *patron* also offers a selection of Belgian and Trappist beers. ● *Sat L, Sun.* ⓰	MC V	●	■		■
EASINGTON: *Mole & Chicken* **£££** Easington Terrace, Chilton Rd, Bucks. 〖 *01844 208387*. Ⓦ www.moleandchicken.co.uk Adventurous cooking is the hallmark of this friendly and efficient restaurant. Specialities include duckling in orange sauce. Now also a B&B. ⓰ 🍴	AE MC V	●	■	●	
GODSTOW: *Trout* **££** Godstow, Wolvercote, Oxon. 〖 *01865 302071*. A trout stream runs past this charming creeper-covered medieval pub north of Oxford. Peacocks strut outside; inside, it is always civilized. ⓰ 🍴	MC V	●		●	■
GORING: *Leatherne Bottel* **££££** On B4009, Goring, Oxon. 〖 *01491 872667*. Ⓦ www.leathernebottel.co.uk A glorious riverside setting accounts for the popularity of this relaxing place. Fresh local ingredients are presented with Pacific Rim touches. ● *Sun D.* ⓰ 🍴	AE MC V		■	●	■
GREAT MILTON: *Le Manoir aux Quat'Saisons* **£££££** Church Rd, Great Milton, Oxon. 〖 *01844 278881*. Ⓦ www.manoir.com Raymond Blanc's gastronomic pleasure palace is a rural idyll. The superb food is fresh, inventive and fully flavoured. A memorable experience, though at a price. Luxurious rooms available. ⓰ 🌿 🍴	AE DC MC V	●	■	●	
GREAT MISSENDEN: *La Petite Auberge* **££££** 107 High St, Great Missenden, Bucks. 〖 *01494 865370*. An intimate restaurant producing reliable provincial French cooking. Service is efficient but unobtrusive. ● *L, Sun, public hols.* ⓰ 🍴	DC MC V	●			
HADDENHAM: *Green Dragon* **£££** 8 Church Way, Haddenham, Bucks. 〖 *01844 291403*. Ⓦ www.eatatthedragon.co.uk A village dining pub with wide range of home-made British food such as scallops. The big dining rooms are open to the bar. ● *Sun D.* ⓰ 🌿 🍴	AE MC V	●	■	●	■
KINTBURY: *Dundas Arms* **£££** 53 Station Rd, Kintbury, Newbury. 〖 *01488 658263*. Ⓦ www.dundasarms.co.uk This old riverside pub serves an imaginative range of bar snacks and traditional dishes. Fresh fish supplied daily. ● *Sun, Mon D.* ⓰ 🌿 🍴	AE MC V	●		●	■
LONG CRENDON: *Angel Inn* **£££** Bicester Rd, Long Crendon, Bucks. 〖 *01844 208268*. Ⓦ www.angelrestaurant.co.uk Antique, listed 16th-century inn offering fresh fish, blackboard specials, mouth-watering puddings and good-value wines. ● *Sun D.* 🌿 🍴	MC V	●	■	●	■

MELBOURN: *Pink Geranium* [W] www.pinkgeranium.co.uk   £££££
Station Rd, Melbourn, nr Royston, Herts. [01763 260215.
Assured cooking is served in this pretty thatched cottage by the church.
The atmosphere is welcoming, the decor pink. ● Sun D, Mon. & limited.

	AE				
	MC				
	V				

MOULSFORD: *Beetle and Wedge*   £££££
Ferry Lane, Moulsford, Oxon. [01491 651381. [W] www.beetleandwedge.co.uk
On the Thames in *Wind in the Willows* country. Eat in the informal Boathouse
or sophisticated dining room. Booking essential. &

| AE |
| DC |
| MC |
| V |

OXFORD: *Nosebag*   £
6–8 St Michael's St, Oxford. [01865 721033.
Excellent salads, soups and imaginative light dishes are served to queues
of hungry students on the upper floor of a quaint building. ● 25, 26 Dec.

| MC |
| V |

OXFORD: *Al-Shami*   ££
25 Walton Crescent, Oxford. [01865 310066. [W] www.al-shami.co.uk
This bustling Lebanese restaurant serves *falafel, tabouleh, ful medames*
and other favourites, with authentic desserts to follow. &

| MC |
| V |

OXFORD: *Browns*   £££
5–11 Woodstock Rd, Oxford. [01865 511995. [W] www.browns-restaurant.com
A lively, informal restaurant serving a tempting range of snacks and fuller
meals amid bentwood furnishings and potted plants. ● 25, 26 Dec. &

| AE |
| MC |
| V |

OXFORD: *Cherwell Boathouse*   £££
Bardwell Rd, Oxford. [01865 552746. [W] www.cherwellboathouse.co.uk
A romantic punting spot on the River Cherwell. The fixed-price menus
are British with a European twist. ● Sun D. &

| AE |
| DC |
| MC |
| V |

SHINFIELD: *L'Ortolan* [W] www.l'ortolan.com   £££££
Old Vicarage, Church Lane, Shinfield, Reading. [0118 9883783.
L'Ortolan is one of Britain's best restaurants. The setting is charming, though
the modern French and British dishes are very pricey. Set menus and lunches
represent better value. ● Sun D, Mon.

| AE |
| DC |
| MC |
| V |

SPEEN: *Old Plow*   £££
Flowers Bottom, Speen, Bucks. [01494 488300.
An informal bistro in a picturesque former pub. Much is home-made,
and all of it is fresh. ● Sat L, Sun D, Mon. & limited.

| AE |
| MC |
| V |

STONOR: *The Flying Pig at the Stonor Hotel*   £££
On B480, Stonor, Oxon. [01491 638345. [W] www.mystonor.com
A restaurant near Henley-on-Thames. Good local organic produce is cooked
with flair then served in the conservatory or outside deck (seats 80). &

| AE |
| MC |
| V |

STREATLEY: *The Swan at Streatley*   £££
High St, Streatley, Berks. [01491 878800. [W] www.theswanatstreatley.com
A Thames-side business and leisure hotel serving carefully prepared dishes
using the finest local ingredients in a delightful setting. ● Sat L. &

| AE |
| DC |
| MC |
| V |

WINDSOR: *Al Fassia*   ££
27 St Leonards Rd, Windsor, Berks. [01753 855370.
Much-praised Moroccan restaurant with traditional North African decor. Try filo
parcels of chicken and almonds; vegetarian dishes also good. ● Sun. &

| AE |
| DC |
| MC |
| V |

WOBURN: *Paris House*   £££££
Woburn Park, Woburn, Beds. [01525 290692. [W] www.parishouse.co.uk
Modern French food stars at this smart mock-Tudor building in the grounds
of Woburn Abbey. Try the hot raspberry soufflé. ● Sun D, Mon, Feb.

| AE |
| DC |
| MC |
| V |

WOBURN SANDS: *Spooners* [W] www.spooners.co.uk   £££
61 High St, Woburn Sands, Milton Keynes, Bucks. [01908 584385.
This Victorian terraced house makes an agreeable place for a light lunch
or a substantial meal in the evenings. The steaks are especially tasty.
Warm, friendly atmosphere. ● Sun, Mon. &

| AE |
| MC |
| V |

WESSEX

AVEBURY: *The Circle Restaurant*   £
Avebury, Wilts. [01672 539514
Wholefood fans rave about the dishes at this counter-service vegetarian
restaurant beside the ancient stone circle. Some lovely soups on the menu.
Vegan and gluten-free diets are catered for. ● D. &

| MC |
| V |

	CREDIT CARDS	CHILDREN WELCOME	FIXED-PRICE MENU	VEGETARIAN	OUTDOOR TABLES

Price categories include a three-course meal for one, half a bottle of house wine, and all unavoidable extra charges such as cover, service, VAT:
£ under £15
££ £15-£25
£££ £25-£35
££££ £35-£50
£££££ over £50

CHILDREN WELCOME
Restaurants which offer smaller portions and high-chairs for children. Special menus sometimes available.
FIXED-PRICE MENU
A good value fixed-price meal, at lunch, dinner or both, usually of three courses.
VEGETARIAN
Vegetarian specialities served, sometimes for both starters and main courses.
CREDIT CARDS
Indicates which credit cards are accepted: AE American Express; DC Diners Club; MC Master Card/Access; V Visa.

BARWICK: *Little Barwick House*   £££
Off A37, Barwick, Som. 01935 423902. www.littlebarwickhouse.co.uk
Non-residents can dine at this Georgian dower-house hotel. The quality of the local ingredients underpins the Modern British menu. limited.
AE MC V — ● ■ ●

BATH: *Hole in the Wall*   £££
16 George St, Bath, B & NE Som. 01225 425242.
The new management has made dynamic changes in this famous cellar. Sample modern British cooking at its best. Sun, public hols.
AE MC V — ■ ●

BATH: *Moon and Sixpence*   £££
6A Broad St, Bath, B & NE Som. 01225 460962. www.moonandsixpence.co.uk
This popular bistro and wine bar serves inexpensive lunchtime dishes and good-value dinners. The downstairs conservatory is particularly pleasant in summer. 26 Dec, 1 Jan.
AE MC V ● ■ ●

BATH: *The Bath Priory*   £££££
Weston Rd, Bath, B & NE Som. 01225 331922. www.thebathpriory.co.uk
This palatial but relaxing country-house hotel in lovely gardens offers French and English Michelin-star cooking in a variety of themed rooms.
AE DC MC V ● ■ ● ■

BEAMINSTER: *Bridge House*   £££
3 Prout Bridge, Beaminster, Dorset. 01308 862200. www.bridge-house.co.uk
This ancient clergy house dishes up old favourites and inventive adaptations in a civilized setting. Good-value rooms.
AE DC MC V — ■ ●

BOURNEMOUTH: *Chez Fred*   £
10 Seamoor Rd, Westbourne, Bournemouth. 01202 761023. www.chezfred.co.uk
Fred's fish and chips and wicked puddings, such as treacle sponge, are his claim to fame. The service is friendly, the atmosphere lively. Sun L.
MC V ● ■ ●

BRADFORD-ON-AVON: *Woolley Grange*   ££££
Woolley Green, Bradford-on-Avon, Wilts. 01225 864705. www.woolleygrange.com
A delightful Jacobean country-house hotel with everything from children's chicken nuggets to enterprising international cuisine. The atmosphere is informal, and the service excellent.
DC MC V ● ■ ● ■

BRISTOL: *Riverstation*   £££
The Grove, Bristol. 01179 144434. www.riverstation.co.uk
A former river police station on the docks near the city centre, this light and airy restaurant and deli specializes in Modern European cuisine. 25, 26 Dec.
DC MC V ● ■ ● ■

BRISTOL: *Lords*   ££££
43 Corn Street, Bristol. 01179 262658.
French and Mediterranean influences combine in the delicious creations on offer in the basement of a bank building. The fish dishes are good, as is the choice of desserts. Sat L, Sun, 25 Dec–2 Jan, Easter week, last 2 weeks Aug.
AE MC V ● ●

CLEVEDON: *Junior Poon*   £££
16 Hill Rd, Clevedon, Som. 01275 341900. www.juniorpoon.com
A relaxed Peking and Szechuan restaurant and wine bar, set in a Grade II listed Georgian building. Try the tiger prawns in garlic butter sauce. Sun.
AE MC V ● ■ ●

COLERNE: *Lucknam Park*   £££££
Off A420, Colerne, Wilts. 01225 742777. www.lucknampark.co.uk
A luxurious country-house hotel offering suitably posh cooking. The atmosphere is discreet and formal. Men are required to wear a jacket and tie. A memorable experience. Mon–Sat L.
AE DC MC V — — — ●

LACOCK: *At the Sign of the Angel*   ££££
6 Church St, Lacock, Wilts. 01249 730230. www.lacock.co.uk
The 14th-century hotel with low beams, wood panelling and open fires serves superb traditional British fare, including steak and kidney pie. Mon L.
AE DC MC V ● — ● ■

MAIDEN NEWTON: *Le Petit Canard* £££ AE MC V
Dorchester Rd, Maiden Newton, Dorset. ☎ *01300 320536.* W *www.le-petit-canard.co.uk*
Modern British dishes prepared using fresh local produce feature in this
candlelit restaurant. ● *Mon, Tue–Sat L, 2nd & 4th Sun of month.*

MONTACUTE: *The King's Arms Inn* ££ AE MC V
Off A303, Som. ☎ *01935 822513.*
This 16th-century inn houses the award-winning Abbey Room, offering
superb modern British cuisine in cosy surroundings.

POOLE: *The Mansion House* £££ AE DC MC V
Thames St, Poole, Dorset. ☎ *01202 685666.* W *www.themansionhouse.co.uk*
Located in a cobbled mews just off Poole Quay, this Georgian townhouse
restaurant uses local produce in good Modern British fare.

SALISBURY: *Harpers* W *www.harpers.restaurant.co.uk* ££ AE DC MC V
6–7 Ox Row, Market Place, Salisbury, Wilts. ☎ *01722 333118.*
Light, friendly, family restaurant offers unpretentious roasts, casseroles
as well as daily specials. Worth a visit for the wonderful views over
historic Salisbury. ● *Sun D (Oct–May).*

SHAFTESBURY: *La Fleur de Lys* ££££ AE MC V
25 Salisbury St, Shaftesbury, Dorset. ☎ *01747 853717.* W *www.lafleursdelys.co.uk*
This unobstrusive place (a wood panelled loft conversion above a stable block)
conceals some accomplished cooking. ● *Sun D, Mon L, 2 weeks Jan.*

SHEPTON MALLET: *Bowlish House* £££ MC V
Wells Rd, Shepton Mallet, Som. ☎ *01749 342022.* W *www.bowlishhouse.com*
A Georgian merchant's house with peaceful gardens. Relaxed dinners;
afternoon teas too. Modern British cuisine.

STON EASTON: *Ston Easton Park* ££££ AE DC MC V
On A37, Ston Easton, Som. ☎ *01761 241631.* @ *stoneastonpark@stoneaston.co.uk*
Straightforward menus characterize this splendid country-house hotel.
The modern European cookery justifies the expense. An experience
that will not be a disappointment.

STURMINSTER NEWTON: *Plumber Manor* W *www.plumbermanor.com* £££ AE DC MC V
Hazelbury Bryan Rd, Sturminster Newton, Dorset. ☎ *01258 472507.*
Oil paintings adorn this hotel dining room, but they won't distract from the
food. The fish is superb, and the desserts are very tempting. ● *Mon–Sat L.*

TAUNTON: *Castle* £££££ AE DC MC V
Castle Green, Taunton, Som. ☎ *01823 272671.* W *www.the-castle-hotel.com*
A dignified but unostentatious wisteria-clad hotel makes a fine setting
for consistently excellent modern British fare.

WARMINSTER: *Bishopstrow House* ££££ AE DC MC V
On B3414, Warminster, Wilts. ☎ *01985 212312.* W *www.vonessenhotels.com/bishopstrow*
Light lunches and dinners in the elegant Georgian surroundings
of this country-house hotel.

WEST BAY: *Riverside* ££ MC V
Off A35 nr Bridport, Dorset. ☎ *01308 422011.* W *www.riverside-restaurant.co.uk*
Fish is the mainstay of this long-established restaurant, but there's a good
selection of casual snacks. Book ahead. ● *Sun D, Mon, Dec–mid-Feb.*

WEST BEXINGTON: *Manor Hotel* £££ AE DC MC V
Beach Rd, West Bexington, Dorset. ☎ *01308 897785.* W *www.themanorhotel.com*
A delightful range of bar and restaurant food in an old stone inn with nice
guestrooms and a garden for children. Close to Chesil Beach. ● *25 Dec D.*

DEVON AND CORNWALL

AVONWICK: *Avon Inn* £££ MC V
Avonwick, nr South Brent, Devon. ☎ *01364 73475.*
A dining pub on the banks of the Avon. The restaurant is English with a
Continental twist, using fish and local meat.

BARNSTAPLE: *Lynwood House* ☎ *01271 343695.* £££ AE MC V
Bishops Tawton Rd, Barnstaple, Devon. W *www.thelynwood.freeserve.co.uk*
Family-run Victorian house hotel offering real home cooking. Good
fish soup and seafood dishes. Comfortable rooms.

Price categories include a three-course meal for one, half a bottle of house wine, and all unavoidable extra charges such as cover, service, VAT:
£ under £15
££ £15-£25
£££ £25-£35
££££ £35-£50
£££££ over £50

CHILDREN WELCOME
Restaurants which offer smaller portions and high-chairs for children. Special menus sometimes available.
FIXED-PRICE MENU
A good value fixed-price meal, at lunch, dinner or both, usually of three courses.
VEGETARIAN
Vegetarian specialities served, sometimes for both starters and main courses.
CREDIT CARDS
Indicates which credit cards are accepted: *AE* American Express; *DC* Diners Club; *MC* Master Card/Access; *V* Visa.

	CREDIT CARDS	CHILDREN WELCOME	FIXED-PRICE MENU	VEGETARIAN	OUTDOOR TABLES
CHAGFORD: *22 Mill Street* (££££) 22 Mill St, Chagford, Devon. 01647 432244. W www.22millstreet.co.uk Exquisite Modern European cooking, such as crab lasagne or seabass roasted with pickled ginger and basil. Sun–Tue L, 2 wks Jan, 1st wk in Jun.	MC V		■	●	
CHAGFORD: *Gidleigh Park* (£££££) Chagford, Devon. 01647 432367. W www.gidleigh.com Imaginative details mark out from the crowd this first-class country-house hotel and restaurant. Pricey; a place for special occasions.	AE DC MC V		■	●	
DARTINGTON: *Cott Inn* (££) Dartington, Devon. 01803 863777. W www.thecottinn.co.uk A restaurant-with-rooms in a 14th-century inn. Good British home cooking with a daily changing menu and a nice garden.	AE MC V			●	■
DARTMOUTH: *Carved Angel* (££££) 2 South Embankment, Dartmouth, Devon. 01803 832465. W www.thecarvedangel.com One of Britain's best restaurants occupies a quayside Tudor building. The menu features local fish and shellfish, and in winter makes use of local game, like wild duck. Sun D, Mon L, 24–26 Dec.	AE MC V	●	■	●	
DODDISCOMBSLEIGH: *Nobody Inn* (£££) Doddiscombsleigh, nr Exeter, Devon. 01647 252394. W www.nobodyinn.co.uk The traditional, beamed restaurant in this dining pub has a stunning wine list and an amazing choice of local cheeses.	AE MC V			●	■
EXETER: *Thai Orchid* (££) 5 Cathedral Yard, Exeter, Devon. 01392 214215. Authentic Thai cuisine is expertly served within a 15th-century listed building which originally housed the stonemasons working on the cathedral. Fresh orchids on every table add to the elegance. Sun, 25, 26 Dec, 1 Jan.	MC V	●	■	●	
KINGSBRIDGE: *Buckland-Tout-Saints Hotel* (££££) Goveton, Kingsbridge, Devon. 01548 853055. W www.tout-saints.co.uk/hotels Refined cuisine served in a handsome Queen Anne house in lovely grounds. British produce is cooked with Gallic finesse. 3 wks in Jan. limited.	MC V	●	■	●	■
LEWDOWN: *Lewtrenchard Manor* (££££) Off A30, Lewdown, Devon. 01566 783256. W www.lewtrenchard.co.uk This Elizabethan manor-house hotel with mouthwatering fixed-price menus makes a gloriously romantic retreat.	AE DC MC V		■		
LIFTON: *Arundell Arms* (££££) Off A30, Lifton, Devon. 01566 784666. W www.arundellarms.com An attractive sporting inn in a peaceful village. Local fish and game appear on the fixed-price menus. Bar snacks are also available for lunch and dinner. Convivial atmosphere.	AE DC MC V	●	■	●	
LYNMOUTH: *The Rising Sun* (££££) Harbourside, Lynmouth, Devon. 01598 753223. W www.risingsunlynmouth.co.uk Fish is unloaded almost on the doorstep of this 14th-century smugglers' haunt, but it excels in cooking other things as well.	AE DC MC V		■	●	■
PADSTOW: *Seafood Restaurant* (£££££) Riverside, Padstow, Corn. 01841 532700. W www.rickstein.com A favourite with fish-lovers, this restaurant has a wonderful harbourside location. Plainer, but good, food in sister hotel-restaurant St Petroc's House. 22–26 Dec, 1 May, 1st Sun in Jul.	MC V		■	●	
PENZANCE: *Harris's* (£££) 46 New St, Penzance, Corn. 01736 364408. W www.harrissrestaurant.co.uk Game, when in season, and locally farmed meat are a match for the fish dishes. The lunch menu is good value. Sun; Mon (winter). limited.	AE MC V		■		

POLPERRO: *Kitchen* £££
The Coombes, Polperro, Corn. ☎ 01503 272780. @ kitchen@polperro.aol.com
A tiny restaurant specializing in fresh local fish which is a sound choice for the
tourists who flock to Polperro in summer. ● *L; Oct–Easter.* 🔌 ▯
MC V

PORT ISAAC: *Slipway* £££
Harbour Front, Port Isaac, Corn. ☎ 01208 880264. ☒ www.portisaac.com
In season, this 16th-century chandlery offers a perfect sample of
North Cornwall's fishy fare. ● *Jan–mid-Feb; mid-Feb–Easter: Sat & Sun.* 🔌 ▯
AE MC V

PORTREATH: *Tabb's* ££
Tregea Terrace, Portreath, Corn. ☎ 01209 842488.
A small restaurant in an old forge. Everything on the deliciously eclectic menu
is home-made. ● *Mon–Sat L, Tue D, 26 Dec, 1 Jan.* ♿ 🔌 ▯
MC V

ST IVES: *Tate St Ives Coffee Shop and Restaurant* ££
Porthmeor Beach, St Ives, Corn. ☎ 01736 791122. ☒ www.tate.org.uk
Admire the views from this art-gallery brasserie while tucking into wholefood
dishes made with fresh local produce, including fish and shellfish.
● *D; Mon (winter).* ♿ 🔌
MC V

ST IVES: *Russets* £££
18A Fore St, St Ives, Corn. ☎ 01736 794700. ☒ www.russets.co.uk
This seafood restaurant in St Ives main thoroughfare is casual, laid-back and yet
surprisingly lively. Local artists' work hangs from the walls. ● *Jan.* ♿ 🔌
AE MC V

ST MAWES: *Hotel Tresanton* ££££
Lower Castle Rd, St Mawes, Corn. ☎ 01326 270055. ☒ www.tresanton.com
This restaurant in one of the best hotels in Cornwall specializes in local fish and
has wonderful views over the sea from the terrace. ♿ ▯
AE MC V

TAVISTOCK: *The Horn of Plenty* ☒ www.thehornofplenty.co.uk £££££
Gulworthy, Tavistock, Devon. ☎ & ☎ 01822 832528.
A 200-year-old building set in almost five acres of gardens. TV cook Peter
Gorton is executive head chef. ● *Mon L, 23–26 Dec.* 🔌 ♿ ▯
AE MC V

TORQUAY: *Mulberry House* £££
1 Scarborough Rd, Torquay, Torbay. ☎ 01803 213639.
This friendly restaurant-with-rooms offers snacks and delicious lunches (dinners
on Fri to Sun). Try the bread and cakes. ● *Mon & Tue (residents only).* ♿ 🔌

TOTNES: *Willow* £
87 High St, Totnes, Devon. ☎ 01803 862605.
Vegetarian specialities from around the globe, including Mexican, Indian,
Caribbean and Italian, make this place cosmopolitan and eclectic. Warm
welcoming atmosphere. ● *Sun, Mon D, Tues D.* ○ *Thurs D (summer only).* ♿ 🔌 ▯

TREBURLEY: *Springer Spaniel* £££
Treburley, nr Launceston, Cornwall. ☎ 01579 370424.
A friendly dining pub with an attractive, beamed restaurant. The menu
changes frequently, reflecting the owners' desire to use local produce,
including home-grown vegetables and salads. ♿ *limited.* 🔌
MC V

VIRGINSTOW: *Percy's* ££££
Virginstow, Devon. ☎ 01409 211236. ☎ 01409 211275. ☒ www.percys.co.uk
Contemporary country cuisine is the fare of this very rural restaurant, situated
some 9 miles from Launceston in the midst of a 130 acre estate. ♿ ▯
AE MC V

THE HEART OF ENGLAND

ABBERLEY: *Brooke Room, The Elms* £££££
Stockton Rd, Abberley, Worcs. ☎ 01299 896666. ☒ www.theelmshotel.com
Finest organic home-grown produce and local specialities at this elegant
Queen Anne mansion. Lovely decor and rooms. ♿ 🔌 ▯
AE DC MC V

BIRMINGHAM: *Chung Ying Garden* ££
17 Thorp St, Birmingham. ☎ 0121 6666622. ☒ www.chungying.co.uk
A flamboyant Cantonese food palace offering a giant range of specialities,
including *dim sum*. Karaoke on request. ♿ ▶
AE DC MC V

BISHOP'S TACHBROOK: *Mallory Court* £££££
Off B4087 nr Leamington Spa, Warw. ☎ 01926 330214. ☒ www.mallory.co.uk
Classic French and British cuisine feature at this manor-
house hotel, with impressive results. Beautiful gardens. ♿ 🔌 ▯
AE DC MC V

	CREDIT CARDS	CHILDREN WELCOME	FIXED-PRICE MENU	VEGETARIAN	OUTDOOR TABLES

Price categories include a three-course meal for one, half a bottle of house wine, and all unavoidable extra charges such as cover, service, VAT:
£ under £15
££ £15-£25
£££ £25-£35
££££ £35-£50
£££££ over £50

CHILDREN WELCOME
Restaurants which offer smaller portions and high-chairs for children. Special menus sometimes available.
FIXED-PRICE MENU
A good value fixed-price meal, at lunch, dinner, or both, usually of three courses.
VEGETARIAN
Vegetarian specialities served, sometimes for both starters and main courses.
CREDIT CARDS
Indicates which credit cards are accepted: AE American Express; DC Diners Club; MC Master Card/Access; V Visa.

BRIMFIELD: *The Roebuck Inn* £££ Brimfield, Here. 01584 711230. W www.theroebuckinn.com A deceptively simple setting (a village pub) and a relaxed atmosphere conceal highly sophisticated British cooking. ● *Mon–Fri (dining room).*	MC V	●		●	■
BURTON UPON TRENT: *Dovecliff Hall* 01283 531818. £££££ Dovecliff Rd, Stretton, Burton upon Trent, Staffs. W www.dovecliffhallhotel.co.uk A Georgian country house in extensive grounds by the River Dove. An elegant setting. Modern British food. ● *Sat L, Sun D, Mon L, bank hols.*	AE MC V		■	●	
CHELTENHAM: *Le Champignon Sauvage* £££££ 24 Suffolk Rd, Cheltenham, Glos. 01242 573449. A two Michelin-starred restaurant serving Gallic dishes with startling ingredient combinations: sardine and *tapenade* (olive and anchovy paste), rabbit and black pudding. A delight to the palate. ● *Sun, Mon, 24 Dec–3 Jan, 3 weeks in June.*	AE DC MC V	●	■	●	
CHESTER: *Francs* £££ 14 Cupping St, Chester, Ches. 01244 317952. W www.francs.co.uk An ever-popular brasserie where French rock beats out over tasty *plats du jour*. Sundays are family days; special low price for children. Book ahead.	AE MC V	●	■	●	
COVENTRY: *Browns* £ Earl St, Coventry. 024 76221100. W www.browns-cafebar.co.uk Located next to Coventry Cathedral, this restaurant and bar have a wide-ranging menu of traditional English food. There is a late-night bar and live music on Friday and Saturday nights. ● *Sun D, 25 Dec.*	DC MC V			●	■
COVENTRY: *Ryton Organic Gardens Restaurant* W www.hdra.org.uk ££ Henry Doubleday Research Assoc., Ryton Organic Gardens, off A45. 024 76307142. Set within 10 acres of organic display gardens, this restaurant offers meat, fish, vegetarian and vegan meals. Many of the vegetables are grown on site. ● *24 Dec–2 Jan.*	MC V	●		●	■
DORRINGTON: *Country Friends* ££££ On A49 nr Shrewsbury, Shrops. 01743 718707. Simple, reliable English cooking in a pleasant mock-Tudor setting. Fixed-price menu available. Log fires burn in winter. ● *Sun–Tue.*	MC V	●	■	●	
KENILWORTH: *Restaurant Bosquet* ££££ 97A Warwick Rd, Kenilworth, Warw. 01926 852463. This Victorian house offers serious classic French food with rich sauces and fresh seasonal produce. ● *Sat L, Sun, Mon.*	AE MC V	●	■		
LEAMINGTON SPA: *Piccolino's Pizzeria* ££ 9 Spencer St, Leamington Spa, Warw. 01926 422988. A jovial family-owned place serving home-cooked Italian favourites – pizza and pasta, of course, and other dishes at inexpensive prices.	MC V	●		●	
LEAMINGTON SPA: *Flynns* ££ 14 The Parade, Leamington Spa, Warw. 01926 421620. Italian dishes predominate in this relaxed brasserie. Stylish decor.	AE MC V	●	■	●	
LOWER SLAUGHTER: *Lower Slaughter Manor* £££££ Off A429, Lower Slaughter, Glos. 01451 820456. W www.lowerslaughter.co.uk Renowned restaurant in a beautiful Cotswolds manor. The menu is based on French and British classics, modernized by the latest influences from all over the globe. Highly recommended.	AE MC V		■	●	
LUDLOW: *Unicorn Inn* ££ 66 Corve St, Ludlow, Shrops. 01584 873555. W www.theunicorninn.com The emphasis is on local produce in the restaurant of this 17th-century inn. The home-made puddings are good. Great bar food available too.	AE MC V	●		●	■

LUDLOW: *Merchant House* £££ DC MC V
62 Lower Corve St, Ludlow. (01584 875438. W www.merchanthouse.org
This highly acclaimed restaurant is based in a charming Jacobean
building which backs on to the River Corve. The eclectic menu is
mostly organic. Vegetarians should call in advance. ● Sun, Mon;
Tue–Thu L. ⚡

PRESTBURY: *White House* £££ AE DC MC V
The Village, Prestbury, Ches. (01625 829376. W www.whitehouse.co.uk
The smart and elegant decor matches the up-market cosmopolitan food
here. There's a conservatory for warm summer evenings. Attractive rooms.
● Sun D, Mon L. ⚡

ROSS-ON-WYE: *Meader's* ££ MC V
1 Copse Cross St, Ross-on-Wye, Here. (01989 562803.
Friendly Hungarian business; you can sample authentic goulash and
galuska (dumplings) without breaking the bank. ● Sun, Mon. ⚡

ROSS-ON-WYE: *The Pheasant* ££££ AE DC MC V
52 Edde Cross St, Ross-on-Wye, Here. (01989 565751.
W www.pheasant-at-ross.co.uk
A cheerful, homely restaurant in a former Tudor tavern offers fine British
cuisine, ancient and modern, and personal service. ● Sun–Wed. ⚡ ♟

SHREWSBURY: *Floating Thai Restaurant* (01743 243123. ££ AE MC V
Welsh Bridge, Frankwell, Shrewsbury. W www.floatingthairestaurant.co.uk
This atmospheric Thai restaurant is located near the city centre, on a boat as the
name suggests. It has an extensive seafood menu. Advanced reservation is
recommended. ● L. ♟

SHREWSBURY: *Cromwells Hotel* £££ AE MC V
11 Dogpole, Shrewsbury. (01743 361440. W www.cromwellsinn.com
A wine bar/restaurant located in a small hotel in the town centre, opposite
the Guildhall. ⚡ throughout. ♟

STRATFORD-UPON-AVON: *The Opposition* ££ MC V
13 Sheep St, Stratford-upon-Avon, Warw. (01789 269980. W www.theopposition.co.uk
A bustling bistro offering simple pre-theatre suppers. The day's specials
are chalked on blackboards. ▶ (Fri–Sat).

STRATFORD-UPON-AVON: *Russons* £££ AE MC V
8 Church St, Stratford-upon-Avon, Warw. (01789 268822.
This rustic 16th-century setting fits the Shakespearean location. A varied menu,
with fish a speciality. Pre-theatre dinners and lunches available and varied
inexpensive meals. ● Sun, Mon. ⚡

TETBURY: *Gumstool Inn* £££ AE DC MC V
Calcot Manor, Tetbury, Gloucs. (01666 890391. W www.calcotmanor.co.uk
The dining area and bar are combined in this popular gastro dining pub.
The eclectic menu ranges from local beer sausages to Moroccan
specialities. ♿

EAST MIDLANDS

BAKEWELL: *Renaissance* £££ AE MC V
Bath St, Bakewell, Derbs. (01629 812687.
French-style cuisine enjoyed in this traditionally beamed house. Despite
lavish ingredients, (truffles and *foie gras*), the prices are reasonable.
● Sun D, Mon, 1–15 Jan, early Aug. ♿ ⚡ ♟

BASLOW: *Fischer's at Baslow* £££££ AE DC MC V
Baslow Hall, Calver Rd, Baslow, Derbs. (01246 583259.
W www.fischers-baslowhall.co.uk
Whether you eat in the smart dining room or more casually at the
adjoining Café Max, the cooking is top notch. Handy for Chatsworth.
♿ ⚡ ♟

BECKINGHAM: *Black Swan* ££ MC V
Hillside, Beckingham, Lincs. (01636 626474.
This award-winning 17th-century coaching inn is intimate, the quality
of the modern British dishes on the gourmet menu or the less formal
café menu is high and the service is always friendly and efficient.
● Mon, Sun D. ♿ ⚡

Price categories include a three-course meal for one, half a bottle of house wine, and all unavoidable extra charges such as cover, service, VAT:
£ under £15
££ £15–£25
£££ £25–£35
££££ £35–£50
£££££ over £50

CHILDREN WELCOME
Restaurants which offer smaller portions and high-chairs for children. Special menus sometimes available.

FIXED-PRICE MENU
A good value fixed-price meal, at lunch, dinner or both, usually of three courses.

VEGETARIAN
Vegetarian specialities served, sometimes for both starters and main courses.

CREDIT CARDS
Indicates which credit cards are accepted: *AE* American Express; *DC* Diners Club; *MC* Master Card/Access; *V* Visa.

	CREDIT CARDS	CHILDREN WELCOME	FIXED-PRICE MENU	VEGETARIAN	OUTDOOR TABLES
BIRCH VALE: *Waltzing Weasel* ££££	AE MC V	●	■	●	■
BOTTESFORD: *Paul's Contemporary Cuisine* £££	MC V	●	■	●	
BURTON ON THE WOLDS: *Langs* £££	AE MC V	●	■	●	
CASTLETON: *Castle Inn* £££	AE MC V	●		●	■
COLSTON BASSETT: *Martins Arms Inn* £££	AE MC V			●	
EMPINGHAM: *White Horse* ££	AE DC MC V	●			■
GAUNTON NEWARK: *Gaunton Beck* £££	AE DC MC V	●	■	●	■
HAMBLETON: *Hambleton Hall* £££££	AE MC V	●	■	●	■
KEYSTON: *The Pheasant Inn* £££	AE DC MC V	●		●	■
LEICESTER: *Bobby's* ££	MC V	●	■	●	
LEICESTER: *The Case* ££££	AE DC V	●		●	
LINCOLN: *Wig and Mitre* £££	AE DC MC V	●	■		

BIRCH VALE: *Waltzing Weasel* ££££
New Mills Rd, Birch Vale, High Peak, Derbs. 01663 743402. W www.w-weazel.co.uk
Hearty English fare (roasts, chops, game pie and Stilton) is served, accompanied by panoramic views of Kinder Scout. Attractive rooms.

BOTTESFORD: *Paul's Contemporary Cuisine* £££
1 Market St, Bottesford, Leics. 01949 842375. W www.paulsrestaurant.co.uk
Local supplies of game in season is one reason for this bistro's success; attractive beamed decor is another. Sun D, Mon.

BURTON ON THE WOLDS: *Langs* £££
147 Melton Rd, Burton on the Wolds, Leics. 01509 880980. W www.langsrestaurant.com
Smartly furnished barn conversion offering inventive dishes and startling arrays of classic treatments of fish and meat. Sun D.

CASTLETON: *Castle Inn* £££
Castle St, Castleton, Derbs. 01433 620578.
Relaxing pub restaurant in the heart of the Peak District. Traditional British food with Mediterranean influences served in an oak-beamed room.

COLSTON BASSETT: *Martins Arms Inn* £££
School Lane, Colston Bassett, Notts. 01949 81361.
Situated in a former farmhouse, this traditional English pub includes a comfortable dining room that serves much more than standard pub fare. The cooking is in the modern British style. Sun D, 25 Dec.

EMPINGHAM: *White Horse* ££
Empingham, Rutland. 01780 460221. W www.the-white-horse.co.uk
This delightful, 17th-century stone-built courthouse now holds a bar and bistro. It also serves morning croissants and afternoon teas.

GAUNTON NEWARK: *Gaunton Beck* £££
Main St, Gaunton Newark, Notts. 01636 636793.
An eclectic menu of French, British and Eastern dishes are served in this 1750s beamed building. Nice patio in summer.

HAMBLETON: *Hambleton Hall* £££££
Off A606 nr Oakham, Rutland. 01572 756991. W www.hambletonhall.com
Splendid views over Rutland Water are a good start to the menu of outstanding fresh cooking with lobsters and *foie gras*. Such memorable feasts don't come cheap. Smart accommodation.

KEYSTON: *The Pheasant Inn* £££
Off A14, Keyston, Northants. 01832 710241. W www.huntsbridge.co.uk
Light or full-menu options are available in this delightful thatched inn. The menu is eclectic and modern; the home-made ices are delicious. limited.

LEICESTER: *Bobby's* ££
154–156 Belgrave Rd, Leicester. 0116 2660106. W www.eatatbobbys.com
Vegetarian Gujarati and South Indian dishes make an interesting, good-value treat. The combinations of freshly ground spices make this place unique. Licensed, but you can also bring your own wine. Mon.

LEICESTER: *The Case* ££££
4–6 Hotel St, Leicester. 01162 517675. W www.thecase.co.uk
Stylish, light restaurant serving Modern European dishes such as home-made brie Sun, 24–27 Dec, 1, 2 Jan.

LINCOLN: *Wig and Mitre* £££
30–32 Steep Hill, Lincoln. 01522 535190. W www.wigandmitre.com
This operates on similar lines to its sibling, Gaunton Beck, in Newark. French and British dishes. Diners appreciate its flexibility and long opening hours.

LINCOLN: *Jew's House* ££££ AE DC MC V
15 The Strait, Lincoln. **(** 01522 524851. **W** www.thejewshouse.co.uk
A fascinating old building close to the cathedral, serving Modern European and international food. Wonderful, calorific hand-made chocolates. **●** *Sun & Mon.*

NEWARK: *Gannets Café* £
35 Castlegate, Newark, Notts. **(** 01636 702066.
A cheery ground-floor café by the castle with a garden extension and an upstairs bistro. It is plain, simple and affordable. The staff are very friendly and the atmosphere is bohemian. **●** *D, 25–26 Dec, 1 Jan.*

NOTTINGHAM: *Saagar* ££ AE MC V
473 Mansfield Rd, Sherwood, Nottingham. **(** 0115 9622014.
North "Indian" cookery from the Punjab, Kashmir and Pakistan. Menus change frequently and new recipes spice up the choice. **●** *Sun L.*

NOTTINGHAM: *Sonny's* £££ AE MC V
3 Carlton St, Hockley, Nottingham. **(** 0115 9473041.
Blend of simple snack-bar and restaurant offering Modern European food with Eastern touches. The atmosphere is laid-back and fashionable.

PAULERSPURY: *Vine House* ££££ MC V
100 High St, Paulerspury, Northnts. **(** 01327 811267. **W** www.vinehousehotel.com
Seventeenth-century house just off the A5. Unusual ingredients, modern British influences and informal, pleasant rooms. **●** *Sat L, Sun, Mon–Wed L.*

PLUMTREE: *Perkins Restaurant* ££ AE DC MC V
Old Railway Station, Plumtree, Notts. **(** 0115 9373695. **W** www.perkinsrestaurant.co.uk
This bistro serves a mix of British game and fish with French sauces. Good bar snacks. **●** *Sun D, Mon.*

REDMILE: *Peacock* ££££ AE MC V
Church Corner, Redmile, Leics. **(** 01949 842554.
An excellent dining pub offering a changing menu of modern and traditional British and European dishes. Menu changes regularly.

RIDGEWAY: *Old Vicarage* ££££ AE MC V
Ridgeway Moor, Ridgeway, Derbs. **(** 0114 2475814. **W** www.theoldvicarage.co.uk
High-quality meat, vegetables and fresh herbs produce insistent flavours at this stone-built Victorian house. With three- and four-course menus, and plenty of vegetarian choices. **●** *Sun D, Mon.*

ROADE: *Roade House* **W** www.roadehousehotel.co.uk ££££ AE MC V
16 High St, Roade, Northnts. **(** 01604 863372.
This family business offers seasonal British cooking. Most dishes have complex sauces. Game features during winter. **●** *Sat L, Sun D, Mon L.*

STOKE BRUERNE: *Bruerne's Lock* ££££ AE MC V
5 The Canalside, Stoke Bruerne, Northnts. **(** 01604 863654. **W** www.bruerneslock.co.uk
A fast-evolving modern British restaurant by the side of the Grand Union Canal. Personal service is the keynote. **●** *Sat L, Sun D, Mon.*

STRETTON: *Ram Jam Inn* **W** www.rutnet.co.uk/customers/ramjam £££ AE MC V
Great North Rd, Stretton, Rutland. **(** 01780 410776.
This roadside haven has provided hospitality since 1750. Hearty snacks and freshly prepared hot dishes are served all day, every day. **●** *25 Dec.*

LANCASHIRE AND THE LAKES

AMBLESIDE: *Sheila's Cottage* ££ MC V
The Slack, Ambleside, Cumbria. **(** 015394 33079.
Tasty baking takes place in this converted stable-block cottage. Tea breads and cakes supplements savoury dishes such as Cumbrian sugar-baked ham or Westmorland ramekin. Children at lunchtimes only. **●** *25, 26 Dec, 2 wks in Jan.*

AMBLESIDE: *Zeffirelli's* ££ MC V
Compston Rd, Ambleside, Cumbria. **(** 015394 33845. **W** www.zeffirellis.co.uk
An unusual enterprise combining shops, café, a cinema and a trendily decorated pizzeria serving pizzas, salads and pasta. **●** *Mon–Fri L.*

AMBLESIDE: *Rothay Manor* ££££ AE DC MC V
Rothay Bridge, Ambleside, Cumbria. **(** 015394 33605. **W** www.rothaymanor.co.uk
This elegant Regency hotel mainly serves traditional English dishes. Lunch and splendid teas are excellent value.

Price categories include a three-course meal for one, half a bottle of house wine, and all unavoidable extra charges such as cover, service, VAT:
£ under £15
££ £15-£25
£££ £25-£35
££££ £35-£50
£££££ over £50

CHILDREN WELCOME
Restaurants which offer smaller portions and high-chairs for children. Special menus sometimes available.

FIXED-PRICE MENU
A good value fixed-price meal, at lunch, dinner or both, usually of three courses.

VEGETARIAN
Vegetarian specialities served, sometimes for both starters and main courses.

CREDIT CARDS
Indicates which credit cards are accepted: AE American Express; DC Diners Club; MC Master Card/Access; V Visa.

	CREDIT CARDS	CHILDREN WELCOME	FIXED-PRICE MENU	VEGETARIAN	OUTDOOR TABLES
APPLETHWAITE: *Underscar Manor* £££££ Off A66 nr Keswick, Cumbria. 017687 75000. A sumptuous Italianate house in peaceful gardens sets the scene for ambitious food. Beautifully decorated rooms make a romantic retreat.	AE MC V		■	●	
BLACKPOOL: *September Brasserie* £££ 15–17 Queen St, Blackpool. 01253 623282. @ pat.wood@cyberscape.net Amid the flotsam of Blackpool's eateries, this brasserie is a beacon of hope. It produces some highly innovative robust dishes. ● Mon, Sun.	AE DC MC V	●	■	●	
BOWNESS-ON-WINDERMERE: *Porthole Eating House* £££ 3 Ash St, Bowness-on-Windermere, Cumbria. 015394 42793. Summer crowds fail to jade this Italian restaurant. It maintains its pleasing simplicity of style and provides good value. ● Sat L, Tue, mid-Dec–mid-Feb.	AE DC MC V	●		●	■
BRAITHWAITE: *Ivy House* £££ Off A66 nr Keswick, Cumbria. 017687 78338. W www.ivy-house.co.uk This Georgian hotel is in the centre of the village. Striking decor. Dinners have panache. Comfortable accommodation. ● Jan.	AE DC MC V		■	●	
CARTMEL: *Uplands* £££ Haggs Lane, Cartmel, Cumbria. 015395 36248. W www.uplands.uk.com This peaceful hotel serves excellent-value set lunches of local produce; the views towards Morecambe Bay are delightful. A place to come back to, year after year. ● Mon; Tue–Thu L.	AE MC V		■		
CARTMEL: *L'Enclume* £££££ Cavendish St, Cartmel, Cumbria. 015395 36362. W www.lenclume.co.uk This much-talked of Michelin-star restaurant run by chef Simon Rogan offers ultra-modern Continental cuisine. Open for breakfast. ● Mon, 1st 2 wks Jan.	AE DC MC V	●			■
COCKERMOUTH: *Quince and Medlar* £££ 13 Castlegate, Cockermouth, Cumbria. 01900 823579. Adventurous vegetarian cooking in a modest house near the castle. The award-winning menu is well worth sampling. ● L, Sun, Mon.	MC V			●	
CROSTHWAITE: *Punch Bowl Inn* @ enquiries@punchbowl.fsnet.co.uk ££ Crosthwaite, nr Kendal, Cumbria. 01539 568237. People come from miles around to eat at this 17th-century coaching inn. There is a choice of several rooms. The menu is eclectic and special diets are catered for. ● Sun & Mon (except bank hols), 25 Dec, 26 Dec D, 1 Jan D.	MC V	●	■	●	■
GRASMERE: *White Moss House* ££££ On A591 at Rydal Water, Cumbria. 01539 435295. W www.whitemoss.com Classy set dinners are served unpompously in this comfortable country-house hotel. A traditional setting and attentive service in a house that once belonged to William Wordsworth. ● L, Sun.	MC V	●			
KENDAL: *Moon* 01539 729254. ££ 129 Highgate, Kendal, Cumbria. @ moon@129highgate.freeserve.co.uk Modern contemporary cuisine using fresh local produce. The atmosphere is pleasantly informal and relaxed. ● L; Mon, Tue; 25, 26 Dec.	MC V	●	■	●	
LANGHO: *Northcote Manor* £££££ On A59 nr Blackburn, Blackb with Darwen. 01254 240555. W www.northcotemanor.com Nigel Howarth cooks with regional flair including several Lancashire specialities. Also more gastronomic dishes served in the evenings. Highly recommended food and wine.	AE MC V	●	■	●	
LIVERPOOL: *Left Bank* £££ 1 Church Rd, Liverpool. 0151 734 5040. W www.theleftbankrestaurant.co.uk French restaurant located off Penny Lane of Beatles fame, in a wood-panelled intimate setting. Book well in advance for weekend meals. ● Sat D.	AE MC V	●	■	●	

LIVERPOOL: *60 Hope St* ££££
60 Hope St, Liverpool. (0151 707 6060. FAX 0151 707 6016. W www.60hopestreet.com
Spread over three floors of a Georgian building with a modern interior.
Quality service, superb food. ● Sun, Mon; 25, 26 Dec, 1 Jan, bank hols.
MC
V

LONGRIDGE: *The Longridge Restaurant* ££££
104–106 Higher Rd, Longridge, Lancs. (01772 784969. W www.heathcotes.co.uk
The relaxed style of this British restaurant is deceptive, as the food is prepared
with slick technique and innovative talent. ● Mon L. & limited.
AE
DC
MC
V

MANCHESTER: *Siam Orchid* ££
54 Portland St, Manchester. (0161 236 1388.
Manchester's best Thai restaurant has a great range of dishes, including many
vegetarian choices. There are also influences from other parts of south-east
Asia. Beware the fiery sauces; quell them with Singha beer. ● Sat L, Sun L.
AE
MC
V

MANCHESTER: *Restaurant Bar & Grill* £££
14 John Dalton St, Manchester. (0161 839 1999.
This modern eaterie offers fine Modern European dishes in impressive
surroundings, with glass walls and a long bar downstairs. ● 25 & 26 Dec.
AE
MC
V

MANCHESTER: *Moss Nook* £££££
B5166 nr airport, Manchester. (0161 437 4778.
Moss Nook offers a superb presentation of gastronomic medleys. Try the
vast *menu surprise*, or one of the many desserts. ● Sat L, Sun, Mon.
AE
MC
V

MELMERBY: *Village Bakery* ££
On A686 nr Penrith, Cumbria. (01768 881811. W www.village-bakery.com
An 18th-century barn is the setting for this shop and eaterie. Organic
and vegetarian meals are available all day. ● D. &
DC
MC
V

NEAR SAWREY: *Ees Wyke* £££
On B52 nr Hawkshead, Cumbria. (015394 36393. W www.eeswyke.co.uk
The views towards Esthwaite Water are one attraction; charming hosts and
excellent, good-value dinners are others. This country house hotel is a place
that you will not forget in a hurry. ● L; Jan–Feb.
MC
V

POULTON-LE-FYLDE: *River House* ££££
Skippool Creek, Thornton-le-Fylde, Lancs. (01253 883497. W www.hotel-lakedistrict.com
This restaurant-with-rooms prides itself on its details (cheeses,
teas and *petits fours*) being as good as the main courses. ● L, Sun; 25, 26 Dec.
MC
V

SADDLEWORTH: *The Old Bell Inn Hotel* £££
Huddersfield Rd, Delph, Oldham. (01457 870130.
A seasonally changing menu is offered in the main restaurant,
with informal meals and snacks served in the bar.
AE
MC
V

ULLSWATER: *Sharrow Bay* £££££
Nr Pooley Bridge, Ullswater, Cumbria. (017684 86301. W www.sharrow-bay.com
This is one of Britain's greatest country-house hotels. Even the teas
are a banquet. ● Dec–Feb. &
MC
V

WATERMILLOCK: *Rampsbeck Country House Hotel* £££££
On A592 nr Pooley Bridge, Cumbria. (017684 86442.
Rampsbeck's dining room occupies a fine stretch of lakeshore, but
the modern British food is ambitious enough to hold the attention
and the service is pleasant. Book for lunch. ● 4 Jan–mid-Feb.
MC
V

WHITEWELL: *Inn at Whitewell* £££
Whitewell, Forest of Bowland, Clitheroe, Lancs. (01200 448222.
Full of atmosphere and very friendly, this old coaching inn's restaurant
offers an above-average menu of predominantly English dishes.
MC
V

WINDERMERE: *Miller Howe* £££££
Rayrigg Rd, Windermere, Cumbria. (015394 42536. W www.millerhowe.com
This restaurant is also a beautiful hotel, but the elaborate and theatrical
dishes are the main reason for visiting.
AE
MC
V

WITHERSLACK: *Old Vicarage* £££
Church Rd, Witherslack, Cumbria. (015395 52381.
W www.oldvicarage.com
Dinner at this idyllic country-house hotel is a mouthwatering affair using local
produce. Book ahead. Early bird half-price dinner until 7pm. ● L. &
AE
MC
V

<table>
<tr><td>Price categories include a three-course meal for one, half a bottle of house wine, and all unavoidable extra charges such as cover, service, VAT:
£ under £15
££ £15-£25
£££ £25-£35
££££ £35-£50
£££££ over £50</td><td>CHILDREN WELCOME
Restaurants which offer smaller portions and high-chairs for children. Special menus sometimes available.
FIXED-PRICE MENU
A good value fixed-price meal, at lunch, dinner or both, usually of three courses.
VEGETARIAN
Vegetarian specialities served, sometimes for both starters and main courses.
CREDIT CARDS
Indicates which credit cards are accepted: AE American Express; DC Diners Club; MC Master Card/Access; V Visa.</td></tr>
</table>

Column headers: CREDIT CARDS · CHILDREN WELCOME · FIXED-PRICE MENU · VEGETARIAN · OUTDOOR TABLES

YORKSHIRE AND THE HUMBER REGION

ASENBY: *Crab and Lobster* £££ — AE MC V — Children ●, Fixed-Price ■, Vegetarian ●, Outdoor ■
Off A168 nr Thirsk, N Yorks. 01845 577286. www.crabandlobster.com
A great seafood pub just off the A1. Blackboards reflect the unpredictability of fresh catches. The place hums with activity. Rooms available. ♿ ⚡ ▯

BOLTON ABBEY: *Devonshire Arms Country House Hotel* £££££ — AE DC MC V — Children ●, Fixed-Price ■, Vegetarian ●
Just off A59 nr Ilkley, N Yorks. 01756 710441. www.thedevonshirearms.co.uk
A luxurious country-house hotel. All types flock in to enjoy the smart restaurant, excellent bar snacks and luscious teas. ● Mon–Sat L. ♿ ⚡ ▯

BRADFORD: *Koh-I-Noor* £ — MC V — Children ●, Fixed-Price ■, Vegetarian ●
Simes St, Bradford. 01274 737564. www.kohinoor.co.uk
This up-market Indian restaurant specializes in Balti and vegetarian dishes, although the menu offers plenty of variety for all. Tandooris are an especially strong point. ● Mon–Sat L. ⚡ ▯

BRADFORD: *Guide Post Hotel* £££ — AE DC MC V — Children ●, Vegetarian ●
Common Rd, Low Moor, Bradford BD12 0ST. 01274 607866. www.guideposthotel.net
The location of this restaurant may not be ideal – a warehouse district surrounds the building – but it is definitely worth a visit for the quality of the English and continental food and for the service. ● Sat L, Sun D. ♿ ▯

BREARTON: *The Malt Shovel* £ — Children ●, Vegetarian ●, Outdoor ■
Brearton, N Yorks. 01423 862929.
Varied blackboard menu featuring British, European and Oriental influences, served in a 16th-century beamed pub. ● Mon; Sun D; 25, 26 Dec. ♿

ELLAND: *La Cachette* ££ — MC V — Fixed-Price ■, Vegetarian ●
31 Huddersfield Road, Elland, Calderdale. 01422 378833.
Modern British food served in an Edwardian interior from an extensive menu, which may include deep-fried brie, rib-eye steaks, game and sticky toffee pudding. Fish a speciality. ● Sun, bank hol Mon, last 2 weeks of Aug.

HARROGATE: *Betty's* ££ — MC V — Children ●, Vegetarian ●
1 Parliament St, Harrogate, N Yorks. 01423 502746. www.bettysandtaylors.co.uk
Betty's serves breakfasts, lunches and dinners as well as an eye-popping range of cakes, teas and coffees, all in a refined atmosphere of Edwardian living. ● 25, 26 Dec, 1 Jan. ♿ ⚡

HARROGATE: *Drum and Monkey* ££ — MC V — Children ●
5 Montpellier Gardens, Harrogate, N Yorks. 01423 502650.
The Drum and Monkey is a town-centre pub which has now achieved a more elevated status as a smart seafood restaurant. It's fish or nothing here. ● Sun.

HAWORTH: *Weaver's* ££ — AE DC MC V — Children ●, Fixed-Price ■, Vegetarian ●
15 West Lane, Haworth, W Yorks. 01535 643822. www.weaverssmallhotel.co.uk
Hearty Yorkshire home cooking is given a modern accent at Weaver's, to the delight of literary pilgrims seeking sustenance after tramping Heathcliff's moors. ● Sun D, Mon; 26 Dec–1 Jan. ⚡

HEADINGLEY: *Bryan's* £ — MC V — Children ●, Fixed-Price ■, Vegetarian ●
9 Weetwood Lane, Headingley, Leeds. 0113 2785679.
A traditional fish and chip restaurant of the best Yorkshire sort. Beef dripping and fresh fish are the secrets behind perfect results. Traditional, delicious desserts like treacle pudding round off the meal. ♿ ⚡ ▯

HETTON: *Angel Inn* ££££ — AE MC V — Children ●, Fixed-Price ■, Vegetarian ●
Off B6265 nr Skipton, N Yorks. 01756 730263. www.angelhetton.co.uk
This convivial beamed restaurant-with-rooms is more than a village pub, but the bar and brasserie food stay down to earth. ● 25 Dec. ♿ ⚡ ▯

ILKLEY: *Box Tree* £££
35–37 Church St, Ilkley, W Yorks. ☎ 01943 608484. 🆆 www.theboxtree.co.uk
Cuisine is definitely haute in this 18th-century farmhouse, recently
revitalized by a new and creative chef. Desserts and cheeses do
not disappoint. ● Sun D, Mon. 🔣 🔣 🔣 🔣
AE MC V

KNARESBOROUGH: *Carriages Wine Bar* £££
89 High St, Knaresborough, N Yorks. ☎ 01423 867041. 🆆 www.carriageswinebar.co.uk
The Australian owner and chef serves mainly Pacific Rim cuisine
in summer and French and Mediterranean food in winter. A lovely
garden overlooks the quiet, pretty railway station and the viaduct
over the Nidd Gorge. ● 25, 26 Dec, 1 Jan. 🔣 limited. 🔣
MC V

LEEDS: *Brasserie Forty-four* ££££
44 The Calls, Leeds. ☎ 0113 2343232. 🆆 www.brasserie44.com
This waterfront warehouse complex combines bright, sophisticated
cooking with stylish accommodation at No. 42. The lively atmosphere
makes this a fun night out. Especially pleasant in summer.
● Sat L, Sun. 🔣 limited. 🔣 Fri & Sat.
AE DC MC V

LEEDS: *Haley's* £££
Shire Oak Rd, Headingley, Leeds. ☎ 0113 2784446. 🆆 www.haleys.co.uk
A peaceful Victorian hotel in the university district produces
Anglo-French cuisine with exquisite presentation. Light, modern
bedrooms. ● L. 🔣 limited. 🔣
AE MC V

RIPLEY: *Boar's Head* £££
Ripley Castle Estate, Ripley, N Yorks. ☎ 01423 771888. 🆆 www.boarsheadripley.co.uk
This coaching inn provides luxury accommodation and fine dining as well as a
bistro. Fine wines and a great selection of ales. 🔣 🔣 🔣
AE DC MC V

SHEFFIELD: *Greenhead House* ££££
84 Burncross Rd, Chapeltown, Sheffield. ☎ 0114 2469004.
Four-course menus give a taste of France in the smart
dining room of this stone house. Home-made soups
a speciality. ● Sun–Tue, Wed L, Sat L. 🔣 🔣 🔣
AE MC V

WATH IN NIDDERDALE: *Sportsman's Arms* £££
Wath in Nidderdale, Pateley Bridge, nr Harrogate, N Yorks. ☎ 01423 711306.
This restaurant-with-rooms also has a bar, but it is the well-cooked food
that attracts customers. Local produce features on the menu. ● 25 Dec. 🔣 🔣
MC V

WHITBY: *Magpie Café* £
14 Pier Rd, Whitby, N Yorks. ☎ 01947 602058. 🆆 www.magpiecafe.co.uk
This house by the harbour serves superlative fish and chips with good cheer.
Don't miss the diverse and unusual puddings. ● Jan–early-Feb. 🔣
MC V

WINTERINGHAM: *Winteringham Fields* £££££
Winteringham, N Lincs. ☎ 01724 733096. 🆆 www.winteringhamfields.com
Superlative modern British cooking is served in this restaurant-with-rooms,
in a setting of opulent Victoriana. *(See also p563.)* ● Sun, Mon. 🔣 🔣 🔣
AE MC V

YORK: *Little Betty's* ££
46 Stonegate, York. ☎ 01904 622865. 🆆 www.bettysbypost.com
A wide range of Yorkshire and Swiss specialities, home-made cakes
and light lunches are served in this medieval building. 🔣
MC V

YORK: *Melton's* £££
7 Scarcroft Rd, York. ☎ 01904 634341. 🆆 www.meltonsrestaurant.co.uk
This small restaurant in a Victorian terrace is good value and welcoming,
serving varied Anglo-French food. ● Sun; Mon L. 🔣 limited. 🔣 🔣
MC V

NORTHUMBRIA

BELFORD: *The Blue Bell Hotel* ££
Market Place, Belford, Northum. ☎ 01668 213543. 🆆 www.bluebellhotel.com
The walled gardens of this old coaching inn shelter a profusion of organic
produce, complementing local meat and fish on seasonally changing menus. 🔣
AE MC V

CONSETT: *Pavilion* ££
Iveston, Consett, Durham. ☎ 01207 503388.
Bustling Cantonese restaurant serving generous helpings from an extensive
Chinese menu. Friendly atmosphere and good value. 🔣 🔣
AE DC MC V

Price categories include a three-course meal for one, half a bottle of house wine, and all unavoidable extra charges such as cover, service, VAT:
£ under £15
££ £15-£25
£££ £25-£35
££££ £35-£50
£££££ over £50

CHILDREN WELCOME
Restaurants which offer smaller portions and high-chairs for children. Special menus sometimes available.

FIXED-PRICE MENU
A good value fixed-price meal, at lunch, dinner or both, usually of three courses.

VEGETARIAN
Vegetarian specialities served, sometimes for both starters and main courses.

CREDIT CARDS
Indicates which credit cards are accepted: *AE* American Express; *DC* Diners Club; *MC* Master Card/Access; *V* Visa.

	CREDIT CARDS	CHILDREN WELCOME	FIXED-PRICE MENU	VEGETARIAN	OUTDOOR TABLES
DARLINGTON: *Cottage Thai* £££ 94–96 Parkgate, Darlington, Durham. 01325 361717. Handy for the station and theatre, this simple place offers Thai classics like *tom yum* soups, and red and green curries.	AE MC V	●		●	
DURHAM: *Bistro 21* £££ Aykley Heads House, Aykley Heads, Durham. 0191 3844354. Eclectic modern cooking with menus that include enough variety to satisfy just about any taste. Relaxed atmosphere. *Sun, 25 Dec, bank hols.*	AE DC MC V	●	■	●	■
DURHAM: *Shaheens Indian Bistro* @ shaheens_durham@yahoo.com ££ Old Post Office, 48 North Bailey, Durham. 0191 386 0960. This Indian bistro is located in the historic part of Durham, with a range of good traditional Indian dishes on its menu. *L.*	DC MC V	●	■	●	
EAST BOLDON: *Forsters* www.forsters-restaurant.co.uk £££ 2 St Bedes, Station Rd, East Boldon, Tyne and Wear. 0191 5190929. A family enterprise run on classic British lines, welcoming and unpretentious but with plenty of sparkle. The food is never disappointing. *Sun, Mon, Tue–Sat L.*	AE DC MC V		■	●	
GATESHEAD: *Eslington Villa* £££ On A6127, Low Fell, Gateshead. 0191 4876017. Reliable classic cooking figures in this attractive, graciously furnished hotel. Guests are greeted with bonhomie. *Sat L, Sun D.*	AE DC MC V	●	■	●	
HAYDON BRIDGE: *General Havelock Inn* ££ Radcliffe Rd, Haydon Bdge, Northum. 01434 684376. www.northumberlandrestaurants.co.uk Good food at sensible prices, both for the evening four-course menu and the lunchtime specials. Gardens run down to the River Tyne. *Mon, Sun D.*	DC MC V	●	■	●	■
HEXHAM: *The Valley Connection 301* £££ 19 Market Pl, Hexham, Northum. 01434 601234. www.thevalleyrestaurant.co.uk Luxurious interior and top-quality Indian cuisine using unusual herbs and spices. Good views of Hexham Abbey, floodlit at night. *Mon; L; 25 Dec.*	MC V			●	
NEWCASTLE UPON TYNE: *Café 21* www.cafetwentyone.co.uk £££ 19–21 Queen St, Princes Wharf, Quayside, Newcastle upon Tyne. 0191 2220755. Much more than just a café, this is a warm, welcoming bistro with a cosy feel. The menu changes on a daily basis. Unruffled service. *Sun.*	AE DC MC V		■	●	
NEWCASTLE UPON TYNE: *Treacle Moon* ££££ 5–7 The Side, Newcastle upon Tyne. 0191 2325537. www.treaclemoonrestaurant.com Fresh local meat, game and exotic fish feature in this brasserie. Modern-international cuisine gives flavour and colour. A laid-back atmosphere with jazz in the background. *L; Sun. limited.*	AE MC V	●		●	
NEWCASTLE UPON TYNE: *Fisherman's Lodge* £££££ Jesmond Dene, Jesmond, N'castle upon Tyne. 0191 2813281. www.fishermanslodge.co.uk Situated in the centre of Jesmond Dene park, serving excellent food of the highest quality. Fish is a speciality. *Sun, 25, 26 Dec, bank hols.*	AE MC V	●	■	●	■
ROMALDKIRK: *Rose and Crown* £££ On B6277 nr Barnard Castle, Durham. 01833 650213. www.rose-and-crown.co.uk This handsome coaching inn offers a splendid mix of pub with good-value bar meals and undaunting restaurant. Well worth making a detour. Good selection of ales. *24, 26 Dec.*	MC V	●	■	●	
SEATON BURN: *Horton Grange* 01661 860686. ££££ Off A1 at Ponteland, Northum. www.hortongrangehotel.sageweb.co.uk This pleasant country house hotel offers local English produce. Decor and cooking are sophisticated, light and elegant. *L, Sun.*	AE MC V		■	●	

STOKESLEY: *Chapters* £££
27 High St, Stokesley, N Yorks. (01642 711888. W www.chaptershotel.co.uk
A successful duo of informal bistro and more serious dining room.
Cooking is French with global cross-currents. ● *Sun, 25 Dec, 1 Jan.*
AE DC MC V

NORTH WALES

ABERDYFI: *Penhelig Arms* £££
Aberdyfi, Gwynedd. (01654 767215. W www.penheligarms.com
Freshly caught fish features strongly on the menu at this hotel-restaurant
right by the sea. *(See also p564.)* ● *25, 26 Dec.*
MC V

ABERSOCH: *Riverside Hotel* £££
On A499 nr Pwllheli, Gwynedd. (01758 712419. W www.riversideabersoch.co.uk
Morning coffee, light lunches and afternoon teas are served in the lounge and
garden. Restaurant evening meals ooze with Mediterranean charm. ● *Nov–Easter.*
MC V

ABERSOCH: *Porth Tocyn* ££££
Abersoch, Gwynedd. (01758 713303. W www.porth-tocyn-hotel.co.uk
Few fail to be charmed by this coastal hotel. There are light alternatives
to the menu on offer. *(See also p564.)* ● *Nov–wk before Easter.*
MC V

BEAUMARIS, ANGLESEY: *Ye Olde Bulls Head* ££££
Castle St, Beaumaris, Anglesey. (01248 810329. W www.bullsheadinn.co.uk
This handsome coaching inn has a restaurant and a brasserie, both of which
feature its wonderful fish specialities. Book ahead. *brasserie only.*
AE MC V

CAPEL COCH: *Tre-Ysgawen Hall* £££
On B5111 nr Llangefni, Anglesey. (01248 750750. W www.treysgawen-hall.co.uk
A firm classical training tailors the modern French cooking at this
massive country-house hotel. Service is courteous and attentive.
AE MC V

COLWYN BAY: *Café Niçoise* £££
124 Abergele Rd, Colwyn Bay, Conwy. (01492 531555.
This French-style bistro comes complete with jazz and blues and Parisian
scenes. Modern European cooking inspires the menus. ● *Mon; Tue L, Sun.*
AE MC V

CONWY: *Old Rectory* W www.oldrectorycountryhouse.co.uk ££££
Llanrwst Rd, Llansanffraid Glan, Glan Conwy. (01492 580611.
Great care is lavished on the three-course dinners here. Inside, there
are many paintings and antiques. Rooms available. ● *30 Nov–1 Feb.*
MC V

DEGANWY: *Paysanne* ££
Station Rd, Deganwy, Conwy. (01492 582079.
This bustling Gallic bistro serves daily specials and three-course provincial dinners.
Special dietary needs catered for by arrangement. ● *L, Sun, Mon.*
MC V

DOLGELLAU: *Dylanwad Da* £££
2 Ffôs-y-Felin, Dolgellau, Gwynedd. (01341 422870. @ dylanwadda@aol.com
Bistro serving Welsh lamb and port, plum and ginger pie. Serves coffee and cakes
during day. ● *L; Nov–Apr: Sun–Wed; Feb–mid-Mar; May–Oct: Mon.* *limited.*

EYTON: *The Plassey Shippon Restaurant* ££
Eyton, nr Wrexham. (01978 780905. W www.theplassey.co.uk
Set amid a complex of Edwardian farm buildings and craft workshops,
Plassey offers good bar snacks and blackboard specials. Slow-roasted
Welsh lamb is a delicious speciality. ● *Sun & Mon D.*
DC MC V

GLANWYDDEN: *Queen's Head* ££
Off B5115 nr Llandudno Junction, Conwy. (01492 546570.
Popular country pub offering Welsh lamb, local mussels and soups.
Traditional puddings appear on a long list of sweets. *limited.*
MC V

HARLECH: *Castle Cottage* £££
Pen Llech, Harlech, Gwynedd. (01766 780479. W www.castlecottageharlech.co.uk
This is one of the oldest buildings in Harlech. Menus have Welsh and
English elements. Fresh local produce gives the dishes an authentic
flavour. Bedrooms available. ● *L, Jan.*
MC V

LLANARMON DYFFRYN CEIRIOG: *West Arms Hotel* ££££
Llanarmon Dyffryn Ceiriog, nr Llangollen, Denbighs.
(01691 600665. W www.thewestarms.co.uk
Superb cooking and excellent presentation await at this restaurant in an idyllic
16th-century inn. Local fish dishes are good. Afternoon teas available. *limited.*
MC V

	Credit Cards	Children Welcome	Fixed-Price Menu	Vegetarian	Outdoor Tables
Price categories include a three-course meal for one, half a bottle of house wine, and all unavoidable extra charges such as cover, service, VAT: £ under £15 ££ £15-£25 £££ £25-£35 ££££ £35-£50 £££££ over £50	**CHILDREN WELCOME** Restaurants which offer smaller portions and high-chairs for children. Special menus sometimes available. **FIXED-PRICE MENU** A good value fixed-price meal, at lunch, dinner or both, usually of three courses. **VEGETARIAN** Vegetarian specialities served, sometimes for both starters and main courses. **CREDIT CARDS** Indicates which credit cards are accepted: *AE* American Express; *DC* Diners Club; *MC* Master Card/Access; *V* Visa.				
LLANBERIS: *Y Bistro* £££ 43–45 High St, Llanberis, Gwynedd. ☎ 01286 871278. w www.ybistro.co.uk Hungry walkers flock to this restaurant at the foot of the Snowdon railway. A good range of hearty main courses. ● *L, Sun.* ♿ ⌸	MC V			●	
LLANDRILLO: *Tyddyn Llan* ££££ On B4401 nr Corwen, Denbigh. ☎ 01490 440264. w www.tyddynllan.co.uk This Georgian country house hotel produces distinctive, high-quality cooking using local ingredients such as Welsh Black beef and fish. *(See also p565.)* ● *Mon L.* ♿ ⌸	MC V	●	■	●	■
LLANDUDNO: *Richard's* £££ 7 Church Walks, Llandudno, Conwy. ☎ 01492 877924. This bistro in a Victorian town house is deservedly popular. The menu has plenty of options. ● *L, Sun–Mon, 25–26 Dec.*	AE DC MC V	●	■	●	
LLANGOLLEN: *Gales* ££ 18 Bridge St, Llangollen, Denbighs. ☎ 01978 860089. w www.galesofllangollen.co.uk A wine bar, restaurant and guesthouse. Cosmopolitan menu changes daily, and is served in a panelled bar with church pews. ● *Sun, 25 Dec–2 Jan.* ♿ *limited.* ▯	AE DC MC V	●			
NORTHOP: *Soughton Hall* £££ Off A5119, Northop, Flint. ☎ 01352 840811. w www.soughtonhall.co.uk Grand cooking matches this hotel's palatial setting: an 18th-century bishop's palace in parkland. Restaurant in bar and hotel restaurant. ⌸ ▯	MC V			●	■
PORTMEIRION: *Hotel Portmeirion* w www.portmeirionvillage.com ££££ Off A487, signposted from Minffordd, Portmeirion. ☎ 01766 770000. Elegant restaurant in a smart seaside hotel using local produce in a Modern British menu. The nearby Castell Deudraeth brasserie is an offshoot. ⌸ ▯	AE DC MC V	●		●	■
PWLLHELI: *Plas Bodegroes* ££££ Nefyn Rd, Pwllheli, Gwynedd. ☎ 01758 612363. w www.bodegroes.co.uk This elegant Georgian country house takes full advantage of excellent local ingredients to produce accomplished British cooking for its three-course dinners. Fish especially good. ● *Tue–Sat L; Mon, Dec–Feb.* ♿ ⌸ ▯	MC V	●	■		
SOUTH AND MID-WALES					
ABERAERON: *Hive on the Quay* ££ Cadwgan Pl, Aberaeron, Cardiganshire. ☎ 01545 570445. w www.hiveonthequay.co.uk Honey ice-cream is the speciality at this summertime café, which serves wholesome teas and lunches (dinners too, in high summer) in a welcoming setting of stripped pine and lots of pot plants. ● *mid-Sep–Apr.* ⌸ ♿	MC V	●		●	■
BRECHFA: *Ty Mawr* £££ Brechfa, Carmarthen. ☎ 01267 202332. w www.tymawrhotel.co.uk Small, luxury rural hotel with fine dining. Local produce is treated to international flourishes. ♿ ⌸ ▯	MC V	●	■	●	
BROAD HAVEN: *Druidstone Hotel* w www.druidstone.co.uk £££ Druidston Haven, Broad Haven, Pembroke. ☎ 01437 781221. This informal family hotel combines local produce with international spices. Set in vast grounds with clifftop views. ● *Sun D (phone for winter opening hours).* ♿ ⌸	AE MC V	●		●	■
CARDIFF: *La Brasserie/Champers/Le Monde* ££ 60–62 St Mary St, Cardiff. ☎ 029 20234134. w www.le-monde.co.uk Bustling complex of French brasserie (fish and grills), tapas bar and seafood restaurant with friendly atmosphere and good wines. ♿ ▯	AE DC MC V	●	■		
CARDIFF: *Woods Brasserie* £££ Pilotage Building, Stuart St, Cardiff. ☎ 029 20492400. Minimalist but comfortable, serving Modern British food, with an emphasis on fish and Welsh chicken and lamb. ● *Sun D, 25, 26, 31 Dec, 1 Jan.* ♿	AE DC MC V	●		●	■

CLYTHA: *Clytha Arms* £££
Nr Abergavenny, Monmouth. 01873 840206. www.clytha-arms.com
Country pub where France and Wales meet in fare such as laverbread *(see p36)*
or oysters with leeks. ● *Sun D, Mon.*
AE DC MC V

COWBRIDGE: *Off the Beeton Track* ££
1 Town Hall Sq, Cowbridge, V of Glam. 01446 773599.
Home-baked cakes, simple lunches and afternoon teas. ● *Sun & Mon.*
DC MC V

CRICKHOWELL: *Nantyffin Cider Mill Inn* £££
Brecon Rd, Crickhowell, Powys. 01873 810775. www.cidermill.co.uk
This unpretentious, 16th-century stone-built inn proffers Modern British and
European dishes, plus local game and seafood. ● *Mon or Tue (phone first).*
AE MC V

CRICKHOWELL: *The Bear* £££
High St, Crickhowell, Powys. 01873 810408. www.bearhotel.co.uk
Traditional British food using local produce, especially fish and game.
Bar meals or dining room. Rooms available. ● *25 Dec.* limited.
AE MC V

FISHGUARD: *Three Main Street* ££££
3 Main St, Fishguard, Pembroke. 01348 874275.
In a Georgian building overlooking the harbour the Modern British menu may include
crab soufflé and roast breast of guinea fowl. ● *Sun–Mon, Feb, 2 weeks end Nov.*

GWAUN VALLEY, NR FISHGUARD: *Tregynon Country Farmhouse* £££
Off B4313, Gwaun Valley, Newport. 01239 820531. www.online-holidays.net/tregynon
The food here is delicious and carefully considered (home-smoked bacon
and wholefoods). Best to book. ● *L, Sun, Thu.*
MC V

LAMPHEY: *Dial Inn* £££
The Ridgeway, Lamphey, Pembroke. 01646 672426.
Hearty fare such as Lamphey lamb and home-made beef and Guinness pie
keeps the customers happy. Fish and vegetarian choices too. ● *25 Dec.*
MC V

LLANDEWI SKIRRID: *Walnut Tree Inn* £££
On B4521 nr Abergavenny, Monmouth. 01873 852797. www.thewalnuttree.com
This popular, informal bistro offers a vast selection of Italian cuisine,
unpretentiously served but carefully prepared. ● *Sun D & Mon (except bank hols).*
MC V

LLYSWEN: *Griffin Inn* £££
On A470, Llyswen, Powys. 01874 754241. www.griffin-inn.co.uk
Shooting and fishing are the attractions in the Wye Valley, home of this
15th-century inn; the fare reflects this. Rooms available. ● *Sun D.*
AE DC MC V

MUMBLES: *Claude's* ££
93 Newton Rd, Mumbles. 01792 366006. FAX 01792 368931. www.claudes.org.uk
Modern European cuisine is the style of fare here, using fresh local produce.
● *Mon & Sun D, 26 Dec–1 Jan.*
AE MC V

NANTGAREDIG: *Four Seasons, Cwmtwrch Farm* £££
On B4310, Carmarthen. 01267 290238.
Local produce receives honest farmhouse treatment in this family-run
restaurant. Welsh lamb and smoked salmon feature prominently. ● *Sun, Mon.*
MC V

NEWPORT: *Cnapan* £££
East St, Newport, Pembroke. 01239 820575. www.online-holidays.net/cnapan
This Georgian restaurant-with-rooms includes Welsh specialities
in its lunch and dinner menus. ● *Tue, Jan–Feb.*
MC V

ST DAVID'S: *Morgan's Brasserie* £££
20 Nun St, St David's, Pembroke. 01437 720508. www.morgan-in-stdavids.co.uk
Fish is the main attraction at this family-run brasserie. Local beef and
lamb also feature. ● *Jan & Feb: daily; Mar: Sun–Tue; Nov & Dec: Mon–Thu.*
AE MC V

SWANSEA: *La Braseria* £££
28 Wind St, Swansea. 01792 469683. www.labraseria.com
This Spanish restaurant is especially popular at lunchtime for good-value
set lunches garnished with chips, salads and garlic bread. ● *Sun.*
AE DC MC V

TENBY: *The Plantagenet* £££
Plantagenet Hse, Quay Hill, Tenby. 01834 842350.
This partly medieval restaurant next to the Tudor Merchant's House is also open
for breakfast and snacks. It specializes in seafood, serves organic meat and is
very child-friendly. ● *L Mon–Fri, D Sat & Sun; Jan–mid-Feb.* limited.
AE MC V

For key to symbols see back flap

<table>
<tr><td>

Price categories include a three-course meal for one, half a bottle of house wine, and all unavoidable extra charges such as cover, service, VAT:
£ under £15
££ £15–£25
£££ £25–£35
££££ £35–£50
£££££ over £50

</td></tr>
</table>

CHILDREN WELCOME
Restaurants which offer smaller portions and high-chairs for children. Special menus sometimes available.
FIXED-PRICE MENU
A good value fixed-price meal, at lunch, dinner or both, usually of three courses.
VEGETARIAN
Vegetarian specialities served, sometimes for both starters and main courses.
CREDIT CARDS
Indicates which credit cards are accepted: *AE* American Express; *DC* Diners Club; *MC* Master Card/Access; *V* Visa.

	CREDIT CARDS	CHILDREN WELCOME	FIXED-PRICE MENU	VEGETARIAN	OUTDOOR TABLES
WELSH HOOK: *Stone Hall* £££ Off A40 nr Wolf's Castle, Pembroke. 01348 840212. www.stonehall-mansion.co.uk French cooking with unusual touches reigns in this hotel-restaurant in wooded grounds. ● *L, 25 & 26 Dec.*	AE DC MC V	●	■	●	
WHITEBROOK: *Crown at Whitebrook* ££££ Whitebrook, Monmouth. 01600 860254. www.crownatwhitebrook.co.uk This 17th-century outpost of modern French and British cuisine in the Wye Valley is now run as a restaurant-with-rooms. ● *Sun D, Mon L, Christmas & New Year.*	AE DC MC V		■	●	

THE LOWLANDS

	CREDIT CARDS	CHILDREN WELCOME	FIXED-PRICE MENU	VEGETARIAN	OUTDOOR TABLES
ANSTRUTHER: *Cellar* ££££ 24 East Green, Anstruther, Fife. 01333 310378. One of this fishing port's oldest buildings. Only top-quality produce is used; fresh seafood dominates the menu. ● *Sun & Mon in Nov–Mar; 24–28 Dec.*	AE MC V		■	●	
AYR: *Fouters Bistro* £££ 2A Academy St, Ayr, S Ayrshire. 01292 261391. www.fouters.co.uk Lively bistro in a vaulted basement. Ingredients are Scottish, cooking mostly provincial-French, with vegetarian dishes. ● *Sun, Mon.*	AE MC V	●	■	●	
CUPAR: *Ostlers Close* ££££ Bonnygate, Cupar, Fife. 01334 655574. www.ostlersclose.co.uk Fish plays a large part in the menus at this tiny place, but plenty of meat or game dishes get expert French treatment too. Wild mushrooms are one of their delicious specialities. ● *Sun, Mon, Tue–Fri L.* limited	AE MC V	●		●	
DIRLETON: *Open Arms Hotel* £££ Dirleton, E Lothian. 01620 850241. www.openarmshotel.com On the edge of the village green overlooking the 13th-century castle the well-established hotel-restaurant enjoys a deserved reputation for good food. Choose between formal restaurant or the brasserie.	MC V	●	■	●	■
EDINBURGH: *Henderson's* ££ 94 Hanover St, Edinburgh. 0131 2252131. www.hendersonsofedinburgh.co.uk This institution has a wide range of vegetarian specialities. Cakes and unusual cheeses accompany filling salads and hot dishes.	AE MC V	●	■	●	
EDINBURGH: *Indigo Yard* ££ 7 Charlotte La, Edinburgh. 0131 220 5603. An informal café/bistro with outdoor tables, combining restaurant and bar services. Popular in the evenings. Great atmosphere.	AE MC V	●		●	■
EDINBURGH: *Susie's Diner* £ 53 West Nicolson St, Edinburgh. 0131 6678729. A friendly wholefood vegetarian café centrally located near Edinburgh University. Good-quality ingredients, impeccably flavoured. limited.		●		●	■
EDINBURGH: *Daniel's* ££ 88 Commercial St, Leith, Edinburgh. 0131 5535933. www.daniels-bistro.co.uk One of the best of the new conservatory restaurants, situated opposite the Scottish Office. Serves hearty Alsace cuisine.	AE MC V	●	■	●	
EDINBURGH: *Kalpna* ££ 2–3 St Patrick Sq, Edinburgh. 0131 6679890. Indian vegetarian cookery in a calming environment near the university. Flavours are mild and service variable. ● *Sun L.*	MC V	●	■	●	
EDINBURGH: *Atrium & Blue Bar Café* ££££ 10 Cambridge St, Edinburgh. 0131 2288882. www.atriumrestaurant.co.uk A stylish interior by the Traverse Theatre complements the simple but exciting cooking here. Modern British with a Mediterranean influence. ● *Sat L, Sun.*	AE MC V	●		●	

EDINBURGH: *Martin's* @ martinirons@fsbdial.co.uk £££££
70 Rose St, North Lane (between Frederick St and Castle St), Edinburgh. (0131 2253106.
This central restaurant offers a range of imaginative, contemporary Scottish
cooking. ● Sat L, Sun, Mon; Christmas & New Year, end May, beg. Oct. ⚑ ☐ | AE DC MC V

EDINBURGH: *Vintners Rooms* ££££
87 Giles St, Leith, Edinburgh. (0131 5546767. W www.thevintnersrooms.demon.co.uk
This unusual candlelit restaurant is housed in a wine warehouse. Both
cooking and service are admirably unpretentious. Light lunches are
served in the wine bar. ● Sun, last week Dec, first week Jan. ⚑ ☐ ☐ | AE MC V

EDINBURGH: *Waterfront Wine Bar* ££££
1C Dock Place, Leith, Edinburgh. (0131 5547427. W www.sjf.co.uk
Best of the Leith waterfront bar-restaurants with a cosy bar, excellent wine list,
and conservatory restaurant serving modish fare. ● 25 & 26 Dec. ☐ ⚑ ☐ | MC V

GLASGOW: *Brian Maule at Chardon d'Or* £££££
170 West Regent St, Glasgow. (0141 248 3801. @ info@lechardondor.com
French and Mediterranean flavours combine with Scottish produce at this
restaurant in a traditional stone building close to the centre. ● Sun. ⚑ ☐ | AE MC V

GLASGOW: *The Buttery* £££££
652 Argyle St, Glasgow. (0141 2218188.
Attractive turn-of-the-century pub converted into an elegant dining room.
● Sat L, Sun & Mon, 25 Dec, 1 Jan. ☐ | AE MC V

GLASGOW: *Camerons, Glasgow Hilton* £££££
1 William St, Glasgow. (0141 2045511. W www.hilton.com
This is theme-park Scotland, but both food and service are beyond
reproach at this business hotel and restaurant. ● Sat L, Sun D, Mon. ☐ ☐ | AE DC MC V

GLASGOW: *Ubiquitous Chip* £££££
12 Ashton Lane, Glasgow. (0141 3345007. W www.ubiquitouschip.co.uk
The lighthearted individuality suggested by the name reveals itself most
in the upstairs bistro. The food throughout is good, with well-rehearsed
and hugely varied treatments of Scottish fare. ☐ ☐ ☐ | AE DC MC V

KIPPFORD: *The Anchor Hotel* ££
Kippford, Dalbeattie, Kirkcudbrightshire. (01556 620205
Situated on the waterfront, with views of the boating activity, this friendly
hotel and pub offers good bar food. ● 25 Dec. ☐ limited. ⚑ ☐ | MC V

LARGS: *Nardini's* ££
The Esplanade, Largs, N Ayrshire. (01475 674555. W www.nardini.co.uk
A splendid Art Deco interior sets the scene of this seafront lounge café.
Breakfasts, cakes, Italian and British dishes are served all day. This is
the perfect place in which to sit back, read the paper and relax. ☐ ⚑ ☐ | AE DC MC V

LINLITHGOW: *Champany Inn* £££££
Champany, nr Linlithgow, W Lothian. (01506 834532. W www.champany.com
Wines are exceptional, but the food is good too, whether an Angus steak, or more
ornate dishes. There is an informal chop house here too. ● Sat L, Sun. ☐ ☐ | AE DC MC V

MOFFAT: *Well View* ££££
Ballplay Rd, Moffat, Dumfries & Galloway. (01683 220184. W www.wellview.co.uk
Modern French cooking with some Scottish elements is served in this family-run
hotel. Peaceful atmosphere. No children under five at night. ● Sat L. ⚑ | AE MC V

PORTPATRICK: *Knockinaam Lodge* (01776 810471. £££££
Off A77 nr Portpatrick, Dumfries & Galloway W www.prideofbritainhotels.com
An idyllic location overlooking the sea. Modern British cooking with
international touches. ☐ limited. ⚑ | AE DC MC V

ST ANDREWS: *Brambles* ££
5 College St, St Andrews, Fife. (01334 475380.
Popular self-service café specializing in wholefood and vegetarian recipes,
though meat and fish also appear. Cakes are freshly baked on the
premises. ⚑ | MC V

ST ANDREWS: *The Peat Inn* £££££
On B940 nr St Andrews, Fife. (01334 840206. W www.thepeatinn.co.uk
Highly accomplished modern cooking with regional produce and
seasonal vegetables has established this fine hotel-restaurant as one of the
best in Britain. Lunch is a bargain. ● Sun, Mon. ☐ ⚑ ☐ | AE MC V

Price categories include a three-course meal for one, half a bottle of house wine, and all unavoidable extra charges such as cover, service, VAT:
£ under £15
££ £15–£25
£££ £25–£35
££££ £35–£50
£££££ over £50

CHILDREN WELCOME
Restaurants which offer smaller portions and high-chairs for children. Special menus sometimes available.
FIXED-PRICE MENU
A good value fixed-price meal, at lunch, dinner or both, usually of three courses.
VEGETARIAN
Vegetarian specialities served, sometimes for both starters and main courses.
CREDIT CARDS
Indicates which credit cards are accepted: *AE* American Express; *DC* Diners Club; *MC* Master Card/Access; *V* Visa.

	CREDIT CARDS	CHILDREN WELCOME	FIXED-PRICE MENU	VEGETARIAN	OUTDOOR TABLES
SWINTON: *Wheatsheaf* £££ Main St, Swinton, Borders. 📞 *01890 860257.* 🖥 www.wheatsheaf-swinton.co.uk This country inn offers imaginative cooking served in a traditional dining room or conservatory. Bedrooms available. ● *Dec & Jan D.* ♿ ⚡	MC V	●		●	▪
TROON: *Highgrove House* £££ Old Loans Rd, Troon, S Ayrshire. 📞 *01292 312511.* 🖥 www.costley-hotels.co.uk Watery prospects over the Firth of Clyde accompany informal meals from a wide-ranging menu in this retired sea-captain's house. Bedrooms available.	AE MC V	●	▪	●	

THE HIGHLANDS AND ISLANDS

	CREDIT CARDS	CHILDREN WELCOME	FIXED-PRICE MENU	VEGETARIAN	OUTDOOR TABLES
ABERDEEN: *The Silver Darling* £££ Pocra Quay, Footdee, North Pier, Aberdeen. 📞 *01224 576229.* Located on the north side of Aberdeen Harbour, this restaurant offers superb seafood, which varies with the daily catch. ● *Sat L, Sun, 24 Dec–mid-Jan.* 🍴	AE DC MC V	●			
ALEXANDRIA: *Georgian Room, Cameron House* £££££ Off A82, Loch Lomond, Alexandria, W Dunbar. 📞 *01389 755565.* 🖥 www.cameronhouse.co.uk This large, comfortable hotel caters for the well-heeled leisure market of fishing and golf with three fine restaurants. ● *Mon.* ♿ ⚡	AE DC MC V		▪	●	
ALYTH: *Drumnacree House* ££ St Ninian's Rd, Alyth, Perthshire. 📞 *01828 632194.* 🖥 www.drumnacreehouse.co.uk The smokehouse and garden provide produce for a mixed bag of cooking styles used with great enthusiasm and flair. An eclectic range of original ideas to tempt any palate. ● *Mon.* ♿ ⚡ 🍴	MC V	●			
AUCHMITHIE: *But 'n' Ben* ££ Off A92 nr Arbroath, Angus. 📞 *01241 877223.* Twin cottages in a working fishing village. The day's catch figures at lunch and dinner, and there are splendid high teas. ● *Tue.* ♿ ⚡	MC V	●		●	
BALLATER: *Green Inn* ££££ 9 Victoria Rd, Ballater, Aberdeenshire. 📞 *013397 55701.* 🖥 www.green-inn.com Scottish produce is given the full works at this refurbished restaurant-with-rooms. Service is friendly and informed. ● *L, 25–27 Dec.* ♿ ⚡	AE MC V	●		●	
BALLATER: *Darroch Learg* ££££ Braemar Rd, Ballater, Aberdeenshire. 📞 *013397 55443.* 🖥 www.darroch-learg.co.uk A Victorian shooting lodge with a fine restaurant. The food is Modern British using a wide range of ingredients. ● *23–27 Dec, 10 Jan–1 Feb.* ♿ ⚡ 🍴	AE DC MC V	●	▪	●	
CAIRNDOW: *Loch Fyne Oyster Bar* 🖥 www.loch-fyne.com ££ Clachan Farm, Ardkinglas, Cairndow, Argyll & Bute. 📞 *01499 600236.* This splendid place offers a warm welcome with platters of shellfish, overlooking the lochside oyster beds. ♿ ⚡	MC V	●		●	
COLBOST BY DUNVEGAN: *The Three Chimneys* £££££ Colbost, nr Dunvegan, Isle of Skye. 📞 *01470 511258.* 🖥 www.threechimneys.co.uk Situated a few miles from Dunvegan, on the western shore of Loch Dunvegan. Once a stone-built crofter's cottage, this award-winning restaurant offers seafood and game lovingly prepared with fresh local ingredients. The atmosphere is peaceful and relaxed. Accommodation is also available. ● *Jan.* ♿ ⚡ *throughout.* 🍴	AE MC V	●		●	
DRYMEN: *The Pottery* ££ The Square, Drymen, Stirlingshire. 📞 *01360 660458.* Friendly restaurant and coffee shop, serving good home-cooked food all day and delicious afternoon teas. Delightful terrace. ● *1 Jan, 25 Dec.* ♿ ⚡ *throughout.*	AE DC MC V	●		●	▪

DUNKELD: *Kinnaird* w www.kinnairdestate.com £££££
Kinnaird Estate, off B898 nr Dunkeld, Perthshire. [01796 482440.
This estate hotel produces ornate food of great originality.
Lunch is more affordable. ● Jan–Feb: Mon, Tues, Wed. 🔲 ●

AE MC V

FORT WILLIAM: *Crannog Seafood Restaurant* £££
Town Pier, Fort William, Highland. [01397 705589. w www.crannog.net
Nothing detracts from the simple pleasure of eating exquisitely fresh
seafood overlooking a panoramic loch view. Helpings are generous.
The atmosphere is warm and welcoming, and the service efficient. 🔲 ●

MC V

INVERNESS: *Culloden House* £££££
Off A96 at Culloden, Highland. [01463 790461. w www.cullodenhouse.co.uk
The food is Scottish country-house style, with sauces, jellies, sorbets and
mousses interspersing hearty meat, game and fish dishes. Rooms available.

AE MC V

KILBERRY: *Kilberry Inn* ££
Kilberry by Tarbert, Argyll & Bute. [01880 770223. w www.kilberryinn.com
This small, white croft (former post office, now pub) in a quiet coastal village
serves traditional British home cooking at its best, with a constantly changing
blackboard menu. Rooms available. ● Sun D, Mon (except public hols). throughout.

MC V

KILLIECRANKIE: *Killiecrankie House Hotel* £££
Off A9 nr Pitlochry, Perthshire. [01796 473220. w www.killiecrankiehotel.co.uk
Excellent bar food and dinnertime fare in this attractive hotel. Hearty stuff, with
some Oriental dishes. ● at times from Nov–Mar – phone to check. 🔲 limited.

MC V

KINCLAVEN: *Ballathie House* £££££
Off B9099 nr Stanley, Perthshire. [01250 883268. w www.ballathiehousehotel.com
A warm, hearty hotel in a huge estate on the Tay. The restaurant
serves appropriate fare like venison and, of course, salmon. 🔲

AE DC MC V

KINCRAIG: *The Boathouse Restaurant* ££
Loch Insh, Kincraig, Invernesshire, Highland. [01540 651272. w www.lochinsh.com
Food is served all day at this log-cabin restaurant overlooking the loch – fresh fish,
haggis or steak. A bar and a gift shop can also be found here. 🔲

MC V

KYLESKU: *Kylesku Hotel* £££
On A894 by Lairg, Highland. [01971 502231. @ kyleskuhotel@lycos.co.uk
Lochs and mountains provide a splendid backdrop to this hotel. The menu is
extensive, with fresh fish always a good option. Bar meals and restaurant.

MC V

OBAN: *Knipoch Hotel* ££££
On A816 nr Oban, Argyll & Bute. [01852 316251. w www.knipochhotel.co.uk
Dinners range from three to five courses. Huge arrays of vegetables and
flamboyant puddings are features.

AE DC MC V

PERTH: *Let's Eat* £££
77 Kinnoull St, Perth. [01738 643377. w www.letseatperth.co.uk
Local ingredients – fish, game, beef and lamb – are the mainstay of the modern
cooking here. ● Sun, Mon, 25–26 Dec, 1–2 Jan, 2 weeks mid-Jan, 2 weeks mid-Jul.

AE MC V

PLOCKTON: *Off the Rails* w www.off-the-rails.co.uk ££
Old Station, Plockton, Wester Ross, Highland. [01599 544423.
Traditional Scottish food, such as local seafood and juicy steaks, with an
international flavour. Delightful atmosphere in an old railway station
waiting-room. ● limited winter opening – phone to check. 🔲

MC V

PORT APPIN: *The Airds Hotel* £££££
Port Appin, Appin, Argyll & Bute. [01631 730236. w www.airds-hotel.com
This hotel restaurant has a fine waterfront location and cheerful interior
to complement the splendidly flavoured dinners. (See also p573.)

MC V

ST MARGARET'S HOPE: *The Creel Restaurant* ££££
Front Rd, St Margaret's Hope, S. Ronaldsay, Orkney. [01856 831311. w www.thecreel.co.uk
Excellent, honest cooking. Seafood predominates, but you might try the
seaweed-fed lamb. ● Jan–Feb, 2 weeks mid-Oct.

MC V

ULLAPOOL: *Ceilidh Place* £££
14 West Argyle St, Ullapool, Highland. [01854 612103. @ info@theceilidhplace.com
An interesting building with great atmosphere, incorporating a restaurant,
bars and bookshop, as well as rooms above. Imaginative menus at various
prices. 🔲 throughout.

AE MC V

British Pubs

No TOUR OF BRITAIN could be complete without some exploration of its public houses (see pp34–5). These are a great social institution, descendants of centuries of hostelries, ale-houses and stagecoach halts. Some have colourful histories or fascinating contents, and still occupy a central role in the community, staging quiz games and folk dancing. Many of those listed below are lovely buildings, or have attractive settings. Most serve a variety of beers, spirits and wine by the glass.

A "free house" is independent and will stock several leading regional beers, but most pubs are "tied" – this means that they are owned by a brewery and only stock that brewery's selection.

Many pubs offer additional attractions such as live music and beer gardens with picnic tables. Traditional pub food is often served at lunchtime, and increasingly food is served in the evenings too. Traditional pub games take many forms, including cribbage, shove ha'penny, skittles, dominoes and darts.

LONDON

BLOOMSBURY: *Lamb*
94 Lamb's Conduit St, WC1.
Unspoilt Victorian pub with cut-glass "snob screens" and theatrical photographs. Small courtyard at the rear.

CITY: *Black Friar*
174 Queen Victoria St, EC4.
Eccentric inside and out, with intriguing Art Nouveau decor. Attentive service.

CITY: *Olde Cheshire Cheese*
Wine Office Court, Fleet St EC4.
Authentic 17th-century inn haunted by the shades of Johnson, Pope and Dickens. Restored to its plain, bareboarded glory with open fires in winter.

HAMMERSMITH: *Dove*
19 Upper Mall, W6.
One of the most attractive of West London's riverside pubs, where you can watch rowing crews from the terrace. Very crowded in fine weather.

HAMPSTEAD: *Spaniards Inn*
Spaniards Lane, NW3.
Famous Hampstead landmark dating from the 18th century, once part of a tollgate. Attractive garden.

KENSINGTON: *Windsor Castle*
114 Campden Hill Rd, W8.
A civilized Georgian inn with traditional oak furnishings and open fires. The walled garden attracts well-heeled, youngish crowds in summer. Hearty English food.

SOUTHWARK: *George Inn*
77 Borough High St, SE1.
Quaint coaching inn with unique galleried courtyard, now owned by the National Trust. Rooms ramble upstairs and downstairs, and the overspill sits outside. Morris men and Globe Players may be seen at times (see p122).

THE DOWNS AND CHANNEL COAST

ALCISTON: *Rose Cottage*
Off A27 nr Lewes, Sussex.
Charming, creeper-covered cottage inn decorated with rustic bygones. Limited room inside.

ALFRISTON: *Star*
Alfriston, Sussex.
This quaint old inn, once a pilgrim hostel, is now a smart hotel but is full of character.

CHALE: *Wight Mouse Inn*
On B3399, Chale, Isle of Wight.
Cheerful, family-oriented inn with large gardens. Bric-a-brac dangles from the ceilings.

FLETCHING: *Griffin*
Off A272, Fletching, Sussex.
Sophisticated but very laid-back country inn with a 1930s air, which serves imaginative food. Attractive accommodation.

RYE: *Mermaid*
Mermaid St, Rye, Sussex.
Famous historic building in a steep cobbled street, full of panelling, frescoes and antiques.

SMARDEN: *Bell*
Off A274, Smarden, Kent.
An ancient brick-and-beam pub among orchards. Traditional games, inglenook fireplaces and flagstone floors.

WALLISWOOD: *Scarlett Arms*
Off A29 nr Ewhurst, Surrey.
Workers' cottages converted into a relaxing pub with beams, log fires and trestle tables.

WINCHESTER: *Wykeham Arms*
75 Kingsgate St, Winchester, Hants.
Classy, idiosyncratic town centre pub/hotel with fascinating decor. Excellent food, wine and accommodation (see p547).

EAST ANGLIA

CAMBRIDGE: *Boathouse*
14 Chesterton Rd, Cambridge.
One of the best of Cambridge's waterside pubs, overlooking Jesus Green. For entertainment in summer, sit and watch barges and punts glide past; oars hang in the bars.

HOLYWELL: *Olde Ferry Boat*
Off A1123 at Needingworth, Cambs.
The Great Ouse reaches almost to the door of this picturesque thatched pub. Inside it is comfortably modernized, with cosy bedrooms. Wide range of food, and a resident ghost called Juliette.

LITTLEBURY: *Queens Head Inn*
High St, Littlebury, Essex.
This Tudor village pub has kept plenty of its original character. It offers outstanding real ales and food in a welcoming atmosphere.

SNAPE: *Golden Key*
Priory Lane, Snape, Suffolk.
Pretty gardens, stylish interior and appetizing food are a draw at this inn. Very popular during the Aldeburgh Festival (see p63).

SNETTISHAM: *Rose & Crown*
Off A149 nr Heacham, Norfolk.
Former coaching inn with three attractive bars and plenty of room for children to play in the garden.

SOUTHWOLD: *Crown*
High Street, Southwold, Suffolk.
Popular seaside haunt with nautical decor and oak panelling. Excellent food, wine list and Adnam beers.

STIFFKEY: *Red Lion*
On A149, Norfolk.
Traditional English pub with open fires in winter and the garden overlooking the Stiffkey River on the North Norfolk Coastal Path.
🚶 🍴 🚭 ↗

TILLINGHAM: *Cap & Feathers*
South St, Tillingham, Essex.
Smoked meat, homemade pies and sausages, and fish are on offer at this 16th-century pub near the salt marshes. 🚭 🍴 ↗ 🎵

THAMES VALLEY

BARLEY: *Fox & Hounds*
High St, Barley, Herts.
Look for the tall chimney and the hunting scene sign. Both food and real ales are excellent. Disabled visitors welcome. 🚶 🍴 🚭 ↗ 🎵

BROOM: *Cock*
23 High St, Broom, Bedfordshire.
Charming 17th-century inn called "the pub with no bar" (place your orders at the hatch, and the beer comes straight from the cellar casks). 🚶 🍴 🚭 ↗

BURFORD: *Lamb*
Sheep St, Burford, Oxon.
This picture-postcard Cotswolds inn has roses round the door and mullioned windows. Food is good, as is the service and atmosphere.
🚶 🍴 🚭

FAWLEY: *Walnut Tree*
Off B4155 nr Henley, Buckinghamshire.
A splendid base for enjoying the Chilterns. You can even hitch your horse up in the car park.
🚶 🍴 🚭 ↗ 🎵

GREAT TEW: *Falkland Arms*
Off B4022 nr Chipping Norton, Oxon.
This partly thatched and creeper-covered inn is in an idyllic corner of rural England. It is delightfully straightforward and simply decorated, with mugs and jugs and gleaming horsebrasses.
🚶 🍴 🚭 ↗ 🎵

OXFORD: *Turf Tavern*
Bath Pl, St Helen's Passage, Oxford.
Tiny pub in the heart of the old collegiate quarter gives you an idea of cloistered quadrangles. Sit outside in fine weather. 🍴 🚭

WATTON-AT-STONE:
George & Dragon
High St, Watton-at-Stone, Herts.
Attractive pink building dating back to 1603. Smart but also welcoming; plenty of locals use it, and there are newspapers to read.
🚶 🍴 🚭 ↗

WEST ILSLEY: *Harrow*
Off A34 nr Newbury, Berkshire.
A stylish, white, tiled inn by the village pond, catering for walkers and racing folk. Up-market food.
🚶 🍴 🚭

WESSEX

ABBOTSBURY: *Ilchester Arms*
Market St, Abbotsbury, Dorset.
The pub is a main feature of this honey-coloured village near Chesil Beach. Warm, rambling rooms are smartly done up with prints. The restaurant has a conservatory extension. 🚶 🍴 🚭 ↗

BATHFORD: *Crown*
2 Bathford Hill, Bathford, Avon.
This hilly village has enjoyed its namesake hostelry since its 18th-century heyday. Now it is stylish inside, with ambitious food.
🚶 🍴 🚭 ↗ ❤

CROSCOMBE: *Bull Terrier*
On A371 nr Wells, Somerset.
One of Somerset's oldest pubs (originally a priory), this inn is much loved for good food, and has welcoming service. Try the Bull Terrier best bitter, and the walk to the Bishop's Palace at Wells.
🚶 🍴

FORD: *White Hart*
On A420 nr Chippenham, Wiltshire.
A delightful trout-stream setting adds a lot to this lovely 16th-century pub-hotel. It is very popular in summer. Good walks nearby. 🚶 🍴 🚭

NORTON ST PHILIP: *George*
On A366, Somerset.
This famous old pub sheltered the Duke of Monmouth before the Battle of Sedgemoor. It is a splendid half-timbered building with good food and an ancient galleried courtyard. 🚶 🍴 🚭

SALISBURY: *Haunch of Venison*
1 Minster St, Salisbury, Wiltshire.
Once the church house for St Thomas's, this ancient pub dates back 650 years. The severed, mummified hand of an 18th-century card-player is on display among more cheerful clutter in its genuinely antique interior.
🚶 🍴

STANTON WICK:
Carpenters Arms
Off A368, Avon.
A row of pretty converted miners' cottages contain this welcoming place with log fires. Excellent food is a major attraction. 🚶 🍴 🚭

DEVON AND CORNWALL

BROADHEMBURY: *Drewe Arms*
Off A373, Devon.
Fresh fish is one reason to come to this thatched village pub, but the West Country ales, garden and atmosphere add to its appeal.
🚶 🍴 🚭 ↗

DARTMOUTH: *Cherub*
13 High St, Dartmouth, Devon.
Dartmouth's oldest building, dating from 1380 and once a wool-merchant's house. Local fish prominent on the menu. 🍴

KNOWSTONE: *Masons Arms*
Off A361 nr South Molton, Devon.
One of Devon's favourite inns, with plenty of local life and welcoming hosts. The rustic decor includes farm tools. The big fireplace has a bread oven. Good bar food.
🚶 🍴 🚭 ↗

LYDFORD: *Castle Inn*
Off A386, Devon.
Pretty, pink-washed Tudor inn by a ruined castle and scenic river gorge. Staff are friendly, food is imaginative, and there's lots of historic interest. Good value rooms.
🚶 🍴 🚭 ↗

MYLOR BRIDGE: *Pandora Inn*
Off A39 nr Penryn, Cornwall.
Medieval thatched pub by the waterside. Popular with boating folk and crowded in summer. Bags of atmosphere. 🚶 🍴 🚭 ↗

PORT ISAAC:
Port Gaverne Hotel
Off B3314 nr Pendoggett, Cornwall.
Gorgeous seafront setting. A 17th-century building with panelling and maritime decor. Local seafood and excellent wine list. Good rooms available. 🚶 🍴 🚭

TREGADILLETT: *Eliot Arms*
Off A30 nr Launceston, Cornwall.
Cluttered with horsebrasses, old postcards, prints, books and china, and a curious collection of clocks.
🚶 🍴 ↗

THE HEART OF ENGLAND

ALDERMINSTER: *Bell*
On A34 nr Stratford-upon-Avon, Warwickshire.
Coaching inn conveniently near Stratford. A civilized place to stop for a meal with well-kept beers. Good wines too. 🚶 🍴 🚭 ↗

For key to symbols see back flap

BICKLEY MOSS:
Cholmondeley Arms
On A49, Cholmondeley, Cheshire.
Food draws the crowds to this
Victorian school room pub near
the castle grounds. Lots of period
interest inside.

BLOCKLEY: *Crown*
High St, Blockley, Gloucestershire.
Smart Elizabethan pub in a
gorgeous Cotswolds village. The
food and courtyard gardens are
a great draw.

BRETFORTON: *Fleece*
The Cross, Bretforton,
Hereford & Worcester.
Astonishing medieval house
owned by the National Trust, first
licensed in 1848. A living museum
of rural antiquities such as dough-
proving tables and cheese moulds.
Food is simple, but beers are
excellent. Lots of community
gatherings for Morris dancing.

CAULDON: *Yew Tree*
Off A523 Waterhouses, Stoke-on-
Trent, Staffs.
An extraordinary collection of
musical machines is on display
(working polyphones, pianolas,
symphonions), along with many
other fascinating bygones. The
interior is homely, with traditional
pub games. Simple snacks and
beers.

TUTBURY: *Dog & Partridge*
On A50 nr Burton-on-Trent, Staffs.
Imposing Tudor coaching inn,
agreeably modernized into bars
and family-oriented eating areas.
Pleasant service.

WENLOCK EDGE:
Wenlock Edge Inn
Hilltop, Much Wenlock, Shropshire.
There's a wood-burning stove and
friendly bar owner; Monday night
is story night. Good walks nearby
and rooms available.

EAST MIDLANDS

BIRCHOVER: *Druid Inn*
Main St, Birchover, Derbyshire.
Creeper-covered village pub with
a large menu of good fresh food.
Excellent walking centre with Row
Tor Rocks (allegedly a place of
Druid rituals) and Stanton Moor
nearby.

FOTHERINGHAY: *Falcon*
Main St, Fotheringhay, Northants.
A splendid pub, now modernized
to serve a range of excellent food.
The public bar keeps its original
character and local clientele.

GLOOSTON: *Old Barn Inn*
Andrews Lane, Glooston, Leicestershire.
Sixteenth-century inn with
tastefully renovated interior and
several cosy rooms. A la carte
menu and hand-pumped ales.
Rooms available.

MONSAL HEAD:
Monsal Head Hotel
On B6465, Derbyshire.
Former stable block with horsy
decor. Magnificent view of the
steep Wye valley from the hotel
lounge; good walks all round.

NOTTINGHAM:
Olde Trip to Jerusalem
Brewhouse Yard, Nottingham.
Unique pub built into sandstone
caverns once used as a meeting
place for crusaders. One of the
oldest in Britain.

STAMFORD: *George*
St Martins, Stamford, Lincolnshire.
Splendid old coaching inn with
vestiges of a Norman pilgrim hos-
pice. Now very elegant, it offers
an excellent range of food with
Italian wines. Pretty cobbled courtyard and gardens.

UPTON: *Cross Keys*
Main St, Upton, Nottinghamshire.
Beamed pub with hanging baskets
and pictures. Good bar food with
fresh fish. The restaurant is in the
old dovecote.

LANCASHIRE AND
THE LAKES

CARTMEL FELL: *Mason's Arms*
Off A5074 at Bowland Bridge sign,
Cumbria.
Lively, characterful pub with an
immense range of bottled beers,
real ales, cider and country wines.
Good walks nearby.

ELTERWATER: *Britannia Inn*
Off A593 nr Ambleside, Cumbria.
Unadorned rustic interior and
open fires in the Langdale valley.
An excellent walking or touring
base with rooms.

GARSTANG: *Th'Owd Tithebarn*
Off Church St, Garstang, Lancashire.
A converted barn by the canal
with rustic decor, popular with
walkers.

GREAT LANGDALE:
Old Dungeon Ghyll
On B5343, Langdale, Cumbria.
Dramatic setting near waterfalls in
the Langdale Pikes. A walking and
climbing base with rooms, plain
but cosy.

LIVERPOOL: *Philharmonic*
36 Hope St, Liverpool.
One of the most characterful
Merseyside haunts, a Victorian
setting with plasterwork, stained
glass and mahogany.

MANCHESTER: *Lass o' Gowrie*
36 Charles St, Manchester.
Popular student dive with a gaslit
bar and its own brewery in the
cellar. Lively at weekends.

NEAR SAWREY:
Tower Bank Arms
B5285, Near Sawrey, Cumbria.
This pretty village is a mecca for
Beatrix Potter fans. The pub backs
on to her house, Hill Top. Well-
preserved interior.

YORKSHIRE AND
HUMBERSIDE

ASKRIGG: *Kings Arms*
Off A684 nr Bainbridge, N Yorks.
The rustic interior is used as the
set in a TV series. Good bar food,
wines and beers are other reasons
to find it.

COXWOLD: *Fauconberg Arms*
Coxwold, N Yorks.
"Olde worlde" pub with antique
oak settles and Windsor armchairs
to sit on, and plenty of beer, wine,
and good food.

FLAMBOROUGH: *Seabirds*
On B1255, Flamborough, N Yorks.
The white chalk cliffs nearby are a
marvellous place for birdwatching.
Interesting interior. The fish is the
highlight of the menu.

GOATHLAND: *Mallyan Spout*
Off A169, Goathland, N Yorks.
Traditional moorland inn with a
relaxing air and good food. The
open fires make it popular with
walkers. Good rooms.

HULL: *Olde White Harte*
Off 25 Silver St, Hull, E Yorks.
This ancient tavern lies behind a
modern "White Hart". The interior
sports inglenook fireplaces and
copper-topped bar.

LOW CATTON: *Gold Cup*
Off A166 at Stamford Bridge, E Yorks.
The farm animals around add an
authentic touch to this rural pub
with comfortable, relaxing bars
and good food.

MOULTON: *Black Bull*
Off A1 nr Scotch Corner, N Yorks.
This pleasant old place puts
masses of energy into the food,
bar snacks and good wines. The
atmosphere is upmarket.

NORTHUMBRIA

BLANCHLAND: *Lord Crewe Arms*
Blanchland, Northumb.
Moorland hotel with priests' holes, 13th-century fireplaces and ghosts. Popular with walkers; good food and rooms. 🚶 🍽 🛏

CRASTER: *Jolly Fisherman*
Off B1339 nr Alnwick, Northumb.
Unassuming local pub with beautiful sea views. Home-made crab soup and seafood are specialities. Excellent cliff-top walks. 🚶 🍽 🛏 ✈

GRETA BRIDGE: *Morritt Arms*
Off A66 nr Scotch Corner, Co Durham.
A fine stone coaching inn with a splendid, spacious interior with oak settles. Attractive riverside setting. 🚶 🍽 🛏

NEW YORK:
Shiremoor House Farm
Off A191, New York, Tyne & Wear.
A skilful conversion from some derelict farm buildings, it is now comfortable and stylish. Has interesting food, and families welcome. 🚶 🍽 🛏

NEWCASTLE UPON TYNE:
Crown Posada
31 The Side, Newcastle upon Tyne.
A Victorian real ale pub with an ornate interior of gilt mirrors and stained glass. It is a city pub for drinkers, so no children are allowed.

SEAHOUSES: *Olde Ship*
On B1340, Seahouses, Northumb.
Maritime curiosities festoon this harbour-front inn. From the window you can see the Farne Islands. Good coastal walks. 🚶 🍽

NORTH WALES

BEAUMARIS: *Olde Bulls Head*
Castle St, Beaumaris, Anglesey.
A 500-year-old building with fascinating details inside including a 17th-century water clock, cutlasses and a witch's ducking stool. 🚶 🍽

BODFARI: *Dinorben Arms*
Off A541, Bodfari, Denbighshire.
Hillside pub with excellent bar food, lots of whiskies and a pleasant range of terraces for admiring the views. 🚶 🍽 🛏 ✈

CAPEL CURIG: *Bryn Tyrch Hotel*
On A5 nr Betws-y-Coed, A & C.
This inn is popular with walkers and climbers exploring the Snowdonia National Park. 🚶 🍽 🛏 ✈

GLANWYDDEN: *Queen's Head*
Off B5115, The Glanwydden, A & C.
Excellent pub food is a major draw at this village pub. It can get crowded in season. 🚶 🍽 🛏

MAENTWROG: *Grapes Hotel*
On A496, Maentwrog, A & C.
Coaching inn with lovely views and a walled garden. Much of the furniture was salvaged from disused chapels. 🚶 🍽 🛏

SOUTH AND
MID-WALES

ABERYSTWYTH: *Halfway Inn*
On A4120, Pisgah, Cardiganshire.
Rheidol Valley pub with stunning views. Comfy rooms, and free camping for customers. 🚶 🍽 🛏 ✈

CRICKHOWELL: *Bear*
Brecon Rd, Crickhowell, Powys.
Old inn with splendid food and excellent range of drinks. Period features and interesting decor. Bedrooms available. 🚶 🍽 🛏

EAST ABERTHAW: *Blue Anchor*
On B4265, East Aberthaw, V of Glam.
Charming thatched pub with low-ceilinged, intimate warren-like rooms and open fires. Estuary walks nearby. 🚶 🍽 🛏 ✈

HAY-ON-WYE: *Old Black Lion*
26 Lion St, Hay-on-Wye, Powys.
A 13th-century inn with restaurant food and 10 rooms. Lots of local sporting activities (fishing, riding, golf), plus bookshops. 🍽 🛏

NEVERN: *Trewern Arms*
On B4582, Nevern, Pembrokeshire.
Appealing riverside inn in a pretty village. The slate-floored bar is crammed with agricultural and domestic bygones. 🚶 🍽 🛏 ✈

PENALLT: *Boat Inn*
Long Lane, Penallt, Monmouthshire.
A mecca for music and ale right on the border; drinks are served in Wales. Disused railway cycle tracks and canoeing. 🚶 🍽 🛏 🎵

THE LOWLANDS

EDINBURGH: *Bow Bar*
80 West Bow, Edinburgh.
Bar of mahogany and mirrorglass, with malts and real ales. No children, games or music.

EDINBURGH:
Cafe Royal Circle Bar
West Register St, Edinburgh.
Refurbished in Victorian style –

tiled portraits of Scottish worthies, leather seating and chandeliers. Oyster bar and restaurant.

ELIE: *Ship Inn*
The Harbour, Elie, Fife.
Atmospheric quayside pub with nautical decor and attractive views. Summer barbecues are a feature. 🚶 🍽 🛏

GLASGOW: *Horseshoe*
17–19 Drury St, Glasgow.
Busy Victorian pub with a long bar and plenty of period features. Good value bar snacks. Karaoke in the evenings. 🚶 🍽 🎵

ISLE OF WHITHORN:
Steam Packet
Isle of Whithorn, Dumfries & Galloway.
Superb setting on a lovely harbour scene. Pleasant eating areas and real ales. Boat trips from the harbour. 🚶 🍽 🛏 ✈

THE HIGHLANDS
AND ISLANDS

APPLECROSS: *Applecross Inn*
Shore St, Applecross, Wester Ross, Highland.
Spectacularly located beyond Britain's highest mountain pass, this pub overlooks Skye. Local seafood is served, and there is music some evenings. 🚶 🍽 🛏 ✈ 🎵

DUNDEE: *Fishermans Tavern*
10-16 Fort St, Broughty Ferry, Tayside.
Award-winning real ales and lots of malts too. Good seafront and Tay rail bridge views. Rooms available. 🚶 🍽 🛏 ✈ 🎵

ISLE OF SKYE:
Tigh Osda Eilean Iarmain
Off A851, Isle Ornsay, Isle of Skye.
Welcoming hotel bar. Lots of malts and good bar food. Gorgeous setting. 🚶 🍽 🛏

LOCH LOMOND: *Oak Tree Inn*
Balmaha, Loch Lomond (east side).
Traditional stone inn with bar, restaurant and bed & breakfast; open fires in winter and good bar food served all day. 🚶 🍽 🛏 🎵

PORTSOY: *The Shore Inn*
The Old Harbour, Portsoy, Banffshire.
A 300-year-old seafaring inn nestling in a picturesque harbour. Traditional cask ale and a real open fire. 🚶 🍽 🛏 🎵

ULLAPOOL: *Ferry Boat*
Shore St, Ullapool, Highland.
Good whiskies and bar lunches, and fine views over the harbour. Coal fires and big windows overlooking the loch. 🚶 🍽 🎵

For key to symbols see back flap

SURVIVAL
GUIDE

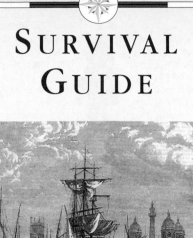

PRACTICAL INFORMATION

MILLIONS ANNUALLY seek out what the British often take for granted – the country's ancient history, colourful pageantry, and spectacularly varied countryside. The range of facilities on offer to visitors in Britain has expanded and improved considerably over the last few years. To enjoy Britain fully it is best to know something about the nuts and bolts of British life: when to visit, how to get around, where to find information and what to do if things go wrong. Whether or not you find Britain an expensive country will depend a lot on the exchange rate between the pound and your own currency. Prices vary within Britain; regional differences in some items are very noticeable. London, not surprisingly, is the most expensive. The knock-on effect extends to most of southern England, Britain's most affluent region. Entertainment, food, hotels, transport and consumer items in shops are generally cheaper in other parts of the country.

A mounted sentry, London

Weymouth beach, Dorset, on a busy public holiday weekend

WHEN TO VISIT

BRITAIN'S TEMPERATE maritime climate does not produce many temperature extremes (see p68). There are many fine days but it is impossible to predict rain or shine reliably in any season. Weather patterns shift constantly, and the climate can differ widely in places only a short distance apart. The southeast is generally drier than elsewhere. But wherever you are going be sure to pack a mix of warm and cool clothes and an umbrella. Always get an up-to-date weather forecast before you set off on foot to remote mountain areas or moorland. Walkers can be surprised by the weather, and the Mountain Rescue services are often called out due to

A sign for the Mountain Rescue

unexpectedly severe conditions. Weather reports are given on television and radio, in newspapers, or by phone services (see p637).

Britain's towns and cities are all-year destinations, but many attractions open only between Easter and October. Some hotels are crammed at Christmas and New Year. The main family holiday months, July and August, and public holidays (see p65) are always busy. Spring and autumn offer a compromise between some good weather and a relative lack of crowds. The information at the beginning of each attraction listed in this guide gives opening days.

INSURANCE

IT IS SENSIBLE to take out travel insurance to cover cancellation or curtailment of your holiday, theft or loss of money and possessions, and the cost of any medical treatment (see p620). It is better to arrange this in advance, although you can organize it once on your trip if necessary. If your country has a reciprocal medical arrangement with Britain (for example Australia, New Zealand and the EU), you can obtain free treatment under the National Health Service, but there are a number of forms to fill in. Certain benefits covered by medical insurance will not be included. North American and Canadian health plans or student identity cards may give you some protection against costs, but check the small print. If you want to drive a car in Britain, it is illegal to drive without third-party insurance and it is advisable to take out fully comprehensive insurance.

ADVANCE BOOKING

OUT OF SEASON, you should have few problems booking accommodation or transport at short notice, but in the high season, if you have set your heart on a popular West End show, luxury hotel, well-known restaurant, or specific flight or tour, always try to book ahead. Contact **VisitBritain** in your country, or a travel agent for advice and general information.

TOURIST INFORMATION

TOURIST INFORMATION is available in many towns and public places, including airports, main rail and coach stations and at some places of historical interest. These bureaux will be able to help you on almost anything in their area. Look out for the tourist information symbol, which can indicate anything from a large and busy central

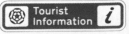

The most common English tourist information sign

◁ **Fishing boats in Scarborough port, North Yorkshire**

office to a simple kiosk or even an information board in a parking area.

Free leaflets are generally offered but a charge may be made for more detailed maps and booklets. Most tourist offices can suggest guided walks, places of interest and nearly all will reserve accommodation for you on request. During the busy holiday periods it is worth asking about the *Book-a-bed-ahead* scheme to places you intend to visit. Tourist office addresses and phone numbers are listed wherever possible in this guide. **VisitBritain**'s monthly magazine *In Britain,* available from tourist offices, contains articles about worthwhile places to visit and also includes a useful events diary.

VisitBritain's magazine

DISABLED TRAVELLERS

THE FACILITIES on offer for disabled visitors to Britain are steadily improving: recently designed or newly renovated buildings and public spaces now offer lifts and ramps for wheelchair access (information given in the headings for each entry in this book); specially designed toilets; grab rails, and for the hearing impaired, earphones. Given advance notice, British Rail *(see p638),* ferry or bus

staff will help any disabled passengers. Ask a travel agent about the Disabled Persons Railcard, which entitles you to discounted rail fares. Many banks, theatres and museums can now provide aids for the visually or hearing impaired. Specialist tour operators, such as **Holiday Care Service,** cater for the physically handicapped visitor. If renting a car, Hertz offers hand-controlled vehicles for hire without any extra cost *(see p637).* For permission to use any of the disabled parking spaces, you need to display a special sign in your car. For more general information contact **RADAR** or **Mobility International**.

One of the best series for disabled travellers is *Access* by Pauline Hephaistos, published by Survey Projects. You could also try *Holidays in the British Isles: a Guide for Disabled People* (RADAR), and *The World Wheelchair Traveller* by Ann Tyrrell and Susan Abbott (AA).

RADAR
📞 020-7250 3222.
🔲 www.radar.org.uk

Mobility International
North America 📞 541 343 1284.

Holiday Care Service
📞 08451 249971.
🔲 www.holidaycare.org.uk

Lorna Doone Cottage and National Trust Information Centre, Somerset

A visit to HMS Victory (p157)

TRAVELLING WITH CHILDREN

BRITAIN IS NOT the easiest or most welcoming place for young children, but things are slowly changing.

Peak holiday times – Easter, July and August – and school holidays have most to offer in the way of entertainment for children. Many places have something child-centred going on at Christmas too, particularly pantomimes. Discounts for children, or family tickets, are now widely available for travel, theatre shows and other entertainments.

Choose accommodation that welcomes children, or opt for self-catering solutions with hard-wearing furnishings and room in which to run around. Many hotels now provide baby-sitting or baby-listening services, and may offer reductions or free accommodation for very young children (see pp538–73).

Restaurants are becoming less child-phobic than they used to be and many now provide highchairs and special child menus (see pp574–607). Italian eateries are often the most friendly and informal, but even the British pub, once resolutely child-free, is now relenting with beer gardens and family rooms. Under-18s are not permitted near the bars and must not buy or consume alcohol. The annual publication *Family Welcome* (HarperCollins) is available from newsagents and lists those places where children are made welcome.

PUBLIC TOILETS

ALTHOUGH MANY older-style supervised public toilets still exist, these have largely been replaced by the modern free-standing, coin-operated "Superloos". Young children should never use these toilets on their own.

STUDENT TRAVELLERS

FULL-TIME STUDENTS who have an International Student Identity Card (ISIC), are often entitled to discounts on things like travel, sports facilities and entrance fees. North American students can also get medical cover but it may be very basic (see p620). If you don't have an ISIC, they are available from **STA Travel**, or the **National Union of Students**.

An **International Youth Hostel Federation** card enables you to stay in Britain's hundreds of youth hostels. Inexpensive accommodation is also available (out of term) at many of the university halls of residence – such as the **University of London** – a good way of staying in city centres on a tight budget. If you are exploring the wilder regions of Britain, sleeping quarters can be found in camping barns (dormitory-style bunkhouses) which, though spartan, cost very little. For information on working in Britain, contact **BUNAC**.

Great British Heritage Pass

BUSINESS HOURS

MANY BUSINESSES and shops are closed on Sundays, though trading is now legal. Monday to Friday hours are generally 9 or 10am to 5 or 5:30pm, but shop hours can vary, with late shopping one evening a week, and lunch-time or even half-day closing – usually a Wednesday.

Museums in London often open late one day a week, but those outside the capital may have more inflexible hours, sometimes closing during the morning, or for one day a week – often on Mondays.

On public holidays, known as bank holidays in Britain, banks, offices, most shops, restaurants and attractions will generally close.

ADMISSION CHARGES

THESE VARY WIDELY from a nominal 50p to over £10 for the popular attractions, although many of the major national museums are now free. Museums now combine entertainment with education, and are livelier than ever before.

Alongside this move, however, there is sometimes a rise in admission charges. But reductions are often available for groups, senior citizens, children or students (proof of identity will be required). Visitors from overseas may buy a

The privately owned, admission-charging, Hever Castle (see p177)

A Cotswold church, one of hundreds of parish churches open to the public free of charge

Great British Heritage Pass, which gives access to over 600 sights, available from VisitBritain offices abroad and, in the UK, from the Britain Visitor Centre in London's Lower Regent Street and some ports of entry and Tourist Information Centres *(see p615)*. A few local authority museums and art galleries are free, but dona-tions are always welcome. Other sights are in private hands, run either as a commercial venture or on a charitable basis. Stately homes open to the public may still belong to the gentry who have lived there for centuries; a charge is made to defray the enormous costs of upkeep. Many of these beautiful houses have added safari parks or garden centres to encourage and attract more visitors, such as Woburn Abbey *(see p218)*.

Britain's thousands of small parish churches are among the country's greatest archi-tectural treasures. None of the churches charge an entrance fee, although some, sadly, are locked because of vandalism. Increasingly, many of the great cathedrals expect a donation from visitors.

Information leaflets, National Trust

ENGLISH HERITAGE AND THE NATIONAL TRUST

M ANY OF BRITAIN'S historic buildings, parks, gardens, and vast tracts of countryside and coastline are cared for by **English Heritage** (EH), the **National Trust** (NT) or the **National Trust for Scotland** (NTS). We identify EH, NT and NTS properties at the beginning of each entry. Entrance fees are often high, so if you wish to visit several stately homes it may be worth taking out annual member-ship, which allows free access thereafter to any of their properties (remember many are closed in winter)

Many of the NT's properties are "listed". These are buildings or sites that are recognized as having special architectural or historical interest and therefore fully protected from alterations and demolition.

ENGLISH HERITAGE

The sign and symbol of English Heritage

USEFUL ADDRESSES

BUNAC
16 Bowling Green Lane, London EC1R 0QH. ☎ 020-7251 3472.
🗔 www.bunac.org

English Heritage (EH)
PO Box 569, Swindon SN2 2YP.
☎ 0870 333 1181.
🗔 www.english-heritage.org.uk

International Youth Hostel Federation
☎ 0870 770 8868.
🗔 www.hihostels.com

National Trust (NT)
PO Box 39, Bromley, Kent, BR1 3XL. ☎ 0870-458 4000.
🗔 www.nationaltrust.org.uk

National Trust for Scotland (NTS)
28 Charlotte Sq, Edinburgh EH2 4ET. ☎ 0131 243 9300.
🗔 www.nts.org.uk

National Union of Students
☎ 020-7272 8900.
🗔 www.nusonline.co.uk

STA Travel
Priory Hse, 6 Wrights Lane, London W8 6TA.
☎ 0870 160 0599.
🗔 www.statravel.co.uk

University of London
Malet St, London WC1.
☎ 020-7862 8880.
🗔 www.housing.lon.ac.uk/looking/short stay

USEFUL PUBLICATIONS

BOTH THE REGIONAL and national tourist boards produce comprehensive lists of local attractions and registered accommodation. For route planning, excellent, clear, large-format motoring atlases are produced by the RAC and AA *(see p637)*. For rural exploration, *Ordnance Survey* maps are ideal.

MEDIA

BRITISH NATIONAL newspapers fall into two categories: broadsheets – quality papers, such as *The Times* or *The Guardian* – and tabloids, heavy on gossip, such as *The Sun* or *The Daily Mirror.*

The weekend newspapers are more expensive than dailies but are packed with supplements of all kinds, including sections on the arts, motoring, entertainment, travel, listings and reviews.

Specialist periodicals are available from newsagents on just about every topic from hamster-keeping to hi-fi. For a more in-depth analysis of current events buy *The Economist, New Statesman & Society* or *The Spectator,* while *Private Eye* cocks a satirical snook at public figures. There are a few foreign magazines and newspapers available in large towns, often at main railway stations, but mostly in London. One of the most popular is the *International Herald Tribune,* which is available on the day of issue.

Television is undergoing an upheaval in Britain as satellite and cable networks invade the airwaves. Still more influential,

Some of Britain's national newspapers

A local newsagent and sub-post office at Arisaig, Scotland

however, is the state-run BBC (British Broadcasting Corporation), which operates two terrestrial channels and maintains its reputation for producing some of the best television in the world without commercial breaks. The BBC's three commercial rivals are ITV, Channel Four and Channel 5, the first tending toward popular soap operas and game-shows, Channel Four catering for trendy and minority tastes (art films, offbeat chat shows, game-shows and documentaries), and the last relying on US imports and TV movies. There are also regional variations.

The BBC has a number of radio stations, ranging from pop music (Radio One) to the middlebrow Radio Four. There are many local commercial radio stations.

Full TV and radio schedules are listed in daily newspapers and several listings magazines; one of the best is the *Radio Times,* a weekly publication found in most newsagents.

SMOKING

IT IS NOW forbidden to smoke in many public places in Britain. These include most public transport systems, taxis, theatres and cinemas. The exception to the anti-smoking trend is pubs. ASH (Action on Smoking and Health) can advise on smoke-free venues (020-7935 3519).

WORKING RESTRICTIONS

RESIDENTS OF THE EU can work in Britain with no permit, while Commonwealth citizens under the age of 27 may work part-time for up to two years in the UK. North American students can get a blue card through their university, which enables them to work for up to six months – get this before arrival in Britain. BUNAC *(see p617)* is a student club which will organize exchange schemes for students to work abroad.

ELECTRICITY

THE VOLTAGE IN Britain is 220/240 AC, 50 Hz. Electrical plugs have three square pins and take fuses of 3, 5 and 13 amps. Visitors will need an adaptor for North American or continental appliances which have been bought from home, such as portable computers, hairdriers and tape recorders. Most hotels will have two-pronged European-style sockets for shavers only.

Standard British three-pin plug

Clock, the Royal Observatory, Greenwich *(see p133)*

TIME

BRITAIN IS ON Greenwich Mean Time (GMT) during the winter months, five hours ahead of Eastern Standard Time and ten hours behind Sydney. From the middle of March to October, the clocks go forward one hour to British Summer Time (equivalent to Central European Time). To check the correct time, you can dial 123 to contact the Speaking Clock service.

Customs and Immigration

A VALID PASSPORT is needed to enter Britain. Visitors from the European Union (EU), the United States, Canada, New Zealand and Australia do not require visas to enter the country. Nor are inoculations or vaccinations necessary. When you arrive at any British air or seaport you will find separate queues at immigration control – one for European Union nationals, and several others for everyone else. As a result of Britain's membership of the European Union, anyone who arrives in Britain from a member country can pass through a blue channel – but random checks are still being made to detect entry of any prohibited goods, particularly drugs, indecent material and weapons. Never, under any circumstances, carry luggage or parcels through customs for someone else.

Highland malt

Travellers entering from outside the EU still have to pass through customs channels. Go through the green channel if you have nothing to declare over the customs allowances for overseas visitors, and the red channel if you have goods to declare. If you are unsure of importation restrictions go through the red channel.

Limits on the quantities of alcohol are: two litres of still table wine plus one litre of alcoholic drink over 22 per cent vol or two litres of alcoholic drink not over 22 per cent vol; for tobacco products the limits are: 200 cigarettes or 50 cigars. You are allowed up to £145 worth of other goods

Green and red customs channels at Heathrow airport *(see p634)*

including gifts, souvenirs, cider and beer. No live animals may be imported without a permit as Britain is free of rabies. Any animals found will be impounded and may be destroyed. Non-EU residents can obtain a VAT refund on goods bought in Britain *(see p626)*.

HM Customs and Excise

Thomas Paine House, Angel Square, Torrens St, London EC1.
█ *020-7865 3000; advice line 0845 0109000. Contact for information regarding import or export restrictions.* W *www.hmce.gov.uk*

The mosque in Regent's Park *(see p105)*, **London**

Religious Organizations

Baptist

London Baptist Assn, 235 Shaftesbury Ave., London WC2. █ *020-7692 5592.* W *www.londonbaptist.org.uk*

Buddhist

Buddhist Society, 58 Eccleston Sq, London SW1. █ *020-7834 5858.* W *www.thebuddhistsociety.org.uk*

Church of England

Great Smith St, London SW1.
█ *020-7898 1000.*
W *www.cofe.anglican.org*

Evangelical Alliance

Whitefield Hse, 186 Kennington Park Rd, London SE11.
█ *020-7207 2100.* W *www.eauk.org*

Jewish

Liberal Jewish Synagogue, 28 St John's Wood Rd, London NW8. █ *020-7286 5181.* W *www.ljs.org*

United Synagogue (Orthodox), Adler House, 735 High Rd, North Finchley, London, N12.
█ *020-8343 8989.*
W *www.unitedsynagogue.org.uk*

Moslem

Islamic Cultural Centre, 146 Park Rd, London NW8. █ *020-7724 3363.*
W *www.icc.uk.org*

Quakers

Friends Hse, 173–177 Euston Rd, London NW1. █ *020-7663 1000.*
W *www.quaker.org.uk*

Roman Catholic

Westminster Cathedral, Victoria St, London SW1.
█ *020-7798 9055.*
W *www.westminstercathedral.org.uk*

Embassies and Consulates

Australian High Commission

Australia Hse, the Strand, London WC2.
█ *020-7379 4334.*
W *www.australia.org.uk*

Canadian High Commission

Canada Hse, Trafalgar Sq, London SW1.
█ *020-7258 6600.*
W *www.canada.gc.ca*

New Zealand High Commission

New Zealand Hse, 80 Haymarket, London SW1.
█ *020-7930 8422.*
W *www.nzembassy.com*

United States Embassy

24 Grosvenor Sq, London W1.
█ *020-7499 9000.*
W *www.usembassy.org.uk*

Conversion Chart

Britain is officially metricated in line with the rest of Europe, but imperial measures are still in common usage, including road distances (measured in miles). Imperial pints and gallons are 20 per cent larger than US measures.

Imperial to metric
1 inch = 2.5 centimetres
1 foot = 30 centimetres
1 mile = 1.6 kilometres
1 ounce = 28 grams
1 pound = 454 grams
1 pint = 0.6 litres
1 gallon = 4.6 litres

Metric to imperial
1 millimetre = 0.04 inch
1 centimetre = 0.4 inch
1 metre = 3 feet 3 inches
1 kilometre = 0.6 mile
1 gram = 0.04 ounce
1 kilogram = 2.2 pounds

Personal Security and Health

BRITAIN IS A DENSELY POPULATED COUNTRY which, like any other, has its share of social problems. However, it is very unlikely that you will come across any violence. If you do encounter difficulties, never hesitate to contact the police for help. Britain's National Health Service can be relied upon for both emergency and routine treatment. However, you may have to pay if your country has no reciprocal arrangement with Britain.

HOSPITALS AND MEDICAL TREATMENT

ALL VISITORS to Britain are strongly advised to take out medical insurance against the cost of any emergency hospital care, repatriation and specialists' fees, especially for those visitors from outside the European Union (EU). Emergency medical treatment in a British National Health Service (NHS) casualty ward is free, but any kind of additional medical care could prove very expensive.

Residents of the European Union and nationals of some other Commonwealth and European countries are entitled to free medical treatment under the NHS, though the process is bureaucratic. Before travelling, you should obtain a form confirming that your country of origin has adequate reciprocal health arrangements with Britain. But some treatments are not covered and repatriation is not included, so medical insurance is preferable.

If you need to see a dentist while staying in Britain, you will have to pay. The cost varies, depending on your entitlement to NHS treatment, and whether you can find an NHS dentist to treat you. Emergency dental treatment is available in some hospitals, but if you would prefer a private dentist, try looking in the *Yellow Pages (see p622)*.

PHARMACISTS

YOU CAN BUY a wide range of proprietary medicines without prescription from chemists in Britain. Boots is the best-known and largest

supplier, with branches in most towns. Many medicines, however, are only available with a doctor's prescription, which you must take to a chemist or pharmacist. If you are likely to need drugs, either bring your own or get your doctor to write out the generic (as opposed to the brand) name of the drug. If you are entitled to an NHS prescription, you will be charged a standard rate; without this you will be charged the full cost of the drug. Do ask for a receipt for any insurance claim. Some pharmacies are open until midnight; for emergencies contact the local hospital. Doctors' surgeries are normally open mornings and early evenings. You can call NHS Direct 24-hour helpline (0845 4647), or go to a hospital casualty department any time. In an emergency, dial 999 for an ambulance.

Pharmacy sign

CRIME

BRITAIN IS NOT a dangerous place for visitors, and it is most unlikely that your stay will be blighted by crime. Practical advice to help you avoid loss or injury is given below. Due to past terrorist attacks, there are occasional security alerts, especially on the Underground, but these are mainly false alarms often due to people accidentally leaving a bag or parcel lying around. Always co-operate with the authorities if your bag has to be searched or if you are asked to evacuate a building.

SUITABLE PRECAUTIONS

TAKE GOOD CARE of your belongings at all times. Make sure your possessions are adequately insured before you arrive. Never leave them unattended in public places.

Keep your valuables well concealed (particularly mobile phones), especially in crowds. In all public places, keep handbags on your lap, not on the floor. It is always advisable not to carry too much cash or jewellery with you; leave it in your hotel safe instead. Pickpockets love crowded places like markets, busy shops and all modes of transport during rush-hour.

Female police constable

Traffic police officer

Male police constable

If you are travelling alone at night try to avoid deserted and poorly lit buildings and places such as back streets and car parks. By far the safest way of carrying large amounts of cash around is in traveller's cheques *(see p625)*.

Begging is an increasingly common sight in many British cities, and foreign visitors are frequent targets for hard-luck stories. Requests for money are usually polite; but any abuse should be reported to the police immediately.

WOMEN TRAVELLING ALONE

IT IS NOT UNUSUAL in Great Britain for women to travel unaccompanied, or visit a bar or restaurant with a group of female friends. Nor is it especially dangerous, but caution is advisable in deserted places, especially after dark. Try to avoid using public transport when there is just one other passenger or a group of young men. Summon a licensed taxi *(see p642)* rather than walk through a lonely area at night, especially if you do not know the district very well.

Legally, you cannot carry any offensive weapons around with you in Britain, even for self-defence. This include knives, coshes, guns or tear-gas; however, personal alarm systems are allowed.

POLICE

THE SIGHT of a traditional British bobby patrolling the streets in a tall hat is now less common than the police patrol car, sometimes with wailing sirens and flashing lights. But the old-fashioned police constable does still exist, particularly in rural areas and in crowded city centres, and continues to be courteous, approachable and helpful.

Unlike in many countries, the police force in Great Britain do not carry guns. If you are lost, the advice to

Police car

Ambulance

Fire engine

ask a policeman or woman still applies. Traffic wardens may also be able to help you with directions.

In a crisis, dial 999 to get the police, fire and ambulance services which are on call 24-hours a day. Calls are free from any public or private phone, but they should only be made in real emergencies. Along the coastal areas of Great Britain this number will also put you in touch with Britain's voluntary coastguard rescue service, the Royal National Lifeboat Institute.

Royal National Lifeboat Institute logo

LOST PROPERTY

IF YOU ARE UNLUCKY enough to lose anything or have anything stolen, go straight to the nearest police station and make a report of your loss. If you plan to make a claim on your insurance for any theft, you will need a written report from the local police. All of the main bus or rail stations have lost property offices. Don't leave your valuables on display in your room: hotels usually disclaim all responsibility for valuables not kept in their safe.

Communications

Modern BT phone box

W ITH CONTINUOUSLY IMPROVING telecommuni-
cation systems and the spread of e-mail,
staying in contact and making plans while
travelling has never been easier. The telephone system in Britain is efficient and
inexpensive. Charges depend on when, where
and for how long you talk. The cheapest time
to call is between 6pm and 8am Monday to
Friday, and throughout the weekend. Local
calls made on public payphones, however,
are charged at a fixed rate per minute.

PAYPHONES

Y OU CAN PAY for a payphone
using coins or a card.
Payphones accept 10p, 20p,
50p and £1 pieces, while
newer phones also accept £2
coins. The minimum cost of a
call is 20p. If you expect a
call to be short, use 10p or
20p pieces, as payphones
only return unused coins. You
may find a phone card more
convenient than coins. BT
(formerly British Telecom)
has now stopped issuing its
own prepaid phone cards,
but other phone companies'
cards are available from
newsagents and post offices.
If you use a credit card, be
warned that it carries a
minimum charge and your
phone calls will be charged
at a higher rate.

TELEPHONE DIRECTORIES

D IRECTORIES, SUCH as *Yellow
Pages* and *Thomson Local*,
list local businesses and services. They can be found at
local Post Office branches, libraries and often at your hotel.

USING A CARD AND COIN PHONE

1 Lift the receiver and wait
for the dial tone.

2 Insert your phone card into
the slot or deposit any of the
following coins: 10p, 20p, 50p, £1,
£2. The minimum amount is 20p.

3 Dial the number and
wait to be connected.

4 The display indicates how
much credit you have
left. A rapid bleeping noise
means your money has run
out. Deposit more coins or
insert another phone card.

5 If you want to make
another call and you have
money left in credit, do not
replace the receiver, press
the follow-on-call button.

6 When you have finished
speaking, replace the
receiver and retrieve your
card or collect your change.
Only wholly unused coins
are refunded.

£1   50p   20p   10p

USEFUL NUMBERS

A number of telephone services
exist to help you find or reach a
specific phone number. You will
be charged more for enquiries if
calling from a mobile phone.

Emergency Calls
🕻 *999. Police, Fire,
Ambulance, Coastguard,
Mountain and Cave Rescue.*

BT Directory Enquiries
🕻 *118 500 (charge applies).*

**International Directory
Enquiries**
🕻 *118 505 (charge applies).*

International Operator
🕻 *155 (charge applies).*

Operator Assistance
🕻 *100.*

Overseas Calls
🕻 *00 followed by country code:
Australia (61), Canada (1), Ireland
(353), New Zealand (64), South
Africa (27), United States (1).*

Yellow Pages
🕻 *118 247. Provides numbers
for specific kinds of shops or
services in any area.*

ACCESSING THE INTERNET

M OST CITIES AND towns now
have some form of
public access to computers
and the Internet, including
payphones in the street. Free
Internet access is often available at main library branches,
although you may have to
book a time slot. Hotels are
increasingly including Internet
facilities as part of their
service. Internet cafés usually
charge by the minute for
computer use. Charges tend
to build up quickly, especially
when including the cost of
printed pages. Internet access
is generally very cheap and is
most reasonable during off-
peak times.

**24-hour Internet access at the
Europe-wide chain EasyEverything**

Sending a Letter

Red and gold Post Office logo

BESIDES MAIN POST OFFICE branches that offer all the mail services available, there are many Post Office outlets in newsagents, grocery stores and general information centres, particularly in more isolated areas. In many villages the Post Office outlet is also the only shop. Post Office branches are usually open from 9am to 5:30pm Monday to Friday, and until 12:30pm on Saturday. Post boxes – in all shapes and sizes but always red – are found throughout cities, towns and villages.

A Cotswold Post Office outlet

POSTAL SERVICES

STAMPS CAN BE BOUGHT at many outlets, including supermarkets and petrol stations. Hotels often have post boxes at their reception. When writing to a British address always include the postcode, which can be obtained from either the **Royal Mail** enquiry line or

All air letters are 1st class

1st-class stamp   2nd-class stamp

Greetings stamps featuring characters from children's fiction

website. Letters and postcards can be sent either first or second class within the UK. First-class service is more expensive but quicker, with most letters reaching their destination the following day (except Sunday); second-class mail takes a day or two longer.

Royal Mail
0845 7740740.
www.royalmail.com

POSTE RESTANTE

LARGE URBAN Post Office branches have a *poste restante* service where letters can be sent for collection. To use the service be sure to print the surname (last name) clearly so it will be filed correctly. Send it to P*oste Restante* followed by the address of the Post Office branch. To collect your post you will have to show your passport or other form of identification. Post is kept for one month. London's main Post Office branch is in William IV Street, WC2. The American Express office at 30–31 Haymarket, London SW1 has a *poste restante* for customers.

POST BOXES

THESE MAY BE either freestanding "pillar boxes" or wall safes, both painted bright red. Some pillar boxes have separate slots, one for overseas and first-class mail, another for second-class mail. Collections are usually made several times a day during weekdays (less often on Saturdays and Sundays); the last collection time is marked on the box.

A rural mailbox, embedded in a stone wall

MAILING ABROAD

Pillar box

AIR LETTERS go by Royal Mail's airmail service anywhere in the world; the cost depends on the destination. On average, it takes 3 days for them to reach cities in Europe, and 4 to 6 days for destinations elsewhere. Sending post by surface mail may be economical, but it can take up to 8 weeks for it to reach its destination. Royal Mail offers an express airmail service called **Airsure**. Available from all Post Office branches, mail goes on the first available flight to the country of destination. **Parcelforce Worldwide** offers courier-style services to most destinations and is comparable in price to **Crossflight**, **DHL**, **Expressair** or **UPS**.

Airsure (Royal Mail)
08457 740740.
www.royalmail.com

Crossflight
01753 776000.
www.crossflight.co.uk

DHL
08701 100300. www.dhl.com

Expressair
020-8897 6568.
www.expressair.co.uk

Parcelforce Worldwide
08708 501150.
www.parcelforce.com

UPS
08457 877877. www.ups.com

Banking and Local Currency

VISITORS TO BRITAIN usually find that the high-street banks offer them the best rates of exchange. However, if you do find yourself having to use one of the hundreds of privately owned bureaux de change that are found at nearly every major airport, rail station and tourist area, care should be taken to check the commission and minimum charges before completing any transaction. Traveller's cheques are by far the safest method of bringing currency to Britain with you.

Lloyds Bank with bureau de change facilities

BUREAUX DE CHANGE

SMALL PRIVATE bureaux de change may be more conveniently located and open when banks are closed. But rates of exchange can vary considerably and commission charges can be high, so it may be worth looking around.

The reputable firms such as **Exchange International**, **Travelex**, **American Express** and **Chequepoint** usually offer good exchange facilities and have branches throughout Britain.

British Banks
All these high-street banks have branches in most of Britain's towns and cities. Most will also offer exchange facilities, but proof of identity may be required.

Barclays Bank logo

HSBC Bank logo

Lloyds TSB Bank logo

BANKS

BANKS GENERALLY offer the best rates of exchange for visitors, though commissions may vary considerably.

Every large town and city in Britain will have a branch of at least one of these five high-street clearing banks – **Barclays**, **Lloyds TSB**, **HSBC**, **National Westminster**, and the **Royal Bank of Scotland**. Many banks have an ATM (cash dispenser) from which you can obtain money with a credit card and your personal identification number (PIN); arrange this before you leave home. Some of the most modern machines have easy-to-read computerized instructions in several languages. American Express cards may be used at all ATM cash machines. Once again you will need a PIN number to access your personal account. There is a 2 per cent handling charge for each transaction that you make.

If you run out of funds, another way to get money is to contact your own bank

National Westminster logo

The Royal Bank of Scotland logo

and ask them to wire the cash to the nearest British bank. You can also ask branches of Travelex or American Express to do this for you. North American visitors can get cash dispatched through **Western Union** to a bank or post office. Take along your passport to claim the money.

Banking hours vary, but the minimum opening times are 10am to 3:30pm, Monday to Friday. Many will stay open longer, especially in cities, and some open Saturday mornings. All banks close on Public Holidays *(see p65)*.

CREDIT CARDS

CREDIT AND STORE cards are widely accepted throughout Britain, and you will definitely need a credit card in order to rent a car and usually for hotel bookings. But many smaller shops, markets, guesthouses and cafés may not accept them, so it is always wise to check in advance. Cards that are accepted are usually displayed on the windows of the establishment. The main card used throughout Britain is Visa, but other credit cards include Diners Club, American Express, Access and Mastercard.

You can get cash advances with a credit card (up to your credit limit) at any bank and ATM cash machine displaying the appropriate card sign. You will be charged the credit card company's interest rate for obtaining cash, which will appear on your statement with the amount advanced when you return home.

Exchange International
[020-7630 1107.

Travelex
[07333 18901.

American Express
[020-7834 5555.
[w] www.americanexpress.co.uk

Chequepoint
[020-7373 0111.
[w] www.chequepoint.com

Western Union
[0800 833 833.
[w] www.westernunion.com

CURRENCY AND TRAVELLER'S CHEQUES

Britain's currency is the pound sterling (£), which is divided into 100 pence (p). There are no exchange controls in Britain, so you may bring in and take out as much cash as you like. Scotland has its own notes, which, though legal tender throughout Britain, are not always accepted in England and Wales. Traveller's cheques are the safest alternative to carrying large amounts of cash.

A Scottish one pound (£1) bank note

Always keep the receipts from your traveller's cheques separately from the cheques themselves because it makes it easier to obtain a refund if your cheques are lost or stolen. Some high-street banks issue traveller's cheques free of commission to their account holders, but the normal rate is about 1 per cent. When changing money ask for some smaller notes, as these are easier to use.

Bank Notes
English notes are produced in denominations of £5, £10, £20, and £50. Always get small denominations as some shops may refuse the larger notes.

£50 note

£20 note

£10 note

£5 note

Coinage
Coins currently in use are £2, £1, 50p, 20p, 10p, 5p, 2p and 1p (shown here at actual sizes).

2 pounds (£2)

1 pound (£1)

50 pence (50p)

20 pence (20p)

10 pence (10p)

5 pence (5p)

2 pence (2p)

1 penny (1p)

Shopping in Britain

WHILE THE WEST END OF LONDON *(see pp124–5)* is undeniably Britain's most exciting place to shop, many regional centres offer nearly as wide a range of goods. Moreover regional shopping can be less stressful, less expensive, and remarkably varied, with craft studios, farm shops, street markets and factory showrooms adding to the enjoyment of bargain-hunting. Britain is famous for its country clothing: wool, waxed cotton and tweed are all popular, along with classic prints such as Liberty or Laura Ashley and tartan. Other particularly British goods include antiques, floral soaps and scents, porcelain, glass and local crafts.

Antiques stall at Bermondsey Market

SHOPPING HOURS

IN GENERAL, you can assume most shops in Britain will open during the week from 9am or 10am, and they will close after 5pm or 6pm. Hours on Saturdays may be shorter. Few town centre shops open on Sundays, unless it is near Christmas. Some stores open late for one evening a week – Thursday in London's West End – while village shops may close at lunch-time, or for one afternoon each week. Market days vary from town to town; some markets *(see pp124–5)* are held on Sundays.

HOW TO PAY

MOST LARGE SHOPS all over the UK will accept well-known credit cards such as Access and VISA. Charge cards such as American Express or Diners Club are acceptable in some places, but Marks & Spencer, markets and some small shops will not take credit cards. Traveller's cheques can be used in larger stores, though exchange rates for non-sterling cheques may be poor. Take your passport with you for identification. Few places will accept cheques drawn on foreign banks. Cash is still the most popular way to pay for small purchases.

RIGHTS AND REFUNDS

IF SOMETHING YOU BUY is defective, you are entitled to a refund, provided you have kept your receipt as proof of purchase and return the goods in the same condition as when you bought them, and preferably in the same packaging. This may not always apply to sale goods clearly marked as seconds, imperfect, or shop-soiled. Inspect these carefully before you buy. You do not have to accept a credit note in place of a cash refund.

Vivienne Westwood's designer label

Sign for the Lanes, Brighton *(see p163)*

ANNUAL SALES

TRADITIONALLY, sales take place during January, and in June and July, when nearly every shop cuts prices to get rid of slow-selling or imperfect stock. But you may well find special offers at any time of the year. Some shops begin their winter sales just before Christmas. Department stores and fashion houses have some excellent bargains for keen shoppers; one of the most prestigious sales is at Harrod's *(see p99)*, where queues will usually form long before opening time.

VAT AND TAX-FREE SHOPPING

VALUE ADDED TAX (VAT) is charged on most goods and services sold in Britain – exceptions include food, books and children's clothes. It is usually included in the advertised price. Visitors from outside the European Union who stay less than three months may claim this tax back. Take your passport with you whenever you go shopping. You must complete a form in the shop when you buy your goods and give a copy to the customs authorities when you leave the country. You may have to show your goods as proof of purchase. If you arrange to have the goods shipped from the store, the VAT should be deducted before you pay.

OUT-OF-TOWN SHOPPING CENTRES

THESE LARGE COMPLEXES, built along the lines of North American malls, are rapidly increasing around Britain. The advantages of car access and easy, cheap parking are undeniable, and most centres are accessible by public transport too. The centres usually feature clusters of popular high street stores, with many services on offer such as toilets, cafés, crèches, restaurants and cinemas.

A traditional shop front in Stonegate, York *(see p390)*

DEPARTMENT STORES

A FEW BIG DEPARTMENT stores, such as Harrod's, are only found in London, but others have provincial branches. John Lewis, for example, has shops in 22 locations. It sells a huge range of fabrics, clothing and household items, combining quality service with good value. Marks & Spencer, with branches in most major towns and cities in Britain, is famed for its good-value clothing and pre-prepared food. Debenhams and British Home Stores (BhS) are other well-known general stores with inexpensive clothing and home furnishings. Habitat is a reputable supplier of modern furniture. The sizes of all these stores, and the range of stock they carry, will differ from region to region.

Local Teesdale cheeses

CLOTHES SHOPS

ONCE AGAIN, London has the widest range, from *haute couture* to cheap and cheerful items ready-made. Shopping for clothing in the regions, however, can often be less tiring. Many towns popular with tourists – Oxford, Bath and York for instance – have independently owned clothes shops where you receive a more personal service. Or you could try one of the chain stores in any high street such as Principles or Next for smart, reasonably priced clothes, and Top Shop and Miss Selfridge for younger and cheaper fashions.

SUPERMARKETS AND FOODSHOPS

SUPERMARKETS are a good way to shop for food. The range and quality of items in stock is usually excellent. Several large chains compete for market share and as a result prices are generally lower than smaller shops. Sainsbury, Tesco, Asda, Safeway and Waitrose are some of the national names. However, the smaller town-centre shops such as local bakeries, greengrocers or farm shops, may give you a more interesting choice of fresh regional produce, and more personal service.

SOUVENIR, GIFT AND MUSEUM SHOPS

BUYING PRESENTS is a must for most travellers. Most reputable large stores can arrange freight of high-value

The Mustard Shop *(see p189)*, Norwich

items. If you want to buy things you can carry back in your suitcase, the choice is wide. You can buy attractive, well-made, portable craft items all over the country, especially in areas tourists are likely to visit. For slightly more unusual presents, have a look in museum shops and the gifts available in National Trust *(see p25)* and English Heritage *(see p617)* properties.

SECONDHAND AND ANTIQUE SHOPS

B RITAIN'S LONG HISTORY means there are many interesting artifacts to be found. A visit to any of Britain's stately homes will reveal a national passion for antiques. Most towns will have an antique or bric-a-brac (miscellaneous second-hand items) shop or two. Look for auctions – tourist information centres *(see pp614–15)* can help you to locate them. You may like to visit a jumble or car boot sale in the hope of picking up a bargain.

Book stall, Hay-on-Wye, Wales *(see p447)*

MARKETS

L ARGE TOWNS AND CITIES usually have a central covered market which operates most weekdays, selling everything from fresh produce to pots and pans. The information under each town entry in this guide lists market days. Many towns hold weekly markets in the main square. While you browse among the stalls, look out for local fresh produce and the jams and cakes of the Women's Institute stalls.

Entertainment in Britain

Punch and Judy show

LONDON IS WITHOUT DOUBT the entertainment capital of Britain *(see pp126–9)*, but many regional theatres, opera houses and concert halls have varied programmes. Edinburgh, Manchester, Birmingham, Leeds and Bristol in particular have a lot to offer and there are a number of summer arts festivals around the country such as those at Bath and Aldeburgh *(see pp62–3)*. Ticket prices are often cheaper outside the capital.

SOURCES OF INFORMATION

IN LONDON, check the listings magazines, such as *Time Out*, or the *Evening Standard*, London's evening newspaper. All of the quality broadsheet newspapers *(see p618)* provide comprehensive arts reviews and listings of the cultural events and shows throughout the country, with the largest sections at the weekends. Local newspapers, libraries, or tourist offices *(see p615)* can supply details of regional events. Specialist magazines such as *NME* or *Melody Maker* give up-to-date news of the pop music scene and are available from any newsagent.

THEATRES

BRITAIN HAS AN enduring theatrical tradition dating back to Shakespeare *(see pp312–15)* and beyond. All over the country, amateurs and professionals tread the boards in purpose-built auditoriums, pubs, clubs and village halls. Productions and performance standards are generally high, and British actors have an international reputation.

London is the place to enjoy theatre at its most varied and glamorous *(see p126)*. The West End alone has more than 50 theatres *(see p127)* ranging from elaborate Edwardian, upholstered in red plush, to exciting modern buildings such as the National Theatre on the South Bank in London.

In Stratford-upon-Avon, the Royal Shakespeare Company presents a year-round programme of Shakespeare, as well as avant-garde and experimental plays. Bristol also has a long dramatic tradition, the Theatre Royal *(see p244)* being the oldest working theatre in Britain. Some of the best productions outside the capital can be found at the West Yorkshire Playhouse in Leeds, the Royal Exchange in Manchester *(see p360)* and the Traverse in Edinburgh.

Street entertainer

Open-air theatre ranges from the free street entertainment that is to be found in many city centres, to student performances on the grounds of Cambridge or Oxford colleges or a production at Cornwall's spectacular clifftop amphitheatre, the Minack Theatre *(see p264)*. Every fourth year, York also stages a series of open-air medieval mystery plays called the York Cycle. Perhaps the liveliest theatrical tradition in Britain is the Edinburgh Festival *(see p495)*. Seaside resorts put on summer programmes of lighthearted entertainment, traditionally stand-up comedy.

Ticket availability varies from show to show. You may be able to buy a ticket at the door, especially for a mid-week matinee, but for the more popular West End shows tickets may have to be booked weeks or even months in advance. You can book through agencies and some travel agents, and most hotels will organize theatre tickets for you. Booking fees are often charged. Beware of tickets offered by touts *(see p67)* – these may be counterfeit. There are no age restrictions in Britain's theatres. It is left to your discretion to decide whether a show is suitable for children.

MUSIC

A DIVERSE musical repertoire can be found in a variety of venues. Church choral music is a great national tradition and many churches and cathedrals host concerts. London, Manchester, Birmingham, Liverpool, Bristol and Bournemouth all have their own excellent orchestras.

Rock, jazz, folk and country-and-western concerts are staged periodically in pubs, clubs and sometimes in outdoor auditoria. Wales has a strong musical tradition which you will come across in many Welsh pubs; northern England is renowned for its booming brass and silver bands; and Scotland, of course, has its famous bag-pipers *(see p466)*.

The Buxton Opera House, the Midlands

The multiplex Warner West End cinema, Leicester Square, London

CINEMAS

THE LATEST FILMS can be seen in any large town. Check the local papers or the tourist office to find out what is on.

Cinemas are having a revival, with luxurious multi-screen cinemas taking over from the local, single-screen cinemas. In larger cities a more diverse range of films is often on offer including more foreign-language productions. These tend to be shown at arts or repertory cinemas. Mainstream English-speaking films are usually shown by the big chains. Age limits apply to certain films. Young children are allowed to see any feature film which is graded with a U (universal) or PG (parental guidance) certificate. Cinema prices vary widely; some are cheaper at off-peak times, such as Mondays or afternoons. For new releases it is advisable to book in advance.

CLUBS

MOST CITIES have some sort of club scene, though London has the most famous venues (see p129). These may feature live music, discos, or DJ or dance performances. Some insist on dress codes or

members only, and most have doormen, or "bouncers". Apart from the major cities, Brighton and Bristol have lively clubs.

DANCE

THIS COVERS a multitude of activities: everything from classical ballet and acid-house parties to traditional English Morris dancing or the Scottish Highland fling, which you may come upon in pubs and villages around the country.

Dance halls are rarer than they were, but ballroom dancing is alive and well. Other dance events you may find are ceilidhs (pronounced kay-lee), which is Celtic dancing and music; May Balls often held at universities (invitation only); dinner or tea dances and square dancing.

Birmingham is home to the Birmingham Royal Ballet and is the best place to see performances outside London. Avant-garde contemporary dance is also performed.

GAY

MOST LARGE communities will have some gay meeting places, mostly bars and clubs. You can find out about them from publications such as the free *Pink Paper* or *Gay Times* on sale in some newsagents, and in gay bars and clubs. London's gay life is centred around Soho (see p82) with its many European-style cafés and bars. Outside London, the most active gay scenes are in Manchester and Brighton. Gay Pride is the largest free outdoor festival in Europe.

Three revellers, Gay Pride Festival

CHILDREN

LONDON OFFERS children a positive goldmine of fun, excitement and adventure, though it can be expensive. From the traditional sights to something more unusual such as a discovery centre, London

has a wide range of activities, many interactive, to interest children of all ages. The weekly magazine *Time Out* has details of children's events.

Outside London, activities for children range from nature trails to fun fairs. Your local tourist office or the local library will have information on things to do with children.

Pirate Ship, Chessington World of Adventures, Surrey

THEME PARKS

THEME PARKS in Britain are enjoyed by children of all ages. Alton Towers has conventional rides plus a motor museum. Chessington World of Adventures is a huge complex south of London. Based on a zoo, it includes nine themed areas, such as Calamity Canyon and Circus World. Legoland, the latest park, opened in March 1996. Thorpe Park is a large watery theme park full of model buildings and a peaceful pet farm.

Alton Towers
Alton, Staffordshire.
☎ 0870 444 4455.
🌐 www.altontowers.com

Chessington World of Adventures
Leatherhead Rd, Chessington, Surrey.
☎ 08704 447777.
🌐 www.chessington.com

Legoland
Winkfield Rd, Windsor, Berkshire.
☎ 08705 040404.
🌐 www.legoland.co.uk

Thorpe Park
Staines Rd, Chertsey, Surrey.
☎ 08704 444466.
🌐 www.thorpepark.com

Specialist Holidays and Outdoor Activities

BRITAIN OFFERS MANY special interest holidays or courses where you can learn a new sport or skill, practise an activity you enjoy, or simply have fun and meet people. If you prefer less structured activities, there is a variety of sports you can participate in, from walking in Britain's national parks to sailing on the many waterways and skiing in Scotland, or exploring the country on horseback. Another option is volunteer work on a nature or bird reserve, or an archaeological dig or conservation project.

Sailing, Cardigan Bay, Welsh coast

Horse riding on a country bridleway *(see p33)*

SPECIALIST HOLIDAYS

A GREAT ADVANTAGE to these holidays is that you can attend the courses alone but without feeling too solitary. There are hundreds of options: any kind of sport – boating, golf, skiing, riding, tennis; arts and crafts such as painting, pottery, calligraphy, jewellery-making; and educational courses on everything from Shakespeare to ecology.

The British Tourist Boards *(see p615)* have lists and pamphlets on some of these activities, and can tell you who to contact for more information. Look out for their publication, **Activity Holidays** (Jarrold), available from some bookshops.

You can book direct with the organizers, or through a travel agent. Introductory courses generally provide you with all the equipment you need plus accommodation and sometimes transport.

Courses are available at all levels of expertise, for all ages. If you are fit and interested in the countryside, you may like to work on a conservation project for a few days. It can be hard work but worthwhile. Contact the tourist board.

WALKING AND CYCLING

WALKING ALLOWS YOU to experience at first hand the spectacular variety of the British landscape, by yourself or with a club. There is a network of long-distance foot-paths and shorter trail routes all over Britain *(see pp32–3)*.

Cyclists may use designated cycle routes and bridleways *(see p643)* and the quieter rural roads can be a delight. Choose a flat or hilly one depending on your energy and fitness. Be sure to take spare parts with you.

GOLF AND TENNIS

THERE ARE ABOUT 2,000 golf courses in Britain and many clubs welcome visiting players. Weekends are usually busy. Specialist operators will book packages for you. Green fees vary widely; many clubs offer temporary membership.

You will find tennis courts in every town and many hotels and some clubs offer temp-orary membership, but courts in summer are in demand. The **Lawn Tennis Association** can provide more information.

BOATING AND SAILING

MESSING ABOUT IN BOATS is a British obsession. You can sail at many places – the Isle of Wight and the south coast are full of pleasure craft. Inland, the network of rivers, lakes and canals can offer a calmer sort of pleasure. Canal-cruising is very popular *(see p641)* and the Norfolk Broads *(see p186)* provides one of the best inland boating experi-ences (the **Broads Authority** will provide information). Elsewhere, the Thames and the canals slice through lovely landscape. The Lake District *(see pp342–57)* is another area which is popular with boating enthusiasts.

OTHER WATER SPORTS

WITH SO MUCH coastline, Britain is a place for enjoying the water, even if temperatures are low. The best areas for surfing are the

Walkers and rock climbers, Yorkshire Dales National Park *(see pp370–71)*

West Country and South Wales. Windsurfing is also popular, both on the coast and on lakes. Tuition and equipment hire are available at many resorts, and several also offer water-skiing facilities. Most towns and resorts have public swimming pools, many with water tunnels, slides and wave machines. Scuba diving is popular around rocky parts of the West Country.

FISHING

Fishing in the sea and on rivers is Britain's biggest participation sport. Regulations are very strict, so check for

Solitary sea fisherman, England's southeast coast

details of rod licences, close seasons and other restrictions at tourist offices or tackle shops. You may have to join a club, or buy a temporary permit. The best game fishing (salmon and trout) is in the West Country, the Northeast, Wales and Scotland.

SPECTATOR SPORTS

Football (soccer) is a passion for a large section of the population. League fixtures are held at many large towns once or twice a week in the season. If you want to see a game, ask at the local tourist office, or check the local papers. Rugby Football also has a good following and games are played in cities such as London, Cardiff and Edinburgh. Cricket is the English national game, and matches are played from April to September on village greens throughout the land. Both flat-racing and steeplechasing are very popular and betting is big business. You can find details of race meetings in most national newspapers.

Paragliding over the South Downs *(see p169)*

ADVENTURE SPORTS

Adventure sports are well-catered for and popular. Among the options are rock-climbing and mountaineering; aeronautical sports and gliding; ice-skating in many major cities and horse riding throughout the country. Although expensive, it is also possible to try go-karting. Facilities for skiing are limited in the UK but there are winter sports facilities at Scottish resorts such as the Cairngorms.

TRAVEL INFORMATION

As IT IS AN international gateway for air and sea traffic, travelling to Britain poses few problems. By air, travellers have a very large choice of carriers serving North America, Australasia and Europe. Coach (bus) travel is a cheap, albeit rather slow, form of transport from Europe, while travelling by train has been transformed thanks to the Channel Tunnel – less than three hours from Paris to London on

British Airways passenger jet

Eurostar. Travelling within Britain itself is fairly easy. There is an extensive network of roads to all parts of the country and hiring a car is often the best way of travelling around. The rail network is efficient and the network to the smaller towns, especially around London, is good. Travelling by coach is the cheapest option; the coach network serves most areas but can be slow. If time is short, air travel is possible but expensive.

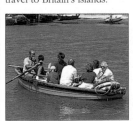

Passenger concourse, Waterloo Station, London

TRAVELLING AROUND BRITAIN

CHOOSING THE BEST way to travel around Britain depends very much on where and when you want to go, although the quickest and most convenient methods are generally the most expensive.

Distances between any two points within mainland Britain are relatively small (at least by American or Australian standards) so air travel usually makes sense only between the extremes, such as London to Edinburgh. For shorter journeys, the time spent getting to and from airports often outweighs any savings in actual travelling time. Rail services are the best alternative if you want to visit Britain's major cities, though fares, especially at peak times, can be quite expensive. If you plan to do much travelling within Britain, a rail pass can be very good value. You can buy a pass before you arrive in the UK as several schemes cater for overseas visitors (see p638).

Coach (bus) networks cover a wide number of UK destinations, and are cheaper than trains, but take longer and may be less comfortable (see p640). Taxis are available at all main coach or rail stations to take you to your hotel; without a car you will avoid the stress of driving in city centres.

If you plan a more flexible touring holiday, hiring a car is more feasible than relying on public transport. Car rental can be arranged at major airports, large railway stations and city centre outlets (see p637). To get the best deals, book from abroad. Small local firms often undercut the large operators in price, but may not be as reliable or convenient.

For detailed exploration of smaller areas such as Britain's National Parks or popular

regions like the Lake District (see pp342–57) you may prefer more leisurely transportation offered by bike, horse or narrowboat. Sometimes there are picturesque local options like a rowing-boat ferry, such as the one between Southwold and Walberswick on the Blyth Estuary (see p190). There are also larger car ferries which travel to Britain's islands.

Rowing-boat ferry on the River Blyth, Southwold, Suffolk

CHANNEL TUNNEL

This historic landlink between France and Britain opened for business in late 1994 and closed one of the "missing links" in the European transport system. The sleek new rolling-stock is high-tech and very comfortable, producing an experience more akin to air travel than rail. Passengers on buses and cars get onto a freight train run by **Eurotunnel** which takes 35 minutes to travel between Calais and Folkestone.

EURO TUNNEL

Eurotunnel logo

For those travelling by rail there are about 40 scheduled passenger-only **Eurostar** services, operated by the French, Belgian and British. They run direct services between Brussels, Lille, Paris, Frethun, Calais and London/Ashford. There are two passenger tunnels – and one service tunnel – which lie 25–45 m (82–147 ft) below the sea bed. All the tunnels are made of concrete and iron, and are 50 km (31 miles) long.

Arriving by Sea, Rail and Coach

IF YOU ARE travelling from Europe by foot, car, coach (bus) or rail you will have to cross the English Channel or North Sea either by ferry or the Channel Tunnel. Ferry services operate from a huge number of ports on the European mainland and have good link-ups with international coaches, with services from most European cities to Britain. The Channel Tunnel has meant there is now a non-stop rail link between Europe and Britain. Prices between the ferries and the tunnel services remain competitive.

A Eurostar train, which takes less than 3 hours from Paris to London

Ferry arriving at Dover

FERRY SERVICES FROM EUROPE

A COMPLEX NETWORK of ferry services operate to over a dozen British ports, with around 20 car and passenger ferry services that travel regularly across the Channel and North Sea routes from many ports in northern and southern Europe *(see pp10–15)*.

Because of the number of areas they reach, ferries can be convenient and economical for those travelling in cars or on foot, depending on your destination. Fares vary greatly according to the season, time of travel and duration of stay. The shortest crossings are not always the cheapest: you pay for the speed of the journey.

CROSSING TIMES

CROSSING TIMES VARY from just over an hour on the shortest routes to a full 24 hours on services from Spain and Scandinavia. If you take an overnight sailing, you may have to pay extra for sleeping accommodation, but it is often worth booking a cabin on the longer trips to avoid feeling exhausted when you arrive. Fast **Seacat** (catamaran) services between Calais and

Dover, Ostend and Dover, and Dieppe and Newhaven are run by **Hoverspeed**. These are the fastest routes across the Channel, taking just under an hour, and catamarans can carry vehicles. The crossings lack the dip and sway of a conventional ship, and so may be less painful for poor sailors.

SEAPORT BUREAUCRACY

THOSE VISITORS from outside the European Union should allow plenty of time for immigration control and customs clearance at British seaports *(see p619)*. You are not allowed to bring pets into Britain because of rabies.

INTERNATIONAL COACH TRAVEL

ALTHOUGH COACH (BUS) travel is comparably cheaper than other methods of travel, it is not the most comfortable way of travelling across Europe. But if you have a lot of spare time and want to stop off en route it can be convenient. Once you have paid for your ticket you will not have to pay again to use the ferry or the Channel Tunnel.

INTERNATIONAL RAIL TRAVEL

WITH THE ADVENT of the Channel Tunnel, there is now access to Britain via **Eurostar** and **Eurotunnel** from the French and Belgian high-speed rail networks. Rail travel can be an efficient, comfortable and fast way of travelling across Europe to Britain – in France and Belgium, trains reach speeds of up to 186 mph (300 kmph). The cost is comparable to flying, although it is much more convenient.

Arriving by Air

BRITAIN HAS ABOUT 130 licensed airports but only a handful of these are equipped for long-haul traffic. The largest is London's Heathrow, the world's busiest international airport and one of Europe's central routing points for international air travel. It is served by most of the world's leading airlines with direct flights from nearly all the major cities. The other major international airports include Gatwick, Stansted, Manchester, Glasgow, Newcastle, Birmingham and Edinburgh. Smaller airports such as London City, Bristol, Norwich and Cardiff have daily flights to European destinations.

Platform sign for express railway service to London

which flies to Western Europe.

The main American airlines offering scheduled services to Britain include **Delta**, **US Air** and **American Airlines**. From Canada, the main carrier is **Air Canada**. From Australasia, the national carriers **Qantas** and **Air New Zealand** vie with many Far Eastern rivals.

Britain imposes an airport tax on all departing passengers – currently £10 for domestic and EC routes, and £20 for non-EC and long-haul flights.

A British Airways 747 jet at Heathrow Airport

BRITISH AIRPORTS

THE MAJORITY of Britain's largest and best known airports are run by the British Airports Authority – the rest are owned by a local authority or are in private hands. All BAA airports offer up-to-date facilities, including 24-hour banking, shops, cafés, hotels and restaurants. Security is strict at all British airports and it is important never to leave baggage unattended.

If you are starting your visit in London, flights to Gatwick, Heathrow or Stansted are equally convenient. But if you plan to visit northern England, there are an increasing number of flights going to Birmingham,

Newcastle and Manchester, while for Scotland you can fly to Glasgow or Edinburgh.

Heathrow has four terminals and some others have two. Before you fly, check with the airport from which terminal your flight leaves.

During severe weather conditions in the winter months, your flight may be diverted to another airport. If this happens, the airline will organize transportation back to your original destination.

British Airways has flights to nearly all the world's important destinations. Other British international airlines include **Virgin Atlantic**, with routes to the USA and the Far East, and **British Midland**,

TRANSPORT FROM THE AIRPORT

BRITAIN'S INTERNATIONAL airports lie some way from city centres, but transport to

Arrival terminal at Heathrow Airport

AIRPORT	ℂ INFORMATION	DISTANCE TO CITY CENTRE	TAXI FARE TO CITY CENTRE	PUBLIC TRANSPORT TO CITY CENTRE
Heathrow	08700 000123	14 miles (23 km)	£40–45	Rail: 15 min Tube: 45 min
Gatwick	08700 002468	28 miles (45 km)	£75	Rail: 30 min Bus: 70 min
Stansted	08700 000303	37 miles (60 km)	£80	Rail: 45 min Bus: 75 min
Manchester	0161 4893000	10 miles (16 km)	£15–16	Rail: 15 min Bus: 30 min
Birmingham	0870 733 5511	8 miles (13 km)	£12–15	Bus: 30 min
Newcastle	0191 2860966	5 miles (8 km)	£10–12	Metro: 20 min Bus: 20 min
Glasgow	0141 8871111	8 miles (13 km)	£12–15	Bus: 20 min
Edinburgh	0131 3331000	8 miles (13 km)	£17–18	Bus: 25 min

and from them is efficient. Every airport has taxis and these are the most convenient form of door-to-door travel, but they are also expensive and can be slow if there is traffic congestion – very likely if you travel in the rush hour (see p636). This can also be a problem with taking a coach or bus, although they are a lot cheaper than taxis.

Heathrow and Newcastle are both linked to the centre of the city by the Underground (see p643). These are efficient, quick and cheap. Manchester, Stansted, Gatwick and Heathrow (see p638) have regular express trains which are not too expensive and are a reliable method for travelling into the heart of the city.

National Express Coaches (see p640) provide direct connections from major airports to many British destinations. They have a regular service between Gatwick and Heathrow.

CHOOSING A TICKET

FINDING THE RIGHT FLIGHT at the right price can be difficult. Promotional fares do come up and it is always worth checking with the airlines direct. Cheap deals are often available from package operators and are advertised in newspapers and travel magazines. Students and under 26s, senior citizens and regular or business travellers may be able to obtain a discount through student travel agencies. Children and babies also travel at cheaper rates.

The bar at the popular Posthouse Heathrow hotel

AIR FARES

FARES TO BRITAIN are usually seasonal, the highest being from June to September. The best deals are available from November to April, excluding the Christmas period – if you want to travel then, be sure to book well in advance.

APEX (Advance Purchase Excursion) fares are often the best value, though they must be booked up to a month ahead, and are subject to restrictions. Charter flights offer even cheaper seats, but are not usually flexible.

If you choose a discount fare, always buy from a reputable operator, and do not part with cash until you have seen your ticket and ensured your seat has been confirmed.

Packages may be worth considering, even if you enjoy independent travel, as sometimes car rental or rail travel is included. This can be cheaper than arranging it yourself when you have arrived in Britain.

TRAVELLING WITHIN BRITAIN BY AIR

Britain's size means that internal air travel only makes sense over longish distances, where it can save a great deal of time – for example, London to Scotland, or to one of the many offshore islands. Air fares can be expensive, but if you book well ahead, fares can be up to three times cheaper than if you just turn up at the airport – although you are still always guaranteed a seat. The British Airways shuttle flights that operate between London and cities such as Glasgow, Edinburgh and Manchester are extremely popular with business travellers. At peak times of the day, flights leave every hour, while at other times there is usually a flight every two hours. Bad weather can cause delays or diversions during the winter months. Even on domestic flights, security is stringent, and you should never leave your bags unattended.

Award-winning exterior of Stansted Airport

Travelling Around by Car

THE MOST STARTLING difference for most foreign motorists is that in Britain you drive on the left, with corresponding adjustments at roundabouts and junctions. Distances are measured in miles. Once you adapt, rural Britain is an enjoyable place to drive, though traffic density in towns and at busy holiday times can cause long delays – public holiday weekends near the south coast can be particularly horrendous. An extensive network of toll-free motorways and trunk roads has now cut travelling time to most parts of the country.

WHAT YOU NEED

TO DRIVE IN BRITAIN you need a current driving licence with an international driving permit if required. In any vehicle you drive you must carry proof of ownership or a rental agreement, plus any insurance documents.

ROADS IN BRITAIN

PEAK RUSH-HOUR traffic can last from 8–9:30am and 5–6:30pm on weekdays in the cities; at these times traffic can grind to a halt. In the country a good touring map is essential; the AA or RAC motoring atlases are fairly straightforward to use. For exploration of more rural areas, the Ordnance Survey series is the best. On all road maps B roads are secondary roads and A roads, often dual carriageways (two lanes in each direction), are main routes. B routes are often less congested and more enjoyable to use. Rural areas are crisscrossed by a web of tiny lanes. Motorways are marked with M followed by their identifying number.

A motorway sign in miles

London 32
Cambridge 25
Newmarket 30
M 11
Bishops Stortford 4
Dunmow (A120) 8

ROAD SIGNS

SIGNS are now generally standardized in line with Europe. Directional signs are colour-coded: blue for motorways, green for major routes and white for minor routes. Signposting in Britain is not consistent and city suburbs can be confusing. Brown signs indicate places of interest. Advisory or warning signs are usually triangles in red and white, with easy to understand pictograms. Watch for electronic notices on motorways that warn of road works, accidents or patches of fog. Level crossings, found at rail lines, often have automatic barriers. If the lights are flashing red it means a train is coming and you must stop. The *UK Highway Code Manual* – available from most bookshops – is an up-to-date guide to all the current British driving regulations and traffic signs.

RULES OF THE ROAD

SPEED LIMITS are 30–40 mph (50–65 kmph) in built-up areas and 70 mph (110 kmph) on motorways or dual carriageways – look out for speed signs on other roads. It is compulsory to wear seat-belts in Britain. Drink-driving penalties are severe – see the *UK Highway Code Manual* for legal limits.

The A30 dual carriageway going through Cornwall

No stopping **Speed limit applies**

No entry **No right-turn allowed**

Railway level crossing **Give way to all vehicles**

One-way traffic **Gradient of a road**

PARKING

THIS IS THE BANE of the British motorist's life. Parking meters operate during working hours (usually 8am–6:30pm Mon–Sat); keep a supply of coins for them. Some cities have "park and ride" schemes, where you can take a bus from an out-of-city car park into the centre. Other towns have parking schemes where you buy a card at the tourist office or newsagents, fill in your parking times and display the card. Avoid double yellow lines at all times; single lines sometimes mean you can park in the evenings and at weekends, but check carefully. Traffic wardens will not hesitate to ticket, clamp or tow your car away. If in any doubt, find a car park *(see pp642–3)*. Outside urban areas and popular tourist zones, parking is easier. Look out for signs with a blue P, indicating parking spaces. Never leave any valuables or luggage in your car: thefts are common, especially in cities.

Sign for a car park

Petrol

Nᴏʀᴛʜ ᴀᴍᴇʀɪᴄᴀɴ visitors may find fuel (gas) very expensive in Britain. Large supermarkets often have the cheapest petrol; look out for branches of Tesco or Sainsbury with petrol stations. Motorway service areas are generally more expensive. Petrol is sold in three grades: diesel, LRP (lead replacement petrol) and unleaded. Most modern cars in Britain use unleaded petrol – any vehicle you hire will probably do so. Unleaded and diesel are cheaper than LRP. Most petrol stations in Britain are self-service but instructions at pumps are easy to follow.

Breakdown Services

Bʀɪᴛᴀɪɴ'ꜱ ᴍᴀᴊᴏʀ motoring organizations, the **AA** (Automobile Association) and the **RAC** (Royal Automobile Club), provide a comprehensive 24-hour breakdown service for members, as well as many other motoring services. Both offer reciprocal assistance for members of overseas motoring organizations – before arrival check with your own group to see if you are covered. You can contact the AA or RAC from the roadside SOS phones found on motorways. **Green Flag** is the other major rescue service in Britain, which can sometimes be quicker and cheaper since it makes greater use of local garages.

Most car hire agencies have their own cover, and their charges include membership of either the AA, the RAC or Green Flag while you are driving. Be sure to ask the rental company for the service's emergency number.

Even if you are not a member of an affiliated organization you can still call out a rescue service, although it will be expensive. Always follow the advice given on your insurance policy or rental agreement. If you have an accident that involves injury or another vehicle, call the police as soon as possible (see p621).

A small rural petrol station in Goathland, North Yorkshire

Car Hire

Hɪʀɪɴɢ ᴀ ᴄᴀʀ in Britain can be expensive. One of the most competitive national companies is **Autos Abroad**, but small local firms may undercut even these rates. Many companies prefer you to leave a credit card number; otherwise you may have to part with a substantial cash deposit. You need your driving licence and a passport when you hire. Most companies will not hire to novice drivers, and set age limits (usually 21–74). Automatic cars are now generally available for hire. If you are touring Britain for three weeks or more, you may find a leasing arrangement cheaper than hiring. Remember to add VAT and insurance costs when you check hire rates.

Hitchhiking

Hɪᴛᴄʜʜɪᴋɪɴɢ is a common practice in Britain, and you are likely to thumb a long-distance lift if you stand near a busy exit road junction. In rural or walking areas like the Lake District, tired hikers may well be offered a lift. It is illegal to hitch on motorways or their approach roads. As anywhere, there is a risk in hitchhiking alone, especially for a woman. Lift-sharing is now a common practice. The small-ads magazine *Loot* (sold in newsagents in London, Manchester and Bristol) has a large section for lift-seekers.

Travelling Around by Rail

BRITAIN HAS a privatized rail network which covers the whole of the country. It is divided into regional sections which serve over 2,500 stations throughout Britain. The system is generally efficient and reliable. Parts of the network are occasionally closed for repairs, mostly at weekends, so check before travelling. Journeys across the country, rather than out of London, may involve a number of changes as most lines radiate from London, which has seven major terminals. There is a rail link with Continental Europe on Eurostar, from Waterloo Station in London and Ashford in Kent (see p632).

Mainline train speeding through countryside

TICKETS

LARGE TRAVEL AGENTS and all railway stations sell rail tickets. First-class tickets cost about one-third more than standard fares, and generally return fares are cheaper than two singles.

Allow plenty of time to buy your ticket and always ask about any special offers or reduced fares. There are four types of discounted fares for adults. Apex tickets are available in limited numbers on some long-distance routes and have to be booked at least a week in advance. SuperApex fares have to be purchased 14 days in advance and again are available in limited numbers on a few mainline services. Savers can be used at weekends and on most weekday trains outside rush hours. Finally, Supersavers cannot be used on Fridays, or any peak-hour service to, from or through London.

Ticket offices in rural areas may close at weekends, but small branch lines have a conductor on board who sells tickets. Otherwise buy a ticket beforehand as inspectors can levy on-the-spot fines if you do not have a valid ticket. Many stations have automatic ticket machines.

RAIL PASSES

IF YOU PLAN to do much train travelling around Britain, buy a rail pass. These can be bought from many agents abroad, such as **Rail Europe** or **CIE Tours International**. An All Line Rail Rover gives adults unlimited travel throughout England, Scotland and Wales for 7 or 14 days. Children under 16 travel half price, or a Family Rail Card is available. It can be used for up to four adults and four children. Discounts are also available for 16- to 25-year-olds or full-time students attending a UK educational establishment with a Young Person's Rail Card. For those over the age of 60, the Senior Rail Card entitles you to a one-third price discount on most fares. There are special passes for London transport

and a pass that covers London, Oxford, Canterbury and Brighton. Children of 5–15 years pay half fare; the under-5s travel free. Family tickets are also available. Disabled travellers qualify for many discounts. Keep a passport-sized photo handy for buying passes. If you have a pass, make sure you always show it when you buy a ticket.

GENERAL TIPS

BRITAIN'S FASTEST and most comfortable trains are those on the mainline routes. These are very popular services and get booked up quickly. It is always advisable to reserve your seat in advance, especially if you want to travel at peak times such as Friday evenings. Mainline trains have dining cars, air-conditioning and are fast, travelling to Edinburgh from London, for example, in just over four hours.

For those arriving at Heathrow Airport and travelling into London (see pp634–5), an alternative to the Underground (see p643) is the Heathrow Express, the fast train to Paddington Station (www.heathrow express.com or 0845 600 1515). Trains run every 15 minutes from 5am until around midnight, and take 15 minutes (8 minutes more to and from Terminal 4).

Rail terminal, Liverpool Street Station

Porters are rare on British stations, although trolleys are often available for passengers to help themselves. If you are disabled and need help, call to book assistance at least 24 hours before your journey. A yellow line above a train window indicates a first class compartment. You cannot use these without paying the full fare, even if the train is full. Check which section of the train to join as they sometimes split through the journey and proceed to different destinations. Trains stop for only a minute at each station, so be ready to get on and off. Some stations are a little way from town centres, but are well signposted and nearly always on a bus route. Sunday trains and public holiday services are often a lot slower than normal.

SCENIC TRAIN RIDES

As MOTOR TRANSPORT made many rural railways redundant in the mid-20th century, picturesque sections of track, as well as many old steam engines, were rescued and restored to working order by enthusiasts. These services are often privately run: the local tourist office, railway station ticket office or travel agents will provide you with information. Most of the lines are short – around 20 miles (32 km) – but cover some of the prettiest parts of the country and are one of the best ways to enjoy its spectacular scenery. Lines include: the Ffestiniog Railway *(see pp438–9)* in North Wales; the North York

Moors Railway *(see p380)*; the Strathspey Steam Railway in the Cairngorm Mountains of the Scottish Highlands *(see p530)* and the La'l Ratty Railway in Cumbria *(see p352)*.

A reconditioned steam train, North Yorkshire

NATIONAL RAIL NETWORK

KEY

— Principal routes

— Other routes

● Rail junction

○ Rail station

☐ London area

LONDON
Euston
King's Cross
St Pancras
Paddington
Liverpool Street
Victoria
Charing Cross
Waterloo

Kyle of Lochalsh
Inverness
Fort William
Aberdeen
Oban
Perth
Dundee
Stirling
Edinburgh
Glasgow
Stranraer
Carlisle
Newcastle
Durham
Windermere
Harrogate
Scarborough
Lancaster
York
Preston
Bradford
Hull
Liverpool
Leeds
Holyhead
Manchester
Chester
Sheffield
Bangor
Crewe
Lincoln
Shrewsbury
Nottingham
Leicester
Norwich
Wolverhampton
Peterborough
Birmingham
Coventry
Cambridge
Hereford
Luton
Ipswich
Fishguard
Swindon
Stansted
Milford Haven
Cheltenham
Swansea
Bristol
Cardiff
Bath
LONDON
Canterbury
Barnstaple
Taunton
Salisbury
Dover
Gatwick
Exeter
Southampton
Brighton
Hastings
Plymouth
Weymouth
Portsmouth
Torquay
Penzance

DIRECTORY

UK RAIL NUMBERS

Disabled Travel
📞 0845 744 3366 (call 24 hrs before journey to book help).

First North Eastern Railways
📞 08459 505000 (bookings).

Great Western Trains
📞 08457 000125 (bookings).

Lost Property
📞 020-7387 8699 (Euston) or contact train company.

Midland Mainline
📞 08457 221125 (bookings).

National Rail Enquiries Timetables
📞 08457 484950.
🖥 www.nationalrail.co.uk

Rail Europe
📞 08705 848848 (London).
🖥 www.raileurope.co.uk

Virgin Trains
📞 08457 222333 (bookings).

OVERSEAS RAIL NUMBERS

CIE Tours International
📞 (201) 292-3438 or (212) 319 0561 (United States); (800) 243 8687 (Canada).

Rail Europe
📞 (914) 682-2999 (United States); (800) 848-7245 (Canada).

Travelling around by Coach

IN BRITAIN, coaches refer to the long-distance express buses and those used for sightseeing excursions. What the British refer to as buses, however, covers those vehicles that operate on regular routes with scheduled stops around or between villages, towns and cities. Many coach services duplicate rail routes, but are generally cheaper. Journey times, however, are longer and much less predictable on crowded roads. Modern coaches are comfortable, sometimes with refreshments and toilets on board. Some city to city routes, especially at weekends, are so popular that it is a good idea to buy a reserved journey ticket, which guarantees you a seat.

A coach tour, the Royal Mile, Edinburgh

NATIONAL COACH NETWORK

THERE ARE A LOT OF regional coach companies, but by far the largest British coach operator is **National Express** with a nationwide network of over 1,200 destinations *(see pp12–15)*. On the more popular routes – particularly on Friday evenings – it is best to book ahead.

Discounts are available for full-time students or anyone under 25. Anyone aged 50 or over can also qualify for a discount coach card, saving up to 30 per cent on many fares. Britexpass cards lasting 30 days and Tourist Trail Passes are also available for those planning to cover many destinations in a limited period. You can buy these from most coach travel agents in North America – via **British Travel Associates** – or while in the UK, at the major international airports, **Victoria Coach Station** and most large travel agents. The

Oxford Tube runs between Oxford and London, and is a frequent, wheelchair-friendly coach service. **Scottish Citylink** is a major operator running regular services between London, the North and Scotland. Some services run direct from Heathrow, Gatwick and Stansted airports. Allow plenty of time to buy your ticket before boarding. Luggage is stowed in the vehicle hold.

British Travel Associates
☏ 800 327 6097 *(in North America).*

National Express
☏ 08705 808080.
W www.nationalexpress.com

Oxford Tube
☏ 01865 772250.
W www.stagecoach-oxford.co.uk

Scottish Citylink
☏ 08705 505050.
W www.citylink.co.uk

Victoria Coach Station
☏ 020-7730 3466.
W www.victoriacoachstation.com

COACH TOURS

DOZENS OF COACH TOURS are available in the UK, for all interests, age groups and destinations. Some include a tour guide. They may last anything from a couple of hours to two weeks or more, touring coast or countryside and visiting places of interest. Some are highly structured, organizing every last photo opportunity or cup of tea; others leave you to sightsee or shop at your own pace. You can opt for a prearranged route, or commission your own itinerary for a group.

Coach tours are popular, but may leave you feeling somewhat herded. Groups always travel at the pace of their slowest member, which can mean a lot of waiting. But at the same time all the stress of organizing a similar trip for yourself is taken away. Some coach operators will pick up passengers from their hotels and then drop them back.

Any large town will have a selection of coach companies. Check the local *Yellow Pages* *(see p622)*, or ask your hotel or the local tourist office. You can also book coach trips direct from overseas through a specialist travel agent.

Seaside resorts and tourist sites are destinations for many day trips, especially in high season. In some of the more popular rural areas, such as the Lake District, special small buses operate for ease of movement. You can book

A National Express coach

these in advance, or just turn up before the coach leaves, although the tour is likely to be fully booked, especially in high season. The local tourist information point or travel agent will be able to tell you where these trips leave from, the cost and may even sell you tickets. It is customary to tip the guide after your tour.

REGIONAL BUSES

REGIONAL BUS SERVICES are run by a large number of companies, some private and some operated by local authorities. Less economic services to remote rural areas tend to be sporadic and expensive, with some buses running just once a week and many isolated villages having no service at all. Only a few rural buses are equipped for wheelchairs.

As a general rule, you can assume that the further you get from a city, the fewer the buses and the more expensive the fare. It is therefore unwise to rely on local buses for transport, and if you want to see a lot of the country, renting a car is a better option. But if you do have the time, local buses can be a pleasant and often sociable way of travelling around Britain's lovely countryside.

Most buses run with just one operator – the driver. All drivers prefer you to have the correct fare, so always have a selection of low denomination coins handy. Some routes do not operate on Sundays and public holidays, and those that do are much reduced.

Always check your routes, schedules and fares at the local tourist office or bus station before you depart on a bus. This will prevent your being stranded somewhere with no return transport.

The Postbus provides transport in remote parts of the Highlands

Travelling Britain's Coasts and Waterways

BRITAIN HAS THOUSANDS OF MILES of inland waterways and hundreds of islands scattered along its coastline. Cruising along a canal in the beautiful Midlands countryside or travelling on one of the small local ferries to a remote Scottish island are both wonderful experiences. Canal boats can be hired and scores of ferries run between Britain's offshore islands.

A barge on the Welsh Backs, Bristol, Avon

CANALS

AS INDUSTRIAL PRODUCTION grew in the 18th century, it became vital to find a cheap and effective way of transporting heavy loads. Canals fulfilled this need and a huge network was built, linking most industrial areas in the north and sea ports.

The arrival of the railways and their immediate success for freight made most canals redundant, but there are still some 3,200 km (2,000 miles) left, most in the old industrial heartland of the Midlands.

Today these canals lure the travellers who are content to cruise on old-fashioned, slow narrowboats, taking their time to enjoy the views and the canalside inns, originally built to satisfy the bargees' thirsts and to supply stabling for the barge horses. These canal holidays can be very relaxing if you have the time.

If you wish to hire a narrow-boat, you can book with a specialist travel firm or contact **British Waterways**.

British Waterways
📞 *01442 235400.*
W *www.britishwaterways.co.uk*

LOCAL FERRIES

BRITAIN'S LOCAL FERRIES can offer anything from a ten-minute river journey to a seven-hour sea cruise.

Many of Scotland's ferries are operated by **Caledonian MacBrayne**. They sail to lots of different destinations, such as the Isle of Skye to the Kyle of Lochalsh, or the five-hour journey from Oban to Lochboisdale in the Western Isles. They offer a variety of different ticket types, from unlimited rover tickets for a specific period of time, to island-hop passes or all-inclusive coach tour and ferry tickets. Not all the island ferries take cars.

A car ferry travelling from Oban to Lochboisdale

River ferries make an interesting alternative to the more usual forms of transport. The ferry across the Mersey, between the cities of Liverpool and Birkenhead, is still used by many commuters. London's river trips, such as the one that runs from Westminster to Tower Bridge (see p75), offer a different perspective on the city and make a change from tubes, buses and cars. Local tourist information centres can give you information about ferries in their area.

Caledonian MacBrayne
📞 *01475 650100.*
W *www.calmac.co.uk*

Travelling within Cities

URBAN PUBLIC TRANSPORT in Britain is efficient and can be fun – children love London's double-decker buses. Fares are good value, bearing in mind that you avoid the expense and difficulty of parking a car. Most of the larger cities have good bus services. London, Newcastle and Glasgow also have an underground system, while Manchester and Blackpool have trams. Taxis are available at every railway station and at ranks near hotels and city centres. The best way to see many cities is on foot, but whatever transport you choose, try to avoid the rush hours from 8am to 9:30am, and 4:30pm to 6:30pm.

Local buses travelling along Princes Street, Edinburgh

LOCAL BUSES

THE DEREGULATION of bus services has led to a complex system with many buses often duplicating services on the busiest routes. On most buses you pay the driver as you enter. They will not always accept notes so keep a selection of coins handy. Credit cards and cheques are not accepted. The fare depends on the distance you travel. If you are exploring a city by bus, a daily pass is a good idea. Many of the larger cities have daily or weekly passes that can be used on all public transport in that city; these can often be bought from newsagents. Check with the tourist office for schedules and fares. All-night services are only available in major cities, from about 11pm until early morning. You cannot use a day pass on these.

A London double-decker bus

In London night buses are prefixed with the letter N and all of them pass through Trafalgar Square.

Be on your guard when travelling home alone late at night, when there may be few other passengers aboard.

Bus designs have become more innovative in the last few years. The old "big red bus" with a conductor still exists in London, but has been joined by a plethora of modern vehicles of all shapes, colours and sizes, with automatic doors and comfortable interiors. Many are small single-deckers, able to weave in and out of traffic more easily.

Many cities have bus lanes, intended to bypass car traffic jams during the rush hours. These can be effective but your journey could still take a long time. Schedules are hard to keep to, so regard timetables as advisory. At some stops, called request stops, the driver will not halt unless you signal that you want to get on or off. If you want to board, raise your arm as the bus approaches the stop; if you want to get off, ring the bell once before your stop.

Destinations are shown on the front of buses. If you are not sure which stop you need, ask the driver or conductor to alert you and stay on the lower deck. Always keep your ticket until the end of the journey in case an inspector boards, who can impose an on-the-spot fine if you are without a valid ticket. Stops can often be quite a long distance apart.

DRIVING IN CITIES

DRIVING IN CITY CENTRES is being increasingly discouraged, most notably in London with the introduction of the congestion charge in spring 2003. If you drive or park within the congestion zone covering central London from Monday to Friday, 7am to 6:30pm, you will need to pay a £5 fee before 10pm that day at a newsagent, petrol station or Post Office. Not paying the charge will lead to a large fine. Go to www.cclondon.com for more information. Other cities are considering similar steps to keep drivers out of the centres.

A traditional parking meter

Parking in city centres is also strictly controlled to prevent congestion (*see p636*).

TAXIS

IN LARGE TOWNS there are plenty of taxis to be found at taxi ranks and train stations. Some operate by radio so you have to phone. The local *Yellow Pages (see p622)*, pubs, restaurants and hotels will all have a list of taxi numbers. Prices are usually controlled. Always ask the price before you start your journey if there is no taxi meter. If you are not sure of the correct fare ask the local tourist information point.

Licensed taxi drivers undergo strict tests and all licensed cabs must carry a "For Hire" sign, which is lit up whenever they are free. Care is needed if you use unlicensed minicabs – some may be mechanically

An illegally parked car immobilized by a wheel clamp

unsound or even uninsured. Do not accept an unbooked minicab ride in the street. The famous London black cabs are almost as much of an institution as the big red bus. These are the safest cabs to use in London as all the drivers are licensed. They also know where they are going. Even these are changing, however, and you will see cabs of many colours, many covered with advertising. The newer cab designs are equipped to carry wheelchairs. If a cab stops for you in London, it must by law take you anywhere within a radius of 6 miles (10 km) so long as it is within the Metropolitan Police District. This includes most of London and Heathrow Airport.

One of London's black cabs

All licensed cabs have meters that start ticking as soon as the driver accepts your custom. The fare will increase minute by minute or for each 311 m (1,020 ft) travelled. Surcharges are added for each piece of luggage, each extra passenger or unsocial hours. Most drivers expect a tip of between 10 and 15 per cent of the fare. If you have a complaint, note the serial number found in the back of the cab.

GUIDED BUS TOURS

IN MOST MAJOR tourist cities, sightseeing bus tours are available. Weather permitting, a good way to see the cities is from a traditional open-topped double-decker bus. Private tours can be arranged with many companies. Contact the tourist information centre.

TRAMS

AFTER A LONG ABSENCE (apart from a few nostalgic remnants in Blackpool), trams are making a comeback in clean, energy efficient and more modern guises. One of the best tram schemes in Britain is Manchester's Metrolink.

LONDON UNDERGROUND

THE UNDERGROUND in London, known as the tube, is one of the largest systems of its kind in the world. It has over 270 stations, each of which are marked with the London Underground logo. The tube can get very overcrowded during the rush hour. The only other cities with an underground system are Glasgow and Newcastle, but both are small. London tube trains run every day, except Christmas Day, from about 5:30am until just after midnight. Fewer trains run on Sundays.

The 11 tube lines are colour-coded and maps called *Journey Planners* are posted at every station, while maps of the central section are displayed in each train. Most tube journeys between central destinations in London can be completed with only one or two changes of train. Smoking is not permitted on the Underground.

Newcastle's tube system is limited to the city centre but Glasgow's skirts around the centre. Both are clean and efficient, running the same hours as London's.

A tram along Blackpool's famous promenade

WALKING IN CITIES

ONCE YOU GET USED to traffic on the left, Britain's cities can be safely and enjoyably explored on foot.

There are two types of pedestrian crossing: striped zebra crossings and push-button crossings at traffic lights. At a zebra crossing traffic should stop for you, but at push-button crossings cars will not stop until the lights change in your favour. Look for instructions written on the road; these will tell you from which direction you can expect the traffic to come. More and more cities and towns are creating traffic-free zones in the city centre for pedestrians.

A London Underground sign outside a station

Cycling under the Bridge of Sighs, Oxford

CYCLING

Cycling is a popular pastime in Britain. Even in the smallest town there is often somewhere you can hire bikes. Whether you cycle in towns or the countryside, a helmet is recommended. Cyclists may not use motorways or their approach roads, nor can they ride on pavements, footpaths or pedestrianized zones. Many city roads have cycle lanes and their own traffic lights. You can take a bike on most trains (phone to check). Never leave your bike unlocked.

General Index

Acknowledgments

DORLING KINDERSLEY would like to thank the following people whose contributions and assistance have made the preparation of this book possible.

MAIN CONTRIBUTOR

Michael Leapman was born in London in 1938 and has been a professional journalist since he was 20. He has worked for most British national newspapers and now writes about travel and other subjects for several publications, among them *The Independent*, *Independent on Sunday*, *The Economist* and *Country Life*. He has written 11 books, including the award-winning *Companion Guide to New York* (1983, revised 1995) and *Eyewitness Travel Guide to London*. In 1989 he edited the widely praised *Book of London*.

ADDITIONAL CONTRIBUTORS

Paul Cleves, James Henderson, Lucy Juckes, John Lax, Marcus Ramshaw.

ADDITIONAL ILLUSTRATIONS

Christian Hook, Gilly Newman, Paul Weston.

DESIGN AND EDITORIAL

MANAGING EDITOR Georgina Matthews
SENIOR ART EDITOR Sally Ann Hibbard
DEPUTY EDITORIAL DIRECTOR Douglas Amrine
DEPUTY ART DIRECTOR Gaye Allen
PRODUCTION David Proffit
PICTURE RESEARCH Ellen Root
DTP DESIGNER Ingrid Vienings
MAP CO-ORDINATORS Michael Ellis, David Pugh
RESEARCHER Pippa Leahy
Eliza Armstrong, Sam Atkinson, Moerida Belton, Josie Barnard, Hilary Bird, Louise Boulton, Julie Bowles, Roger Bullen, Deborah Clapson, Elspeth Collier, Gary Cross, Cooling Brown Partnership, Guy Dimond, Danny Farnham, Joy Fitzsimmons, Fay Franklin, Ed Freeman, Charlie Hawkings, Martin Hendry, Andrew Heritage, Paul Hines, Annette Jacobs, Gail Jones, Steve Knowlden, Nic Kynaston, Esther Labi, Kathryn Lane, Pippa Leahy, James Mills Hicks, Rebecca Milner, Elaine Monaghan, Marianne Petrou, Chez Picthall, Clare Pierotti, Andrea Powell, Mark Rawley, Jake Reimann, Carolyn Ryden, David Roberts, Mary Scott, Alison Stace, Hugh Thompson, Simon Tuite.

ADDITIONAL PHOTOGRAPHY

Max Alexander, Peter Anderson, Apex Photo Agency: Simon Burt, Steve Bere, Deni Bown, June Buck, Michael Dent, Philip Dowell, Mike Dunning, Chris Dyer, Andrew Einsiedel, Philip Enticknap, Jane Ewart, DK Studio/Steve Gorton, Frank Greenaway, Stephen Hayward, John Heseltine, Ed Ironside, Dave King, Neil Mersh, Robert O'Dea, Stephen Oliver, Vincent Oliver, Roger Phillips, Kim Sayer, Karl Shone, Chris Stevens, Jim Stevenson, Clive Streeter, Harry Taylor, David Ward, Mathew Ward, Alan Williams, Stephen Wooster, Nick Wright, Colin Yeates.

PHOTOGRAPHIC AND ARTWORK REFERENCE

Christopher Woodward of the Building of Bath Museum, Franz Karl Freiherr von Linden, Gendall Designs, NRSC Air Photo Group, The Oxford Mail and Times, and Mark and Jane Rees.

PHOTOGRAPHY PERMISSIONS

DORLING KINDERSLEY would like to thank the following for their assistance and kind permission to photograph at their establishments: Banqueting House (Crown copyright by kind permission of Historic Royal Palaces); Cabinet War Rooms; Paul Highnam at English Heritage; Dean and Chapter Exeter Cathedral; Gatwick Airport Ltd; Heathrow Airport Ltd; Thomas Woods at Historic Scotland; Provost and Scholars Kings College; Cambridge; London Transport Museum; Madame Tussaud's; National Museums and Galleries of Wales (Museum of Welsh Life); Diana Lanham and Gayle Mault at the National Trust; Peter Reekie and Isla Roberts at the National Trust for Scotland; Provost Skene House;

Saint Bartholmew the Great; Saint James's Church; London St Paul's Cathdral; Masters and Wardens of the Worshipful Company of Skinners; Provost and Chapter of Southwark Cathedral; HM Tower of London; Dean and Chapter of Westminster; Dean and Chapter of Worcetser Cathedral and all the other churches, museums, hotels, restaurants, shops, galleries and sights too numerous to thank individually.

PICTURE CREDITS

t = top; tl = top left; tlc = top left centre; tc = top centre; tr = top right; cla = centre left above; ca = centre above; cra = centre right above; cl = centre left; c = centre; cr = centre right; clb = centre left below; cb = centre below; crb = centre right below; bl = bottom left; b = bottom; bc = bottom centre; bcl = bottom centre left; br = bottom right; d = detail.

Works of art have been reproduced with the permission of the following copyright holders: © ADAGP, Paris and DACS, London 1995: 159t; © Alan Bowness, Hepworth Estate 265bl; © DACS, London 1995: 93c; © Patrick Heron 1995 all rights reserved DACS: 228cb; © D Hockney: 1970–1 93tr, 1990–3 397t; © Estate of Stanley Spencer 1995 all rights reserved DACS 223t; © Angela Verren-Taunt 1995 all rights reserved DACS: 265br.

The work of Henry Moore, *Large Two Forms*, 1966, illustrated on page 399b has been reproduced by permission of the Henry Moore Foundation.

The publisher would like to thank the following individuals, companies and picture libraries for permission to reproduce their photographs:

ABBOT HALL ART GALLERY AND MUSEUM, Kendal: 358b(d); ABERDEEN ART GALLERIES 526t; ABERDEEN AND GRAMPIAN TOURIST BOARD 465ca; ACTION PLUS: 67t; 466t; 420c; David Davies 67cr; Peter Tarry 66cla, 67bl; Printed by kind permission of MOHAMED AL FAYED: 99t; ALAMY: Gina Calvi 361tl; Angus Palmer 205b; AMERICAN MUSEUM, Bath: 249tl; ANCIENT ART AND ARCHITECTURE COLLECTION: 42cb, 44ca, 44clb, 45ca, 45clb, 46bl, 46br, 48crb, 51ca, 220tl, 223br, 425t; THE ARCHIVE & BUSINESS RECORDS CENTRE, University of Glasgow: 469t; T & R ANNAN AND SONS: 502b(d); ASHMOLEAN MUSEUM, OXFORD: 47t.

BARNABY'S PICTURE LIBRARY: 60tr; BEAMISH OPEN AIR MUSEUM: 410c, 401b, 411ca, 411cb, 411b; BRIDGEMAN ART LIBRARY, LONDON AND NEW YORK: Agnew and Sons, London 311t; Museum of Antiquities, Newcastle upon Tyne 44tl; Apsley House, The Wellington Museum, London 26tl; Bibliotheque Nationale, Paris *Neville Book of Hours* 310t(d); Birgmingham City Museums and Gallery 307t; Bonham's, London, *Portrait of Lord Nelson with Santa Cruz Beyond*, Lemeul Francis Abbot 54cb(d); Bradford Art Galleries and Museums 49clb; City of Bristol Museums and Art Galleries 244c; British Library, London, *Pictures and Arms of English Kings and Knights* 4t(d), 39t(d), *The Kings of England from Brutus to Henry* 26bl(d), Stowe manuscript 40tl(d), *Liber Legum Antiquorum Regum* 46t(d), *Calendar Anglo-Saxon Miscellany* 46–7t(d), 46–7c(d), 46–7b(d), *Decrees of Kings of Anglo-Saxon and Norman England* 47clb, 49bl(d), *Portrait of Chaucer*, Thomas Occleve 49br(d), *Portrait of Shakespeare*, Droeshurt 51bl(d), *Historia Anglorum* 40bl(d), 224tl(d), *Chronicle of Peter of Langtoft* 273b(d), *Lives and Miracles of St Cuthbert* 405tl(d), 405cl(d), 405cr(d), *Lindisfarne Gospels* 405br(d), *Commendatio Lamentabilis intransitu Edward IV* 422b(d), *Histoire du Roy d'Angleterre Richard II* 424t(d), 523b; Christies, London 431t; Claydon House, Bucks, *Florence Nightingale*, Sir William Blake Richmond 150t; Department of Environment, London 48tr; City of Edinburgh Museums and Galleries, *Chief of Scottish Clan*, Eugene Deveria 470bl(d); Fitzwilliam Museum, University of Cambridge, *George IV as Prince Regent*, Richard Cosway 167cb, 200bl, *Flemish Book of Hours* 338tl(d); Giraudon/Musee de la Tapisserie, with special authorization of the city of Bayeux 47b,169b; Guildhall Library, Corporation of London, *The Great Fire*, Marcus Willemsz Doornik 53bl(d), *Bubbler's Melody* 54br(d), *Triumph of*

Steam and Electricity, The Illustrated London News 57t(d), *Great Exhibition, The transept from Dickenson's Comprehensive Pictures* 56–7, *A Balloon View of London as seen from Hampstead* 107c(d); Harrogate Museum and Art Gallery, North Yorkshire 374t; Holburne Museum and Crafts Study Centre, Bath 53t; Imperial War Museum, *London Field Marshall Montgomery*, J Worsley 27cbr(d); Kedleston Hall, Derbyshire 24br; King Street Galleries, London, *Bonnie Prince Charlie*, G Dupré 468tl; Lambeth Palace Library, London, *St Alban's Chronicle* 49t; Lever Brothers Ltd, Cheshire 337cra; Lincolnshire County Council, Usher Gallery, Lincoln, *Portrait of Mrs Fitzherbert after Richard Cosway* 167b; London Library, *The Barge Tower from Ackermann's World in miniature*, F Scoberl 55t; Manchester City Art Galleries 361b; David Messum Gallery, London 433b; National Army Museum, London, *Bunker's Hill*, R Simkin 54ca; National Gallery, London, *Mrs Siddons the Actress*, Thomas Gainsborough 54t(d), 151ca; National Museet, Copenhagen 46ca; Phillips, the International Fine Art Auctioneers, *James I*, John the Elder Decritz 52b(d); Private Collections: 8–9, 26ca(d), 34tl, 48–9, 55cla, 55bl, 56clb, Vanity Fair 57br, 151t, *Ellesmere Manuscript* 176bl(d), *Armada: map of the Spanish and British Fleets*, Robert Adam 281t, 382t, 408b; Royal Geographical Society, London 151cb(d); Royal Holloway & Bedford New College, the *Princes Edward and Richard in the Tower*, Sir John Everett Millais 123b; Smith Art Gallery and Museum, Stirling 482b; Tate Gallery, London: 56crb, 225t; Thyssen-Bornemisza Collection, Lugo Casta, *King Henry VIII*, Hans Holbein the Younger 50b(d); Victoria and Albert Museum, London 24t(d), 56b, 99c, 192t, 339cr, 379b, *Miniature of Mary Queen of Scots*, by a follower of Francois Clouet 497br, 523t(d); Walker Art Gallery, Liverpool 364c; Westminster Abbey, London, *Henry VII Tomb effigy*, Pietro Torrigiano 26br(d), 40bc(d); The Trustees of the Weston Park Foundation, *Portrait of Richard III*, Italian School 49cla(d); Christopher Wood Gallery, London, *High Life Below Stairs*, Charles Hunt 25c(d); reproduced with permission of the BRITISH AIRWAYS: Adrian Meredith Photography 632t; BFI LONDON IMAX CINEMA WATERLOO: Richard Holttum 127c; BRITISH LIBRARY BOARD: *Cotton Faustina BVII folio 85* 49cb, 111cl; © THE BRITISH MUSEUM: 42cr, 43cb, 73tl, 83c, 105, 108–9 all except 109t and 109bl; © THE BRONTE SOCIETY: 398 all; BT PAYPHONES: 622tl, 622bla; BURTON CONSTABLE FOUNDATION: Dr David Connell 388t.

CADOGEN MANAGEMENT: 86b; CADW – Welsh Historic Monuments (Crown Copyright) 460t; CAMERA PRESS: Cecil Beaton 94bl; CARDIFF CITY COUNCIL: 458tr, 459t, 459c; FKB CARLSON: 35bcl; CASTLE HOWARD ESTATE LTD: 385tl; COLIN DE CHAIRE: 185c; TRUSTEES OF THE CHATSWORTH SETTLEMENT: 322b, 323b; MUSEUM OF CHILDHOOD, Edinburgh: 496b; BRUCE COLEMAN LTD: 31br; Stephen Bond 282b; Jane Burton 31cra; Mark N. Boulton 31cl; Patrick Clement 30clb; Peter Evans 530tl; Paul van Gaalen 238tl; Sir Jeremy Grayson 31bl; Harald Lange 30br; Gordon Langsbury 531t; George McCarthy 30t, 31bl, 230b, 273br; Paul Meitz 514clb; Dr. Eckart Pott 30bl, 514t; Hans Reinhard 30cb, 31tc, 282t, 480tl; Dr Frieder Sauer 520t; N Schwiatz 31clb; Kim Taylor 31tl, 514cra; Konrad Wothe 514ca; COLLECTIONS: Liz Stares 26tr,Yuri Lewinski 361tl; CORBIS: Angelo Hornak 119tc, Bill Ross 633tr, John Heseltine 113br; JOE CORNISH: 389b; DOUG CORRANCE: 471b; JOHN CROOK: 159b; EASYEVERYTHING: James Hamilton 622br; 1805 CLUB: 27t; 1853 GALLERY, Bradford 397t; EMPICS LTD: Nigel French 66bl; Tony Marshall 66tl, 66c; ENGLISH HERITAGE: 134b, 196c, 196b, 197b, 236–7b, 251b, 338br, 339b, 380t, 405tr, 405c; Avebury Museum 42ca; Devizes Museum 42br, drawing by Frank Gardiner 409br; Salisbury Museum 42t, 42bl; Skyscan Balloon Photography 43t, 250b; 380t; 409bl; ENGLISH LIFE PUBLICATIONS LTD, Derby: 330tl, 330tr, 331t, 331b; ET ARCHIVE: 41tc, 41cr, 52cb, 53clb, 58crb, 150b; Bodleian Library, Oxford 48crb; British Library, London 48tl, 48ca; Devizes Museum 42cl, 43b, 250c; Garrick Club 422tl(d); Imperial War Museum, London 58clb(d), 59br; Labour Party Archives 60hr; London Museum 43cla; Magdalene College 50ca; National Maritime Museum, London 39b; Stoke Museum Staffordshire Polytechnic 41bc, 52tl; Victoria & Albert Museum, London 50t(d); MARY EVANS PICTURE LIBRARY: 9 inset, 34tr, 40br, 41tl,

41cl, 41bl, 41br, 44bl, 44br, 46cb, 47cla, 51t, 51cb, 51br, 53crb, 54bl, 55br, 56tl, 58ca, 59ca, 59clb, 59crb, 81cb, 106t, 107t, 145 inset, 150cb, 151b, 175c, 177c, 183b, 194c, 210bl, 216tl, 219c, 219bl, 219br, 222bl, 227 inset, 267t, 285 inset, 324b, 337t, 337cla, 406t, 433tl, 468b, 485b, 498bl, 500b, 501t, 521b, 613 inset. CHRIS FAIRCLOUGH: 283b, 340b, 640b; FALKIRK WHEEL: 487b; PAUL FELIX: 222c; FOTOGRAFF © Charles Aithie: 421t; FISHBOURNE ROMAN VILLA: 45t; LOUIS FLOOD: 470br; FOREIGN AND BRITISH BIBLE SOCIETY: Cambridge University Library 423c; FOTOMAS INDEX: 107cra. GARDEN PICTURE LIBRARY: J S Sira 23crt; John Glover 23rb; Steven Wooster 22–23t; GLASGOW MUSEUMS: Burrell Collection 507ca, 506–7 all except 506tl; Art Gallery & Museum, Kelvingrove 505t, 517b, 529b(d); Saint Mungo Museum of Religious Life and Art 503tl; Museum of Transport 504cr; JOHN GLOVER: 62cr, 148ccb, 193b; THE GORE HOTEL, London: 540c.

SONIA HALLIDAY AND LAURA LUSHINGTON ARCHIVE: 395t; ROBERT HARDING PICTURE LIBRARY: 170t, 534t; Jan Baldwin 275b; M H Black 276t; Teresa Black 621cb; Nigel Blythe 632ca; L Bond 325b; Michael Botham 32br; C Bowman 62c; Lesley Burridge 292tr; Martyn F Chillman 293bc; Philip Craven 105t, 188b, 313b; Nigel Francis 207b, 635b; Robert Francis 66–7; Paul Freestone 214b; Brian Harrison 515b; Van der Hars 524t; Michael Jenner 45b, 515c; Norma Joseph 65b; Christopher Nicholson 241t; B O'Connor 33ca; Jenny Pate 149bc; Rainbird Collection 47crb; Roy Rainsford 33b, 156t, 286b, 36cr, 356t, 372t, 461b; Walter Rawling 21t; Hugh Routledge 2–3; Peter Scholey 287t; Michael Short 293br; James Strachen 370b; Julia K Thorne 472bl; Adina Tovy 61tl, 472br; Andy Williams 167t, 222br, 334c, 418t, 510; Adam Woolfitt 20t, 20c, 44tr, 45crb, 248b, 260, 275ca, 293bl, 425bl, 454tl, 530tr; HAREWOOD HOUSE: 396c; PAUL HARRIS: 32t, 62cl, 289bl(d), 326b, 355b, 612–3, 630c, 630b; HARROGATE INTERNATIONAL CENTRE: 375b; HEATHROW AIRPORT LTD: 619b; Crown copyright is reproduced with the permission of the Controller of HMSO: 73br, 120bl, 120br, 121tl; CATHEDRAL CHURCH OF THE BLESSED VIRGIN MARY AND ST ETHELBERT IN HEREFORD: 304b; HERTFORDSHIRE COUNTY COUNCIL: Bob Norris 58–9; JOHN HESELTINE: 74t, 104, 109t, 110, 238tr, 238c, 455tl; HISTORIC ROYAL PALACES (Crown Copyright): 161, 223 all; HISTORIC SCOTLAND (Crown Copyright): 483c, 492tr, 492c, 493bl; PETER HOLLINGS: 336bl; NEIL HOLMES: 246b(d), 248c, 274t, 359b, 415tl, 415tr, 437b, 631t; ANGELO HORNAK LIBRARY: 392tl, 392bl, 392br, 395br; Reproduced by permission of the CLERK OF RECORDS, HOUSE OF LORDS: 469c; DAVID MARTIN HUGHES: 144–5, 152; HULTON-DEUTSCH COLLECTION: 22tr, 27cl, 27cr, 53cla, 54c, 56c, 57cb, 58tl 58tr, 58b, 59t, 60ca, 60bl, 150ca, 157c, 221b, 288t, 336c, 337crb, 338bl, 363b, 383b, 384br, 423t, 481b, 508tl, 522b; HUNTERIAN ART GALLERY. 505b; HUTCHISON LIBRARY: Catherine Blacky 34cb; Bernard Gerad 467t; HUTTON IN THE FOREST: Lady Inglewood 346t.

THE IMAGE BANK, London: Derek Berwin 538t; David Gould 345b; Romilly Lockyer 74bl; Colin Molyneux 455bl; Stockphotos/Steve Allen360c, Trevor Wood 274b; Simon Wilkinson 168b; Terry Williams 114tc; IMAGES COLOUR LIBRARY: 30cla, 43c, 209b, 222t, 237t, 238bl, 239b, 324t, 326cl, 327t, 341c, 638t, 638b; Horizon/Robert Estall 424c; Landscape Only 33cb, 236, 353, 425br; IRONBRIDGE MUSEUM: 303b. JARROLD PUBLISHERS: 200br, 217t(d), 292bl; MICHAEL JENNER: 292tl, 328b, 514b; JORVIK VIKING CENTRE, York: 391tl.

FRANK LANE PICTURE AGENCY: 386b(d); W Broadhurst 242b; Michael Callan 230crb; ANDREW LAWSON: 23c, 23cb, 232br, 233tl, 233tr, 233br; LEEDS CASTLE ENTERPRISES: 153b; LEIGHTON HOUSE, Royal Borough of Kensington: 130br; published by kind permission DEAN AND CHAPTER OF LINCOLN 328t, 329cb, 329bl; LINCOLNSHIRE COUNTY COUNCIL: USHER GALLERY, Lincoln: c 1820 by William Ilbery 329bl; LLANGOLEN INTERNATIONAL MUSICAL EISTEDDFOD 436c; LONDON AMBULANCE SERVICE: 621ca; LONDON FILM FESTIVAL: 62t; LONDON TRANSPORT MUSEUM: 82t; LONGLEAT HOUSE: 254t; THE LOWRY COLLECTION, Salford: *Coming From the Mill*, 1930, L.S. Lowry 359tr.

MADAME TUSSAUDS: 106b; MAGNA: 341b; MALDOM MILLENIUM TRUST: 197t; MANSELL COLLECTION, London: 27clb, 40tr, 52ca, 55cb, 249tr, 311bl, 337clb, 388b; NICK MEERS: 18t, 226–7;

METROPOLITAN POLICE SERVICE: 621t; ARCHIE MILES: 228ca; SIMON MILES: 340tr; MINACK THEATRE: Murray King 264b; MIRROR SYNDICATION INTERNATIONAL: 76b, 89b, 114; BTA/Juilian Nieman 34ca; MUSEUM OF LONDON: 44crb, 115t; NATIONAL EXPRESS LTD: 640bl; NATIONAL FISHING HERITAGE CENTRE, Grimsby: 389t; NATIONAL GALLERY, London: 73tr, 84–5 all; NATIONAL GALLERY OF SCOTLAND: *The Reverend Walker Skating on Duddingston Loch*, Sir Henry Raeburn 490c(d); NATIONAL LIBRARY OF WALES: 422tr, 425c(d), 453b; NATIONAL MUSEUM OF FILM AND TELEVISION, Bradford: 397c; Board of Trustees of the NATIONAL MUSEUMS AND GALLERIES ON MERSEYSIDE: Liverpool Museum 365t; Maritime Museum 363t; Walker Art Gallery 334b, 364tl, 364tr, 364b, 365c; NATIONAL MUSEUMS OF SCOTLAND: 491t, 497bl; NATIONAL MUSEUM OF WALES: 422c; By courtesy of the NATIONAL PORTRAIT GALLERY, London: *First Earl of Essex*, Hans Peter Holbein 339t(d); NATIONAL TRAMWAY MUSEUM, Crich: 327c; NATIONAL TRUST PHOTOGRAPHIC LIBRARY: *Bess of Hardwick (Elizabeth, Countess of Shrewsbury)*, Anon 322tl(d); Mathew Antrobus 290br, 376cl, 377bl; Oliver Benn 25br, 266c, 281bl, 376b; John Bethell 267c, 267bl, 267br, 291t; Nick Carter 243b; Joe Cornish 442; Prudence Cumming 255c; Martin Dohrn 50crb; Andreas Von Einsidedel 25bl, 290cb, 291ca; Roy Fox 259t; Geoffry Frosh 277t; Jerry Harpur 232t, 232bl; Derek Harris 232clb, 255t; Nadia MacKenzie 24cl; Nick Meers 254b, 255b, 308b, 615b; Rob Motheson 280t; Cressida Pemberton Piggot 540t; Ian Shaw 446t; Richard Surman 291br, 350b; Rupert Truman 291br, 365b; Andy Tryner 290bl; Charlie Waite 377t; Jeremy Whitaker 291bc, 379t, 446b; Mike Williams 290ca, 377c; George Wright 232crb, 280c; NATIONAL TRUST FOR SCOTLAND: 464b, 486b, 487c, 494b, 508tr, 509tl, 509tr, 509br; Glyn Satterley 503tr; Lindsey Robertson 509bl; NATIONAL WATERWAYS MUSEUM at Gloucester: 289bc, 289br; NHPA: Martin Garwood 381ca; Daniel Heuclin 270la; NATURE PHOTOGRAPHERS: Andrew Cleave 230cla; E A James 31cla, 348t; Hugh Miles 407t; Owen Newman 31ca; William Paton 514crb; Paul Sterry 30crb, 30br, 31cb, 31crb, 222c, 243t, 373t, 514cla; Roger Tidman 185b; NETWORK PHOTOGRAPHERS: Laurie Sparham 466b; NEW SHAKESPEARE THEATRE CO: 127t; NORFOLK MUSEUMS SERVICE: Norwich Castle Museum 189b; OXFORD SCIENTIFIC FILMS: Okapia 270lb.

'PA' NEWS PHOTO LIBRARY: John Stillwell 61 cr. PALACE THEATRE ARCHIVE: 126c; PHOTOS HORTICULTURAL: 149tlc, 149cra, 149cb, 149crb, 232ca, 233c; PICTURES: 632t; PLANET EARTH PICTURES: David Phillips 23crca; POPPERFOTO: 27br, 59bl, 60clb, 60crb, 61bl, 88tl, 148tr, 191t, 272cl, 430b; AFP/Eric Feferber 61br; SG Forester 67br; PORT MERION LTD: 440tl; THE POST OFFICE: 623tl, 641bl; PRESS ASSOCIATION: Martin Keene 62b; PUBLIC RECORD OFFICE (Crown Copyright): 48b.

ROB REICHENFELD: 162t, 163c, 163b, 288b, 626b, 631t; REX FEATURES LTD: 27ca, 41tr, 60tl, 61bc, 224c, 225br; Barry Beattie 247cl; Peter Brooke 27bc, 624br; Nils Jorgensen 26c, 629t, 636c; Eileen Kleinman 629bn; Hazel Murray 61tr; Tess, Renn-Burrill Productions 257b; Brian Rasic 63t; Nick Rogers 61tc; Tim Rooke 64cr, 66tr; Sipa/Chesnot 27bl; Today 21c; Richard Young 60tl; THE RITZ, London: 83t; ROYAL ACADEMY OF ARTS, London: 86ca; ROYAL COLLECTION © 1995 Her Majesty Queen Elizabeth II: *The Family of Henry VIII*, Anon 38(d), 87c, 88tr, 88bl, 89t, 224tr, 225tl(d), 225tr, 225bl, *George IV, in full Highland dress*, Sir David Wilkie 471t; David Cripps 89c; John Freeman 88br; ROYAL COLLEGE OF MUSIC, London: 98c; ROYAL PAVILION, ART GALLERY AND MUSEUMS, Brighton: 166c,

166bl, 166br, 167cl, 167cr; ROYAL BOTANIC GARDENS, Kew: 76ca;ROYAL SHAKESPEARE THEATRE COMPANY: Donald Cooper 315c(d).

ST. ALBAN'S MUSEUMS: Verulamium Museum 220b; SARTAJ BALTI HOUSE: Clare Carnegie 397b; SCOTTISH NATIONAL GALLERY OF MODERN ART: Roy Lichtenstein In the Car 493c; SCOTTISH NATIONAL PORTRAIT GALLERY: on loan from the collection of the Earl of Roseberry, *Execution of Charles I*, Unknown Artist 52–3; S4C (Channel 4 Wales): 423b; SIDMOUTH FOLK FESTIVAL: Derek Brooks 277b; SKYSCAN BALLOON PHOTOGRAPHY: 250t; JOHN SNOCKEN: 23c, 23ra; SOUTHBANK PRESS OFFICE: 128t; SPORTING PICTURES: 66ca, 66bc, 66br, 67cl, 346b; STILL MOVING PICTURES: Doug Corrance 534b; Wade Cooper 469b; Derek Laird 468c; Robert Lees 65t; STB 530br, 531c, Paisley Museum 501b, Paul Tomkins 515tr; SJ Whitehorn 481t; DAVID TARN: 375tl; TONY STONE IMAGES: 34–5, 536–7; Rex A.Butcher 83c; Richard Elliott 64b; Rob Talbot 341ca; David Woodfall 426; © TATE, LONDON 2002: 73bl, 93 all except c and tl, 93c with kind permission of the Henry Moore Foundation, *Standing by the Rags*, 1988 © Lucian Freud 125tr; *Death from Death Hope Life Fear* (d) 1984 © Gilbert and George 125 cl; *Soft Drain Pipe – Blue (Cool) Version*, 1967 © Claes Oldenburg 125cr, 125bc, 265c, 265bl, 265br; ROB TALBOT: 341cb; TULLIE HOUSE MUSEUM, Carlisle: 346c; URBIS: 360c; courtesy of the Board of Trustees of the VICTORIA AND ALBERT MUSEUM, London: 72b, 100–101.

CHARLIE WAITE: 535t; © WALES TOURIST BOARD: 419c, 420b, 424–5, 454br, 455tr, 455br; Roger Vitos 454tl, 454bl; THE WALLACE COLLECTION, London: 106cb; DAVID WARD: 511b, 529t; FREDERICK WARNE & CO: 355t(d); Courtesy of the Trustees of THE WEDGWOOD MUSEUM, Barlaston, Staffordshire, England: 299b; DEAN AND CHAPTER OF WESTMINSTER: 95bl; Tony Middleton 94bc; JEREMY WHITAKER: 216tr, 216c, 217b; WHITBREAD PLC: 34bl; WHITWORTH ART GALLERY, University of Manchester: courtesy of Granada Television Arts Foundation 361c; CHRISTOPHER WILSON: 390bl; WILTON HOUSE TRUST: 253b; WINCHESTER CATHEDRAL: 159t; WOBURN ABBEY – by kind permission of the Marquess of Tavistock and Trustees of the Bedford Estate: 50–1, 218t; TIMOTHY WOODCOCK PHOTOLIBRARY: 5b; Photo © WOODMANSTERNE, Watford, UK: Jeremy Marks 116t, 117t.

YORK CASTLE MUSEUM: 391cb; YORK CITY ART GALLERY: 393bl; DEAN & CHAPTER YORK MINSTER: 395cla, 395ca, 395cl; Peter Gibson 395cra, 395cr, 395cl; Jim Korshaw 392tr; Reproduced couresty of the YORKSHIRE MUSEUM: 394c; YORKSHIRE SCULPTURE PARK: Jerry Hardman Jones 399t. ZEFA: 64t, 128b, 251t, 257t, 472c, 627t, 634c, 636bl; Bob Croxford 63cr; Weir 185t.

Front Endpaper: All special photography except ROBERT HARDING PICTURE LIBRARY/Andy Williams tl, Adam Woolfitt bl; DAVID MARTIN HUGHES brl; NATIONAL TRUST PHOTOGRAPHIC LIBRARY/Joe Cornish clc; TONY STONE IMAGES/David Woodfall cl. Back Endpaper: All special photography except JOHN HESELTINE tl, br.

JACKET
Front - GETTY IMAGES: main image; DK PICTURE LIBRARY: Peter Anderson crb; Rob Reichenfeld bc; GETTY IMAGES: Derek P. Redfearn clb. Back - GETTY IMAGES: Peter Irish t; Glyn Kirk b. Spine - GETTY IMAGES.

All other images © Dorling Kindersley. For further information see www.DKimages.com

---

DORLING KINDERSLEY SPECIAL EDITIONS

DORLING KINDERSLEY books can be purchased in bulk quantities at discounted prices for use in promotions or as premiums. We are also able to offer special editions and personalized jackets, corporate imprints, and excerpts from all of our books, tailored specifically to meet your own needs.

To find out more, please contact:
(in the U.K.) Sarah.Burgess@dk.com or
Special Sales, Dorling Kindersley Limited,
80 Strand, London WC2R 0RL;
(in the United States) Special Markets Dept.,
DK Publishing, Inc., 375 Hudson Street,
New York, NY 10014.

EYEWITNESS TRAVEL INSURANCE

FOR PEACE OF MIND ABROAD,
WE'VE GOT IT COVERED

DK INSURANCE PROVIDES YOU
WITH QUALITY WORLDWIDE
INSURANCE COVER

Central London

**REGENT'S PARK
AND BLOOMSBURY**
See pp104–109
Street Finder maps 3, 4

REGENT'S
PARK

EUSTON

MARYLEBONE ROAD

GLOUCESTER PLACE

BAKER STREET

HARLEY STREET

PORTLAND PLACE

GREAT PORTLAND STREET

CLEVELAND STREET

TOTTENHAM COURT

GOWER STREET

MORTIMER STREET

WIGMORE STREET

OXFORD STREET

WARDOUR STREET

SOHO SQUARE

REGENT STREET

SHAFT

MARBLE ARCH

BROOK STREET

CONDUIT ST

BAYSWATER ROAD

MOUNT ST

BERKELEY ST

PICCADILLY

ST JAMES'S ST

PALL MALL

THE MALL

KENSINGTON PALACE GDNS

KENSINGTON

Round Pond

GARDENS

HYDE PARK

PARK LANE

SERPENTINE ROAD

Serpentine

ROTTEN ROW

HYDE PARK CORNER

GREEN PARK

ST JAMES PARK

KENSINGTON ROAD

KNIGHTSBRIDGE

KNIGHTSBRIDGE

BUCKINGHAM PALACE GARDENS

Buckingham Palace

BUCKINGHAM GATE

EXHIBITION ROAD

Victoria and Albert Museum

BROMPTON ROAD

GROSVENOR PLACE

LOWER GROSVENOR PLACE

VICTORIA STRE

ROCHESTER ROW

VAUXHALL BRIDGE

**SOUTH KENSINGTON
AND HYDE PARK**
See pp96–103
Street Finder maps 2, 5

**WEST END AND
WESTMINSTER**
See pp78–95
Street Finder maps 3, 4, 5, 6